MACAULAY.

MACAULAY

Statue of Lord Macaulay by Thomas Woolner (1863), antechapel of
Trinity College, Cambridge (Photograph by Jonathan Smith; repro-
duced with the kind permission of the Master and Fellows of Trinity
College). The inscription on the pedestal reads in part: Baron
Macaulay of Rothley: "India litteris et legibus emendanda."

Macaulay

The Tragedy of Power

ROBERT E. SULLIVAN

THE BELKNAP PRESS OF
HARVARD UNIVERSITY PRESS
Cambridge, Massachusetts
London, England
2009

Library of Congress Cataloging-in-Publication Data

Sullivan, Robert E.

Macaulay : the tragedy of power / Robert E. Sullivan.

p.   cm.

Includes bibliographical references and index.

ISBN 978-0-674-03624-6 (alk. paper)

1. Macaulay, Thomas Babington Macaulay, Baron, 1800–1859.   2. Historians—Great Britain—
Biography.   3. Authors, English—19th century—Biography.   4. Statesmen—Great Britain—
Biography.   5. Great Britain—Politics and government—1800–1837.   I. Title.

DA3.M3S85 2009

941.081092—dc22   2009019983

Ai miei amici di Lilliano

CONTENTS

MACAULAY

INTRODUCTION

An irony governs the reputation of Thomas Babington Lord Macaulay 150 years after his death. Within living memory much of the English-reading world has demoted him from an Eminent Victorian properly mentioned in the same breath with John Stuart Mill and George Eliot to a name known only to liberal-arts graduates of a certain age and to students of nineteenth-century culture. Meanwhile, his legacy flourishes in South Asia, where he detested living but relished power. The Latin inscription below his statue in Trinity College, Cambridge University, acclaims him for reforming the letters and laws of India. The tribute sounds like imperial hyperbole until you hear the voice of a fluent English-speaker in a call center in what was recently Bangalore (Bengalooru) and consider that in 1835 Macaulay, not yet thirty-five, was instrumental in launching English as the subcontinent's shared language. A glance at his Wikipedia entry will inform you that his penal code remains the law there and elsewhere in the former British Empire. Then remember that fifty years ago Britain—the nation that Macaulay compressed into "England"—still ruled an empire and preserved the nationalist ethos that Macaulay, as the best-selling nineteenth-century historian writing in English, helped to invent and popularize. His *History of England from the Accession of James II* is now seldom read even in his beloved Cambridge. But there George Macaulay Trevelyan, his grandnephew, propagated his style of history, which thrives in two hemispheres.

There are many twentieth-century books about Macaulay, all useful and some distinguished, but the only full account remains the double-decker *Life and Letters of Lord Macaulay* (1876), by Sir George Otto Trevelyan, O.M., his devoted nephew and intellectual heir. Living mainly in the world Macaulay helped to invent and writing his kind of history, Trevelyan died in 1928, but his virtually filial piety colors and distorts everything later published about his uncle. Until 1962 G. M. Trevelyan, also O.M., a more formidable historian than his father and an academic eminence first as Regius Professor of Modern History at Cambridge and then as Master of Trinity College, controlled access to Macaulay's letters in his college's library, where he also deposited and guarded the eleven-volume manuscript of his granduncle's journals. Appended to volume one is a handwritten note addressed from the Master's Lodge in December 1945, in which Trevelyan declared that he felt "strongly . . . that they ought never to be published as a whole, or any large continuous section of them," because they had "already been put to their full literary use" by his father, and "Wholesale publication would be very unfair to . . . [Macaulay's] memory."[1] In "excerpting" the diaries, Sir George routinely used tendentious discretion and sometimes pure imagination. There were family secrets, but above all Professor Trevelyan was concerned to forestall the publication and sensationalizing of Macaulay's unconsummated passion for his two youngest sisters. One of these was Trevelyan's grandmother, Hannah Lady Trevelyan.

Macaulay kept his journal from October 1838 until May 1839, during June 1840, and then—apart from a spell during 1855 and 1856 while finishing the second installment of his *History*—almost daily from late October 1848 until the eve of his death at the end of 1859. Thousands of scrawled entries expose the emotional consciousness of the unknown Macaulay, a powerful and representative leader of a tenacious and resourceful caste that governed England when England was on top. He wrote quickly, usually at the end of the day but sometimes for several days at a time in a retrospective flurry, and primarily for his own pleasure: "No kind of writing is so delightful, so fascinating, as this minute history of a man's self." Perhaps more than many, he had his secrets and thus occasionally regretted what he had committed to paper. On 28 July 1849, after a largely idle day and dining alone at home, he wrote: "In ye evening"—almost two lines following are obliterated. His final sentence remains: "How my hieroglyphics will throw out any prying person." Lest these fail, he occasionally resorted to a code in Greek letters, usually to designate "the short titles of popular novels which he knew were 'trash' but often reread." In the beginning he wrote only for himself. But William Thomas, the editor of Macaulay's recently published journal, persuasively maintains that he increasingly wrote with a view to Lady Trevelyan's "properly" using it as a "record"—presumably for an official biography. Knowing there were aspects of his life and opinions that would shock her, Macaulay "omitted or disguised" them. He also censored his journal by defacing unseemly material, and after his death both Hannah and her son, George, defaced more, or occasionally tore out an offending page.[2]

In 1973 John Clive began to explore the unknown Macaulay in a masterful biography that ends before his return from India and remains definitive for the years 1800–1837. *Macaulay: The Shaping of the Historian* discreetly reveals the secret the Trevelyans fearfully guarded. Trying to rewrite Clive's work would be impertinent and redundant. Rather, my account of Macaulay's childhood, adolescence, and young adulthood highlights what it slighted or overlooked.

Despite the revelation of Macaulay's passion for his two youngest sisters, he continues to be depicted as an almost transparent man. He was more protean, subtle, and effective than G. O. Trevelyan and those who followed him allowed. Macaulay's aptitude for power and subversion challenges our illusion that people became uniquely complex during the twentieth century. From adolescence onward he needed to conform and be accepted, as well as to simulate and dissimulate. The old word "doubleness" encapsulates better than "duplicity" or "deviousness" the ambivalent sensibility that underlay his virtuosic ability to exercise power as a cultural warrior, a front-bencher, a nationalist historian, and a proselytizing imperialist.

Macaulay's doubleness took charge when he wrote and talked subversively about religion, which is a major achievement of the unknown Macaulay. At once a nominal Anglican and an unbeliever, he presented himself publicly as a "Christian," but on his own terms, which he kept to himself. Because the supersession of religion was long held to be inevitable, the impact of Macaulay's religious subversion of it has never before been studied. During his lifetime he won widespread acceptance as a sage because he could make his opinions seem familiar, even commonsensical. But what explains the long Anglo-American afterlife of his reputation? Decisive were the slow waning of Macaulay's England and his ability to sustain, articulate, and perhaps sometimes half-believe enduring contradictions. Macaulay lived several lives, some of them known, others unknown or irretrievable. My subject is the tragedy of power that killed him and confounds us today.

During the winter of 1919 the social theorist Max Weber lectured on the cost of "Politics as a Vocation": power must imperil humanity. He spoke of the "ethical paradoxes" that bedevil the vocation. Primary were "the diabolic forces lurking in all violence," because, ultimately, the "tasks of politics can only be solved by violence." Those who sought "the salvation of the soul," both their own and others', should avoid the "avenue of politics." It was the domain of a "genius or demon" that "lives in an inner tension with the god of love" and with "the Christian God." In defeated and revolutionary Munich Weber captured the tragedy that Richard Holbrooke discerned in McGeorge Bundy a generation ago. A uniformed noncombatant during World War II and thereafter self-confidently one of "the best and the brightest," Bundy became an architect of the Vietnam War. During his only visit to the combat zone he dined in Saigon with a group of notables. Holbrooke recalled the occasion. At the American ambassador's table, "Bundy quizzed us in his quick, detached style for several hours, not once betraying emotion," distant "from the realities of Vietnam," and either hostile or indifferent to "far less intelligent" people around him who nonetheless knew more about those realities than he, unless they could "present their views in quick and clever ways."[3] Bundy's encompassing emotional "detachment" depended on his ability to reduce groups and individuals to bloodless abstractions. Macaulay could do the same.

Schooled to call "tragedies" everything from monstrous crimes to playground accidents, we have largely forgotten the somber reality that Weber sought to evoke. Aristotle, who taught Macaulay the meaning of tragedy, captured the essence of his life: "A perfect tragedy should imitate actions which excite pity and fear." It is not a matter of a virtuous person being "brought from prosperity to adversity," nor "of a bad man passing from adversity to prosperity" or "the downfall of the utter villain." Rather, Aristotle's "tragic hero" is "one who is highly renowned and prosperous," whose fortune changes "from good to bad," not as the result "of vice, but of some great error or frailty." His "unmerited misfortune" arouses our pity, and that he is someone "like ourselves" makes us fearful.[4] Neither a conspicuously "virtuous man" nor an "utter villain," Macaulay was afflicted with the "great frailty" of conjoining the narrowest human sympathies with a genius for power. It enabled him to embrace "the diabolic forces lurking in all violence," while his sympathies narrowed until he wanted only Hannah Trevelyan's care and, threatened with its loss, longed for the death without leave-taking that he was granted. More unknown than transparent, his was a tragic life.

But Macaulay, and particularly the unknown Macaulay, has cast a long and sometimes sinister shadow. His origins and education shaped his uncommon mingling of the typical, the idiosyncratic, and the spectacular. Both a stern evangelical Anglicanism—imposed at home but rejected at school—and his classical rhetorical education—also imposed but ultimately irresistible—marked him permanently. They inform everything from his doubleness to the method and style of *The History of England from the Accession of James II*. Even more decisive for Tom Macaulay's formation were his increasingly fraught relations with Zachary, his implacably pious father, best known as a leading abolitionist. Zachary's hapless parenting taught his heir to see human sympathy as circumscribed and human relations as mostly a matter of power and competition. Entering Cambridge at eighteen, Tom, still a boyish prodigy, found liberation in a blend of doubt, Hellenism, duplicity, and Utilitarianism. When his enthusiasm cooled into skepticism, he was poised to fight and finally prevail in the cultural and political wars that defined the 1820s and early 1830s. At issue was how to remake England after the unraveling of the counterrevolutionary regime that overcame Napoleon. Evangelizing for a modern because post-Christian England, Macaulay seemed to outgrow his ardor for the classics. There was, however, no outgrowing his two youngest sisters. Enthralled with them and refusing to form any other "serious attachment," he was left "with nothing else to love."[5] Margaret, the younger, became the emotional anchor of his young adulthood, and when she married his already-stunted capacity for human sympathy began shrinking.

Margaret once heard her idolized brother declare "that in politics right and might [are] very much the same thing." Then a member of Parliament, he was establishing himself as the premier spokesman for modernizing English politics by admitting "the middle class to a large and direct share in the representation." But India gave him the opportunity for real political power, first at long distance in Westminster and then on the ground in Calcutta. Seeking money as well as mastery, he browbeat Hannah into joining him there as his companion. He soon lost her to marriage and Margaret to death and came to loathe the subcontinent and to disdain its people. The brilliant, farsighted legislator whom Clive so learnedly and readably evoked was also an evangelizing imperialist and again, but now enduringly, an ardent classicist. Convinced that "Greek literature" kept him sane after his double loss, Macaulay read Greek and Latin from five to eight almost every morning for more than three years in Calcutta. It amounted to the second and permanent of his classical conversions. Although he was now a chronic depressive shadowed by a death wish, he started prophesying a happy future propelled by "Progress" and "Utility" and resolved to write the *History* that would narrate its English origins and worldwide growth.[6]

Helping to rule India left him with time for writing as well as reading. In 1837 he published over 100 pages on Francis Bacon. Once famous on three continents and still controversial, his essay has never been closely read. A learned and cunning insinuation of his vision of England as progressive, calculating, nationalist, materialistic, and only culturally Protestant, "Bacon" is an achievement of the unknown Macaulay. What Macaulay wrote and implied there both illuminates everything he subsequently taught and predicts much that was widely accepted as common sense during Britain's century and afterward.

In Calcutta the unknown Macaulay also projected what became his most chilling achievement: he appears to have been the first responsible European to advocate publicly what the mid-twentieth century learned to call "genocide." From London during the summer of 1838, he wrote about Sir William Temple, a second-tier seventeenth-century politician and writer. Zachary had died on 13 May. Tom despised his father and, even more, the scheme of Zachary's antislavery allies to protect endangered native peoples against various European and American civilizing imperial projects. He turned "Sir William Temple" into a preemptive strike against those meddlesome "philanthropists." The essay proved to be as prescient as "Bacon." More than ever an enthusiast for human progress and English power, he insisted that "it is in truth more merciful to extirpate a hundred thousand human beings at once, and to fill the void with a well-governed population, than to misgovern millions through a long succession of generations." Presented as a counterfactual history of modern Ireland, his ethic of civilizing and imperial slaughter was embraced globally before World War I and practiced into the second half of the twentieth century. During all those murderous years no one publicly objected to what he advocated in "Temple" and reiterated elsewhere.[7]

Macaulay's diary during a sojourn in Italy in the autumn of 1838 and the early winter of 1839 exposes the brittle iron of his self-absorption. For almost a decade afterward his inner world is largely inaccessible, but the public record of his career of political and cultural power reveals much about the unknown man. Whether as a cabinet minister, a compelling orator, or a molder of the public mind, he regularly embellished his realistic calculations with lofty professions. Above all, Macaulay sold the British Empire. His thumping *Lays of Ancient Rome* instructed modern Britons in the bellicose virtues that made the Romans both imperial and great. In 1857 rebellion in India transformed his ballads into a bestseller and the surrogate national epic. Having long diagnosed Ireland as "the diseased part of the empire," he clinically monitored its depopulation by famine, disease, and emigration during the late 1840s.[8] Finally detaching himself from routine politics, he finished the first volumes of his great book. Informed by classical models, this modern history is at once pellucid and artful. Because Macaulay wanted to persuade different audiences to identify their nation with the state and themselves with its interests, he wrote in several voices, some of which have gone undetected.

The *History*'s immediate success matured into sustained and unrivaled popularity, in part because he was often misread as liberal-minded. Scared by revolutionaries and would-be revolutionaries in 1848, Macaulay in fact wrote as a fierce counterrevolutionary. His triumph made him anxious about falling short in future volumes, but seeing the famine-stricken Irish during his only visit to their island did not cause him to reappraise the human cost of his imperial ethic. It was, in any case, already gaining acceptance as the way of the world, perhaps unfortunate but likely the law of nature. Alive with concern about honor and respectability and devoid of any sense of guilt, Macaulay's intense classicism was widely shared. Its values therefore counted publicly as well as personally during his last decade; interconnected elites found in the ancients both refuge from contemporary theological divisiveness and an adjunct to—perhaps even a surrogate for—Christianity. Now wealthy, honored, and famous, Macaulay began living out his own cliché about the self-destructiveness of power: "ruinous to powerful himself."[9]

The Great Exhibition of 1851 validated his hope that progress would become England's common faith without motivating him to finish the even more rhetorical and amusing second installment of his book. Although he was widely accepted as a national sage, the discrepancy between his public voice—all eloquent optimism—and his experience became palpable. A potentially lethal medical regime too much in thrall to antiquity ravaged his last years. Surviving maltreated heart attacks, he completed two more volumes of his book, now a consensus history as well as a great commercial success. Neither his return to the House of Commons nor his subsequent elevation to the House of Lords rallied him to reengage domestic politics. But there could be no neglecting India. After managing the re-creation of its British bureaucracy for the benefit of the classically educated alumni of the ancient universities, he endured the trauma of the 1857 rebellion. In declining health and working as he pleased, he felt his death wish more insistently until the atrophied emotional consciousness that had stunted his humanity ceased to sustain his will to power.

[1]

HEIR

More than most of us, Thomas Babington Macaulay never outgrew his upbringing. He was the firstborn of Zachary. Tom rejected much in that autodidactic, arriviste, evangelical, and abolitionist authoritarian while assimilating at least as much. Zachary's success story was classically Scots. Nearing thirty in 1797, he wrote confessions that looked backward to St. Augustine's to edify himself and his fiancée, Selina Mills. Born with partial sight and later maiming an arm, he endured a hardscrabble childhood in a western fishing village as one of a Church of Scotland minister's dozen children. At fourteen apprenticeship in a Glasgow countinghouse ended his formal education and left him with "great regret" at losing the "hope of academical honors" that had energized him. He grew into a tough and anxious man. Almost on his own he acquired mathematics and modern English literature, French, and "a pretty general knowledge of the Latin language, and . . . such a tincture of Greek learning as enabled me to read Homer." For a lifetime he emulously respected classical learning and imposed it on his reluctant heir. Zachary's religion was less stable. In Glasgow he converted to freethinking under the influence of "men of wit and taste," hard-drinking coworkers, and the kind of "trashy" novel that Tom later devoured. Zachary also anticipated Tom's religious doubleness. In a society in which religion was normative and public doubt could be dangerous, hypocrisy was the compliment that any prudent freethinker paid to respectability. Zachary disguised his unbelief because he needed his father's Glasgow connections.[1]

The skeptical crisis that has ebbed and flowed in Europe and its extensions since the Renaissance touched first the father and then the son. For almost five hundred years doubts about the scope and limits of human knowledge, especially about the possibility of knowledge of the divine, have been variously embraced, resisted, and sublimated by luminaries such as Michel de Montaigne, René Descartes, David Hume, Friedrich Nietzsche, A. J. Ayer, and Jacques Derrida, along with countless unknowns. Both the nineteenth-century "Darwinian crisis of faith" and late twentieth-century "postmodernism" are episodes in the history of modern skepticism, not epiphanies. A witty twenty-first-century undergraduate blogs about her own condition: "At one point I called my mother and told her I was having an existential crisis. 'Oh no!' she cried. 'What's wrong?' I explained that I was stricken with doubt about the possibility of knowledge and whether my life had any meaning. 'Oh,' she said, sounding a little relieved. 'An actual existential crisis. I can't help with that.'"[2] The crisis becomes solvent not when skepticism afflicts individuals—Montaigne and the rest mostly led interesting and useful lives —but when it seems to permeate whole societies and melt their sense of collective meaning and, hence, of identity and purpose.

Shadowed by Descartes's doubt, an eighteenth-century Italian philosopher of history called that shared predicament "the barbarism of reflection." Grappling with the skeptical crisis decades earlier, a great contemporary of Descartes first wrote, "Whatever is, is in God, and without God nothing can be, or be conceived," and then added, "there does not exist a vacuum in nature . . . but all parts are bound to come together to prevent it."[3] No more can whole societies long endure emotional, moral, and intellectual vacuums. Because fundamental and ramifying doubt is irrefutable on its own terms, there is no transcending it. And so the recurrent skeptical crisis has spawned a parallel history of philosophical responses, religious revivals, ethical crusades, and political religions that have served to hold at bay, or at least disguise, the threat of enervating collective doubt. Zachary would respond to his crisis religiously and ethically. Personally as well as publicly, his firstborn discovered meaning and identity in a fervor for English civilization and imperial power that he helped to propagate.

At sixteen Zachary found work as a bookkeeper on a Jamaican plantation. Becoming "callous and indifferent" to the misery of the slaves, he maintained "an unbroken spirit" despite "extreme illness." His "outward conduct" was "sober and decorous" by local standards, but he looked back with a sense of shame on "a period of most degraded servitude to the worst of masters": Satan. His reading consoled him. Worldly-wise and charming, "Horace was my constant companion," providing a congenial "philosophy" as well as amusement; he also admired a poem by Voltaire. Soon he was regarded as "a kind of prodigy" by "my brother book-keepers and overseers, and even among planters and merchants." At the time he believed that his books provided him with "motives to support me from sinking under my trials," but later he attributed his survival to his own "constitutional firmness of nerve and to vanity." Zachary preserved his gloss on a line in Virgil's *Aeneid* in which a father encourages his son to battle by reminding him that life is short, death is ordained, and valor spreads renown: "however empty 'fame' may be considered in the eye of speculative philosophy, of all sublunary motives it certainly is the strongest, and properly directed, the desire of it becomes the source of the most brilliant actions."[4] He transmitted his steady faith in "fame" as a motivator to Tom, along with his reliance on reading as a therapy.

After returning to Britain in 1789 Zachary looked upward. Some of his siblings already inhabited worlds bigger than their parents'. Although they were innocent of the verb "to network," they cultivated proliferating ties of mutual support, constraint, and usefulness among family and friends to advance their ambitions. Zachary's bachelor brother Colin became a major general in India and eventually bequeathed a small fortune to his favorite nephew, Tom. More immediately, the husband of Zachary's sister Jean, an evangelical country gentleman named Thomas Babington, welcomed his brother-in-law to his Leicestershire estate and helped convert him to "vital religion" and the crusade to abolish slavery. Theirs was a relationship of tutelage and dependence. Babington coolly detailed Zachary's "chief faults," which were attributable to his "natural ardour of mind and firmness of character"—above all to his stubbornness—but he also recommended Macaulay to one of the leaders of the Clapham Sect, a group of mostly rich evangelical Anglicans living in a pious commune in that southwestern London suburb. Disciplined, resourceful, and well-connected, they wanted to use the state's power to impose their morality on the public and, by abolishing the trade, to strangle slavery throughout the empire.[5] Despite Zachary's increasingly English veneer, he remained culturally Scots.

At the end of 1790 leading Claphamites sent Zachary to Sierra Leone to investigate the failing settlement of freed slaves that they maintained there. His report earned him an appointment to the council of the company recently chartered to govern the colony and, more importantly, a place in the sect. By 1794 he was the governor of Sierra Leone, now more a business than a philanthropic venture. Returning home to recover from physical collapse, he sailed partway on a slaver to witness the horror of the passage. In Somerset Hannah More, the formidable doyenne of the Claphamites, provided him with hospitality and an introduction to Selina Mills, a daughter of a Quaker bookseller in Bristol and a protégée. After Zachary finished another tour in Africa, they married. Thomas Babington Macaulay was born on 25 October 1800 in Rothley Temple, the Babington manor house. By 1803 the Macaulays lived in Clapham as members of a privileged quasi-family, an arrangement that continued to advance Zachary's career. Ruling like a stern son of the manse when he was at home, he imposed an austere version of Scottishness on his family, particularly on his firstborn. Shrewd, efficient, and warm, Selina was also private and retiring—qualities that fostered her historical effacement. Bookish and often effectively a single parent, she doted on Tom. He was a prodigy, reading at three and talking like a book by four. Memorably, his father visited a great house to show him off, and a servant "spilt some hot coffee over his legs." When his hostess sought to comfort him, the little boy replied: "Thank you, madam, the agony is abated." Zachary wrote to Selina, "yours is the sole merit of his acquirements."[6]

An artifact of overreaching American social science captures something of the boy's intellectual power and promise. Published in 1926, when nature last trumped the claims of nurture among students of human development, *The Early Mental Traits of Three Hundred Geniuses* awarded Tom, along with Jeremy Bentham, Blaise Pascal, J. W. Goethe, and G. W. Leibniz, a childhood "IQ of 180 to 190." Only John Stuart Mill outranked them. "Macaulay's phenomenal precocity is well known. His AI IQ is rated on early intellectual brilliance and extraordinary literary production, combined with a memory the power of which has seldom been equaled and scarcely exceeded by any individual in the study." On the eve of adulthood, Selina's firstborn, who "reigned" at home whenever Zachary was away, adored her. Between 1802 and 1813 eight siblings—five sisters and three brothers—were born. Tom assumed the role of big brother to all of them. His two youngest sisters, Hannah and Margaret, whom he came to love uniquely, were toddlers when he left home for school.[7]

While trading with West Africa, first profitably and then disastrously, Zachary became a crusader against slavery. Alone among the leading British abolitionists, he commanded fluent French. It enabled him to establish an international reputation as the movement's ambassador-at-large and backstage technician. The Claphamite abolitionists understood that hope may be audacious, but successful politics is the art of the possible. They carefully managed their godly endeavors, adopting a top-down strategy to neutralize suspicions of them as pesky enthusiasts and radicals. To court worldly and powerful allies, they minimized their distinctively Christian language and beliefs and instead marketed their great cause with anodyne words like "liberty," "civilisation," and "philanthropy." Exploiting and popularizing a robust language of national uplift while also appealing to a calculus of economic self-interest, they advertised an appealing version of authentic Englishness. Their secular antislavery rhetoric succeeded in changing the public mind, but it risked depriving their religion of a public face. When Tom was thirteen, Zachary taught him that the Claphamites' philanthropy was "our political program."[8] During the 1820s and 1830s Tom promoted himself by exploiting many of Zachary's connections and championing elements of his politicized religion. Liberated from the faith of his father, he made himself famous as the champion of English civilization, liberty, and progress. More than the evangelical God, that trinity promised to supply a new moral consensus for the nation.

Coherent religious attitudes, opinions, and practices united the Clapham Sect during its prime between the 1790s and the late 1820s. Years later Tom corrected his pious sister Fanny's assertion that they "were too obscure."[9] After enumerating the religious and philanthropic societies they founded, their contributions to popular education, their role as "the destroyers of the Slave trade and of Slavery," and their political impact in India as well as Britain, he insisted that the "whole organization of the Evangelical party was their work." He found it "needless to speak of Wilberforce" (William "the Emancipator") and instead explained to her the centrality of Wilberforce's Cambridge mentor, Charles Simeon, whose "real sway in the Church was far greater than any primate."[10]

Over decades as a Cambridge don and vicar of Holy Trinity Church there, Simeon developed a genius both for converting likely young men like Wilberforce and for playing church politics. Simeon's theology provides a convenient window onto the Claphamites' distinctive beliefs. Daniel Wilson, a disciple who long served as the minister of the London chapel frequented by the Macaulays and their circle, wrote an appendix to Simeon's *Memoirs* that summarizes his characteristic doctrines. It suggests something of both their appeal and their vulnerability. Genteelly Anglican, Simeon and his Clapham friends disdained public displays of enthusiasm and emotion.[11] Deep feeling nonetheless infused their religion. Two hundred years on, their language and sensibility may seem glib, alien, or odd, but it rested on a certain realism about the human prospect and an internal logic that evoked in believers powerful motives for action. Simeon's assurance that by embracing his own suffering he shared in Christ's cross of atonement energized him. Original sin ravaged the moral economy of the universe, and personal sin intensified its effects, but Christ, by voluntarily substituting himself for sinful humanity, atoned for sin, bearing and sparing us the ultimate punishment our race deserves. For Simeon and like-minded believers, it was in Christ crucified that the invisible God dealt personally with men and women.

Sustained discipline made devout evangelical Anglicans activist and long-suffering Christians. In Christ's cross they found meaning in their individual and collective miseries, which became for them more than arbitrary afflictions or inklings of final nullity. Simeon, for example, "meekly bore for Christ's sake the cross imposed upon him. He returned good for evil. He subdued the old man within him. He looked above creatures and instruments to the hand which sent them." Such discipline was hard-won personal knowledge as well as the fruit of conversion. It could be preached and modeled by one person for another's benefit but never inherited or imposed. Once redeemed by Christ, a believer had to continue living not as she wanted but on God's terms, which by human standards routinely seemed unfair and often cruel. By doing everything she could but then surrendering and embracing what life gave her, she gained the reassurance that hers was the grace of authentic conversion to her crucified Savior. She learned to trust Him. When Tom was twenty-two, manifestly unconverted, and a provocateur, Zachary railed but then told Selina, "I desire to receive it as a part of my merited chastisement at the hand of God."[12]

Evangelical Anglicans cooperated with Dissenters and others in various godly and philanthropic projects but were sensitive to the difference between themselves as insiders and the rest as outsiders. One of Simeon's clerical protégés sniffed, "Popery is the religion of Cathedrals—Protestantism of houses—Dissenterism of barns." The sentence condenses his party's idea of the church. Unlike the Roman Catholics' formalism and priestcraft ("Cathedrals"), evangelical Anglicans' religion (real "Protestantism") was lay and only lightly invested in sacraments and institutions. Shunning the Dissenters' potentially wild subjectivity ("barns"), evangelical Anglicans insisted on respecting social distinctions and upheld the social and political order embodied in the establishment. Moving from Eton to King's College, Cambridge, Simeon was a lifelong snobby old boy. In his *Memoirs,* he lavishly excoriated himself for the sins of "my early life"—"my vanity, my folly, my wickedness"—while carefully showing that he possessed a proper gentleman's classical education. Immune to self-hatred, Simeon knew his place and took it as God-given: "I might live as my servants do, but I should be wrong." The Claphamites for their part understood that rank mattered, not least because it gave them political standing: "Constituted as the world is, example and influence will be the more efficacious, the more personal consequence is attached to them; and personal consequence will be measured by strangers, nay, insensibly by those who are not strangers, in a certain degree by external appearances."[13] It was a life lesson for Tom Macaulay.

Decrying the prevalence of nominal Christianity within the "higher and middle classes," William Wilberforce sought to reclaim them for vital religion: "The general notion appears to be, that, if born in a country of which Christianity is the established religion, we are born Christians. We do not therefore look out for positive evidence of being out of that number; but putting the *onus probandi* (if it may be so expressed) on the wrong side, we conceive ourselves such *of course,* except our title be disproved by positive evidence to the contrary." Hypothetically, Wilberforce and his friends had three options for resolving the tension between increasing the number of top-drawer "real Christians" and reducing the population of Anglicans who were nominally Christians. They could secede from the establishment and constitute themselves as a separate denomination, or disestablish the church and transform it into a less numerous but generally more committed group, or strengthen the church by using state power to enforce the kind of discipline that would make Britain a home fit for saints. Wilberforce found secession unthinkable and abhorred disestablishment because it would "greatly endanger our civil institutions."[14] Tom Macaulay would learn to assent.

In 1797 it seemed possible for the state, waging a counterrevolutionary war with France and repressing internal dissent, to enforce the regimen the Claphamites wanted to grow vital Christianity. Thus invigorated, the church could propel Britain into the "millennium of the future." When Wilberforce died in 1833, both that possibility and the Anglican religious monopoly belonged to history. Divisions within the establishment were multiplying, and Zachary Macaulay and his generation increasingly seemed like anachronisms. By 1847 Daniel Wilson recalled that the "moderation and comprehension of the Church of England was [Simeon's] joy—as it is of all her best members. A thousand—ten thousand—opinions on difficult or subordinate questions are all equally compatible with a conscientious obedience to her rules of discipline and form of sound words." Using Simeon as a mouthpiece, Wilson accepted that a comprehensive church must now mirror a permanently diverse nation. After the Claphamite moment, England was still in the market for a viable, culturally Protestant moral consensus. By renaming as "progress" the millennium Zachary Macaulay hoped would usher in Christ's Second Coming and compellingly preaching its "wonders yet unseen," Tom, safely anchored in the present along with his father, helped to create a substitute here.[15]

Often the evangelical Anglicans appeared more discriminating socially than theologically. Simeon favored *"Moderation on contested and doubtful points of theology,"* which meant admitting "man's profound ignorance" and refusing "to proceed one step beyond the fair and obvious import of Divine Revelation." Keeping "the Bible as his perpetual standard" and with due respect for "all the apparent difficulties" in trying to reconcile texts, he "never ventured to push conclusions from Scripture into metaphysical refinement." Determined not to "speculate on matters placed far above human comprehension," Simeon refused to try reasoning from revealed premises to theological inferences. His was a bounded view of our knowledge of God. For him and other evangelical Anglicans, the private judgment of every believer who read the Bible was reasonable and inviolate. The real church would remain invisible until the end of time. Meanwhile, the Word of God enlightened individuals rather than informing them as members of a visible communion. In 1823 Zachary Macaulay visited the aged novelist Fanny Burney in Paris. His report captured his sense of the limited utility of any church. She was now "a thorough Roman Catholic in heart": "Poor thing! She seems utterly lost amid the mazes of controversy, and what she seems to desire is an infallible authority on which to repose. All ends in this: to be saved the trouble and risk of deciding for oneself and judging of one's own state."[16] Burney was responding in her own way to the skeptical crisis that shaped both Zachary and Tom Macaulay.

Instead of pursuing the chimera of "an infallible authority," the Claphamites sought to root their theological parsimony in the terra firma of English reason: the opinions of most practical-minded gentlemen. Simeon was sometimes compared to Francis Bacon. Both considered "not theories, but facts; not what agreed with principles, but principles themselves; not hidden matters, but phenomena; not speculation, but practice, as the points of greatest moment." The evangelical Anglicans' resistance to elaborate theology depended on a division of mental labor already ancient when Bacon wrote. Philosophy, he asserted, belonged to reason, while religion, including "divine poesy," was the province of the imagination: "poetry relieves us by unexpected turns and changes, and thus not only delights, but inculcates morality and nobleness of soul. Which it may be justly esteemed of a Divine nature, as it raises the mind, by accommodating the images of things to our desires, and not, like history and reason, subjecting the mind to things."[17] Tom would also learn those lessons and adapt them to his own purposes.

By anchoring Christian faith in the domain of imagination, evangelical Anglicans found mental security. Nurtured and regulated through Bible-reading and prayer, it enabled them to control both the images they formed of external reality and their own conduct. Revelation worked on believers' imaginations to direct their wills. After Zachary's first conversion he knew that if "a man can once be persuaded to make the Bible his rule of acting and judging, he will become a Christian of course." The secular complement of revelation was knowledge of polite letters, which inculcated decorum. Zachary and his friends created collective and personal structures that enabled them to achieve an uncommon, seemingly objective personal discipline. It trumped speculation and exorcised doubt. Because their sense of their own selfhood was irreducibly subjective—God and me—enthusiasm and antinomianism scared them, and they battled "the pleasures of imagination." Despite Zachary's conversion, he often found himself distracted by "wandering thoughts." He counterattacked with his vigorous literacy. "On principle" he was "quite a peripatetic" while he read. Walking helped him to "derive a greater fixedness of mind to any object which I wish to contemplate." To fix on God, Zachary paced the room, "pronouncing at the same time distinctly my thoughts as they arise, but not of course audibly."[18] Tom grew up to be a walking though skeptical reader.

The Clapham Sect's resistance to thinking deeply about their Christianity deprived them of the intellectual capital they needed to transmit their religious meaning and identity to their children. By locating Christianity in their houses and treating their public doctrine as essentially a "political program," they worked to confine their beliefs to the private domain and to merge them publicly with respectability as well as with civilization, liberty, and progress. With care, their children could acquire the "sense of abiding responsibility" and know what to do and avoid. There was, however, no transmitting the subjective essence of faith from one generation to the next. Not mere reason and persuasion but the personal conversion that an inscrutable God either gave or withheld and its practical fruits yielded saving faith in Jesus Christ.

Believing that good works followed justification by faith in Christ, the Claphamites were moralistic. Conversion was usually progressive rather than a single transforming experience and the promised victory rarely certain in anyone. Disciplines that inculcated self-regulation enabled self-transcendence and formed repentant converts into saints. Thus Zachary controlled his days by allotting exact periods to his every activity, from dressing ("about half an hour") to a series of specialized spiritual labors: "About five minutes more may be taken up in a general anticipation of the work of the day, and in calling up proper considerations to strengthen me to meet with foreseen difficulties." Though devoid of his father's aptitude for time management, Tom imbibed and shared his yen for respectability. The Claphamites' high earnestness provoked some of their contemporaries to derision and a few of their descendants, including Virginia Woolf, to condescension.[19] But she lived in twentieth-century Bloomsbury, not in Tom Macaulay's Westminster.

The same drive to achieve consistent personal responsibility that made the Claphamites hard on themselves made them hard on other people. When, for example, Prime Minister William Pitt ("the Younger"), a friend of Wilberforce, counterrevolution, and abolition, died in 1806, Zachary, though a political supporter, broadcast his "very deep regret that a regular attendance upon the duties of public worship did not constitute a part of the character of this illustrious politician." Knowing that in a hierarchical society like Britain the great must be conspicuously good and pious to uplift their inferiors, Zachary insisted that "the general course" of a life "must be allowed to be the least fallible test of human character." It amounted to accepting the rule of cause and effect in life: was a person regularly willing and able to take care of himself and to accept the consequences of his actions, both here and in the hereafter? In public policy, the Claphamites seemed to turn self-reliance into a virtual gospel. Generally opposed to state intervention in the marketplace—the nation's moral economy was another matter—they also accepted as a causal law the Reverend Thomas Malthus' prophecy of inevitable mass starvation brought on by improvident breeding.[20] In puffing self-reliance, Tom was enduringly Zachary's son.

Families like the Macaulays were economic as well as emotional and cultural units. Their complex interdependence belied the vocabulary of autonomous selfhood that proliferated in much of the nineteenth-century Atlantic world. Notwithstanding exhortations to adult ("manly") self-reliance, cultivating and multiplying connections that both supported and constrained individuals remained a moral, social, and economic imperative. The Macaulays, along with their kin and friends, were not closed nuclear families supporting an "affective individualism" that encouraged everyone to pursue her own happiness. Their interdependence extended to minutiae. When Tom was thirty-two, an M.P., and secretary to the Board of Control of the British East India Company, Zachary routinely used his son's official mailing privilege to send personal letters to his Babington in-laws. Family cohesion was a reality that shaped Tom Macaulay's life and hastened his death. For all that, the Claphamites' language of affection could be almost clinical in its tentativeness. On their seventeenth wedding anniversary, Zachary wrote to Selina detailing his defects and insisting on his "great and growing happiness." Its foundations were his "fond domestic enjoyment," "the children whom God has given us, and the pleasing hopes He allows us to indulge respecting them," and her "undeviating care and kindness, and forbearance and devotion." He also assured her "of the undiminished warmth of my attachment, and of my *increasing* regard and affection."[21]

The trend was preferable to a decrease, but their oldest son grew up craving an effusion. Writing as an absent paterfamilias after twenty-one years of marriage, Zachary reminded Selina that he valued "the course of regular and consistent discipline, applying chiefly to the state and temper of the mind, which it is in the power of parents to pursue; the affectionate but decisive check imposed upon bad dispositions; the vigilance exercised to all indications of bad humour shown by pouting, harsh tones, and quick and unkind replies." Understandably, he associated the words "discipline" and "affectionate" when describing the proper relations between parents and children and among siblings. Control in Selina's and Zachary's house tightened on Sundays, which they observed as a Scottish Sabbath. Between morning and evening church services he read sermons to his whole household and decreed that "walking, for walking's sake was never allowed."[22] Resenting that stern regime for a lifetime, Tom relished his Sunday power walks.

Christian charity had little to do with Zachary's treatment of his heir. It worked to belie the metaphor of God's loving paternity and instead taught the boy to regard human affection as a dear and mostly fraught thing. Socially ambitious and presiding over a vigorously literate household, Zachary and Selina wanted their children to receive the formal education Zachary lacked. Above all, Tom's father worked to form him into a prodigy who would grow up to lead the conversion of England into a godly nation. The precocious boy-man he nurtured became a kind of missionary, but his evangel would not be Zachary's. By first cosseting Tom and then favoring him with noisy reproof and sere affection, Zachary made him the center of the family's home: self-conscious, ambitious, and increasingly resentful. Tom spent a lifetime trying to recapture or replicate the happiness of his childhood when his father was absent. He saw his family as a virtual church, the haven of unique devotion, support, and obligation. But even out of sight, his father was inescapable. When the boy was seven, Zachary reproved his handwriting: "Your last letter I think, is still worse written than the two former. When you write you ought to take pains to do it well. Indeed whatever you do, it shd. be the g[oa]l. to do well." Zachary insisted that pleasing him was the condition for enjoying God's favor: "Unless you are thus docile and obedient, you cannot expect, my dear children, that Jesus Christ shd. love you or give you his blessing."[23]

An image Tom retained from infancy captures Zachary's rule: "He remembered standing up at the nursery window by his father's side, looking at a cloud of black smoke pouring out of a tall chimney. He asked if that was hell; an inquiry that was received with a grave displeasure which at the time he could not understand. The kindly father must have been pained, almost against his will, at finding what feature of his creed it was that had embodied itself in so very material a shape before his little son's imagination."[24] The story was retold by Tom's adoring nephew and biographer. Its substance belies his cheerful gloss. For the child, the eternal punishment due chronically irresponsible behavior readily "embodied itself" in smoky perdition. But the "kindly father" offered his son no more powerful image of enjoying paradise with his Savior, which was the essence of his own faith. For a lifetime Tom recalled Zachary's "grave displeasure." It taught him about the inexorability of power and control in both politics and human relations.

Tom read "incessantly," memorizing many pages, and talked and wrote prodigiously. Before he was seven he produced "a compendium of Universal History," and more followed; but he rebelled against the schoolroom's drill. His beloved youngest sister Margaret heard the pious version of his being sent to a day school in Clapham during his sixth year: "'Now, my dear Tom,'" Selina warned, "'you must not expect to have bread and butter given to you at school; I hope you will learn to do without' . . . After a moment's pause, he said with great energy:—'No mamma, industry shall be my bread and application my butter.'" Here his nephew did not gloss the reality: "no one ever crept more unwillingly to school. Each several afternoon he made piteous entreaties to be excused from returning" after the noon meal. At twelve he was shipped in tears to be bullied in a small private school near Cambridge run by one of Simeon's clerical disciples: "I do not remember being ever more gloomy in my life than when I first left Clapham." Already intimidated by the heir he had wrought, Zachary wanted him out of the house but under tight control in order to correct his faults and preserve him from evil influences. He rejected Hannah More's sensible plan to send Tom as a day student to Westminster, a great London public school, where he would have intelligent competition and companionship, along "with the safety of the paternal hearth during all the intervals of study." Then and in the future he was disposed to be what the twentieth century called a "loner": "a person who avoids company and prefers to be alone."[25]

As much as Tom's family and their religion, his education marked him for the rest of his life. What he studied and how he studied had more in common with the Renaissance, indeed with late antiquity, than with the early twenty-first century. In Clapham his primer was the *Eton Latin Grammar,* which began as a sixteenth-century textbook. Years of repetitive exercises lay ahead: parsing, scanning, memorizing, and translating. At thirty, he mocked a foe by recommending that he improve his learning and manners by giving "an hour every morning to our old friend Corderius." That was Mathurin Cordier, whose sixteenth-century manual led boys of nine or ten from construing simple Latin sentences to more demanding fare, often moralizing and socializing. "Corderius" taught privileged schoolboys the theory that justified their backward-looking education. Learning decorum in a dead language, they also learned to associate politeness with learning good letters: Latin and later perhaps Greek. The ancient texts instilled polished words and behavior into well-disposed boys. After antiquity Latin became primarily a male language, often beaten into youths who misbehaved during their drills or botched them. Docility and accuracy spared them from blows. Competence in Latin helped them to sublimate their aggression into stylized combat with words and to make their routine behaviors sociable.[26] But such gentlemen were also jealous of their honor, and, when provoked, they could revert to physical violence. In 1838 Macaulay barely avoided a duel.

During his schooldays the preeminence of the classical educational regime was widely questioned. Its defenders successfully counterattacked by urging the intellectual benefit of devoting years to the study of one or two dead languages: the old curriculum instilled in boys the mental discipline they needed to compete and win in a modern society in which gentlemen were increasingly made as well as born. In Corderius' pages class mattered, but there it was usually ascribed, a family legacy rather than a man's own achievement. In Macaulay's Britain birth also mattered, but many individuals were socially outgrowing their families. He often

depicted himself as "a parvenu," a self-made man who harbored "a profound contempt for rank, fashion, power, popularity, and money."[27] He
neither was nor did, but he convinced himself that he owed everything
to the talents and education that enabled him to compete and win. Eventually, he acquired the cultural and political power he needed to help
turn a theory about the utility of classical studies into an imperial policy.

Fueled by ambition for the prodigy, fear of him, and memories of his
own godless youth, Zachary's direction of Tom's education was dangerously intrusive and unsystematic. A busy autodidact, he failed to establish
an educational program for his son apart from the schoolroom, effectively leaving Tom to indulge his bibliophagy. After shipping the boy off
to Matthew Preston's school in February 1813, Zachary tried to control his education at long distance. It would be classical, with Greek taking pride of place, and rhetorical. Tom would learn how to manipulate
words to engage, persuade, and control. In a series of letters, Zachary
blamed his heir, small, delicate, and ungainly, when he complained about
being beaten by "big boys." Selina played the good cop: "You have hitherto been the only topic of conversation since you left us." After itemiz-
ing his "very busy week" as one of those "who are much concerned in
doing good to their fellow creatures" and hectoring Tom for sundry intellectual and moral faults, Zachary closed a letter by exhorting him to
learn Greek well. It was "the very finest language extant." As usual, Tom
tried to obey his father, though that language "intimidated" him. It is
possible to trace his growing estrangement from his implacable father by
contrasting the wary, mostly factual letters that Zachary required of him
with the long, affectionate, and playful ones he composed for Selina.[28]

Studying the classics was inseparable from classical rhetoric, still "a basic tool of power and cultural integrity" in nineteenth-century Britain.
Strikingly bashful and homesick, but also articulate, retentive, and often
underworked, Tom helped to establish "a spouting club" modeled on his
grammar-school debating society. The press alerted him to the parliamentary debate over revising the charter of the East India Company,
which provided for teaching Indians English "in order to promote Science and Christianity." Exercises in English and Latin composition took
the form of writing "letters from persons renowned in history to each
other." He also learned how to manipulate the requisite "specious arguments" to compose speeches in which he "spoke against my conscience"

and, by imitating Cicero's "masterly Oration against Catiline," how to acquire "the art of the Climax."[29]

Tom was so dutiful and bright that Preston indulged his intense and random self-education. Although plane geometry, like all other mathematics, bored and tried him, half-yearly examinations introduced Tom to male competitiveness and the pleasures of victory. A "Greek examination, in which, as I beat all the others in the class I am to receive a prize" left him in "very high spirits." But the classroom was safer than outside, where "the big boys" continued bullying him. He came to depend on a respected older boy: "I am completely safe under his protection." It taught him a permanent lesson about the necessity of patronage in hierarchical societies. There were other lessons that would serve him for life. Desiring to return home happy and "triumphant," he knew that his success "depends much on myself," on being "up and fagging before five in the morning," and that failure would be "my fault." His schedule included a weekly afternoon of privacy. He read a translation of Plutarch, an ancient who decades later helped him to write modern English history, and learned "a chapter in the Greek Testament . . . with the aid of our bibles, and without doing it with a dictionary"—it was how he came to learn all foreign languages. But Mr. Preston's effort to control his reading by allowing him to borrow only "one book at a time . . . till I have read it through" failed.[30] He carried a habit of diffusion with him to the grave.

A teary and self-dramatizing letter to his mother after returning from summer holiday brought down his father's rebuke. Zachary commanded him to "pray to God" for "that calm fortitude and serenity of mind which it is our duty to cultivate under all circumstances": "fix your eyes on that meek and patient Lamb of God whose language and whose life exhibit one uniform and striking example of self denial and resignation and holy and cheerful obedience." Then he decreed, "It is the will of your parents, and therefore the will of God, that you should be placed where you are; and you must be sensible that it is for your own benefit and advantage, not for their pleasure, that they have made that arrangement." Zachary's arrogation of divinity would eventually boomerang against himself and his God, but in the short run it inhibited Tom. Reading "ten times as much as I did at home," he found contentment in books, not in people. Although he enjoyed walking and began "to sit and joke with the boys in the school-room," he delighted in a room of his own, where behind a locked "monstrous oak door" he could exclaim, "I am King here," and read at will.[31]

In what he knew as social graces and we call social skills he remained backward. John Clive thought that Tom, emotionally delicate and greedy for admiration and affection, forged a cover of toughness that protected "him as a battering ram as well as a shield." Perhaps, but Zachary's hectoring continued—"a loud and boisterous tone," "proneness unduly to estimate talent in others," "a tendency to laugh at whatever is capable of being made ridiculous in others," and so on—and Tom's political education deepened. He became more adept at fighting with words, at placating or evading his father, and at positioning himself to anticipate the winning side. When he was fourteen, his letters to his parents sounded ever more erudite and mature and sometimes suggest furtiveness and distancing. He reported home that he was the target of a bully—"I was generally beaten or taunted by him ten times a day"—but only after his tormentor left school. In quoting Latin to his mother, he condescended to her: "Papa must construe it to you." French served as the second language in which he occasionally communicated with her and other educated women.[32]

Tom mounted his first public offensive in his battle of wills with his "Papa" just before Christmas 1816 in the pages of the *Christian Observer,* which Zachary then edited. It was a clever exercise in requital. Almost two years earlier Zachary had punished Tom's manifold indiscipline—Preston was an avid reporter—by requiring him to index the journal's thirteenth volume. With characteristic shrewdness, Hannah More cautioned Zachary that it was a wise but rather cruel way of dulling "his genius." Tom's account to her of what he felt suggests wry anger: "Index-making, though the lowest, is not the most useless round in the ladder of literature; and I pride myself upon being able to say that there are many readers of the Christian Observer who could do without Walter Scott's works, but not without those of, My dear madam, Your affectionate friend." Zachary, remembering his own misspent youth, scorned reading novels as a time-wasting source of temptation. In the early winter of 1816 he received a letter defending the practice signed only "Candidus." It was from Tom, who already knew his Voltaire, including *Candide.* His moralistic defense duped Zachary, who published it to a largely hostile

reaction. Apprehending his heir's mischief and feeling "betrayed," he re-
taliated by requiring him to write a long retraction. John Clive found "in
all this a prankish strain of gaiety and panache." Perhaps, but two years
later while reading "Cicero's Epistles" Tom reported to Zachary a hor-
rifying discovery: "duplicity." He reproachfully quoted many examples
that illustrated Cicero's dictum that "we must dissemble if we would live
in the world." After a last blast against him—"baseness, profligacy and
hypocrisy"—he proposed to bid "farewell to Cicero": "My heart relents
over him while I abuse him.—He was such a man, such a genius!" Then
he offered Zachary an excursus on the worthy theology of "that Prince
of Ancient poets, the Sublime, the Incomparable Eschylus."[33] Tom's doctrinal parsimony would be as constant as his reliance on Cicero.

Tom was assimilating other commonplaces that perpetuated the authority of the ancients among modern gentlemen. He faulted Hume for
his hostility toward religion, assuring his mother that it was "the most
important topic in every point of view that ever occupied the attention
of man." Hume was, however, the first writer in English to "produce a
History equal to any of the Classical Models in elegance" and "superior
to them in authenticity." Tom regarded the ancient historians' authority
as uneven and finally limited, because Christian Europe had superseded
their moral world. For all his success with the ancients, he remained their
reluctant student. At sixteen he faulted his education in familiar terms:
"far greater attention . . . is paid to the ancient than the modern classics."
"England," he knew, "can boast of a literature which . . . need not shrink
from a contest with those of Athens or of Rome; and which . . . deserves
to be as much attended too [sic]." When Zachary heard of this assertion—Tom could not trust the discretion of others—he was not amused,
and Tom again backed down: "you see that my doubts as to the expediency of Classical literature are merely speculative. Indeed were it only
that a certain degree of respectability is attached by common consent to
proficiency in the languages of Greece and Rome, it would be the duty
of every person who desired to qualify himself for extensive usefulness
to devote a certain degree of attention to them." Even as he wondered
why "we spend the ten most important years of our life" learning about
an extinct and narrow world, classical allusions began shaping how he
talked about not only contemporary politics but also one of his father's
real estate deals.[34] Against his will the ancients were beginning to own
his mind as well as his words.

Rhetoric ensured their control. Tom read the great Demosthenes "in a good humour," weighing his speeches against those of Cicero, duplicitous but still "the greatest prose writer that the world has produced." Demosthenes possessed an "eloquence which consists in the force and energy of ideas simply but nervously expressed . . . the eloquence of all countries, of all ages, of all assemblies. At the bar, in the senate, from the pulpit, from the chair of the professor, from the hustings of palace yard, Demosthenes would have been heard with attention and delight." And again: "Eloquence and history are the two branches of literature which . . . we must yield to the ancients," and he attributed the enduring superiority of their speeches to "the negligence of our orators." It was anomalous that modern historians "have not far excelled" the ancients, because "moral philosophy is closely connected with history," and "immense advances" had occurred there since antiquity. Tom assured Zachary that "the superior advances which we have made in moral sciences must be wholly ascribed" to Christianity, which both Hume and Edward Gibbon, "our most admired historians," scorned.[35] Tom said much the same thing about history at twenty-seven, only to reverse himself seven years later after rediscovering the ancients' power.

Always the master of what he read, he was the heir of centuries of Christians who evacuated or effaced the specifically "pagan" religious content of ancient texts in order to discover their permanent interest. Evacuation and effacement were among the techniques Macaulay would later use to marginalize the Christianity of writers such as John Milton and John Dryden and of modern England's history in an effort to modernize the nation. His serious reading became more wide-ranging. In volumes by Zachary's acquaintance J. C. L. Simonde de Sismondi, a Genevan polymath, he discovered the vernacular literatures of the Continent. He "sate for hours considering and resolving" and memorizing Sismondi's vision of the eclipse of Europe, "which is now the Empire of the arts and sciences, of Civilization and of greatness." In future centuries, it could "sleep in the dust" like ancient Rome, reflected on and moralized about by civilized people "of other languages, other manners, other religions" from the other side of the globe.[36] That pessimistic vision lingered in his mind, deeper and perhaps more credible than the hope in progress that he trumpeted for most of his adult life.

Like Zachary, Tom possessed a formidable memory, but his was schooled in the ancient arts of mnemonics. His nephew remembered

his "extraordinary faculty of assimilating printed matter at first sight."
His sister reported that he once told her that his practice of "castle-
building" explained his factual accuracy and enabled him to construct
history "into romance." Contemporaries who lacked Tom's rhetorical
education were baffled, and one scholar has treated his mental architecture as a psychological need fed by trauma or by a longing to escape the
uncertain present for a secure past made in his mind. His practice of
castle-building owed more to the psychology of cognition than to the
psychology of personality. As much as the sixteenth-century Italian Jesuit Matteo Ricci reinventing himself as a Chinese mandarin, he along
with countless others trained in classical rhetoric knew how to memo-
rize words and concepts by linking chains of images.[37] Cicero taught all
of them how to construct and describe a place so that its mental architect virtually saw it and retained it accurately. Translated back into words,
the rhetorician's images became accessible to his audience.

Although the technique fostered a vivid accuracy, its classical practi-
tioners were innocent of modern notions of objectivity. In *De Oratore*
Cicero tried to subject all humane learning to rhetoric. As much as oratory, philosophy, history, and literature were liberal arts of persuasion. The
ethical responsibility of those who practiced any of them was to teach, to
please, and to move—always to some useful end. Whether reading, speaking, or writing, the artful rhetorician must exercise control over both
himself and his materials. It was an office incompatible with detachment but, as Niccolò Machiavelli understood three centuries before Tom
Macaulay, entirely consistent with imposture. Looking forward to Cambridge, he knew that "in oratory, in philosophic writing, and I think
above all in criticism, (witness the Treatise De Oratore,) . . . [Cicero] tran-
scends any writer that any country has seen."[38]

Tom kept his political bridges to Zachary in good repair. It was otherwise with religion. During the late winter and early spring of 1814 Tom
worked on an epic, "The Conquest of Ireland," twenty-seven pages of
which survive in a transcription made by his favorite niece. The opening
parroted *The Aeneid,* Virgil's epic of the birth of imperial Rome—"Arms
and the man I sing." Tom's poem, like its model, meant to do justice to
the vanquished, but it depicted the enmity between the English and the
Irish as primordial, reminiscent of that between the Romans and the
Carthaginians. At about the same time he wrote an "Essay on Patrio-

tism," which tempered Englishness with Christian universality. It was another judgment he would reverse under classical influence. In 1814 he
also composed a hymn that was music for his father's ears: "But that
Lord so great so high / Has sent his Son for man to die." His pious voice
proved unsustainable. Three years later he copied out for Zachary a poetic exercise "on the idea of Horace's Carmen Seculare; which is, you
know, a series of blessings upon the Roman people, and wishes for their
grandeur and prosperity during the coming century." The muse of his
"lay" was "the mighty theme" of "my country's fame, my country's fates,"
and he assimilated the greatness of "Albion" (or "Britannia") to that of
"Rome and Athens." His patriotism only intensified and decades later
animated his own hugely popular "Roman" ballads. God, however, was
absent from the three closely printed pages of verse he shared with Zachary in 1817. Five months later, with matriculation at Trinity College,
Cambridge, approaching, Tom quoted for him a passage from "the Incomparable Eschylus" preserved "by one of the Christian fathers . . . from
a tragedy now lost"—it was a misattribution. By now he had embraced
Cicero's worldly-wise dissembling. In Tom's translation, God "controuls,
pervades, inspires, Creation's frame" while remaining unknowable to a
"vain mortal." He assured his father that Aeschylus' vision of the all-
pervading but hidden "nature of the Deity" was "well worthy of a Christian poet."[39]

At seventeen Tom sought to accommodate what he read as Aeschylus'
acceptably vague theology to his single-minded father's faith. Zachary
indulged his son's experiments because he saw in Tom's unblemished
character and punctilious deference signs of openness to religious enlightenment. On 24 November 1818 Zachary passed along to Hannah
More a letter from Tom in Cambridge addressed to one of his sisters—
again there was no privacy—and commented: "May God preserve him
in his present apparent purity and simplicity of mind." Zachary would
soon learn more about unanswered prayers but nothing about parenting.
A life-threatening fever that spring had left Tom "fat . . . and his figure
was always bad since, which was made worse by his inattention to dress":
another gaucherie that provided grist for his father's mill of rebuke. John
Clive located the origins of Tom's persistently "unconverted state" in
Preston's school and traced it to "a temperamental difference between
father and son." But it was Zachary's heedlessness and hectoring that

worked to turn his heir against him and away from the God for whom he claimed to speak. Clapham, however, remained as inescapable as Cicero.[40]

Cambridge

For more than two years Tom dwelled outside the charmed walls of Trinity, academically and socially the most prestigious of Cambridge's colleges. To protect the purity his heir would need to lead England's re-generation, Zachary compelled him to lodge with some other sons of the converted in—almost inevitably—Jesus Lane. Lacking intimacy apart from his family and their circle, understanding books better than people, homely, and physically awkward, Tom afterward remembered subordi-nating himself to other students in order to court their affection. Then by speaking his own mind fluently, confidently, and often, he learned how to master his fellows through persuasion or intimidation. In Octo-ber 1818 the establishment was omnipresent in the university. Its roots in the medieval church showed in the names of its colleges and in the celibate divines who governed them and taught their students. Until the 1850s only Anglicans could take Cambridge degrees. In 1818 the established churches of England, Scotland, and Ireland dominated the United Kingdom. Within a decade, however, Dissenters and Roman Catholics were included in the political nation, though on an unequal footing. Apart from Quakers, only those who swore "upon the true faith of a Christian" could sit in Parliament. Jews were excluded until 1858. Though a huge institutional presence, the Anglican establishment was on the defensive. During Tom's first year at Trinity continuing fears of revo-lution sustained the assault on the publicly irreligious. In the spring of 1819 the Society for the Suppression of Vice, of which Zachary was an ornament, initiated the prosecution of the veteran radical Richard Car-lile on charges of sedition and blasphemy for republishing Tom Paine's *The Age of Reason* and another freethinking tract. In Cambridge an un-derground of privileged and clever students disillusioned with Christi-anity became adept at subterfuge. Tom Macaulay would join it.

Mapping the surface of his university years is easy, but their depths require careful excavating. Within days of moving into Jesus Lane, Tom pledged his resolve to Zachary. The "evils of Cambridge . . . were evils which must be sought," and he trusted that "the goodness of God, my own education, and the connections which I have formed will preserve me." Then he confided what he needed from his father and summarized the beliefs they shared. He understood that to earn Zachary's "quiet approbation"—"I am sure that I never valued any human applause so much"—he must self-reliantly and successfully compete to perfect "those weapons of assault and that armour of defence which literature furnishes for such contests" with "the enemies of humanity." They would first "triumph together," and then Tom would "inherit your public objects . . . and succeed to your benevolent enterprises." He was already treating as down-to-earth causes much of what his father privately read as signs of God's grace. For Tom religion now amounted to an extension of philanthropy by other means. He wrote a few weeks later of "motives [that], if they spring from earth, tend to heaven." During his first weeks in Cambridge he read only "grave Latin and Greek." Despite interruptions—"the chapel breaks upon my morning studies"— he was now eagerly assimilating ancient texts whole. Zachary's Christianity remained powerless to convert Tom, whereas Homer's "effulgence casts a shade on every other creation of Human genius." Early in the next term Tom competed for an English verse medal and asked his father to "criticize it with the utmost severity." When Zachary obliged at length, Tom asked rhetorically if "no literary employment is estimable or laudable which does not lead to the inculcation of moral truth or the excitement of virtuous feeling" and answered "that it is an employment in itself laudable *to communicate pleasure innocently.*"[41] Winning the medal, he read his verse before the university and its royal chancellor and continued pushing against the cocoon Zachary sought to weave around him.

Insofar as Tom could, he ignored the reality that Cambridge was more mathematical and less classical than Oxford. He became a keen competitor, writing Latin epistles and English declamations and scouting out the system of examinations and his likely rivals. Luckily, the rise of competitive university athletics came later. Although he endured Latin composition in order to win honors—he took that declamation prize in 1820 —mastering the ancients riveted him and promised greater rewards. In his world, a good degree in classics from one of the ancient universities was a marketable commodity. A half-century later G. O. Trevelyan, Zachary's grandson and Tom's nephew, could "never remember the time when it was not diligently impressed upon me that, if I minded my syntax, I might eventually hope to reach a position which would give me three hundred pounds a year, a stable for my horse, six dozen of audit ale every Christmas, a loaf and two pats of butter every morning, and a good dinner for nothing, with as many almonds and raisins as I could eat at dessert." Cambridge's curriculum fostered the treacherously diffuse reading that Tom relished. There was no classical honors track until 1824, and he resented intrusions on reading and writing as he chose, soon declaring his "abomination" of algebra and trigonometry: "starvation, confinement, torture, annihilation of the mind." Written to amuse his mother, his self-mockery was a portent. And he remained almost immune to "scientific subjects." After his first Greek examination, however, the Regius professor told him that "I had done myself very high credit" and recommended that he "addict myself particularly to Classics." Needing little encouragement, Tom thought it "would be the most prudent course." Mathematical cramming enabled him to finish high in the freshman class.[42]

But the classics were coming to mean something personal, virtually spiritual, to him. Briefly, Tom lost sight of the unbridgeable historical and ethical distance between ancient Greece and modern England. Sharing in the philhellenism stirred by the Greek revolt against Turkey, he looked backward and discovered unique and abiding inspiration: "And what an incalculable debt we owe to that little speck of land, Greece.—The principles of taste, the finest models of composition, the doctrines and the glorious examples to which we owe political freedom, the arts, the sciences, architecture, sculpture, everything that is great and splendid in literature and politics, must be considered as ultimately derived from that little peninsula." Bracketing off monotheism, he made Homer the exemplar of "literary immortality." Even more, the "preeminence" of his legacy helped to explain some of the "immense advances" in moral philosophy since antiquity: "What a superior rank is to be assigned to the man who through six and twenty centuries has influenced the feelings, interested the sympathies, governed and fixed the standard of taste of vast and enlightened empires."[43]

There was no taking an honors degree without mastering basic mathematics, but Tom insisted that the requirement would not cause him "to abandon Classical studies." He would "read the Classics as a real pleasure;

proceeding regularly at the rate of two or three hours a day, for some years to come, through their most celebrated works." His aim was to make himself, "if not a medallist, something much better, a man who has got a few *ideas* from Antiquity, though he may not know much of the critical peculiarities of *words.*" Nine months later he was "deep in Plato, Aristotle, and Theocritus . . . and admiring more and more every day the powers of that mighty language which is incomparably the best vehicle both for reasoning and for imagery that mankind have ever discovered, and which is richer both in abstract philosophical terms and poetical expressions than the English, French, and Latin tongues put together." Endowing the Greek language with consummate rationality and some of its masters with permanent authority, he read the Authorized Version's translation of the Hebrew scriptures poetically for Zachary's benefit and contrasted "Christian hymns . . . poor both in thought and language" with "all the Pagan hymns . . . full of poetry and elegance."[44]

An aesthetic reader, Tom looked to writers to *"communicate pleasure innocently"*—he meant beauty—and evaluated books by their capacity to produce in him what he desired. The Renaissance historian James Hankins has captured Macaulay's lifelong way with books: "The aesthetic reader has a strong sense of the literary work as an object, and tries to relate its parts to the artistic effect of the whole. He also has a strong sense of the author as a literary personality. He tends to read the bare text without notes at the pace of oral delivery and relies on his native *virtù* and his classical education to understand it. Ready understanding is also enhanced by the fact that the aesthetic reader prizes clarity above all other literary virtues in the authors he reads and patronizes." Ancient in origin, aesthetic reading reemerged in early-modern Europe, but the tide of Cambridge classics during the early nineteenth century flowed toward what Tom called "the critical peculiarities of *words.*" Still, during the winter of his third year he won a Craven University Scholarship "for knowledge of the languages and civilisations of ancient Greece and Rome." The other two scholars went on to teach classics. He "was as proud of it as a peacock of his tail," and the stipend reduced his dependence on his father. That was almost his last success as an undergraduate. Finally, his contempt for mathematics undid him. Cramming for the exclusively mathematical honors examination during the Christmas holidays of his last year was much too little and much too late. After "two days struggle," he quit the examination—"gulfed"—and in humiliation took an ordinary degree.[45]

In January 1822 he also faced "a vigorous plan of retrenchment" because of Zachary's deteriorating finances. He needed to earn his keep. After admission to Lincoln's Inn with a view to the bar, Tom seemingly toyed with ordination. For a prize of ten pounds, he eulogized "The Conduct and Character of William Third." Harkening back to Plutarch, the exercise prefigured *The History of England*. In July 1822 he contracted to coach two brothers for Cambridge for 100 guineas—with a 2007 purchasing power of just under £8,000. Too optimistically, he told his father that he was cultivating "the regularity of habits necessarily produced by a periodical employment which cannot be procrastinated." What failure meant to Tom emotionally is irretrievable, but he needed to change the subject and later to forget it. His nephew recalled that "he loved to dwell long after the world had loaded him with its most envied prizes" that his first successes "were the fruit, not of favour or inheritance, but of personal industry and ability."[46] When we fail, all of us at least flirt with self-delusion.

During Tom's last months in Cambridge his education became more vocationally rhetorical. Long intimidated by his intelligence, Zachary came to envy his eloquence. "Often in later years," Hannah remembered, "I have heard my father, after expressing an earnest desire for some object, exclaim, 'If I had only Tom's power of speech!'" Speaking seventeen times in the Cambridge Union between February 1822 and December 1824, he learned how to win an audience "composed partly of future senators"—his classicizing variant for M.P.'s. He remembered that he sometimes used his "supreme" power there "tyrannically." It was a foretaste of his great career. Among the rules of the union's game were inventiveness and impersonation. Debaters regularly defended positions they personally rejected, and the university required them to discuss politics only before 1801. Tom was soon noticed where notice mattered. In 1823 Henry Brougham, Whig parliamentarian, legal and literary eminence, and then both Jeremy Bentham's disciple and Zachary's philanthropic colleague, favored Zachary with fulsome advice for his heir. Brougham reduced "general learning" to the acquisition of "classical propensities." To improve "the great talent for public speaking which . . . [Tom] happily possesses," he "earnestly" entreated him "to set daily and nightly before him the Greek models." To become "a great orator, he must go at once to the fountain head, and be familiar with every one of the great orations of Demosthenes," who "must positively be the model." Of course Tom had memorized Cicero's orations: "very beautiful but not very useful." Brougham insisted that "in courts of law and Parliament, and even to mobs, I have never made so much play (to use a very modern phrase) as when I was almost translating from the Greek" and solemnly warned against "speaking off-hand": "even to the end of a man's life he must prepare word for word most of his finer passages." In an aside, he pronounced that "a familiar knowledge of Dante" would also promote verbal economy and purity: "I do not council any imitation, but only an imbibing of the same spirit." It was a version of the ancient technique of mimesis, the creative adaptation of an exemplar. For all that great oratory required artifice and craft, it aimed to exercise the "almost absolute power of doing good to mankind in a free country."[47] Tom had already known all that when he entered Cambridge. As much as worldly-wise duplicity, it was pure Cicero.

But at the university he gained the hard knowledge that "no . . . food is so bitter as the bread of dependence, and no ascent so painful as the staircase of a patron." As he paraphrased Dante, he was preparing to launch a career whose success required that he garner the patronage of powerful older men. Deferentially, he offered Brougham private thanks and public homage: "the most eloquent statesman of the age." A few months later Tom published an essay "On the Athenian Orators," which reaffirmed the linkage between "the educated classes throughout Europe" on the one hand and classical learning and modern rhetoric on the other. He understood that anyone imitating the ancient exemplars must adjust to "modern feelings and acquirements." But he never forgot their timeless lesson that "the object of oratory . . . is not truth but persuasion."[48]

The essay appeared in the new *Knight's Quarterly Magazine,* published by a group of old Etonians, including some of his Cambridge friends. As in the union, Tom's words soon overcame his appearance. Twenty years later a poet who was there recalled his effect:

A presence with gigantic power instinct,
Though outwardly, in truth, but little graced
With aught of manly beauty—short, obese,
Rough-featured, coarse-complexioned, with lank hair,

And small grey eyes . . .
. . .—his voice abrupt,
Unmusical;—yet, when he spake, the ear
Was charmed into attention, and the eye
Forgot the visible and outward frame
Of the rich mind within; with such swift flow
Of full, spontaneous utterance the tongue
Interpreted the deep impassion'd thought,
And pour'd upon our sense exhaustless store of multifarious
    learning.

Less high-flown contemporaries had a similar experience of Tom achieving ascendancy. Compared with, say, Lord Byron's *Don Juan, Knight's* seems tame: a confection of classical allusions, quotations, and pastiches, which testified that the young writers were of "the educated classes," leavened by patches of bookish raciness suggesting unrequited desire. Tom's contributions show him again cleverly pushing the envelope and trying to appease his implacable father. In the first issue, for example, he balanced "Fragments of a Roman Tale" with an attack "On West Indian Slavery."[49]

He had been refining his double game. In the September 1820 issue of the *Christian Observer* he published "The Lamentation of the Virgins of Israel for the Daughter of Jephthah: A Hebrew Eclogue." William R. McKelvy, an American literary scholar, has detected and decoded in it Tom's "duplicitous opportunity" publicly to subvert Zachary's authority and prejudices. In the "Lamentation" he discerns the interplay of eroticism, Tom's "role as the hero of his own Oedipal romance," and the renewal of a year-old quarrel with Zachary about the "Peterloo Massacre." In September 1819 troops charged into a crowd of thousands in a Manchester field in order to arrest an orator who was urging parliamentary reform and the repeal of tariffs on grain. They killed several people and injured hundreds more. In full counterrevolutionary mode, Zachary blamed the incident on the government's failure to suppress the freethinking publications of Carlile and others. In the aftermath Tom wrote a letter to his mother, now lost, which gave her and his father "uneasiness," and Zachary struck back. Much concerned, Tom tried to reassure him that he was not a member of "any democratical societies here" and had "long made it a rule never to talk on politics except in the most general manner." The latter assertion was certainly false. Ostensibly a riff on a passage in the Hebrew Bible, Tom's "Lamentation" imitated the third-century B.C.E. sophisticate Theocritus' eclogue on the love-death of the shepherd Daphnis. His most sophisticated experiment to date in using the apparently familiar to subversive ends failed at least in part. Zachary caught the Peterloo subtext in the idyll and prefaced the published version with a chastened prose introduction drawn from his son's letter. Tom continued to write poetry compounding "religion, politics, sex, and irony."[50]

Duplicity abounded in his Cambridge. When he wrote his "Hebrew Eclogue," a heady blend of Jeremy Bentham's "Philosophic Radicalism" and romantic Hellenism was voguish, particularly in Trinity College. Bentham taught that pleasure is good and pain evil, that people are motivated to maximize their pleasure and minimize their pain, and that every government should act to promote the well-being of all whom it touches. He, too, was responding to the skeptical crisis and in 1802 coined a name for those who embraced what he called his "new religion": "Utilitarian." More than his moral theory, his atheism made him widely objectionable. Like every other Cambridge student, Tom understood that "it is the utility of any moral rule alone which constitutes the obligation of it." All of them learned their "*Moral* and *Political Philosophy*" from "the incomparable Archdeacon Paley," a pillar of the establishment. Only philosophers bothered themselves with the differences between Paley's principle of utility and Bentham's. The university offered its undergraduates few resources to cope with skepticism, much less with atheism. They were examined on John Locke's "*Philosophy of the Mind,*" but "*theological lectures*" were optional for undergraduates not aspiring to ordination. In 1826 the commencement preacher, himself an adept theologian, complained "that the University had lost its way as a religious institution and had become dominated by the search for 'knowledge of the material universe.'" The following year an evangelical clergyman coined a name for Bentham's surrogate religion: "Intent only upon the present . . . men will . . . devote themselves . . . to a life . . . of sordid godless Utilitarianism."[51]

James Mill, Bentham's chief interpreter, linked the self-conscious modernity of utilitarianism and atheism with democratic politics and devotion to classical Athens. Through a lens borrowed from Cicero, Mill read Plato as a skeptic who showed how to clear the ground in order to make Britain less religious and more rational and democratic. Mill had no time for Platonic speculation. Instead, he found permanent value in Socrates' puncturing questioning and deflating irony and taught that lesson to a number of bright young men, beginning with his oldest son, John, an even greater prodigy and far more systematically educated than Tom Macaulay.[52] That James Mill was both Bentham's associate and friendly with Zachary Macaulay is another example of the incongruous networking among the sundry philanthropists who were working to change England during the 1820s. Their fundamental differences of opinion have tended to overshadow their agreement about the need to promote civilization, liberty, and progress.

Charles Austin, who proselytized in Cambridge for "the Benthamic & politico-economic form of Liberalism," brilliantly profited from religious duplicity. When Tom entered Cambridge, Zachary naïvely fantasized that he could determine "the entire circle of" his son's friendships. A "king among his fellows," Austin "certainly was the only man who ever succeeded in dominating Macaulay," bringing "him nearer to Radicalism than he ever was before or since." No woman ever dominated Macaulay either. The four closest relationships of his adult life were all unequal, although in the cases of those that mattered most to him he failed to achieve the domination he desired. His subordination to Austin "created some consternation in the family circle." Temperamental and intellectual complements, they became almost inseparable. When Austin was old, rich, and comfortable, he told a confidant that "he had never desired universal suffrage . . . In this matter . . . there was in his Benthamism a dash of Hobbism. He was a great admirer of Hobbes" and suggested that another philosophic radical edit Hobbes's complete works. His admiration extended to ecclesiastical affairs—"He had no wish to see the Church disestablished"—and he was partial to Hobbes's definitions of superstition ("tales and fables not allowed by the authorities") and religion ("allowed"). He combined utilitarianism "with pessimism" and a firm belief in progress, and "his chief passion was for the classical writings." Tom Macaulay did not need Austin to teach him the value of the classics or the principle of utility, but it was perhaps from Austin that he imbibed his own lifelong but insinuating Hobbism. Once more, James Mill acted as the unmoved mover. In the 1820s, when "Hobbes was almost a forgotten man," he took him up and disseminated his steely philosophy of power among his own protégés.[53]

An articulate nonbeliever, Austin as a fourth-year student won the university's Hulsean Prize for the best essay on the evidences for the truth of the Christian religion. Offering an erudite, lucid, and ingenious defense of the Bible against the accusation of forgery, it amounted to a 148-page riff on the skeptical principle that Christian faith is inaccessible to human reason. On page two Austin prompted alert readers to his subtext: "The real account of the origin and causes of religious conviction has, if we suppress the epithets and passages marked in *italics* intended to prejudice the statement, been accurately described by Montaigne and Hume in the following singular passages." Years later a friend heard Austin say, "'I could have written a much better essay on the other side.' At the time Mr. Austin defended his juvenile *tour de force* on the principle of *Audi* (or rather *Dic*) *alteram partem*": "Hear (or rather Say) the other side."[54]

The extent of Tom's "conversion" to Benthamism seemingly eluded Zachary, who concerned himself with evidence of immorality. Back in 1820 he was pained to hear that his heir was called "the novel-reader." Then Tom showed ostentatious docility: "Nothing that gives you disquietude can give me amusement." Three years later he read two of Tom's lyrics in the latest issue of *Knight's*. The closing stanza of "Oh Rosamond" captures its tone:

> How gay would be the fireside light, how sweet the kettle's moan,
> Joined to the lustre of thy smile, the music of thy tone!
> How fondly could I play for hours with thy long curling tresses.
> And press thy hand and clasp thy neck with fanciful caresses,
> And mingle low impassioned speech with kisses and with sighs,
> And pore into the dark-blue depths of those voluptuous eyes.

Although the moaning kettle was likely the most realistic part of the poem, Zachary worked himself into a theatrical fury: "a loose, low, coarse and almost blackguard work in *some* of its parts . . . a strain of voluptuousness and even licentiousness which is quite intolerable . . . I am quite shocked and pained that a son of mine should have linked himself with such associates and should countenance and even compose such mischievous effusions . . . I did not want this at present to add to my cares—but I desire to receive it as part of my merited chastisement at the hand of God."[55] He was a philanthropist for whom even his heir's offenses were ultimately all about him.

Selina showed Tom his father's rant and another like it. He replied to Zachary with overt respect and newfound firmness, but also in what Thomas Pinney rightly calls a "misleading" way. Zachary's wrath gave him "deep pain;—but pain without remorse. I am conscious of no misconduct—and whatever uneasiness I may feel arises solely from sympathy for your distress." He mentioned two of his essays in the same number, but evaded his offending verses: "As to the poem . . . I am utterly unable to conceive what poem you mean." He was equally misleading about his involvement with *Knight's:* "If however a bookseller of whom we knew nothing have coupled improper productions with ours in a work over which we had no controul, I cannot plead guilty to any thing more than misfortune—a misfortune in which some of the most rigidly moral and religious men of my acquaintance have participated in the present instance . . . I am pleading at random for a book which I never saw. I am defending the works of people most of whose names I never heard." In concluding, he mingled filial piety and self-assertion: "I await your arrival with great anxiety; unmingled, however, with shame, remorse, or fear. Ever my dear Father affectionately yours T B M." Within two weeks Tom told Knight, the "bookseller of whom we knew nothing," that he was suspending his contributions "for the present": "My father, in particular, is . . . generally known to entertain, in their utmost extent, what are denominated evangelical opinions . . . I need not say that I do not in the slightest degree partake his scruples. Nor have I at all dissembled the complete discrepancy which exists between his opinions and mine. At the same time, gratitude, duty, and prudence, alike compel me to respect prejudices which I do not in the slightest degree share."[56]

Emotionally and financially, Tom could neither declare independence from his father nor break with his family and their religion. Futilely cramming for his honors examination six months earlier, he missed Christmas at home for the first time and dreamt of "that happy fire side which had always been the centre of my hopes and affections." His mind associated "our religion," childhood memories of the holiday, and "those

domestic feelings and enjoyments which that religion has created or pu-
rified." The letter was one of the few he wrote from Cambridge that
showcased religion. "Every peaceful Christmas hearth in England" testified "to the beneficial influence of Christianity on the morals and the
happiness of nations and families." Without it "the portion of domestic
virtue and enjoyment . . . among mankind" would now be "scanty" and
"sullied," and "how degraded would still be the condition of that sex
whose influence has made hostility gentle and vice decorous." Christmas
was "the festival not only of our religion, but of civilization, of morals, of
toleration, of domestic happiness, of social courtesy." Thus Tom joined
the angels in proclaiming Jesus' birth: "'Glory to God in the Highest,
and on earth peace, good will towards men.'" Testifying to his deepest
affections and briefly coloring his vision of how to write modern history, his sentiments owed nothing to doctrine. Four months earlier during a reading party led by the Trinity fellow coaching him for his examination, he refused to join the meeting of a Bible society.[57]

The family's economic interdependence—to say nothing of the demands of living and pursuing a public career "in the world"—also made
a split unthinkable. After Easter 1823 Tom left Cambridge desperate for
"honourable independence and distinction" but with no fixed residence
except his family home. It was a tie that bound him until 1830. Now
Zachary was, in his grandson's euphemism, "under the pressure of pecuniary circumstances." The feckless Babington nephew who managed his
trading firm while he pursued his sundry good causes drove it into the
ground. A dutiful son, Tom "quietly took up the burden which his father
was unable to bear," and "throughout the coming years of difficulty and
distress, his brothers and sisters would depend mainly upon him for comfort, guidance, and support." Money preoccupied him for the rest of his
life. Eager to avoid his father's public humiliation, he would die a rich
man. Zachary tried first to ignore the shifting balance of power between
himself and Tom, and then to resist its implications. As 1823 ended, his
vulnerability became undeniable. On 18 December *The Times,* in re-
printing some Jamaican slaveowners' charges that Zachary had oppressed
slaves there, sneered: "We are sure he was a very good tempered boy, if
he did not throw stones at his godfathers and godmother whenever he
saw them." Tom formulated a lucid defense for his inarticulate father.
The two remained interdependent, not least because of Zachary's formi-

dable and useful network of philanthropic and political allies in Britain and on the Continent.[58]

The end of 1823 also saw Zachary relent on Tom's contributing to *Knight's*. In the next issue he published three pieces. Set in the fifth century B.C.E., "Scenes from 'Athenian Revels'" is a charming satire on the recent dustup with Zachary. Both technically and colloquially, it is a closet drama about the inexorability of power in human relations, the limits of affection, and the necessity of prudence. Balancing it were two pious if doctrinally vague "Songs of the Huguenots," which also aired "paternal issues." "Speusippus," the protagonist and Tom's mouthpiece in "Scenes," was the name of Plato's nephew, who revised his uncle's doctrine by treating sense perception as an accurate source of knowledge. In "A Street in Athens," his impoverished and pious father, Callidemus—or "Beautiful People," a dig at the power of popular religious prejudices—berates him as a "reprobate." His alleged profligacy includes "marching in state . . . to thunder with your hatchet at the doors" of the stews. They squabble for pages over religion and money. When the son calls his father "unreasonable," he demands to know whether the youth is "not afraid of the thunders of Jupiter." The son proposes to enter "politics,—the general assembly," a course that involves becoming "an orator," and his enraged father blames himself in terms evocative of a polytheistic Zachary: "Oh, all ye gods and goddesses, what sacrilege, what perjury have I ever committed, that I should be singled out from among all the citizens of Athens to be the father of this fool?" After the father mocks Speusippus as "an universal genius; sophist,—orator,—poet," he lists possible subjects for his first tragedy, with one exception all mythical parricides, beginning with "OEdipus." He then announces that he will rewrite Aeschylus' "Prometheus," whose protagonist hated "all the gods," but "anew upon the model of Euripides," the most naturalistic of the great Greek tragedians whose plays Tom then "could not bear."[59]

While mocking his father, he did not spare himself. Conceited and callow, the Greek son, like the English son who created him, awkwardly begins to learn public prudence. In the second scene Alcibiades, the *monstre sacré* of fifth-century Athens, hosts a banquet. Planning one of the sacrileges that disgraced him, he makes Speusippus the butt of his zesty irreligion. Asked whether he fears the fertility deities whose rites Alcibiades plans to profane, he stammers: "No—but—but—I—that is I—but

it is best to be safe—mean—Suppose there should be something in it."
Mocked, he becomes defensive: "How can you talk so, when you know
that I believe all that foolery as little as you do?" Alcibiades proposes to
appoint him the crier of the mock rite, but it is finally unclear whether
Speusippus participates. Whatever the outcome of the story, the ironical
distance Tom achieved from his own situation and beliefs enabled him to
cultivate the prudent self-restraint that breeds success. An adult sense of
the absurd was not the least important of Tom's debts to the ancients.
Though abounding in pious works and childlike fun, Clapham was innocent of wit and irony.[60]

Macaulay's satire also twitted James Mill's style of classicizing radicalism. The late summer of 1823 seems to have been a turning point in
the history of his opinions. A quarter-century later, in acknowledging
the gift of a translation of Immanuel Kant's *Critique of Pure Reason,*
he affirmed that his "metaphysical system is and will, I think, continue
to be the ακαταληψία of the second Academy . . . For I am exactly of
Arcesilas's mind." Among the densest sentences he ever wrote, they repay unpacking. In 1605 Francis Bacon had Englished the Greek word
as "acatalepsy": "Incomprehensibility:—a term of the Sceptic philosophers." Arcesilaus (Tom's "Arcesilas") of Pitane (ca. 315–242 B.C.E.)
founded the second or middle Academy in Athens. Cicero, his distant
philosophical descendant, summarized his teaching. Arcesilaus denied

> that anything could be known, not even the residual claim . . . [of]
> the knowledge that he didn't know anything. He taught that every-
> thing was hidden so deeply and that nothing could be discerned or
> understood. For these reasons, he thought that we shouldn't assert
> or affirm anything, or approve it with assent: we should always curb
> our rashness and restrain ourselves from any slip. But he considered
> it particularly rash to approve something false or unknown, because
> nothing was more shameful than for one's assent or approval to out-
> run knowledge or apprehension. His practice was consistent with
> his theory, so that by arguing against everyone's views he led most
> of them away from their own.

In the family it was remembered that Tom "very probably never formulated [his religious convictions] to himself": "Perhaps the term 'agnostic,'

in the stricter sense of that misused word, might have fitted him."[61] Whatever he really believed or thought he knew, he never heard the term; "agnostic" was first used ten years after Macaulay died. A precise writer, George Macaulay Trevelyan meant his caveat: "'agnostic,' in the stricter sense of that misused word." Far from wanting to indulge in self-assertive and destabilizing public doubt, his granduncle knew only that "we shouldn't assert or affirm anything, or approve it with assent: we should always curb our rashness and restrain ourselves from any slip." Hence Macaulay prudently adopted classical "acatalepsy."

How did Zachary's heir come to identify himself "exactly" with "Arcesilas's mind"? In 1855 while rereading Cicero's philosophical works for at least the fourth time—he did so again the year before he died—he reported, "I . . . think, as I thought at twenty two, when I read him under the chestnuts at Trinity, that De Finibus is the best, that then comes the De Natura Deorum, and that the Tusculan Disputations are the least valuable,—mere anointing for broken bones." The third work's Stoic apathy—"the healthy soul is the soul without affections"—made it inaccessible to Tom, boy and man a connoisseur of his own emotions. During the tense late summer of 1823 he informed Zachary of his preparation for the upcoming Trinity fellowship examination, which he correctly expected to fail: "[a] month will pass away usefully and pleasantly in reading Cicero, Juvenal, and Locke."[62]

Unlike Tom Paine and Richard Carlile, Cicero presented the respectable face of skepticism. De Finibus (On the Ends of Goods and Evils) is a dialogue about living philosophically. It sets up and quickly knocks down the Epicureans, who either disdained or flaunted the virtues that made Rome great. Stoicism, in contrast, was consistent with such Roman values as self-control, patriotism, property, civic duty, friendship, and noble suicide. Because human well-being encompasses both the right state of mind and soul and physical well-being, Stoicism needs the leavening of Plato's wisdom and Aristotle's ethics. Virtue consists in making proper choices according to nature—the sum of our desires higher and lower—but it is not the sole human good. As a devoted Cockney indifferent to sky-gazing, Macaulay was unlikely to be moved by Cicero's argument that contemplating the divine universe refined souls and lives. But contemplation also included using leisure to gain worthwhile knowledge. By enabling contemplatives to pursue mental pleasures and to behave moderately and honorably, reading and conversation could elevate them and insulate them against fortune's whims. Macaulay's tireless marginalia—"that species of running conversation which he frequently kept up with his author for whole chapters together"—amount to a record of his spiritual exercises. Antiochus of Ascalon (d. ca. 68 B.C.E.), Cicero's teacher, dominates book five of *De Finibus*. Cicero's mouthpiece identifies himself as "a mitigated skeptic." Rejecting the Stoic effort to practice apathy, the sadder but wiser skeptic avoids intellectual commitments that render him vulnerable to error and its consequences. For him, the certainty accessible to us is small, the borderlands of conjecture extensive, and the frontiers of error immense. However Macaulay interpreted *De Finibus* during the late summer of 1823, the book helped him to survive a decade later in India.[63]

James Mill's style of classicizing radicalism was exceptional when Macaulay found enlightenment in Cicero "at twenty two." The close limits that classical skepticism imposed on human knowledge endowed it with a conservative potential. If it excluded much that was mistaken for truth, it could also recommend upholding the conventions of one's own people rather than deploying uncertain arguments to assault them. Hume, for example, championed monarchical government and established churches. In *De Natura Deorum (On the Nature of the Gods)* Cicero discussed our possible knowledge of and relation to divinity. Except among the Jews and sundry philosophers and mystics, religion in most of the ancient Mediterranean world involved neither personal faith nor ethical behavior. As Macaulay knew, it was cultic, political, and ethnic. When the gods were offered proper worship, they would favor their votaries. To withhold it was to court divine requital. Insofar as Roman religion was a businesslike affair of giving to the gods in order to receive back from them in return, it risked courting practical cynicism and philosophical doubt. Cicero gave the best lines in *De Natura Deorum* to the skeptic who also served as a high priest of the Roman cult. Reason is impotent, and the gods are indifferent to humanity, letting the good suffer and the wicked prosper. Justifying their ways (or God's) to men is, in any case, ethically beside the point. Instead, the skeptical priest recommends looking for suitable direction about worship in Rome's cultic rules and popular opinion, which amounts to reaffirming the utility of conforming to the state's religious ceremonies.[64]

In thus interpreting Cicero Macaulay stood on the shoulders of giants. Edward Gibbon found in the "admirable work of Cicero de Naturâ Deorum . . . the best clue we have to guide us through the dark and profound abyss. He represents with candour, and confutes with subtlety, the opinions of the philosophers." In an elegant aside a couple of pages earlier Gibbon captured how many enlightened Britons misread Cicero on the gods: "The various modes of worship, which prevailed in the Roman world, were all considered by the people as equally true; by the philosopher, as equally false; and by the magistrate, as equally useful." Cicero was a philosopher as well as a magistrate, while Gibbon and Macaulay were philosophical M.P.'s. Living in less tolerant times than Gibbon, Macaulay more sedulously upheld the ancient "magistrate's" view of religion.[65] His Ciceronian Anglicanism—nonbelieving, nominal but always insisted upon and increasingly visible—guaranteed him respectability and preserved him from disrepute and the risk of prosecution.

Along with many of his contemporaries, Macaulay discovered a means of reanimating Rome's "old civic piety." It made "no real distinction between the political and the religious. The loyalty men owed to their state was equally a loyalty to their civic gods." That was generally "conceived to be an ultimate loyalty from which there could be no appeal to any higher norm." During Macaulay's lifetime the word "nationalism" was coined to define a theological proposition (the "doctrine that certain nations . . . are the object of divine election") and then quickly translated to define a political commitment ("devotion to one's nation"). A heady brew of politics and religion that Gibbon lived to apprehend, nationalism became nineteenth-century England's civil religion and Macaulay one of its high priests.[66] In adolescence he found incredible Christianity's narrative and the doctrines that both inform it and derive from it. Beginning at "twenty two . . . under the chestnuts at Trinity," his religious opinions and behavior—what he said and left unsaid, and did and failed to do—increasingly modernized the practice of "acatalepsy." For the benefit of the "multitude" of British Christians, nationalism inverted the ancient formula, so that the loyalty they owed God was at least equally a loyalty they owed to their state. Along with Macaulay, many religious skeptics clung to the ancient formula but sometimes with heartfelt fervor for the nation. Their predecessors in doubt who prized the state and their own security routinely chose either winking and nodding conformity or taking the leap of faith. By 1859, when Macaulay died, he and many others had found in nationalism a common meaning powerful enough to motivate collective action.

Selling himself as an oracle of modern cultural Protestantism mattered for his success in promoting English nationalism. It required that he win at least the acquiescence of readers in stories that effectively evacuated Christian belief and theology from modern English culture and history. In *Knight's* he experimented in an essay on Dante. Anticipating the Anglo-American Dante boom, it fused a traditional Christian way of religiously neutering and expropriating the "pagan" classics and a traditional Protestant view of Catholicism as pagan. As much as Homer, Dante was the product of "dark and half barbarous times." "Fanaticism" is an evil, but in the case of his Catholicism its effect was creative. Not "only a sincere, but a passionate believer," Dante still appealed because he believed in "his wildest fictions": "The fact is, that supernatural beings, as long as they are considered merely with reference to their own nature, excite our feelings very feebly." Notwithstanding the power of the poetic imagination, the "noblest earthly object of the contemplation of man is man himself." Dante therefore belongs to a past superseded by the march of reason: "Euripides and Catullus believed in Bacchus and Cybele as little as we do. But they lived among men who did. Their imaginations, if not their opinions, took the colour of the age. Hence the glorious inspiration of the Bacchæ and the Atys. Our minds are formed by circumstances: and I do not believe that it would be in the power of the greatest modern poet to lash himself up to a degree of enthusiasm adequate to the production of such works."[67] By mixing the first person singular and plural, he invited his readers to share his state of mind.

Macaulay's story about the *Divine Comedy* pointed backward to baroque tomes decoding all myths and forward to Carl Jung's murky collective unconscious. Animating the poem is "a vague and awful idea of some mysterious revelation, anterior to all recorded history, of which the dispersed fragments might have been retained amidst the impostures and superstitions of later religions. Indeed, the mythology of the Divine Comedy is of the elder and more colossal mould. It breathed the spirit of Homer and Æschylus." Dante's mind was thus not only obsolete but also essentially pagan. Macaulay's version enabled his readers to enjoy Dante on familiar terms rather than instructing them in the intricate theology that ordered the "passionate" beliefs which informed his poem. In much the same way, Macaulay at fourteen knew that the ancient historians Livy and Herodotus "believe [a]ll the stories of their Jupiters and [Minerva]s," but moderns "can separate between what is true and what is false."[68]

He prefaced "Dante" with an epigraph from Milton. It pointed to an essay that he published twenty months later in which he refined his secularizing techniques. "Milton" would make him famous, but in 1824 Tom was still churning out pieces for *Knight's* and toiling to redeem himself by winning election to a Trinity fellowship. Full of delight, exhaustion, and "nervous depression," he informed his father on 1 October that he thought he "stood first of the Candidates." He then came to the financial point. Although "the pecuniary emolument" would be small until he became a master of arts in a few months, for "seven years from that time it will make me almost an independant man." His adverb mattered. Between 1825 and 1831 the meticulously hierarchical system of dividends that apportioned stipends to the master and fellows brought him an average of £209 a year—with a 2007 purchasing power of under £15,000. Living under Zachary's roof, however, Tom had limited expenses and by living frugally usually paid his bills. His situation fell far short of the gentleman's privilege "not to have to work for his bread," which his discredited father had promised to provide him "in a modest way."[69]

On the eve of Tom's successful fellowship examination, he put his mother and, through her, his father on notice about the future: "But if those who are excluded from the blessings of the family circle are still to feel its restraints and hear only its reproofs—I tremble for the consequences. I have seen hundreds of families made miserable by these means." Zachary ceased raining down noisome reproofs on him and nineteen months later received from him "some lines which I made in bed last night—An Inscription for a picture of Voltaire." They capture both the increasingly inverted power relationship between son and father and the ironic outcome of Zachary's heedless parenting.

> From all that God revealed,—that jugglers feigned,—
> That crippled reason,—that restrained from sin,—

His venturous wit a fettered race unchained,
And left them slaves to nothing—but a grin.

. . .

In very wantonness of childish mirth
He puffed Bastilles and thrones and shrines [away]
Insulted Heaven, and liberated earth;—
Was it for good or evil?—Who shall sa[y?][70]

The money, the sense of independence, the social prospects, and the religious liberation that Macaulay's classical rhetorical education brought him are easier to assess than how it shaped him. At forty-three he told his closest male friend that men should bring "away from Cambridge self-knowledge, accuracy of mind, and habits of strong intellectual exertion." It was the platitude of a middle-aged eminence. More tellingly perhaps, a month after his victorious fellowship exam he published an effusive tribute to his studies. His target was William Mitford's *History of Greece*, which as its volumes multiplied became a polemic against the Athenian premonition of French revolutionary democracy. Among Mitford's outrages was demeaning "one of the greatest men that ever lived, Demosthenes."[71]

In the last three paragraphs Macaulay hailed the abiding power of "the great works of Athenian genius": "that splendid literature from which has sprung all the strength, the wisdom, the freedom, and the glory, of the western world." Athens' cultural authority was still "manifested at the bar, in the senate, in the field of battle, in the schools of philosophy." It was the sufficient cause of the best of everything: "All the triumphs of truth and genius over prejudice and power, in every country and in every age." There was no allowing any noble creations in Israel, much less in South and East Asia. Cicero, to whom Macaulay owed his mature outlook, headed his catalogue of the heirs of Athens, followed by Juvenal, Dante, Cervantes, Bacon, Samuel Butler, Shakespeare, Erasmus, Pascal, Mirabeau, Galileo, and Algernon Sidney. Those disparate intellects were linked with one another mainly in Macaulay's fertile imagination: "Wherever a few great minds have made a stand against violence and fraud, in the cause of liberty and reason, there has been her [Athens'] spirit in the midst of them; inspiring, encouraging consoling."[72]

That spirit's "influence on private happiness" was even greater, making "many thousands . . . wiser, happier, and better, by those pursuits in which she has taught mankind to engage." Macaulay breathlessly avowed that about ancient Athens "I cannot speak with fairness. It is a subject on which I love to forget the accuracy of a judge, in the veneration of a worshipper and the gratitude of a child." Even when allowance is made for rhetorical contrivance, his peroration breathes an unsustainable intensity. It depended on the conjunction of his disenchantment, his infatuation with Philosophic Radicalism, and the lightening of Zachary's grip, which he would soon almost outgrow. He closed the essay by envisioning a future after "the sceptre shall have passed away from England," when "travellers from distant regions" would behold the wreck of her former greatness. His image captures the sense of the pathos of all human achievements that the ancients taught. But he was still a very young man who knew that home truth only at a distance. Exile, death, depression, and rediscovering "Greek literature with a passion quite astonishing to myself" would teach him about his own implication in the human predicament of necessity and limits.[73] But all that came a decade later in Calcutta when he was famous and powerful.

[2]

STAR

During the next decade Thomas Babington Macaulay succeeded in crafting an intricate and winning public face that often belied him. He became a prominent spokesman for abolishing slavery in the British Empire who lacked any taste for the cause, a forceful theoretician and practitioner of reforming Whig politics who was a Machiavellian realist, a soaring parliamentary orator who avoided debate, a self-declared Christian who was a committed skeptic and a masterly secularizer of English history and culture, and a stern public moralist in love with his two youngest sisters.

Crucially, his family taught him to be Janus-faced. He returned from Cambridge with ancient resources—above all Cicero—that enabled him to accommodate his parents' incredible religion. They minded his dalliance with Benthamism because of its democratic turn and support for the only secularization they knew: ending state endowment of and perhaps disestablishing the Church of England. But Tom envisioned nothing less than the transformation of English culture. As he launched his public career, he shared the goals of "secularism" almost a generation before the word was coined. He believed that "morality should be based solely on regard to the well-being of mankind in the present life, to the exclusion of all considerations drawn from belief in God or in a future state." He also believed that ideally "education . . . should . . . concern the present or visible world as distinguished from the eternal or spiritual world." He was, however, also an elitist who believed that "the multitude" required the discipline and consolation of religion. Macaulay's reading of pre-Christian antiquity provided him with the model for disenchanting the

world. Decades later he told himself that he had outgrown its complement, Benthamism, which had provided him with a vision of England's
future and later a blueprint for modernizing India. Like many aging luminaries, he was embarrassed by his youthful radicalism.[1] As much as his
classicism, however, his Benthamism proved inescapable.

Yet Clapham was also inescapable. Zachary's leadership in the Anti-
Slavery Society brought Tom an invitation to address its first general
meeting in late June 1824. With a royal duke presiding, he made politic
nods to God and Christianity before invoking England's "peculiar glory,
not that she has ruled so widely, not that she has conquered so splendidly,
but that she has ruled only to bless, and conquered only to spare." Repeating "ruled" and "conquered" was more important than repeating
"only." The speech was a triumph, and Brougham publicized it in the
Edinburgh Review, the journal of enlightened Whiggism. The *Quarterly
Review,* its Tory rival, complimented his speech by attacking it. Zachary
was himself. Riveted as Tom spoke, he afterward rebuked him for folding
his "arms in the presence of royalty." With Brougham's endorsement and
perhaps because of the verve of the articles in *Knight's,* Tom began writing for the *Edinburgh Review.*[2]

Macaulay never heard the phrase "cultural and intellectual hegemony"
and likely would have groaned at the academic jargon describing it: "Intellectuals are a social group that organize and elaborate culture in its
widest sense, and the function of intellectuals is precisely to formulate
and proliferate a culture and a system of thinking and valuing throughout society." But Macaulay was a rhetorician who believed that words, if
they do not quite constitute reality, regularly shape how it is perceived
and determine whether an account of it is accepted or rejected. As a
rhetorician, he helped to define an acceptable middle-class version of the
identity of the modern English people. It required abandoning a youthful scruple: "The editorial *we* has often been fatal to rising genius; though
all the world knows that it is only a form of speech, very often employed
by a single needy blockhead."[3] As much as vituperation, naturalism, and
Whiggism, "we" belonged to the *Edinburgh Review's* corporate voice. In
its pages, Tom Macaulay was always "we," less to suppress his individuality
than to seem to teach, exhort, and censure magisterially if not quite ob-
jectively.

"We" was a cultural warrior—Macaulay described his role as "intellectual gladiatorship"—who knew that especially in unsettled times literature was inextricable from both politics and religion. The end of the Anglican monopoly in 1828–29, the parliamentary reform bills of 1831–32, and the rest of the political drama of the period are the stuff of textbooks. But, as historians recognize, the "public mind"—a favorite term of Macaulay's—also "experienced uncertainty and opportunity . . . The mental crisis was probably longer in the making, perhaps somewhat shorter in duration, but it had like effects—liberation and creativity, unease and failure, and an unusual burst of individual accomplishment." The combatants were numerous. Notwithstanding their bellicose rhetoric, among them alliances of convenience abounded and genuine fondness was possible. Henry Brougham, a deistic Whig, and James Mill, an atheistic Benthamite, maintained a placid friendship for decades. Zachary Macaulay also worked with Mill and fervently prayed for Brougham in his sickness. Their alliances suggest the comparative narrowness of England's ideological spectrum and the rules regulating warfare among its chattering classes. Visiting in 1835, the cosmopolitan Alexis de Tocqueville contrasted English radicals ("they are recognised as gentlemen") and French ("almost always very poor,""often boorish,""often presumptuous," and "profoundly ignorant"): "an enlightened man, of good sense and good will would be a Radical in England. I have never met those three qualities in a French Radical."[4]

By the spring of 1826 Tom was already speaking as a partisan Whig, and thereafter he was—and is—routinely seen as simply that. His Whiggism was, however, accommodating rather than dogmatic, an attitude that eventually made him a bellwether, leading and signaling the equipoise that ended the culture and political wars of his young manhood. Meeting him on a London street in July 1838, a political sophisticate "walked with him for some time": "Said . . . that he was as great a Radical as anybody, that is, that if ever the voice of the nation should be as clearly and universally pronounced for reform of the H[ouse] of Lords, or any other great change, as it had been for the Reform Bill, he should be for it too." Macaulay's ear for the "voice of the nation" testified to his determination to follow the dominant minority as well as to lead it, but neither too far nor too fast. His changing positions on the secret ballot, a staple radical demand, typify his politics. In 1830 he was undecided. Ten months later he was favorable but not aggressively so. In 1840 he pub-

licly supported the ballot. In 1848, with the Continent upended by revolution and Britain seemingly imperiled, he opposed it. Privately he admitted that his "opinions on that question have undergone some change,"
but he assured voters in Edinburgh four years later of his constancy. It
was a reasoned and circumstantial inconsistency. During the last months
of the long debate over the Reform Bill of 1832 he reminded his fellow
M.P.'s that "the science of government was essentially an experimental
science—that is, its conclusions were so wholly the creatures of experience, and its application so dependent upon ever-changing circumstances, that nought could be predicated of them of universal applicabil-
ity. Political doctrines were not like the axioms and definitions of the
geometer—of intrinsic truth, wholly uninfluenced by time and place;
their worth and force depended on experience and were necessarily as
changing as the circumstances on which all experience was founded."
Here as so often in his political and literary career, he was recycling
the teaching of earlier essays. Macaulay attracted readers and exercised
cultural authority over them because he peddled an increasingly congenial message. It was "antirevolutionary," "broadly Benthamite," "militantly
middle-class," and animated by an "aggressive faith in things English."[5]

But the Simmering Twenties as well as "the 'Angry Thirties' and the
'Hungry Forties'" preceded equipoise. In 1825 an attentive reader of the
three smartest British journals would likely have foreseen permanent
conflict. The Whig *Edinburgh Review* debuted in 1802, the Tories entered
the lists with the *Quarterly Review* seven years later, and the Benthamites
launched the *Westminster Review* in 1824. The *Edinburgh* and the *Quarterly* each sold under 14,000 copies during the mid-1820s, but they circulated throughout Great Britain and were read by thousands more. With
sales of 2,000–3,000 an issue, the *Westminster* was a more precarious venture. Competition for readers drove the hunt for new talent.[6]

A tough-minded Dutch historian who survived Buchenwald discerned in Macaulay's style "a projection of certain features . . . of his temperament: of his passion for straight, unhesitating phrasing, for surprising
effect, for sharp, dramatic contrasts. There was in him no sympathy with
his fellow men, no instinctive understanding of them." Macaulay viewed
the larger world "with the eye of the zealot for public virtues and for
progress and for the cause of liberty. But he was incapable . . . of establishing . . . [empathy] with the human being in historic or even literary per-

sonages." Macaulay's style perhaps imaged his temperament, but the essays he published between 1825 and 1832 clearly reflected the conventions of highbrow journalism and his theory of it. The reviewers often sounded like "paranoid readers": "there is no moment when there is not something crucial at stake. They always find what they expect to find yet when they find it they react with outrage." Even "an unpromising subject" evoked "a hysterical embittered tone and the suggestion of extreme emotions barely under control."[7] The appraisal slights both Macaulay's rhetorical virtuosity and the curious impersonality of much of the reviewers' venom. They were mostly rhetoricians skilled at targeted fulmination.

In contrast, Macaulay's feelings toward Francis Jeffrey, the *Edinburgh Review*'s founding editor, ran deep. Jeffrey gave him the care that he craved and that his father denied him, and Macaulay reciprocated: "I loved him as much as it is easy to love a man who belongs to an older generation—and how good & kind & generous he was to me. His goodness too was the more precious because his perspicuity was so great—He saw through & through you—He marked every fault of taste, every weakness, every ridicule—& yet he loved you as if he had been the dullest fellow in England." Jeffrey appreciated the originality of Macaulay's style, and Macaulay for his part knew that his verbal fireworks captured an audience. Artful sneers and tight reasoning, however, were at least as frequent as contrived "outrage."[8]

In January 1825 Tom debuted before the *Review*'s approximately 50,000 readers with a rehash of his speech to the Anti-Slavery Society. "The West Indies" appealed to the "friends of humanity and freedom" and the "spirit" of Christianity, but it also included an analysis of honor that paraphrased without referencing Thomas Hobbes: "The desire which we feel to obtain the approbation, and to avoid the censure of our neighbours, is no innate or universal sentiment. It always springs, directly or indirectly, from consideration of the power which others possess to serve or injure us."[9] Hobbes's analysis subverted Tom's invocations of philanthropy and Christianity. He never acknowledged the essay. Slavery was Zachary's concern, not his own.

Tom's next contribution, published in the August number, owed nothing to his father. Surmounting the anonymity that the *Edinburgh Review* imposed on its contributors, "Milton" began to make him famous. Although he later deprecated it along with his other literary criticism, it exemplifies his subversive cultural intentions and capability. Assigned the just-published edition and translation of Milton's *Treatise on Christian Doctrine,* he adopted the *Review's* iconoclastic tone, quickly dismissing as obsolete the book and, by implication, Milton's complex and idiosyncratic theology: "The men of our time are not to be converted or perverted by quartos. A few more days, and this essay will . . . [be consigned] to the dust and silence of the upper shelf." Instead, Macaulay proposed to explore Milton's contemporary significance for his country: "the poet, the statesman, the philosopher, the glory of English literature, the champion and the martyr of English liberty." The public context of his reevaluation was the movement to repeal three pillars "of the old system of intolerance": the legal disabilities on non-Anglican Protestants, Catholics, and Jews. Its probable target was the Tory pundit Samuel Johnson's "Life of Milton," which scorned the republican politician but engaged the religious sublime of *Paradise Lost.*[10]

Macaulay's achievement revealed an intolerant society fostering its own subversion. In 1825, foreseeing that the inclusion of non-Anglicans would recenter England's culture along with its politics, he adopted a breezy theological indifference. It was then easier to enunciate than to live. Milton's effective editor and translator, another contributor to *Knight's,* decided that his own doubts about hell were incompatible with ordination and was legally obliged to resign as a fellow of Macaulay's college. He died insane and destitute, leaving a sister who became one of Macaulay's charities.[11] His reviewer possessed a more pliable conscience and a stronger instinct for survival.

But what did Macaulay make of *Paradise Lost,* complete with Adam and Eve, angels and the Serpent, as well as God? By writing a great epic in "modern times," Milton defied the rule "that, as civilisation advances, poetry almost necessarily declines." Although the imagination, which for Macaulay meant not creativity but the power to invent compelling images, passed for thought before human beings could reason, it lacked any probative capacity: "In proportion as men know more and think more, they . . . make better theories and worse poems." Skeptical and literal-minded, Macaulay found in the Bible clear and bounded stories rather than open-ended symbols and metaphors. He also detested the Romantic poets of his day—"the old flimsy philosophy . . . the old crazy mystical metaphysics." Macaulay's commonplace story about the progress of reason—an idea to which James Mill subscribed—enabled him to deploy a hopeful prophecy as if it were a datum of history. His story explained, moreover, why, despite the moderns' victory over the ancients in the late seventeenth-century "battle of the books," even in enlightened Britain the losers continued to dominate what we call the humanities: the ancients were the better poets. His story, finally, encouraged his readers' faith in their intellectual superiority over the multitude: "Logicians may reason about abstractions. But the great mass of men must have images."[12] By implication most people were incorrigibly irrational.

Because religion belonged to the imagination, the notion of "God, the uncreated, the incomprehensible, the invisible" was a "noble conception" but unimaginable and thus incomprehensible. Macaulay adapted a theory about the degeneration of Christianity invented by the first Protestants and later expropriated by skeptics. "Soon after Christianity had achieved its triumph, the principle which had assisted it began to corrupt it": "Deity embodied in human form." True Christianity was peripheral to the modern imagination because it was "pure Theism" not idolatry and incapable of generating compelling images: "What is spirit? . . . We observe certain phenomena. We cannot explain them into material causes. We therefore infer that there exists something which is not material. But of this something we have no idea . . . We can reason about it only by symbols. We use the word; but we have no image of the thing; and the business of poetry is with images, and not with words." Ignoring Christ, for Christians God incarnate, Macaulay divorced Milton's theology from his literary achievement.[13]

Scorning everything "mystical," Macaulay as an adult determined "to write nothing which he does not fully understand, and which he cannot make intelligible to his readers." Unlike Dante, Milton "wrote in an age of philosophers and theologians." To avoid shocking his contemporaries, when representing spirits he "left the whole in ambiguity," avoided "metaphysical abstractions," and endowed them with "a certain dim resemblance to those of men but exaggerated to gigantic dimensions and veiled in mysterious gloom." Macaulay discovered the sources of Milton's poetry in the Greek and Roman classics rather than in the Bible. It was autobiography masked as criticism. For him, passages from *Paradise Lost,* which he knew by heart, and some other poems worked like "charmed names," forming links "in a long chain of associated ideas." They evoked "all the dear classical recollections of childhood, the school-room, the dog-eared Virgil, the holiday, and the prize." Otherwise the associations with the poem were impersonal, belonging "to a remote period of history" or "a distant region." Just as Macaulay discerned in "the book of Job . . . a considerable resemblance to some of [Aeschylus'] dramas," he converted Milton, a great classicist, into a non-Christian writer.[14]

Macaulay lavished twenty-two pages on Milton's place in modern England's history, especially in the upheavals of 1642–1649 and the ensuing military dictatorship, which in his reckoning dwarfed the "Glorious Revolution" of 1688–89. Milton "was not a Puritan." Although like them he "kept his mind continually fixed on an Almighty Judge and an eternal reward," he was as "free from the contagion of their frantic delusions" as "the coolest sceptic or the most profane scoffer." What counted in 1825 was that Milton "fought for the species of freedom which is the most valuable, and which was then the least understood, the freedom of the human mind." He was thus an ideological ancestor of the *Edinburgh Review* and other "friends of liberty" in "the great conflict between . . . liberty and despotism, reason and prejudice . . . The destinies of the human race were staked on the same cast with the freedom of the English people." Despite Macaulay's invocation of eternal principles, he judged political actions according to their impact on the national interest. Charles I was "'a tyrant, a traitor, a murderer, and a public enemy,'" but beheading him was wrong because the deed harmed England. In contrast, Macaulay hailed Oliver Cromwell, Charles's successor and a shaky friend of individual liberty, because during his rule "never before had the national honour been better upheld abroad."[15]

Macaulay's extrusion of the Bible from Milton's life and art eluded his pious and doting patron Hannah More, also a vociferous patriot. Her reaction signaled a sea change in cultural perception. The more than fifty reviews of Milton's *Treatise* displayed "an evolving cult of national literary veneration colliding with the doctrines of orthodox Protestantism." Squabbling divines fostered the cult. Reviewing the book in the *Quarterly Review,* the Reverend Henry Hart Milman, doctrinally broadminded and suspicious of Catholicism, called Milton "the greatest religious poet of the Christian world," to the disgust of at least one fierce

High Churchman. Within a few years Milman, who knew his Macaulay, presented Geoffrey Chaucer as "resolutely, determinedly, almost boastfully English" and endowed him with "strong Teutonic good sense," which enabled him to see through "the whole monastic and sacerdotal system."[16] By implication, the nation was the repository and creation of England's literature and the rest of its culture, including the Christian religion.

Macaulay's version of Milton scarcely affected subsequent interpretations of his poetry. But his decision to confine the religious imagination to humanity's prerational past and to ignore or evacuate the religious content of sundry usable persons and achievements prefigured a tenacious and appealing theory of secularization. Vulgarizations of the arguable philosophy of history that envisioned the progressive and virtually inevitable "disenchantment of the world" endure. Here it may be instructive to contrast the obituaries of Dr. Cicely Saunders, O.M., who founded today's hospice movement, in *The Times* and the *New York Times*. Her London obituarist simply noted that "her conversion to evangelical Christianity" heightened her "dedication." The New York writer eagerly offered secular reassurance: "Dame Cicely, a Christian, included a chapel and provided for prayer time but made it clear that religion, even when proffered tactfully, was no substitute for clean, well-lighted rooms, a comfortable day room, a homelike setting and a caring staff."[17]

Many English aristocrats felt at home with a "tradition of indifference masquerading as a form of rational religion." They tended to embrace Whiggism, and "it was generally held that to offer religion to a Whig was the equivalent of offering garlic to a vampire." By 1826 Macaulay had assimilated their style. He was also developing the "skeptical politics" that lasted a lifetime: "power politics of so-called 'realism' in international relations and the pluralism of 'interests' in domestic politics." Encountering him at a dinner in the autumn of 1826, a sophisticate concluded, "His opinions are quite liberal and yet he is by no means a vulgar radical." Macaulay drifted away from the Benthamites, briefly playing the role of a quiet fellow traveler. The small band of committed Philosophic Radicals was splintering. Bentham, who was interested mainly in legal reform, squabbled with James Mill, who wanted to reform Parliament. Remaining loyal to Mill, Charles Austin continued to look back to ancient Athens for guidance about organizing a modern democracy. Even at the height of Macaulay's collegiate enthusiasm for the ancient Greeks, he marked self-deception in those who "consider all the Classics as contemporaries."[18] The crucial word was "all."

In March 1826 Macaulay began discovering everyday life as a barrister on the Northern Circuit Court, based in Lancaster and York. He keenly felt his continuing financial dependence on his father. Thirty years later he would associate it with "indecency," "servility," and "mendicancy." Although circuit-riding was unprofitable, it offered consolations. Traveling by horse-drawn carriage was slow—he considered seven miles an hour a good pace—but the camaraderie pleased him. Crucial for the future was the beginning of his intimate friendship with Thomas Flower Ellis, his older contemporary at Cambridge, who found him "a very amusing person—somewhat boyish in manner but very original." A letter from Tom to his sister Hannah may suggest how Ellis heard him: "But I must go back to court. There is a highwayman to be tried for his life who interests the ladies very much; a stout handsome swaggering fellow, the very image of Macheath ['Mack the Knife']. He has been twice tried since we came hither and has got off by alibi both times. If he is convicted the Lancaster witches will be inconsolable—'such a nice gentleman;—and if he did rob the folks, why it is hard to hang such a pretty young man for that' . . . Pretty creatures! But in spite of their prettiness and of their pity I would not give two pence for the life of this Adonis if he should be convicted." He left the circuit in the spring of 1830 to enter Parliament, more adult in manner and with some knowledge of the North and its people and an abiding affection for old-fashioned English inns.[19]

As the editor of Macaulay's letters observed, his "real life in these years was in his writing." Although his essays provided him with a lifetime supply of language and opinions, they were occasional pieces and must be read in their context. "The London University," which he never acknowledged, offered both his coolest verdict on classical education and his fullest argument for restricting Christianity to the domestic sphere. On 9 February 1825 an open letter in *The Times* to Henry Brougham recommended creating a metropolitan university where "the youth of our middling rich people" could study "the liberal arts and sciences." Brougham then launched a campaign to establish such an institution, enlisting the support of Whigs and Benthamites along with leading Dissenters, Catholics, and Jews. He also persuaded Zachary to represent the largely hostile evangelical Anglicans on its governing council.[20] Funding the university required selling hundreds of shares in it, and Tom wrote his essay to refute Tory and Anglican critics of the campaign.

In this case, posing as the voice of the middle classes enabled him to speak "for the sake of this country, and of the whole human race." The ancients had taught him the necessity of putting down and censuring his opponents. The new university's refusal to impose religious tests or to teach religion incensed partisans of Oxford and Cambridge, eager to restore an epoch when "all men should be dunces together": "filthy and malignant baboons." More than religion, Macaulay insisted, class divisions threatened to split the nation. From ancient sources he fashioned a forward-looking social analysis. Borrowing from Aristotle—"perhaps" the greatest philosopher—taught him to separate England's population into three groups: the rich, "the middling rich," and the poor. The nation had entered into "the most dangerous state in which a country can be placed," an "iron age"—he owed the term to another ancient Greek— "in which the lower classes . . . [were] rising in intelligence, while no corresponding improvement was taking place in the rank immediately above them." In these circumstances, it was necessary that the rich accommodate the middling rich in order to create a class "deeply interested . . . in the prosperity and tranquillity of the country . . . too numerous to be corrupted by government . . . too intelligent to be duped by demagogues," and "not likely to carry its zeal for reform to lengths inconsistent with the security of property and the maintenance of social order."[21] Macaulay would ride his analysis into political power.

Tory propagandists, churchmen, and dons attacked a "University without religion!" But in fact the establishment's doctrinal wrangles and declining authority in an era of burgeoning knowledge rendered it impotent either to arouse or to compel national unity. As part of his argument Macaulay contrasted "theology"—the lower case was significant—ancient and contentious, with the modern "science of Political Economy." Capitalization imparted to it the dignity of "a science of considerable intricacy, a science, we may add, which the passions and interests of men have rendered more intricate than it is in its own nature." Cambridge and Oxford were hotbeds of impiety and dissipation. The new university's students would live at home, where their womenfolk would both inspire their ambition and help to make their lives "deco-

rous." He knew from experience. Like all monopolies, Oxbridge had resisted adapting to "the change which daily takes place in the state of
knowledge"—"even the comparative value of languages." He renewed
his schoolboy complaints about "a glut of Greek, Latin, and Mathematics, and a lamentable scarcity of every thing else." It was possible for "clever men of four and five-and-twenty, loaded with academical honours
and rewards"—he himself had left Cambridge on the eve of his twenty-
fourth birthday—to need real education. Invoking Francis Bacon, he assessed the harm done by excluding "histories, modern languages, books
of policy and civil discourse" from the curriculum. He then went on to
settle an old score and reassert his intellectual limitations. Cambridge's
cult of mathematics "is peculiarly dangerous, unless diluted by a large
admixture of" other studies: "on questions of religion, policy or common life, we see these boasted demonstrators either extravagantly credulous, or extravagantly skeptical."[22] Two years later he would elaborate his
argument as an indictment of the Philosophic Radicals.

Macaulay presented himself as "impartial" before launching an attack
on the traditional primacy accorded to learning "the Latin tongue." Latin
"is principally valuable as an introduction to . . . Greek, the insignificant
portico of a most chaste and majestic fabric." To master a foreign language and know its literature was to experience education as uprooting.
"The remains of Greece" were "peculiarly calculated to produce" in a
student the discovery of the relativity and limitations of the "principles
of politics and morals . . . which he has hitherto supposed to be unquestionable, because he never heard them questioned." His appreciation of
learning Greek was autobiographical: "He doubts where he formerly
dogmatised. He tolerates where he formerly execrated."[23]

But learning Greek typically required eight years of study, and for "a
man who is to enter into active life" the cost in time was prohibitive. It
was more sensible to master a useful modern European language "in less
than half the time." The market governed education as much as it governed real estate. "Classical knowledge" was rightly "valued by all intelligent men" because it remained useful. Ensuring that the ancients remained "prized by the public" required that they "be refined from . . .
[their] grosser particles, burnished into splendour, formed into graceful
ornaments, or into current coin."[24]

Though never a cultural democrat, Macaulay proposed to widen access to education by organizing curricula appropriate to each of England's three classes. Those who could afford to study into their twenties should learn the classical languages. All who left school at twenty-one, including most of those enrolled at the ancient universities, must "be satisfied with the modern languages." Anyone employed by the age of sixteen "should confine himself almost entirely to his native tongue, and thoroughly imbue his mind with the spirit of its best writers." Free competition among schools and within schools would preserve classical knowledge for a smaller but abler elite. The "great body" of university men were competent and respectable, but their "foundations are unsound": "They hate abstract reasoning. The very name of theory is terrible to them. They seem to think that the use of experience is not to lead men to the knowledge of general principles, but to prevent them from ever thinking about general principles at all."[25] A classical education might teach men how to question and criticize, but it yielded no reasonable answers. Within three years Macaulay would anathematize theory and later, in India, reverse himself on downsizing classical education.

During 1827 Macaulay wrote about politics. The March issue of the *Edinburgh Review* included both his studied vindication of the "Social and Industrial Capacities of Negroes" and his insinuating analysis of "Machiavelli," which worked to change minds. Sensing "the Machiavellian flavor of Macaulay's outlook," an astute scholar concluded that "much" of it was "in the nineteenth century, no longer distinctive." During the twentieth century that seemed obvious, just as it had been two hundred years earlier, when the widespread practice of Machiavellianism in England rendered Machiavelli otiose. Macaulay, however, wrote earlier in the nineteenth century against counterrevolutionary and philanthropic politics informed by religious imagery, language, and even faith. For Zachary's sake he pleaded the case of the abolitionist "philanthropists," denying both any inherent antipathy between whites and blacks and the incompetence of freed slaves in the tropics. But he argued on his own terms: "We have treated the question as a question purely scientific. We have reasoned as if we had been reasoning, not about men and women, but about spinning-jennies and power-looms."[26]

Macaulay's Machiavellianism helped to change the nation's political language. In 1837 the Tories provoked him because they invested policies he opposed—"civil abuses"—with "the sanctity of religion." Six years

later he sniffed at "Machiavelli" as a "juvenile essay written while I was in
my full honey-moon with the Tuscan Muse." But he regretted its "errors
and faults," not his choice of a muse. Now "even the Tories" thought the
"old Florentine was much . . . cleverer" than their leader, Sir Robert Peel.
They, too, had become Macchiavellians.[27]

Macaulay opened his seminal and subversive 1827 essay by rhetorically conceding that Machiavelli's "character and writings" were "generally odious": "Principles which the most hardened ruffian would scarcely
hint to his most trusted accomplice, or avow . . . are professed without
the slightest circumlocution, and assumed as the fundamental axioms of
all political science." He then began to insinuate a more knowing interpretation of "the Tuscan Muse." A real though not necessarily deserved
hatred—"odium"—was the reaction of "ordinary readers." In contrast,
the wise "have always been inclined to look with great suspicion on the
angels and dæmons of the multitude." Macaulay questioned "the justice
of the vulgar decision." *The Prince* was the exception among Machiavelli's writings, which in general "exhibit so much elevation of sentiment,
so pure and warm a zeal for the public good, [and] so just a view of the
duties and rights of citizens." Ethically, moreover, he surpassed his Italian
contemporaries, who provided the proper benchmark for judging him
and his works. Here Macaulay's historical relativism was unequivocal:
"Succeeding generations change the fashion of their morals, with the
fashion of their hats and their coaches."[28] With age his public voice grew
more circumspect.

But in 1827 he insisted that even *The Prince* taught a rhetorical aesthetics of power, because "propriety of thought, and propriety of diction,
are commonly found together . . . The judicious and candid mind" of
Machiavelli shows itself in his "luminous, manly, and polished language."
Whereas *The Prince* "traces the progress of an ambitious man," the *Discourses on Livy* traces "the progress of an ambitious people. The same
principles on which, in the former work, the elevation of an individual is
explained, are applied in the latter, to the longer duration and more complex interest of a society." There could be no "denying" both books'
"peculiar immorality," but neither was it possible to deny "the highest
and the most peculiar praise to the precepts of Machiavelli": "they may
be of real use in regulating conduct . . . because they can be more readily
applied to the problems of real life." Machiavelli's flaw was insufficient

realism. He paid "more attention to means than to ends" and failed to give proper weight to the "great principle, that societies and laws exist only for the purpose of increasing the sum of private happiness." Informed by Macaulay's conviction that rivalry among states and classes was permanent, the essay updated the clever "old Florentine" for future reference. A year later he reprised his argument for the genius of Machiavelli's *Discourses:* "they are strikingly practical, and teach us not only the general rule, but the mode of applying it to solve particular cases."[29]

Published in June, "The Present Administration" championed a coalition government led by the Tory George Canning. Long the masterly peacekeeper among the Tory factions, Lord Liverpool resigned the premiership after an incapacitating stroke. His party was divided over reducing protective tariffs on imported corn (wheat) and "emancipating" the Catholics by repealing the Test Act and permitting them to sit in the House of Commons. At stake was pacifying alienated, heavily Catholic Ireland. Thirty years later Macaulay remembered those days with a vehemence that suggests their bitterness. Long after making his peace with Peel, he still blamed him for refusing to see as late as 1827 that, minus emancipation, "the state would have been in great danger." Instead Peel had waited to concede, "acted most culpably in deserting & persecuting Canning," and incurred "the disgrace of yielding to agitation and to the fear of insurrection."[30]

Stylish, eloquent, painstaking, and the possessor of a sterling résumé, Canning was the heir of William Pitt the Younger's reforming politics. When George IV appointed him prime minister in April 1827, the duke of Wellington, along with other arch-Tories and the nondoctrinaire Peel, boycotted the government. Canning's cabinet consisted mainly of liberal Tories and a group of Whig moderates led by Lord Lansdowne. Both sides vowed silence about parliamentary reform and repealing the Test Act. Lord Grey captained the Whig "malignants" who opposed the government. Several of Macaulay's formative political and personal associations were at least briefly Canningites. In 1830 Lansdowne would bring him into the House of Commons. Also in the cabinet were the future Lord Melbourne, who as prime minister would appoint Macaulay to a Whig cabinet in 1839; and Lord Palmerston, then a long-marginalized Pittite but by the 1850s almost Macaulay's ideological soul mate. Brougham moved to the government benches. Canning was, moreover,

Zachary's kind of liberal Tory: pro-Catholic and antiprotectionist. On the transcendent question of abolition Canning also had his uses. At one time a convinced supporter of ending the slave trade, he remained well disposed toward if not always reliable about Zachary's projects.[31]

Tom's essay combined a visceral tone and a calculating message. The high Tories resembled aborted and drowned whelps, "at once transferred from the filth in which they were littered to the filth with which they are to rot." Canning's government upheld "liberty," "toleration," and "political science" and represented both "the people, who are entitled to expect . . . many judicious reforms," and "the aristocracy, who unless those reforms be adopted, must inevitably be the victims of a violent and desolating revolution." Macaulay carefully distinguished between "the real and the imaginary" Pitt the Younger. The Pitt of history anticipated his own Whiggism: "a Parliamentary reformer, and enemy of the Test and Corporation Acts, and advocate of Catholic Emancipation and of free trade." Macaulay was never a Whig malignant. Decisive for the success of Catholic emancipation were the realities of class. Most of "the higher classes" supported it, and the lower classes—"corrupt," "servile," "rude," "uneducated," "dissolute," and "turbulent"—opposed it. The task was to win over "the People of England"—"the great body of the middling orders." That cool analysis complemented his matter-of-fact reference to "this tragicomic world of ours." As much as his hostility to democracy, his instinctive disillusionment endured.[32]

Parliamentary reform was for the moment "evidently unattainable," but he predicted that if the Tory "seceders" regained power they would provoke a revolution. It was imperative to prevent "the majority of the middling orders" from joining "with the mob." A would-be revolutionary vanguard already existed. They "profess to derive their opinions from demonstration alone . . . Metaphysical and political science engage their whole attention . . . It has made them arrogant, intolerant, and impatient of all superiority." He was referring to a claque of Benthamites, who possessed both "real claims to respect" and a vitiating weakness. They disdained rhetoric and objected to having their opinions expressed in an appealing form. Canning died four months into his premiership, leaving Macaulay "extremely shocked" and Brougham scrambling to explain away his protégé's truculent essay and his own alliance with Canning: "Two great divisions of the community will . . . soon be far more generally known; the *Liberal* and the *Illiberal*." Immediately, Lansdowne thought "highly" of the essay, which offered him a deferential nod. The long term vindicated its political insight. By 1849 "pre-1832 liberal Toryism" was blending into "post-1848 liberal conservatism."

> Their principles were the same—an inclination rather to support the prerogatives of Government than to give any great extension to popular power; but a strong conviction that the Government as constituted should be conducted with justice and intelligence; that all monopolies, whether in trade or religion, ought to be abolished, and that the general policy of our civil administration at home, and of our affairs abroad, should be in accordance with the character of a great Empire, eminently commercial, and under the sway of free, but not democratic institutions.
>
> These opinions, though not precisely Whig or Tory, were in reality . . . becoming about this time, the opinions of the day.[33]

But a partisan melee defined the late 1820s and 1830s. In those days Tom was on the make and dependent, "a young fellow, fighting my way uphill." On Brougham's recommendation and partly out of regard for Zachary, the Tory lord chancellor who survived Canning in office appointed him a commissioner of bankrupts. Tom insisted to his father that "it implies no political obligation." During his three years in office his annual earnings averaged £253 6s 8d, with a 2007 purchasing power of £18,273. The money was "welcome." But writing persuasively and often iconoclastically on all manner of topics without benefit of deep learning enabled him to transcend his barely genteel station. Revisiting Edinburgh in the spring of 1828 for the first time in eleven years occasioned a small epiphany: "I seem to myself here another being from what I was. Between me and the schoolboy of sixteen there is nothing in common—absolutely nothing."[34]

His assiduous wordsmithery refuted his insistent adverb. In "Machiavelli" he had appealed to historical circumstances to vindicate his subject. Nine months later he used the tactic to deprecate the poet John Dryden, who, living in an unpoetic age, "succeeded only in an inferior department of his art, but . . . succeeded pre-eminently." Bracketing the literary impact of Dryden's complex religious itinerary from Puritanism through

Anglicanism to Catholicism, he digressed to disparage the "creations of the great dramatists of Athens" as "cold, pale, and rigid, with no bloom on the cheek, and no speculation in the eye." Increasingly confident about the originality of the modern era, Macaulay had already weighed its implications for writing history. One great classical historian's works "may almost be called romances founded in fact." The story was "in all its principal points, strictly true," but "the imagination of the author" enlivened it with "numerous little incidents which heighten the interest" and "imprinted on the mind for ever." Modern histories were "more exact," but the ancients conveyed "a more vivid and a more faithful impression of the *national* character and manners." Machiavelli's "elegant, lively, and picturesque" *History of Florence* belonged "rather to ancient than to modern literature."[35]

In May Macaulay expanded his musings into forty pages on writing a "perfect" modern history. Once famous and occasionally remembered even now, "History" testified to his abated "passion" for the classics and to his interest in creating a modern historical style that was recognizably Protestant, because it was domestic and more cultural and social than political. In addition to accommodating the religion "of houses," his essay sought to mediate between the rhetorical panache of classical historians and the analytical rigor of up-to-date philosophical historians. Conjuring "imaginary models," he located history "on the confines of two distinct territories": "Instead of being equally shared between . . . the Reason and the Imagination, it falls alternately under the sole and absolute dominion of each." The historian's dilemma was that as philosophy grew "in soundness and depth, the examples generally lost in vividness."[36] He refused to republish "History" and in practice repudiated it in *The History of England*.

Self-consciously modern, Macaulay faulted all the ancient rhetorical historians. Herodotus, "the father of history," was "a delightful child," whose "simple and imaginative mind" led him to tell stories worthy of "servants." More sophisticated, Thucydides was like a portraitist who transcended the "merely mechanical" craft of producing a recognizable likeness to "condense into one point of time, and exhibit, at a single glance, the whole history of turbid and eventful lives." He understood that history is an art of perspective and arrangement: "No picture, then, and no history, can present us with the whole truth: but those are the best pictures and the best histories which exhibit such parts of the truth as most nearly produce the effect of the whole." Thucydides' failure lay in not theorizing: "Facts are the mere dross of history. It is from the abstract truth which interpenetrates them, and lies latent among them like gold in the ore, that the mass derives its whole value." In the end, he remained "simply an Athenian of the fifth century before Christ." Macaulay thus purposed writing history in the present-minded way in which he read all the ancients, so that his own contemporaries could "form just calculations with respect to the future": "No past event has any intrinsic importance."[37] He died believing that good history was about the usable past.

The other Greek historians of the golden age lacked "comprehensive minds," and their successors like Plutarch were nostalgic pedants. In a voice sounding both cosmopolitan and Christian, Macaulay scouted the ancients' "exclusive attachment to a particular society." It "has turned states into gangs of robbers whom their mutual fidelity has rendered more dangerous, has given a character of peculiar atrocity to war, and has generated that worst of all political evils, the tyranny of nations over nations." Three permanent realities differentiated late antiquity from the modern world: its liberty was the freedom not of individuals but of polities; its "ordinary rules of morality are deduced from extreme cases" rather than from universal principles; and its historians "paid little attention to facts, to the custom of the times of which they pretend to treat, [and] to the general principles of human nature." For all that, Macaulay's exclusive attachment to the particular society of England infused his essay: "Our liberty . . . [is] essentially English. It has a character of its own,—a character which has taken a tinge from the sentiments of the chivalrous ages, and which accords with the peculiarities of our manners and of our insular situation." And England's insularity was more than geographic. Again Macaulay hailed "the yet loftier genius of Cromwell" because of what he did for his nation and to its enemies.[38]

Among the Romans, Livy formed "a class by himself": "no historian with whom we are acquainted has shown so complete an indifference to truth. He seems to have cared only about the picturesque effect of his book, and the honour of his country." But his art was a bad thing done superbly. Unlike his backward-looking Greek contemporaries, his loyalty went to the imperial present. Tacitus was "certainly the greatest" of the

Romans, not because of his dense Latin but "in the delineation of character," which was "unrivalled among historians . . . with very few superiors among dramatists and novelists." He exemplified the talent for dramatization required "to write history."[39]

Because of the progressive nature of "the science of government," the moderns excelled "in the philosophy of history," one of "the experimental sciences" along with "legislation and political economy." At the same time, as much as the ancients Macaulay believed that an essentially unchanging human nature permitted the discovery of timeless truths about ourselves and our behavior. Of course, technological, intellectual, and moral change was undeniable. Printing "diffused knowledge widely" and "introduced into reasoning a precision, unknown in those ancient communities, in which information was, for the most part, conveyed orally." Narrow communication fostered narrow sympathies. The spirit of both the Greeks and the Romans "was remarkably exclusive": "the Greeks admired only themselves, and the Romans admired only themselves and the Greeks." Cultural inbreeding led them to persecute Jews and Christians and to disdain the "sublime poetry . . . curious history . . . [and] striking and peculiar views of the Divine nature and of the social duties of men" found in the "Jewish scriptures." As a result, the vast and despotic Roman Empire risked achieving "a tottering, drivelling, paralytic longevity" worthy of "Chinese civilisation." Then Christianity overthrew "the old system of morals; and with it much of the old system of metaphysics . . . It stirred the stagnant mass from the inmost depths. It excited all the passions of a stormy democracy in the quiet and listless population of an overgrown empire": "It cost Europe a thousand years of barbarism to escape the fate of China." After religion and barbarism finished their purging, "the second civilisation of mankind commenced," eclipsing Asia and the rest.[40] In India Macaulay would perfect his Eurocentric voice and drop its Christian overtones.

Moderns surpassed the ancients in "depth and precision of reason," but "the best historians of later times have been seduced from truth, not by their imagination but by their reason." It led them to "distort facts to suit general principles." Practicing all the "arts of controversy" caused them to neglect "the art of narration, the art of interesting the affections and presenting pictures to the imagination." Looking to "excellent biographical works" that outsold novels, Macaulay imagined a history that would make the voices of the Long Parliament (1640–1649) speak again and achieve popularity. It would exhibit the "history of the government, and the history of the people" in "inseparable conjunction and intermixture." Penetrating beneath high politics—"the surface of affairs"—it would reveal the "mighty and various organisation which lies deep below" and "the noiseless revolutions" that usually yield profound change. Here Macaulay echoed the founders of the *Edinburgh Review*, who themselves popularized what they had learned from some of their enlightened Scottish professors. But in their view "the revolution of 1688" rather than the earlier Civil War and Commonwealth was decisive. It brought England a "commercial government" and fostered "the subsequent increase of expense and of public revenue, the influence of the Crown upon one hand, while it has promoted the cause of freedom, on the other, by the general increase of riches and knowledge, and the gradual diffusion of political information among people."[41] Eventually Macaulay adopted their interpretation.

Reviewing Henry Hallam's *Constitutional History of England* from 1485 to 1760 a few months later, he outlined his own *History*. A Whig though no liberal, Hallam was an arid writer who confirmed Macaulay's conviction that impressing "general truths on the mind by a vivid representation of particular characters and incidents" required prose that was both "eminently judicial" and "a compound of poetry and philosophy." Only a rhetorical history accommodated both levels of truth: "Every political sect has its esoteric and its exoteric school, its abstract doctrines for the initiated, its visible symbols, its imposing forms, its mythological fables for the vulgar." Rhetoric, finally, enabled a historian to adjust his voice to his readers' changing capacities and moods. That said, Macaulay accepted most of Hallam's story. At heart, England's Reformation was a secular and political affair. Its medieval constitution survived into the seventeenth century because weak monarchs failed to create a professional military. The Civil War was the turning point. Devious and incompetent, King Charles I presented "an extreme case" that demanded a "remedy which is in its own nature most violent." Insistent as always on the supremacy of England's interests, Macaulay again trumpeted Oliver Cromwell. He "possessed, in an eminent degree, that masculine and full-grown robustness of mind, that equally diffused intellectual health, which, if our national partiality does not mislead us, has peculiarly characterised the great men of England. Never was any ruler so conspicuously born for sovereignty . . . he was punctilious only for his country."[42]

Macaulay's *History of England* would also follow "Hallam" in depicting the Stuart Restoration as a reaction against Puritan stringency, which killed "almost all national feelings" in the sundry mercenaries who enjoyed power. But in 1828 Macaulay's enthusiasm for the Revolution of 1688–89 remained tempered: "It was assuredly a happy revolution, and a useful revolution; but it was not, what it has often been called, a glorious revolution. William, and William alone, derived glory from it. The transaction was, in almost every part, discreditable to England." His reign was "the Nadir of the national prosperity. It was also the Nadir of the national character." Progress followed, however, and the elements of modern parliamentary government were in place by 1760.[43]

Unlike Hallam, Macaulay championed parliamentary reform, and the essay echoed its radical genealogy by emphasizing the Civil War. It also refined what became the stock argument of the seven speeches on reform that brought him acclaim in 1831–32. It was imperative to reconcile "the two great branches of the natural aristocracy, the capitalists and the landowners." Therefore it "will soon again be necessary to reform that we may preserve, to save the fundamental principles of the Constitution by alterations in the fundamental parts." Although the public was distracted, class warfare and revolution loomed. His insistence on the necessity of reform was lucky guesswork. In retrospect, enacting it seems a contingency. As Boyd Hilton has recently noted, "no petitions calling exclusively for reform were presented between 1825 and 1829 . . . Even [the Whig leader] Grey abjured reform in 1827, and the issue seemed dead. Moreover, its eventual revival was more a consequence than a cause of Wellington's fall [in November 1830], which was due to discontent within his party rather than in the country at large."[44]

However congenial, practice on the Northern Circuit was a drain on Macaulay's income—in 1829 £700, with a 2007 purchasing power of £49,506. The support of his parents, two brothers, and five sisters fell on him. When Jeffrey resigned as editor of the *Edinburgh Review* in April 1829, Macaulay was offered the editorship, but the post went instead to Macvey Napier, perhaps because of Brougham's opposition to Tom. Macaulay considered withdrawing his services. During 1830 Brougham's harassment continued, but the future belonged to Macaulay. Parliament had become permanently sensitive to "a politically educated public opinion," which intensified the competing reviews' ambitions and aggressiveness: they played to their base. By 1833 Napier, who initially underestimated and mismanaged him, recognized that he was essential to the magazine. Its sales rose when he contributed and fell in his absence.[45]

Macaulay's best-studied essays are three published in 1829 savaging James Mill's political theory. They raised his profile and foretold his future. He brought complex purposes to his "review" of a set of Mill's encyclopedia articles, some dating back to 1816. It was necessary to rebuke Mill's "intolerance toward piecemeal, moderate reform" of Parliament, which Macaulay and his colleagues favored. He also wanted publicly to divorce himself from the Philosophic Radicals and to repay Mill's reported disdain for him. Finally, there was a score to settle on behalf of the *Edinburgh Review*. Five years before, Mill had launched the *Westminster Review* with a "merciless denunciation" of the Whig magazine for pretending "interest in the people in order to advance their own interests." When Macaulay struck back, the factional quarrels rending the *Westminster* made it an invitingly weak target.[46]

While branding the Utilitarians as mostly "ordinary men, with narrow understandings and little information," Macaulay carefully deferred to the "illustrious" Jeremy Bentham. His objection was to Mill's dogmatic anticipation of something like what we call "rational choice theory": "Any scientific theory worthy of the name must proceed from a finite set of assumptions about human nature, with the self-interest axiom at their center. From these one can deduce conclusions about the ways in which rational political actors will (or at any rate ought to) behave." The political reasoning of Bentham, whom Macaulay dubbed "the founder of the sect," was more empirical.[47]

Macaulay's first critique was virtuosic: "the *à priori* method is altogether unfit for investigations of this kind and . . . the only way to arrive at truth is by induction." Because humans are not only calculators but also "imaginative beings," understanding their affairs required either "history or experience." Instead of pioneering "behavioral economics," Mill confused reality with a "hubbub of unmeaning words" and practiced "the verbal sophistry which flourished during the dark ages" before Francis Bacon achieved "the great deliverance of the human mind." All governments were historically contingent, and no system of government was normative. Practically, Macaulay objected that Mill's theory necessarily implied universal manhood suffrage, needled him for exclusivity—"But why not the women too?"—and prophesied that democracy would destroy civilization. Because "the interest of the majority" lay in plundering "the rich," within a couple of centuries "a few lean and half-naked fishermen may divide with owls and foxes the ruins of the greatest European cities—may wash their nets amidst the relics of his gigantic docks, and build their huts out of the capitals of her stately cathedrals."[48] Again the prospect of eventual desolation shadowed his evocation of the "natural progress of society."

Anonymously, a third-tier disciple of Bentham defended the "'Greatest Happiness' Principle"—"History is nothing but the relation of the sufferings of the poor from the rich"—and accepted Macaulay's premonition of class warfare. Macaulay rejoined, believing that Bentham—"the father of the philosophy of Jurisprudence" and "a truly great man"—was the author. He wrote cautiously, "in a state of perfect skepticism" and without any "complete theory of government," much less theorymaking. The burden of "Mr. Bentham's article" was "an exposition of the Utilitarian principle, or, as he decrees that it shall be called, the 'greatest happiness principle'": "We never said a syllable against it." Macaulay's earlier silence became assent. The principle was so commonplace as to seem commonsensical, "at best no more than the golden rule of the Gospel without its sanction." Reclaiming Utilitarianism for Christian England, he asserted that the principle presumed the sanctions of religion, because people "will not and cannot" act "to promote the happiness of others, at the expense of their own." Bentham himself only taught people "*how,* in some most important points to promote their own happiness." Macaulay's sticking point remained the Utilitarians' advocacy of manhood suffrage, which would make "parliamentary reform" the "object of disgust to the majority of the community."[49]

In a coda Macaulay declared himself "truly happy" to find that Bentham—"this illustrious man"—had had "so small a share" in the article, which, "for his sake, we have treated with far greater lenity than it deserved." His refutation provoked a reply from his Utilitarian critic, who mocked him as a refractory member of the extended Benthamite family, "a thoughtless little boy" guilty of "unadvised assault upon the venerable father of the flock." Macaulay vituperatively responded that parliamentary reform must not be conflated with "universal suffrage." In passing he also sneered at a Tory paternalist whom he was soon to vivisect and revisited the recent history of his own opinions. The Utilitarians erred in trying "to revive" "the worse parts" of the "nonsense" of "that shallow dogmatist, Epicurus," who "shrank from the keen and searching scepticism of the second Academy."[50] Eight years later in India Macaulay would cling to his skepticism while revising his dismissal of Epicureanism.

In the aftermath many Philosophic Radicals considered themselves discredited, but the controversy proved to be a creative impetus for John Stuart Mill. He recalled that his father "felt" Macaulay's attack "keenly ... but with a quite impersonal feeling, as he would have felt anything that he thought unjustly said against any opinion or cause which was dear to him." The son was more deeply affected: "this gave me much to think about ... there was truth in several of his strictures on my father's treatment of the subject ... my father's premises were really too narrow, and included but a small number of the general truths on which, in politics, the important consequences depend ... there was really something more fundamentally erroneous in my father's conception of philosophical method, as applicable to politics, than I had hitherto supposed there was." His reevaluation bore fruit of lasting importance. As for James, his capacity for "quite impersonal feeling" served Macaulay well. He respected Macaulay's political skills and thought his "accurate acquaintance with the Greek writers" peerless. It perhaps mattered more to Mill that Macaulay, despite his abjuring the Benthamite "sect," remained an orthodox, indeed literal-minded, advocate of its creed of utility. The only competing moral system imaginable to him was the "Sentimental," whose claims, apart from rhetorical convenience, began and mostly ended in the domestic sphere.[51]

Utility was also the only language of public morality available to most of Macaulay's Edinburgh Review colleagues. An occasional contributor to the magazine, the Reverend Thomas Robert Malthus was no secular Benthamite but a "theological utilitarian, on morals" who sought to deflate revolutionary utopianism and to direct human hopes upward rather than onward: "The view of human life which results from the contemplation of the constant pressure of distress on man from the difficulty of subsistence, by shewing the little expectation that he can reasonably entertain of perfectibility on earth, seems strongly to point his hopes to the future." Macaulay adapted that lesson and many others from Malthus in order to cudgel the Tory paternalists, the "wets" of their day. Inspired by Samuel Johnson, Robert Southey became perhaps the most conspicuous of them. Having abandoned his youthful revolutionary enthusiasm and been appointed the poet laureate in 1813, he remained "Sentimental" in his social vision but now looked to retrieve a better world from the late Middle Ages. His prominence invited Macaulay's assault.[52]

The conceit of *Sir Thomas More; or Colloquies on the Progress and Prospects of Society* was that More's ghost appeared to the naïve young radical Southey to discuss the condition of England. In an essay that would sound almost contemporary in 2009, Macaulay began by acknowledging the laureate as "a mind which has exercised considerable influence on the most enlightened generation of the most enlightened people that ever existed"—in fact he invented the historical essay that Macaulay perfected—but condemned him as "utterly destitute of the power of discerning truth from falsehood." He mingled his vituperation with praise for Edmund Burke, "a much greater man." Macaulay's insistence that there was nothing personal in "any of the remarks which we have made on the spirit of . . . [Southey's] writings" was probably accurate. It was all "just business" of *The Godfather* sort. Assaulting Southey's paternalism enabled him to stigmatize as irrational competing notions of public reason and the state's role in the economy. He distinguished between reason and argument on the one hand—an "account of the way in which he has arrived at his opinions"—and imagination and taste on the other— what he called "will and pleasure." The strategy enabled him to assert both that civil government was "quite distinct from religion" and that his own unspecified version of reason was a "matter of science," the only acceptable form of political talk.[53]

He barbed his tribute to Burke. In prosecuting Warren Hastings, the Indian empire-builder, and opposing the French Revolution, Burke "chose his side like a fanatic, and defended it like a philosopher": "His reason, like a spirit in the service of an enchanter, though spell-bound, was still mighty. It did whatever work his passions and his imagination might impose." "Imagination" was the key word. Burke's *Reflections on the Revolution in France* (1790) had famously assailed "this new conquering empire of light and reason" and championed the "moral imagination, which the heart owns, and the understanding ratifies, as necessary to cover the defects of our naked, shivering nature, and to raise it to dignity in our own estimation." Macaulay learned to call such altruistic reasoning "philanthropic cant" and worked systematically and with much success to discredit it.[54]

A major issue between himself and Southey was the establishment's public role after Catholics and Protestant Dissenters received the franchise in 1828. Macaulay, whom Southey scorned as a deadly serpent hatched by "dogmatic atheism," now assigned a circumscribed utility to Christianity. Far from initiating a moral revolution in public life, both the religion and the moral imagination it fostered belonged to domestic life: "The whole history of Christianity shows, that she [that is, Christianity] is in far greater danger of being corrupted by the alliance of power, than of being crushed by its opposition." Although "she"—the feminine pronoun effectively domesticated the religion—properly "sanctions government, as she sanctions every thing which promotes the happiness and virtue of our species," Christianity no more provided the basis of government than it provided the basis of "eating, drinking, and lighting fires in cold weather." Rather, the state's legitimacy rested on "public opinion"—the point of view "of some class which has power over the rest of the community"—and the state could not "train the people in the ways in which they should go."[55] Max Weber was not original, only blunter about the fundamental amorality of power.

Insisting on the state's incompetence to relieve the English people's distress, let alone guarantee their well-being, Macaulay summarized the difference between Southey's economics and his own: "Rose-bushes and poor-rates, rather than steam-engines and independence." He ridiculed Southey's regime as "a jack-of-all-trades, architect, engineer, schoolmaster, merchant, theologian, a Lady Bountiful in every parish, a Paul Pry in every house, spying, eavesdropping, relieving, admonishing, spending our money for us, and choosing our opinions for us." Informing Macaulay's prophecy of endless progress was the "technological sublime," a vision of machines as not merely productive and proliferating but virtually supernatural. It was the "improvements of machinery" that raised the standard of living far above what had obtained in Southey's fanciful golden age before the Reformation and made England "now the richest and the most highly civilized spot in the world."[56]

To succor "the lower orders in England . . . [who] suffer severe hard-

ships," Macaulay invoked the "natural tendency of society to improvement." He was redirecting earthward and onward Malthus' advice
"strongly to point" the hopes of the distressed "to the future." Though
refusing to "prophesy," Macaulay introduced "this natural progress of society" as one of "those general laws" by which God—in whom he did
not believe—regulated "the moral world" and improved English life in
scarcely imaginable ways. Progress worked not "by the intermeddling of
Mr. Southey's idol, the omniscient and omnipotent State, but by the prudence and energy of the people." The policy implications of that God-
given law were clear: "leaving capital to find its most lucrative course,
commodities their fair price, industry and intelligence their natural reward, idleness and folly their natural punishment, by maintaining peace,
by defending property, by diminishing the price of law, and by observing strict economy in every department of the state."[57] The appeal of
Macaulay's market utopia exemplifies how popularizing the opinions "of
some class which has power over the rest of the community" can legitimate its rule.

However retrograde Southey's views, he received a certain politeness
as a member of the power elite. In contrast, a few months later Macaulay
skewered a popular enthusiast's response to England's distress. According
to one assessment, the Anglican poetaster Robert Montgomery "appealed to a (largely evangelical) taste for grandiose restatements of traditional Christian wisdom, generally with an apocalyptic bent, in a decade
troubled by the prospect of imminent social and political catastrophe";
his "very banality" made him "one of the two or three best-selling poets
of the second quarter of the nineteenth century." Recognizing that
Montgomery's success depended on a huge class of new readers who
were, often unhappily, "now the patron, and a most liberal one," Macaulay
ridiculed his poems as semiliterate absurdities. His fusillade hit home.
Twenty years later Montgomery protested the republication of the review and in 1854 threatened to bring suit. Macaulay found him "a fool"
and "a coxcomb" but amusing as an occasional whipping boy.[58]

Macaulay's next evangelical target was also a godsend: Michael Sadler,
an autodidact, failed businessman, and abolitionist, but also a Tory, anti-
Catholic, foe of parliamentary reform, and paternalist. Over nearly thirteen hundred pages Sadler labored to overturn Malthus' theory of almost
inevitable overpopulation and dearth, insisting that, all things being equal,

people reproduce in inverse proportion to their numbers. He knew that Malthus' prophecy was "inconsistent with Christianity, and even with the purer forms of Deism." After heaping ridicule, Macaulay statistically eviscerated Sadler's "wretched trifling" and "ludicrous absurdity" in order to vindicate Malthus' "law of geometrical progression." He aimed to block the imposition of "blundering piety" on political economy: "A man who wishes to serve the cause of religion ought to hesitate long before he stakes the truth of religion on the event of a controversy respecting facts in the physical world." Sadler published a refutation, and Macaulay refuted his "foolish pamphlet." Despite Macaulay's best efforts he could not avoid the "guer[r]illa war" of theology. His stance was cleverly skeptical: "Of the puzzles of the [ancient] Academy, there is not one which does not apply as strongly to Deism as to Christianity, and to Atheism as to Deism. There are difficulties in everything. Yet we are sure that something must be true." A warm enmity was born, and a year later in Leeds he defeated Sadler for a seat in Parliament.[59]

Politician

It was Macaulay's first contested election and his second constituency. In mid-January 1830, Lord Lansdowne, whom he had saluted in the Canning essay, offered him a seat that he controlled. One radical denounced Calne, a market town in Wiltshire, as the "rottenest, stinkingest, skulkingest of boroughs." A landed magnate of refined tastes, reforming disposition, and equable temperament, Lansdowne became Macaulay's greatest patron apart from Jeffrey: "I owe more to him than to any man living; and he never seemed to be sensible that I owed him anything." In early February 1830 Macaulay was summoned to Bowood, a "magnificent palace," to await his election—"All the votes have been promised to me" —and was sworn in as an M.P. on the eighteenth. But why choose Tom Macaulay? Lansdowne reportedly told him that he admired the essays against James Mill, as he had the Canning piece, and approved of his "high moral and private character." There were also personal connections. Zachary and Lansdowne collaborated in the Anti-Slavery Society and other philanthropic activities. The marquess was said to have also noticed Tom's continuing friendship with Charles Austin, his own acquaintance and still a firm Benthamite.[60] Lansdowne's sense of balance

perhaps enabled him to intuit that Tom, exceptionally talented, constitu-
tionally realistic, and improbably connected with both Zachary and Austin, could mature into an effective partisan of equipoise. If so, time vindicated his insight.

Lansdowne's choice infuriated Brougham, who had favored a friendly
senior Whig politician for the seat. Largely oblivious to other people and
disposed to a "psychopathic egotism," Brougham began taking his revenge. Tom described for his sister Margaret being sworn in with him:
"As I turned from the table at which I had been taking the oaths . . . he
cut me dead. We never spoke in the House, excepting once, that I can
remember, when a few words passed between us in the lobby." The
bankruptcy post was not renewed, but there could be no breaking with
Brougham, on his way to becoming lord chancellor when the Whigs returned to power after decades in opposition. Tom's family depended on
his largesse. Before 1830 ended Brougham arranged for John, recently
ordained an Anglican priest, to receive a country benefice said to be
worth £300 a year, with a 2007 purchasing power of £21,912. In 1831
he was instrumental in securing for the threadbare Zachary appointment as, ironically, a commissioner of public charity at £800 a year—
with 2007 purchasing power of £57,702—and cleared the way for his
son Henry to receive a post in Sierra Leone with an annual salary of
£2,000—£144,255 in 2007. There was at least one row over Brougham
between Zachary and Tom. Margaret's eyewitness account illustrates how
they could joust. Tom "as usual abused" Brougham "as the most profligate, faithless scoundrel in England, and Papa defended him with his
usual warmth." Zachary insisted that Tom must no longer go about "talking in the violent manner in which he had spoken . . . he was extremely
angry. Tom's voice trembled with passion and agitation." Over the years
there would be truces between Brougham and Tom, whose "warmth"
cooled into disdain for a has-been: "His friendship has caused me more
vexation in a fortnight than his enmity in seventeen years."[61]

Catholic Emancipation had been enacted in the spring of 1829, destroying the old regime and resurrecting the issue of parliamentary reform. It was a textbook case of the rule of unintended consequences.
Fearing civil war in Ireland, the duke of Wellington flew in the teeth of
resentful Tory peers and rammed Catholic emancipation through the

House of Lords. In June 1830 William IV's accession necessitated a general election—Macaulay was returned for Calne on 2 August. Lord Grey, onetime Whig malcontent and now leader of the party, emerged from a long funk to denounce Wellington's government, which was "in terminal disarray." The disfranchised made themselves heard in many constituencies, a reality that compelled many candidates to pledge themselves to expand the electorate. Appalled at Wellington's treachery and mindful of the nation's solid anti-Catholicism, many staunch Anglicans joined with some Dissenters to support reform for "illiberal and populist reasons." The spectacle of agrarian vandalism "terrified landed society as a whole, and added to the sense that ministers had lost control." Wellington refused to concede even a measure of parliamentary reform to Palmerston, the Canningite leader, and thus alienated that Tory faction. In the House of Commons Peel lost control of his backbenchers. On 15 November the government was swamped on a procedural issue. Thinking to forestall parliamentary reform, Wellington resigned, and Grey formed a government containing an abundance of liberal Tories, moderates, and reformers and a few Whigs.[62]

In July 1830 another French revolution permanently evicted the Bourbons. The event was widely interpreted in Britain as presaging upheaval at home, and after spending September in Paris—his first trip abroad—Macaulay decided to write about Napoleon's fall. When Brougham succeeded in blocking the publication of the essay in the *Edinburgh Review,* Macaulay proposed a history that would culminate in the latest revolution. *Napoleon and the Restoration of the Bourbons* was advertised, and 6,000 title pages were printed. Macaulay wrote with his mind on revolution and his eye on England: "There are two portions of modern history pre-eminently important and interesting—the history of England from the meeting of the long parliament to the second expulsion of the Stuarts; and the history of France from the opening of the states-general at Versailles to the accession of the house of Orleans . . . neither of these portions of history will ever be thoroughly comprehended by any man who has not often looked at them in connexion, and carefully examined the numerous points of analogy and of contrast which they present."[63] That his unfinished draft lay unpublished until 1977 was a portent.

Orator

Macaulay embodied three attributes of a certain kind of old-regime M.P.: he owed his seat to a patron rather than to independent electors; because he did not belong to the elite and was unpaid, he needed to support himself—there was no profit from the law and too little from his reviewing; and his rhetorical education had prepared him to "speak brilliantly and according to classical standards of oratory," talents that went "a long way toward establishing a political reputation." Orating was easier than moneymaking. When he was famous and almost rich he remembered that he "made my way in the world by haranguing" and saw "parliamentary government [as] . . . government by speaking." While an undergraduate, he already knew that M.P.'s targeted public opinion when they spoke: "They think less of the few hearers than of the innumerable readers." But he was no instinctive House of Commons man. During his first year he found it "surely a very strange place" but imagined that he would adjust to his colleagues. Within a couple of years he had refined the litany of complaint about the place that he would rehearse for nearly thirty years: "I begin to wonder what the fascination is which attracts men who could sit over their tea and their books in their own cool quiet room to breathe bad air, hear bad speeches, lounge up and down the long galley and doze uneasily on the green benches till three in the morning. Thank God, these luxuries are not necessary to me." The Commons still met in St. Stephen's Chapel, a cramped and stifling retouched Gothic pile, but its denizens were an uncommonly interesting group, whom Macaulay largely ignored. He preferred to immure himself in the library and then leave the House quickly after speaking.[64]

On 5 April 1830 he delivered his maiden speech in favor of a Jewish petition "for relief from the absurd restrictions which lie on them—the last relique of the old system of intolerance." It was a controversial subject, and he nobly attacked as "religious persecution" the principle "that no one who is not a Christian is to be intrusted with power." He urged it as an "experiment whether, by making Englishmen of . . . [the Jews], they will not become members of the community . . . as long as they are not Englishmen they are nothing but Jews." The motion passed the House of Commons, failed in the Lords, and Jews continued to be excluded from Parliament until 1858. He judged the speech a success, and it found favor with Isaac Lyon Goldsmit, a financier, philanthropist, and assimilationist, who maintained that "Anglo-Jewish political emancipation . . . would come only when Judaism was seen to discard its nationalistic elements and its 'foreign' overtones."[65]

No philo-Semite, Tom held an Enlightenment notion of religious toleration: it was less a way of protecting religious minorities than of subordinating their diversity to the authority and control of the state. The nineteenth century was learning to call it the nation. For the Jews and the rest, following the rules of Englishness was the price of becoming English. Fourteen months later Goldsmit invited Tom and his brother Charles to a fancy-dress ball, and Tom wrote an outlandish account to amuse their sister Hannah. The guests were "mixed," but the Jews' foreignness struck him. Charles, "dressed like a sailor in a blue jacket and check shirt marched up, and asked a Jewish-looking damsel near me to dance with him . . . most knowingly . . . did he perform a quadrille with Miss Hilpah Manasses, or whatever her name is." When he learned the young woman's actual name—"Miss Levi"—and realized that Charles was smitten, he pronounced her "the most beautiful young women [*sic*] that I have almost ever seen, a splendid specimen of the Jewish breed." At the end of 1830 he recycled the argument of his maiden speech in a "short and carelessly written" essay and took up the cause again in Parliament a decade later.[66]

Becoming prime minister at sixty-six, Grey looked to refight the battles of his prime. He and the other senior Whigs wanted parliamentary reform in order to decrease royal power, not to share power with more of their inferiors. His goal was consistent with his strongly held aristocratic principles, which involved "the denial of 'democracy and Jacobinism'"; indeed, he regarded aristocratic rule as "a guarantee for the safety of the state and of the throne." The government efficiently drafted reform bills for the three kingdoms. Although the House of Commons received the English bill as early as 1 March 1831, it took fifteen months to enact the legislation, a delay that in the end mattered more than the limited scope of reform. In 1831 there were not quite 13.9 million people and about 370,000 electors in England and Wales, and the initial proposal was to increase their ranks by as much as 80 percent on the basis of property, occupied as well as owned.[67] On 23 March the bill passed its second reading by one vote, only to be overturned on 19–20 April. The king agreed to dissolve Parliament, the Whigs won a commanding majority in the ensuing election, and Grey formed his second government. On 6–7 July the Commons passed the second bill by 136 votes. After considerable amendment it reached the Lords, which defeated it on 7–8 October, with the bishops overwhelmingly in opposition.

Widespread rioting caused Tory moderates to seek a compromise and the "Ultras" to dig in their heels more deeply. After the House of Commons passed the third bill on 22 March 1832, King William promised, if necessary, to swamp the Tory majority in the upper house by creating well-disposed peers. The threat temporarily succeeded. Although the Lords narrowly passed the bill on second reading, on 6–7 May the Whigs were defeated on an opposition amendment, and the king reneged on his promise to create new peers. After Grey resigned, William turned to the Tories, further dividing them. Supporters of reform massed in the provinces: "The May crisis marked the high point in cooperation between middle- and working class reformers." But their amity was scattered and ephemeral. Overwhelmed and conceding the inevitability of reform, Wellington ceded office to Grey. With the king once again under control and the Lords subdued, the bill easily passed on 4 June, and the December general election gave the Whigs a majority of more than three hundred. Reform legislation came to Scotland in July and to Ireland a month later. The complexity of the legislation reflected its serpentine history. The electorate increased only to about 653,000, and their impact was essentially conservative: the middling classes "remained as deferential as ever . . . as reluctant to engage in agitation" and determined "not to allow the workers a greater influence in politics." In the short run the Reform Act strengthened the landed interest.[68]

Alarmed by rumors of revolution and the reality of mass agitation and uncertain about the future, contemporaries regarded the act as epochal. Speaking first on 2 March 1831, Macaulay soared and shone thereafter. All his speeches were carefully prepared, but only in his mind, where he formulated, revised, and retained them; his words spread in *Hansard* and the newspapers. He had spoken four times since his maiden speech, including in defense of Henry Brougham—now "Our Lord Chancellor" —with a vehemence that caused him to be called to order: "I was in no good humour with B. But . . . [John Wilson] Croker exasperated me beyond all patience." A lasting hatred had begun. Macaulay's attack on West

Indian slavery was equally contrived and notable only because it flirted with images of violence as the concomitant of every great movement: "though nobody supposed violence is good, what good cause had escaped being disfigured by violence? The Christian religion itself . . ." For over a decade he had been practicing the abolitionists' style of jeremiad: "The political world, in the same manner, often derives great advantage from those fierce and destroying visitations, which lay in the dust for ever the dark and infected haunts where a great moral malady has fixed itself in irremediable malignity. Still we most earnestly desire that a change . . . should be produced by the mildest means." Religionists had no monopoly on such talk. Before 1830 James Mill was already teaching his disciples how to deploy a secular "language of menace" in pursuit of reform.[69]

On the second night of debate Macaulay spoke on the initial reform bill with a voice "injured" by a "bad cold" and at a speed that made it "impossible for the reporters to do justice to it." The ministers had barely mentioned what Macaulay described as their "principle . . . plain, rational, and consistent . . . to admit the middle class to a large and direct share in the representation, without any violent shock to the institutions of our country." Borrowing from the essays on London University and James Mill and to immediate cheers, he reprised Aristotle's analysis of class. It informed his unequivocal rejection of universal suffrage. Ill-educated, rash and volatile, and susceptible to demagogues—especially in times of "distress"—"the poorer class of Englishmen" should not be allowed to vote, for their own "sake." He went on to sharpen the government's case for the union of government and "property," unlike Mill, who spoke of the "middle rank" and proposed instead to unite government and brains.[70]

Macaulay rejected attempts to justify the existing scheme of representation by appealing to history, only to invoke history in behalf of change. Once a weak group "becomes strong" and "demands a place in the system," it must be placated to avoid "the struggle between the young energy of one class and the ancient privileges of another." That was "the struggle which the middle classes in England are maintaining against an aristocracy of mere locality." He also nodded at Grey and other Whigs who wanted to reform Parliament in order to check the monarchy's power, but he did so drily by invoking the Tory icon Burke. Peel's flip-flopping on the rights of Dissenters and Catholics made him an irresistible target. Macaulay linked it with parliamentary reform and urged Peel to "concede with grace" now, lest "property and order, and all the institutions of this great monarchy . . . be exposed to fearful peril." Clear and finally hopeful, his message was "Reform, that you may preserve" and "Renew the youth of the State." But as the debate over reform dragged on and overheated, Macaulay sometimes predicted "that blood will flow in this city." Margaret knew that his "imagination . . . often exaggerates evil."[71]

A generation later a sophisticated and well-connected barrister who heard him still remembered a "great speech" on reform: "The House was entranced, almost breathless: and I recollect that, when I overtook him the same night walking home, I could hardly believe that the little draggled, ordinary man plodding by himself up the Strand was the same creature whom I had seen holding the House of Commons absorbed as the Opera House is by a first-rate singer." Later on the morning of 3 March 1831—the House sat between 3:00 P.M. and 2:00 A.M. for seven days running—a connoisseur noted in his diary a "very brilliant" speech. Macaulay thought it a "great success" and quickly wrote it out for publication.[72]

Today his first speech on the Reform Bill still reads well, and its logic seems clear if somewhat forced. What accounted for its powerful effect on contemporaries? Even halfway-original political arguments are at least as rare as similar jokes, rarer still if they become accepted as common sense. It seemed clear to Macaulay's contemporaries that his class analysis framed the rest of the debate over parliamentary reform, and historians relied on it into the 1970s. To the extent that he set the terms of the debate, and to the extent that it, in turn, helped to make credible "the complete and unabridged narrative of the ever-rising 'middle class,'" he became at thirty-one a principal inventor of modern England. Throughout the Atlantic world others announced a similar dispensation of prosperity, law, commercial rectitude, and technological improvement, which later elevated Macaulay above parochialism. Ensuring that he and his Trevelyan collaterals joined the governing class, he practiced the accommodation he preached. Into the twentieth century it remained "small" and "close-knit," never amounting in total to much more than about 2,500 families, only a few hundred of whom sent members to Parliament.[73] History ratified Macaulay's appeal to "Reform, that you may preserve."

"Literary intellectual": Macaulay would have despised the term, but it may be the most accessible description of him as a rhetorician, in Parliament as well as in print. He achieved long-lasting fame because during his lifetime words—sometimes even ideas—seemed to be the lifeblood of British politics. While still at Cambridge, Macaulay already understood the magic: "Men of great conversational powers almost universally practice a sort of lively sophistry and exaggeration, which deceives, for the moment, both themselves and auditors." A close reader of nineteenth-century speeches detected in Macaulay's "the style of his first reviews": "The diction is of flawless lucidity, slightly touched with an amplitude which reminds us that the speaker was born in the eighteenth century . . . The movement of thought is slightly ahead of the audience, but not too far ahead: each paragraph has its own keynote, its appropriate cadences, and the language rises and falls from narrative to declamation, and back to straight hard-hitting argument, without effort, or interruption, or display." After Tom became a theatergoer—Zachary disapproved—he saw that "the genuine mimetic genius" was the secret of great actors. Credibly and appealingly, they embodied the reality their lines spoke. It was not his art. Even when in good health and at the top of his form, he never projected himself physically as more than "a little draggled, ordinary man": "muscularly uncoordinated, stiff and immovable"; "rapid delivery"; "voice although monotonous and inflexible . . . unquestionably loud enough"; "delivery lacked grace, variety, and warmth." A clever, moderate Tory peer who heard Macaulay for the first time on 28 February 1833 and later became one of his warmer enemies studied him as he spoke: "Macaulay's enunciation is very inferior to his language. His manner too is not perfect."[74]

Listening for his words and his ideas, most of his auditors in the Commons forgot his appearance and his voice as he spoke. To his primary audience, reading his speeches in newspapers or hearing about them, he was silent and invisible. However he communicated to his several audiences, most of them appreciated his tone. He admired in the elder William Pitt's words "the air of sincerity, of vehement feeling, of moral elevation" and cultivated the same tone. A wealthy, long-serving M.P. reported on one of Macaulay's later speeches on reform: "without comparison the most powerful I ever heard . . . It had more of argument and profound philosophy, given in the most appropriate language and delivered with a fervency of manner than I ever before witnessed . . . It produced an immense sensation, and the cheers that followed were the longest I remember."[75]

Like Pitt, Macaulay was never a "great debater." He thought it an "art" that was always acquired after "long practice," and no more than Pitt could he bother himself to haunt St. Stephen's Chapel, "speaking, well or ill, at least once every night." His deficiency shaped him as a politician and colored him as a writer. In one debate Macaulay endured wounding ridicule from John William Croker, his Tory counterpart, but instead of extemporizing he took a long revenge in print. A couple of months later Croker committed "extraordinary blunders" in replying to Macaulay, who remained silent, priming a cabinet member with the wanted corrections, which his colleague delivered the next day in the course of "one of the most satisfactory and splendid speeches I had ever heard."[76] Macaulay would not try to frame a refutation overnight.

More important for the future were his relations with Peel. They skirmished and twitted each other without provoking mutual hatred or contempt. One connoisseur marked Macaulay's speeches as "harangues and never replies" and presciently compared him with his rival: "Peel's long experience and real talent for debate give him a great advantage in the power of reply, which he very eminently possesses. Macaulay, however, will probably be a very distinguished man. Their debates have elicited a vast amount of talent, and have served as touchstones to try real merit and powers." But his early triumphs also set a high bar, which perhaps came to intimidate him. William Ewart Gladstone, who knew him and his oratory well, thought that "it was only on very rare occasions that Macaulay achieves such results."[77] Subsequent acclaim for other successes would similarly daunt him.

Whig

Macaulay worked hard inside and outside the Palace of Westminster. Between his first address on parliamentary reform in March 1831 and leaving for India in February 1834 he delivered eighteen speeches in the Commons and twenty-one elsewhere. In the same period he also published nine essays—nearly 250 closely printed pages—in the *Edinburgh Review*. His review of a biography of Lord Byron, poet and harbinger of celebrity culture, showed his rhetorical spears and pruning hooks at work. He both mocked and accommodated the prudery that was emerging as the nation's ethos, virtually its surrogate religion. If some Whig grandees insisted on perpetuating their youthful frolics, Lord Holland, an acquaintance of Byron and himself no stranger to scandal, knew that the "higher classes" must learn self-restraint in order to command the respect of the nation and maintain their privileges. In an effort to mediate between the Whigs' proclivities and middle-class morality, Macaulay painted Byron sympathetically: "He came into the world; and the world treated him as his mother had treated him, sometimes with fondness, sometimes with cruelty, never with justice." After his wife left him spreading tales of his wicked ways, he became a permanent exile. Macaulay's verdict was lapidary: "We know of no spectacle so ridiculous as the British public in one of its periodical fits of morality." It was, however, "public opinion," not legislation, that "should be directed against" the "vices which destroy domestic happiness," and the repression should be applied "uniformly, steadily, and temperately."[78]

Living in Venice, Byron went native: "They were a race corrupted by a bad government and a bad religion, long renowned for skill in the arts of voluptuousness, and tolerant of all the caprices of sensuality." As a result, his "verse lost much of the energy and condensation which had distinguished it"—here Macaulay was telescoping as well as moralizing. After a "brilliant and miserable career," Byron died "at thirty-six, the most celebrated Englishman of the nineteenth century." Byron's "enthusiasts" derived from his poetry, much of which would be rejected in the future as "worthless," an ethic whose "two great commandments were to hate your neighbour and to love your neighbour's wife." Tom told his sister Hannah that he "never wrote anything with less heart" and that he disliked both the poet and his biography but wrote "civilly" of both because he knew the biographer: "I shall be abused, I have no doubt, for speaking so coldly of Lord Byron." Two weeks later the author and he breakfasted amicably with a common friend. "Excessively pleased with my review," he showed Macaulay "very marked attention." Placation was an art Macaulay continued using in calmer times, even as prudery became more fashionable.[79]

Published a few months later, his review of Croker's edition of Boswell's *Life of Samuel Johnson* was venomous. Croker first endowed the word "conservative" with its political meaning. Detestable both ideologically and personally—"more than cold boiled veal"—Macaulay ridiculed him as ill-educated and error-prone. That seventeen years later they still publicly wrangled over a "grossly corrupt passage" in a Greek tragedy hints at antiquity's improbable sway over two representative nineteenth-century English politicians. Underlying it were the rites of passage that had shaped their education and fears about their status, even their manhood: Macaulay evoked "flogging" twice in three paragraphs and reduced Southey to "a schoolboy." Although Croker proved to be right about the passage, Macaulay never conceded. His assault on Croker's Greek prefaced his critique of Dr. Johnson's classicism. Anglican and prolific as well as Tory, Johnson was a national icon and a target of Macaulay since "Milton." He was also one of those eighteenth-century eminences who believed that the ancients' defeat by the moderns in the battle of the books had dissipated their moral and intellectual authority. Even as an undergraduate, Macaulay had marked Johnson as "perhaps, the most ridiculous character in literary history." Seven years later he declared that of "remote countries and past times . . . [Johnson] talked with wild and ignorant presumption." Johnson imagined that the "'Athenians of the age of Demosthenes were a people of brutes, a barbarous people,'" because they were mostly illiterate. Seeing the rising literacy of modern Londoners, Johnson inferred, "in defiance of the strongest and clearest evidence, that the human mind can be cultivated by means of books alone." Three years earlier Macaulay, like Johnson, had insisted that printing had elevated the public mind. Lacking any more evidence in 1831 but needing an argument, he concocted a tale about an illiterate Athenian civilized by passing "every morning in conversation with Socrates," by listening regularly to Pericles, and by otherwise being a dutiful citizen.[80]

Not yet thirty-one and still on the make, Macaulay exuded callow hauteur. His goal was to impugn the learning, manners, and ethics of Johnson, who, like his friend Burke and his disciple Southey, argued politically out of his moral imagination. Aware that a skillful rhetorician should avoid demonizing a widely venerated opponent, Macaulay offered a bit of faint praise that worked to underline his ad-hominem indictment. Johnson's politics displayed "the lowest, fiercest, and most extravagances of party spirit." His churchmanship was "altogether inconsistent with reason or with Christian charity." Macaulay was unsparing toward the Christianity that motivated Johnson's antislavery opinions and much else: "He began to be credulous precisely at the point where the most credulous people begin to be sceptical"; "He could discern clearly enough the folly and meanness of all bigotry except his own." Macaulay avoided repeating his earlier praise for Christianity's contribution to "the superior advances which we [moderns] have made in moral sciences," not least toward abolishing slavery. Ultimately, Johnson was "likely to be remembered as long as the English language is spoken in any quarter of the globe" not for his writings, many of which were now "treated with indiscriminate contempt," but for his biographer's vivid portrayal of his "peculiarities of manner" and "careless table-talk," remembered in effect as a "most ridiculous character." As retouched in 1856, Macaulay's caricature outweighed fuller depictions of Johnson into the late 1950s.[81]

He treated John Bunyan's art more carefully. His review of Southey's edition of *The Pilgrim's Progress* began with high praise—"eminently beautiful and splendid"—but it was barbed. A few pages later he inserted a seeming digression comparing Bunyan with Percy Shelley, author of *On the Necessity of Atheism*. The point was to depict modern religious fervor like Bunyan's as crazy and atavistic. Both poets enjoyed the imaginative power needed "to make individuals out of generalities." Some of Shelley's "metaphysical and ethical theories . . . were certainly most absurd and pernicious," but he was "a bard," possessing "some of the highest qualities of the great ancient masters." Had Shelley "lived to the full age of man," he might perhaps "have given to the world some great work of the very highest design and execution." Macaulay elegized him in classical Greek and then exclaimed: "But alas!" A learned and imitative classicism fed Shelley's genius. Bunyan, in contrast, was "an illiterate man"—"ignorant of literature or letters"—"who was under the influence of the strongest religious excitement": "his mind was constantly occupied by religious considerations"; "his imagination exercised despotic power over his body and mind. He heard voices from heaven." Half-mad, Bunyan also spoke with a bumpkin's voice: "There is not an expression, if we except a few technical terms of theology, which would

puzzle the rudest peasant." Juxtaposing Shelley with Bunyan neatly insinuated the contrast between religious emancipation, civilization, and
gentility on the one hand and religious enthusiasm, primitivism, and vulgarity on the other. Macaulay's matter-of-fact digression artfully implied
that he shared with his audience tacit knowledge that needed no proof.
The essay shaped "one of two principal responses to Bunyan" in the Victorian period.[82]

Macaulay understood that engaging the establishment required greater
subtlety. In January 1831 the freethinking propagandist Richard Carlile
received a sentence of two years' imprisonment. Discussing his prosecution for seditious libel with liberal-minded friends, Macaulay "was surprised at the way in which we divided on the matter." He was "against
prosecuting" in all such cases but expressed himself "somewhat doubt-
fully." A similar indirection characterized what he wrote about the
church. As the year ended, he recast as "in part a narrative"—"a sort of
composition which I have never yet attempted"—the analysis of the origins of modern English constitutional history he offered in "Hallam."
Encouraged by his editor to continue using the new medium, he then
wrote a story embodying his theory that England's Reformation was
primarily a secular and political affair. The sixteenth-century English
were not "irreligious" but "sometimes Protestants, sometimes Catholics;
sometimes half Protestants half Catholics." Their Reformation was above
all a "movement" directed, regulated, and arrested by the government.
It was not an edifying tale. The "great Queen" Elizabeth persecuted in
a way "even more odious than the persecution with which her sister
['Bloody Mary'] had harassed the Protestants," setting the nation on a
course not toward "perfect freedom of conscience" but rather toward a
repression that "brought the state to the very brink of ruin." After the
"exclusions and disabilities" were removed, they "left behind them a ran-
kling which may last for many years." Predominantly Catholic Ireland
was on Macaulay's mind. An inflammation "in one of my eyes" slowed
his writing, and he accurately judged the result "a strange rambling performance." Its lesson, however, was obvious: more than divisive Anglicanism, shared Englishness unified the modern nation.[83]

Even when Macaulay wrote about abroad, his mind and heart stayed
at home. An essay on the origins of the first French Revolution followed
the passage of the Reform Act. It began by praising Jeremy Bentham as

"a great original thinker" and "a sincere and ardent friend of the human race." Even more indicative of Macaulay's current politics was his tribute a few pages later to "Mr. Canning," even in death a great favorite of the "friends of popular government." He was the disciple of William Pitt the Younger, and, like his master, he had "changed with the nation." Once a reformer, Pitt became "something very like a Tory" in response to "the calamities produced by the French Revolution." Canning, in contrast, began as a counterrevolutionary and died "something very like a Whig." Had Pitt "lived in 1832, it is our firm belief that he would have been a decided Reformer." More generally, Macaulay wrote about France in order to praise England as the exceptional nation: "If we look at the magnitude of the reform, it may well be called a revolution. If we look at the means by which it has been effected, it is merely an act of Parliament, regularly brought in, read, committed, and passed." The act testified to "the unparalleled moderation and humanity . . . [of] the English people . . . the fruits of a hundred and fifty years of liberty.[84]

For all that Macaulay now happily and usefully frequented Holland House, the fashionable and droll salon of pure Whiggism, the cult of partisan memory practiced there never tempted him. His politics owed more to the prerevolutionary Pitt as channeled by George Canning. Dropping in on Lord Holland, down with the gout, he told his sister Hannah: "I was grateful . . . for many pleasant evenings passed there when London was full and Lord Holland out of bed. I therefore did my best to keep the house alive." On that Saturday solitude was the reward of his dutifulness: "I had the library and the delightful gardens to myself during most of the day; and I got through my visit very well." Holland upheld the pro-French politics of his uncle, Charles James Fox. For Macaulay, however, the revolutionary National Assembly was "in truth, what Mr. Burke called them in austere irony, the ablest architects of ruin that ever the world saw."[85]

The year before leaving to assume high office in India he published three essays about the eighteenth century, where he felt at home. The first reviewed a history of the War of the Spanish Succession (1701–1714) by Lord Mahon, a Tory peer who became a friend. Electioneering in Leeds slowed his writing, and he described his account as "long" and "very dull." Importantly, however, it forecast the political inclusiveness that he would practice as the historian of modern England. Forward-looking Whigs usually led the way, and laggard Tories brought up the rear: "The tail is now where the head was some generations ago." But he also commended the Tories for ending the war in the teeth of fierce Whig opposition: the move was "beneficial to the state." Eight months later he etched a portrait of Horace Walpole, favored son of Britain's longest-serving prime minister. Macaulay worked "from morning to night on it," and the result pleased him—"a hit"—though he rightly suspected that it would annoy people friendly to Walpole's memory who were helpful to him. Now he was significant and secure enough not to care. Macaulay's feel for power colored even that entertainment, which offers a close and nuanced analysis of mid-eighteenth-century high politics innocent of the Whig pieties favored in Holland House. Nearly three years in the House of Commons had confirmed for him that a "life of action, if it is to be useful, must be a life of compromise."[86]

He intended an essay on the elder Pitt to advance his account of the eighteenth century through the Seven Years' War (1756–1763). Rushing to finish and "stupid with disease and physic," he wanted it to be "amusing," just as he "had much amusement in writing it." Macaulay portrayed Pitt both sympathetically as if from within and ironically from a distance. His verdict on the Seven Years' War, "the most glorious war in which England had ever been engaged," was nuanced. "It must be owned that some of our conquests were rather splendid than useful . . . [Pitt] was proud of the sacrifices and efforts which his eloquence and his success had induced his countrymen to make. The price at which he purchased faithful service and complete victory . . . was long and severely felt by the nation." But Macaulay warmed to the spectacle of Pitt's words rousing England. "The success of our arms was perhaps owing less to the skill of his dispositions than to the national resources and the national spirit. But that the national spirit rose to the emergency, that the national resources were contributed with unexampled cheerfulness, this was undoubtedly his work. The ardour of his soul had set the whole kingdom on fire . . . They, like him, were disposed to risk every thing, to play double or quits to the last, to think nothing done while any thing remained undone, to fail rather than not to attempt." Pitt used the supreme art of rhetoric minus God-talk to fire the English "national spirit" to support the state. In 1827 Macaulay had recommended as much in comparing two books by

Machiavelli. England was a society with "complex" interests, and in India he determined to write an amusing history of its modern progress infused with maxims beneficial to the state.[87]

Big Brother

Tom was permanently celibate. Years before 1830 his emotional life centered on his youngest sisters, Margaret—twelve years his junior—and Hannah—ten years younger. The three lived in their parents' Bloomsbury house from 1823 until the early winter of 1829–30, when Tom moved into rooms in Gray's Inn. Their mother died on 3 May 1831, leaving him first "thunderstruck" and then distracted, not least by politics. Ailing and hard up, Zachary sold the house and moved with Hannah and her two older sisters to Leamington Spa in the Midlands until November. Margaret stayed in London, living first with a cousin and then with the Buxtons, close family friends. Separation made Tom a tireless letter-writer.[88]

Thomas Pinney, who edited his correspondence, cautiously evaluated his letters to Margaret and Hannah, "beginning in 1830 and swelling to a flood in the years from 1831 through 1833." They are

> most striking and curious for their amorous language and their evidence of Macaulay's almost complete dependence for emotional satisfaction upon his relation to these two girls. At times, these letters seem strongly self-pitying, almost maudlin, as though Macaulay were indulging in them every obscure and unacknowledged impulse he had ever felt. At other times sentimental indulgence is set off in sharp contrast against perfectly judicious self-awareness or almost jaunty matter-of-factness. The effect is not ironic but contradictory . . . these letters are perplexing. It is very difficult to venture a confident opinion about them . . . it seems doubtful that, on the evidence of the letters alone, the case can be adequately diagnosed. Macaulay himself, so far as I can judge, never betrays the least consciousness that his relation to his sisters was latently incestuous; to suppose that it was ever overtly so, I think absurd. There was, unquestionably, a need in Macaulay to have someone whom he could

exalt without reservation. In his younger years it was his two sisters whom he converted, in his imagination, into paragons of womanly virtue.

Among the Macaulays, as in many respectable nineteenth-century families, the incest taboo, though technically inviolable, was supple.[89]

Before examining an aspect of his relations with Margaret that illuminates rather than perplexes, it is useful to hear Tom addressing her and Hannah. During the summer of 1831 he wrote to "Nancy" (Hannah) in Leamington:

My dear dear girl,

I am sorry to find that there is any chance of your having to go to a place which you dislike. I will do all in my power to prevent it. But at any rate do not think that you will miss seeing me. You will go to no place to which as soon as Parliament rises, I shall not follow you. My dear dear girl, my sister—my darling—my own sweet friend,—you cannot tell how, amidst these tempests of faction and amidst the most splendid circles of our nobles, I pine for your society, for your voice, for your caresses. I write this with all the weakness of a woman in my heart and in my eyes. We have difficulties to pass through. But they are not insurmountable; and, if my health and faculties are spared, I feel confident that, however the chances of political life may turn, we shall have a home, perhaps a humble one, but one in which I can be happy, if I see you happy.— Farewell my dearest, and believe that there is nothing on earth that I love as I love you.

T B M[90]

Sometimes he wrote more effusively and furtively. Even so, his ambition to possess "a home . . . in which I can be happy, if I see you happy" more than his pining "for your caresses" hints at the emotional core of their relationship. On the evidence of Tom's letters to her and Margaret, his "need to have . . . someone whom he could exalt without reservation" demanded a return. He needed at least as much exaltation as he could give to his younger sisters or anyone else. Despite his assurances to

Hannah that he loved her like "nothing on earth," he was with Margaret daily for "an hour or two" and wrote at least as fulsomely to her: "I am sure that no change of situation or lapse of time can alter a love like that to which I bear to you and which you have always shewn to me."[91] His fascination with both of them and, later, with one of his nieces testifies to his lifelong immersion in masculine society, his desire for the company of women, his segregation from them outside his family and their circle into early adulthood, his residence with his sisters into his thirtieth year, and his need to dominate.

In mid-August 1832 Margaret announced her engagement to Edward Cropper, a widower about Tom's age from a wealthy mercantile family that belonged to the Macaulays' set. Tom assured her that "my love for you is not so selfish that I should repine at your decision. In a pecuniary point of view the connection is highly advantageous. It is no disrespect to Edward to say that in other things I do not consider him worthy of my Margaret." But "repine" Tom loudly did, both then and later: "God bless you, my own dear Margaret—and make you as happy as I wish you to be. I had much more to say—but I can scarcely see the paper for weeping." The wedding was scheduled for 11 December, when Macaulay would be campaigning in Leeds against Sadler. He departed London without taking "leave of you" lest he lose "all my firmness." In another letter for her he again pledged not "to repine," only to do so volubly, yet mingling it with "perfectly judicious self-awareness": "During the years when the imagination is most vivid and the heart most susceptible, my affection for my sisters has prevented me from forming any serious attachment. But for them I should be quite alone in the world. I have nothing else to love."[92]

Tom's rhetoric was self-dramatizing and hyperbolic, but the phrases "prevented me from forming any serious attachment" and "nothing else to love" delimit his capacity for human affection and sympathy. As much as his sisters, he seemed younger than his years. Margaret and Hannah were on the edge of adulthood and sheltered, but Tom was thirty-two, moving in the corridors of power and celebrated there for his "genius, eloquence, astonishing knowledge, and diversified talents." His social immaturity remained obvious. In early October 1832 he dined with some fellows of Trinity College, one of whom reported: "Much brilliant convers[ation] from Macaulay . . .—Macaulay's manners amazingly im-

proved: he was very agreeable & full of anecdote & quot[ation]." The
next morning he "breakfasted alone with Macaulay & his 2 sisters (agreeable girls with sweet voices: not pretty but clever and conversible & very
young)." For all that Tom in 1832 struck a longtime acquaintance as
"amazingly improved" socially, at first gape he still seemed more a boy
prodigy than a notably successful young man. A few months earlier a
diner at Holland House also admired Tom's table talk—"quotation, illustration, anecdote, seemed ready in his hands for every topic"—but
judged "his manner . . . not pleasing . . . unembarrassed yet not easy, un-
polished yet not coarse." His off-putting manner betrayed his stunted
feelings. In the wake of their mother's death, he and his grieving sisters,
Margaret recalled, "talked of *her* and of death in general. He spoke much
of what he should have felt if it had been Hannah or myself, his two
dearest on earth, who had been taken" and, generalizing from his own
emotional parsimony, insisted that sympathy could exist only in small
groups. Inverting their father's combination of global philanthropy and
domestic chill, it was a rule that Tom applied to high politics as well as to
human relations.[93]

Margaret recorded those comments and many others in a memoir that
was published long ago. Uniquely illuminating her brother and his opinions before 1838, it has never been studied. Younger than Hannah, seeing
herself as a girl, and cosseted by Tom, she exalted him: "But the idea of
being separated from him is what I cannot support. He has given me
tastes which no other person can satisfy, he has for years been the object
of my whole heart, every occupation almost has had him for its object
and end in some manner, and without him would be void of interest."
Worshiping "my hero," she applied her native alertness to preserving
many of their conversations from the years 1830–1832. At seven she first
became aware of Tom, bound for Cambridge: "rather afraid of him."
When she was twelve and he returned home, she "became very fond of
him, and from that time my affection for him has gone on increasing
during a period of seven years." Because of his "habit of talking a great
deal with very young people, and with people to whom he has a great
deal to explain," she found him fun, accessible, and informative: "His
manner indeed was very flattering to such a child as I was, for he always
seemed to take as much pains, and exert himself as much to amuse and
please me, to explain anything I wished to know, or inform me on any

subject, as he could have done to the greatest person in the land." Sometimes they flirted: "He was very agreeable this evening. He and I acted a scene between John and Miss L., which ended in a rupture between the lovers." Tom confessed to being plagued by "extreme idleness": "He said he had never really worked, and at Cambridge was more idle than the men who were plucked." Self-congratulation underlay his self-deprecation—"If there had not been really something in me, idleness would have ruined me." Even so, he once "dawdled with us all day and did nothing."[94] Yet his productivity then and later would shame many confirmed workaholics.

Whether Tom was exultant or sad, his sister sympathized with him. She found him quick-tempered but sweet, because "he will be sorry the moment" he offended. She also caught glimpses of a shadow side. "Tom," she wrote, "is a more amiable man than Dr. Johnson, and a much pleasanter friend." But

> He is not as generous a man as the Doctor. No consideration in earth would make him take disagreeable people into his house for charity, neither would he give away as Dr. Johnson did when he was poor.
>
> He is, however, extremely pitiful. The sight of pain puts him into an agony, but he is, I think, a little too fond of reasoning himself out of feeling, and tries too much to forget unpleasant things. I believe, however, he feels as much as other people do in half the time.

She also diagnosed the cause of his protracted social immaturity: "He disliked company, and therefore gave little chance of improvement to manners naturally embarrassed and awkward."[95]

Often they talked of religion. She heard both his skepticism and his recognition of a basic human need to believe: "If a man will not believe anything he cannot prove, he must believe nothing." He taught her that "it was not on the question alone we might then be considering that this uncertainty remained, when followed out to the end; but on all questions of morals, on all speculations upon this strange theatre upon which we have appeared, just to play a part and then vanish." All religions—Jewish and Catholic as well as Protestant—were primarily concerned with "the duty of obeying God." Understanding that notoriously "infidel" opinions worked to create "prejudice" and deflate reputations, he exercised an irrecoverable verbal magic to persuade her that he was helping her to see beyond unsparing naturalism and to glimpse divine light: "By no one have my conceptions of the majesty, goodness, and benevolence of God been so elevated; there is never anything low or vulgar in his ideas on this great subject, one on which he has never 'filtered his notions through other men's minds.'" Margaret's hero was a man "enlightened enough to comprehend the meaning latent under the emblems of . . . [Christian] faith." Enlightenment, for example, informed his interpretation of original sin: "we came into the world liable from the constitution of mind and body to certain temptations, and led by their power to do wrong. He thought that quite sufficient for practical purposes, and all that the Bible laid down." What did she make of the viscerally anticlerical doggerel he wrote about their reverend brother?

> My brother John is made a parson,
> But small, I fear, will be his tithes,
> While peasants are committing arson,
> and slay the clergy with their scythes,
> Sure to John will be a beacon
> To those will live for ease and feast,
> If having thriven while still a deacon,
> He's murdered when a tithe-pig priest.[96]

Might Makes Right

Margaret also preserved her brother's talk about politics. It was clear to her that his classicism and rhetorical formation shaped him as a politician. During the early 1830s he was trapped into speaking against the government in support of the abolitionist demand for the total and immediate end of slavery in the British Empire. The unmoved mover was Zachary, "for whose sake alone he takes any part at all in it." Worrying that "the Anti-Slavery people will think him too cold," he nurtured a permanent grievance against their father and his abolitionist allies. Once Margaret suggested that Ireland should be allowed to dissolve its union with England on the same grounds that England was reforming Parliament, and he explained his first principle to her. Their conversation "ended in his saying that *in politics he thought right and might very much the same thing.*" She judged that he "discussed it very well, and completely routed the rights of man, at least my feeble defence of them. I did not, indeed, defend them long, for it is impossible not to see that when looked into it is a mere cant phrase." Long before Machiavelli, Thrasymachus of Chalcedon had forcefully argued the same case, and British authors from Thomas Hobbes through Jeremy Bentham to James Mill wrote variations on the theme.[97]

On 6 February 1833 Macaulay spoke in the Commons defending the United Kingdom of Great Britain and Ireland. Protest and violence had plagued the other island for two years. The government was well-meaning, "well-informed, and determined to take advantage of the goodwill which they hoped had been created by emancipation" and "advanced nineteen bills for solving the country's social and economic problems." Daniel O'Connell, the Irish Catholic parliamentary leader, would have none of it. In the Commons Macaulay sounded judicial until he evoked the "civil war" raging in Ireland and the Irish ingratitude toward the Whigs. One of the ministers responsible for Ireland had already privately concluded that, "Until that unhappy and insane people be reconquered there will be no peace." Also privately, Macaulay was heard about the same time advocating something like reconquest: "if he had had to legislate he would . . . have suspended the laws for five years in Ireland, given the Lord-Lieutenant's proclamations the force of law, and got the D. of W[ellingto]n to go there." Told of the recommendation, the duke "seemed very well pleased." Speaking in the Commons about the policy of coercion, Macaulay defended "suspension of the Habeas Corpus Act, and the suspension of trial by juries" and the blanket prohibition of public meetings. Although the cabinet was divided over the measures, he was remorseless: "In departing from the law, he would rather err on the side of rigour than of lenity." He recalled Scotland after 1745, when his father's people had endured ethnic cleansing because of their participation in the failed Stuart insurrection: "Let the Highlanders be asked; there would not be found one among them who did not bless the severity used towards them at the period mentioned, and the salutary wisdom that directed that severity."[98]

When he spoke on Ireland, he was in his eighth month as a commis-

"House of Commons, 1833" and detail of Thomas Babington Macaulay (center), by George Hayter (© National Portrait Gallery, London). "What is the best arrangement for the country to which I can induce six hundred and fifty-seven other persons to accede?" (TBM to Smithson, 11.viii.32, *L*2:177)

sioner of the Board of Control for India, which represented Parliament
in its dealings with the East India Company. As 1831 ended, he needed
money, and both his dependent sisters and the government knew it. Lord
Holland confided to his diary: "an offer to employ him does not come
too soon." It was necessary to find Macaulay a suitable post and wait for
a safe time for him to resign Calne and perhaps find another constituency. At the beginning of 1832 Lord Lansdowne heard him describe
himself "as a poor man" who "had as much as he wanted, and as far as
he was personally concerned had no desire for office." The death of Sir
James Mackintosh opened a place on the board; his demise would bring
Macaulay other advantages. When he was appointed secretary in December 1832, the annual salary of the post was raised to £1,500—equivalent to £112,152 in 2007—and he enjoyed numerous privileges. He
wanted an additional £500. Resenting his dependence and unwilling to
show a weak hand when bargaining with his betters, he bristled at the
prime minister's "insolence of sending to him to come and show off before he was hired"—we would call it an interview. On 22 June 1832 he
became a member of the parliamentary committee inquiring into the
renewal of the company's charter: "There are wheels within wheels,—
mines under mines,—intrigues crossing intrigues."[99]

Joining the board obliged him to be returned once more for Lansdowne's pocket borough. In the week before the elections, the king assented to the act reforming the House of Commons, which stripped
Calne of one seat and gave Leeds two. For months Macaulay had been
negotiating with prominent liberals "to represent Leeds in a reformed
Parliament" at their expense in the upcoming general election. The day
Calne voted, he faced a scheduling conflict and resolved it in a way that
shows him both innocent of reformed electioneering and preoccupied
with India: "The people at Calne fixed Wednesday for the election
there;—the very day on which I wished to be at Leeds. I shall therefore
remain here [Bath] till Wednesday morning, and read Indian politics in
quiet. I am already deep in Zemindars, Ryots, Polygars, Courts of Phous-
dary, and Courts of Nizamut Adulut . . . Am I not in fair training to be as
great a bore as if I had myself been in India?—that is to say as great a
bore as the greatest."[100]

He described his first brush with Leeds as "a violent struggle and a
complete victory"; his handlers failed to protect him from aggressive

questioners. He was running with a local Whig industrialist and against Michael Sadler, who worked "on behalf of agricultural labourers, Irish poor and above all factory children": "The choice of actual candidates to stand at the first Leeds election accelerated the alienation of working men from the middle-class commercial and industrial interest. A Tory-Radical alliance born out of elements of class cleavage, which character-ized but did not dominate Leeds society, was nurtured by candidates whose views crystallized the campaign into a test of opinion on the fac-tory question." During the 1832 campaign Macaulay unwittingly helped to wreck the improving "Whig position on factory reform."[101]

A rude education, campaigning confirmed his aversion to democracy. In early August he sniffed to a radical correspondent, "I hope to see the day when an Englishman will think it as great an affront to be courted and fawned upon in his capacity of elector as in his capacity of juryman." By early September he was praising an audience for their dynamism and intellect, in contrast to "the squalid misery, the dependence, and I may say the comparative stupidity, which I regret to know, characterizes the agricultural population of that part of the country in which I have gen-erally resided." His total experience of country life amounted to a few weeks. In a bare-knuckled campaign, he compared Sadler to a "Hyaena" and once had to flee for safety. Religious rhetoric was inescapable. Macaulay warned the lower orders—"lower!—I ought to apologize for using the word, for they are lower only because Providence has decreed that some of us should earn our bread by the sweat of our brows"—against "the great delusion" of expecting help from the government. For Macaulay to talk of the divine on the stump amounted to playing with fire. At another rally a Methodist minister called out demanding "to know the religious creed" of Macaulay and his Whig colleague. Macaul-ay's improvisation was brilliant, successful, and false: "I do most deeply regret that any person should think it necessary to make a meeting like this an arena for theological discussion . . . My answer is short, and in one word. Gentlemen, I am a Christian." When the crowd cheered, he plunged onward:

No man shall speak of me as the person who, when this disgrace-ful inquisition was entered upon in an assembly of Englishmen, brought forward the most sacred subjects to be canvassed here, and be turned into a matter for hissing or for cheering. If on any future occasion it should happen that Mr. Carlile should favor any large meeting with his infidel attacks upon the Gospel, he shall not have it to say that I set the example. Gentlemen, I have done; I tell you, I will say no more; and if the person who has thought fit to ask this question has the feelings worthy of a teacher of religion, he will not, I think, rejoice that he has called me forth.[102]

Macaulay succeeded both in his impersonation and in helping to define a British political language that routinely excluded "theological discussion" except when rhetorical necessity required it. Although the election yielded "a clear Whig victory," Macaulay soon railed against "my villains at Leeds" for demanding that he pay £120 in election expenses: "It is well I am in office. But I will be wise another time." Within a year his mind was already elsewhere: "On the 6th of Novr. I am to dine at Leeds and to make a harangue. I think it a foolish business: but our people will have it so. Before that time I shall probably know something decisive about India." After receiving the longed-for appointment there, he resigned his seat, forcing a by-election. In Leeds there was a widespread feeling of having "been 'used' by an ambitious outsider."[103]

[3]

LEGISLATOR

India made Macaulay a political power, first at home and then in the subcontinent. Even before becoming the secretary of the East India Company's Board of Control, he advised its chairman, a Clapham "saint." Marking him as "idle," Macaulay soon became the power behind the chair, framing the terms of the 1833 bill that renewed the charter of the company and overseeing its passage: "I have to sit on the Treasury Bench the whole time, watching every word that is said, and ready to answer every objection." On 10 July 1833 he led on the second reading and intervened on seven other occasions. It was, he insisted to Hannah, "the best speech, by general agreement, and in my own opinion, that I ever made in my life." Tom went on to confide that he pined "for a few quiet days, a cool country breeze, and a little chatting and fondling with my own Nancy."[1]

He had, however, no enthusiasm for the government's bill to abolish slavery throughout the British Empire, which was also before the House —"miserably bad." To appease Zachary and his abolitionist colleagues he again offered to resign from the Board of Control in order to oppose it. There was no danger; Tom's work for the charter made him irreplaceable. On 24 May 1832 he dutifully indicted West Indian slavery as "a foul blot to this country" and fourteen months later in the final debate expressed "insurmountable doubts" about delaying immediate emancipation. Rumors of his offer to resign confirmed his reputation as a committed abolitionist. It proved useful throughout his career. The vast eastern empire for which he legislated was expanding. Robert Clive, its pioneer, regarded the company as primarily a trading firm and confined his conquests to Bengal. By 1833, nonetheless, the company "had established control over 500,000 square miles of territory in India, containing 93.7 million 'British subjects' who paid £22,718,794 a year in taxation," with a 2007 purchasing power of £1,771,617,531. Beginning in the 1820s a coalition of evangelicals and Utilitarians successfully advocated policies to promote the "welfare of India—the happiness of its immense population and the blessings of British rule."[2] Though growing, the company's thin bureaucracy was ill equipped to effect such improvements.

The would-be improvers included James Mill, Macaulay's "old enemy" and chief examiner of Indian correspondence. His modest title belied his control over information and hence policy at East India House. On 21 February 1832 he testified before the parliamentary committee charged with drafting the bill. His major concern was legal reform, specifically codifying and generalizing a system of laws for the subcontinent. He proposed that a small legislative committee prepare a code. The president should be no old India hand but a British lawyer "capable of bringing to the great work the aid of general principles . . . a person thoroughly versed in the philosophy of man and of government." Although the act tinkered with some of Mill's recommendations, it mandated a uniform legal system for India and ended the company's monopoly on the China trade. As a result, "its functions were little more than cosmetic. Real power was now shared between the Board of Control at home and a new Supreme Council in Calcutta, though the façade of Company Rule was maintained until 1858."[3]

On 10 July Macaulay's primary task was justifying the "façade," which emerged from a compromise with the company's directors that he helped to engineer. Acknowledging that the plan was "beset by difficulties," he presented India as an English experiment in solving "one of the hardest problems of politics. We are trying to . . . give a government to people to whom we cannot give a free government." After acclaiming Mill's *History of British India* as "the greatest historical work which has appeared in our language since that of Gibbon"—his earlier assaults on Mill left him with much to atone for—he declared that England must "engraft on despotism those blessings which are the natural fruits of liberty." But he recommended caution, "even to the verge of timidity," because there was no access to the "light of political science and history." Everything depended on the wisdom of those on the ground, feeling their way forward one step at a time.[4]

William Thomas, the most recent editor of Mill's history, has described it as "a scissors-and-paste performance stiffened by pure utilitarian dogma. Mill repudiated as reliable evidence the firsthand observations of travelers in India, ridiculed the scholars who translated its indigenous literature, and claimed to be more objective because he had *not* visited the country whose laws and government he analysed. His book . . . turned out to be well-suited to the outlook of those top British administrators who went out to India determined not to stay for long." It was, in other words, the perfect cram for Macaulay, eager to accelerate "the reconstruction of a decomposed society" on the subcontinent and alert to Mill's disguised critique of English institutions.[5]

Transforming India depended, Macaulay told his fellow M.P.'s, on filling "the magistracies of our Eastern Empire with men who may do honour to their country, with men who may represent the best part of the English nation." His compromise retained the directors' patronage by permitting them to nominate four candidates, from whom the best would be selected by competitive testing modeled on Cambridge's "examinations in Latin, in Greek, and in mathematics." He conceded "that too exclusive an attention is paid in the education of young English gentlemen to the dead languages" and instead offered a practical justification for examining candidates in the subjects that dominated the great public schools and ancient universities. Refusing to attribute any intrinsic merit to the ancient languages, he urged the value of competition: "If, instead of learning Greek, we learned the Cherokee, the man who understood the Cherokee best . . . would generally be a superior man to him who was destitute of these accomplishments. If astrology were taught at our Universities, the young man who cast nativities best would generally turn out a superior man. If alchymy were taught . . ." By the time he reached India, he knew that some languages—Greek, Latin, and English—possessed intrinsic merit. No more than Cherokee were Sanskrit and Arabic among them. His compromise with the company failed in practice, and he lived to override it.[6]

Macaulay's peroration envisioned the empire as evolving into self-government in the very distant future. Including the best of the governed

among the governors was key: "I am far, very far, from wishing to proceed hastily in this most delicate matter. I feel that, for the good of India
itself, the admission of natives to high office must be effected by slow
degrees. But that, when the fulness of time is come, when the interest of
India requires the change, we ought to refuse to make that change lest
we should endanger our own power, this is a doctrine of which I cannot
think without indignation." In India the goal was "the pacific triumphs
of reason over barbarism," which would render England's "the imper-
ishable empire of our arts and our morals, our literature and our laws."
Conjuring Macaulay's vision while chaotically liquidating British rule
over the subcontinent in 1947, Prime Minister Clement Atlee declared
that the time had come.[7]

Macaulay had emphasized "by slow degrees" rather than "the fulness
of time," a biblical allusion to Christ's birth presaging the end of time. In
a still bibliolatrous nation a prudent imperialist cited scripture for his
own purpose. Macaulay's experience informed his recommendation. In
1831 he wanted to meet Ram Mohan Roy, the paradigm of those promising "natives," recently arrived in Britain as the agent of the Mughal
court: "He seems by all that I can learn of him to be a very remarkable
man. He is it appears . . . more struck by our political and moral state,—
than almost any foreigner that I have ever heard of." Two years later and
a few weeks before he prophesied the distant end of empire he felt
"plagued out of my life" by, among others, "Ramohum Roy." Now enjoying political as well as cultural power, Macaulay exhibited signs of a
trait that psychologists and the rest of us observe in many of the powerful: "Individuals primed with power anchor too heavily on their vantage
points and demonstrate reduced accuracy when assessing the emotions
and thoughts of others." Convinced that sympathy can exist only in small
groups, Macaulay was unusually vulnerable to "a power-induced impediment with experiencing empathy."[8] The shortcoming would foster not
only his social ineptitude but also his lethal policy recommendations.

To the Commons, Macaulay defined British India as a foreign military
despotism. Echoing James Mill's testimony, he urged "digesting and reforming the laws of India, so that those laws may, as soon as possible, be
formed into a code": "It is a work which especially belongs to a government like that of India, to an enlightened and paternal despotism." Force
and the threat of force were also necessary to govern England. In an aside

he quipped: "A broken head in Cold Bath Fields produces a greater sensation among us than three pitched battles in India." It was an airbrushed allusion to a riot in London a few weeks earlier that ended in both deaths and wounds after police charged workers demanding higher wages. Macaulay became the empire's publicist, but in 1833 he welcomed "the strange indifference of all classes of people," including both houses of Parliament, "to Indian politics." It enabled the drafting committee to "effect some most valuable improvements with little or no opposition."[9] The multitude was as unfit to exercise imperial power as the squeamish.

Money would follow power, but in India. Versifying his balance sheet to amuse Hannah, he reminded her of her dependence on him:

> So if my debtors pay their debts,
> You'll find, dear sister mine,
> That all my wealth together makes
> Seven hundred pounds and nine.

Prosaically, its 2007 purchasing power was £54,621. He was maneuvering to be appointed the legal member of the Supreme Council for India in Calcutta (now Kolkata): Mill's "person thoroughly versed in the philosophy of man and of government." Paying £10,000 a year—with a 2007 purchasing power of £799,520—the post would enable him to support his dependent family, build capital, and escape from the Whigs' political morass. He looked forward to amassing "a fortune of thirty thousand pounds." Crucially, he made his peace with James Mill. In 1834 Macaulay told the assistant undersecretary of the Colonial Office, their common acquaintance James Stephen, "I did great injustice to him," and noted that when he pilloried Mill in 1829 he had not yet "read his history of India": "a very extraordinary performance." He was indirectly thanking Mill, who two months earlier had "very handsomely" advised the chairman of the company "to take me." Over dinner as 1833 ended, they "were extremely friendly." Unlike a disciple who a couple of weeks later derided Macaulay as an apostate from Benthamism, Mill understood Macaulay's unshakable commitment to utility as a legal and ethical lodestar.[10] Macaulay possessed no alternative scheme of political morality.

The mandate of the fourth member of the governing council for India was originally confined to legislation: "he had no power to sit or vote except at meetings for the purpose of making laws and regulations; and it was only by courtesy, and not by right, that he was allowed to see the papers or correspondence, or to be made acquainted with the deliberations of Government upon any subject not immediately connected with legislation." Macaulay desired a greater role and won it in Calcutta. After the swearing-in ceremony on 8 January 1834 the Court of Directors hosted a celebratory dinner for him. A guest recalled that he "rather gave himself the airs of a Lycurgus, and spoke as if he were to bestow on the swarming millions of India the blessings of rudimentary legislation." But about India, too, Macaulay could speak in different voices to different audiences. He told Hannah that it was his "peculiar" charge to act as "the guardian of the people of India against the European settlers." He went on to warn her to take great care in selecting the maid whom she brought with her. Such servants "generally treat the natives with gross insolence—an insolence natural enough to people accustomed to stand in a servile relation when, for the first time, they find a great population placed in a servile relation towards them."[11] It was a characteristically astute analysis of the human susceptibility to "a power induced impediment with experiencing empathy," but in other people.

Hannah's New "Papa"

Macaulay's ambitions were stronger than his self-control. Before Margaret married, he wanted both her and "Nancy" to live with him. Afterward he started cocooning Hannah and fretting that she, too, would likely abandon him. For Margaret's benefit he quoted the Bible: "The heart knows its own bitterness." If he lost Hannah, he would be left with nothing "in this world but ambition." Seventeen months of courting her rendered him even more emotionally dependent. Over seventy manipulative and seductive letters to her from the period survive. In one of them, she is his "dearest love," "my own darling," "my dear girl," and he "ever dearest yours." A year into the campaign he reiterated his complex motives for going to India: "poverty, unpopularity, and the breaking up of old [political] connections." Warning that debtors' prison might otherwise await their father and writing "through the tears that force themselves into my eyes," he told her that her presence with him would determine "whether the period of my exile shall be one of misery or comfort, and, after the first shock, even of happiness." For her benefit he called on "God to witness that . . . [your happiness] is as dear to me as my own—that I love the ground that you tread on—that, if I shrink from poverty, it is more for your sake than for my own." When she replied with "an agonised appeal to him entreating him to give it up," he professed to hesitate "principally on your account" but again insisted that he was sacrificing himself "that I may have a home for my Nancy, that I may surround her with comforts, and be assured of leaving her safe from poverty." He was relentless.[12]

As late as 2 January 1834 Tom wrote again to his "Dearest love." After gossiping and previewing the luxuries awaiting them in Calcutta—two carriages—he recounted a "most extraordinary scene" with Lady Holland, cast as the frustrated rival for his affections. That great hostess and diva echoed his appeal to Hannah's sense of obligation but as an indictment: "'You are sacrificed to your family . . . I see it all. You are too good to them. They are always making a tool of you . . . now sending you to India to make money for them. Your sister is to go with you . . . Is she pretty?'—'I think her so—' I said. 'But I am a great deal too fond of her to be a judge. I have watched her face ever since she was a month old.'" Cassandra-like, Lady Holland then "cried": "'She will marry some rich Nabob within six months after she reaches Bengal . . .—no three.'" After reporting his defense of Nancy's devotion to him "in a voice trembling with anger," he promised to protect her from becoming "such a woman as my Lady": "I am your papa now." He knew that Hannah felt herself to be a suffering and powerless woman, but Margaret, married to a wealthy and doting man, now enjoyed a life apart from him. The same day he wrote abjectly to her—"Dear dear Margaret"—assuring her both that "no successor comes to occupy your place" and that she remained "necessary to me."[13]

Two realities condition any effort to interpret the words of the recently appointed member of the Supreme Council of India: all of us have expressed our emotions in hyperbole that makes us seem both ridiculous and sad when it is embalmed in print; establishing what words from a vanished world likely raised eyebrows there is a tentative business. In 1876 Hannah's son published his biography of Uncle Tom. It included an abridgment of the letter in which Macaulay told his sister, "I am your

Hannah Macaulay Lady Trevelyan (Photograph by Andrew McGregor; at Wallington, Northumberland, © The National Trust). "My love" (TBM to HMT, 30.xi.33, *L*2:347).

papa now." There G. O. Trevelyan vindicated the stereotype of the proper late Victorian squeamish about sex and money. He omitted Macaulay's declaration, changed the salutation from "Dearest love" to "My dear Sister," and edited his report of Lady Holland's effusion by dropping both her gibe about Macaulay going to India "to make money" for his family and their banter about Hannah's prettiness.[14]

During the long voyage to India Macaulay planned to enjoy "Literature . . . in abundance." It was remote preparation for the decision he proposed to make after returning to England as a rich and independent man: either to choose between "the paths of literature and politics" or to pursue both. During the last months of 1833 he greedily bought "books

. . . good books for a library." His own choices were mostly early-modern. In his brief catalog Gibbon, Voltaire, Cervantes, and the rest preceded "Homer in Greek" and "Horace in Latin." For an outbound high official of the Raj, however, initiation "in Persian and Hindostanee" counted more than the ancient European books that had first oppressed and then shaped his youth. He trusted his friend Ellis to make "a little collection of Greek classics for me."[15]

Neither Tom nor Hannah was flourishing. Years later one of his friends recalled their parting: "his complexion was foul, his aspect jaded, his skin blotched, and I felt the strongest persuasion that he was going to sacrifice his life." Afterward, however, Tom felt "infinitely better than I have for months" and assured Margaret that "Dear Nancy has behaved like an angel." The same day Hannah wrote to her sister, "If I could have conceived the sufferings of the last twenty-four hours beforehand never would I have placed myself here. It is impossible that I could be called upon to such a sacrifice as I have really made." She and their younger brother Charles spent "the night before she left" for India "in each others arms."[16]

Sailing Away

The voyage was a microcosm of empire. In a coincidence made to delight postcolonial scholars, Hannah and Tom sailed around Africa with a servant apiece on a ship called the *Asia*. Leaving Gravesend on 15 February and delayed by gales in the Channel for almost a month, they finally arrived in Madras on 10 June. A good sailor, Tom became not just a loner but a virtual recluse. Hannah endured violent seasickness. He noticed that she "suffered terribly—thought she was dying—and seemed to care very little whether she died or lived" but viewed her suffering as transient. Her depression—"I have no human soul to speak to and I must relieve the dreadful oppression"—was tinged with resentment toward her heedless brother: "Tom has no conception what I am feeling." He distanced himself: "Society indeed I had none . . . I shut myself up in my cabin with my books, and found that the time on the whole passed easily and pleasantly. I was in almost utter solitude. Except at meal times I scarcely exchanged a word with any human being. I never was left for so long a time so completely to my own resources . . . I found them quite sufficient to keep me cheerful.""Nancy" appeared happy and "extremely social" during the day in a women's book club and on the dance floor at night.[17] She was beginning to find her way without him.

Five days after landing he wrote a letter to their sister that fills more than eight printed pages: "Again, and again dearest Margaret farewell and love me." Reading "insatiably and with keen and increasing enjoyment" on the *Asia,* he "devoured" first the "Greek [and] Latin" books, and only then books in four modern European languages. Though capable of quickly learning the rudiments of any new language whose literature he wanted to read, he ignored his "Persian and Hindostanee" grammars. The European books seemed to him more interesting, perhaps more real than the people whom he met at table: "The society, though not such as I have been used to, has nothing to disgust." Living again with the long-familiar ancients, he discovered in them fresh delight and new under-standing. As serious as a child's intense play, his aesthetic reading provided diversion, gratification, and inspiration. He conducted open-ended con-versations with the dead, first in his mind and by January 1835 in mar-gins free of scholarly impedimenta. The old words were fixed on the page, but his relation to their authors changed according to his needs. Bewildered and increasingly alienated in the "new world" of India, Macaulay found a home in his books.[18] It was as delightful as Clapham minus Zachary, when he had lain for hours on the hearthrug reading and eating buttered bread.

To Ellis he later reported that even after years of neglect his classical languages remained "in good condition enough." The frequency and content of Macaulay's letters to him, first from India and then back in England, are striking. Their shared devotion to the classics, especially to the ancient Greeks, was cementing their friendship as well as reshaping his mind. As early as 1 July 1834 it already seemed to be working half-time in Attic. A hybrid word in his first surviving letter to Ellis from In-dia jumps off the page twice. He told Ellis that on his arrival Governor-General Lord William Bentinck summoned him to a mountain resort: "this sana$\tau\eta\rho\acute{\iota}o\nu$"—"I always spell the word sana$\tau\eta\rho\acute{\iota}o\nu$." He graded what he read: the *Iliad,* seemingly accessible, was slightly down from col-lege, and the *Odyssey,* full of depth and shadows, greatly up. His reading fortified his provincialism. He now scorned Ellis' study of "ethnological questions" concerning the Amerindians, recommending that he instead take up the "serious and worthy pursuit" of translating Herodotus.[19] It was of a piece with his neglect of his own Asian grammars on the voyage out.

An Englishman Abroad

Macaulay came to India as "the interpreter of the Act of 1833," in whose drafting he had been decisive, and armed with detailed instructions from the company. They were perhaps drafted by James Mill. Macaulay also carried with him a seaborne disdain for India and its people. Nearly "ten hours a day" with the West's primordial literature reinforced in his mind the rift between the languages of Europeans, informed by the Greek legacy of reason, and the languages of non-Europeans. When they entered the port of Madras (now Chennai), "the first glimpse that I caught of the people among whom I am to live" was a "little black boatman beating the water with his paddle":"He came on board with nothing on him but a pointed yellow cap, and walked among us with a self-possession and civility which, coupled with his colour and nakedness, nearly made me die of laughing." Now more deeply though not more widely learned, and supremely confident of his power to ignore and disparage all that he had failed to learn, he immediately tasted difference:"As to the fish and fruit which they regularly put on the table, I do not trouble them. The fish is insipid: and all the tropical fruits together are not worth any of our commonest English productions."[20]

Less than two weeks later he visited the court of the young nabob of the Carnatic. Humanly he was unimpressed—"a nest of blackguards," "beggarly Musselmans," "scare-crows"—until he met the "interpreter of the court, a handsome, intelligent-looking man, whose mind has evidently been enlarged by much intercourse with Englishmen." A few days later he was summoned to call on the deposed rajah of Mysore:

> The whole thing indeed was better managed than at the Court of the Nabob of the Carnatic. The soldiers were not better dressed or drilled, but their costume was oriental, and had on the whole a striking effect. An elephant richly harnessed, led the procession. Then followed a long stream of silver spears and floating banners. Music, detestable like all the music I have heard in India [after less

than three weeks], preceded the carriage and the whole rabble of Mysore followed my train. We came at last to a square surrounded by buildings less shabby than Indian houses generally are . . . The Durbar fronted the square . . . The pillars were gaudily painted and carved, and the whole look of the thing was like that of a booth for strolling players on a large scale . . . Everywhere I saw that mixture of splendour and shabbiness which characterizes the native courts . . . Having seen his Highness's clothes, and his Highness's horse, I was favoured with a sight of his Highness's Gods, who were much of a piece with the rest of his establishment. The principal deity was a fat man with a paunch like Daniel Lambert's ["the fattest man in England"], an elephant's head and trunk, a dozen hands, and a serpent's tail.

"The principal deity" was Ganeśa, revered throughout the subcontinent as the personification of *Brahman* (the Absolute) under the aspect of "Lord of Obstacles" and "Lord of Beginnings." Had Macaulay inquired, he would perhaps have grasped the ex-rajah's devotion. Although England had made him a king as a child, neglected his upbringing, and then deposed him as unfit, he retained a "strong attachment to the English government" and begged to "be restored to his power": "I felt indeed much pity for him and some shame for my country. He has little reason to thank us."[21]

For the first time in years Macaulay lacked a responsive audience that would daily listen to—perhaps hang upon—his words. Turned in on himself in a strange land, he wrote home voluminously. Because the turn-around time for mail was initially over seven months, and delivery uncertain, his letters, above all to Margaret and Ellis, became monologues. Crafted but often self-revelatory, they amount to a quasi-diary, complementing his marginalia. From the beginning he wrote to his sister not only to entertain and to inform but also to repine. "Oh my dear, dear Margaret, if you knew how fondly, in this distant country, amidst ten thousand new objects my mind turns to you, how much more you are to me than all the rest that I have left, how many tears the thought of you draws from my eyes every day, how lightly all other afflictions fall on me, compared with that stroke which separated us, you would feel more than I wish you to feel." She was now married and a young mother, but he still needed to infantilize her. Writing letters early in the morning "to my dear, dear, little, Margaret, or to some other person," required him to observe widely and watch closely in order to report amusingly. For five months he sent her imperial panoramas evoking the wonders, grotesquerie, and comedy he saw in India. Stereotyping the unfamiliar came more easily to him than studying it: "As to the European villas . . . There is a want of repair—a slovenliness—a sort of Simon O'Doherty way of taking things *asy*—which marks that the rulers of India are pilgrims and sojourners in the land." When a letter from her arrived on 10 October, all seemed well.[22]

In India only Hannah and a few others seemed as real to him as the books he studied and his invisible correspondents. In his letters Indians soon became faceless or caricatures and the bulk of the English variously nonentities, nuisances, or ridiculous, like his former shipmates on the *Asia*. He mocked a religious zealot who tried to construe the meaning of the biblical mark of the beast—"666"—without knowing a word of Greek. Uniquely alive for him was his first valet, Peter Prim, honest, priggish, and "a half caste and a Catholic"; but he died within six weeks. When he fell ill, Macaulay "sent my palanquin for the priest" and experienced his agony: "The struggle continued for near ten days. The sick man's room opened into mine, and I heard his gaspings and moanings plainly through the door. At last, after a hard battle, he sank. I ordered him to be decently buried." The small Indian Catholic community included both converts to the Roman rite made by the Portuguese and members of eastern rites that retained their own languages and liturgies. It registered with Macaulay only that the priest who attended Peter spoke no Latin and that the funeral "service," if it was really in Latin, was pronounced "very strange": "I cannot tell you how curious an effect was produced by the contrast between their oriental dresses and complexions and the European character of their rites." He was as incurious witnessing a group of Indian Catholics worship as before Ganeśa's statue in the rajah of Mysore's shrine. But some of the mourners touched him deeply and memorably. They "praised my attention to the poor fellow; and I saw a letter from one of them in which I was called *the benefactor of my servant*. This says little for the general conduct of masters in India. For I did absolutely nothing more than common humanity required, and had been sometimes inclined to fear that I had done less."[23]

Whether Macaulay possessed a limited capacity for human sympathy or an intense but transient susceptibility to human pain, as his sister Margaret believed, he never again empathized with an Indian. No half-caste, his next valet was "such a Christian as the missionaries make in this part of the world,—that is to say a man who superadds drunkenness to the other vices of the natives." He once visited an Indian's house. Without naming his host, he notified his two pious sisters: "a very wealthy native . . . proposes to entertain us with a shew of fire-works." Up to a point his host was an ersatz European: "a liberal, intelligent, man, a friend to education, and in opinions an Englishman, though in morals, I fear, a Hindoo." On 30 November 1836 that Calcuttan entrepreneur, eager Anglicizer, and grandfather of the future Nobelist Rabindranath Tagore hosted 300 guests at a ball. Macaulay attended in the new governor-general's "train of retainers." Decades later Macaulay remembered his host with a precision that conveys his keen attention to the nuances of class: "You ought not to call Dwarkanauth [sic] Tagore a high caste Hindoo. His ancestors lost caste in the days of Surahah Dowla; and he was a mere Pariah." It was perhaps less the dancing and fireworks that etched Tagore in his memory than Tagore's opposition to his plan for mitigating the dual legal system that privileged Europeans over Indians. Macaulay drafted legislation to subject Europeans to the company's civil jurisdiction and to limit their direct access to the Supreme Court in Calcutta to criminal cases, unless they were British-born and resident there. Feeling threatened by Indian competition and increasingly given to "racialist stereotypes," many in the English community denounced it as the "Black Act" and pilloried Macaulay with "their invectives."[24]

Tagore perhaps supported their protest against an antidiscriminatory measure because he rejected the anachronistic British project of trying to govern the subcontinent through the company. Macaulay's task was to help refashion it into something like a legal state responsible for protecting all its subjects. Was it Tagore's example which convinced him that the Indian national character was helpless? "There is no helping men who will not help themselves. The phenomenon which strikes an observer lately arrived from England with the greatest surprise, and which more than any other damps his hope of being able to serve the people of this country, is their own apathy, their own passiveness under wrong. He comes from a land in which the spirit of the meanest rises up against the insolence of the richest and the most powerful. He finds himself in a land where the patience of the oppressed invites the oppressor to repeat his injuries."[25] His bias only deepened.

Macaulay never bothered learning any Persian, the official language of the Mogul Empire, or "Hindostanee." At first he blamed Hannah for his lack of Hindi: "her knowledge of the language has been a hindrance to me . . . she acts as interpreter." There was, however, an advantage to speaking English in front of uncomprehending retainers: "The servants indeed are so constantly about us here—fanning us—pulling punkahs— and so forth—that if they understood all that we might say, we should be under constant restraint." Despite his vise of a memory, he never directly quoted any of their words nor tried to fathom their speech beyond the snatches he needed to command them: "Coop tunda pawnee" (Very cold water). But in September 1834 during a week's voyage from Madras to Calcutta, he acquired enough Portuguese to read *The Lusiads*, Luis de Camões' poem about the birth of his nation's Indian empire, long since recommended to the English as "the epic of those who hold possession" of the subcontinent.[26]

The Indians to whom he would speak became almost invisible to him unless they were repugnant or amusing. In announcing his acquisition of Portuguese to Margaret, he complained about a row involving his name-less, "very worthless" new manservant. The incident required him to sit through a trial. Uncomprehending, he fumed at the "jabbering" natives, not at his own ignorance of their language: a "rabble . . . remarkable for profligacy, ferocity and impudence." His condescension toward Indians sometimes mellowed into drollery. Passing again through Mysore, he was visited by "one of the princes of the blood, who speaks English very de-cently": "The illustrious person who was in attendance on me amused me very much. He had never been out of Mysore, and his questions about England were very diverting." Did Macaulay not recall that, apart from a month in Paris in 1830, he had never been out of Britain until he boarded the *Asia?* In any case, he lacked both his father's easy French and his unshakable if authoritarian belief that he shared a common humanity with the rest of a single redeemable human race.[27]

Macaulay's first task in India was to join Lord William Bentinck, the governor-general of Bengal, recuperating at Ootacamund, a mountain spa in the south of Madras province. He stayed from 26 June through 31

August 1834. The twelve Indian bearers who in rotation carried him 400 miles on their shoulders through jungle and over mountain streams were "a very fine race of men." But as much as the "ten porters" who carried his baggage—"I brought no more than absolutely necessary"—and the two "police officers with swords and badges" who "ran by my side," they were merely useful instruments, otherwise to be ignored. Carried "on men's shoulders" and attended by a numerous retinue, he found the journey "agreeable . . . on the whole." In September, when he was carried from Ootacamund to Calcutta, he thought about the "peculiar chaunt of the bearers." A colleague who knew Indian dialects once heard a group of them singing: "There is a fat hog—a great fat hog—how heavy is is [sic]—hum—shake him—hum—shake him well." Macaulay told Margaret, "Whether they paid a similar compliment to me I cannot say. They might have done so, I fear, without any breach of veracity." It was a passing wry insight, not a prod to meditate on the dynamics of dominance and subordination. The tangible disparity between his power and the Indians' only grew. A few days earlier, when confronting the "gang of blackguards" who were persecuting his new servant—"like most of his countrymen, he is a chicken-hearted fellow"—Macaulay ensured that they "retained a great respect for my race and station," despite their rage.[28] He saw his own "race" more in terms of his Englishness than in terms of his skin color, and the biases he acquired in India were seemingly more cultural and social than racialist. He still believed in the reality of unequal, sometimes obnoxious, but possibly changeable national and class characteristics more than in immutable biological differences among peoples.

At Ootacamund he paid court to Bentinck and others of "high importance"—"many others of inferior note" deserved no mention—doing business, and adapting to his new position: "half a dozen bearers are always in attendance in case I should want my palanquin, which I find very useful when it rains; and it rains . . . eighteen hours in the twenty-four." Hannah was left in "very unhealthy" Calcutta until 25 September. Although he greedily received letters from her, none to her survive from their more than three-month separation. It was "very disagreeable" to him, but she was making a life of her own without him: "Lady William Bentinck . . . has taken a very great liking to her. They are very gay . . . and the Bishop [with whom she resided] puts no restraint on

Nancy. She goes with Lady William to Balls and Operas." He wrote often to Margaret—"my love," "my darling." But was he changing in how
he related to her? In his first letters he signed off with profuse expressions of affection as usual: "T B M." After six weeks of transacting "public
business" at the governor-general's "sana$\tau\eta\rho\iota o\nu$," his profusions continued, but he was now invariably to her, as to all his correspondents, not
the familiar shorthand "T B M" but "T B Macaulay."[29]

Lord William Bentinck was a duke's younger son, a soldier, an old India hand, and a Whig—Canning had appointed him governor-general.
His wife's evangelicalism dovetailed "with his own evolving ideas of
imperial trusteeship." He also considered himself a pupil of James Mill,
whom he promised: "I shall not be governor-general. It is you that will
be governor-general." Awaiting Macaulay's arrival in June 1834, he understood his potential usefulness. Major General Sir Samuel Ford Whittingham, Bentinck's military secretary and confidant, informed him that
he had

> no knowledge of Mr. Macaulay save as a man of superior abilities,
> raised by their possession from insignificance and poverty to be one
> of the rulers of India. It is not in human nature that a man so con-
> stituted should be free from a very great share of vanity. The aristoc-
> racy which rests upon station alone, is of necessity, full of conceit of
> that ability which has gained the battle.
>
> It would I should think, be highly desirable that Mr. Macaulay
> should be led to imagine that he was taking the initiative in your
> discussions. If a man in his position, once adopts a child as his, the
> world is not wide enough to contain its marvelous virtues! . . .
> Composed as your council will, in part, be, of a *novus homo* [new
> man] on the one side, and of a legitimate child of Madras and its
> prejudices on the other, no directing hand should appear even at
> the greatest distance, but your own.[30]

Widely disliked within the English community, Bentinck distrusted
the East India Company's bureaucrats and routinely ignored their advice.
He found Macaulay agreeable, and both favored limiting Christian proselytizing. They also wanted the government to end subsidizing instruction of natives in their classical languages and apply the money to teach-

ing them in English. Bentinck's objectives were those of a practical administrator: to ensure that Indians enjoyed access to modern knowledge, which for him was Western; to replace Persian as the official language of government; and to train a cadre of Indian civil servants who would do the same work as Britons but more cheaply. While in Bentinck's entourage at Ootacamund, Macaulay began composing poems that would vindicate the practicality of his cultural warfare. The *Lays of Ancient Rome* are his imaginative re-creation of lost ballads celebrating the city's heroic period, when it acquired the ruthless might that enabled it to win an empire almost as vast as modern England's.[31] As long as India was Britain's, they were popular wherever English was spoken.

Still learning at thirty-three how to exercise political power, "Mr. Macaulay" knew more about the theory of Machiavellianism than about its practice. With decades of experience in both hemispheres, Major General Sir Samuel Ford Whittingham knew how Governor-General Lord William Bentinck should play him. By the autumn of 1834 Macaulay imagined that he had "induced Lord William to declare himself" on the language question, accepted appointment as president of the governing council's education committee, and began working to break the longstanding deadlock within the Supreme Council of India. Enjoying his newfound role, he was at least as cocksure as any of his "Orientalist" opponents, who supported teaching only the Hindu and Muslim classics. Simultaneously radical and backward-looking, his position owed more to cultural prejudices than to ideology. Back in East India House John Stuart Mill sided with the Orientalists and urged continuing to subsidize the teaching of the subcontinent's classical languages, while his chief, James Mill, despite his ardent classicism and bias against the subcontinent's traditional cultures, favored educating Indians in their own vernaculars. Even some Christian missionaries shared the elder Mill's judgment.[32] At the same time Macaulay's notion of the ideal curriculum betrayed his own old-fashioned education. Unlike James Mill, he wanted Indians to learn literature unleavened by the natural sciences.

Calcutta welcomed him by celebrating his power. Arriving before dawn at Government House, a neoclassical pile centered by a triumphal arch erected at the turn of the century at a cost of £87,000—with a 2007 purchasing power of almost £6.3 million—he found Hannah "surprisingly well and cheerful." As "soon as the first gleam of daylight was

Government House, Calcutta, before 1870. Daguerreotype from [George Nathaniel] Marquis Curzon of Keddleston, *British Government in India: the Stories of the Viceroys and Government Houses*, 2 vols. (London: Cassell, 1925), 1:84. "A salute of fifteen guns thundered from Fort William to announce my arrival to the good people of the capital" (TBM to MMC, 17.x.34, *L*3:90).

discernible, a salute of fifteen guns thundered my arrival." He looked forward to more substantial perquisites, including a rented house "said to be the best in Calcutta": "Two rooms, the dining room and the great drawing room, are really magnificent. I have dined there with a party of forty; and there was not the smallest crowding or inconvenience." For Margaret he conjured the style to which he was becoming accustomed. Most afternoons he and Hannah took a carriage ride with Lady William Bentinck: "We are attended by two of the governor general's body-guard, in blazing uniforms and with drawn swords. It is certainly very agreeable and refreshing particularly after a warm day." Impending affluence was beginning to change how he saw himself. To pay for relocating to India he had borrowed from Margaret's husband £600, with a 2007 purchasing power of £47,971. But that was in England. In India, "If I live, I shall get rich fast. I quite enjoy the thought of appearing in the new character of an old hunks [miser] who knows on which side his bread is buttered,— a warm man—a fellow who will cut up well. This is not a character which the Macaulays have been much in the habit of sustaining. But I can assure you that, after next Christmas, I expect to lay up an average of about seven thousand pounds a year while I remain in India." The exchange rate, moreover, was "very favourable indeed."[33]

Calcutta's imperial colony reflected and reinforced the English social hierarchy, just as its increasing ethnic segregation manifested Britain's economic and technical predominance. Soldiers constituted the vast majority of the ruling population. Despite Uncle Colin the general, Tom managed to ignore that "the most striking feature of Anglo-India before 1858 was that it was a military society." Upward-bound, Hannah and Tom occupied a "splendid house" staffed by "an army of servants." It was located in the small, tony English enclave—"the May Fair . . . of Calcutta," separated from the "nearly half a million" Indians in "the Black Town": "I know no more of the Black Town . . . than what I have seen in a drive by night through one great street,—and . . . till the cold season comes, I am not likely to know more of it." He left no description of the place. But from a distance he quickly saw enough to make "death and everything connected with it . . . familiar subjects": "Six months ago I could not have believed that I should look on with composure while the crows were feasting on a dead man within twenty yards of me." His new vantage inspired him to make finer English class distinctions than when he championed the Reform Bill. He was barely two weeks in-country when the ex-rajah of Mysore eagerly led him into "a little room which had more of an English look than any that I had seen in India." It was, alas, "not much unlike the drawing room of a rich, vulgar, Cockney cheesemonger who has taken a villa at Clapton or Walworth, and has shewn his own taste in the furnishing of the apartments."[34] Neither of those London suburbs could be confused with Mayfair.

As Macaulay hovered over his sister, the prophecy he had attributed to Lady Holland was almost fulfilled. Two months after he reached Calcutta, Hannah became engaged to Charles Trevelyan, not "some rich Nabob" but at twenty-seven already the "Deputy Secretary to the Supreme Government in the political" department. Marriage would liberate her from her brother's domination. On 7 December 1834 Tom informed Margaret in a letter filling more than eight pages. From an old, moneyed family, Trevelyan possessed a "literary merit which, for his opportunities, is considerable"—he was an alumnus of a great public school but had attended the East India Company's training college rather than university. Marking Trevelyan's "religious feelings"—"ardent . . . even to enthusiasm"—his "faults," and his "odd" manners, Macaulay nonetheless judged him to be educable. He was spearheading the campaign to transfer the government's annual subsidy of "native education" from studies in "Sanscrit or Arabic," but their goals differed. A self-confessed proponent of "ultra radicalism," Trevelyan wanted to transliterate all the indigenous languages into the Roman alphabet, so that within a generation, "All the existing Muhammadan and Hindu Literature will be cut off at the root." Lacking his "religious feelings," Macaulay wanted only to open "the whole knowledge of the western world" for the benefit of an Indian elite." Intuiting Hannah's attachment to Trevelyan "before she knew it herself," he subordinated his own happiness to hers. Had he offered the "smallest rebuff" to Trevelyan, there would have been no marriage. During a crucial debate that autumn Trevelyan had been "a little rash in his expressions," but after Macaulay "threw all my influence in the scale," it was possible to "consider the victory as gained" over the Sanskrit- and Arabic-loving Orientalists. He was certain that "Lord William . . . intends, very speedily, to pronounce a decision in our favour in the points at issue."[35]

For five pages he sounded self-possessed and self-congratulatory. Then his composure seemed to dissolve. At least seventy times on a single printed page he used the pronouns "I," "me," or "myself": "Now I have nothing . . . I am alone in the world. I have lost everything." In the course of that litany he declared what he needed from Hannah: "She was everything to me: and I am henceforth nothing to her—the first place in her affections is gone." Losing "the first place" suggests that possessing her had reassured him that he was not merely loved by someone but was supremely lovable. His notion of the meaning of "separation" from her says as much. At first he welcomed her proposal that the three of them form a household: "I have not fortitude enough to relinquish her society at once in this strange country." But within a couple of weeks doubt set in: "It is the moral much more than the physical separation which I dread: and the very course which she has taken for the purpose of preventing the physical separation will make the moral separation a slow torture instead of a quick decisive pang." For "moral" we would substitute "emotional," a word just coined by John Stuart Mill. Macaulay nonetheless depicted—perhaps saw—himself as a martyr to his fraternal generosity: "For her sake more than my own . . . For her sake far more than my own." He tried to restrain his feelings—"I do not repine . . . I have gone on"—only to declare himself "unable even at Church or in the Council-room to command my voice or to restrain my tears . . . I never knew unhappiness before." Two pages earlier he had insisted to Margaret that "my parting from you almost broke my heart." After his homey evocation of churchgoing and the Bible, he announced what he wanted from Margaret: "there is a pleasure in reposing confidence somewhere, in exciting sympathy somewhere. I shall write in a very different style to my father."[36] His rhetorical capability was resilient.

During those weeks Macaulay used yet another style to describe his condition to Ellis, an educated and prudent man like himself. He was reading "much—and particularly Greek . . . however, not as I read at College, but like a man of the world." Bypassing unknown or unimportant words and intractable passages, "I thoroughly enter into the spirit." The minutiae that had preoccupied him when he was grubbing for success and reputation were now irrelevant. In India the old Greek and Roman authors spoke directly to him, helping him to escape into himself as he did onboard the *Asia*. His renewed devotion to the classics, above all to Greek literature, would be both permanent and contagious. It was a

manly affair with public implications. Planning to live with Hannah under Tom's roof—"I have a house about as large as Lord Dudley's in Park
Lane, or rather larger, so that I shall accommodate them without the
smallest difficulty"—Charles sought his advice about reviving his own
neglected Greek. "With perfect rapture," he read aloud from Homer and
proposed that together they study the great works of the language.
Macaulay found him to be "not a bad brother-in-law for a man to pick
up in 22 degrees of North Latitude and 100 degrees of East Longitude."[37] Twenty years later those tutorials helped to reshape the government of British India.

The actual of an avid and smart reader, Margaret was excluded from what
drew her unnerved brother to read "Æschylus," immeasurably superior
"to every poet of antiquity." He told her only: "Books are becoming everything to me ... I would bury myself in one of those immense libraries
that we saw at the Universities." She was barred from studying there, but
Ellis could understand the drift of Macaulay's mind: "Greek reminds me
of Cambridge . . . From one Trinity Fellow to another—(This letter is
quite a study to a metaphysician who wishes to illustrate the law of association.)." Macaulay's friend was also more interested in the public
world, where able and ambitious men competed, than in family values
like churchgoing and the Bible. As much as the law, the church belonged
to that world. The college's high-Tory clerical master had forced out
Connop Thirlwall, an assistant tutor and historian of Greece, for championing measures that would have diluted its Anglican character: "unutterable baseness and dirtiness."[38]

The classicism that marks Macaulay's letters to Ellis inhibited his words
and perhaps what he could feel. Rationing terms of endearment to safe-
guard the distance proper to English gentlemen, he was Ellis' "affectionate friend," but they were not on a first-name basis. He sometimes signed
off with variations on "affectionately" but always as "T B Macaulay,"
never as "Tom." Before one another, gentlemen of course avoided tears
—or at least mentioning them—and abbreviated their expressions of
emotion. It would have been weak and dishonorable to excite Ellis' sympathy, much less to demand it, as he did Margaret's. Reserve that had
become habitual seemed to cauterize Macaulay's affections: "My spirits
are not bad; and they ought not to be bad": "I *have* health, affluence, consideration, great power to do good, functions which, while they are hon-

orable and useful, are not painfully burdensome." His calculating words to Ellis mirrored his economic mindset, which as much as the language of gentlemen worked to turn other humans into objects. In Macaulay's public world whatever could not be calculated seemed fuzzy and likely irrational. To treat all that as somehow not quite real tended to minimize the human dimension, privately as well as publicly. At length Macaulay itemized for Ellis all that he possessed, ending with "warm affections, and a very dear sister."[39] Once again writing of Hannah—perhaps half-regarding her—as a supremely precious commodity was a more objective restatement of his repining about having "lost everything" when she became engaged.

But however phrased, his repining was palpable. He created a regimen of reading Greek and Latin "for three or four hours" every morning before breakfast, which he sustained throughout his Indian exile. Daily his father read his Bible at that time. Fresh in India, Macaulay had written letters home early in the morning, a practice that required him to observe the world in front of him widely, if not deeply. His introverting classical regimen changed his mind. He quietly buried his advocacy of reforming higher education by modernizing its curriculum and diversifying its population and later adroitly helped to perpetuate the classical stranglehold on elite education that had vexed his own youth. Contrasting admonitions illuminate his changing educational theory. Just before leaving England, he urged that young Frank Ellis be sent to Cambridge and win a prize for his English verse. From India he now admonished Ellis, "Tell Frank that if he is not a better Greek scholar than I when I come back, I shall hold him in great contempt." That admonition became a refrain. What may fairly be called Macaulay's second and definitive classical conversion was no quirk. His younger American contemporary Henry David Thoreau captured its rigor and its naïveté: "The student may read Homer or Æschylus in the Greek without danger or dissipation or luxuriousness, for it implies that he in some measure emulate their heroes, and consecrate morning hours to their pages . . . For what are the classics but the noblest recorded thoughts of man? They are the only oracles which are not decayed . . . To read well, that is, to read true books in a true spirit, is a noble exercise which the customs of the day esteem. It requires a training such as the athletes underwent, the steady intention almost of the whole life to this object."[40]

Macaulay read Aeschylus' *Libation Bearers,* a tragedy about Elektra and Orestes' plotting matricide to revenge their slain father and Orestes' subsequent flight from the wrathful Furies. After Hannah rejected him as her "new papa," he did not need Sigmund Freud's instruction to understand the plot. Nine days later he again repined to Margaret. It was Christmas Eve. Instead of alluding to the Furies, he broke off after two paragraphs of level reportage to identify his agony with Christ's before his Passion: "My soul is exceeding sorrowful even unto death." Foreseeing that Hannah must outgrow him, he nonetheless worked to possess her always. Now he was locked in the emotional prison he meant for her and feared that he would be left possessing nothing "in this world but ambition." Another invocation of his unrequited sacrifice on behalf of his family justified both his identification of his victimhood with Christ's and his anger at Margaret's primal betrayal in marrying: "my feelings will govern my pen. I shall give you pain, I know. But you will forgive me for the sake of what we once were to each other in pleasant times that are gone and that will return no more." He went on to frame perhaps the coolest attempt at self-analysis he ever committed to paper.

> I am a changed man. My sense and my humanity will preserve me from misanthropy. My spirits will not easily be subdued by melancholy. But I feel that an alteration is taking place. My affections are shutting themselves up and withering. I feel a growing tendency to cynicism and suspicion. My intellect remains and is likely, I sometimes think, to absorb the whole man. I still retain not only undiminished, but strengthened by the very events which have deprived me of everything else . . . my power of forgetting what surrounds me, of living with the past, the future, the distant, and the unreal . . . I know this state of mind will not last . . . Ambition will again spring up in my mind. I may again enjoy the commerce of society and the pleasures of friendship. But a love like that which I bore to my two youngest sisters, and which, since I lost my Margaret, I felt with concentrated strength for Nancy, I shall never feel again.[41]

The day before, Hannah and Charles had married in Calcutta's cathedral. Macaulay "gave her away," and they left for a two-week honeymoon in a villa about twelve miles outside the city. For the benefit of his unmarried sisters back home he was all phlegm, expressing "the fullest confidence that the event will be for her happiness." He wrote to the new Mrs. Trevelyan what she remembered as "the most fearful letter of misery and reproach," which she destroyed along with "one begging me to forgive it." On her wedding night the Bentincks visited him. They wrote imploring the newlyweds "to return as soon as we could, as they were frightened about him," but the Trevelyans continued their honeymoon.[42]

"The History of Progress"

During December 1834 Macaulay's anger was driven outward as well as inward. His official duties left him time for some writing along with much reading. A scalding attack on the inept editor of Sir James Mackintosh's fragmentary, posthumous *History of the Revolution in England, in 1688* provoked its target to issue challenges to Macaulay and the editor of the *Edinburgh Review.* Carefully dispatched in duplicate, the piece offered both light and heat. Some block quotations in Latin and Greek hinted at how deeply his classical regimen had affected him. As much as Mackintosh's Whiggish book, the ancients now persuaded him to accept what he had eloquently rejected a decade earlier: that history was mainly dead politics. Now for Macaulay, 1688, not the Civil War, had set England on the path of self-sustaining progress and greatness, which was "felt, not only throughout our own country, but in half the monarchies of Europe, and in the depth of the forests of Ohio."[43] Unlike the Civil War, the "Glorious Revolution" was a generally accepted turning point among Tories and Whigs.

But Macaulay's admiration for Cromwell, who had made England "more respected and dreaded than any power in Christendom," remained unbounded. Troweling flattery on his compatriots enabled him to invite them to make England's power the barometer of their condition. A "brave, proud, and high-spirited race, unaccustomed to defeat, to shame, or to servitude," the English were "the greatest and most highly civilised people that ever the world saw," who "have spread their dominion over every quarter of the globe, have scattered the seeds of mighty empires and republics over vast continents . . . have produced a literature which may boast of works not inferior to the noblest which Greece has bequeathed to us." They were, moreover, "at heart a religious people," fun-loving but viewing "gross profaneness and licentiousness . . . with gen-eral horror." He would continue experimenting to perfect the rhetoric which could persuade that "brave, proud, and high-spirited race" to identify themselves and their interests with those of "the State"—duly capitalized—the ultimate guarantor of their order.[44]

If the anglicized Indian elite were to filter Western knowledge to their benighted masses, the historian of England must also enlighten his back-ward readers. Because "the history of the national mind" was ultimately the history of the nation, the "highest intellects, like the tops of moun-tains, are the first to catch and to reflect the dawn. They are bright, while the level below is still in darkness. But soon the light which at first illu-minated only the loftiest eminences, descends on the plain, and pene-trates the deepest valley. First come hints, then fragments of systems, then defective systems, then complete and harmonious systems. The sound opinion, held for a time by one bold speculator, becomes the opinion of a small minority, of a strong minority, of a majority of mankind."[45]

Macaulay endorsed Mackintosh's conciliatory partisanship along with his emphasis on 1688–89. It was decisive for modern England that after the Glorious Revolution the "Whig party had, during seventy years, an almost uninterrupted possession of power." Their "fundamental doc-trine" was "that power is a trust for the people; that it is given to magis-trates, not for their own, but for the public advantage; that, where it is abused by magistrates, even by the highest of all, it may lawfully be with-drawn." The Tories during their long opposition also embraced "doc-trines favourable to public liberty," which now informed "the national mind." Mackintosh failed, however, to sustain the combination of "new and curious information" and rhetorical flair that made a history persua-sive as well as "sound." Writing such a book required an author to imitate a "real model" by choosing and crafting the available materials into a work of art.[46]

James Mill's *History of British India* was also shaping Macaulay's histori-cal imagination. By demonstrating that progress alone confers meaning, Mill showed how to craft a modern English history. "He eagerly culls from old dispatches and minutes every expression in which he can dis-cern the imperfect germ of any great truth which has since been fully developed. He never fails to bestow praise on those who, though far from coming up to his standard of perfection, yet rose in a small degree above the common level of their contemporaries. It is thus that the annals of past times ought to be written. It is thus, especially, that the annals of our own country ought to be written." The history of England was "emphatically the history of progress." Macaulay offered one qualification: its history, "when examined in small separate portions . . . may with more propriety be called a history of actions and reactions." Although the forward "direction" of society was incontestable, a "recoil . . . regularly follows every advance and a great general ebb." Macaulay's sunny dogma was for public consumption. Privately, he wrote: "The world is a tragi-comedy."[47]

Mill taught another lesson that Macaulay embraced: "Exactly in proportion as Utility is the object of every pursuit, may we regard a nation as civilized. Exactly in proportion as its ingenuity is wasted on contemptible or mischievous subjects, though it may be, in itself, an ingenuity of no ordinary kind, the nation may be denominated barbarous." Because Macaulay spoke for progress in "Mackintosh," he endorsed Utilitarian schemes "to improve the discipline of prisons, and to enlighten the minds of the poor": Jeremy Bentham's monitorial jail, the Panopticon, and Joseph Lancaster's monitorial charity schools.[48] Before leaving India, he would embrace "Utility" as the second hallmark of modern England's ascent to supreme greatness.

Classicist

A few letters survive from the Christmas season, when Macaulay, alone except for the small army of retainers on whom he depended from rising "at six in the morning," mourned Hannah: "These you must understand are not the servants of the Government House, but our own." There was no exposing his rawness to either his friends or the rest of his family: "My domestic life is very agreeable." Solace came instead from "renewing my acquaintance with old friends with whom I never expected to fall in again—the Greek poets and philosophers." Then, early in January, he was again staggered. Scarlet fever had killed Margaret before she received any of his letters. For over six months he had been trying to amuse, inveigle, and love a dead woman, who now became a permanent source of his grief and fear. A journal entry twenty-three years later evokes his sense of injury. He remembered repeating to himself an Italian sonnet about losing everything "when I lost M & H at once." The association of what he read and felt during the early winter of 1835 was etched in his brain. Cognitive-behavioral psychiatrists have established the "functional relationship" between the two long-term memory systems that capture events and words: "left lateral temporal regions involved in semantic memory play an important role in accurate episodic memory retrieval."[49]

Henceforth Macaulay associated the loss of "M & H at once" above all with his Greek "old friends." Hannah recalled that after she and Charles rushed to him, "We spent many months in great unhappiness." They lived together in his "palace," the Trevelyans perhaps less economically dependent on him than he was becoming emotionally dependent on them. The brothers-in-law worked in tandem and would continue to do so in Britain, particularly in crisis. Family conversations are irretrievable, but reading his journals after he died, Hannah remembered that his "former lighthearted vivacity" never returned and a "certain amount of depression remained, and to his last day." He had predicted as much for himself. His habit of tearfully rereading poems associated with those days reflected his "depression" but also helped to ensure that "my affections are shutting themselves up and withering. I feel a growing tendency to cynicism and suspicion."[50]

On 8 February 1835 he wrote to Ellis. Meandering but finally confluent, his letter is one of the most artless of his adult life. Fearing after three pages that "I shall run on for ever," he tried to stop, only to continue for almost two more pages. Here uniquely, he exposed for Ellis something of his emotional rawness. January "has been the most painful month that I ever went through." Now he "knew . . . what it was to be miserable." He evoked his damaged sensibility with a classical reference. For the first time feeling the power of Euripides, the rational and perhaps misogynistic dramatist of extravagant passion and suffering, he quoted from *Hippolytus,* a tragedy about thwarted incest and death:

> If only mortals would mix the bowl of friendship for each other
> only to a moderate strength

and not touch the deepest marrow of their soul.
The loves of our hearts should be easy to untie,
easy to push away, easy to tighten fast.

The obvious inference seems right. The tragedy "certainly constitutes
the most powerful enacted articulation of the ancient Greek perception
that eros 'is the most dangerous of all relations' and poses 'a serious threat
to the boundaries of the autonomous self by putting it in another's power
under the magnetic pull of desire." Two other themes in the play may be
pertinent: "The plot emphasizes above all the power of language to reveal and silence to conceal . . . A feminist reading can hardly fail to see
the drama as a charter text for patriarchy: a 'male-bonding' play." Now
Euripides' *Bacchae* and *Medea,* which stereotyped Asians as irrational and
barbarous, also resonated with Macaulay: "what a poet!"[51]

Time, he told Ellis, had perhaps started to exercise its "healing office."
Even so, "I cannot write about her without being altogether unmanned."
Fearful of regressing into primal childishness and taking comfort where
he could find it, he was "recovering my mental health": "That I have not
utterly sunk under this blow, I owe chiefly to literature": "Greek literature." The ancient tragedians described madness and its relief in similar terms. That Greek offered a rich "vocabulary for anger-like states"
and that its literature was alive with "psychological complexity" may
have prevented Macaulay's collapse. Offering him hitherto-unknown intellectual enjoyment, Euripides and the other great ancients occupied
his solitude, where as a boy he had been taught to locate heartfelt religion. That a mawkish poem titled "To Margaret in Heaven" indescrib-
ably "moved" him testifies that, despite his return to the classics, he
remained a nineteenth-century man, savoring various irrational, over-
powering "emotions" which the ancients taught Christians to distrust as
"passions."[52]

For him and some of his contemporaries, reading provided a form of
"cognitive-behavioral therapy," which seeks to use words to help depressives overcome—or at least mitigate—defective or destructive ways of
thinking. Capitalizing "Literature," one of Macaulay's critics "was sure
that, in proportion as we master it . . . and imbibe its spirit, we shall ourselves become in our own measure the ministers of like benefits to others, be they many or few, be they in the obscurer or more distinguished

walks of life,—who are united to us by social ties, and are within the sphere of our personal influence." Macaulay was more succinct: "I have gone back to Greek literature with a passion quite astonishing to myself." It sustained his desire for human society, though on his now even more exacting and restrictive terms. To Ellis he apologized, "You must excuse all this. For I labour at present, under a suppression of Greek; and am likely to do so for at least three years to come." If by "suppression" Macaulay meant stifling, putting down, or excluding, the sentence sounds incoherent. But "suppression" understood as keeping something secret or private explains the unhappy solitude of his passion for Greek. Macaulay craved but lacked sympathetic, classically educated men with whom to talk in a shared idiom. A Cambridge contemporary of Ellis and Macaulay, Benjamin Heath Malkin had recently been appointed judge of the Supreme Court in Calcutta. He delayed arriving until early October 1835, when he and Macaulay worked together to re-create the Indian penal laws on Utilitarian lines. But Malkin's marriage precluded extensive society apart from the world of couples, and he was one of those who "have the most particularly disagreeable wives, who must be asked with them." In any case, he died a gruesome death—"three abscesses in the stomach, and the whole œconomy of the brain disarranged"—before Macaulay returned to England.[53]

His unsparing portrait of the English elite of Calcutta outside "a little circle of people whose friendship I value" suggests that neither his "sense" nor his "humanity" was preserving him from depressive "misanthropy." A year after learning of Margaret's death, he told his unmarried sisters, Selina and Frances: "I avoid all these amusements,—if they deserve the name,—the dinners excepted. I am forced now and then to be a guest, and now and then to be a host . . . The conversation is the most deplorable twaddle that can be conceived; and as I always sit next to the lady of the highest rank—or in other words next to the oldest, ugliest, proudest, and dullest woman in the company—I am worse off than my neighbours." Many of "the English settlers" reciprocated his disdain: "'Soon we hope they will recall ye / Tom Macaulay, Tom Macaulay.'"[54]

The classics were also preparing him to escape Calcutta. In Hesiod's *Theogony* he discovered hints about how to flourish in public life back home. To Ellis he quoted in Greek six lines evoking the visitation of the Muses as the poet, suffering fresh grief, sat silently "with sorrow-stricken heart." After they restored to him the gift of song, "at once he forgets his melancholy and remembers not at all his grief." Divine eloquence endowed those possessing it with authority. Macaulay, who had looked to ambition as a refuge should he lose Hannah and Margaret, "repeated to myself" those six lines "many times during the last few weeks," like a prayer. Now he "loved" some of his old books so intently that their authors came alive for him, enabling him "to converse with the dead and to live amidst the unreal."[55]

On 25 October 1835, his birthday, he was reading Aeschylus' *Seven against Thebes,* a tragedy rich in gore, but his mind wandered from the afflictions of Oedipus' children—who were also his half-siblings—to Sophocles' *Oedipus at Colonus.* The play begins with Oedipus wandering, self-blinded in remorse for his unwitting incest, and ends with his death. In a margin of Aeschylus' tragedy Macaulay wrote out from memory in Greek a chorus of Sophocles: "'The happiest destiny is never to have been born; and the next best, by far, is to return, as swiftly as may be, to the bourn whence we came.'" Although his unhinging grief subsided, he continued to present textbook symptoms of chronic, low-level depression: shunning public functions and eating himself fatter. Official work never filled his days, and he seemed almost to be living outside real time in his own head. Except for the comfort of seeing the Trevelyans and "the books which I read . . . I should have no mark to distinguish one part of the year from another." He kept track by dating the marginalia he lavishly penciled in the classics he read and reread, checking them to determine "when an event took place." He "was generally astonished to see that what seemed removed from me by only two or three months really happened nearly a year ago."[56]

Macaulay's desolate meditation on his thirty-fifth birthday belonged to the Sunday regimen that he kept from 18 October 1835 to 5 June 1836. English Calcutta kept the Sabbath, though for him it was usually a churchless one. For thirty-four weeks he faithfully read a different Greek tragedy. While writing his essay on Bacon, so assertively modern and upbeat, he reported, "Euripides has made a complete conquest of me." After each of the tragedies he penciled an appreciation. Of *Prometheus Bound,* about a giant persecuted by the tyrant Zeus and unrepentant in his hatred of the gods, Macaulay wrote: "One of the greatest human compositions." Such was the power of its beauty and his memory that he knew it

and some other tragedies by heart. Despite the appeal of the great tragedians, he flinched at their stark vision of human destiny. Early in 1835 he
quoted to Ellis a passage from Lucretius' *De Rerum Natura* reiterating the
denial of any hope beyond our world that he had first accepted while at
Cambridge. There was no reconsidering Christianity, and he now spared
his father, who had once claimed to be God's surrogate, and his surviving
siblings the pieties he had once bestowed on Margaret and Hannah. His
mature classicism resembled the second naïveté often observed in adults
who revisit and learn to reclaim a chastened form of the religious faith
of their lost childhood. But two residues of Clapham tinged it. Trumping
his skepticism, his self-dramatizing sensibility and desire not for salvation
but for a happy ending in this world endured.[57]

Despite the thousands of hours Macaulay devoted to the ancients,
even his devoted nephew, whom he formed to share his enthusiasm, assumed that, apart from a few published pages, he derived from them only
immense learning and private solace and amusement. The academic clas-
sicists who explored some of the records of his daily communion interpreted them as curious remains of an erudite amateur's pastime. One don
condemned him for reading in "a typically wrong way": "one of the
most interesting things about these marginalia [to Lucretius] is that they
show so clearly his very deep lack of what we call a historical sense." The
word "inconsistent" better evokes Macaulay's unstable but creative oscil-
lations between feelings of closeness to and distance from antiquity. It
also captures him selectively learning from the ancients with whom he
maintained a "daily communion" that seemed to annihilate time and
distance.[58]

The affronted scholar studied ancient things and persons that for him
were irretrievably gone. Understanding that Macaulay's reading was subjective, he failed to recognize that it was spiritual in the basic sense of the
word: in "distinction to bodily, corporal, or temporal." Macaulay's classicism formed his personal spirituality. After saving his sanity, a profusion
of Greek and Latin authors helped him to buffer life's afflictions. In India
the elegance of the best of them permanently recaptured him, always
aesthetically stunted. But Macaulay's classically informed spirituality had
public implications. Strengthening his belief that rhetoric is constitutive
of society and politics, his engagement with some of the ancients inspired him to adapt them for the future world he was imagining.[59]

In the winter of 1835 Thucydides seemed to be the most important of his rediscoveries. Seven years earlier he had marked him as "simply an Athenian of the fifth century before Christ." Now *The History of the Peloponnesian War* came as a revelation: "A young man, whatever his genius may be, is no judge of such a writer . . . I have now been reading him with a mind accustomed to historical researches and to political affairs; and I am astonished at my own former blindness, and at his greatness." By the end of the month Thucydides was "the greatest historian that ever lived." Rereading him again and again in Calcutta confirmed that "there never was a historian, ancient or modern, who could bear a comparison with Thucydides"; every judicious historian "should make Thucydides his model." He tried to explain why he saw Thucydides as nonpareil: "a certain πρέπον [seemliness]" and "judicial gravity." The pages of Macaulay's late seventeenth-century edition of *The History of the Peloponnesian War* reveal Thucydides' arduous Greek captivating him, enabling him to see antiquity come alive, and making him a virtual participant. Early in the morning while a barber shaved him, he, "always with a pencil in his hand," read Thucydides oblivious to the soap trickling onto the page, the razor cuts, his blood dripping, and his fingerprints on the stains. When Macaulay wrote his *History of England* during the 1840s, he applied lessons about what is now called "cultural history" from Herodotus, whom he read and read "again," lessons about adapting ancient characters to satisfy the modern taste for biographies, to both Plutarch— "greatly risen in my opinion"—and Tacitus, also read and reread, and lessons about national history from Livy—"I admire him greatly."[60] But it was Thucydides, the inventor of political history, whom he resolved to imitate.

"India Litteris et Legibus Emendanda"

A cliché of thanatology depicts intense ambition as an expression of the denial of death. Whatever its truth, during late December 1834 and early 1835 Macaulay, though mourning, was waging successful imperial battles by means of intrigue and polemic. Bentinck stayed in the background while Macaulay lobbied the Council of India for votes to direct the government's funding of indigenous education to English-language instruction. By December 1834 his side appeared to be on the verge of winning, but in January the Orientalists proposed a compromise. Full of anger, Greek, and ambition, he counterattacked on 2 February with a "Minute" blackguarding India's cultures and implicitly all the others lacking roots in classical Greece and Rome. Many schoolboys used to know perhaps the most notorious lines Macaulay ever wrote: "a single shelf of a good European library was worth the whole native literature of India and Arabia." He immediately explained why: "The intrinsic superiority of the Western literature is, indeed, fully admitted by those members of the Committee who support the Oriental plan of education."[61]

Provocatively misrepresenting the Orientalists' convictions and barely acknowledging the "already existing desires and felt needs of forward looking gentry in India" to learn English, Macaulay's inflammatory hyperbole was deliberate. But why? Even when emotionally raw and in full throat, he usually remained the master of his words. Echoing the evangelical polemics against Hindu idolatry and idolaters that he had devoured as a boy and expressing his visceral disdain for India and nearly all its works, his vehemence testified to his sincerity. At the beginning of his paper he issued a serious threat to his colleagues. The Orientalists' strongest argument was a provision in the India Charter Act of 1813, never repealed, that obliged the government to support both Indian and European learning. After awkwardly parsing it, the legal member of the council told the other members that if they disagreed with his interpretation, "I will prepare a short Act rescinding that clause of the Charter of 1813 from which the difficulty arises."[62]

Macaulay's vehemence also confirmed his secularizing genius. He accepted the evangelical ambition to convert the subcontinent through education—Indophobia minus God and the Bible. He wedded it to the Utilitarian project of transforming India through legal reform. Dismissing the "whole" of South Asian and Middle Eastern civilization was the major premise of his moral justification for Britain's Indian empire. Much as his father believed that Christianity was the one true religion, he posited one civilization informed by a rational language and a humanizing literature. Sanskrit, Arabic, and the like were intrinsically defective languages, fostering ignorance and barbarism manifested in "false taste and false philosophy": "History, abounding with kings thirty feet high, and reigns thirty thousand years long—and Geography, made up of seas of treacle and seas of butter." English, however, was a very rational

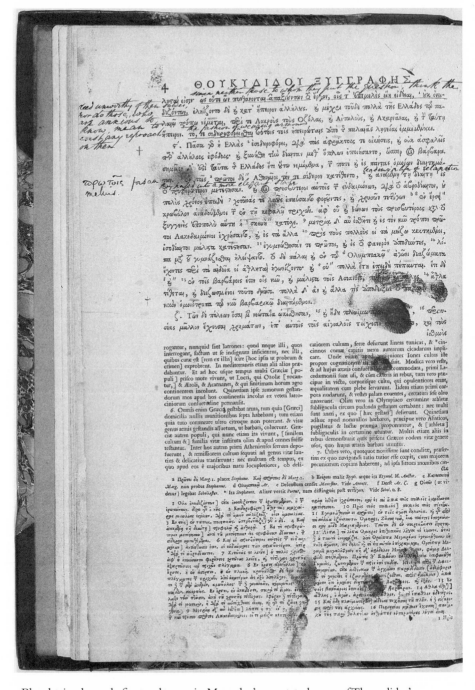

Bloodstained, much-fingered pages in Macaulay's annotated copy of Thucydides' *History of the Peloponnesian War* (Photograph by Andrew McGregor; at Wallington, Northumberland, © The National Trust). "I pass the three or four hours before breakfast in reading Greek and Latin . . . Before six the barber comes to shave me" (TBM to TFE, 30.xii.35, *L3*:160; and TBM to SM and FM, 9.v.36, *L3*:173).

language, encouraging accurate knowledge and abounding "with works of imagination not inferior to the noblest which Greece has bequeathed to us": "Whoever knows [English], has ready access to all the vast intellectual wealth, which all the wisest nations of the earth have created and hoarded in the course of ninety generations."[63]

Admitting that he had "no knowledge of either Sanscrit or Arabic," he nonetheless insisted that he had formed "a correct estimate of their value." In fact Macaulay's ignorance of both Islamic and Hindu cultures was profound, willed, but vincible. When the Indian rebellion of 1857 caused him to study Islam for the first time, "I was quite astonished." But an old, worldly-wise realism informed his ignorant hyperbole: "language declines with political power." His inquisitive and learned Orientalist opponents failed to understand that dividing languages between civilized and uncivilized provided their Indian empire with an ethical justification for continuing to consolidate and expand. England's mission of civilizing others authorized violence and the threat of violence against barbarous and recalcitrant peoples. At home Macaulay liked "to see abuses die out quietly," but in Calcutta he worked to transform subject Indians.[64]

Writing to Zachary, he conflated the Christianizing mission, which he privately rejected, with England's real mission: "the effect of this education on the Hindoos is prodigious ... It is my firm belief that, if our plans of education are followed up, there will not be a single idolater among the respectable classes in Bengal thirty years hence." In the "Minute" Tom explained how to convert them into civilized English men and women: "We must at present do our best to form a class who may be interpreters between us and the millions whom we govern; a class of persons, Indian in blood and colour, but English in taste, in opinions, in morals, and in intellect." His vision of a quick and "prodigious" transformation was grandiose. The amount of money allocated for Indian education just equaled his annual salary. Change would come, but slowly and incrementally. In the near term, however, Macaulay contributed to making the identification of civilizing and Christianizing India English common sense. A couple of decades after his "Minute" the archbishop of Canterbury blessed the combination.[65]

Far from being "simple-minded," Macaulay offered a carefully meditated, deeply felt transvaluation of a fragile principle: ethical universalism. By the end of the eighteenth century the belief that even England must "do unto others" was the precarious achievement of Britons as diverse as Sir William Jones, the greatest of the Orientalists; Samuel Johnson; and Edmund Burke. Incompatible with winning empires and in tension with governing them, that ethic invited Macaulay's assault. Deferring to the habits of his family and the English public mind and savoring the greatness of the Authorized Version, Macaulay treated Christianity discreetly. But the born-again classicism that fostered his belief in the unity of modern civilization also renewed his conviction that Athens and Rome were superior and had precious little in common with Jerusalem. Besides intensifying his disdain for India and its people, his resurgent classicism biased him against the mass of humanity: deposed Mysorean rajahs and rich Cockney cheesemongers were of a piece.[66]

At home Macaulay had once applauded Christianity for overthrowing "the old system of morals," especially for stirring "the stagnant mass from the inmost depths." In those days the swirl of "crowded senates and fine drawing-rooms" had also given him a certain respect for Stoicism, some of which was interpreted as a virtually Christian ethical universalism. It vanished along with his applause for the demise of "the old system of morals." The books of the most famous Stoics, the freedman Epictetus and the Emperor Marcus Aurelius, were absent from his annual catalogs of his "connected course of study" of Greek literature. Insisting on a civilizing "radical universalism," Macaulay returned home denying that humanity possessed a common ethical dignity and positing intractable differences among certain national characters or races. From that perspective he would write England's imperial history and help frame its imperial policy.[67]

Although the draft resolution that Macaulay ghosted for Bentinck was businesslike, news leaked out that his "Minute" urged closing "the Sanscrit college at Calcutta." Protest petitions were "signed by no less than 10,000 people. On 7 March 1835 Bentinck endorsed the "Minute's" argument with a notable modification: "it is not the intention of His Lordship in Council to close a College or School of Native Learning, while the Native Population shall appear to be inclined to avail themselves of the advantages which it affords." Bentinck was already on his way home, where official reaction to his resolution was "decidedly hostile." Almost a year later, Macaulay welcomed news of Lord Auckland's appointment as governor-general. They got along famously—"an excellent Governor General . . . The sensible manly w[ay] in which he looks at every subject,—the liberality of his views"—and Auckland worked to uphold Bentinck's decision.[68]

As president of the Committee on Public Instruction, Macaulay was activist and single-minded, interesting himself in everything from sketching an English primer to permitting Christian schoolchildren at Agra "not to be mingled with the *natives.*" After Macaulay left India, Auckland framed a compromise restoring "some of the patronage of government to classical Indian learning, while retaining and encouraging the new system of English education." By 1840 English was the dominant language in Calcutta, but into the 1850s "syncretic education in Indian language" prevailed. Meanwhile Hindi was growing in prestige and popularity. With the advent of nationalism it seemed to be the wave of the future. The Indian constitution of 1950 allowed the use of English in public business until 1965, when Hindi in the Devanagari script would become normative. In the twenty-first century the transition continues.[69]

An Indian historian recently tried to locate Macaulay in his nation's memory. He is "revered by some and reviled by others. In his four years in this country, he made two notable contributions. One was to draft the Criminal Procedure Code . . . This aspect of his legacy remains relatively uncontentious . . . Macaulay's second, and more controversial contribution, was a Minute . . . It is reviled by nativists, who think it condemned India and Indians to centuries of mental servitude; but revered by modernists, who argue that it allowed Indians to take advantage of the modern economy and thus emancipate themselves from the burdens of a traditional and hierarchical society."[70]

Macaulay's code prevailed slowly. James Mill expected the "person thoroughly versed in the philosophy of man and of government" to ensure that India became "the first country on earth to boast a system of law and judicature as near to perfection as the circumstances of the people will admit." Macaulay did not disappoint him. On 25 May 1835 he was named president of the Indian Law Commission, although as the legal member of the council he must evaluate the document whose drafting he oversaw. Appointed "at his own instigation," he already had "immense reforms in hand . . . such as would make Old Bentham jump in his grave—oral pleadings—examination of parties—single-seated justice—no institution fees—and so forth." The task did not prevent him from being up "every morning at five over my folio Plato, covering the margins with annotations." On 4 June his colleagues received his instructions on the foundation of the code: "We agree perfectly as to all the general principles on which we ought to proceed, and differ less than I could have thought possible as to details." In late August, after assuring Mill that they were "most vigorously at work," he reported in detail: "it is really important that you should know exactly how matters stand, and that, whenever a favourable opportunity may occur, you should do what may be in your power in order to procure good assistance for us."[71]

Unwavering clarity about England's imperial burden informed Macaulay's code: "We know that India cannot have a free Government. But she can have the next best thing—a firm and impartial despotism." Reflecting Bentham's authoritarian side, the form and structure of the code appeared to bulldoze tradition. The code was not "a digest of any existing system, and . . . no existing system has furnished us even with a groundwork," and individual acts without preamble were framed "as purely imperative rather than argumentative." In fact the carefully crafted "illustrations" he attached to each act indicate that he grasped the limits of even enlightened despotism: "They are merely instances of the practical application of the written law to the affairs of mankind." In effect, they were meant to "fit the Code's laws to the frame of Indian society" and to "reconcile the Utilitarian view of justice with indigenous conceptions of acceptable social behaviour." His gradualist approach toward eliminating Persian as India's official legal language was similarly accommodating. Instead of trying to substitute English, he advocated using the predominant local vernaculars. Unlike the mythical Spartan lawgiver Lycurgus, Macaulay worked from precedents. By winning "so many conceptual battles," previous enactments by Bentinck and his predecessors had cleared the ground for the substance of his code.[72]

Because of the illnesses of Macaulay's four colleagues during 1836, "it seems likely that I may have to do the whole my self." Simultaneously he was laboring over "an article of prodigious length" on Francis Bacon, which contains the fullest statement of Macaulay's own "philosophical speculations"—our term is "ideology." In early March 1837 he looked forward to bringing "our first great work to a conclusion," and on 2 May he formally submitted his code. A day earlier, he notified the Supreme

Council that he intended "to resign my situation and to return to Europe in the course of the next cold season." On the eve of the code's publication in Calcutta at year's end, he assessed his enterprise: "It has cost me very intense labour; and, whatever its faults may be, is certainly not a slovenly performance. It is full of defects which I see, and has no doubt many which I do not see. Yet I think that it is, as a whole, better than the French [Napoleonic] Code . . . Whether the work proves useful to India or not, it has been of great use, I feel and know, to my own mind."[73]

When the code reached Britain, James Mill was dead, but John Stuart Mill, eventually his successor in East India House and no admirer of Macaulay, welcomed it for "eminently successfully" framing "adequate definitions of offences, expressed in general language: definitions sufficiently accurate, to leave no doubt that complete accuracy is attainable." Mill summarized the code for his readers. Chapters one through four comprised "all those explanations and directions which may be given once for all." The remaining twenty-one chapters treated "separate classes of offenses," beginning with "Offenses against the State" and concluding with "Criminal Intimidation, Insult and Annoyance."[74]

While writing the code, Macaulay assured Zachary that capital punishment would be abolished "except in cases of aggravated treason and willful murder" and promised that he would "also get rid indirectly of everything that can properly be called slavery in India." He was as good as his word. Recognizing Macaulay's style "distinctly visible" everywhere in the code where it "was possible that style should be discernible," John Mill faulted it for not leaving "any immoralities whatever exempt from legal punishment." He sounds like a contemporary liberated voice rebuking an early nineteenth-century reforming project. As much as Mill, Macaulay believed that, in theory, law should start with a blank tablet, express the sovereign's command, depend on sure punishments, and rarely enforce moral norms. Macaulay, however, better understood the art of the possible and sometimes amused himself while playing politics in the code. The result was the one section that today provokes outrage. As a recent headline announced, "Gay Activists in India Want British Apology for Sex Law."[75]

In the "Notes" printed without the text of the code in his collected *Works,* he appeared to succumb to a paroxysm of pre-Victorian Victorianism over clauses 361 and 362, which "relate to an odious class of offenses respecting which it is desirable that as little as possible should be said." Without naming them, he again execrated them: "revolting subject." The crime whose name dared barely be spoken was treated in chapter eighteen of the code ("Of Offences Affecting the Human Body"): "Unnatural Offences." Macaulay's harrumphing parodied the eighteenth-century French jurist Charles-Louis Baron de Montesquieu's lead-up to arguing against making homosexual acts a capital crime. Macaulay proposed to subject consensual relations to imprisonment for a term of two to fourteen years and a fine and nonconsensual ones to imprisonment for seven years to life and a fine. Since 1562 "Buggery commyttd with mankynde or beaste" had continuously been a capital offense in England, and in 1835 three men were "hanged for sodomy." In 1861 the Elizabethan statute was repealed, but "sodomy" became a "crime punishable by penal servitude for life or for any term not less than ten years."[76]

Irony marked the reception of the code. Unlike the imposition of English-language instruction, it was a Utilitarian project, meant as much to model legal reform at home as to codify penal laws on the subcontinent. Macaulay understood that such thoroughness could not be replicated in Britain: "A code is almost the only blessing, perhaps it is the only blessing, which absolute governments are better fitted to confer on a nation than popular governments." But enacting the Indian code remained impossible as long as it clashed with English criminal law, backward-looking and sometimes pell-mell. A particular obstacle was its intermingling of civil and ecclesiastical statutes and jurisdictions. Because of the glacial progress of efforts to achieve standardization in England, the Indian code was introduced only in 1862. But the social vision animating Macaulay's code shaped domestic penal legislation, because there, too, it was widely accepted that "a traditional society entering the modern age needed a rational legal system, and someone had to provide it." In both hemispheres it seemed urgent to establish "clear and reliable rules of behavior" for increasingly uprooted individuals.[77]

The Indian penal code is Macaulay's most enduring and perhaps greatest achievement. Of a piece with the Black Act and the 1836 act abolishing the "indefensible" press censorship throughout the subcontinent, the code testifies to his genius and suggests the amalgam of humanity and violence that was the British imperial project. A statue of Lord William Bentinck opposite Calcutta's town hall captures both dimensions. In 1835 it fell to Macaulay to compose the inscription. He eulogized government for the people, though neither of them nor by them, and endorsed some eighteenth-century public virtues—universal benevolence, the tolerance of inevitable cultural and religious diversity, and the aspiration to create states well policed but nonetheless ensuring a tolerable measure of personal freedom. The Romanizing frieze at the base of the statue suggests the power undergirding those ideals. Macaulay never forgot the connection between the base and the superstructure of all empires, but he also appreciated the necessity of adorning their foundations. Not for him the *Aeneid's* "cautionary tale . . . [a]bout the terrible ills that attend empire—its war-making capacity, the loss of blood and treasure." Rather, Macaulay's *Lays of Ancient Rome* would celebrate Rome's martial virtues as exemplary for his England.[78]

Homeward Bound

Between 25 July and 12 August 1836 and busy with the penal code, Macaulay composed a long letter to Ellis. He projected that he was fifteen months away from returning to England and counted the days: "The time is fast drawing near . . . It is really worth while to go into banishment for the pleasure of going home again. Yet that home will, in some things, be a different home—oh how different a home . . . But I will not stir up the bitterness of sorrow which has at last subsided." He knew that it would never disappear, and that "every day renders it more unlikely that I should marry." He wrote much about his reading and reported on a debate within himself that recurred almost until death. Yearning for both study and power, he projected his alternatives as the ancient choice between the contemplative and the active life: "Whether I have learned philosophy enough to free me from political ambition remains to be seen." It mattered that his "uncle General Macaulay who died last February has left me 10000£." But it mattered more that he was "becoming every day fonder and fonder of my little niece." Almost ten months old, Hannah's first-born was named Margaret. Minutely observing her gradual development was "a source of great and almost painful pleasure to me."[79]

In Calcutta Macaulay worked mainly at home and led a life of "the most peaceful monotony" and virtual agoraphobia. He rose by five in the morning for his classics, his toilet, and breakfast and never went to his office before nine, usually leaving in the late afternoon. Back home he walked "with a book," took a carriage ride, dined, drank coffee, and retired early. His life centered on the Trevelyans, particularly on Margaret, who embodied both his memories and his hope for future happiness. With her he began reenacting his earlier courtship of both her mother and the dead aunt who was her namesake: "She is exceedingly fond of me, and, if am by, will never take breakfast from any other person's hand." Fonder of the baby "than a wise man, with half of my experience, would chuse to be of anything except himself," he had her carried to his room every morning in order to dote on her. Imported into the nursery by servants, India's babel of languages was "not favourable to the early development of the power of speech in children," and so he taught "Baba"—her babyish name for herself, which stuck for a lifetime—her English words. Once more he worked to create an exclusive love that would prove his own lovability. Years later he vividly remembered being almost blinded by a "whirlwind of red sand" while he searched for her after she ran outside.[80]

During the summer of 1837 Macaulay endured a brief, "smart touch of fever," which left him "very languid and exhausted for nearly a fortnight": "This was my first, and I hope my last taste of Indian maladies." His emotional health was more fragile. After finishing "Bacon," he told his brother Charles: "In another year my banishment will be over . . . I already begin to feel the pleasure of returning from exile. That pleasure ought to be very great to compensate for the bitter pain of so long and so complete a separation from home. And it is very great. For though England is not all that it once was to me yet I have no hopes or wishes but what point to England; and I would rather go home with the knowledge that I should die there next year than live here till seventy in the midst of whatever splendour or comfort India affords." Like Odysseus, Macaulay "was willing to forego [sic] everything to see once more the smoke going up from the cottages of his dear island. Few people I believe have the feeling so strongly as I have it."[81] And his love for England was exclusive.

Another death interrupted his inconclusive ruminations about a political or literary future. In early May Hannah lost a younger daughter, "a little thing only 3 months old, but as engaging as a baby of that age can be": "I did not feel the loss as I should have felt the loss of her sister who begins to prattle in a *lingua franca* made up of a dozen languages . . . Still I was a very sincere mourner for the poor little creature, both on her mother's account and her own. Since I heard of the death of my sister Margaret, my spirits have never been what they once were, and a lighter domestic calamity than this would have been sufficient to depress them." "Calcutta" became his shorthand for "exile" to the end of the world. Leaving "all my furniture, plate, and carriages to be sold immediately after my departure," as if they were contaminated, he sailed for England on 21 January 1838, eager to discover the reception of "Bacon": "by many degrees, the best thing that I ever wrote.[82]

[4]

SINISTER PROPHET

"Bacon" and a projected essay on Sir William Temple, a seventeenth-century Anglo-Irish politician and litterateur, broadcast what became the catchwords of Britain's century—utility, progress, and civilization—as well as the convictions that supported them: materialism, cultural Protestantism, nationalism, and imperialism. To understand the essays is to understand the genesis of the core beliefs of several generations of ruthlessly successful idealists and millions of their subjects. An idea of England informed Macaulay's Indian projects, but enjoying power on the subcontinent clarified for him both the benefits that modern Englishness could provide and the sacrifices it could demand. His vision was surer at long range than close-up. Disposed to shun public life, he discerned at home "the signs which have, in all ages, preceded the downfall of ancient institutions." The "crisis . . . at hand" was warfare between the rising "commercial and manufacturing classes" and the entrenched "great landed proprietors." About the outcome he professed indifference. But the prospect persuaded him of the wisdom of passing "the rest of my life in quiet study," which then consisted mostly of his classical exercises. He left India both reaffirming that he was finished with politics and feeling "some strong temptation that draws me again into" it. The "crisis" was imaginary. His indecision lasted.[1]

He labored over the essay for almost a year. Not quite the "interminable" piece he described, it fills 111 pages in his *Works.* Macaulay's personal task in "Bacon" was to make the case for a studious retirement and to reassert his emotional distance from antiquity and modern England's superiority over it. Although the classics reminded him that the ultimate questions of life are unanswerable, they provided no compelling vision of the future. Rereading Plato's *Euthyphro,* a send-up of piety as deal-making with divinity, he marked its "superstitions, and odious opinions about the divine nature" while relishing its inconclusiveness and "enchanting" irony. In the spring of 1837, as when he had read all the dialogues after learning of Margaret's death, he thought that sturdy empiricism exploded Plato's gossamer. Macaulay's enduring problem was how to construct an uplifting and compelling public vision on the basis of his conviction that ultimately we can know little. Plato confirmed that a credible vision must be down-to-earth. His teaching that death releases just souls to the care of a welcoming divinity "conveys no satisfaction to my mind." But Socrates' "example of benevolence, patience, and self-possession . . . is incomparable and inestimable."[2] They were modern English values that even Zachary Macaulay tried to live by.

If his son found "more depth and acuteness in Plato than my college recollections led to expect," he knew that he must look to rhetoric for the tools with which to articulate his vision of modern Englishness. He read and reread the great Athenian orators "with interest and admiration indescribable" and Cicero's *De Oratore,* including a "memorable sentence" that contained "my creed": how to compose a speech. Macaulay's instinctive utilitarianism provided him with the method and buzzwords he wanted. News of James Mill's death reached him as he polished "Bacon." A "sincere mourner," he never republished his three assaults on Mill's political philosophy. But partial agreement and tactical alliances with the Benthamites left unshaken Macaulay's conviction that their disdain for the power of human emotions was deluded. He clung too tightly to the Trevelyans and depended too much on letters from his "affectionate friend" Ellis to imagine otherwise.[3]

"Bacon" began in the third person with Macaulay owning his "incalculable" debt as "a man of liberal education" to "the great minds of former ages." It was both a tribute to how much he then lived with and through his books and an assertion of his cultural authority. Those immortals with whom he enjoyed "daily communion" seemed more real to him than most of the living and more tractable than those whose adoration he craved. The "highest of human intellects" were his "old friends" with whom he conversed and who "guided him to the truth," "filled his mind with noble and graceful images," and "stood by him in all vicissi-

tudes, [as] comforters in sorrow, nurses in sickness, companions in solitude." In the third paragraph he paraded ten famous ancient and modern
authors whom he had studied and largely remembered.[4]

Pen in hand, Macaulay read them as stimulants to his creativity. Above
all, he used Francis Bacon, Baron Verulam, as an authoritative mouthpiece for his own version of Englishness: a modernized Epicureanism.
With Locke's reputation in eclipse, Bacon was the national philosopher.
Although scholars debated his meaning, Macaulay acclaimed him as "the
great apostle of experimental philosophy," "the great English teacher,"
and the prophet of its progress and empire. Among the most rhetorical
and least technical of major philosophers, Bacon seemed malleable as
well as accessible. Macaulay, who found Kant "utterly unintelligible, just
as if it had been written in Sanscrit"—the damning obscurity—expurgated what he disliked in Bacon in order to emphasize his worldliness.
Suppressing riotous India, he wrote the piece as from emphatically progressive England but with nuances that belied his thumping adverb.
Macaulay rejected the supernatural "reasoning" of Socrates but needed
to believe and prophesy that human endeavors, perhaps even human life
itself, could end happily. He desired "reasonable hopes."[5]

His intended audience was diverse. Because almost every sentence
in "Bacon" seems clear, the essay can be misconstrued as transparent.
Counting on its popularity "with the many," Macaulay was unsure of the
reaction of "the few who know something about the matter." Front-
loaded for the benefit of his superficial readers, nearly sixty-nine pages
contain the "historical and political part," which seems to make easy
reading. The remaining forty-two pages contain his exposition of "Bacon's philosophy." They demanded the attention of his sophisticated
readers. Understanding his allusions and then making connections and
extrapolations that he hinted at enabled them to share fully the essay's
mixed messages.[6]

A reference to Thomas Hobbes illustrates how "the few who know
something about the matter" were invited to read between the lines. It
also suggests the essay's underlying disillusionment. In closing a seemingly digressive paragraph on Bacon's taste for the company of bright
young men, Macaulay observed that it was improbable that he "fully appreciated" Hobbes, his disciple, "or foresaw the vast influence, both for
good and for evil, which that most vigorous and acute of human intel-

lects was destined to exercise on the two succeeding generations." He did
not analyze the impact of Bacon's much-demonized and long-neglected
disciple, now become a magnet for young Benthamites, because he, like
them, sought to reorder England after the establishment forfeited its monopoly and traditional deference began eroding.[7] The problem underlay
what Macaulay in Calcutta imagined to be the looming "crisis" of the
nation melting into a battlefield where all fought all, restrained only by
interests, passions, and the marketplace.

Even more than with Machiavelli, Macaulay always teased about his
debt to Hobbes. An 1852 manuscript catalogue of his library included
"Hobbes's, T., Leviathan." In 1843 he had declined an invitation to review a new edition of Hobbes's collected works: "On the whole I think
a subject which would hardly suit me." Five years later, in the first volume of *The History of England,* he applauded Hobbes for maintaining "in
language more precise and luminous than has ever been employed by
any other metaphysical writer . . . that the will of the prince was the standard of right and wrong." Carefully, he went on to rebuke Hobbism,
the cynical amorality of late seventeenth-century "fine gentlemen" who
were "incompetent to appreciate what was really valuable in his speculations." Those bloods "relaxed the obligations of morality, and degraded
religion into a mere affair of state."[8]

It was a delicious irony. Throughout his career Macaulay himself similarly "degraded religion," insisting that history demonstrated that the
Anglican principle was "Erastianism," or state supremacy. For him, "prevailing immorality" meant above all sexual impropriety: "prevailing licentiousness," "pandar of every low desire," "formidable shafts against in-
nocence and truth"—here he clearly enjoyed his moralistic sputtering.
The mission of "the Church" was to enforce national propriety rather
than a set of doctrines, and it sometimes conspicuously failed to perform.
Macaulay manhandled his ideological opponent Samuel Johnson to discredit his vision of Englishness as essentially Christian but dared only
tease about what made Hobbes "that most vigorous and acute of human
intellects." Like Hobbes, Macaulay guarded his religious beliefs. His former Greek tutor at Cambridge became a bishop. Reading him in Calcutta, Macaulay scored his pining for the seventeenth century, when religion could not be insulted "with impunity": "In those days, that is in the
days when Hobbes's books came out, there was a censorship. Does the

Bp wish to restore it?" For an ambitious new man the informal pressures could be almost as intimidating as official censorship. Macaulay's conflicts with his impossible father had taught him that prudence demanded religious conformity, and his doubleness required him to conceal what he believed and felt and to pretend to believe and feel what he could not.[9]

Macaulay therefore enveloped his debt to Hobbes in plausible deniability. Defining modern Englishness required him to distinguish statecraft, the supple rules of politics informed by true Hobbism, from the tight proprieties that informed daily respectability. Government depended "on the great art of inspiring large masses of human beings with confidence and attachment." The goal was to arouse in them devotion to something greater than themselves and to convince them to pursue something more tangible than the incredible hope of heaven. The moral cost was to imitate the ancients by fostering an exclusive and stratified Englishness: "This [ancient Greek and Roman] public interest was the public interest of a single city, and indeed of the minority of the inhabitants of that city, which was pursued at the expense of all the rest of mankind. Why is this sort of patriotism more laudable than the attachment of a Jesuit to his order?"[10] Macaulay had raised the question in 1828. Flourishing in a society in which those on top enjoyed much and those at the bottom routinely went without and helping to rule tens of millions of "Asiatics" against their will persuaded him to recalculate the utility of "this sort of patriotism" and to propagate it.

More obviously than Hobbes, Plato colored the rhetorical strategy of "Bacon." On 3 July 1835 Macaulay finished Plato's *Republic* with appreciation. "Socrates'" discussion of the "necessary lie" triggered a telling association: "See Swift's *Art of Political Lying* for a discussion of this point." Plato wrote: "The rulers then of the city may, if anybody, fitly lie on account of enemies or citizens for the benefit of the state; no others may have anything to do with it. But for a layman to lie to rulers of that kind we shall affirm to be as great a sin, nay greater, than it is for ... a man to deceive the pilot about the ship and the sailors as to the real condition of himself or a fellow sailor, and how they fare ... If then the ruler catches anybody else in the city lying ... he will chastise him for introducing a practice as subversive and destructive of a state as it is of a ship." Then attributed to Swift, the pamphlet had in fact been written by his close friend and ally John Arbuthnot: "in these brief phantom proposals . . . Arbuthnot's satiric temper reaches its most ingenious expression, ending on an ironical consideration of the spin-doctor's basic problem, 'whether a lie is best contradicted by truth or another lie.'"[11]

Plato recommended and Arbuthnot satirized "the necessary lie." But Macaulay, who before he was eighteen learned from Cicero that "we must dissemble if we would live in the world," applied the lesson, above all for the good of the state but also for his own success—his survival was never at stake. Because he aimed to promote good government and England's interests as he understood them, his standard of public truthfulness was rhetorical. When handling serious or dangerous topics, he often teased, insinuated, alluded, evaded, and sometimes lied. Opened in classical antiquity, the school of politic liars closed for several dark centuries but reopened in early-modern Europe, when politic lying became identified with "Tacitism." In "younger days" Macaulay had "always thought the Annals [of Tacitus] a prodigiously superior work to the History" of Thucydides. It moved him to experiment with multiple feats of translation, itself an art of accommodation and simulation. In India, he again thought that "Tacitus was a great man" and the *Annals* his best work. Both Macaulay and Bacon studied him on the Caesars' handling of the secrets of empire. Tiberius, "the most artful of dissemblers," interested Macaulay. Bacon expounded his version of Tacitism in a short meditation, "Of Simulation and Dissimulation," on some passages in the *Annals* and the *Histories*. Never referencing it in "Bacon," Macaulay mentioned that Bacon's "historical work and his essays prove he did not hold, even in theory, very strict opinions on points of political morality."[12] Tongue-in-cheek, he expertly deployed some of Bacon's recommended techniques in writing about him.

Bacon began by declaring that "dissimulation is but a faint kind of policy, or wisdom," a maxim that he proceeded to complicate, dilute, and subvert.[13] There exists a fundamental distinction between "arts or policy" and "dissimulation or closeness": "For if a man have that penetration of judgment as he can discern what things are to be laid open, and what to be secreted, and what to be shewed at half-lights, and to whom and when, which indeed are arts of state, and arts of life, as Tacitus well calleth them, to him a habit of dissimulation is hindrance and a poorness." The

habit not the practice is objectionable. At the end of the paragraph Bacon noted that even "the ablest men that ever were" sometimes find
themselves in situations that "required dissimulation." Circumstances and
consequences determine when "this hiding and veiling of a man's self" is
necessary and which of its forms to employ: "first, closeness, reservation,
and secrecy, when a man leaveth himself without observation, or without hold to be taken, what he is. The second dissimulation in the negative, when a man lets fall signs and arguments, that he is not that he is."
And the third, "simulation in the affirmative, when a man industriously
and expressly feigns and pretends to be that he is not." Bacon recommended "an habit of secrecy" as "both politic and moral," because "dissimulation . . . followeth many times upon secrecy, by a necessity: so that
he that will be secret must be a dissembler in some degree." When "beset" by insistent questions about important matters, a public figure cannot sustain "an absurd silence," "equivocations, or oraculous speeches."
But Bacon distinguished between practicing "a little scope of dissimulation" and the habit, which brands one a dissimulator. As for "the third
degree, which is simulation and false profession," he held it "more cul-
pable and less politic, except it be in great and rare matters." As "a general custom," nonetheless, simulation is "a vice" revealing the simulator's
falseness, cowardice, or madness.

Bacon helpfully summarized both three "great advantages of simulation and dissimulation" and their "three disadvantages." When announcing one's intentions amounts "to an alarm to call up all that are against"
one, it is prudent "to lay asleep opposition, and to surprise." The second
advantage is the chance to execute a "fair retreat" from an insupportable
position. Bacon saved his most subtle advantage for last: "For to him that
opens himself, men will hardly shew themselves adverse; but will fair let
him go on, and turn their freedom of speech to freedom of thought.
And therefore it is a good shrewd proverb of the Spaniard, Tell a lie and
find a truth. As if there were no way of discovery but by simulation."
Bacon ran through the disadvantages of the practices: creating "a shew of
fearfulness, which in any business doth spoil"; repelling possible collaborators who find the practitioner incomprehensible; and, most important,
forfeiting the "trust and belief" that are "the most principal instruments
for action." In sum, Bacon counseled his readers "to have openness in

fame and opinion; secrecy in habit; dissimulation in seasonable use; and a power to feign, if there be no remedy."

In "Of Simulation and Dissimulation" Bacon, it has been asserted, meant to discourage his readers from viewing current knowledge as more than fragmentary and instead to encourage them to undertake their own inquiries.[14] Perhaps. But insisting on the primacy of Bacon's readers' response implausibly excludes his inviting and directive voice from the conversation he led and modeled for them. He taught that although habitual simulation is self-destructive, we should avoid full disclosure lest it alarm our antagonists and foreclose our options. But he also advised sometimes letting "fall signs and arguments" that indicate that our words are not really what they seem to be. Doing so can enable us to "discover" another's mind, win us a friendly hearing, and perhaps change her mind. Our interlocutor may be moved to attend to us, and she, by speaking freely, can learn to think more freely and perhaps by reexamining her own point of view come to adopt the "truth" that we convey by our "seasonable use" of lying. It is, however, the dissimulator's truth, not his interlocutor's. As Macaulay assured voters in Leeds, "Gentleman, I am a Christian . . . I will say no more."

Playing to and on several audiences is the classical rhetorical technique of persuasion. On the principle that knowledge is eclectic, hierarchical, and dynamic, Macaulay welcomed superficial knowledge and accepted specialization. But his reconversion to the classics in India persuaded him to oppose wide educational diversity among gentlemen. In undemocratic societies like India and Britain, mastering difficult and rational foreign languages helped to maintain the coherence and cultural ascendancy of men who upheld order and property. The ancient distinction between esoteric and exoteric knowledge was useful to him, particularly when handling Christianity. He did not, however, seek to ban destabilizing knowledge from the popular story he was fabricating about modern England's rise. His aim rather was to discover such knowledge and to diffuse it as widely as possible, according to his readers' differing capacities. The technique looked backward to the Christian strategy of accommodation—adapting preaching and teaching to the circumstances and capacities of different audiences—and forward to the "filtration" method of uplfting Indians "through the operation of intermediate agents." Near the end of "Bacon" he explained:

The *Novum Organum* and the *De Augmentis* . . . have produced indeed a vast effect on the opinions of mankind; but they have produced it through the operation of intermediate agents. They have
moved the intellects which have moved the world. It is in the Essays
alone that the mind of Bacon is brought into immediate contact
with the minds of ordinary readers. There he opens an exoteric
school, and talks to plain men, in language which every body understands, about things in which every body is interested . . . the
great body of readers have, during several generations, acknowledged that the man who has treated with such consummate ability
questions with which they are familiar may well be supposed to
deserve all the praise bestowed on him by those who have sat in his
inner school.[15]

Macaulay judged the first section of the *New Organon* to be Bacon's
supreme achievement: "No book ever made so great a revolution in the
mode of thinking, overthrew so many prejudices, introduced so many
new opinions." It succeeded because "it truly conquers with chalk and
not with steel. Proposition after proposition enters into the mind, is received not as an invader, but as a welcome friend, and, though previously
unknown, becomes at once domesticated."[16] Here he was paraphrasing
without a footnote a great lesson he had learned in youth from Bacon:
"For to him that opens himself, men will hardly shew themselves adverse; but will fair let him go on, and turn their freedom of speech to
freedom of thought," or "Tell a lie and find a truth."

Insinuating Lucretius

Macaulay applied that lesson in writing the history of modern England,
increasingly emancipated from misty superstition and bathed in the dry
light of realistic earthly hopes. Viewing the best history as "a compound
of poetry and philosophy," he harked back to Lucretius' *De Rerum Natura
(On the Nature of Things),* which versified Epicurus' doctrines to liberate
more people from the fear of death and the gods. Grieving to distraction
in January 1835, Macaulay rediscovered that ingenious, playful, and finally majestic poem. He associated his "intellectual enjoyment" in returning to Greek literature with "the same expression which Lucre-

tius has employed about the victory over superstition—'Primum Graius homo' [the first man to understand the things of nature]": Epicurus. Before him humanity had lived oppressed by superstition, but his intelligence punctured fables about divine thunder and lightning. After exposing the secrets of nature, he exalted humanity to the heavens, and Lucretius proposed to teach others the same freedom. By 24 March 1835 Macaulay had read the poem twice. His marginalia scorned its physics and cosmology, "but in energy, perspicuity, variety of illustration, knowledge of life and manners, talent for description, sense of the beauty of the external world, and elevation and dignity of moral feeling, he had hardly ever an equal."[17]

Elsewhere, Macaulay channeled Bacon on the primordial limit on all optimism: "Men fear *Death,* as Children feare to goe in the darke . . . Certainly, the Contemplation of Death, as the *wages of sinne* and Passage to another world, is Holy and Religious; But the Feare of it, as a Tribute due unto Nature, is weake. Yet in Religious Meditations, there is sometimes, Mixture of Vanitie, and of Superstition." Making the obvious association, Macaulay noted in the margin that "Lucretius gave him a hint of this." But he also detected naïveté in Bacon about another constant reality: "*Atheisme* is rather in the *Lip,* then [*sic*] in the Heart of Man." He noted: "There is truth in this. But in every age there are many concealed atheists who keep their opinions to themselves." Bacon thought that Epicurus was not among them. Macaulay scoffed: "I think that he dissembled. He is a great fool if he believed in a God, for he believed in none of those things in wh. the belief could be grounded. He did not believe that God had made & governed the world, & gave no reason whatever except the universality of the opinion for entertaining it."[18]

Macaulay avoided naming Lucretius in print, once praising the power of his imagination but never his "elevation and dignity of moral feeling." Lucretius was not a writer for any would-be English public moralist courting popularity to endorse. In 1810 the *Encyclopaedia Britannica* marked him as "one of the most celebrated Latin poets," who, driven mad "by a philtre given him by his wife," died a suicide. A tentative rehabilitation minus the aphrodisiac was visible in the 1842 edition. Although his "philosophy is that of the atheist" and "he represses all hopes and stifles all fear, yet all ages have admired this poem of Lucretius, as one of the most wonderful productions of human genius." Debates over scientific naturalism after 1860 put him on the Victorians' cultural map as a protoscientist.[19]

In "Bacon" Macaulay mounted for the benefit of serious readers an insinuating display of erudition on the subject of good ethics: "There was one sect which, however absurd and pernicious some of its doctrines may have been, ought, it should seem, to have merited an exception from the general censure which Bacon had pronounced on the ancient schools of wisdom. The Epicurean, who referred all happiness to bodily pleasure, and all evil to bodily pain, might have been expected to exert himself for the purpose of bettering his own physical condition and that of his neighbours. But the thought seems never to have occurred to any member of that school." Without naming "their great poet," he quoted Lucretius to illustrate their static outlook and lumped them with the Stoics as teachers of "a garrulous, declaiming, canting, wrangling" philosophy.[20]

Macaulay faulted the Epicureans not for referring "all happiness to bodily pleasure" but for adding "little to the quantity of pleasure." They taught a stunted and impotent Epicureanism. After again quoting Lucretius anonymously and in Latin, now in praise of Epicurus—"Primum Graius homo"—he insisted that it "is on the pedestal of Bacon not on that of Epicurus, that those noble lines ought to be inscribed." The association of Bacon with Epicurus via Lucretius was fixed in literate English memories, but not to teach Epicureanism. Near the end of "Bacon" Macaulay referenced the source. In 1667 Abraham Cowley, a divine, paraphrased *De Rerum Natura* in hailing Bacon as the inspiration of the new Royal Society of London for the Improvement of Natural Knowledge:

> Bacon at last, a mighty man, arose
> Whom a wise King and Nature chose
> Lord Chancellor of both their laws . . .

In 1837 Bacon remained the new Epicurus but with Macaulay as his Lucretius. Macaulay, however, did not quote Lucretius on Epicurus' "divine mind" teaching indifference to the indifferent gods, courage in the face of inevitable death and dissolution, and confidence that life endures from one generation to the next.[21]

Transvaluing English Values

For over 170 years the debate over Macaulay's portrait of Bacon has distracted attention from the essay's clever subversion of English Protestantism. It is not a modern biography reconstructing a unique person's
life history through his words and deeds. Rather, it is an example of a
character, an ancient literary form revived during the seventeenth century and popularized by eighteenth-century novelists. A character was
more about a human type than about an individual. In Calcutta Macaulay
read Plutarch's *Lives* "over and over," "prodigiously" enjoying them as
artful stories revealing the moral nature of famous Greeks and Romans:
"I have never till now rated him fairly." But he also modernized Plutarch,
who, innocent of Christian moral dudgeon, usually dappled his characters. In Alcibiades, for example, Plutarch saw "many great inconsistencies
and variations . . . in accordance with the many and wonderful vicissi-
tudes of his fortunes." Macaulay professed to believe it wrong to "take a
man's character for granted, and then from his character to infer the
moral quality of all his actions," but he also loved melodrama, once bawl-
ing "as if my heart would break" over a passage in Dickens. Like many of
the readers they shared, both relished flamboyant villains. Macaulay cast
Bacon as a very naughty politician. Often contested, his verdict was canonized in standard reference books and can still provoke massive indignation.[22]

Macaulay's Bacon began as a type of the corrupt tyrant, much as
Ebenezer Scrooge began as the heartless miser. In retirement, however,
Bacon became his own antitype—the virtuous scholar—just as Scrooge,
by keeping Christmas daily after he met the ghosts, became his own antitype: a generous man. Echoing the Authorized Version, Macaulay in-
toned:

> his conduct was not justifiable according to any professional rules
> that now exist, or that ever existed in England; [t]he moral qualities
> of Bacon were not of a high order. We do not say that he was a bad
> man. He was not inhuman or tyrannical . . . He seems to have been
> incapable of feeling strong affection, of facing great dangers, of
> making great sacrifices. His desires were set on things below; Bacon
> had sullied his integrity, had resigned his independence, had vio-

lated the most sacred obligations of friendship and gratitude, had
flattered the worthless, had persecuted the innocent, had tampered
with judges, had tortured prisoners, had plundered suitors, had
wasted on paltry intrigues all the powers of the most exquisitely
constructed intellect that has ever been bestowed on any of the
children of men.[23]

His torrent of obloquy perhaps distracted readers from the contradiction between his indictment—"not inhuman or tyrannical"—and his
charge: "persecuted the innocent . . . tampered with judges . . . tortured
prisoners . . . plundered suitors." Impeachment and brief imprisonment
redeemed Bacon: "Those noble studies for which he had found leisure
in the midst of professional drudgery and of courtly intrigues gave to
this last stage of his life a dignity beyond what power or titles could bestow." Bacon the moustache-twirler embodied the ruinousness of politics awaiting Macaulay back home. Had Bacon avoided public life, he
would likely have "deserved to be considered, not only as a great philosopher, but as a worthy and good-natured member of society." Put another way, "All power tends to corrupt." Here Macaulay both feinted and
presented himself as a sound public moralist. It was a case of "Tell a lie
and find a truth." Bristling with aggrieved rectitude, he invited his audience to assimilate his values: in politics, England's national and imperial
interests; and in everyday life, ancient Epicureanism adapted and generalized to sustain respectable modern economic women and men.[24]

England's eternal professional rules were fictions. Indicting Bacon for
violating them amounted to charging him with political failure. In contrast, the successful politicians of the generation before him were guilty
of nameless offenses, but "their fidelity to the State was incorruptible":
"they committed many acts which would justly bring on a statesman of
our time censures of the most serious kind. But, when we consider the
state of morality in their age, and the unscrupulous character of the adversaries against whom they had to contend, we are forced to admit that
it is not without reason that their names are still held in veneration by
their countrymen." That the Spanish were "unscrupulous characters"
justified English preventive warfare, including state-sponsored piracy, a
policy as contemptible among seagoing nations in the sixteenth century
as in the nineteenth. It was all forgivable for Macaulay, whose casuistry in

defense of the transcendent principle of reason of state was as slippery as that of the Jesuits whom he mocked. Pillorying Bacon, however, he harrumphed: "if a man does that which he and all around him know to be bad, it is no excuse for him that many others have done the same."[25] He relied on knowing readers to notice the discrepancy.

Establishing his moral authority also required that he insinuate his heartfelt Protestantism. There could be no reciting a creed or broadcasting that the religion he wanted for England was Protestantism minus Christianity. After announcing that he was not someone who "confounds right and wrong with all the dexterity of a Jesuit," he sneered at a life of Cicero—"a lying legend in honour of St. Tully"—written by Conyers Middleton, a famously heterodox eighteenth-century divine: "The great Iconoclast was himself an idolater." More orthodox authors deserved to be flaunted, if not necessarily believed. And to propagate new and sometimes subversive values for the benefit of his Protestant readers, there was always a verse from scripture at hand. It was his rule that anyone seeking to master "the delicacies of the English language ought to have the Bible at his finger's end."[26]

Macaulay's detestation for India energized him to inspire in others something of his attachment to their "dear island." In "Bacon" English homes, self-regulating and regulated but also emotionally fulfilling, mediated between the sovereign and amoral state and self-interested and unruly individuals. The Elizabethan politicians exemplified that fusion of realpolitik and domesticity: "Their private morals were without stain." Macaulay insisted that only self-discipline could sustain the properly functioning families that ensured public order. He acted properly, but his private voice remained worldly-wise and equivocal. Writing to Ellis with a Greek tag, he laughed about the likely public outcry to a scandal involving Lord Melbourne, the louche prime minister. A year earlier, after finishing "all Ovid's poems," Macaulay penciled in a margin: "He seems to have been a very good fellow; rather too fond of women; a flatterer and a coward; but kind and generous: and free from envy, though a man of letters . . . The Art of Love, which ruined poor Ovid, is, in my opinion, decidedly his best work."[27] Augustus Caesar, a public moralist with teeth, banished him in part because of that witty how-to-do-it manual for seducers.

Astounding and frightening, India helped to renew Macaulay's faith in the political utility of personal moral absolutes, perhaps even to half-believe in them at home and in the marketplace. But enjoying power there also confirmed what he had told Margaret in 1830: in politics might is usually right. While he finished "Bacon," "extraordinary discoveries" revealed "the usages and the constitution of a vast fraternity of assassins which has existed here for many centuries." Infesting the country, the Thugs were "a phænomenon without a parallel in history," and he "set" Trevelyan to write an exposé of them. Although Macaulay insisted on proper evidence in trying cases of alleged "thuggee," he exaggerated the marauders' cohesion and numbers. Imagining the subcontinent as a vast temple of doom vindicated England's civilizing rule there, along with the history and threat of violence on which it rested.[28]

Enforcing English morality did not entail restoring the church's civil authority. A story about England's evolution into a modern nation emancipated from superstition runs through "Bacon." To confect it, Macaulay added an anticlerical and Erastian twist to the philosophical history of the Reverend William Robertson, an eminent eighteenth-century Scots whom he had first read in adolescence. Macaulay's nation-builders were his successful Elizabethan politicians and their great queen. By eclipsing loutish warriors and sinister priests as the guardians of England's destiny, they achieved a transfer of power and caused a mental revolution. Macaulay personified the medieval church as a prelate: "calm and subtle," "trained in the Schools to manage words, and in the confessional to manage hearts," "practicing on the superstition of others," "false," "selfish," "more attached to his order than to his country, and guiding the politics of England with a constant side-glance at Rome." After again reassuring superficial readers that he was authentically Protestant, he also signaled his cool rhetorical game to knowing readers. Though famously celibate and childless, he insisted that such prelates were, excepting a few saints, "hypocrites, selfish, as it was natural that a man should be who could form no domestic ties and cherish no hope of legitimate posterity."[29]

In *The History of England* he would expand his secular, nationalist, and political story of the Reformation. Bleeding on his copy of Thucydides in Calcutta, he reconsidered what counts in history and how history moves. Instead of trying to identify and highlight the sources of fundamental change in "noiseless revolutions" in society and culture, he made politics essential and powerful politicians his stars, just as he used a composite prelate to personify the medieval church. Thus, Elizabeth's lay, civilian, and learned ministers ensured that modern religion would serve the state. Impelled by the "increase of wealth, the progress of knowledge, and the reformation of religion," that new class in turn became the agents of progress. Besides leashing "the ferocious chieftains of Scotland," they founded "the maritime greatness of their country," which eventually made it richer than any other: "how dexterously, how resolutely, how gloriously they directed the politics of England."[30]

The Elizabethan church lacked such dynamism. Projecting a forensic and forward-looking history that excluded supernatural claims and deprecated the past role of religion, Macaulay exploited and enriched the lush rhetoric of English anticlericalism. The churchmen who managed "the reformation of religion" were shadows of his medieval prelate, and history eventually outpaced their faith. A "narrow-minded, mean, and tyrannical priest, who gained power by servility and adulation, and employed it in persecuting," Elizabeth's archbishop of Canterbury upheld predestination. Neither a Puritan nor a priest, James I was both "a witty, well-read scholar" and "a nervous drivelling idiot." As "a Canon of Christ Church, or a Prebendary of Westminster . . . [the king] would have left a highly respectable name to posterity." Exceptionally, "honest Hugh Latimer" spoke truths that shamed rascally officials like Bacon. But it was Bishop Latimer's down-to-earth Englishness, not his office, that ennobled him.[31]

The members of the new political class were intellectually progressive and hence "one and all, Protestants." What mattered was not their religion's truth and purity but its contribution to increasing England's power. Elizabeth's new and more tolerant church helped to make her reign "a long career of power, prosperity, and glory." Her politicians, however, wore their Protestantism lightly, submitting to Rome under "Bloody Mary." In praising their versatility, Macaulay echoed the Bible: "No men observed more accurately the signs of the times." Did his readers remember that the gospel passage rebuked the worldly-wise who accurately forecast the weather but ignored God's presence? The point of his paraphrase was to explain how the "warfare" between the "principles of Conservation and Reform" propelled history. It was a dialectic that operated "in the recesses of every reflecting mind." By the end of the sixteenth century "Conservation" was the sign of the time as Protestantism lost its ability to inspire nations to throw off Rome, "the superstition of the ages." The Catholic revival constituted "one of the most curious and interesting problems in history," which he marked "to solve" in the future.[32]

Women's education seemed to defy his rule that modern English history was moving onward and upward. Bacon's mother and other women of her class read and even wrote Greek and Latin, but Macaulay's sisters, like most educated women of the nineteenth century, knew little Latin and less Greek. To dispose of the apparent anomaly he offered a "digression" that vindicated the reality of progress. Elizabethan gentlewomen had no alternative education. Now, "though [the classics'] positive value is unchanged, their relative value . . . has been constantly falling. They were the intellectual all of our ancestors. They are but a part of our treasures." He proceeded to depreciate human culture before the sixteenth century more vehemently than when he was in recovery from his passionate undergraduate classicism. It was mostly rhetoric. A hundred pages on he contrasted feminine fancy with masculine judgment. But his own fancy led him to relieve "Bacon" with a few brief romances, just as he would pepper his *History* with similar tales to amuse female readers. "Bacon" also anticipated the book by offering ambitious young gentlemen crafty maxims that taught the rules for winning the game of life.[33]

Even as Macaulay depreciated the "relative value" of the ancients, they continued building his "mental wealth." His conversation about the timeless issues of politics with his folio of Plato "every morning" intensified his conviction of the urgency of nurturing adroit rulers. If some parts of the *Laws* were "very absurd," others showed "Excellent sense." There was less to fault in the *Republic*. He commented on the scheme in book three for breeding reasonable and learned "guardians" to serve the state: "Interesting, but quite visionary . . . Quis cust. des custodes [who will guard the guardians] . . . the great pol. question." Yet he endowed the Elizabethan new class with the same selfless and sharp capacity for government that imbued Plato's ideal rulers. There were ups and downs as he read the *Republic*—"very little that is satisfactory"; "I remember nothing in Greek philosophy superior to it in profundity, ingenuity and eloquence"—but finally it was a "noble work with all its faults."[34] Years later he helped to create a system designed to produce Platonic guardians for the subcontinent.

"Utility and Progress"

Macaulay reported that he "never bestowed so much care on anything" as on "Bacon," above all on explicating the "Baconian doctrine," which developed much that he only hinted to "ordinary readers" in the biographical section. The simplicity of his thesis—"Two words form the key of the Baconian doctrine, Utility and Progress"—seems to belie his exertions. He avoided philosophical technicalities, and much that he wrote would have been familiar to attentive readers of the *Edinburgh Review* and the *Encyclopaedia Britannica*. But translating his vision of England's future and past into fetching stories required much artifice. Bacon counseled that, when announcing one's intentions became "an alarm to call up all that are against" one, it was prudent "to lay asleep opposition, and to surprise." Macaulay understood.[35]

Eager for experience and observation rather than logic and theory, Bacon discovered the modern way of knowing. Aristotle grasped that induction can yield knowledge, but Bacon revealed its intellectual supremacy and empowered humanity to progress—perhaps indefinitely —by pursuing "Utility": first calculating how to increase the pleasure and reduce the pain of nations and individuals and then acting on those calculations. By 1836 progress and utility already seemed English values to many. By ending their association with materialism and unbelief, Macaulay could use them to write a history of the nation that was both post-Christian and agreeable. It was necessary first to dismiss most of the ancient "pagans" whom he read so admiringly. However beguiling and venerated, they were, on his showing, mostly deluded: impractical contemplatives, aspirants for "moral perfection," and unfeeling. Bacon, a modern Protestant, finally exploded their stagnation. In fact Macaulay's classical passions and sources provided him with the stuff of forward-looking, worldly hope. The accessible stories dotting the first sixty-eight pages of "Bacon" contain only two brief quotations in Latin and, near the end, two Greek words. The opening paragraphs of the second part contain seven Latin quotations, and more follow. Together with the appearance of footnotes—nine on the first full page—they serve to deter "plain readers" while welcoming other classically educated intellects equipped to move the world.[36]

Among the ancient philosophers there was a notable exception to the general airiness: "Our great countryman [Bacon] evidently did not consider the revolution which Socrates effected in philosophy as a happy event, and constantly maintained that the earlier Greek speculators, Democritus in particular, were, on the whole, superior." In India Macaulay began "dipping" into Aristotle and then undertook "a thorough course" in his writings. "Bacon" inverted the history of philosophy that Aristotle invented and made standard, which celebrated as progress the shift from identifying self-sufficient material causes to discovering immaterial ones.[37]

But "incorporeal things" held no interest for either Macaulay or Democritus, a materialist, whom he praised in the voice of Bacon, "our great countryman." Fifteen pages later Macaulay coupled Democritus and Anaxagoras, a philosopher expelled from Athens for impiety, as the tragic opponents of the "abject superstition" that "added the last disgrace to the long dotage of the Stoic and Platonic schools." The pair was linked in William Mitford's *History of Greece,* so familiar to Macaulay and to which serious readers tracing his allusions could easily turn. An amateur theologian as well as a historian, Mitford declared that in Anaxagoras' teaching "the supernatural was struck as by a mortal blow": "But the Mind of Anaxagoras, which in order to organize the world had omniscience and reason, had no knowledge of goodness or justice. It was an intelligent natural force; it was not the personal God of conscience; the moral government of the world was not in its jurisdiction. However, the great builder of the kosmos was found, and a path by which humanity might advance to the conception of the divine unity. It was the work of the Sokratic schools to give to the immaterial principle of Anaxagoras those attributes which the human reason conceives to make up the idea of Providence." Mitford then launched into a criticism of "Demokritos," who by "denying the truth of the perception and senses, prepared the way for the skepticism of Protagoras and Pyrrho" and "rendered the supernatural useless."[38]

By championing Democritus, Macaulay implied that Epicureanism was the road not taken. Although philosophical materialism no more tempted him than any other system, practical materialism followed from his skepticism and seemed to promise England a more reasonable and humane future than any metaphysics. Bacon's genius lay in devising a calculus of happiness suitable for regulating both daily life and the affairs of state. Its "essential spirit" was *"philanthropia"*—the identification of practical benevolence with reducing pain was a cliché of English moral philosophy. Although Plato's "genius is above all praise," Socrates now vexed Macaulay: "The more I read about him, the less I wonder that they poisoned him." Privately, Macaulay rejected Socrates as at best a creatively destructive skeptic, but publicly he followed Mitford and conflated him with his student Plato as the leaders of the turn to the supernatural. Macaulay's simulation allowed him to adapt the venerable Protestant story of heathen Platonism infecting Christianity with the virus that bred Catholicism's theological enormities, so that for a millennium there existed an "ill-starred alliance . . . between the old philosophy and the new faith."[39] It amounted to relegating Christianity's theological and ethical particularities to the backwater of ancient speculation.

Despite Macaulay's rejection of the Reformers' theology, he, like them, was a rhetorician impatient with philosophy. Admiring "Bacon," his confidant Ellis detected the impact of his "early rhetorical education." As much as practical materialism, opting for rhetoric over philosophy followed from Macaulay's formative skepticism. His story of the birth of progress brilliantly buried layers of hidden meaning beneath some obvious ones. The ancients called the technique *adianoeta*. In Gibbon's *Decline and Fall of the Roman Empire* he found a bridge linking the Protestant story of ancient speculation infecting Christianity with the birth of the modern world. For all his disparagement of the book's "rank" style, he studied it in India. Gibbon depicted the revival of learning in the West as the protracted, uneven achievement of many centuries. On Macaulay's showing, it began haltingly in the "sharp and vigorous intellects of the Schoolmen," but the shift of mental energy from contemplation to invention sparked momentum. "Gunpowder" and "Printing"—he capitalized both—pointed forward. New learning also counted. Breaking the grip of Aristotle's dead hand, the rediscovery of "a great variety of ancient writers" began the ruin of woolly-minded philosophy. After outrunning Gibbon's account, Macaulay seemingly reverted to the standard Protestant story: "But it is chiefly to the great reformation of religion that we owe the great reformation of philosophy." By repudiating "the dominion of the Vatican" the Protestants also repudiated "the authority of the Schools." The Reformers' preference for rhetoric over speculation was progressive. They inspired Bacon, who "did not arm his philosophy with the weapons of logic [but] adorned her profusely with all the richest decorations of rhetoric."[40]

Then Macaulay deepened his *adianoeta* by retailing the story of Jacques-Bénigne Bossuet, a Catholic apologist whom he knew well, about the result of the Protestant overthrow of ecclesiastical authority. Macaulay called it mental "anarchy": "the vacant throne was left to be struggled for by pretenders." By raising a new intellectual order on the smoldering ruins of the old, Bacon made himself the "Bonaparte" of philosophy. Macaulay catalogued his originality over eight pages, contrasting his opinions with Plato's on everything from arithmetic to jurisprudence. In every case the ancient Greek's beguiling pursuit of useless "speculations" necessarily failed, while the modern Englishman's drive to extend "the empire of man over matter" succeeded.[41] Macaulay's marginalia tell a different story.

That Protestantism remained necessary to England led him to portray it as safe and practical, a matter of morality and custom more than one of faith and doctrines. Middleton, "the great Iconoclast," provided Macaulay with an appealing definition of being a Christian: "But if *to live and think freely; to practise what is moral and to believe what is rational,* be consistent with the sincere profession of Christianity, then I shall acquit myself like once of its truest professors." Macaulay underlined those words and wrote in the margin: "Haec est absoluta et perfecta philosophia vitae." In that spirit he applied a heavy Christian gloss to Bacon, depicting "our great countryman" as the author of "the humane spirit of the English school of wisdom." A biblical allusion to God as the beneficent "common Father" baptized Bacon's earthbound scheme of abandoning efforts to perfect humanity in favor of making men and women "comfortable." Plato used pagan myths to raise doubts about medicine, which Bacon vindicated by appealing to "the example of Christ . . . the great Physician of the soul . . . also the physician of the body." Macaulay's religiosity had a political subtext. Pious "Bacon" "well knew" that government was ill suited to promote virtue. Unlike ancient philosophers and modern Tories who fancied such regimes, Macaulay upheld a strong state that promoted the "well-being of the people" by governing least and relying on markets to do the rest. It supported the military, secured public order, and enabled "a judicial, financial, and commercial system, under which wealth may be rapidly accumulated and securely enjoyed." Its primary regulatory function was to arrange for the moral and religious education of its subjects.[42]

Popular well-being, however, was measurable as increased accumulation and enjoyment. Knowing the strength and expansiveness of "Vulgar wants," Bacon insisted on "observations" that yielded new "arts" which supplied and multiplied such wants. The word "technology" was coined only in 1859, the year Macaulay died. But the advent of self-sustaining, demand-creating innovation—"the most salutary medicines," "the most powerful machines," and ever-better "guns, cutlery, spy-glasses, clocks"— and the reality of England as an increasingly consuming nation enabled him to tell a story with a happy ending on Earth: a possibility unimaginable to any of the ancients. Once more he borrowed from eighteenth-century luminaries. Midway through the *Decline and Fall* Gibbon paused to inquire "with anxious curiosity, whether Europe is still threatened with a repetition of those calamities which formerly oppressed the arms and institutions of Rome." It now seemed unlikely. Foremost among "the probable causes of our security" were "the plough, the loom, and the forge" and "the invention of gunpowder"—he did not capitalize the word—which, along with "mathematics, chemistry, mechanics, architecture," had changed "the military art" into "the science of war." A few years earlier Adam Smith had insisted, "Consumption is the sole end and purpose of all production; and the interest of the producer ought to be attended to, only so far as it may be necessary for promoting that of the consumer. The maxim is so perfectly self-evident that it would be absurd to attempt to prove it." "Self-evident" and "absurd" are the giveaway. Smith, once a professor of logic, knew how to beg the question when handling weak evidence. Despite Smith and Macaulay the sixteenth-century word "consumer" remained a pejorative until the late nineteenth century: a synonym for "wastrel" among moralists and to economists the antithesis of "producer."[43]

Technologically driven, ever-increasing prosperity and consumption would ensure that an "acre in Middlesex is better than a principality in Utopia." Though dismissing as quixotic the pursuit of eternal verities and general moral uplift, Macaulay projected his own utopia—fairly enough, since he believed that the "true philosophical temperament" consisted in "much hope, little faith: a disposition to believe that any thing, however extraordinary, may be done; an indisposition to believe that any thing extraordinary has been done." Knowing that "this glorious prophecy" would deflate the appeal of the "perverted ingenuity" of philosophers and theologians about the supernatural, he prophesied in his Anglican voice: "Bishop Butler so ably pointed out . . ." In affluent nations Macaulay's vision of lush abundance proved to be widely accurate, but in 1836 it remained a well-informed hunch. The year before he had summarized his reaction to Bacon's works in a margin: "This is a glorious daydream, worthy of a mind so exalted & so full of a good hope for the future destinies of mankind. Improvement has not taken the precise line which he fancied that it might take. But the miracles of steam & of gas, the discovery of vaccination, the near approximation made to the longitude & other things show that if he did not guess rightly as to details, he reasoned rightly as to generals."[44]

However clichéd Macaulay's words sound now, they testify to his revelation in Calcutta. As late as 1830 he had noisily defended that grim refutation of all visions of general progress: Pastor Malthus' "theory of superfecundity." The massive and more accessible prosperity that he was celebrating in 1836 began about 1850. Into the 1860s English life expectancy averaged forty, just over thirty in the burgeoning industrial slums. Both his parents lived more years than he, and his fashionable doctors almost killed him. Depressed in Calcutta, he delighted in an ancient satirist's savaging of canting schemes of human improvement, but "Bacon" overrode all those negatives. Macaulay meant to read the portents of the future rather than to project refutable specifics. He, too, had "a glorious daydream" and seized on improvements as proof of the direction of history. In August 1836, for example, the steam route via Egypt brought the London mail to Calcutta in a mere fifty-seven days: "an unprecedented and astonishing instance of rapidity."[45]

Bacon's vision of humanity's increasing power over nature drove Macaulay's prophecy of limitless innovation. Its "immovable strength" rested on a foundation with pilings driven "down into those parts of human nature, which lie low" and hence could last. Making bodies more comfortable was the precondition of the "elevation and purification of the mind." With biblical flourishes he insisted that Bacon's "common sense" materialism was compatible with "popular notions of good and evil" because it was governed by the unchanging needs of human nature: men "do actually love life, health, comfort, honour, security, the society of friends, and do actually dislike death sickness, pain, poverty, disgrace, danger, separation from those to whom they are attached . . . religion, though it often regulates and moderates these [pleasant and unpleasant] feelings, seldom eradicates them; nor did he think it desirable for mankind that they should be eradicated."[46]

By amplifying Lucretius on the servitude inherent in superstition, Macaulay anticipated objections that his Bacon taught an amoral doctrine which aimed merely "to increase the outward comforts of our species." The multiplication of "bodily comforts" offered no happiness "to a man whose mind was under the tyranny of licentious appetite, of envy, of hatred, or of fear." But apart from utility Macaulay could prescribe only the restraints of English respectability: "popular notions of good and evil." Stressing process and technique rather than content and rejecting theories of natural rights and law, his skepticism forbade extrapolating a theory either of obligation from fact or of meaning from behavior. Once again his rhetoric distracted attention from his ethical situation. Reasserting his credentials as a judge competent to acquit Bacon of seeking to make "a world of water-wheels, power-looms, [and] steam carriages" for the comfort of "sensualists and knaves," he reprised his indictment of Bacon's personal defects.[47]

Utility remained Macaulay's ethical lodestone. Wielding seemingly despotic power in India had shrunk his appreciation that unexpected consequences always threaten and often mock even our best aspirations and efforts, together with his human sympathies. A decade earlier Macaulay had perhaps half-believed that seeing God as the father of a single human family had deepened the ancient moral imagination; believing in such a God was impossible. In India even deferring to ethical universalism ceased to matter to him. Both his "connected course" of classical studies and his project to remake and civilize "the Hindoo" dulled his sense of the circumscribed good that empires can do *for* their subjects, because the possibilities of doing *to* them seemed limitless. When intractable human reality frustrated Macaulay's imperial and progressive ambition, he favored desperate means. That Czar Peter I of Russia began dragging his "vast empire" into a "place among civilized com-munities" outweighed the "stormy rage and hate" of that "barbarous tyrant."[48] Macaulay's calculus turned the nameless, faceless thousands crushed by Peter's civilizing juggernaut into inconsequential collateral damage.

Ultimately, results counted, and Bacon's principle of induction yielded "works" not "words"—an allusion to the Epistle of James. Macaulay even foresaw "a science of which the object was to cure the diseases and per-turbations of the mind . . . by a method analogous to that which has im-proved medicine and surgery." Careful observation and experimentation would disclose "the actual effects produced on the human character by particular modes of education, by the indulgence of particular habits, by the study of particular books, by society, by emulation, by imitation. Then we might hope to find out what mode of training was most likely to preserve and restore moral health."[49] Macaulay's blueprint for psychia-try—a word coined circa 1846—anticipated Ivan Pavlov's conditioning, not Sigmund Freud's psychoanalysis.

Pending such a mind cure, he associated Bacon's soundness with down-to-earth Christianity. He was "a theologian" and "we are con-vinced . . . a sincere believer in the divine authority of the Christian rev-elation," who "loved to dwell on the power of the Christian religion to effect much that the ancient philosophers could only promise. He loved to consider that religion as the bond of charity, the curb of evil passions, the consolation of the wretched, the support of the timid, the hope of the dying. But controversies on speculative points of theology seem to have engaged scarcely any portion of his attention." "We are convinced" was a nervy phrase, but Macaulay was playing for high stakes. To per-suade "the great body of readers" in the "exoteric school" that his treat-ment of "questions with which they are familiar" demonstrated his "consummate ability," it was crucial to use "language which every body understands." Thus they would come to trust him about matters known only "by those who have sat in his inner school." Having banished the supernatural from human ken and privileged "vulgar wants," he reiter-ated his authority to judge others' religious sincerity, the content of Christianity, and the interpretation of the Bible. A long quotation from Bacon contrasting the Hebrew scriptures' bias toward "prosperity" with the New Testament's toward "adversity" testified not only to his religious sincerity but also to the sufficiency of Macaulay's cultural Protestantism, reticent about "speculative points of theology." Some clergymen were unconvinced, others extended the benefit of the doubt, and a few applauded.[50] Their disagreement sufficed to position Macaulay as a Christian participating in the debate that was reshaping English religion.

An erudite but seemingly pointless digression about the evolution of Bacon's prose style also pointed forward. Dusting off the old line about the progress from imagination to reason, Macaulay made an unlikely association: "the history of . . . [Bacon's] mind bears some resemblance to the history of the mind of Burke." Both inverted the normal movement from "fancy" to the "sterner faculties," which Macaulay described using a stereotype that associated women with primitiveness and the irrational: "In general, the development of the fancy is to the development of the judgment what the growth of a girl is to the growth of a boy." But alleged gender differences were not his real concern. Diagnosing two cases of late-onset male fancy enabled him to link a great philosophical revolutionary and a great political counterrevolutionary as essential figures in the making of England, embodiments of the fruitful interplay of "the principles of Conservation and Reform." Already musing on the "historical work which may be at once the business and the amusement of my life," he recommended a dictum of Bacon "to be 'chewed and digested'": "Histories make men wise, poets witty, the mathematics subtle, natural philosophy deep, morals grave, logic and rhetoric able to contend."[51] Offering something for almost everyone, Macaulay's *History of England* would be wise in many ways and hugely rhetorical.

From 1835 onward he presented "Utility and Progress" as the hallmarks of the modern world, giving purpose to the past and direction to the present and making transience bearable without the incredible hope of the supernatural. For Macaulay there was no interpreting history according to the ancients' melancholy doctrine of eternal recurrence—again and again forever—or the Sex Pistols' aimless "I don't know what I want,/But I know how to get it." A nineteenth-century man, Macaulay knew what he wanted and anchored it in "an acre in Middlesex," but as remade by his rhetoric. In his peroration he mustered English religion, science, and patriotism, explicitly referencing Cowley's comparison of "Bacon to Moses standing on Mount Pisgah." As much as the Hebrews' "great Lawgiver," Bacon glimpsed the future but could "not go over thither": "While the multitude below saw only the flat sterile desert in which they had so long wandered . . . he was gazing from a far higher stand on a far lovelier country." Macaulay concluded by alluding to his own irresolution about whether to pursue literature or politics in the future. Had Bacon's "civil ends continued to be moderate, he would have been, not only the Moses but the Joshua of philosophy. He would have led his followers . . . into the heart of the promised land. He would not merely have pointed out, but would have divided the spoil." It would fall to Moses' unsparing successor to slaughter the heathen Canaanites and portion "out all those wealthy regions from Dan to Beersheba."[52]

Fussing over "the precious freight" of "Bacon" to the very end, he also pondered his essay on William Temple, which would consider Joshua's career. When "Bacon" appeared in July 1837, he was still in India, anxious about its reception and eager for home. Expecting "that parts of it will be furiously attacked," he was also sure that it was "in the main unexpungable." The essay annoyed some philosophers and infuriated at least one philosophizer, but Macaulay shifted the public conversation to Bacon's role as the new Moses, leading humanity toward a better future through discoveries that advanced our mastery over nature.[53]

One searching critic chided Macaulay for failing to provide an ethic that obliged all because it included all. A paternalistic Berkshire squire, Tory M.P., and the older brother of a newfangled Oxford High Churchman, Philip Pusey was also a talented agriculturalist, cosmopolitan, and classicist. Prussia's learned ambassador in London found him "a most unique union of a practical Englishman and an intellectual German, so that when speaking in one capacity one might think he had lost sight of the other." Studying the same texts that had engaged Macaulay in Calcutta, Pusey reached a different conclusion. His review of "Bacon" elaborated the contrast between Plato and his recent expositors on the one hand and Jeremy Bentham's Utilitarianism on the other. In the belief that Macaulay had only assembled or rearranged English platitudes, Pusey vivisected the essay. Their country was "sinking yearly more and more into natural and mechanical philosophy" and philistinism. The "Greatest Happiness Principle" had become "the practical canon of most English writers on ethics," especially at Cambridge. Ancient "Grecian ethics, it is well known, were too political, making the State 'all in all.'" Contemporary "theories of government" rested on the same principle as "a Mutual

Insurance Company." They denied that "the Christian Church" was the "type and the greatest of States"; that piety, love, and devotion to place made the nation's identity and spirit; and that "Christianity is the foundation of ethics, [and] ethics the illustration of Christianity." Far from improving "the physical good of the country," machines imprisoned children "in the sweltering din of a Manchester factory for the waking hours of their existence."[54]

Pusey conceded that Macaulay's interpretation of "the Baconian philosophy" was valid and distinguished it and him from both "Utilitarianism as concerns morals" and "the Benthamites" as a party. Far from decrying Macaulay's show of Christianity, Pusey, when at last he named him, praised him as "one among us distinguished for commanding eloquence, not less distinguished for a philosophic spirit from which that eloquence receives its substance." Also revering Thucydides, Pusey went on to "invite," "beg," and "earnestly inquire" of Macaulay as a "statesman" and a "philosopher" to reconsider grounding the "sense of duty and shame" in the community's conscience rather than in individual calculation. Finally, he "put" it to Macaulay to consider that England's "corporate spirit" was embodied "in a land, in its laws, and its institutions" and that it was his "most commanding duty" as a teacher of the nation to join in carrying "onward the pure and steady glow of this national spirit, heightened if possible and brightened, but at least unimpaired and unsullied, from generation to generation; and, so long as England lasts, from age to age."[55] It was a doxology to the nation summoning an "Amen."

Macaulay was poised to win the culture war. Sixteen months after "Bacon" appeared, he was accosted in Florence by "a Yankee clergyman," who "begged to thank me for my writings in the name of his countrymen; that he himself reprinted my paper on Bacon; that it had a great run in the States; and that my name was greatly respected there." In America mentioning "'Lord Bacon' could convey authority to almost any cause."[56] Macaulay's concern, however, was modern England, and Pusey's deference hinted that his interpretation of its origins, ethos, and future would prevail at home. There was no serious alternative, and Pusey's willingness to embrace the state as the "Highest Good on earth" implied that even Tories could accept England not as the replacement of "the Christian Church" as the "the greatest of States" but as a down-to-earth facsimile.

A Death in the Family

Because Macaulay deferred his essay on "the Controversy about the Ancients and Moderns," it became political as well as even more personal. In 1690 William Temple opened the English front of the debate over the authority of the ancients by insisting on their abiding superiority. Championing the moderns in response, Richard Bentley, the greatest classical scholar of the age and an expositor of Newton's science, demonstrated that Greek letters which Temple had praised as products of the sixth century B.C.E. were ineptly forged centuries later. Macaulay thought Temple's book absurd but found him intriguing as the type of an able man who, after abandoning his political vocation, selfishly frittered away a studious retirement.[57] He decided to use Temple to make a case for remaining in public life and to remind himself again that he was helping to create a world better than any the ancients had known or imagined.

To think himself back into the present he studied German: "I have always found that to begin with the Bible, which I know by heart, is the best way of dealing with a foreign language." His audit of his 1837 reading noted German for "an hour or two" every day, above all Friedrich "Schiller's History of the Thirty Years' War": "a great deal of very just and deep thought conveyed in language so popular and agreeable that dunces would be likely to think him superficial." But there was still no escaping the classics: all of "the three great names in the literature of Rome"—Livy, Cicero, and Tacitus—and his favorite Greeks, including the inevitable Thucydides and "a good many of Plutarch's lives over and over." But perusing St. Augustine's *Confessions* for the first time, he told Ellis: "The book is not without interest. But he expresses himself in the style of a field-preacher." It was a put-down that Macaulay had learned in genteel Clapham. In his last letter home from Calcutta, he again mustered his domestic voice, asking his sisters to convey to their father his "most affectionate love" and praying that "God grant that we may find him in tolerable health."[58]

On 21 January 1838, with the Trevelyans in tow and mindful of his overdue essay, he sailed for home on a slow boat "celebrated for the comfort and luxury of her internal arrangements." At sea he struggled with Leopold von Ranke's *History of the Popes* but never mastered German. Unlike the Greek and Latin classics, its literature provided him with knowledge rather than sustenance. There was a layover in Cape Town, and they finally landed in Dartmouth around 1 June. A few days later Tom learned that his father had been dead for almost three weeks. At last he was the head of the family and master of his own house. In the "heyday of masculine domesticity" it was the closest approximation of being fully a man possible for any childless celibate.[59]

Zachary's death also led Tom to embed in "Temple" a case for civilizing slaughter, which received first general acquiescence and then terrible validation. Too delicately, John Clive detected in Tom "repressed hostility" toward his father. It was in fact more inhibited than repressed, personal as well as religious, and permanent. Family honor and Zachary's useful reputation as a philanthropic Christian had made Tom publicly defer to him, but in death as in life Tom showed Zachary little of his boasted sensitivity "where my affections are concerned." Hannah mourned her "beloved father"—"through much tribulation he has entered into the kingdom of heaven"—and his abolitionist friends and colleagues planned to honor him: "At a meeting held on 30 July 1838, with Sir Thomas Foxwell Buxton in the chair, it was agreed to erect a memorial to Zachary in Westminster Abbey. The bust incorporates a figure of a kneeling slave together with the motto 'Am I not a Man and a Brother?'" It was the emblem of the Anti-Slavery Society. The inscription reads in part:

> Zachary Macaulay
> Who during forty successive years,
> Partaking in the counsels and the labours
> which, guided by favouring Providence,
> Rescued Africa from the woes,
> And the British Empire from the guilt,
> of slavery and the slave-trade.

Almost five years after Buxton proposed to memorialize Zachary, Tom belatedly thanked the sculptor on behalf of his family.[60]

A wealthy brewer, an Anglican evangelical with Quaker sympathies, and a long-serving M.P., Buxton felt differently about Zachary. After becoming William Wilberforce's coadjutor in the parliamentary campaign against slavery in 1821, he developed a close friendship with Macaulay:

"And now for those dear to me, for my friends, I pray, especially for poor dear Macaulay, who I know is in much sorrow. Let me plead, O Lord, his sacrifices in the slave question." In early February 1838 he traveled to London, calling "on Zachary Macaulay, who was ill and believed that he would never see Buxton again . . . [Macaulay said to him] that he shared his every opinion about the events in the anti-slavery movement at that time." It was their last meeting. Buxton wanted to fulfill Zachary's utopian ambition, which Tom was countering with his own: "to shape those measures which were to change the structure of society throughout the Western World." That revolution would depend on the sway of the Union Jack. In 1828 a missionary had reported that native people were being terrorized at "the caprice of the Dutch boors in South Africa"— "Beneath this grinding misery their numbers had dwindled"—and he urged the abolitionists to agitate for British intervention to save them: "it is one of the principal stones in the foundation of that temple which Mr. Wilberforce has been so long labouring to rear, for the protection of the oppressed; and it has given a strength and an elevation to the building, which will render the whole more secure, and its future progress more easy."[61]

After the abolition of slavery in the British Empire, Buxton focused on "the wickedness of our proceedings as a nation, towards the ignorant and barbarous natives of countries on which we seize. What have we Christians done for them? We have usurped their lands, kidnapped, enslaved, and murdered them"; "I hate shooting innocent savages worse than slavery itself." His indignation grew. In October 1835 he told Zachary: "I am deeply interested about the savages, particularly the Caffres [in the Cape Colony]. Oh! We Englishmen are, by our own account, fine fellows at home! Who among us doubts that we surpass the world in religion, justice, knowledge, refinement, and practical honesty? But such a set of miscreants and wolves we prove when we escape from the range of the laws, the earth does not contain." Britain's antislavery movement needed a new cause, and protecting native peoples from violent Europeans and Americans seemed urgent and promising. From Tasmania to North America to South Africa, terrorizing "aborigines" threatened to escalate into what we call "genocide" and the Victorians knew as "extirpation" or "eradication." Buxton and his colleagues looked to an ancient and widespread maxim, "All things whatsoever ye would that men should do to you, do ye to them." Practicing a universal and reciprocal ethic was always problematic, not least for Christians. During the sixteenth century a few Spaniards had urged applying the "Golden Rule" to the native peoples of their American empire but failed either to gain widespread support among their countrymen and coreligionists or to prevent the African slave trade.[62]

On 9 February 1836 the House of Commons authorized a select committee chaired by Buxton "to consider what Measures ought to be adopted with regard to the Native Inhabitants of Countries where British Settlements are made, and to the Neighbouring Tribes, in order to secure to them the due observance of Justice, and the protection of their Rights; to promote the spread of Civilization among them, and to lead them to the peaceful and voluntary reception of the Christian Religion." Witnesses testified about conditions not only in the antipodes, South Africa, but also in North and South America. Buxton asked how British colonization was "deleterious to the native populations": "I mean, in the first instance, destructive to their lives, reducing their number." The assumption that spreading civilization depended on propagating Christianity informed the proceedings. Buxton assured Zachary: "The Aborigines Committee went on exceedingly well."[63]

A year later the committee's mandate was renewed, with Buxton continuing as chair. His colleagues now included William Ewart Gladstone, rising as both a High Tory and a newfangled High Churchman. It was another sign that "the Anglican wing of the anti-slavery movement tended towards Toryism." In the United States the Jackson administration sought to remove "all the Indians within the Union . . . to the recently acquired country on the Mississippi." More immediately, evidence abounded that "with the exception of missionary efforts, the lack of a systematic policy in colonial affairs not only impeded the progress of colonization and commerce, but resulted in widespread human destruction following the expansion of British power." The committee heard testimony from Henry, one of Tom's younger brothers, on the plight of Sierra Leone's "aboriginal tribes." Buxton, "well satisfied" with the second round of hearings, considered taking up abuses against the natives of India. Three days after Zachary's death he addressed the first meeting of the British and Foreign Aborigines Protection Society, which he had founded in 1837 primarily "to check the progress of oppression in our colonies." Gladstone signed on. The younger abolitionists wanted to effect a reevaluation of imperial values, much as Zachary Macaulay's generation had invoked a universal and reciprocal ethic to fight slavery: "let us awake to our duty, and, relying on the blessing from on high, let every energy be exerted, and every nerve be strained, to hasten the arrival of that period, when the voice of the oppressor, and the cry of the oppressed, shall no more be heard on our earth: when men shall dwell together as brethren—children of one common Father—heirs of the same glorious immortality." The meeting satisfied Buxton, but a friend in the audience reported that the house was small and that the dominance of Nonconformists would probably cause the Anglican church to "withdraw from exerting its influence."[64] Events justified her skepticism. Another bout of national self-reproach lacked the appeal of Thomas Babington Macaulay's full-throated celebration of England and its empire.

From India to Ireland

Macaulay wanted to finish "Temple" before beginning a long continental tour—Italy was his goal—but he made it a deeply felt tract for the times. Zachary's death and the creation of the Aborigines Protection Society caused him to add a few pages that proved to be as farseeing as "Bacon." Buxton was useful to Tom, but he shared with Zachary the inflexibility that complicated enacting abolition in 1833 and nettled Tom: "It was extremely painful to me to speak against all my political friends, so painful that at times I could hardly go on. I treated them as mildly as I could." Also shepherding the bill renewing the East India Company's charter through the House of Commons, he versified his annoyance to Hannah:

> Oh the hateful month of May
> Now that I am in power
> No longer can I ramble
> In the streets to the east of the Tower.
> The Niggers in one hemisphere
> The Brahmins in the other
> Disturb my dinner and my sleep
> With "An't I a man and a brother?"

His solecism mocked his father's society, which, with abolition enacted, he hopefully noted, had "completed its mission." While publicly toasting Buxton and his cause in 1833, Tom was eager to put paid to humanitarian politics:

> Neither planters nor canters [hypocritical abolitionists] will make
>   my ears tingle
> And West Indian sugar, and East Indian tea
> Will both be forgot as I ride to the Dingle
> Derry Down.

Four years of imperial power and his rediscovery of the ancients worked to deepen his despite for "Niggers in one hemisphere" as well as "Brahmins in the other."[65]

By mixing "a good many thoughts in my head" translated from India with a stew of old scores and biases, he made quick work of "Temple." Such were the "crowd and bustle of the late London season"—for him no seclusion and mourning crepe to honor his father—that he updated himself about events "since August 1837" only after finishing the essay. Macaulay required, however, no news about India and Ireland. Aware of the distorting power of his imagination, he was sometimes unable—perhaps unwilling—to control it, particularly when it focused on either antiquity or the empire. Before seeing either colony, he knew his mind about both and mastered them as he mastered the classics, on his own terms.[66]

"Exile" had intensified his devotion to the nation of his dreams: "I believe that nobody ever loved his country as a place to live in with so exclusive a love as mine for England. I would not go again through what I have gone through for Lord Westminster's fortune." In India he had increasingly seen irreducible differences between the English and subordinate nations or races more than fundamental likeness and shared humanity. That conviction informed his effort in "Temple" and elsewhere to apply the progressive and calculating moral logic of "Bacon" to correct James Mill along with "canters" such as his father and Buxton. Mill, once his target and then his patron, had lived and died enough of an eighteenth-century cosmopolitan to regret the cruelty that empires must employ to subjugate, rule, and civilize native peoples.[67]

Macaulay wrote "Temple" with an idea of Ireland, which he had never seen, as conjectural and fixed as his idea of India. On 28 February 1833 he told the Commons that "he would far rather live in Algiers, in its most despotic day, than he would live in the county of Kilkenny at the present time." In Calcutta he had associated faction, agitation, and tumult with Irish politics. His despised British opponents there had reminded him of "O'Connel"—the Irish parliamentary leader Daniel O'Connell. During his last months in India a letter from an old friend whose husband had been posted to Dublin grieved him: "I cannot conceive what has induced you to submit to such an exile. I declare, for my own part that, little as I love Calcutta, I would rather stay here than be settled in the Phoenix park." He imagined Dublin as "a provincial city on fire with factions political and religious" and the hinterland simultaneously rotting and blazing with "sedition." As much as India and Canada, Ireland was an English colony, not part of a nation called the United Kingdom: "Therefore Calcutta for me in preference to Dublin." When writing about Ireland in "Temple," he remembered India, where he became easy with death.[68]

The challenge to a duel issued to him in Calcutta by Sir William Mackintosh's insulted editor also hung over him. Calculating that his honor as "a public man" required him to accept, he prepared for death on the evening before he was to face his challenger. Their seconds negotiated a modus vivendi, but the prospect of his dying reinforced his capacity to laugh at others suffering violence. In 1839 Macaulay's impudent little nephew was "beaten black and blue" by his cane-wielding father, who himself afterward suffered "a fit of ague": "We have all been laughing till our sides were sore at the adventure." No animus colored Macaulay's laughter. The boy was his beloved Margaret's only child and his own putative intellectual heir: "Ever dear Charley . . . Yours affectionately." Nine years later that "good, clever, promising boy of thirteen" succumbed like his mother to scarlet fever contracted from infected water. Many other Victorians thoughtlessly laughed along with him. A year earlier a fair in Hyde Park celebrating the queen's coronation exhibited a "Hottentot Venus," an African woman with pendulous breasts and protruding buttocks, which precocious English boys could pay to flail with a toy whip.[69]

The brutality of the nineteenth-century West foreshadowed the horrors of the next century. In the aftermath of Napoleon its violence became mostly imperial. Notwithstanding defeat, Napoleon pioneered transforming warfare from a limited fact of the human condition into projects of destroying states and remaking societies. In France the Napoleonic cult flourished; many revered him for continuing the revolution to create "a new world, a new order." The delusion made "all the standards, all the laws of the past . . . antiquated; and . . . it had on its side not power only, but right": "everything must give way and all opposition, if not contemptible, will be criminal." Napoleon had his English admirers, including Macaulay in some voices: "No men occupy so splendid a place in history as those who have founded monarchies on the ruins of republican institutions . . . Their reigns shine with a double light, the last and dearest rays of departing freedom mingled with the first and brightest glories of empire in its dawn . . . In this class three men stand preeminent, Caesar, Cromwell, and Bonaparte." Writing about Napoleon as the twentieth century began, a Liberal imperialist politician explained that humanity delighted in "something that indefinitely raises its conception of its own power and possibilities." By then it was widely accepted that an ethic of imperial and civilizing slaughter was a necessary, though perhaps distasteful, corollary of modern progress.[70]

Abroad, ignorant persons of European stock gave little thought to Napoleon, but they were ready and able to use collective violence to transform or kill their "inferiors." The few days Macaulay spent in Cape Town during his passage from India were memorable, not least because "of the tribes of Southern Africa . . . [being] driven back before the white settlers." The campaign of the London Missionary Society's representative there to permit native peoples to own land and move freely succeeded. In reaction, ten thousand Boers began their Great Trek from the Cape Colony, and evidence of their "driving back" native peoples abounded when Macaulay stopped there. Civilizing slaughter took root in the United States, now summoned, as Macaulay knew, to fulfill its "manifest destiny" in "the states behind the Ohio" and beyond. A novel ideology promising to realize everywhere "democratic equality," "human liberty," "progress," and "civilization and refinement" justified human sacrifice. The expulsion and occasional slaughter of American Indians combined with the slave economy to complicate that noble promise. Evoking the horrors of Andrew Jackson's implementation of the Indian Removal Act of 1830, which uprooted five tribes from their ancestral lands and forced them to march westward or to death, a scholarly admirer of Jackson suggests that it saved them from extirpation.[71]

Macaulay's rediscovery of the classics moved him to rewrite modern Europe's moral history by rooting it in the primal Greek values of winning honor and avoiding shame rather than in the western Christian conviction of personal and collective guilt. In India he reread and hailed the *Odyssey* as the *"speciosa miracula"* (brilliant wonder). At ease with its moral logic, he scorned Augustine's *Confessions,* a formative document of the "introspective conscience of the West." At the same time he identified with Odysseus, who returned in disguise to "his rugged little Ithaca" and vindicated his honor by massacring all his wife's suitors. Macaulay felt less affinity for a minor contemporary English poet: "There is a sort of meekness, half Christian, half Utilitarian, about him, which in the early ages of Greece would have been thought contemptible effeminacy." Similarly, he understood that it was Lord Clive's occasional brutality "for the advantage of his country" that vindicated his use of "power." Incarnated in the victorious East India Company, England properly used "the most oppressive form of barbarian despotism" against the aborigines, because, unlike them, it was "strong with all the strength of civilisation." Machiavelli, another apt modernizer of the ancients, had known as much. "Cruel, treacherous and irreligious deeds increase the prestige of a new master of a country in which humanity, trustworthiness and religion have long ceased to have any force. On the other hand, conduct that is in accordance with humanity, trustworthiness and religion is damaging to one's prestige in a country in which cruelty, treachery and irreligion have been dominant for a long time."[72]

Unlike the founders of the Aborigines Protection Society, Macaulay believed that England's imperial mission was civilizing, not Christian. There was no ignoring religion's baleful impact on contemporary politics. Ireland's fanatical Protestants and Catholics had appalled him in India, but he also detected signs at home of "a most pernicious disposition to mix up religion with politics," as if there were no state church. He predicted "a violent reaction" within a decade against not the church but "Christianity . . . on the hustings." The Anglican confessional monopoly was over, but the Tories remained the church party and sometimes exploited their allegiance. When Macaulay returned home, his critic Philip

Pusey's younger brother, a canon of Christ Church, Oxford, and Regius Professor of Hebrew, was already one of the eponyms for a counterrevolutionary movement within the university and the church. They were variously the "Puseyites" (coined in 1838), the "Newmanites" (coined in 1837 after John Henry Newman, their most intellectually elegant theoretician), or the "Tractarians" (coined in 1839 because of their *Tracts for the Times*). Claiming for the Church of England both divine institution and unique privileges as "the visible church," they looked back "to the ancient Church, instead of the Reformers, as the ultimate expounder of the meaning of our Church." They were in fact English originals.[73]

Ireland suffered from a more fundamental problem than religion. To many Englishmen, including Macaulay, its aboriginal people appeared barbarous, perhaps savage, and hence even lower on the scale of civilization than the natives of the subcontinent. Pullulating, landless, and rebellious, the Irish peasantry seemed to refute Macaulay's prophecy that modern England would become an ever more comfortable and consuming place. As much as the Bengalis, they "had reason to apprehend famine." The 1830s saw unparalleled agrarian violence in reaction to mass evictions by landlords and strikes in Dublin, a backward place that had received its first steam engine only in 1833. Two official committees chaired by the Protestant archbishop of Dublin, famous as a logician and political economist, recommended against importing the English workhouse system, which required paupers to live in mean parish institutions as the condition of relief. The Whig government rejected the recommendations.[74] During the 1840s Macaulay would find Ireland first even more nettlesome and then briefly promising.

Pen in hand, he wrote "Temple" on the foolscap in front of him and in the margins of the relics of the battle of the books, correcting and ranking them but also freely lifting from them. He moved quickly when he wrote from "my own head," but the necessity of research made "slow work of it." Ensuring that the essay would "take" with readers required that it be "superficial"—accessible and apparently clear: "by no means easy writing. I hope that it may be found easy reading." Deciding how to spend the rest of his life remained part of his complex agenda in "Temple." He projected the *History of England* on a huge scale, perhaps extending from 1688 to 1830: "an entire view of all the transactions which took place between the revolution which brought the Crown into harmony with the parliament and the revolution which brought the parliament into harmony with the nation." The project might require him to abandon London and politics.[75]

In mid-September 1838 he dispatched "Temple." It digresses even more than "Bacon," and its many pictorial pages invite turning. Macaulay was ostensibly "reviewing" the *Memoirs of the Life, Works, and Correspondence of Sir William Temple* by Thomas Courtney, a retired Tory politician. After congratulating him on escaping "that closely watched slavery," Macaulay described him as more a dutiful compiler than an author whose book "can be enjoyed by the idle consumer." What annoyed was Courtney's charge that "the new Whigs" failed to admit that their ideological forebears "'never extended their liberality to the native Irish, or the professors of the ancient religion [Catholicism].'" On Macaulay's showing, the real falsifiers of history were the Puseyites, busily suppressing the true origins of English Protestantism. Throughout he rode a horse at least as high as his mount in "Bacon" but to frame a case against abandoning politics: "in truth . . . [Temple's] faultlessness is chiefly to be ascribed to his extreme dread of all responsibility, to his determination rather to leave his country in a scrape than to run any chance of being in a scrape himself . . . valetudinarian effeminacy, this habit of coddling himself." He went on to consign Temple to hell, in which he did not believe.[76] Another bow to readers who identified vehemence with sincerity, it invited them to trust his moral judgment.

Temple belonged to a generation of weak men "whom revolutions produce." Looking back reverently to "the strong lineaments which distinguish the men who produce revolutions" led Macaulay to reflect on their transforming power. Even when depraved, such leaders could exhibit "moral qualities" such as "fixedness of purpose, intensity of will, enthusiasm": "zeal makes revolutions; and revolutions make men zealous for nothing." The failure of the revolutionary zealots' projects rendered Temple's generation impotently self-interested. The pattern illustrated both the old lesson that in politics might makes right and the permanent dialectic between "Conservation" and "Reform." Echoing the Bible, Macaulay indicted the "political immorality" of the timid postrevolutionaries—all "contagion," "malady," and "general corruption."[77] But there was no censuring the often ruthlessly energetic revolutionaries.

Experimenting with writing a history that would amuse consumers, he narrated Temple's family romance. It enabled him to imply to hasty readers that Temple was in Ireland when Oliver Cromwell—"good or bad, he could not be otherwise than great"—came and conquered in 1649. William Temple was "in France . . . from 1648 until winter 1651," but his father, Sir John, politician, judge, and polemicist, remained at home. John had also been there in 1641, when the Irish Catholic gentry rebelled, massacring about 4,000 Ulster Protestants, dispossessing countless more, and setting off the interreligious conflict that helped to precipitate the English Civil War. Contemporary Anglo- and Scots-Irish reports multiplied Protestant fatalities into the tens of thousands. Five years later, John published a *History of the Irish Rebellion,* "which made an immediate and great sensation . . . its statements were received with unquestioning confidence, and the work did much to inflame popular indignation in England against the Irish, and to justify the severe treatment afterwards meted out to them by Cromwell."[78]

Reporting that 300,000 Protestants were either "expelled" or "destroyed," Sir John's book "animated militant English attitudes to Ireland for many years to come"—there were at least ten editions between 1646 and 1812—but it drew on precedents and inspired imitators. The same violent antipathy to the aboriginal Irish and the Old English settlers who went native inflamed the poet Edmund Spenser in *A View of the Present State of Ireland,* first printed in 1633. He asked: "Is not the sworde the moste violent redress that maye be used for anie evil?" Temple's *Irish Rebellion,* in turn, colored a later poet's war propaganda: John Milton's *Observations upon the Articles of Peace with the Irish Rebels* (1649) identified the aboriginal Irish as "indocible and averse from all Civility and amendment, and . . . rejecting the ingenuity of all other Nations to improve and waxe more civill by a civilizing Conquest . . . preferre their own absurd and savage Customes." In this "undistinguished" work, which has largely escaped scholarly attention, Milton anticipated his patron Oliver Cromwell's ambivalent defense of his troops, who at Drogheda a few months later massacred about 3,000 soldiers together with many civilians, including every recognizable Catholic priest and religious: "I am persuaded that this is the righteous Judgement of God upon these Barbarous wretches who have so imbrued their hands in so much innocent blood, and that it will tend to prevent the effusion of blood for the future, which are the satisfactory grounds to such Actions, which otherwise cannot but work remorse and regret." Milton blamed "those Irish Barbarians" for killing "more than 200000." A hostile contemporary of Cromwell anticipated most historians in interpreting his bloodletting as brutal tactics rather than the debut of a strategy of systematic eradication or extirpation.[79]

On John Temple's showing, English weakness had caused the 1641 rebellion. Instead of segregating the natives, the conquerors had mixed with that superstitious and backward lot, thereby debasing themselves and anglicizing too many of them. His remedy was thorough: "Ireland was to be conquered and raped, and a policy of religious apartheid developed to justify the mass expropriation of the native peoples." Temple's brutality did not encompass controlled slaughter, Spenser's book was published posthumously, and Milton never acknowledged his. But Temple provided "the raw material from which Protestant memories were shaped and reshaped over generations."[80] His historical reputation depended on *The Irish Rebellion* and his more famous son.

The English sense of cultural, religious, and ethnic superiority extended beyond Ireland, antedated Cromwell, and survived him. During the sixteenth century, "while sovereigns of the realm were struggling to pacify the tribal Celts, and the Puritan colonists in North America were wrestling with the Red Indian for his soul and his lands, all frontier antagonists looked more or less alike. Whether Irishmen or Pequots, Scots or Iroquois, they were enemies, they were ignorant, and they were animal-like." During the eighteenth century English accusations of savagery triggered extraordinary warfare in the Scottish Highlands, where there was wide support for an uprising led by Charles Edward Stuart, the "Young Pretender." On 16 April 1746 an expeditionary force under the duke of Cumberland defeated the Highlanders at Culloden, and his troops coolly slaughtered their captives en masse. Cumberland was briefly an imperial hero. A year later in London George Frederick Handel identified him with Judas Maccabeus, the deliverer of Israel, saluting him as a "truly Wise, Valiant, and Virtuous Commander" in the chorus "See the Conquering Hero Come." Across the Atlantic, counties, mountains, and a river were named Cumberland. In Scotland and elsewhere he acquired a nickname: "The Butcher." With the Stuart threat ended, calculated terror and selective "clearances" of the natives reduced the Highlands to English notions of civilization. During the first decades of the nineteenth century England lacked both an imperial identity and a coherent imperial program, but it was experienced in empire-building.[81]

Macaulay knew that history. He also knew Machiavelli, who taught that Rome had built an empire "by ruining her neighboring cities, and by freely admitting strangers to her privileges and honors." But first came destruction: "Anyone who becomes master of a city accustomed to a free way of life, and does not destroy it, may expect to be destroyed by it himself, because when it rebels, it will always be able to appeal to the spirit of freedom and its ancient institutions, which are never forgotten, despite the passage of time and any benefits bestowed by the new rule. Whatever he does, whatever provisions he makes, if he does not foment internal divisions or scatter the inhabitants, they will never forget their lost liberties and their ancient institutions, and will immediately attempt to recover them whenever they have an opportunity." Machiavelli recalled the Florentine subjection of Pisa in the fifteenth century. Macaulay could cite more immediate parallels. In British India, populated by tens of millions, he recommended fomenting "internal divisions" between Muslims and Hindus as an aid to empire. In Ireland scattering the aboriginal population now seemed a political and practical impossibility, but Catholics and Protestants needed little instruction in fighting each other. For Machiavelli, seizing the right *occasione* was the great thing: "Men of outstanding ability [*excellente virtù*] are able to recognise opportunities and exploit them." Hence effective cruelty must be quick and politic in order to seem almost merciful.[82]

"Drogheda Was as Jericho"

Knowing all this, Macaulay in "Temple" prescribed imperial and civilizing slaughter. When Oliver Cromwell invaded Ireland in 1649, he exhibited his superior "abilities and the force of his character" to their utmost. He was unable and probably unwilling to rule there "in the best way." To explain Cromwell's policy and vindicate its abiding lessons, Macaulay set off rhetorical "fire-works" lifted from the book of Joshua. As much as Machiavelli, he appreciated how religion "availed" to order the state and extend its reach, and Joshua, Moses' successor, offered a seemingly God-given precedent for "Oliver's" thoroughness. At a time when many Anglicans invested all the Hebrew scriptures with permanent and literal authority, even Henry Hart Milman, Macaulay's moderately critical friend, read Joshua as the history of Israel vanquishing the Promised Land, not as the later theological self-imagining "of the Israelite body politic." The Reverend Milman taught that "tribe after tribe was exterminated."[83]

Here Macaulay shelved his story of England as a Protestant but increasingly post-Christian nation. Instead, his appeal to biblical precedents continued his story of Bacon as the new Moses, who, after teaching England the civilizing truths of progress and utility, led it to the verge of empire. In Ireland the English became as Israel and Cromwell their Joshua.

> The rebellion of the aboriginal race had excited in England a strong religious and national aversion to them . . . [Cromwell] had vanquished them; he knew that they were in his power; and he regarded them as a band of malefactors and idolaters . . . Drogheda was as Jericho; and Wexford as Ai. To the remains of the old population the conqueror granted a peace, such as that which Israel granted to the Gibeonites. He made them hewers of wood and drawers of water . . . Under favourable circumstances, Ireland would have found in him a most just and beneficent ruler. She found in him a tyrant; not a small, teasing tyrant, such as those who have so long been her curse and her shame, but one of those awful tyrants who, at long intervals, seem to be sent on earth, like avenging angels, with some high commission of destruction and renovation . . . The thing most alien from his clear intellect and his commanding spirit was petty persecution. He knew how to tolerate; and he knew how to destroy . . . He had a great and definite object in view, to make Ireland thoroughly English, to make Ireland another Yorkshire and Norfolk.[84]

Dropping his sham-religious voice, Macaulay began calculating. Ireland was then "thinly peopled"—it was not—and had Cromwell's policy been adhered to for fifty years, Britons would have made it their habitat. Thus they would have joined the vanguard of civilization.

> The tide of population ran almost as strongly as that which now runs from Massachusetts and Connecticut to the states behind the Ohio. The native race was driven back before the advancing van of

the Anglo-Saxon population, as the American Indians or the tribes of Southern Africa are now driven back before the white settlers. Those fearful phenomena which have almost invariably attended the planting of civilised colonies in uncivilised countries, and which had been known to the nations of Europe only by distant and questionable rumour, were now publicly exhibited in their sight. The words, "extirpation," "eradication," were often in the mouths of the English back settlers of Leinster and Munster.[85]

In 1838 Macaulay's understanding of race was fluid and rhetorical, defined less by biological distinctiveness than by different national characters shaped by climate, language, and history. What mattered to him was that the "English back settlers" were vanquishing the obstinately uncivilized Irish.

He then considered the most extreme case of a basic political question: apart from self-defense, is it ever right to kill en masse? In this case, enabling future English progress and empire determined the greatest good for the greatest number. When "extirpation" and "eradication" advanced England's greatness, they became a "rational" policy: "cruel words, yet in their cruelty, containing more mercy than much softer expressions which have since been sanctioned by universities and cheered by Parliaments. For it is in truth more merciful to extirpate a hundred thousand human beings at once, and to fill the void with a well-governed population, than to misgovern millions through a long succession of generations. We can much more easily pardon tremendous severities inflicted for a great object, than an endless series of paltry vexations and oppressions inflicted for no rational object at all." He imagined that "Oliver" pursued a strategy of slaughtering droves of Irish aborigines—they were for Macaulay a disembodied abstraction—and he generalized his error into an imperial maxim. But privately and publicly he professed "heartily" to hate slavery. Whatever his real attitude, the abolitionists taught him to use a lethal word in pursuit of a good cause. Six years earlier Zachary had obliged Tom to champion Buxton's motion to appoint a parliamentary committee to study the immediate abolition of slavery throughout the empire. One word captured the "general impression" of the committee's report: "Slavery was an evil for which there was no remedy but extirpation . . . its extirpation would be safe."[86]

Macaulay wrote to persuade his readers that he was articulating common sense about the most merciful way of dealing with recalcitrant aborigines. If parroting the Bible and asserting first-person-plural authority ("We can much more easily pardon . . .") seemed insufficient, he pictured a happy outcome. England approximated the model of universal well-being. Although Cromwell failed to extirpate "a hundred thousand human beings at once" and thereby solve the Irish question, the immediate results of his "iron despotism" were salutary: "Ireland was fast becoming English. Civilisation and wealth were making rapid progress in almost every part of the island." Despite that cheerful fantasy, there was no solving the Irish problem with half-measures in either 1659 or 1838. Religious hatred remained endemic, and Irish peasants refuted Macaulay's vision of the world's becoming a marketplace of growing production and consumption. He insisted that had Cromwell persevered, he "would . . . inevitably have produced the effect which he contemplated, an entire decomposition and reconstruction of society."[87] Unfortunately, such a "high commission of destruction and renovation" no longer seemed possible.

Was Macaulay the first powerful nineteenth-century European to recommend publicly not occasional doses of terror and slaughter but an ethic of civilizing and imperial extirpation? The book he "reviewed" contained only "softer expressions." It mentioned Sir John Temple's history as "still a work of some repute," and its account of William's return to Ireland was essentially domestic. Macaulay ignored William's *Essay upon the Present State and Settlement of Ireland* (1668), which recommended brutalizing the native Irish and pilloried the Scots but without advocating mass slaughter as good policy. Courtenay assumed that his own philanthropic contemporaries would reject "Sir William Temple's views of the fit mode of governing Ireland." Macaulay, however, presented Temple as the type both of the English ascendancy in his day and of the colonists who provoked Buxton and the other founders of the Aborigines Protection Society: "He troubled himself as little about the welfare of the remains of the old Celtic population, as an English farmer on the Swan River troubles himself about the New Hollanders, or a Dutch boor at the Cape about Caffres": barbarians all.[88]

To lighten the piece Macaulay satirized the battle of the books, a "most idle and contemptible controversy . . . touching the comparative merit of the ancient and modern writers." By insisting "that the human race is constantly degenerating, and that the oldest books in every kind are the best," Temple produced a "vast mass of absurdity." Here as elsewhere, how Macaulay read the Greek and Latin classics enabled him to hold in tension his appetite for them and his faith in progress: "I have a strong and acute enjoyment of great works of the imagination; but I have never habituated myself to dissect them. Perhaps I enjoy them the more keenly for that very reason." His aesthetic style of reading beggared him as a critic: "I have never written a page . . . on poetry or the fine arts which I would not burn if I had the power." In contrast, he found "several things on historical, political, and moral questions," including "Temple," of enduring importance.[89]

About civilizing slaughter Macaulay wrote with confidence that he would not shock—"For it is in truth"—and in 1838 readers of "Temple" seemed either to ignore or acquiesce in its argument. The sole complaint he recorded concerned his story about a dalliance of Jonathan Swift. He achieved, however, no immediate conquest of the English public mind. Because it remained indifferent to the empire, he labored to reinforce the lesson of "Temple." During the 1830s and 1840s French opinion showed itself to be more forward-looking. Alexis de Tocqueville exemplified "a striking development in the liberalism of his age": "His political career as a defender of the French conquest and rule of Algeria, even if this meant great violence toward indigenous Algerians, helps us understand the eclipse, during the wave of imperial expansion in the mid-nineteenth century, of the earlier suspicion of empire." Tocqueville's unwillingness "to see the natives exterminated" suggests that, unlike Macaulay, he was morally conflicted or perhaps just muddleheaded. If so, the first great student of American democracy resembled its first great theorist. A quarter-century before "Temple," Thomas Jefferson anticipated its conclusion, but in rebuke. Writing in a superior cosmopolitan voice, the former president insisted of the American Indians: "The confirmed brutalization, if not extermination of this race in our America is therefore to form an added chapter in the English history of the same colored man in Asia, and of the brethren of their own color in Ireland and wherever else Anglo-mercantile cupidity can find a two-penny interest in deluging the earth with blood." As president Jefferson had often privately recommended exterminating Indian tribes that resisted the ad-

vance of American civilization.[90] With bloodless courage Macaulay published the thoughts of many of his eminent contemporaries. Neither
they nor a complacent posterity ever challenged him. As late as 1974 the
Everyman Library reprinted "Temple" in his *Critical and Historical Essays*
whole and without comment.

The essay was no aberration. Macaulay routinely used his ethical calculus to determine when it is right to kill en masse. Six years before
"Temple," for example, he applied it in reviewing a book on the origins
of the French Revolution. That its author was a collaborator of the late
Jeremy Bentham allowed Macaulay to extol Bentham as a man worthy
of comparison with Bacon: "we would at all times speak with the reverence which is due to a great original thinker, and to a sincere and ardent
friend of the human race . . . in the same rank with Galileo, and with
Locke, the man who found jurisprudence a gibberish and left it as a science . . . his opinions formed a system, which, whether sound or unsound, is more exact, more entire, and more consistent within itself than
any other . . . one of the greatest men of the age." Mixing Bentham and
the Bible, he went on to inventory the revolutionary bloodletting. The
book depicted Edmund Burke as the accurate if unbalanced prophet of
the Reign of Terror, but Macaulay framed an artful double-negative to
evaluate it. He was unconvinced "that the French Revolution was not a
great blessing to mankind . . . We can perceive that the evil was tempo-
rary, and the good durable." The Terror was another case of the "high
commission of destruction and renovation." France needed "demolition."
If scripture—here an emollient reference was almost inevitable—revealed that "there is a time for everything,—a time to set up, and a time
to pull down," it was "the natural, the almost universal law" of history
that the establishment of "good government, of temperate liberty, and
liberal order" required "insurrections and proscriptions."[91]

Macaulay's story of civilizing and progressive slaughter as history with
a happy ending was a judgment after the fact rather than a timeless
maxim of politics. It amounted to the secular expropriation of Providence. In the late eighteenth century William Robertson discovered it
working through the events of the 1500s to create the Atlantic world.
His *History of the Discovery and Settlement of America* (1777) retailed an
unsparing version of the Black Legend. Marauders and cutthroats, the
conquistadores destroyed first noble savages almost worthy of Eden and

then the civilizations of the bloodthirsty Aztecs and the gentle Incas. But Robertson discovered happiness as the unintended outcome. If the "first visible consequence" of the Spanish Empire in America "was the diminution of the ancient inhabitants, to a degree equally astonishing and deplorable," it culminated in 1772 with the viceroy of New Spain returning home, not gory and laden with booty but "with the admiration and applause of a grateful people, whom his government had rendered happy."[92]

Where Robertson discovered Providence finally transforming carnage into progress, Macaulay saw history working out the mundane logic of climate, deep structures of language and culture, and the deeds of nations and individuals. He agreed with Robertson that expanding human happiness was the end of history but saw progress and utility driving it. That was how he applied Bentham's principle that the "greatest happiness of the greatest number is the foundation of morals and legislation" in framing both historical verdicts and policy recommendations. Macaulay succeeded in part because the "felicific calculus" seemed only common sense to many pious Britons who lacked his enthusiasm for the atheist Bentham. Over a century earlier an enlightened Scots divine had written, "That action is best, which procures the greatest happiness for the greatest numbers." As Macaulay knew, everything depends on what happiness means in practice—and for whom.[93]

Slaughtering other people to achieve religious, political, and economic goals is timeless. Macaulay was not pioneering a revolution in political ethics but trying to avert one by repackaging sundry atrocities as a modern systematic policy. Throughout the eighteenth-century Atlantic world, philanthropists—the word was coined about 1736—flourished in many hues. The Spanish Royal Academy unanimously elected Robertson a corresponding member because he told his monitory tale of their nation's imperial slaughter by ending happily. More immediately, the history of "eradication," one of Macaulay's two mercifully cruel words, evokes the ethical turn that fostered the sensibility of the members of the Aborigines Protection Society. When coined during the sixteenth century, it meant the killing of nations or groups. Later its meaning broadened to include the lethal uprooting of things, sometimes with virtually human effects—in 1646 a writer asserted that, on eradication, the "Roots of Mandrakes doe make a noyse." By the middle of the eighteenth century the pious Dr. Johnson internalized "eradication" to capture moral self-correction, and during Macaulay's lifetime Jefferson continued using the word to mean the uprooting of vices. But its original meaning has prevailed: "The insane, communist-inspired party, led by Pol Pot, tried to eradicate the entire educated population and turn Cambodia back into a primitive agrarian society. Millions were slaughtered or died of starvation before Vietnam . . . brought the regime down."[94]

In "Temple," Macaulay abruptly turned away from his tale of Swift's unhappy dalliance to explain the "difference . . . between a political pamphlet by Johnson, and a political pamphlet by Swift." It was a digression amusing to superficial readers but starkly meaningful for knowledgeable ones: a rebuke to those who would direct eradication inward or invoke Providence eventually writing straight with crooked lines. Johnson's *Taxation No Tyranny* (1776) showed him to be "a man who has never been out of his study." In contrast, Swift's slash-and-burn Tory polemic exhibited the sureness of "a man who has passed his whole life in the midst of public business." Experience and temperament had equipped Swift to grasp the sometimes brutal imperatives of power. Naïvely, Johnson had insisted on counting its costs. Attacking the rebellious Americans, his tale of "the contest between interest and justice" in the planting of large colonies condemned every imperial project. Johnson identified all of them with primitive and retrograde epochs. He imagined "Huns and Vandals" sailing to the Western Hemisphere after 1492, "by myriads under their several chiefs to take possession of regions smiling with pleasure and waving with fertility, from which the naked inhabitants were unable to repel them." A man born out of time, Christopher Columbus was one of "those candidates of sovereignty" who fostered "vagrant excursion and fortuitous hostility." In 1498, a "year hitherto disastrous to mankind," he reached the American mainland, and the Portuguese Vasco da Gama arrived in India. Europeans conquered widely on both continents, seizing land and booty, slaughtering helpless natives, and planting colonies that were "mere extensions, or processes of empire": "The colonies of England differ no otherwise from those of other nations."[95]

The Tory Johnson's verdict resembled that of his Whig friend Edmund Burke. In 1784 he was working himself into the rage that led him to spearhead the impeachment of Warren Hastings, the steely builder of Britain's Indian empire: "We had already lost one empire, perhaps, as a punishment for the cruelties authorized in another. And men might exert their ingenuities in qualifying facts as they pleased, but there was only one standard by which the Judge of all the earth would try them. It was not whether the interest of the East India Company made them necessary, but whether they coincided with the prior interests of humanity, of substantial justice, with those rights which were *paramount to all others.*" Macaulay admired some of Burke's rhetoric on India, but he grew to revere Hastings as "one of the greatest men that England ever produced."[96] Believing not in the judgment of Providence but in history as a winner's tale, he rehabilitated Hastings' reputation in 1841.

As much as Johnson, Macaulay understood "the violence that persistently attended the expansion and defense of European power over the colonized world," and Johnson haunted him. After finishing "Temple," he toyed with commissioning a painting of "Johnson's literary club—the prominent figures to be Johnson, Burke, Gibbon, Fox, Goldsmith and Boswell": Johnson "should be warm in argument." His indictment of the modern European expansion into India and the Americas challenged Macaulay to sharpen his portrait of the imperial English as inculpable because their advancing progress and civilization made them virtually the new "chosen race." Should their nineteenth-century empire be merely a blameworthy and transient episode, the cheery secular version of Robertson's providential story peddled by the *Edinburgh Review* might suffice: not God but history writing straight with crooked lines.[97] Macaulay, however, did not project history as superseding England's empire. He offered no plan whereby peoples long conquered and territories long settled, though perhaps once exploited, would now be nurtured in order to be efficiently surrendered. In 1838 England's interests demanded that it continue to rule Ireland and expand in India, the imperial project seemed dynamic, and its rules were constant. Violence continued to build empires, just as repression and the threat of violence sustained them.

Macaulay imagined modern empires as civilizing and civilization itself as a single river. It flowed from ancient Athens to modern London onward and now upward, without tributaries or branches. Rational languages and literatures nurtured civilization, which in 1838 was swelling with rational calculation, increased knowledge, and material comfort. Everything impeding civilization's flow was contemptible: "a single shelf of a good European library is worth the whole native literature of India and Arabia." From projecting the eradication of aborigines' languages and literatures, it was a manageable stretch to recommending the eradication of aborigines who resisted the civilization that would uplift future generations. Macaulay did not anticipate Mr. Kurtz's "luminous and terrifying" coda to his "moving appeal to every altruistic sentiment": "Exterminate all the brutes!" But against the Aborigines Protection Society and the memory of his detested father he urged the ethic of killing thousands of nameless and faceless people because they spoke irrational languages, lived primitive lives, and resisted England's civilizing mission. Macaulay was not uniquely responsible for Great Britain's midnineteenth-century "turn to empire," which made it "by far the most persistently bellicose of the European powers." But his fluent and plausible bellicosity, uneasy about the present but discerning favorable "signs of the times" and prophesying a better future, was widely heard.[98]

During the eighteenth century many who accepted an ethic of common humanity had seen civilization as more complex. Robertson's last book was the *Historical Disquisition Concerning the Knowledge Which the Ancients Had of India* (1791). Written to support Hastings' impeachment, it depicted India as an old civilization, not yet superseded, perhaps differing from modern Britain's in degree but not in kind, and Sanskrit as a classical language like Greek. Robertson also believed that human nature was always and everywhere the same, so that in all our variety all of us remain human. At the end of the eighteenth century most Europeans in India marked no essential difference between ordinary life there and at home. By 1834 Asia's prosperity still seemed to differ from the United Kingdom's in degree rather than in kind. From our vantage point, it is easy to associate Bengal, where "naked corpses" were swept away by a filthy "boiling coffee-coloured" river, and Merseyside, where Margaret Macaulay Cropper, an intelligent and privileged woman, died at twenty-two of scarlet fever because she drank from the well that drained her barnyard. There was, however, much greater distance between the two societies than in 1791. It continued growing until many found them essentially unlike: the "East is East, and West is West, and never the twain shall meet" version that excepted shared valor.[99]

The British and Foreign Aborigines Protection Society barely survived its birth. After enjoying for a few years the sympathy of two evangelicals weighty in the Colonial Office—both Macaulay's political friends —it endured phantomlike into the early twentieth century. Even a recent American effort to construct a history for late twentieth-century "humanitarian interventionism" overlooks it. Less than two years after addressing the society's first meeting, Buxton thought of withdrawing from it. Instead, he stayed on at a distance and occupied himself with other uplifting schemes. By 1840 he was focused on mounting an expedition to uproot slavery at its source by Christianizing, enriching, and civilizing the Niger Valley. Informed by "a consciousness of Britain's expanding power and with it that characteristically Victorian dream of creating a new world order," the Niger Expedition ended in disaster. Its widely noticed failure provoked a reaction against philanthropy abroad, especially in Africa. For once Thomas Carlyle and Charles Dickens agreed: "abolitionist and missionary activities were distractions from more appropriate concerns about poverty and misgovernment at home." But the expedition also presaged further imperial and civilizing conquests, particularly in Africa. Political scientists' learned debates about the responsibility of universalistic ethics for the ruthlessness of such projects are inconclusive.[100] They serve, however, as a useful reminder that universalism without reciprocity easily degenerates into the strong's insistence that their might makes right, even lethally.

By speaking what for most imperialists was and remained unspeakable though not unthinkable for decades, Macaulay helped to frustrate the effort to reverse history by acting to save native peoples. Amounting to acquiescence, the universal public silence about his argument in "Temple" sufficed to preserve the ethical status quo. His authorship was known, and the public minded that he was Zachary's son, that philanthropy was a continuing experiment rather than a set of commandments, that the abolitionists who had founded the Aborigines Protection Society regarded him as an ally, and that he seemed to be articulating a nasty piece of common sense. Buxton and his colleagues read in Tocqueville that "the Indian nations of North America are doomed to perish." Tocqueville soon became an honorary member of the society but without changing his mind about the fate of either aboriginal Americans or conquered Algerians. A similar dissonance between noble desire and brutal expectation perhaps led Buxton to decide that the Niger Expedition held more promise of success than reversing "the progress of oppression in our colonies." Instead of demanding a revolution in moral attitudes, the expedition seemed only to require extending Britain's policy of suppressing the African slave trade. It mattered, finally, that Oliver Cromwell was becoming an English icon. Carlyle detested Macaulay, but "Cromwell had been much on Carlyle's mind from 1839 onwards"—a few months after the publication of "Temple." His own vastly popular biography of Cromwell appeared six years later, outdoing Macaulay in shamreligious awe about the 1649 Irish campaign: "Oliver Cromwell did believe in God's Judgments; and did not believe in the rose-water plan of Surgery;—which, in fact, is this Editor's case too!"[101]

At the end of the century Joseph Chamberlain as colonial secretary eschewed awe to restate Macaulay's case as the official justification of progressive, civilizing imperialism: "You cannot have omelettes without breaking eggs; you cannot destroy the practices of barbarism, of slavery, of superstition, which for centuries have desolated the interior of Africa, without the use of force; but if you will fairly contrast the gain to humanity with the price which *we* are bound to pay for it, I think you may well rejoice." Of course, they, not "we," paid the price. Leo Tolstoy knew that there "are no conditions of life to which a man cannot get accustomed, especially if he sees them accepted by everyone around him." While it was so with the human toll of civilizing progress, Macaulay came to seem praiseworthy even in Dublin. In *Portrait of the Artist as a Young Man* James Joyce's alter ego hears a priest declare: "I believe that Lord Macaulay was a man who probably never committed a mortal sin in his life, that is to say, a deliberate mortal sin."[102]

[5]

STATESMAN

"Temple" done, Macaulay left London bound for Rome on 12 October 1838 with no plans except to sketch an essay rehabilitating Lord Clive of India and to return in February. Traveling alone, he suffered the longest separation from his family since Cambridge and started his first journal. His detailed entries are more self-preoccupied than self-searching, but they show a man enduring an emotional crisis that essentially eluded him. It would end in Rome, widen his perspective, and expand his understanding of power without cooling his desire for it. Usually a hindrance to action, self-knowledge was not among the preoccupations of most great Victorians. The trajectory of the exceptionally introspective John Stuart Mill provides a suggestive contrast to Macaulay's. As a young adult, Mill endured what he called a "mental crisis" that was at least as much intellectual as emotional. After reading some of the Romantics whom Macaulay scorned, Mill rethought and rejected a life governed by calculation, eventually discovering both France and his capacity for love. Macaulay proved to be immovably utilitarian, materialist, and insular. Suspicious of foreigners and testy, he haggled over prices and went at tradesmen.[1]

On his thirty-eighth birthday he boarded a steamer for Lyons, thinking "of Job, Swift, and Antony"—all men who rued their birth. The next day his spirits lifted. After dinner and "a bottle of good wine" he wryly endured a flea-infested bed. It would take practice for him to learn from what he found alien. Talking with a Frenchman merely confirmed his opinions about everything from the squalor of the Midi to the difficulty of remaking a society—the implications for what he wished for India and Ireland escaped him. When the conversation turned to the Church of England, Macaulay "set him right": "he asked me if the body of the clergy were not Arians. I told him that . . . I believed the number not to be very great." In 1838 the establishment appeared to him unified and embattled but also dangerous. Alien places were generally as closed to him as their inhabitants. Far from stimulating his curiosity, the papal city of Avignon confirmed that the Middle Ages were about darkness and tastelessness.[2] Mill retired to Avignon, where he died and lies buried next to his wife. Lionized in life, Macaulay would be enshrined in West-minster Abbey surrounded mostly by the remains and monuments of strangers.

Although Englishmen traveled south in their thousands, Macaulay kept aloof from them, which made touring lonelier. The kindness of the British consul in Marseilles, a distant relative, failed to offset the silence from home. He felt "disappointed and a little hurt." Marseilles offered his first serious glimpse of Catholicism. Though Sunday, it was no Sabbath. Seeing through enlightened and evangelical English eyes, he bristled as he walked. Lively crowds and brilliant shops filled the new city, but the old stank "worse than the native town of Calcutta." The churches he wanted to see were there. Moving from one to another and smelling the rank worshipers, he marveled "that so many reasonable beings could come together to see a man bow, drink, bow again, wipe a cup, wrap up a napkin, spread his arms, and gesticulate with his hands, and to hear a low muttering which they could not understand, interrupted by the occasional jingling of a bell." It was all "mummery," but he noted that "the mass seems to have as great attraction for the people of Marseilles" —including men—"as the oratory of the most celebrated Evangelical preachers for the pious ladies of London." Leaving France still without word from home, he took consolation in England's modern superiority.[3]

Italy would enlarge both Macaulay's imagination and his desire, but fog enshrouded Genoa when he arrived. Missing his family, above all "my own little Baba," he found solace in home truths and Marsala, which he drank "too freely"—headache. After going to bed "impatient" for Florence, he awoke to discover Genoa: "one of the most remarkable days of my life." Nine pages in his journal record his sensual awakening. The *palazzi* shamed London's great mansions. There were disappointments, but the interiors of churches were a revelation to him: they "dazzled and pleased me more than I can express. It was like the awakening of a new sense. It was the discovery of a new pleasure . . . a new world." Days earlier in France he had scorned ornamentation and praised buildings that were "useful," "simple," and "regular." The contrast between Genoa's gorgeous patrimony, mostly from the sixteenth century, when it was free and imperial, and its current meanness confirmed that political power feeds the opulence on which thriving civilizations depend.[4]

Approaching Florence on a brightening day, he continued to see Italy with bookish eyes. Olive trees brought to mind Washington Irving, Thucydides, Sophocles, Lorenzo de Medici, and Virgil. On that All Souls' Day beginning to see beyond books for the first time since he was a little boy caused him to forget his plan to prepare for Rome by reading about it. In Santa Croce Michelangelo's tomb and Dante's monument combined to make him feel briefly as provincial as a first-time American visitor to Westminster Abbey. In Florence, however, he remained a tourist confident of his privileged insight into what was necessarily closed to him. All "the pleasure that I have derived from" Dante inspired possessive tears. Largely ignorant of medieval theology, Macaulay knew "that very few people have ever had their minds more thoroughly penetrated with the spirit of any great work than mine is with that of the Divine Comedy." As darkness set in, he stepped on Machiavelli's grave. Back in his hotel for dinner he had "the first tea that I have tasted since I left England—found it tolerable." His days were too short. Although "sights" rather than words fed his imagination, he hungered for "literary and political gossip." Suffering migraines and welcoming English kindness, he still shunned English company. Depression and crippling headaches are comorbid.[5]

Writing to Hannah, he dwelt on his encounter with the comic "Yankee clergyman" who propagated "Bacon" in the States and hinted at his own emotional condition: "I sit quietly an hour or two every morning in the finest churches, watching the ceremonial, and the demeanour of the congregation. I seldom pass less than an hour daily in the Tribune, where the Venus de Medici stands, surrounded by other masterpieces in sculpture and painting." Over the centuries Italy's art has caused innumerable northern Europeans to discover their senses and sometimes briefly to lose their minds. Florentine psychiatrists have diagnosed "la sindrome di Stendhal," a collection of nasty psychosomatic reactions, including some that afflicted the French novelist when he first visited the city.[6] Macaulay's sensual awakening proved to be less traumatizing and finally Victorian in its inhibition.

Architecture began to fascinate him and Catholicism to intrigue him, not primarily as an alien religion but as a mysterious amalgam of power and eroticism. In San Lorenzo on Guy Fawkes Day, sacred to English antipopery, and unable to visit Michelangelo's sculptures, he "lounged about the Church discontentedly, heard mass said, saw several female penitents at Confession, and wished myself in the chair of the priest." Thinking of Rubens' "female figures"—"coarse, hulking, flabby, fish-wives"—he was "impatient to see the Venus de Medici;—found my way to the Tribune—There she was. I never saw so lovely a statue. I have seen perhaps a thousand casts of it, and I never saw any that gave me the faint-est notion of its adorable beauty." His solitary reverie was disturbed by some cold marble nudes unfortunately placed near "a glorious female figure by Titian," richly tinted. "But these [sculptures] were thrown into the shade by the Venus. When I left the Tribune I repaired to the Hall of Niobe. The figure of Niobe clasping her daughter is most pathetic and fine. The other figures disappointed me. I observed an exquisite Leda"—presumably Bartolomeo Ammanati's of her nude, kissing and coupling with Zeus embodied as a swan, now in the Bargello.[7] The rest of that line and the nine that follow are effaced.

Still avoiding English tourists, who "overrun the country," he called on Lord Holland's heir, from 1823 mostly resident on the Continent to escape his mother and his amours. His rented palazzo convinced Macaulay that the English aristocracy must live more ostentatiously. Part of its appeal was Caroline Fox, Lord Holland's formidable sister: "the very jewel of old maids, and a prodigious favourite of mine." Imperial and sexual desire jostled in Macaulay's mind. After reading of "rumors of war in India" and considering who should take charge there, he went to "the Gallery again, and went more attentively through the whole series of Roman Emperors." Then he was "struck again by that exquisite Leda," which seemed to him—in Latin—as "the highest beauty—the highest desire." Soon his reverie snapped: "disgusted by a loathsome Hermaphrodite. To the Tribune to sweeten my imagination with the Ve-nus de Medici. Admired her more than yesterday." Wandering the streets, he was astonished "at the meanness of the shops in Italy," not just sub-

English but "below the shops of the fourth rate towns of France." Gestating a theory about the Protestant origin of modern times, he began to feel "near to content."[8]

The next day he first read Mass: "strange and almost disgraceful that it should be so." He thought the Latin "barbarous," unlike the majestic English of the Prayer Book, but he resolved "to frequent the Romish worship till I come thoroughly to understand the ceremonial." Before dining with the Foxes, he again "pored on that lovely Venus." That night three diners at the Palazzo Amerighi embodied the variety of elite English religious experience and the urgency of fabricating a sense of shared Englishness apart from even a vestigial Anglicanism. Reared "in freethinking Enlightenment circles," the future Lord Holland "had a profound religious experience in Rome in December 1825. It is not clear whether he became a Roman Catholic at this date or . . . on his deathbed." Known for her "high principles and tolerant religious views," Miss Fox was a tenacious radical: "Bentham, not her only suitor, dared to propose marriage and, though refused, retained a romantic attachment to her." Finally, there was Macaulay himself, tenaciously skeptical, tiring of Florence, "impatient to be in St Peter's," and buying and studying Catholic service books: "barbarism." Seeing the Dominican convent of San Marco complicated his developing theory about religion and the progress of civilization. Unlike northern Protestants, sixteenth-century Italian reformers "were already Atheists . . . being more highly educated than their neighbours and living close to the headquarters of a most corrupt form of Christianity in the times of its very worst corruption, had already—that is the learned who dared to think for themselves—got far beyond Protestantism." Sometimes his excruciating headaches made him feel "an invalid."[9]

Before departing, Macaulay received from the prime minister an invitation to reenter Parliament and become judge advocate general, a grand-sounding, second-tier, but lucrative post. It paid £2,500 a year—with a 2007 purchasing power of £168,036. The money was "above the market-price of my services" but insufficient to persuade him "to give up my liberty and my studies." The Reverend Sydney Smith, a catty friend, intuited that Macaulay, "like Ladies who resolve upon celibacy if they have no offers," had his uses and his price. Melbourne wanted him as a mouthpiece, not as an administrator. Responding to the feeler with metaphors of courtship, Macaulay signaled his availability for politics, but "as an independent man" after winning a seat in the House of Commons without "improper expense"—he remembered paying the bill for Leeds. His proposal to serve the government according to his own lights rather than their needs raised the ante. To Hannah he confided that he wanted "the power to effect great things," which meant a seat in the cabinet: "An independent member of parliament,—nay an independent man of letters out of parliament has far more of such power than a Judge Advocate." Outside the family he described his motives in terms of "public duty," "personal sacrifice," and "service to the public."[10]

Roman Inspirations

Passing the site of an ancient battlefield en route to Rome, he read Livy and took in the countryside through the eyes of Virgil and Horace. It was important to arrive in daylight: "to see the neighbourhood, to see the dome of St Peter's from a distance, to see the city disclose itself by degrees." On 15 November Macaulay entered, thinking of power and repulsing a human plague: "I am proud to say that I have given not a single piece of copper to a single beggar in Italy . . . I am very far from going all the lengths of some Utilitarians about almsgiving." The key to his calculating morality was the qualified "some Utilitarians." He never heard of cost-benefit analyses, but now they were virtually instinctual for him. A few weeks later he reacted to news of the defeat of a gang of Americans who had invaded Canada. Fearing a popular cry for "punishments so rigorous as would dishonor the English Govt in the eyes of all Europe and in our own eyes ten years hence," he recalled that the duke of Cumberland in the Highlands "did only what all England was clamouring for," but then "all England changed its mind," discrediting him. To select ten or twelve invaders as "examples" and either transport the others or keep them "on the roads at hard labour" would "do more good than a great wholesale execution."[11]

Having felt the eroticism of art in Florence, Macaulay now began to experience its power. After settling in his hotel and seeing a doctor about his headaches—"prescribed rhubarb and other stomachics"—he

> walked instantly to St Peter's. I was so much excited by the expectation of what I was to see that I could notice nothing else—I was quite nervous. The colonnade in front is noble—very, very noble

—Yet it disappointed me; and would have done so had it been the portico of Paradise. The front of the Church disappointed me, though I expected little . . . a most wretched composition. The outside of the dome, though fine, is decidedly inferior to the outside of the dome of St Paul's. In I went and I was for a minute fairly stunned by the magnificence and harmony of the interior. I never in my life saw, and never, I suppose, shall again see anything so astonishingly beautiful, I really could have cried with pleasure.

The basilica's size mattered: "proportions in architecture are good or bad according as the effect which they produce is sublime or mean . . . One chief ingredient of the sublime in architecture is the notion of great human power exerted—Wherever there is a building of vast extent this ingredient of the sublime is found."[12]

Imperial Rome also attracted him, but the Church of Rome's mysterious empire dominated his imagination. After communing "with Cicero and Caesar and Horace and Virgil" outside the Pantheon and vowing to "return daily" to the Coliseum, "I hastened to St Peter's again. I passed two hours in the Church." Its confessionals embodied living power: "Lingua Hispanica—Lingua Anglica—Lingua Germanica &c—There is something very imperial, very metropolitan, in this." Reviewing the history of the papacy in his mind, he decided that the landscape before him agreed "pretty well" with his description of it in what would become one of the *Lays of Ancient Rome*. Inside the Pantheon, he noted "that its dimensions nearly correspond with those of the Cupola of St Peter's." Powerful popes and the Coliseum's "imperial air" impressed him, but he also saw its Christian shrines as "appropriate . . . because of the number of martyrdoms." The Roman Ghetto, where "the Jewry of Rome"—"these strange people"—were "locked up every night" and the threat of mobs exemplified papal maladministration. British politics remained inescapable: "if I am to be in public life I would rather be with the Whigs in opposition than in power." Free of migraines but edgy and musing about the decline and fall of ancient Rome, he imagined "wealthy Patagonians and New Zealanders" visiting the ruins of London in future centuries.[13]

Now uniquely susceptible to new experience, he did not rethink either his core beliefs or his governing passions. Instead, his mind darted from Rome to India to home. Dining in the English College—"strictly English. Neither Scotch nor Irish are admitted"—he met an "exceedingly absurd" old India hand: "I have since heard what is quite compatible with his absurdity that he is a great orientalist." It was of a piece with his reaction to some statuary in the Vatican: "Hindoo deformity." A disagreeable encounter with a radical English politician reminded him of his own "real sympathy with human suffering" and "dislike of oppression." He also remained sure of his human judgment. Dining in an Englishwoman's apartment, he found his hostess "coarse and bold, and unfeminine, with an affectation of fashion which ten years ago I should perhaps have been taken in by, but which now merely moves my ridicule."[14] He was recovering his primness, shaken in Florence by Venus and Leda.

Grasping his ignorance of Catholicism, he wanted to learn and use what he learned. The Jesuits' global sweep impressed him, but St. Peter's was magnetic: "I looked again into St Peter's with ever new delight and admiration"; "went to St Peter's again—This is becoming a daily visit." The Vatican energized his historical imagination. In the museum's mosaic atelier he had a premonition of the National Portrait Gallery, which he would help invent. Three weeks later he spent a "great part" of the morning in the basilica "meditating on many things, particularly on the plan of my history." He began conflating the imperial and the papal cities. The great Roman churches became "lovely Italian temples." The paradox of the papacy intrigued him. It ran a worldwide government "on the superstition of one half, and on the taste and curiosity of the other half," while systematically misgoverning the Papal States: "a Brahminical Govt—Everything is in the hands of the clergy."[15]

Before Macaulay grasped that theatrics are integral to the artifice of power as well as to the power of art, the Italian ceremonies seemed just entertainments: "Certainly whatever faults the Catholic system may have it has the merit of being an agreeable occupation and diversion. In England religious duties are associated . . . with the notion of dullness. The number of good folks to whom Sunday is not a bore and who are not better pleased when it is over than when it begins I suspect is extremely small. Now in Italy the religious worship of the multitude is the most lively festive thing in the world. I, who am a mere looker on, would a great deal sooner go to any of their fine ceremonies than to Covent Garden Theatre." He began imagining Pope Gregory XVI as an imperial figure. Seeing him in his carriage brought to mind "the Governor General's airing at Calcutta." It was harder for Macaulay to grasp that the pontiff seemed powerful because he was revered as sacred: "half idolatrous." A friendly English Catholic tutored him, but his reaction to the continuity he discovered in Santa Maria in Trastevere owed more to Thomas Hobbes: "The Church is supported on pillars of unequal diameters and different orders pillaged from ancient temples; and with the symbols of the gods of Egypt still visible." The furtive eroticism of Florence continued to recede. Although the "beauty of the sculptures particularly of the female figures charms me more and more," he thought the "admired Domenichino of Susanna sprawling in a bath and the elders peeping . . . vulgar, indecent, and not attractive." After ninety minutes in St. Peter's the next day—"still growing pleasure and wonder"—he bought a breviary, out of which Catholic clerics and religious pray daily, and read it with close attention.[16]

For all that, his vision of the city remained aesthetic and political. Folk Catholicism always repelled him. Empire—especially England's and Rome's—preoccupied him: "Read a good deal of Gibbon—I don't know why I had not looked at the part which related to Rome since my arrival here. It interested me much. I went to St Peter's in the afternoon." Rereading *The Decline and Fall of the Roman Empire* showed Macaulay how a skeptical but patriotic historian should not treat religion in an age of religious revival: "He writes like a man who had received some personal injury from Xtianity and wished to be revenged on it and on all its professors." He considered how and where to begin "my history": "I am more and more in love with the subject, I really think that posterity will not willingly let my book die." But he was also full of Ranke and the history of the papacy: "the still more extraordinary empire which, after all the shocks which it has sustained, is still full of life and perverted energy."[17]

On Christmas Eve he attended Papal Vespers: "I found Gladstone among the crowd and accosted him, as we had met, though we had never been introduced to each other. He received my advances with great *empressement* indeed. We had a good deal of pleasant talk." Disappointed by the service, Macaulay left early. On Christmas Day he returned for the papal Mass. The pope disappointed until Macaulay associated him with a familiar face: "Lord William Bentinck." Despite the incomprehensible Latin, the rite now mesmerized him as a ceremony of power:

> The procession—take it altogether—was the finest thing of the kind that I ever saw . . . The general coup d'oeil was superb. The whole theatre of operations was confined to the high altar & the tribune . . . But the bearing of the performance, the incomparable beauty of the edifice made the sight a very fine one. And the immense antiquity of the Papal dignity which can certainly boast of a far longer clear known and uninterrupted succession than any dignity in the world, and which links together the two great ages of human civilization, adds to the interest. Our modern feudal Kings are mere upstarts . . . The consecration of the host was very fine.

After a few criticisms, he continued:

> Nevertheless the effect was very grand. The trumpet began to sound, and at once the whole congregation sank down . . . The trumpet went on blowing with a violent sweetness which I did not know that it possessed during the elevation of the host . . . I went away soon after; for I could see nothing more of the Pope's proceedings . . . Never before did the grandeur of the Church impress me so much . . . On the whole I think high mass at St. Peter's a finer sight than a coronation at Westminster Abbey . . . The ceremonial too is generally better managed.[18]

On that Christmas Day he also felt alone and angry: "I do not know how it is that I have been in three brawls today, and with low people"— he was not eager for Italian company. Like the other deviations from his usually tidy life on the Continent, the rows owed something to his dawning anxiety over the prospect of losing Hannah and her family in September 1840, when Trevelyan was set to return to India. Years later she remembered that Tom "could never afterwards speak of it without emotion. Throughout the autumn of 1839, his misery . . . was the most painful and hourly trial." In January 1840 Trevelyan was appointed assistant secretary to the Treasury. The family regarded it as "one of the few posts in the English Civil Service which could fully compensate" him for postponing "an Indian career." Macaulay likely helped to arrange the appointment and therefore seemed to be "bound to do all that he could for the government."[19]

What began "like the awakening of a new sense" in Genoa ended not in a heightened aesthetic or erotic consciousness but in the recognition of art's capacity to enhance power. On Boxing Day he was disappointed to discover that the Venus in the Capitoline Museum "was shut up": "The statue is indeed [several words crossed-out and "naked" inserted above], but not more so than the Venus de Medici and many others. It is certainly exceedingly lovely—not so fine a work of art as that at Florence—but more attractive, more like a fine woman of flesh and blood." Because the "little group of Cupid and Psyche, and a Leda ... are imprisoned in the same cell with the Venus. I looked at the busts of the Emperors." In Florence eight weeks earlier he had turned from the imperial to the erotic. Now he felt disgust at human flesh, dying, dead, and decaying. Roman burial urns suggested to him "how much less ghastly death appears when bodies are disposed of in this way than when they are left, as with us, to that process of corruption which turns even the loveliest creatures into objects of unutterable loathing and horror." A utilitarian solution occurred to him: "If science could discover some cheap way of rapidly consuming all the soft and permeable parts of the human body [words crossed out] so that only the ashes should be left, and if these, placed in a silver urn, washed with wine, and daily mixed with fresh flowers and perfume, could be the companions of the survivor, and have a place in some niche of the house of mourning, I really think that death would have a less dreadful appearance to many minds." The depictions of slaughtered martyrs in San Stefano Rotondo appalled the author of "Temple": "I have never seen anything more offensive to [words crossed out] good feeling and good taste than this vast circle of frescoes."[20]

He felt easier considering politics. America's expanding democracy caused him to airbrush his radical past with an adverb: "When I left college it was the fashion of young liberals—I cannot say that it was ever exactly mine—to consider the American institutions as the very model of all good government. Now I find that even the most liberal men hold them exceedingly cheap." He welcomed the shift but, he thought, without fanaticism. On 29 December he went to "St Peter's for the last time.

Rambled about quite sadly. I would not have believed that it could have pained me so much to part from stone and mortar." But his mind soon turned from the power of art in Rome to the pursuit of power at home: "looks more and more like coalition. The violence of the Tory newspapers . . . The strength of the Church." Traveling to Naples, he mused on Horace and Bengal and Rome when it "was what England is now."[21]

His moral imagination remained narrow. From his hotel he enjoyed "a noble view of Vesuvius": "There is an eruption, I am glad to say, and a very considerable one. It began yesterday night, as if in honor of my coming." A cannonade had welcomed him to Calcutta. From "at least six miles off" he relished "the spectacle," mindless of the havoc on the ground. Later he heard of "mischief on the side of the mountain farthest from Naples." On seeing details, he confessed that they "far exceed anything that I had imagined." His thoughts were increasingly directed homeward. Borrowing creatively, he refined a theory about England as the end of history. As much as Adam Smith, he believed that growing commerce and prosperity defined a modern state. But Macaulay was also attentively reading "Bossuet's life." In India he had taken over the Catholic apologist's argument about Protestantism's fissiparous and rationalist tendency but as a hopeful analysis of the dampening of its zeal.[22]

The Protestant ethic, he knew, was more tenacious than its doctrines. English clocks, unlike the Neapolitan ones, illuminated the hours and the minutes, which "surely marks the different value of time—the different degree of importance ascribed to punctuality in Italy and England. On the whole however Naples seems to me the city in Italy where there is most industry and activity." That was before he took a second look at the port of Leghorn (Livorno): "It is a modern commercial place—no antiquities—no paintings . . . or local recollections. It is just such a place as Bradford or Paisley." Other Italian cities came to seem "deathlike" in their want of bustle and progress. Less passionately than in Florence, he recorded something that was later censored, as well as his unrequited curiosity about the antiquities locked in the "mysterious cabinet"—the erotica excavated from Pompeii. But he left Naples with a more serious regret. Heavy weather kept him from seeing Paestum's majestic Doric ruins. Perhaps feeling the tension between the remoteness and the presence of classical antiquity, Macaulay never entertained visiting Greece.[23]

In the end his faith in England's encompassing superiority kept him

from seeing Italy, rich in beauty, charm, and humanity as well as inefficiency, on its own terms. The steamer to France also confirmed what he
knew: "Not a window was allowed to be opened. The taste for fresh air
is, I imagine, quite peculiar to the English, and, no doubt, has much to do
with the superior health which we generally enjoy." Two days later he
reminded himself "of the great necessity of caution in travelers as to the
conclusions which they draw from what they themselves see." But he
forgot his resolution at Versailles a few days later: "I saw enough to satisfy
me that my preconceived notion . . . was quite correct." Louis XIV and
all that remained unforgivable, and the nearness of England restored his
full propriety: "Bought a wretched collection of libertine songs—tired
to death by them—threw them into the fire . . . When there is no restraint of virtue or decency, it should be the easiest thing in the world to
be exceedingly stimulating: and yet they cannot manage it." Thinking
about the French Revolution the next day, he diagnosed the defect of
modern patriotism: "the Jacobins having only temporal motives to hold
out to men, could not long keep up enthusiasm when their system was
felt to be productive of great temporal evil & of little or no temporal
good. But Jacobinism with a fulcrum in the other world is a lever with a
vengeance." He "was only a week from home," where he would continue fashioning such a fulcrum.[24]

Rebarbative Religion

Because literature mattered so much and so widely, many Victorian politicians were serious writers. None of them combined the roles more
successfully than Macaulay. Only William Ewart Gladstone and John
Stuart Mill rivaled him, but Gladstone exercised less cultural authority,
and Mill counted less politically. To Macaulay's dismay, religion was more
embroiled with both culture and politics than when he left for India.
There could be no ignoring it. Back from the Continent on 7 February
1839, he deferred rehabilitating Clive in order to deflate some of the
"strength of the Church" but without damaging its contribution to the
state's "fulcrum in the other world." His target was Gladstone's theocratic
The State in Its Relations with the Church. On his second full day home, he
"looked at Gladstone's book—The Lord hath delivered him into our
hand." He also kept at Ranke's *History of the Popes* in German—"slowly"

—and worked on his *Lays*. After St. Peter's, St. Paul's Cathedral "grievously disappointed" him. His distaste for moral crusaders was undiminished. While others arranged for his father's monument, he marked "a foolish woman who talked nonsense about cruelty to animals." Juggling a crowded social calendar—he was newly elected to the Reform Club, open only to supporters of the 1832 Act—he "worked hard" on his paper: "I think that I shall dispose completely of Gladstone's theory. I wish that I could see my way clearly to a good counter-theory. But I catch only glimpses here and there of what I take to be the truth." Full of Gladstone, Ranke, and his own poems, he resolved to "begin my history immediately." He soon discovered the encumbrance of research: "must verify many statements and turn over many books." Meanwhile he opened informal negotiations with Longman the publisher.[25]

Catching up with five years of English news was another priority. Personally, it mattered that Ellis soon became a permanent widower. Forged by the shared experience of loss, their friendship deepened into indispensability and a near intimacy. They were companions at home and abroad for the rest of Macaulay's life. Political talk abounded. Macaulay and Sir Robert Peel, the Tory leader, began healing their rift. As partisanship eased, a noiseless revolution unfolded. The bawdy of Queen Victoria's uncles was becoming more passé than the rigors of Clapham. Tom took Hannah to see "Her 1st play"—she was twenty-eight. It was, they agreed, "a daub." The next day the aging Sydney Smith "talked most unclerically against chastity—said that our English fashions debarred men from the greatest pleasure of life, that of making love to a round of women, and enjoying each for a short time,—that no man could be a lover to his wife long after the honeymoon—&c—an old prebendary talking in the style of" a Restoration rake. Macaulay was amused, not fazed. More ominously, a clerical revanche seemed to be gathering steam. Over breakfast he "quizzed" his old acquaintance Richard Monckton Milnes about "his Newmanism . . . and Animal Magnetism." The belief that every animate being housed an occult power seemed the less threatening fad: "I laughed at him good-humouredly." He judged Milnes "a prig, but good natured enough." That Milnes had amassed a "choice collection of erotica" is a reminder that Macaulay was scarcely unique in his furtive complexity.[26]

Politics beckoned irresistibly. To avoid turning to the Radicals, Melbourne's Whigs increasingly depended on the Tories for counsel and aid: "Peel's withdrawal of support from Melbourne was almost sadistically gradual and calculating . . . not with an intention to bring the Government down (since he was not ready for office), but . . . to force the ministers into supporting Irish and Radical motions, which in turn would make them look extreme, and damage their prospects at the next election." On 7 May 1839 the "Ministers resigned." Not yet twenty, Queen Victoria—Macaulay thought her "rather a nice girl"—refused to allow the Tories to replace some of her Whig ladies-in-waiting. Correctly, Macaulay "disbelieved" the prediction that the Whigs "will never hold up their heads again" after the "Bed Chamber Crisis," and on 15 May he received a formal invitation to stand for Edinburgh.[27]

Opposed by a reluctant Chartist, he ran as an independent Whig. Although he had no truck with the proposal of the People's Charter to outdo America in democracy, his support for the secret ballot and more frequent elections attracted tamer Radicals. Macaulay also upheld "popular education," free speech, free trade, and religious freedom, including opposition to "civil disabilities," and reaffirmed his opposition to the slave trade and slavery. In his first address to Edinburgh's voters, he closed by identifying himself with the Whigs, the party of "the good old cause," historically the champions of "human freedom and of human happiness": "I entered public life a Whig; and a Whig I am determined to remain." But he added the important qualification "in no narrow sense." A few minutes earlier while lavishing tribute on Wellington and Peel, Macaulay recalled George Canning's 1827 coalition government, the first he had publicly endorsed. His conciliation amounted to a straw in the wind. Within a few years he would link the Tory party of order and the Whig party of liberty as necessary complements. "Never was victory so complete" as in Edinburgh, but he presented his constituents with a hostage to fate by promising them "that I will never hold any office, however high, except under circumstances under which it would be wrong and dishonorable to decline it."[28] The farcical Bed Chamber Crisis enabled Peel to escape forming a government. Melbourne staggered on for nearly two more years, reinforced on the front bench from September 1839 by Macaulay as secretary of state at war.

In "Gladstone on Church and State" he dispatched a theory while wooing the theoretician: "I shall however put him on the hook tenderly, and as if I had a love for him." Macaulay's intuition that the "High Church are throwing the Newmanites overboard" was accurate. Ill-suited to be a castaway, Gladstone outlined the argument of his book:

> That the government is not an optional but a natural institution.
>
> That governments are human agencies: rational: collective: and of functions sufficiently influential for good or evil to render them responsible to God.
>
> If they have a moral being, they must also have a religious profession.
>
> That where there is unity of government, there must be unity of this religious profession.
>
> That this unity need not rigorously apply to circumstantials, even of importance, but of substance.
>
> That it would be absolutely broken were the same government of the same kingdom to maintain & profess in one part of it a form of Christianity which anathematized that which it maintains in the other.[29]

Macaulay's essay proved to be almost as most prescient as "Bacon" and "Temple." His schedule during that Holy Week refuted his pose as an arbiter of Anglicanism. The essay was done. On Good Friday he stayed home reading and writing, and on Easter he skipped church and visited one of his clubs. Well-educated and well-connected, the Tractarians bedeviled Macaulay's aspiration to create a religious common ground to support an emerging political consensus. Whatever party leaders' disagreements over particular issues, they increasingly accepted the necessity of a market economy, individualism, and a hierarchy that perpetuated deference by co-opting talented and amenable parvenus such as Macaulay. The line between the secular and the sacred was shifting, but the state's legitimacy and authority still required that it appear to possess the mandate of heaven. Baffled in his effort to frame "a good counter-theory" to Gladstone's, he sidestepped the insoluble problem of defining the first principles of politics. Macaulay's lodestar remained "expediency, to be decided on a comparison of good and evil effects." Writing for an elite audience, he dealt in facts. In 1828 England had ceased to be a confessional state and became instead a religiously pluralist nation that also maintained an establishment. Along with the other churches, it ensured steady discipline for the dangerous classes and national ballast in hard times. Gladstone later admitted that he had failed to engage those facts.[30]

As usual, Macaulay wrote in the first person plural with a sharpness that implied virtual omniscience but now at a reduced volume and with an amiable tone. He deftly opened by distinguishing Peel, essential to any future coalition government and anathema to Newman and his friends, from Tory zanies baying from the backbenches. Macaulay treated Gladstone as their "rising hope," not one of them but a gifted, promising, confused, and educable young man. With his usual acuteness he diagnosed Gladstone's genius for the Higher Uplift, which helped to make him a popular tribune in his time but now often almost unreadable. To twit Gladstone into distancing himself even more from Tractarian excesses, Macaulay identified him as an incipient theocrat outside the central Anglican tradition. The premises of the review were straightforward. Religious differences are real and irreducible because truth is contested and unknowable this side of the veil. Civil government now performs "secular functions," modern prudence consists in utilitarian calculation, and talk about the organic unity of church and society amounts to retrograde fantasy. Macaulay did not quite anticipate Margaret Thatcher's declaration that "there is no such thing as society," but he denied the existence of "collective personalities." Despite insisting that governments are "moral beings," Gladstone refused to follow Plato and endorse a real daddy state ruled by a clique of wise men.[31]

Other lapses subverted his book. He attempted to bracket the uncertainty of competing claims to truth by obliging every real state "to profess a religion, to employ its power for the propagation of that religion, and to require conformity to that religion, as an indispensable qualification for all civil office." On his principle the Emperor Julian ("the Apostate") had worked for "the extinction of Christianity." More generally, Gladstone was guilty of trying to defend "a particular proposition" by mere generalization. Against him Macaulay appealed to history to prove that not shared religion but common allies and common enemies bind together armies and nations to fight, to kill, and to be killed. Enlightened despots, French liberals, and American democrats all governed effectively without propagating "theological doctrines." After paraphrasing Dr. Johnson on the triumph of imperial power—a "handful of daring adventurers from a civilised nation wander to some savage country, and reduce the aboriginal race to bondage"—Macaulay echoed Hobbes on the origin of the state: "It is in events such as these that governments have generally originated; and we can see nothing in such events to warrant us in believing that the governments thus called into existence will be peculiarly well fitted to distinguish between religious truth and heresy."[32] Once more, Macaulay refused to flinch at the brutality that generates and sustains political power.

Official religion belonged to policy, not to theology. Gladstone's proposal to bar Dissenters from public office would "make hypocrites" and "careless nominal conformists" rather than "produce honest and rational conviction." Practiced in such churchmanship, Macaulay claimed that "the humane spirit" of Gladstone's Christianity would cause him to "shrink with horror" from persecution. His judgment was mirrored by a leading Tractarian, who found Gladstone too utilitarian to be a real theocrat. Macaulay went on to challenge Gladstone "to choose" between joining the nineteenth century and keeping "as far in the rear of the general progress as possible." He also disabused Gladstone about India's situation. Invoking a "treaty" between Britain and its benighted subjects there, Gladstone, who wanted to make Ireland Protestant, flirted with tolerating "the priests of Kalee"—the goddess of annihilating time—and "the Thug." His "treaty" was pure fantasy: "It is by coercion, it is by the sword, and not by free stipulation with the governed, that England rules India." To pretend otherwise "would inevitably destroy our empire." Because England and Scotland maintained different but coexisting establishments, they "are one," just as the imposition of an alien establishment had led to Catholic Ireland's permanent alienation.[33]

Macaulay portrayed Gladstone's Anglicanism as potentially Romish in its claims. The Church of England, however, enjoyed no divine authority embodied in bishops who succeeded Christ's apostles and inherited their powers. A product of the sixteenth century, she aimed only for comprehension, admitting "to her highest offices men who differ from each other." That diversity enabled her to function as the church of the nation and its empire. In the third person, Macaulay recalled how he had secured a priest to attend his dying Indian Catholic servant, for whom he cared. He framed his recollection as a thought experiment involving an Irishman in India. "Here is a poor fellow, enlisted in Clare or Kerry . . . He fights for the Government; he conquers for it; he is wounded; he is laid on his pallet, withering away with fever, under that terrible sun, without a friend near him . . . [and] the state for which he dies sends a priest of his own faith to stand at his bedside . . . the state for which he dies does not abandon him in his last moments to the care of heathen attendants, or employ a chaplain of a different creed to vex his departing spirit."[34] Properly managed, even Catholicism could contribute to England's "fulcrum in the other world."

Macaulay looked behind Clapham's warm religion to the cool light of enlightened Anglicanism and behind that to Cicero's cultic piety. In describing "the alliance of Church and State," he selectively drew on William Warburton, an eighteenth-century bishop, to justify the establishment as the source of the everyday discipline and eternal incentives that foster the private virtues the state requires to survive. The government's end is the protection of "persons and property." It could promote other activities, but it was no "institution for the propagation of religion," apart from educating its subjects in "those principles of morality which are common to all forms of Christianity." Therefore, "all civil disabilities on account of religious opinions are indefensible": harmful to the nation, limiting "its choice of able men for the administration and defence of the state," alienating "from it the hearts of the sufferers," and depriving "it of a part of its effective strength in all contests with foreign nations."[35] Macaulay foresaw the shape of English public religion during the second half of the twentieth century. The Education Act of 1944 introduced into the state schools' curriculum a civil religion after his own heart, legislation essentially confirmed by the Education Reform Act of 1988.

In summary and again speaking in the third person, he imagined "a statesman" who both rejected Gladstone's high churchmanship and fought "all attempts to destroy" the establishment. Accepting the social necessity of religion, that statesman understood the necessity of Anglicanism: "an institution so deeply fixed in the hearts and minds of millions, could not be subverted without loosening and shaking all the foundations of civil society." The "national mind" would suffer: her "civilising influence" would end, the ranks of the irreligious would grow, and even more Britons "would fall under the influence of spiritual mountebanks, hungry for gain, or drunk with fanaticism." Thus would it be in Scotland were the Kirk to be disestablished. Unless the English state "gives a public maintenance to the Catholic clergy of Ireland," thus it would remain in Ireland, where the "minds of men, instead of being drawn to the church are alienated from the state."[36]

"Gladstone" was well received, even by Gladstone. Judging the essay "very kind as well as gentlemanly," he wrote to Macaulay with something of the *empressement* with which he had greeted him in St. Peter's the preceding Christmas Eve: "In these lacerating times one clings to everything of personal kindness in the past, to husband it in the future; and if you will allow me, I shall earnestly desire to carry with me such a recollection of your mode of dealing with a subject upon which the attainment of truth, we shall agree, so materially depends upon the temper in which the search for it is instituted and conducted." Macaulay replied "as if I had a love for him," and within a week they breakfasted together. While he courteously handled Gladstone's first book, Peel, another Erastian, and other Tory leaders ostentatiously ignored it. Half a lifetime later Gladstone remembered feeling like "the last man on the sinking ship." Mostly theological, his next book contained little that Macaulay could not "very consistently" say about the state's proper relations with the church.[37]

The Newmanites, however, were increasingly fissiparous and often cryptopapist. Rome lay in Newman's future, but he was already exiting the pale of respectable Anglicanism. His attacks on the opinions of others were almost testimonials to their sound Englishness. In 1841, for example, while ridiculing Peel's platitudinous tribute to the benefits of secular knowledge, he recalled the young Macaulay's anonymous enthusiasm for the "godless" London University: "a kind of neutral ground, on which every shade of politics and religion may meet together, disabuse each other of their prejudices, form intimacies, and secure cooperation." Newman, however, attributed the noxious opinions not to him but to his bête noire Lord Brougham. Commonplaces and common enemies were fostering an unexpected friendship. While "Gladstone" was in press, Macaulay and Peel dined together and "got on very well." As for Gladstone himself, "growing ecclesiastical liberalism" led him in 1845 to renounce his claim "that a Government should endow only the truth" and to vote for Peel's bill permanently endowing the Irish Catholic seminary at Maynooth.[38]

In print and in Whitehall, Macaulay pursued related domestic and imperial agendas. Thus his published and political work for the empire cohered—often intersected—with "Gladstone" and his advocacy of freer trade. But the elements of his imperial agenda have their own thrust and weight and deserve to be examined as an ensemble. Both a complement to "Gladstone" and a meditation on Rome, his review of Ranke's *History of the Popes* is also his *History of England* as it could have been, had his desire for big royalties and nationalist cheerleading not inhibited his penetrating intelligence. Still only "indifferently skilled in German," Macaulay read sheets of the English translation, which was published in June 1840. He treated "the history of all Christendom during a century and more," and the result is a subtler and more insightful analysis than Ranke's. Relishing the archival research that made him the very model of a modern scientific historian, Ranke proved to be obtuse about the fate of the modern papacy. At the beginning of his career he announced his goal: "To history has been assigned the office of judging the past, of instructing the present for the benefit of future ages. To such high offices this work does not aspire: It wants only to show what actually happened (*wie es eigentlich gewesen*)." A dozen years later, however, his German Lutheranism led him to conclude that papal power "no longer exercises any essential influence, nor does it create in us solicitude of any kind; the times are past in which we had anything to fear; we now feel ourselves perfectly secure. Popery can now inspire us with no other interest than what results from the development of its history."[39]

More skeptical, Macaulay also possessed surer political instincts and a richer historical imagination. He grasped the staying power of religion in a world where states were becoming modern nations by attracting broad and deep loyalty. One staunchly Protestant friend mistook Macaulay's disillusioned realism and muted anti-Catholic clichés for philopopery. Three paragraphs into "Von Ranke" Macaulay offered a meditation on the permanence of human credulity and the transience of civil power, including England's. The papacy "saw the commencement of all the governments and of all the ecclesiastical establishments that now exist in the world; and we feel no assurance that she is not destined to see the end of them all . . . she may still exist in undiminished vigor when some traveller from New Zealand shall, in the midst of a vast solitude, take his stand on a broken arch of London Bridge to sketch the ruins of St. Paul's." First conceived during his adolescence, the image had blossomed in Rome. Gibbon had similarly conceived his history of "the decline and fall" of the city of Rome as he "mused amidst the ruins of the Capitol, while the barefooted friars were singing vespers in the Temple of Jupiter."[40]

Whatever Macaulay wrote elsewhere about England as driving endless human progress, he knew that history is naturally aimless and only unfolds. In "Von Ranke" he reasoned like his favorite ancients about the ebb and flow of human achievements. We belong to nature, and our lives are tales of impermanence, variously comic or sad in their unfolding, but ultimately constrained by limits and necessity. Personally incredulous and certain that theological arguments were inconclusive, Macaulay was impervious to the charms and logic of religion. But human irrationality manifested as the permanent will to believe in what eyes cannot see commanded his wary respect. It was obvious both that Christianity was the otherworldly fulcrum of Europe's success and that fanaticism thrived in modern London. But properly managed fanatics could be useful, because hypercivilization spawned a skeptical decadence that sapped nations. Preserving their vitality sometimes demanded "merciless atrocity" and "exterminating swords"—he alluded again to Cromwell in Ireland and Joshua in Palestine. Recollecting Rome in tranquility and trying to explain what he found perversely seductive there complicated his style. A few of his serpentine sentences have a bite worthy of Gibbon's: "The [Byzantine] Greek, still preserving, in the midst of political degradation, the ready wit and the inquiring spirit of his fathers, still able to read the most perfect of human compositions, still speaking the most powerful and flexible of human languages, brought to the marts of Narbonne and Toulouse, together with the drugs and silks of remote climates, bold and subtle theories long unknown to the ignorant and credulous West."[41] Attentive readers of "Bacon" appreciated the joke: all those Greek subtleties were bogus.

In Rome Macaulay saw as reality what Thomas Hobbes had intuited as a possibility two hundred years earlier. Satirizing the papacy as *"the kingdom of fairies,"* Hobbes depicted it as "the *ghost* of the deceased *Roman empire,* sitting crowned upon the grave thereof." Although the Reformation exorcized England, he envisioned "that this spirit of Rome," now abroad in East Asia, might "return . . . enter, and inhabit this clean swept house, and make the end thereof, worse than the beginning." The resurgence of Rome suggested to Macaulay the problem of how regimes acquire, maintain, and renew their power. Surviving four insurrections of "the human intellect . . . against her yoke," the Church of Rome exhibited "the principle of life still strong within her." The papacy's improbable vibrancy made it a "polity" that "is the very masterpiece of human wisdom" and suggested how religion could animate a regime.[42]

In the thirteenth century, Rome had defeated heretics by sanctioning a "war distinguished even among wars of religion by merciless atrocity" and renewed itself through the complementary exertions of "spiritual police" and winsome friars. As the Middle Ages ended, Rome, "fortified by the love, the reverence, and the terror of mankind," had prevailed over resurgent secular authority, theological assault, and schism. Propelled by the revival of lay classicism, the growth of vernacular literature, and the invention of movable type, Martin Luther had inaugurated "the third and the most memorable struggle for spiritual freedom." But Macaulay's was no complacent story of Protestantism's triumph. Here, too, the ebb and flow of history ruled. Religious regeneration had touched southern as well as northern Europe: "the great outbreak of Protestantism" had caused "an equally violent outbreak of Catholic zeal." When the papacy fought back, the Reformation suffered irreversible losses. The Catholic victories owed less to warfare than "to a great reflux in public opinion." The new Catholic leadership had displayed "sincerity, constancy, courage, and austerity of life," while the Reformers "had become lukewarm and worldly," as well as divided.[43] He remembered Bossuet on the variations of Protestantism along with Hobbes on papal resilience.

Skillfully managing fanatics was essential: "The Catholic Church neither submits to enthusiasm nor proscribes it, but uses it." Anglicanism, in contrast, turned its "ignorant enthusiasts" into "a most dangerous enemy." Slyly, he imagined John Wesley transported to Rome and becoming not the founder of Methodism, but the first "general of a new society devoted to the interests and honour of the Church," and Ignatius Loyola waxing in Oxford not as the first general of the Jesuits, but as "the head of a formidable succession." Rome had also marshaled enthusiastic women. If Teresa of Avila had been English, "her restless enthusiasm" would have turned "into madness, not untinctured with craft." As much as he had been in Naples, Macaulay was confident that the "moral effect" of Protestantism, by outliving its religious vigor, had fostered northern Europe's contemporary economic and cultural superiority, just as the

Catholic revival had stunted progress and prosperity in the south. The German sociologist Max Weber, a solemn reader of Macaulay who imagined history as moving inexorably forward, drew on him to connect *The Protestant Ethic and the Spirit of Capitalism*.[44]

Macaulay evenhandedly assessed the French Enlightenment, which had launched the contemporary struggle between the papacy and progress. Voltaire and his ilk had leavened their derision with more of "that charity towards men of all classes and races which Christianity enjoins" than the church they targeted: "Irreligion, accidentally associated with philanthropy, triumphed for a time over religion accidentally associated with political and social abuses." Revolution, invasion, and calamity had ensued. In 1800 the Church of Rome had appeared shipwrecked. Even then, however, "a great reaction had commenced, which after the lapse of more than forty years, appears to be still in progress." Here progress meant not an agreeably upward and reasonable advance but the power of endurance as history unfolded. For all Macaulay's trumpeting of England, he fretted about its future. Dearth was shaping the 1840s, and the dangerous classes seemed to be flirting with revolution. Apart from "Von Ranke," however, he was usually optimistic in public about what lay ahead. As he appreciated, looking "about for something to believe" was a common modern predicament. The English state needed a virtually supernatural aura that could evoke its subjects' reverence and incite their self-sacrifice unto death. Writing his *History of England,* he reflected on how to promote and manage "national feeling." In 1844 a heartfelt sense of England's superiority and single-minded allegiance to its interests inspired the secularization of the word "nationalism" into "devotion to one's nation."[45] Again Macaulay accurately read the signs of the times.

Back in the Game

Bored by committee "business stupid beyond description" on 5 June 1840, he resumed his journal. The preceding thirteen months had been eventful. "What a change since I left it off—Parliament—office—Cabinet—a house and carriage of my own. My dearest Hannah & Baba settled for life in England comfortably and prosperously. Some drawbacks—Hard work and chequered success in parliament—Doubts whether I shall ever make a debater. Yet the balance greatly in my favour." Soon he again put aside his journal: "But how different my frame of mind from what it was two years ago [in 1838]. Now much domestic happiness has altered my whole way of looking at life. I have my share of the anxieties and vexations of ambition. But it is only a secondary passion now." Choosing an active life over literature required him to delay writing his *History of England*—the first two volumes finally appeared in December 1848. He was a busy man. Enmeshed in politics until the eve of publication, he spoke fifty-four times—usually effectively and sometimes at length—in and out of the House of Commons. Meanwhile he published nine essays in the *Edinburgh Review*. They fill 503 pages, about the length of the first volume of his book.[46]

Joining the cabinet as secretary at war required that Macaulay present himself in Edinburgh for reelection, and he triumphed in January 1840: "Not a breath of opposition or censure." Despite flattering his constituents as residents of "the most beautiful town in the Empire," he remained a prereform M.P., elected but still unresponsive to the electorate. More than a bit full of himself, he dismissed their requests almost from the beginning. Instead of visiting them, he grandly issued a circular letter addressed from "Windsor Castle." The press mocked him as "Babbletongue Macaulay," but he continued preening in private: "I have been commanded to dine at the Palace on Friday." His efforts to manage his press coverage met with mixed success, but experience brought improvement.[47] Edinburgh's indulgence was finite.

In cabinet meetings, he "spoke with his usual volubility and eagerness," especially about the empire and national security. When presenting defense estimates and drafting long memoranda on tedious minutiae became routine, he discovered that he had underestimated the cost of administration. He could snatch a few hours to read and write only when the Commons was not sitting. A stream of begging letters annoyed him: "no Guardian of the poor is more mobbed by widows and orphans than I am; and what I have to give among them is a mere pittance." Taking care of his dependents was easier: "during the time—very short it may be—that I keep my office, I wish you, as well as the rest of the family, to get a little enjoyment out of it." Nepotism became a lifetime habit, but a failed attempt to shoot the queen made for a day of drama. A deranged boy acted alone, not as the agent of a secret society or of a conspiracy hatched by the king of Hanover, Victoria's toxic uncle and heir-presumptive. Macaulay toyed with the "monstrously improbable" idea of a plot with "a German air," operating under "foreign management," probably Hanoverian. Later that day a near riot in the House of Commons left him with a headache.[48] Surrendering office would be a relief.

The churchy wrangles he analyzed in "Gladstone" bedeviled practical politics. In Scotland the Kirk was moving toward schism after years of ferment, ostensibly over whether ministers should continue to be appointed by landlords or be elected by their congregations. More profoundly divisive was the longstanding battle between divines over how literally to interpret and teach the church's sternly Calvinist confession of faith. In November 1840 a friend in Edinburgh warned Macaulay to stay away lest he find himself damaged by the controversy. "Greatly vexed," Macaulay excoriated "violent churchmen." Their feuding reinforced his conviction that "while the State and the Church are connected, the State must control the Church. It ought indeed to exercise its powers in such a way as to make the Church in the highest degree useful to the people. But it must control. And I will never put the State under the feet of that Church which it feeds out of the common funds of the Empire."[49]

Inside the cabinet Macaulay's support for Palmerston's forward policy in the eastern Mediterranean inaugurated an enduring and mutually useful alliance: "Palmerston's wisdom or luck is such that he is always right." As 1841 began, Britain appeared to be winning simultaneous wars in China, Egypt, and Afghanistan: "Glorious news from all corners of the world." But politics remained primarily domestic, and the Whigs edged toward endorsing free trade. During the spring the government staggered on, dependent on Peel's tolerance. On 8 May Macaulay correctly foresaw defeat over a proposal to reduce the tariff privileging colonial over foreign sugar.[50] Instead of resigning as Macaulay preferred, Melbourne's cabinet moved to dissolve Parliament. Ousted by a no-confidence vote, the Whigs went to the voters on a platform of multiple tariff cuts.

Troubled only by radical Chartists, Macaulay was easily reelected for Edinburgh on 1 July. Although the Tories won the national election, the Whigs' shift from an aristocratic to a commercial front anticipated the future center of British politics: "provincial businessmen, manufacturers, and retailers, many of whom were Nonconformists." Macaulay pronounced himself "sincerely and thoroughly contented" in opposition. He also enjoyed domesticity. Throughout 1840 the Trevelyans lived with him, along with his financially dependent maiden sisters, Frances and Selina, and several servants. In September 1841 he left their rented house for bachelor quarters in the Albany, Piccadilly, made fashionable by Byron and Canning: "an entrance-hall, two sitting rooms, a bed-room, a water closet, a kitchen, cellars [he thought the 'Teetotallers' wrote 'crazy' stuff] and two bedrooms for servants." Elizabeth and William Williams, a husband and wife who had served Zachary, lived in, enabling Tom to host frequent power breakfasts, the foundation of his energetic social life. In a world fueled by "buzz," being in the know signaled power, and he routinely circulated in Clubland and often sifted competing dinner invitations to divert and position himself.[51] Macaulay's emotional survival, however, depended on his family—especially Hannah and Baba—and Ellis.

Leaving office made him once more an unpaid M.P. When constituents pestered him requesting donations, he cried poor: "laying down my carriage; leaving my house; breaking up my establishment, and settling in chambers." A few months later he was privately more sanguine—"at present I consider my self as one of the richest men of my acquaintance" —reckoning that it cost him £800 a year to "enjoy every comfort" and that he could "well afford" to spend £1,000 on himself—with respective purchasing power of almost £56,000 and £70,000 in 2007. His growing library already contained between three thousand and four thousand volumes. Moving in 1849 to "much larger, brighter, and better rooms" in the Albany enabled him to buy even more.[52]

Whether in power or in opposition, Macaulay sat on the Whig front benches for almost eight years, tasked with making speeches—he lacked either aptitude or stomach for the thrust and parry of debate. How did he earn his keep in the parliamentary speeches he delivered between his return by Edinburgh and the fall of Melbourne's ministry in the late spring of 1841? All of them were rhetorical, usually resonant if not always accurate. His bravura embellished a coherent ideology. He was consistently antidemocratic, concerned to advance England's national and imperial interests, economically liberal, and, most importantly, predictable in his calculating analysis of issues—specific arguments are a case apart. He debuted championing the secret ballot. The issue was not a matter of party discipline, many aristocratic Whigs opposed it, and passage came only in 1872. If his support made him seem a radical in some eyes, doctrines of human rights never troubled his realism. Politics involved "co-operation," and he knew "that there could be no co-operation without mutual compromise." His support for the ballot, "as in almost every other question of human affairs," depended on "balancing the good with the good, and the evil with the evil." Any proposed amendment of the Reform Bill should be debated on the same principle, and in light of the self-evident truth that "wealth . . . was closely connected with intellectual superiority." Defending the ballot against the charge that secrecy was "un-English" led him to defend "men of high consideration, men of the first distinction" who practiced duplicity as well as equivocation. It amounted to indirect self-disclosure.[53]

In the late 1840s a journalist tried to capture Macaulay orating. His description matches both earlier and later reports, but it seems to defy the law of contradiction. When Macaulay packed the House of Commons, he "boldly asserted the most ultra-liberal, almost democratic opinions"—that was outdated news—and was also "a great reconciler of the new with the old," who delighted in giving "new interpretations to old laws and forms of thought, and by so doing, to restore their original integrity." Although his speeches sounded almost effortless and transparent, they were carefully memorized and "read like essays." Often setting the terms of debate, his words were as "admirable" as his person was unprepossessing: short, plump and expanding, and cursed with a voice "pitched in alto, monotonous, and rather shrill, pouring forth words with inconceivable velocity." On the front bench he displayed the "same abstraction" as when "he walks, or rather straggles along the street." Ignoring strangers there and colleagues in the House of Commons, he appeared an embodied intellect: "His face seems literally instinct with expression: the eye, above all, full of deep thought and meaning." Ultimately, it was a flaw: "He exhibits none of the common weakness of even the greatest speakers. He never entices you, as it were, to help him, by the confession of any difficulty. The intellectual preponderates too much. More heart and less mind would serve his turn better."[54]

The final sentence captures Macaulay's tragedy. Calculation rather than ethical abstractions or generous impulses guided his approach to politics, history, and, for the most part, life. It did not keep him from invoking lofty ideals: "for the reformation and for the preservation of our institutions, for liberty and order, for justice administered in mercy, for equal laws, for the rights of conscience, and for the real union of Great Britain and Ireland." Neither did heaping flattery on Peel keep him from bashing the Tory rank and file. But more and more Macaulay regarded Peel not as a Tory dogmatist but as a like-minded empiricist, who usually formed his political judgments on the basis "of expediency, of place, and of time." Unlike the prime minister, however, Macaulay viewed struggle as humanity's normal condition and politics as its precarious sublimation. He therefore justified violating neutral rights: "If a nation were forced to go to war, it was oftentimes compelled to make the innocent suffer with the guilty." It was another extreme case. For him "expediency" was routine politics. In 1841, for example, he again advocated "admitting Jews to seats in Parliament" and "to civil and municipal offices" as a further adjustment to the reality of religious pluralism. Similarly, ensuring cheaper food at home made him support the Whig plan to reduce tariffs on foreign sugar produced by indentured labor, a measure that penalized both landlords and ex-slaves in the British West Indies. Free trade was economically reasonable, and a better-fed populace at home provided the best defense against the Chartists. For all that Macaulay's realism could turn brutal, his easy sentimentality persuaded him that he was the caring man he saw in his mirror.[55]

When Macaulay put his mind to it, he could charm the House. On 5 February 1841 he helped to defeat a bill extending copyright protection for sixty years after an author's death. On that occasion he disowned mere expediency: "I am not prepared . . . to agree to a compromise between right and expediency, and to commit an injustice for the public convenience." It was another high-flown utterance. Invoking the moralist William Paley, he went on to insist "that property is the creature of the law, and that the law which creates property can be defended only on this ground, that it is a law beneficial to mankind." There was no "natural right to property independent of utility and anterior to legislation," and he derided the competing "mystical and sentimental schools of moral philosophy." Bringing the matter down to earth meant that the House of Commons must "look at this question like legislators, and after fairly balancing conveniences and inconveniences, pronounce between the existing law of copyright and the law now proposed to us. The question of copyright . . . like most questions of civil prudence, is neither black nor white, but grey." It entailed weighing authors' reasonable claims to be "remunerated for their literary labors" against the evil of monopoly.[56]

A beguiling erudition adorned his cost-benefit analysis. He referred to Fielding, Gibbon, Johnson, "My dear and honoured friend, Mr. Wilberforce," and the unforgettable "Mrs Hannah More," the Claphamite doyenne, before warning against extending copyright protection to benefit authors' heirs. Had Samuel Richardson's grandson, a notably prudish clergyman, controlled the rights to his edifying novels, he might have suppressed them. It was the preview of a dazzling speech fourteen months later on a second copyright bill, which proposed to grant protection for twenty-five years after an author's death. Macaulay instead urged authorizing a forty-two-year copyright from the date of publication. Enjoying a "field-day," he delivered one of the rare parliamentary speeches that made "a compromise . . . welcome to all parties." In a bantering voice, he dropped the names of nineteen authors and fifty-one titles over four pages. The act, which remained in force until 1911, helped to shut the "copyright window," which had been closing since 1808. By restricting the supply of unprotected works that could be cheaply reprinted, it served to freeze the canon of British literature.[57]

Managing the copyright legislation provided a welcome diversion from besetting religious and economic disputes. Despite Peel, most Tories clung to agricultural protection and the establishment's claims. The Whigs were generally cautious free traders and "tolerators." When Protestant Dissenters sought to reclaim chapels that had turned Unitarian, Peel's government proposed to enact a twenty-five-year statute of limitations on such reversions. The necessity of defending "the principle . . . that prescription is a good title to property" exasperated Macaulay: "Till very lately . . . I could not have imagined that, in any assembly of reasonable, of civilised men, it could be necessary for me to stand up in defence of that principle." Its opponents seemed to him like escapees from "Bedlam" and arguing against them as frivolous as condemning trial by battle, witch-burning, and ordeal by fire. But argue he did. After advertising his long championship of "the cause of religious liberty," he invoked "rights" in which he disbelieved. Thirteen months later, on 9 July 1845, he defended the Scottish universities against Presbyterians "bent on persecution without having the miserable excuse of fanaticism." Even Peel rejected instituting "an inquisition into the religious opinions of people whose business was merely to teach secular knowledge." Modifying the only kind of knowledge Macaulay recognized, "merely" was ironic. More heartfelt was his tribute to the ancient universities for breeding "English gentlemen" to serve the church. Insofar as their religion was principally an aspect of their nationality and caste, they could guard against religion's regressive potential.[58]

When addressing the economy, Macaulay found the technicalities too boring to master. But he accepted the reigning orthodoxy and was sure of his own judgment. Creating a regime of free trade required ending tariff protection for British corn, and in 1839 a group of laissez-faire utopians formed the Anti–Corn Law League to promote total repeal. As late as 1842, Macaulay wanted to realize free trade piecemeal. Protectionism was a "system," so that "at whatever end we effect a breach, the whole is in danger of ruin." Ideally, there should be a total overhaul of tariffs and, failing that, the elimination of "the greatest evil, the corn monopoly. But it is a good thing to begin to reform anywhere." Expecting failure, he proposed "a tolerable compromise" between the Anti–Corn Law League and the protectionists. The Leaguers objected, and Macaulay sought to keep Peel in power because he found him to be "a more powerful minister than any that we have seen during many years." Macaulay voted for tariff reductions but against the income tax that the government proposed to offset lost revenues. Inconsistently, he insisted on another occasion: "I cannot admit that when a Government wants money, and is under the necessity of raising money by taxation it ought to reject every tax which may interfere with the freedom of trade"; "the friends of perfectly free trade, of whom I am sincerely one, are in general quite mistaken as to their own strength."[59]

Macaulay understood "the instability of every thing" in human affairs, and during the 1840s chance seemed to rule politics. If the Anti–Corn Law League dogmatists annoyed him, the agitators for the People's Charter frightened him. In 1839 Parliament had rejected a Chartist petition signed by hundreds of thousands, and widespread strikes followed, triggering official repression. Softening their "violent platform rhetoric," the Chartists concentrated on organizing and alliance-building. After the House received their second national petition in May 1842, Macaulay addressed its demands. With customary deftness, he both urged rejecting the petition and identified acceptable points. He favored the secret ballot and abolishing the property qualification for M.P.'s and was willing to entertain "some compromise" on the Chartists' proposal for annual parliamentary elections. Although he opposed paying M.P.'s and creating equal-sized constituencies, those were not "vital" matters.[60]

But their call for universal manhood suffrage appalled him: "If you grant that, the country is lost." Such an electorate was "incompatible with property, and . . . is consequently incompatible with civilization." Judiciously widening the franchise was a case apart. Progress depended not on government intervention but on individual initiative, because able people dared to innovate only when their gains were secure. Susceptible to demagogues, the poor could not understand the "reasons that irrefragably prove this inequality to be necessary to the wellbeing of all classes." Enfranchising them would produce "general anarchy and plunder." He equated Chartism with socialism, another new ideology: "Every man of sense knows that the people support the Government. But the doctrine of the Chartist philosophers is that it is the business of the Government to support the people." When some Chartists turned violent in Wales, he denounced clemency for the ringleaders: "rely on it that there will be insurrections enough, if turbulent and designing men are apprised that the penalty of raising a civil war is henceforth to be less than the penalty of robbing a hen roost." Once again Macaulay intuited and helped to shape the public mind. In 1914 a smaller percentage of the adult male population voted in the United Kingdom than in the German Empire.[61]

He was too deep a politician to imagine that resistance and repression alone could forestall another English revolution. Civil prudence taught him that there were no absolute rules governing the state's role in the economy. Unlike many Whigs, he supported a bill to limit the workday of women and minors to ten hours. Instead of the predictions of imminent class warfare with which he had once championed parliamentary reform, he preached reconciliation by depicting "the owners of factories" as national assets: "with their interests the interests of the whole community, and especially of the labouring classes, are inseparably bound up." Requiring industrialists to cut the hours of women and children was an investment in England's human capital: "the improvement of the man will improve all that the man produces." Eleven months later he insisted that "it is the right and the duty of the State to provide means of education for the common people." It was England's best defense against the threat of "much barbarism." His educational scheme was nationalist, confessional, and authoritarian. He envisioned the state as supporting denominational schools, Anglican and otherwise, simultaneously where the demographics permitted it. In smaller communities the state would fund the school of the majority religion. During the eighteenth century David Hume had also taught that a benign and inclusive established church could educate the multitude in self-discipline.[62]

Upholding "a Just Mean"

Inhibition was a project that Macaulay promoted in print, especially for the "ladies." In the autumn of 1840 a newly published collection of some racy Restoration comedies suggested the possibility of "an amusing paper." The editor was Leigh Hunt, a litterateur of equivocal moods and reputation, who deprecated a late seventeenth-century bluenose, the Reverend Jeremy Collier. Ever alert to the drift of public opinion, Macaulay wrote to vindicate Collier, notwithstanding his retrograde churchmanship and politics: "one of the greatest public benefactors in our history." Collier prevailed in his argument that the "business of Plays is to recommend Virtue and discountenance Vice; to shew the Uncertainty of humane greatness, the suddain Turns of Fate, and the Unhappy Conclusions of Violence and Injustice: 'Tis to expose the Singularities of Pride and Fancy, to make Folly and Falsehood contemptible and to bring every thing that is Ill Under Infamy and Neglect." Macaulay aimed "to keep a just mean between Hunt's laxity and the puritan austerity" but judged the piece to be the worst he had "written since I was a boy." Did he cringe at its echoes of Zachary?

> And yet it is not easy to be too severe. For in truth this part of our literature is a disgrace to our language and our national character. It is clever, indeed, and very entertaining; but it is, in the most emphatic sense of the words, "earthly, sensual, devilish." Its indecency, though perpetually such as is condemned not less by the rules of good taste than by those of morality, is not, in our opinion, so disgraceful a fault as its singularly inhuman spirit. We have here Belial

... but with the iron eyes and cruel sneer of Mephistophiles [*sic*]. We find ourselves in a world, in which the ladies are like very profligate, impudent, and unfeeling men, and in which the men are too bad for any place but Pandaemonium ... We are surrounded by foreheads of bronze, hearts like the nether millstone, and tongues set on fire of hell.[63]

Macaulay's tirade advertised that he was a very sound moralist. Humanly, it mattered that he showed Hunt much of the goodness of heart which he valued in other people. A childlike and needy stranger, Hunt asked him for help. Although he proved to be burdensome, Macaulay showed him notable patience and gentleness as both a man "whose spirit seems to be quite broken by adversity" and a client for whom he accepted responsibility. Macaulay's solicitude for Hunt helps to explain why his friends esteemed his "robust spirits, and stout and kind heart."[64] But it was difficult for Macaulay to restrict calculation to public life and to act routinely in private according to his generous instincts. Measuring the costs against the benefits was too deep-seated for that.

He found the eighteenth century more congenial than the Restoration and indulged his preference in a series of essays during the 1840s. The end of 1842 saw a long paper on the *Diaries and Letters* of Fanny Burney, a major English novelist who had married a Frenchman, briefly expatriated, and had distressed Zachary by going native as Madame D'Arblay. More concerned with her biography than with her art, Tom pioneered an unbalanced approach that prevailed into the late twentieth century. If his essay lacks critical penetration, it shows him thinking about how to write a book that could attract women. Burney's increasing imitation of the prose of her friend Samuel Johnson began the ruin of her own style, which her translation into Mme. D'Arblay completed. From writing a "true woman's English, clear, natural, and lively," she ended writing "the worst style that has ever been known among men." Macaulay also relied on the popular English contrast between themselves as manly Protestants and the French as effeminate Catholics.[65] He turned the stereotype on and off according to rhetorical necessity, but it would serve him well in his *History*.

More pertinent to his book was an essay on Joseph Addison, classicizing essayist and poet but reluctant politician. There Macaulay sketched "the political and literary history of England" from William III through George I and praised Addison's "model of pure and graceful writing." His admiration for both the man and his style amounted to self-identification. Addison's example suggested the historian he wanted to become: a "firm but moderate Whig" whose manifest Englishness enchanted members of both parties. Personally, Addison shone in his amiability, rectitude, and cheerful religion. He was almost Macaulay's ideal self, and the trajectory of their reputations converged during the early twentieth century. Macaulay had helped to create what then came to be called "Victorianism." Marked as its ancestor, Addison began to seem unsuitable for modern tastes and needs: sententious, patronizing toward women, and humorous rather than witty.[66] By 1905, when "Victorianism" was coined, Macaulay's own fame had crested.

When Macaulay ventured into the continental eighteenth century, his mind and heart remained in England. A conversation with a French eminence about Bertrand Barère, an architect of the Reign of Terror and accomplished survivor, suggested a cautionary tale of revolutionary excess and failure, which Macaulay turned into a parable about the Chartist menace. Gibbeting "this Jacobin carrion," Macaulay argued that the Glorious Revolution had made England exceptional, the "nation which has combined beyond all example and all hope, the blessings of liberty with those of order." Burying his verdict that the French Revolution was on balance a good thing, he now approved of almost everything until September 1792 and condemned almost everything after Louis XVI's guillotining in January 1793. What the homicidal Jacobins inflicted on France recalled Christ's Passion: "This was their hour, and the power of darkness." Although he branded them as virtual demons for relaxing "the great laws of morality," human calculation rather than divine commandments still ruled his judgment: "It is absurd to say that any amount of public danger can justify a system like this, we do not say on Christian principles, we do not say on the principles of a high morality, but even on principles of Machiavellian policy. It is true that great emergencies call for activity and vigilance; it is true that they justify severity which, in ordinary times, would deserve the name of cruelty. But indiscriminate severity can never, under any circumstances, be useful." "Indiscriminate" and "useful" were his key words. As for the "popular notion" that "the leading Terrorists" were both "wicked" and "great": "We can see nothing great about them but their wickedness." Speaking as the ethical voice "of the great society of mankind," Macaulay denounced the "butchering of a single unarmed man in cold blood, under an act of the legislature" and welcomed the "fortunate circumstance that, during a long course of years, respect for the weak and clemency towards the vanquished have been considered as qualities not less essential to the accomplished soldier than personal courage." The author of "Temple" was exercising the rhetorician's license to use any words that could sway his audience. In the peroration he turned a familiar blessing from St. Paul into a curse on Barère.[67]

The eighteenth century also served Macaulay as a refuge from church squabbles—"The Kirk plagues me out of my life. Those fools will utterly ruin themselves." His visits to his constituents continued to be irregular—"neither pleasant nor prudent." Distracted by the Chartists as well as by the sectaries, he imagined Westminster Abbey as the shrine of national memory: a "temple of silence and reconciliation where the enmities of twenty generations lie buried." In venerating its great dead there, England worshiped itself. Macaulay's aim was to write a history that would generalize the cult. When Lady Holland pressed him to eulogize her husband, a shoot of the purest Whig stump, he reluctantly obliged her with a few artfully mixed pages. They endorsed Holland's domestic politics and purported to assent to his views on "Foreign Policy" except on "two or three great questions." The French Revolution was the sticking point. In championing Charles James Fox's policy of appeasing revolutionary France, Holland failed England. Both he and his uncle—and by implication all such Whigs—displayed "the magnanimous credulity of a mind which was as incapable of suspecting as of devising mischief."[68] It was a courtly euphemism for hopeless, inexcusable naïveté. Though an unwanted distraction, "Holland" enabled Macaulay to reiterate that the touchstone of English history was not abstract principles but the national interest.

[6]

EMPIRE BUILDER

England's empire grew after Napoleon's defeat as a piecemeal and unplanned affair, out of sight and mostly out of the public mind. Macaulay used words to make his compatriots see their empire through his own enchanted eyes. As a politician he helped to govern it, above all India and Ireland. After reeling in Gladstone, he produced a "flashy" essay on Robert Clive's Indian conquests, a subject that was "to most readers, not only insipid, but positively distasteful." Persuading them otherwise necessitated confecting a palatable justification of the necessary cruelty of empire-building: no rich omelets for England without breaking many eggs in India. He led with charm: "Every schoolboy knows" about the Spanish conquest of the Americas, but most of them and 90 percent even of "English gentlemen of highly cultivated minds" were ignorant of "the great actions of our countrymen in the East."[1]

James Mill had disparaged Clive as one "'to whom deception, when it suited his purpose, never cost a pang.'" Macaulay acclaimed him: "our island, so fertile in heroes and statesmen, has scarcely ever produced a man more truly great in arms or in council." Because that great Englishman needed an Indian foil, Macaulay cast Bengal's ruler as an idiot sybarite "arrived at that last stage of human depravity": sadism. He was, however, typical: "Oriental despots are perhaps the worst class of human beings; and this unhappy boy was one of the worst specimens of his class." The Bengalis deserved him. Enervated "by a soft climate and accustomed to peaceful employments," they "bore the same relation to other Asiatics which the Asiatics generally bear to the bold and energetic children of Europe." For Macaulay, the received version of the "Black

Hole of Calcutta" captured the nabob's depravity. In 1756 he had imprisoned 146 English traders in a stifling and airless room, where 123 of them perished: a "great crime, memorable for its singular atrocity, memorable for the tremendous retribution by which it was followed." It was a reminder that the imperial burden required Britons to die as well as to kill. Knowing both "the great difference between Asiatic and European morality" and "Oriental politics as a game in which nothing was unfair," Clive became an avenging angel. England's responsibility to extend its superior civilization made conquest a moral imperative to be rewarded with growing prosperity and power.[2]

Because there was no denying the "distasteful" part of Clive's record, Macaulay promised to examine it with "English veracity." Properly evaluating Clive's achievement required weighing his failures against his ultimate success. His intricate double cross of a wealthy Bengali merchant— "dissimulation surpassing even the dissimulation of Bengal"—appeared almost unforgivable and prompted a self-subverting reference to Machiavelli: "Now, we will not discuss this point on any rigid principles of morality. Indeed, it is quite unnecessary to do so: for, looking at the question as a question of expediency in the lowest sense of the word, and using no arguments but such as Machiavelli might have employed in his conferences with Borgia, we are convinced that Clive was altogether in the wrong [in a 'breach of faith'], and that he committed not merely a crime, but a blunder." Here Macaulay used *concessio,* a rhetorical device that admitted Clive's guilt only in this case. His calculating ethic could then vindicate Clive's heroism and his enshrinement among the persecuted benefactors of humanity. In 1757 at Plassey Clive had vanquished a superior Indian army and a handful of French auxiliaries. It was "the day which was to decide the fate of India," the day when Clive "subdued an empire larger and more populous than Great Britain." Macaulay telescoped history. Plassey had been inconclusive, and Clive for his part had opposed expanding the British East India Company's direct rule beyond Bengal. Macaulay recognized the continuing menace of the western Maratha chieftains, who soon learned to fight the English with European tactics and weapons. It was the future duke of Wellington's triumph over them in 1803 that had ended the native rulers' ability to threaten the English and enabled them to expand their empire throughout India. In "Clive" he alluded to Wellington's victories "in Spain and Gascony"

but not on the subcontinent. The need to predate British India in order to make it seem a steady, almost inevitable, if not quite stately, progress trumped his respect for the duke. The popularity of the essay encouraged him to write one on Warren Hastings, who would finish the
English conquest of India and make himself the ruler of "fifty millions of
Asiatics."[3]

Britain was then waging the First Opium War with China. The naval
career of Charles Elliot illustrates its civilizing mission shifting from philanthropy to conquest. After working to protect slaves in British Guiana,
Captain Elliott became British minister to China in 1835, charged with
overseeing the burgeoning trade in Indian opium. Four years later Chinese authorities burned tons of it and seized British representatives. Revenge was swift. A loud hawk, Macaulay as secretary at war lacked any
responsibility for planning strategy, though he helped to administer and
defend the operation. His office made his words seem more authoritative
than those of a mere writer, and they nurtured first English and then
American imperialism into the twentieth century. Perhaps the saintly
William Wilberforce's laudanum habit enabled Macaulay to evoke addic-
tion for the instruction of the House of Commons: "a physical craving
as fierce and impatient as any to which our race is subject . . . [drugs] are
desired with a rage which resembles the rage of hunger." He no more
wanted to suppress the lucrative trade than to kowtow to affronted mandarins. Rather he insisted that China and "all nations, civilised and uncivilised," should know that "wherever an Englishman may wander, he is
followed by the eye and guarded by the power of England." Theirs was
"a country which had made the farthest ends of the earth ring with the
fame of her exploits in redressing the wrongs of her insulted consul; that
revenged the horrors of the Black Hole on the fields of Plassey; that had
not degenerated since her great Protector [Cromwell] vowed that he
would make the name of Englishman as respected as ever had been the
name of Roman citizen."[4]

Macaulay concluded by praying "that the overruling care of that gracious Providence which has so often brought good out of evil" would
establish "a durable peace, beneficial alike to the victors and the vanquished." It was a shortened version of William Robertson's old argument about the Spanish Empire, now urged by someone with no time
for Providence. Macaulay was predicting events in 1840, not interpreting

the course of history centuries after the fact. England would determine what constituted "beneficial" peace terms, which included the cession of Hong Kong. He judged the speech a "great success" but could not imagine its enduring echo. Palmerston, the foreign minister whose bellicosity Macaulay was defending, listened carefully that night. A decade later he refined Macaulay's allusion to justify the dispatch of a flotilla to threaten Athens with bombardment, explicitly referencing St. Paul but eliminating Cromwell: "As the Roman, in days of old, held himself free from indignity when he could say *'Civis Romanus sum'* [I am a Roman citizen], so also a British subject in whatever land he may be, shall feel confident that the watchful eye and the strong arm of England will protect him against injustice and wrong." Palmerston's dictum lodged in the public mind. The transference exemplified Macaulay's genius for articulating what eventually seemed to be common sense without insisting on the credit. When the Americans coined the term "gunboat diplomacy" in the 1920s, they were naming a practice long familiar on several continents.[5]

Nineteen months after vindicating the Opium War, Macaulay published ninety-six pages on a new biography of Hastings in the *Edinburgh Review*. Because the book, which he had asked to review, amounted to hagiography, he decided to fashion a more credible rehabilitation. Despite Hastings' cruelty and corruption, he seemed "a noble subject": "the hero." To make the case for him, Macaulay again shunned Thucydides' judicial austerity in favor of the pleader's arts. Writing proved hard going. Because of the many gaps in his knowledge of India, he took "advantage of being in hourly intercourse with Trevelyan." As pages multiplied, Macaulay toyed with dividing the piece, and after publication he continued fretting over his prose.[6]

More than ever, the literary marketplace influenced how he wrote. Training himself to be a biographer with a genius for composing and polishing details into glittering set pieces, he failed to master the historian's craft of cantering across large stretches. "Hastings" appealed to a wider public than the normal readership of the *Review*. But Macaulay expected to hold his *History* to a higher standard than his essays and refused to authorize an English collection of them until smuggled American versions were "coming over by wholesale." His publisher offered "terms very favourable to me": they split the profits evenly. During the nineteenth century and afterward, authorized and unauthorized editions of the book sold hundreds of thousands of copies throughout the world.[7]

"Clive's" success enabled Macaulay to express his imperial vision more assertively. Brougham denounced its "most profligate political morality," but he was passé. "Hastings" offered a justification of empire-building to a public still mostly uninterested or critical. The ancients called Macaulay's rhetorical strategy *dicaeologia* (pleading necessity as an excuse). From beginning to end he presented himself as an impartial authority, neither idolizing nor demonizing Hastings but calculating his "great services to the state." Macaulay signaled that, to be respected, England must be feared, as Oliver Cromwell once made it. The Protector had commanded an artist to "Paint me as I am," and the result inevitably showed "scars and wrinkles." Macaulay's task was to tell a story that explained—or explained away—the many "dark spots on [Hastings'] fame." As with Cromwell, his contribution to England's power outshone all his blemishes.[8]

He was an Englishman who kept home in his heart while conquering and governing those "millions of Asiatics." By preventing "the stronger race from preying on the weaker," he helped India as well as England. A civilian, Hastings had followed Clive in learning from necessity the home truth that empires demand human sacrifice. The same school taught him the art of war. After Clive left the subcontinent in 1767 the "master class," breaking "loose from all restraint," unleashed "the most frightful of all spectacles, the strength of civilisation without its mercy" —shades of Cromwell in Ireland but to no rational purpose. Minus the constraints of law and justice, India lurched toward anarchy. Then the hero appeared. Again Macaulay was insinuating an analysis through the stories he told. Hastings personified the genealogy of power taught by Thomas Hobbes, for whom the state was "that great LEVIATHAN," which by creating order out of chaos became "that *mortal god* to which we owe, under the *immortal God,* our peace and defence." In passing, Macaulay introduced Edmund Burke, who became Hastings' nemesis, as one who misunderstood the Orient, including "the lower standard of Indian morality."[9]

A Bengali villain reminiscent of Clive's nabob had plotted the hero's ruin. He was "the Maharajah Nuncomar," who "personified" the national "character." Macaulay experimented with racialist language. The Bengalis were not just dark but "black," and other Indians were of a piece. Because the "dark, slender, and timid Hindoo shrank from a conflict with the strong muscle and resolute spirit of the fair race" of Central Asia, there was no resisting the even fairer English race. Just as the warrior race of the "Rohillas were distinguished from the other inhabitants of India by a peculiarly fair complexion," they were also "distinguished by courage in war, and by skill in the arts of peace." National characteristics sometimes expanded into continental characters—"Asiatic mendacity"—but Macaulay could still attribute them to climate or, in the opinion of Britain's first "racial scientist," to "religion." Race talk was another of his rhetorical ploys, as calculating and selective as his bellicosity. Thus, less than a year after "Hastings" appeared, Macaulay mollified Palmerston, choleric about French ambitions in Africa.[10]

Following a show trial Nuncomar was executed, but Macaulay blamed the judge rather than the hero, whose "conduct was dictated by a profound policy." The natives feared Hastings like a "tiger." The directors of the East India Company betrayed him by demanding that he satisfy both their lust for plunder and their hope for routine commerce. With the rest of George III's empire facing ruin in 1780–81, he won battles and made himself "the real master of British India." English bungling had turned Hyder Ali, the king of Mysore, into a "formidable" enemy. An equal-opportunity connoisseur of power, Macaulay turned color-blind and portrayed him as a medieval European king: "a man born for conquest and command," possessing "ability, severity, and vigilance." Defeating him required the talents of the hero, "a ruler of great talents and few scruples." Here Macaulay again insisted that in politics might finally makes right: "The English government was the strongest in India. The consequences are obvious. The English government might do exactly what it chose." Macaulay cataloged "the barbarities," including "torture," that the East India Company inflicted on helpless Indians to extort money. Because "great public services" offset "great crimes," the hero remained "one of the greatest men that England ever produced." In a nine-page eulogy, he pardoned Hastings even for his deep study of India's classical languages and for having done "little" to introduce "into India the learning of the West."[11]

Recalled to commercial and civilized England, Hastings had almost

undone himself. Superficially, Macaulay's purpled story of the hero's impeachment by Parliament seemed evenhanded. Burke was "the greatest
man then living." For him, "India and its inhabitants were not . . . as to
most Englishmen, mere names and abstractions, but a real country and a
real people," all of whom he saw with "the eye of his mind." Burke insisted, for example, that there was no "more glorious sight than that of
men, separated from a remote people by the material bounds and barri-
ers of nature, united by the bond or a social and moral community;—all
the Commons of England resenting, as their own, the indignities and
cruelties, that are offered to all the people of India." He invited his
compatriots to join him in using "the moral imagination." From experience Macaulay knew that the imperial venture required highly selective
vision—often a steely myopia—rather than wide-eyed attention to the
fate of alien peoples. Burke, however, was a sentimentalist: "His reason,
powerful as it was, became the slave of feelings which it should have
controlled. His indignation, virtuous in its origin, acquired too much of
the character of personal aversion." Macaulay went on to allude to his
own closeness to that "great and good man, the late William Wilberforce," but without mentioning that Wilberforce had been no fan of
Hastings. Here as elsewhere when writing subversively, Macaulay used
camouflage.[12]

His account of the hero's trial was a rich confection of Englishness
and imperialism frosted with tradition, pomp, and celebrity: "There were
gathered together, from all parts of a great, free, enlightened, and prosperous empire, grace and female loveliness, wit and learning, the representatives of every science and of every art." Macaulay put the imperial skeptic Burke in his place. Despite his superiority "to every orator, ancient
and modern," he had refused to adapt "his reasonings and his style to the
capacity and taste of his hearers." Realism informed Macaulay's overripe
rhetoric. He knew that impeachment was an archaism, "not a proceeding
from which much good can now be expected." Despite his trumpeting
of progress, he also understood "the instability of all human things . . . the
instability of power and fame and life . . . the more lamentable instability
of friendship." The seven-year-long trial ended in the hero's acquittal
and eventual apotheosis in the holy city of Benares (Varanasi). That improbable outcome enabled Macaulay to turn Burke against himself by
invoking his dictum that Hindus "worshipped some gods from love [and]
. . . others from fear." Hastings had understood that in India both kinds of

deities were necessary. Although he was "deficient" in basic "social virtue," disregarding "the rights of others" and lacking "sympathy for the
sufferings of others," the hero's "fervent zeal for the interests of the state"
redeemed him.[13]

Shortly after reiterating that it is better for an empire to be feared than
loved, Macaulay received news of victories in Asia and the Levant: "We
have placed England at the head of the world, we may be easy about the
rest." "Hastings" was even more popular than "Clive." In distant Philadelphia Edgar Allan Poe borrowed from it to craft a tale about time travel.
Macaulay's propaganda sometimes foretold policy. In "Hastings" he apparently digressed to note that the East India Company's servants returned to England resenting their reduced status and the deference paid
to "the aristocracy." To relieve that inequity he devised a strategy during
the 1850s for recruiting proper English gentlemen to govern the subcontinent. But history dealt ironically with "Hastings." When Macaulay
wrote in 1841 the Indian empire was still a widely unappealing work in
progress rather than the *fait accompli* he described. He was both its most
articulate booster and one of its principal architects. Even after Victoria
was proclaimed empress in 1877, Britain's South Asian empire consolidated and expanded. An early twentieth-century viceroy denounced
"Hastings" as "most vexatiously inaccurate and misleading." Fearful of
rising Indian nationalism, Lord Curzon rejected any criticism of the hero
as aid and comfort to the enemy.[14] It was perhaps the greatest tribute to
Macaulay's success in rehabilitating Hastings.

King Frederick II of Prussia also deserved Macaulay's attention because he "was with us as an ally" during the Seven Years' War, the European theater of the takeoff of imperial England. Macaulay wrote his life
"after the manner of Plutarch"—"my forte." "The necessity of grubbing
in German memoirs and documents" frustrated him, and he professed to
find the carnage of Frederick's wars repellent—"there is too much cut-
ting of throats." Noting Frederick's violation of solemn treaties in 1740
to launch the War of the Austrian Succession against England's ally,
Macaulay pronounced him guilty of worse than "gross perfidy." But alliance with England, the political equivalent of being born again or a ple-
nary indulgence, brought total forgiveness. In 1756, when Frederick
launched a preemptive war against the Habsburg Empire, England and
Prussia fought together, and he became "the injured party" acting "with
prudent temerity."[15]

Macaulay's happy appraisal of the rise of Prussia showed insight into the future of Europe, as well as curious shortsightedness. He fantasized that the "fame of Frederic" became "a rallying point for all true Germans" and began German nationhood. Passing over Frederick's notorious Francophilia and Germanophobia, Macaulay declared that "he did much to emancipate the genius of his countrymen from the foreign yoke." Although Macaulay discerned that Prussia would unify Germany, the long history of Anglo-French conflict blinded him to Germany's destabilizing potential in Europe. When he read the proofs, his dissatisfaction with the essay vanished. Though superficial, it would be "thought amusing enough." His estimate of Frederick continued to rise. In his masterful unscrupulosity he was a "truly great" ruler, worthy of Elizabeth I and Cromwell. Prussia reciprocated Macaulay's esteem. He received its government's highest cultural decoration, and five years later "Frederic" was published in Germany.[16]

In the long-delayed conclusion of Macaulay's biographical essay on William Pitt the Elder, created earl of Chatham in 1766, he tweaked his genealogy of Victorian England's imperial diplomacy. It was his last contribution to the *Edinburgh Review,* and his judgments were harder, simpler, and clearer: the stuff that can make best-sellers. In 1834 he qualified his praise of Pitt's leadership during the Seven Years' War—"It must be owned that some of our conquests were rather splendid than useful"—and asserted that Pitt had been "admired by all Europe." Now Macaulay acclaimed Chatham as "the idol of England, the terror of France, the admiration of the whole civilised world." Imperial Europe was synonymous with civilization. Possessing the "strange power of inspiring great masses of men with confidence and affection, by an eloquence which not only delighted the ear, but stirred the blood, and brought tears into the eyes," Pitt galvanized England to win the decisive war. Even so, he was blameworthy for neglecting England's interests in the wake of victory.[17]

For all that Macaulay favored hyperbole when evoking the eighteenth-century empire, his analysis of the period's domestic politics in "Chatham" was clear-eyed. The elder Pitt had known both that "modern Toryism" accepted the supremacy of the House of Commons and that the dialectic between order and liberty was "essential to the welfare of nations." Hence he discerned that despite Whig paranoia concerning George III as a would-be tyrant, distinctions between the parties "were almost effaced" at his accession in 1760. When circumstances required, Macaulay still bashed Tories, but his words were not visceral. As much as in 1760, the parties had too much in common to risk rekindling animosity between them. Macaulay, for his part, increasingly venerated Edmund Burke, often regarded as the founder of modern British conservatism, and tried to reclaim him as a Whig. Another strand in "Chatham" also pointed forward. Although the essay was primarily about dead politics, it included romantic vignettes for the benefit of readers easily bored by statecraft.[18]

A National Epic?

Begun in India, continued in Rome, and finally published in 1842, the *Lays of Ancient Rome* did most to popularize the Indian empire. The day after their publication Macaulay recalled that he had conceived them "in the jungle at the foot of the Neilgherry hills" and "during a dreary sojourn at Ootacamund" and a "disagreeable voyage in the Bay of Bengal." The book became an unexpected but enduring best-seller. With a "scholar-like" interest in the theory that written Roman history derived from lost ballads and "historical insight" that even now "seems quite brilliant," Macaulay tried to recreate four of them. His literal-minded nephew regarded the several prefaces to the *Lays* and a few paragraphs elsewhere as "the sole visible fruit of the thousands of hours which he spent over the classical writers during the last thirty years of his life." To ensure that his verses would be recited and remembered, Tom declaimed versions of them to his family and to Ellis. His brother Charles "heard them in the making" during rambles through London's "back lanes": "I never saw the hidden mechanism of his mind so clearly as in the course of these walks. He was very fond of discussing psychological and ethical questions; and sometimes, but more rarely, would lift the veil behind which he habitually kept his religious opinions." The satisfaction of such "unlearned" previewers bolstered his hopes for success.[19]

In the general preface he suavely rephrased the ethical dilemma of the "devastation and slaughter" that attend empire-building: "The old Romans had some great virtues, fortitude, temperance, veracity, spirit to resist oppression, respect for legitimate authority, fidelity in the observing of contracts, disinterestedness, ardent patriotism; but Christian charity and chivalrous generosity were alike unknown to them." His words amounted to "plausible deniability," reassurance to his Christian audience that he shared their virtues before inviting them to push their moral limits, perhaps to transvalue their values as they had with "Bacon." The exercise was delicate, requiring him to sustain the appearance of historical distance from the "old Romans" while evoking feelings of immediacy in his readers. Awaiting the page proofs, he worried that his book was "too modern" and had "a less antique air than I could wish."[20]

Macaulay's pastiches brought the imperial idea, dressed in toga and sandals and armed with a sword and shield, alive to his countrymen, especially to generations of schoolboys who memorized and often delighted in their martial anapests. "Made" in 388 B.C.E. to celebrate a century-old victory, "Horatius" is a plebeian's version of the heroic defense of the Tiber bridge against Etruscan invaders. In contrast to the patrician account, in which the solitary defender perished, Macaulay presented him and his two companions swimming "safe to shore" to be "loaded with honours and rewards." He helpfully noted, "Our own literature . . . will furnish an exact parallel to what may have taken place at Rome." His England was a land of happy endings. The heroes were noblemen, but the "author seems to have been an honest citizen, proud of the military glory of his country, sick of the disputes of factions, and much given to pining after the good old time which had never really existed." Macaulay's bard sounded like an eloquent and patriotic Cockney. Scorning class conflict, he properly deferred to his betters when they behaved:

> Then none was for a party;
> Then all were for the state;
> Then the great man helped the poor,
> And the poor man loved the great.

Within living memory countless English-speaking children from Texas to South Africa memorized at least one passage:

> Then out spake brave Horatius
> The Captain of the Gate:
> "To every man upon this earth

Death cometh soon or late.
And how can man die better
Than facing fearful odds,
for the ashes of his fathers,
And the temples of his Gods."[21]

Set a century later, "The Battle of the Lake Regillus" was "national in
its general spirit," though colored by "Greek learning" and "Greek superstition," above all by the *Iliad*. Here and there Macaulay interjected
his prim and rational Protestant voice. After the king's son raped a no-
blewoman and the ousted sovereign invaded with backing from Rome's
enemies, Rome became a republic. In those days the "licentious passions
of young princes" caused wars, and the Romans "were probably as credulous as the Spanish subjects of Charles V." With an eye toward the Newmanites' abuse of Anglican history, Macaulay quipped that Rome's "high
religious functionaries were, as usual, fortunate enough to find in their
books or traditions some warrant for the innovation." Their "discovery"
in 303 B.C.E. that divine intervention had given Rome victory at Regillus almost two centuries earlier provided them with a religious warrant
for a ceremony that saved Rome from "falling under the dominion either of a narrow oligarchy or of an ignorant and head-strong rabble."
Elements of both sides were accommodated, as in the 1832 Reform Act.
Barely able to mount a horse, Macaulay nonetheless deployed his warlike
vocabulary, depicting "a great lake of gore" over several pages:

For shivered arms and ensigns
Were heaped there in a mound,
And corpses stiff, and dying men
That writhed and gnawed the ground;
And wounded horses kicking,
And snorting purple foam.

Then, as legend had it, the immortals Castor and Pollux appeared, bringing victory:

Let no man stop to plunder,
But slay, and slay, and slay;

"Horatius"; drawing by George Scharf, in Macaulay's *Lays of Ancient Rome* (New York: G. P. Putnam's Sons, [1888]), 74. From "Horatius": "But his limbs were borne up bravely / By the brave heart within."

> The Gods who live for ever
> Are on our side to-day.

Only the very learned caught Macaulay's cryptic swipe at the Newman-ites' theories of apostolic succession in his allusion to the supposed epiphany of the twin sons of Leda and the swan.[22]

"Virginia," "composed" in 372 B.C.E. but set decades earlier, is doubly domestic in its concern with class tensions and gender roles. Mindful of the Chartist threat, Macaulay insisted in a plebeian's voice that, unlike the Greek city-states, where "the streets would have run with blood," Rome held together. Whether aristocrat or commoner, a good Roman stayed calm, law-abiding, and protective of "the lives of his fellow-citizens" in the face of virtual anarchy. Such sensible loyalty fostered "the reconciliation of the orders," which in turn produced two hundred years "of prosperity, harmony, and victory." Macaulay's cheery tale neglected the trauma of three wars with Carthage and stopped before the onset of the republic's paroxysms after 135 B.C.E. "Virginia," however, was more than politics and battle. The leader of a usurping oligarchy tried to use a legal ploy to violate the plebeian beauty. A "brave soldier," Virginia's father saved his honor and hers "by stabbing her to the heart" in public view. A "general explosion" ensued, overthrowing the oligarchs and driving to suicide the would-be violator of the "chastity of a beautiful young girl of humble birth." Macaulay's verses sound like misogynistic kitsch. The lecher

> came with lowering forehead, swollen features, and clenched fits,
> And strode across Virginia's path, and caught her by the wrist,
> Hard strove the frighted maiden, and screamed with look aghast.
>   Men destined Virginia for chastity or death:
> Still let the maiden's beauty swell the father's breast with pride;
> Still let the bridegroom's arms infold an unpolluted bridge.
> Her father loved her to death:
> "Farewell, sweet child! Farewell!
> Oh! How I loved my darling! . . .
> And how my darling loved me! . . .
> And now mine own dear little girl, there is no way but this."
> With that he lifted high the steel, and smote her in the side,
> And in her blood she sank to earth, and with one sob she died.

His clever sister Hannah thought it poor stuff, but their devout, aging, and unmarried sister Fanny and many men liked it best of all his ballads.[23]

"The Prophecy of Capys" is cast as an after-the-fact prophecy sung in

"Virginia"; drawing by George Scharf, in Macaulay's *Lays of Ancient Rome* (New York: G. P. Putnam's Sons, [1888]), 171. From "Virginia": "With that he lifted high the steel, and smote her in the side, / And in her blood she sank to earth, and with one sob she died."

the wake of the Romans' near defeat of a Greek army in 279 B.C.E. Later Romans learned to think of King Pyrrhus' near thing as the birth pangs of their new empire, and a generation after Macaulay Britons described it as a Pyrrhic victory. He transposed the ballad to the era of Rome's legendary founder Romulus (ca. 753 B.C.E.) to evoke "the patriotic enthusiasm of a Latin poet" anticipating the imperial future. Prefacing the poem were allusions to both Horace's celebration of the defeat of Anthony and Cleopatra and the *Aeneid*'s prophecy of Roman victories. Absent from Macaulay's ballad were the humane ends that for Virgil might have excused imperial brutality:

> But, Rome, 'tis thine alone, with awful sway,
> To rule mankind, and make the world obey,
> Disposing peace and war by thy own majestic way;
> To tame the proud, the fetter'd slave to free:
> These are imperial arts, and worthy thee.

Disdainful of "the lazy arts of peace," Macaulay presented his Romans as men from Mars:

> "Hurrah! For the good weapons
> That keep the War-god's land.
> Hurrah! For Rome's stout pilium
> In a stout Roman hand.
> Hurrah! For Rome's short broadsword
> That through the thick array
> Of levelled spears and serried shields
> Hews deep its gory way."[24]

Closing drawing by George Scharf, in Macaulay's *Lays of Ancient Rome* (New York: G. P. Putnam's Sons, [1888]), 210. From "The Prophecy of Capys": "'Where Atlas flings his shadow / Far o'er the western foam, / Shall be great fear on all who hear / The mighty name of Rome.'"

The *Lays* taught that Rome's invented traditions inspired its citizens to devotion, slaughter, and sacrifice. For Macaulay, those primal qualities rather than "Christian charity and chivalrous generosity" also defined modern "ardent patriotism." Taken together, the Christian centuries and the abundance of documentation complicated his task of fabricating a history of England that could similarly inspire the nation.

The initial run of 750 copies was respectable for a scholarly work. Disdaining "puffing of any sort," Macaulay enjoyed "the success of my little book." It grew wider and deep. In Oxford Arthur Hugh Clough, a restless don reinventing himself as an experimental poet, wrote out twelve lines from "The Battle of the Lake Regillus" in his commonplace book. The *Lays* charmed John Stuart Mill, whose liberal imperialism trumped his dislike of Macaulay. Elsewhere in London, Leslie Stephen, a clever boy of ten and the son of the permanent undersecretary at the Colonial Office, recited "them with the utmost glee." Virginia Woolf's father grew up to be famously no fan of Macaulay. By 1855 the *Lays* had sold 23,000 copies. The suppression of the 1857 Indian rebellion made their message current. Three years later the cumulative sales amounted to 38,000. By the summer of 1875 they exceeded 100,000 copies. Verses that Macaulay in certain moods considered learned and perhaps obscure —"the whole work is Hebrew to the crowd of penny-a-line men"— enabled him to spread his imperial enthusiasm wherever English was spoken. During the nineteenth century the French rediscovered *The Song of Roland,* the Germans *The Song of the Niebelung,* and the Spanish *The Song of the Cid.* The *Lays of Ancient Rome* provided England with a surrogate national epic. Their Englishness fed "a belligerent militarism which borrowed its rhetorical style, and its political culture if not its colonial policies, from the same Roman imperial imagery which had driven the earlier European empires." Despite highbrow condescension the *Lays* thrived into the next century because they inculcated "the nobler spirit of Roman heroism,—absolute devotion to the state" to schoolboys who might be called upon to die for crown and country.[25]

For Macaulay it was unthinkable that the classical Romans, however deficient in charity and chivalry, could have been uncivilized. He had invested too much of himself in them and their literature. In 1847 he, Robert Peel, and a common friend discussed whether the Romans still sacrificed human beings after 228 B.C.E., when the Greeks welcomed them up from barbarism. At issue was "how far the practice of human sacrifices can possibly coexist with any high degree of civilisation and refinement." Peel and Macaulay agreed that there was no credible evidence of the survival of the practice. Having studied the sources, Peel sounded judicial. Reading little, Macaulay pronounced it "absurd" to credit later Christian reports "in contradiction to the whole literature and history of antiquity." They were as incredible as the Catholic archbishop who "tells the Irish that the English government starved two millions of them last year." A demographic calamity was unfolding in Ireland, England's prematurely overpopulated, almost feudal colony. In the autumn of 1845 late blight devastated the potato crop, which fed much of the population. It struck again in 1847, 1848, and 1849. Probably correct about the Irish prelate, Macaulay was wrong about the civilized Romans: they had sometimes practiced human sacrifice.[26]

The poet remained an active imperialist politician. In November 1842 Lord Ellenborough, the Tory governor-general of India, whom he despised, ordered the restoration of Hindu temple gates supposedly carried by medieval Muslim invaders to Afghanistan, where the British captured them. Mocking Ellenborough in March 1843, Macaulay explained to the Commons that governing the subcontinent depended on courting the "warlike" Muslim minority. For all that his Indian essays portrayed England as almost omnipotent there and endorsed official neutrality "in disputes among the false religions of the East," he intuited that the empire depended on ruling Hindus and Muslims not as a body of 100,000,000 Indians but as members of inimical religions. Hinduism was supremely "unfavourable to the moral and intellectual health of our race," but Islam was almost an offshoot of Christianity and a potential counterpoise to the idolatrous majority.[27] Macaulay lost the vote and only later comprehended that Hinduism was the more accommodating religion.

That performance was relatively straightforward, but his speech against the sugar duties almost twenty-three months later was another exercise in impersonation. During the early 1840s Parliament debated whether to continue subsidizing sugar produced by Jamaican freedmen by imposing heavy duties on the cheaper product of Brazilian and Cuban slaves. On 26 February 1845 Macaulay claimed standing in the debate. As a young M.P. he "shrank from no personal sacrifice" in championing the

abolition of slavery throughout the empire, while the ministers who supported more expensive Jamaican sugar opposed it. He was silent about
his lingering bitterness at his father's irresistible pressure. Insisting that his
moral authority had endured although "my especial obligations in respect of negro slavery itself ceased," he declared American slavery to be
worse than Brazilian—perhaps the worst—because it was essentially rac-
ist. Two years earlier Macaulay had publicly contrasted "the gibberish of
the Negroes of Jamaica" with "the English of the House of Lords." In
late February 1845, however, he claimed to speak for "my lamented
friend, Sir Thomas Fowell Buxton"—the founder of the Aborigines Protection Society had died a week earlier. Macaulay absolved England of
any obligation to use its tax code "for the purpose of correcting vices in
the institutions of independent states," whatever the damage to freed Ja-
maicans. But even here brilliance touched his rhetoric. Anticipating a
theory widely accepted by mid-twentieth-century historians of slavery
in the Americas, he attributed the Brazilians' kinder slavery to the influence of their Catholicism.[28]

"The Diseased Part of the Empire"

With one exception Macaulay's calculating realism informed his recommendations for Ireland. England's first conquest remained the "diseased
part of the empire." He sometimes spoke of England's "great injustice"
toward Ireland, but what mattered was the failure to attach property-
holding Catholics to the crown by integrating them into the Anglo-Irish
elite. Enacting Catholic emancipation when the two kingdoms were
united in 1801 would have dissipated confessional resentment. Now the
best hope lay in tying the Catholic church to the state with golden chains
and thus move propertied Catholics to identify with the interests of their
class rather than with the mass of their coreligionists. It amounted to a
plan to buy the priests in order to control the people. In the spring of
1845 Macaulay joined Peel in advocating tripling the government's annual grant to Maynooth, the primary Irish Catholic seminary, and ap-
propriating £30,000 to rebuild it. But he also memorably twitted Peel
for too long opposing Catholic Emancipation: "There you sit, doing
penance for the disingenuousness of years." The debate was protracted.
All "eager, honest, hotheaded" Protestants opposed the measure, includ-

ing many of his Presbyterian constituents. He bravely defied them: "I have no apologies or retractions to make. I have done what I believed and believe to be right. I have opposed myself manfully to a great popular delusion. I shall continue to do so. I knew from the first what the penalty was; and I shall cheerfully pay it."[29] Macaulay always served England's national interests as he saw them even at political risk to himself.

Without knowing the term "social control," he understood its meaning. In the case of the Irish, "I heartily wish that they were Protestants. But I had rather that they should be Roman Catholics than that they should have no religion at all." Left unchurched, they would "live and die like the beasts of the field, indulge their appetites without any religious restraint, suffer want and calamity without any religious consolation, and go to their graves without any religious hope." Catholicism was corrupt, but after St. Peter's Macaulay reckoned that "the good seems to me greatly to predominate over the evil." He proposed to fund Maynooth by disestablishing the "most absurd" Protestant Church of Ireland and expropriating its endowment income. But the "Established Church of England" must be maintained for "the working man": "A Church exists to be loved, to be reverenced, to be heard with docility, to reign in the understandings and hearts of men."[30]

In 1845 Macaulay presented himself as misgoverned Ireland's friend: "I have done, and propose to do, my best to redress her grievances." His concern was calculating. When he had surveyed the "State of Ireland" in the House of Commons a year earlier, he had spoken with the voice of "Temple." The root of the Irish question was that the English race had conquered the Irish, but that the "Aborigines alone" among northern Europeans remained Catholics. He still regretted that the "great" Cromwell's "wise, and strong, and straightforward, and cruel" policy had died with him. He meant "to make Ireland thoroughly Anglo-Saxon and Protestant. If he had lived twenty years longer he might perhaps have accomplished that work"—again Macaulay projected onto Cromwell his own dystopian fantasy of decomposing a subject people in order to reconstruct their society. Unfortunately, the policy of William III, "or, to speak more correctly, of those whose inclinations William was under the necessity of consulting, was less able, less energetic, and though more humane in seeming, perhaps not more humane in reality. *Extirpation* was not attempted. The Irish Roman Catholics were permitted to live, to be fruitful, to replenish the earth: but they were doomed to be what the Helots were in Sparta, what the Greeks were under the Ottoman, what the blacks now are at New York." In the course of the debate that night Benjamin Disraeli, then a Tory backbencher, had disagreed: "the primary cause of the evils of Ireland is undoubtedly the manner in which that country became annexed to the English Crown . . . It was a conquest of a different kind, well known in ancient times, and down to our own days practiced in rude or semi-civilized nations—the conquest of race over race." In power a generation later Disraeli was less squeamish, exhibiting "sovereign contempt for anything that smacked of cant, especially religious cant."[31]

Macaulay disdained the aboriginal Irish without quite hating them. Except for his glimpses of hordes of them in 1849, they remained for him an abstraction—the primordial imperial problem. Unlike Burke, he could not imagine them with "the eye of his mind." The same one-dimensional calculation that he had once condemned in James Mill bounded his own human sympathies, much as it permeated the dogmas of classical political economy, which he and the Utilitarians accepted as self-evident truths.[32] A demographic, social, economic, and religious conundrum, the Irish question now seemed insoluble to Macaulay. If "extirpation" remained desirable in the abstract, the "sentimental moral philosophy" spread by "philanthropists" like Zachary Macaulay foreclosed it. Now, trying to manage the recalcitrant "Aborigines" required expediently mixing carrots and sticks.

Also a sound political economist, Peel seemed to be looking to eliminate the Corn Laws. In early November 1845 news of the blighted Irish potato crop caused him to urge their suspension. At the end of the month Lord John Russell, leader of the Whig opposition, announced his conversion to unconditional free trade in corn, and Peel resigned a few days before Christmas. Tom told Hannah: "If . . . Peel should still try to patch up a Conservative administration, and should, as the head of that administration, propose the repeal of the Corn Laws, my course is clear. I must support him with all the energy that I have till the question is carried. Then I am free to oppose him." On 2 December 1845 Macaulay spoke in Edinburgh in favor of a resolution that "corn laws press with special severity on the poor." Presenting himself as a steady opponent of "the principle of protection to agriculture" and predicting an extraordinary "crisis," Macaulay rejected the Tory government's adherence to sliding-scale tariffs, but without criticizing Peel. "Different stages of civilisation" produced different economic systems even "in the same climate." The future of his England—it subsumed Scotland even in Edinburgh—was industrial. In contrast, Macaulay foresaw "famine" in agrarian and regressive Ireland. When Russell failed to form a government, Peel resumed the premiership in late December. Macaulay deemed it imperative to "get the country safe through a very serious and doubtful emergency." Relying on Radical and Whig votes, Peel carried the abolition of the Corn Laws as well as a customs law in the Commons on 15 May 1846, and Wellington maneuvered the legislation through the Lords. The legislation replaced "the hegemony of a governing order and a set of political ideas that had preponderated since 1783" with a free-trade regime and ideology.[33] At the end of June estranged Tory backbenchers dumped Peel, who never again belonged to a cabinet.

Famine and disease plagued Ireland through 1849, killing hundreds of thousands of people and impelling more than a million to emigrate. Charles Trevelyan was instrumental in formulating and administering the government's policy there. Knighted in his services, he was praised by historians into the mid-twentieth century for his "outstanding administrative achievement." Although Peel appointed him overseer of Irish operations, Trevelyan opposed Peel's relatively interventionist policy. The economic orthodoxy to which Russell's government adhered after returning to office in July 1846 seemed more scientific. Then, in 1962 the gifted British narrative historian Cecil Woodham Smith (née FitzGerald) indicted Trevelyan, "virtually dictator of relief in Ireland," for refusing to close the ports to stop the export of Irish grain while thousands starved. Until the day before yesterday he was widely reviled as the evil genius of famine nonrelief. During the autumn of 1847 the Whig government effectively refused to pay to avert mass starvation. The basic Irish problem ceased to be dearth and became the maldistribution of food. Ingenious counterfactual scenarios imagine different government strategies saving countless lives, perhaps ending the famine. Their very complexity suggests that demonizing Trevelyan fails to explain the British government's indifference to the starving Irish. Invested with great power, he made a derisory "there but for the grace of God goes God" kind of man, but his economics were the common sense of his time, place, and class. Assured of his own rectitude, he merely obeyed its "laws." Like most of those in charge in England during the hungry 1840s, he deferred to the free market and relied on a benign Providence ultimately to bring good out of evil. An Invisible Hand worth capitalizing, Trevelyan's God punished Ireland for its archaic landlords and its feckless peasants. In time, even Peel hailed Trevelyan's achievement.[34]

Although Trevelyan helped to make and direct policies for starving Ireland, he never dictated them. His meticulous letter books from the famine years capture him at work. Lord Lansdowne, Macaulay's old patron, recommended using public money to assist the emigration of more Irish paupers to North America. Trevelyan disagreed: "The true test of fitness for an emigrant's life is the circumstance that the person selects that life without any artificial inducement and provides his own means for embarking in it." Three months later, with winter approaching, the mother superior of a convent school in Galway wrote asking where she could find food for her young charges. Trevelyan replied: "I do not know of any available resources except a Balance still remaining in the hands of the Relief Committee of the Society of Friends & I doubt whether they could make a grant."[35] "The survival of the fittest" was both an ideology and a reality years before it became a catchphrase.

Trevelyan made himself the best enemy of his own historical reputation. His decision to preserve his objectivity by visiting Ireland only once during those years did not make him discreet. In January 1848 he anonymously published a book-length essay in the *Edinburgh Review*. The premise of "The Irish Crisis" was that "posterity will trace up to that famine the commencement of a salutary revolution in the habits of a nation long singularly unfortunate, and will acknowledge that on this, as on many other occasions, Supreme Wisdom has educed permanent good out of transient evil." Mingling piety, uplift, and obliviousness, Trevelyan drove home the point in his peroration:

> The deep and inveterate root of social evil remained, and this has been laid bare by a direct stroke of an all-wise and all-merciful Providence, as if this part of the case were beyond the unassisted power of man. Innumerable had been specifics which the wit of man had devised; but even the idea of the sharp but effectual remedy by which the cure is likely to be effected, had never occurred

to any one. God grant that the generation to which this great opportunity has been offered may rightly perform its part, and that we may not relax our efforts until Ireland fully participates in the social health and physical prosperity of Great Britain, which will be the true consummation of their union.[36]

The essay fostered recurrent accusations that Trevelyan and the Whigs pursued an ideologically driven policy of using the famine to remake Ireland in England's image and likeness. If the claim is true, then Trevelyan was a notably unselfconscious engineer of eradication. He told Macaulay's publisher that many were urging him to repackage "'The Crisis' in a cheap form to circulate in Ireland," where it could "be freely purchased and would do a great deal of good." Trevelyan's most learned advocate discovered that his "draft was vetted and amended by . . . [the] head of the commissariat in Ireland and other senior officers, who were all asked for suggestions & emendations. It was read, commented upon, and edited by, among others, Sir Charles Wood, Sir George Grey, and T. B. Macaulay, each of whom assisted with the final version. This famous article was, in effect, co-authored by several ministers whose anonymity was assured." Charles assured his editor that he had consulted "Tom" while writing the essay, and "Macaulay was widely believed to have been its principal author."[37]

There is no determining where in "The Irish Crisis" Trevelyan stopped and Macaulay and his colleagues started. As events unfolded, Macaulay spoke infrequently in public, on subjects ranging from freeing imprisoned Welsh Chartists to relations with Portugal. About the famine he was nearly silent. Although he invoked calculation and Trevelyan Providence, they agreed about the desirable outcome in Ireland: uprooting or eradicating the cause of a "social evil." Macaulay translated the Reverend William Robertson's interpretation of Spanish imperial history as a story of God's bringing happiness out of carnage into one about the mundane logic of history. In defending the Opium War, Macaulay showed that he also knew how to back-translate his calculating words into those of faith: "that the overruling care of that gracious Providence which has so often brought good out of evil." He may have only read the assertion in "The Irish Crisis" that "even the idea of the sharp but effectual remedy by which the cure is likely to be effected, had never occurred to any one."

Or he may have written it. In either case, the author of "Temple" could appreciate the joke. The essay reflected how he regarded starving non-English subjects. In 1843 he insisted that in time of dearth "I would not give up the keys of the granary, because I know that, by doing so, I should turn a scarcity into a famine." In writing about India, he defined the imperial principle that guided him as he counseled and defended Trevelyan during the Irish famine. John Mill made it a cliché that "those who know something of India, are . . . those who will understand Ireland best."[38] The traffic of imperial ideas sometimes flowed in both directions.

There was no plan to "solve" the Irish question by denying sick and starving peasants adequate relief. But Trevelyan and his like-minded colleagues expected quicker results from God than Robertson had discerned in the late eighteenth century. On his showing, it took centuries to fathom how Providence ultimately brought good out of the conquistadores' brutality. Many progressive Victorians saw themselves as God's agents, competent to read His mind and hence to do His will in their own day, and they anticipated a quick payoff in return for their labors: "God grant . . . that we may not relax our efforts until Ireland fully participates in the social health and physical prosperity of Great Britain, which will be the true consummation of their union." The confidence that on Earth God's work properly belonged to England accustomed the public mind to acquiesce in the toll of "devastation and slaughter" that was, as Macaulay knew, the burden of civilizing empire. As the nineteenth century unfolded, other nations joined in with similar results.

Macaulay's deeds were consistent with his words. In August 1846 two Whig peers vetted a distinguished economist's essay on the Irish Poor Law. They joined Macaulay in urging a tougher bill. Jeffrey, the emeritus editor of the *Edinburgh Review,* thought that their scheme would likely "excite the bitterest resentment in all zealous Irishmen," because it breathed the "very contempt and distrust and dislike of their race, which we have always abused the Tories for entertaining." In toning it down, Russell eliminated the Macaulay-like assertion "that Ireland would be better under a despotism than a free government." During the late winter of 1847 Ellis asked Macaulay to ask Trevelyan how he could help alleviate "this Irish distress," and was told to send his money to either a reliable "Irish proprietor" or "the Committee in London." In good faith

Ellis entrusted his donation to his friend. Macaulay hoped that "I have used your ten pounds well. I have sent it to the Highlands where it will do good rather than to Ireland where it would probably have been useless." Scotland also briefly opened his own wallet.[39]

The Irish crisis would shadow his *History of England*. Basking in the success of its first installment and desiring to soak up atmosphere for the second, Macaulay made his only visit to Ireland during the late summer of 1849. While he was there, Trevelyan appealed to him: "the good you may do by placing on your *National record* just & liberal views of Irish history & policy—and it possibly may have the same effect on you—the present is a period of great change in Ireland; the elements of the social & political system of that country are in a state of Solution—and nothing would have more influence in giving a beneficial impress[ion] to the unsettled & susceptible mass than a striking & truthful statement of Irish affairs in your history." Six years later, when it was clear that the famine had yielded no "salutary revolution in the habits of a nation long singularly unfortunate," Macaulay obliged his brother-in-law in the next volume of his "National record," but on his own terms. "In the eyes of the peasantry of Munster the colonists were aliens and heretics. The buildings, the boats, the machines, the granaries, the dairies, the furnaces, were doubtless contemplated by the native race with that mingled envy and contempt with which the ignorant naturally regard the triumphs of knowledge. Nor is it at all improbable that the emigrants had been guilty of those faults from which civilised men who settle among an uncivilised people are rarely free. The power derived from superior intelligence had, we may easily believe, been sometimes displayed with insolence, and sometimes exerted with injustice."[40]

History Man

Reluctantly, Macaulay broke with politics in 1848, nine months after he was "completely beaten" in Edinburgh. He blamed his defeat mainly on his constituents' annoyance at his earlier support for the government's funding of Maynooth, a resentment stirred up by a leaked letter in which he dismissed as impracticable his prefamine proposal that the government pay Irish Catholic priests. Another cause lay deeper than he acknowledged—perhaps could see. When Russell became prime minister

THE ENGLISH LABOURER'S BURDEN;

OR, THE IRISH OLD MAN OF THE MOUNTAIN.

[See *Sinbad the Sailor.*

"The English Labourer's Burden," *Punch*, 17.ii.49. "No man of English blood then regarded the aboriginal Irish as his countryman. They did not belong to our branch of the great human family" (*HOE* 2:199–200).

in July 1846, he appointed Macaulay paymaster general of the army, which required him to resign and stand for reelection. He worried about the opposition of "these stupid fanatical [Presbyterian] brutes." Victory proved to be easy, and he relaxed. The cabinet post was worth £2,400 a year (with a 2007 purchasing power of over £166,000) and required no exertion—he spoke in the House of Commons "five times in all during the sessions of 1846 and 1847." During the 1846 campaign Henry Lord Cockburn, a Scottish Whig pundit, diagnosed his weakness as a modern politician: "Macaulay with all his admitted knowledge, talent, eloquence, and worth, is not popular. He cares more for his History than for the jobs of his constituents, and answers letters irregularly, and with a brevity deemed contemptuous; and, above all other defects, he suffers severely from the vice of over-talking, and consequently of under-listening."[41]

The most eloquent advocate of the Reform Bill of 1832, Macaulay remained a politician of the old regime. Reelection in 1846 failed to improve his constituency service. Feuding religionists made themselves more noisome than Chartists. According to Cockburn, Macaulay's opponents in the 1847 election were united "in nothing except in holding their peculiar religion as the scriptural, and therefore the only safe, criterion of fitness for public duty." As early as the 1841 election Macaulay had faced the problem: "I am surrounded by the din of a sort of controversy which is most distasteful to me.—'Yes, Mr. Macaulay; that is all very well for a statesman. But what becomes of the headship of our Lord Jesus Christ?' And I cannot answer a constituent quite as bluntly as I should answer any body else who might reason after such a fashion." The largest number of votes went to an ornament of the secessionist Free Church of Scotland, who was recommended because "Christian men ought to send Christian men to represent them." Macaulay's Whig colleague, a conspicuous Kirkman, won the second seat, and he polled third. His first public failure since Cambridge hurt. During the night of 30 July 1847 he wrote a long poem. It was mostly a high-minded meditation on renouncing "gain, fashion, pleasure, power, / And all the busy elves to whose domain / Belongs the nether sphere, the fleeting hour," and on devoting his remaining years to literature. But he also skewered Edinburgh's ingratitude: "For truth, peace, freedom, mercy, dares defy / A sullen priesthood and a raving crowd." Tom reassured Hannah that he was "as cheerful as ever I was in my life." When offers of other constituencies came in, he doubted that he could "follow my own inclination and . . . relinquish politics, for letters."[42]

But how real was his "inclination"? He spent September in the Netherlands with Ellis, touring and doing a little archival research for his book. Similar work occupied him back in London. Only when none of the bruited constituencies materialized did he resign his sinecure on 23 April 1848. Events made finishing his *History* seem urgent. During the winter and spring, revolutions shook most of Europe. The Irish famine dragged on. England's economy chronically ailed—a severe recession in 1845, a sharp financial downturn in the autumn of 1847, and an agricultural depression that lasted into 1851. It was all fodder for the Chartists. Two weeks before Macaulay resigned, tens of thousands of them peacefully but menacingly demonstrated across the Thames from Whitehall. Forgeries included, the petition to Parliament stating their demands contained over a million fewer signatures than its predecessor in 1842. Even so, Macaulay continued to fear "a crisis." Trevelyan pleaded with him to "make a powerful statement—*such as you alone can make*" against "the stoppage and breaking down of *this wonderfully artificial and complicated fabric of society*"—the regime of free markets and new men—and proposed to plant it as a leader in *The Times*.[43] Macaulay saw wider and further. Anticipating present-day scholars, he imagined "a long eighteenth century." The category enabled him to write a counterrevolutionary *History of England,* which would show that, far from being "artificial," the nation created by Catholic Emancipation, the Reform Bill, and the repeal of the Corn Laws was the logical consequence of the Revolution of 1688 and the fulfillment of everything good in England's past.

When Macaulay at last surrendered office, he was seven busy months away from publishing the first installment. Contracted ambitions and procrastination shaped it. In the summer of 1841 he shelved his plan to begin with the Revolution of 1688 and finish on the eve of the Reform Bill of 1832, reluctantly committing himself to writing "a history of England from the revolution to the accession of the House of Hanover" in 1714. He began serious research only a few months later. But the eighteenth century preoccupied him until the end of 1844, when he stopped writing for the *Edinburgh Review.* Budgeting his time and his attention proved less congenial than casting up his accounts. As early as 1842, Russell was reproving him for his frequent absences from the front bench.

Although Macaulay replied that literature not society kept him away, he remained a fixture of the London circuit.[44]

Learning to write for more audiences led him to experiment with different voices in his later essays. He scorned Fanny Burney's late prose because good English, like a good Englishman, was direct, clear, and accurate. His own distinctively English voice could be trusted to narrate his modern nation's story. But he also wanted a market share that Gibbon had courted before him: "something which shall for a few days supersede the last fashionable novel on the tables of young ladies." That ambition required him to entertain, but he also wanted a bigger audience than Gibbon's and knew that the "tendency of the vulgar is to embody everything." He knew how to smudge the line between history and biography. Historical characters became his *"Dramatis personæ."* Artfully evoking them required "seizing peculiarities which do not amount to deformity" while portraying "characters in which no single feature is extravagantly overcharged." Clapham had taught him how to appeal to Christian readers, resolutely prim if often light on dogma. He stopped treating powerful men's "immoderate appetite for sensual gratifications" as merely "a blemish." But when Macaulay identified a suitable villain, the conventions of melodrama could be irresistible. During the early 1840s he sometimes wanted volume control, railing against Alexander Pope—"all stiletto and mask," whose "life was one long series of tricks" —and damning Barère as one who "approached nearer than any person mentioned in history or fiction, whether man or devil, to the idea of consummate and universal depravity." By the late summer of 1848 he had refined his technique and was "working intensely, and I hope, not unsuccessfully" to bring his first installment "to print": "My third chapter which is the most difficult part of my task is done, and I think not ill done."[45] It was one of ten.

[7]

THE LAST
ANCIENT HISTORIAN

Chutzpah was not in Thomas Babington Macaulay's rich and polyglot vocabulary, but the first sentence of *The History of England* exudes the word's daring and ambition: "I purpose to write the history of England from the accession of King James the Second down to a time which is within the memory of men still living." Beginning an epic story and trying to attract, persuade, and instruct several audiences, he needed to connect with all of them and command their trust. With diversion, instruction, and authority, he exhorted his readers to expand the confidence they had invested in him as a statesman, orator, and essayist and to embrace him as a historian. Three cascading sentences declared his great themes: "I shall recount"; "I shall trace"; "I shall relate": "how, from the auspicious union of order and freedom, sprang a prosperity of which the annals of human affairs had furnished no example." His self-assertiveness testified to the sincerity of his story of England's rise. Also encompassing Wales, Scotland, and Ireland, his "England" others knew as "Great Britain." Scots in a way foreign to Macaulay, David Hume had established the practice of subsuming the stories of the other nations into "the narrative of English history." Macaulay was writing not *a* but *the* modern history of "our country," the definitive book in which future generations could see their past, maybe a book for the ages. Sharing the promise of England's power, glory, and wealth, his audiences would make their own his story of how England became "an empire" superior to Alexander the Great's. Knowing readers perhaps heard an echo of the beginning of Virgil's epic about the origin of another great empire: "Arms and the man I sing . . . And the long glories of majestic Rome."[1]

Macaulay did not purpose to write an objective history. His book was the product of a classically trained orator inspired by the art of Thucydides and the other great ancients. As much as any of them, Macaulay identified truthfulness with persuasiveness. More *chutzpah* two pages later indicated another of his classical affinities. The ancient historians were ignorant of footnotes, and modern novelists avoided them. Although serious modern historians referenced their sources, Macaulay absolved himself of that responsibility for the first two hundred pages of the *History:* "the facts which I mention are for the most part such that a person tolerably well read in English history, if not already apprised of them, will at least know where to look for evidence of them." A modern antiquarian and philosophical historian, rhetorical but no orator, Edward Gibbon had meticulously footnoted *The Decline and Fall of the Roman Empire* and learnedly defended his interpretations of his sources. Macaulay never bothered to establish rules for when and how to cite his. After asserting his self-evident credibility, he eschewed the humbling pronoun "I" except at the beginning of his third chapter and in footnotes that proved that he knew the homeland he and his readers loved.[2] It was another way of presenting himself as the omniscient narrator of English history.

The three major goals of ancient rhetoric informed his book. He aimed to teach his audiences by defending or accusing (judicial), to move them by persuading them to or dissuading them from opinions and actions (deliberative), and to please them by playing on their prejudices, beliefs, fears, and desires to praise heroes and their achievements and blame villains and their crimes (ceremonial). At seventeen Macaulay had understood that "eloquence which consists in the force and energy of ideas simply but nervously expressed, is the eloquence of all countries, of all ages, of all assemblies. At the bar, in the senate, from the pulpit, from the chair of the professor, from the hustings of palace yard . . ." He also knew that "eloquence and history are the two branches of literature which . . . we must yield to the ancients." Eleven years later, in his essay "History," he had proposed to modernize the practice of history, only to rediscover Thucydides and the others in Calcutta: "I did not much like Thucydides formerly. I have now no hesitation in pronouncing him the greatest historian that ever lived."[3]

The History of England from the Accession of James II is Macaulay's great-

est homage to his classicism. He read "like a man of the world": "during
the last fortnight, before breakfast, three books of Herodotus." No longer
did he celebrate the "victory of Christianity over Paganism" on account
of its energy, populism, and ethics. Rereading the ancients during the
late 1840s in dread of democratic revolution also convinced him to see
the past from their vantage and to look down on ordinary people as "politically too insignificant for history." Refusing to emphasize downstairs
over upstairs made his research easier and his life more comfortable. Most
great events had already been amply and accessibly documented. Con-
centrating on them spared him the uncongenial labor of trying to exca-
vate the records of the "stormy democracy" now threatening violence. In
his *History* the progress wrought by "noiseless revolutions" occurring below mattered less than "what historians are pleased to call important
events" directed from above. Apart from intimations in chapters one and
three, he identified such revolutions with political events whose long-
term consequences were unforeseen at the time. He therefore barely
nodded at the combination of plague and fire that made 1666 London's
annus horribilis et mirabilis, despite the abundant evidence of those "two
great disasters, such as never in so short a space of time, befell one city."
Instead he immediately paraded his chief specimen of noiselessness: the
"great English revolution of the seventeenth century, that is to say, the
transfer of the supreme control of the executive administration from the
crown to the House of Commons." High politics was now his story, and
political actors were his characters. After eulogizing Isaac Newton—"his
mind reacted with tenfold force on the spirit of the age"—he treated
him not as a revolutionary scientist but as a walk-on in his nation's revolution. More than Walter Scott or even the hero-worshiping Thomas
Carlyle, Macaulay depicted the powerful movers of great events as the
agents of historical change.[4]

In India he also buried Christian and enlightened cosmopolitanism.
He had once faulted the ancient historians for their "exclusive attachment to a particular society"; it had seemed to him then that English
freedom and civilization were pointless if "we grudge to any portion of
the human race an equal measure of freedom and civilization." Privately,
he elaborated his public critique of ancient patriotism. Helping to rule
Indians on their soil had made him a celebrant of empire and killed his
abstract sympathy for subject peoples, at home and abroad. When he de-

nounced hyperpatriotism for turning "states into gangs of robbers," he may not have known that St. Augustine had anticipated him in *The City of God*. Reading it in Calcutta, he had twitted it as "the most indecent book . . . in the Latin language." As a historian, Macaulay celebrated the tribalism he had once condemned in the ancients, who saw Athens and Rome as the proper objects of civic piety. England's "opulence and her martial glory" had raised her "from a state of ignominious vassalage to the place of umpire among European powers," made her the supreme "maritime power," incorporated Scotland, acquired American colonies "far mightier" than those won by the Spanish conquistadors, and enabled "British adventurers" like Clive and Hastings to acquire a matchless Asian empire. He designed his *History* to be "intensely English": "There is nothing cosmopolitan about it."[5] For him, England superseded Christianity as the font of national unity.

A late twentieth-century British scholar who resembled Macaulay in temperament, outlook, talent, and achievement concluded that "his most permanent contribution to the study of politics—what makes his *History,* in spite of all its blemishes, so difficult to fault—is his unerring grasp of political reality. Uninterested in abstract ideas, insensitive in his approach to persons, Macaulay had nevertheless an unfailing appreciation of political situations." Insert "almost" before "unfailing," and Hugh Trevor-Roper's verdict is lapidary. Writing history as "dead politics" for the instruction of living readers, Macaulay stands at the head of a formidable line of modern historians of power, usually committed nationalists, extending into the American century. He told a story about the making of English liberty, but his nation's power gave it liberty, and its power fascinated him. Trying to explain how during his lifetime England became the top nation, he grasped many of the causes that later professors made the stuff of textbooks. He knew that the eighteenth century, which he preferred, was decisive. England enjoyed relative political stability from the 1720s and immunity to invasion and domestic warfare after 1745; England came to rule a profitable seaborne empire, above all India, and achieved naval supremacy; England possessed rich supplies of iron ore and coal—"perhaps more important than iron itself"—as well as an edge in manufacturing that became commanding, producing "populous and opulent hives of industry"; and sometimes England was simply lucky.[6] Become a storyteller and mythmaker, Macaulay failed to meld his insights and intuitions into systematic analyses. His sheer intellectual power makes the loss palpable.

How he imagined himself as a historian controlled what he wrote and failed to write. Because he aspired to be the "perfect" modern historian, his *History* stopped at the threshold of the eighteenth century. Instead of trenchantly instructing elite readers, he wrote as a "poet-philosopher-prophet" eager to attract, to inspire, and to teach even nonreaders. That had been his ambition when he theorized about writing history in 1828. He drew on and promoted the transatlantic "sustained cultural fashion" of trying to explain people and their affairs historically. A market for usable history existed. But modern and analytically sophisticated historians failed to garner a mass audience: "History, it has been said, is philosophy teaching by example. Unhappily, what the philosophy gains in soundness and depth the examples generally lose in vividness." In Britain novelists told stories that were building a modern nation and teaching the public mind an undogmatic—the word was coined in 1857—and moralistic cultural Protestantism.[7]

Even in 1828, Macaulay had wanted to upend the rule "that history begins in novel and ends in essay." In order to reclaim the past from the novelists he proposed to infuse it with some of the broad human appeal of their stories. Then the "history of the government, and the history of the people, would be exhibited in that mode in which alone they can be exhibited justly, in inseparable conjunction and intermixture." The "perfect historian" must control his readers from the inside: "The instruction derived from history thus written would be of a vivid and practical character. It would be received by the imagination as well as by the reason. It would be not merely traced on the mind, but branded into it." He knew that "interesting the affections and presenting pictures to the imagination" required him to master "the art of narration." He also suspected that branding a story into his several audiences' minds required showing the life of the "nation" as well as that of "the court, the camp, and the senate." Therefore, nothing "which is not too insignificant to illustrate the operation of laws, of religion, and of education, and to mark the progress of the human mind" was too insignificant for him as a historian.[8]

Although his novelistic goal remained constant, his focus began to shift. Four months later he published the next installment in his careful thought experiment about how to write a useful and appealing modern history. Reviewing Hallam's *Constitutional History of England,* he admired and later imitated its "judicial" air of "impartiality" and basically disagreed only with its interpretation of Charles I's reign and Cromwell's Commonwealth. Hallam also confirmed that because "man . . . is always the same," an up-to-date historian could still craft historical details to present "speculations in a practical manner" for the benefit of "the initiated," as in "the Discourses of Machiavelli." "The vulgar" he would engage and instruct with colorful stories of life upstairs: "The favourite Duchess stamps about Whitehall cursing and swearing." Macaulay, finally, deduced from Hallam's book the importance of locating "national feelings" not primarily in political actors but "in the body of the people." The next year savaging James Mill's bloodless theory of human behavior deepened his conviction that history was applied political science, teaching "that noble Science of Politics . . ,—which of all sciences is the most important to the welfare of nations." Real English history, therefore, was mostly a story about the political nation.[9]

Macaulay realized that by dramatizing events he could mix the "history of the government, and the history of the people" without dwelling on what the late twentieth century would call history from below. He had always regarded Thucydides as the master of "the art of producing an effect on the imagination." Riveted to *The History of the Peloponnesian War* in Calcutta, Macaulay learned how the ancient historians turned readers into seers. Then he understood that both by personifying the English nation as for, with, or against their leaders' decisions and actions and by dishing up gossip from "the court, the camp, and the senate," he could attract a wide readership. Quietly, he buried his scruples about celebrating nations tyrannizing other nations: "In 1660 the whole nation was mad with loyal excitement."[10]

Above all, the ancient historians taught Macaulay that stories about the past should aspire to verisimilitude: "no history, can present us with the whole truth . . . History has its foreground and its background: and it is principally in the perspective that one artist differs from another." But objectivity—just the facts—was as impossible as it was undesirable. A fan of Walter Scott from boyhood, he wanted to make history lively. Anticipating modern historical and realistic novelists, ancient rhetoricians had fabricated a persuasive version of reality by arranging true or plausible

material. Early on, Macaulay understood that by dramatically representing life, an artist could surface the moral reality underneath persons and
events. At eleven he had composed a long "pathetic ballad" for his "dear
Mamma," a pastiche of famous English poems in which he dramatized
an everyday event:

> Fierce woxe the Knight and smote with rage,
> His hand upon the table;
> But all I now have wrote;
> And all that I am able.

"This incident really happened in our neighbourhood some little time
ago." It was a permanent lesson about the artful representation of reality.[11]

Writing history only increased Macaulay's appreciation of both classical rhetoricians and modern novelists. Imitating some of the ancients'
epic conventions—for example, looking backward and forward to unite
past, present, and future—reaffirmed his conviction that historians were
primarily artists, not scholars. In time Macaulay discovered that he owed
less to Thucydides than to the father of history. Feeling "somewhat anxious about the fate of my book" on its publication, he decided that
Thucydides' "dry parts are dreadfully dry" because he had followed
"mere chronological order," unlike Herodotus, a livelier "artist." Mostly
implicit, chronology is often blurry as Macaulay's *History* moves from
subplot to subplot. The drier classic came to seem inimitable. Rereading
Herodotus gave "great enjoyment," but Thucydides was "a more interesting writer": "read my book & Thucydides's which, I am sorry to say, I
found much better than mine."[12] Would-be "poet-philosopher-prophets"
must choose models. Unlike Thucydides' profound disillusionment,
Herodotus' liveliness seemed within Macaulay's grasp. But Herodotus'
encompassing human interest held no appeal.

The Medium

Macaulay wrote a huge book with an apparently simple theme: "The
history of England during the seventeenth century is the history of the
transformation of a limited monarchy, constituted after the fashion of the

middle ages, into a limited monarchy suited to that more advanced state of society in which the public charges can no longer be borne by the estates of the crown, and in which the public defence can no longer be entrusted to a feudal militia." He borrowed the interpretation from David Hume and other enlightened Scots.[13] Without either a blueprint or a timetable, Macaulay wrote first slowly and then reluctantly. He would never finish. Imitating *The History of the Peloponnesian War,* he began with the remote background, but his prehistory is seven times longer and nonetheless stops a quarter-century before James II's accession. He finally became king 200 pages later. The next volume ends with the proclamation of King William and Queen Mary less than four years later in 1689. The ten chapters of the first installment fill more than 1,000 pages. The second installment appeared in 1855. Detailing the next eight years, volumes three and four contain chapters eleven through twenty-two and total almost 1,200 pages—an average rate of production of less than a half-page a day, had Macaulay written daily for seven years. A brief third installment—just over 200 pages—the posthumous fifth volume closes with William's death in 1702. Macaulay devoted a couple of thousand pages in three installments to the years from 1685 to 1702. In comparison, Gibbon's stately account of the decline and fall of the Roman Empire from 180 to 1453 seems almost breathless.

Though a massive fragment, Macaulay's *History* triumphed, first as a commodity and then as a classic and an inspiration. Impressively analytic, its tight prehistory is also an exercise in self-congratulatory foreshadowing. A summary risks sounding like *1066 and All That,* which satirizes the teaching and learning of English history in early twentieth-century schools. In the beginning it acknowledges "the Great British People without whose self-sacrificing determination to become top Nation there would have been no (memorable) history." Though unschooled in the Middle Ages, Macaulay located the beginning of "the great English people" in the thirteenth century: "Then it was that . . . the national character began to exhibit those peculiarities which it has ever since retained, and that our fathers became emphatically islanders . . . in their politics, their feelings, and their manners." A century later "the amalgamation of the [Anglo-Saxon and Norman] races was all but complete," and "a people inferior to none existing in the world had been formed by the mixture of the great Teutonic family with each other, and with the aboriginal Britons." Within decades that great people was asserting itself in "so splendid and imperial a manner." The late medieval English, moreover, "were by far the best governed people in Europe," because Parliament constrained monarchical power. After six hundred years "of gradual development, not of demolition and reconstruction," the "polity" enjoyed unique continuity—"what the tree is to the sapling, what the man is to the boy." He honed the image from Edmund Burke, an exemplary celebrant of the Glorious Revolution. Macaulay promised to fulfill his "duty faithfully to record disasters . . . and great national crimes and follies far more humiliating than any disaster." But he quickly dismissed worry: "the general effect of this chequered narrative will be to excite thankfulness in all religious minds, and hope in the breasts of all patriots. For the history of our country during the last hundred and sixty years is eminently the history of physical, of moral, and of intellectual improvement."[14] The pious looked gratefully backward, but patriots found hope in the future.

From the outset Macaulay took aim at the pretensions of the newfangled High Churchmen to independence from the state. Depicting English history as the triumph of reason and the state over barbarism and the church, he extolled medieval Catholicism as a political system: "It is better that mankind should be governed by wise laws well administered and by an enlightened public opinion than by priestcraft: but it is better that men should be governed by priestcraft than by brute violence." From the thirteenth century the nation moved onward and upward "to the age of Elizabeth." While elsewhere in Europe ambitious monarchs came to control professional armies and to suppress "great national councils," England's "medieval parliamentary institutions" remained vigorous. Equally important for the future, England underwent "the great rebellion of the laity against the priesthood" known as "the Reformation." It produced that prodigious "compromise" the Church of England, subordinate to the state from its creation. During the reign of "the great Queen" Puritans, a species of hyper-Protestants, began to threaten the religious equilibrium.[15]

In 1603 she was succeeded by her Scottish cousin James, the first of those bad things called the Stuarts: "On the day of the accession of James the First our country descended from the rank which she had hitherto held, and began to be regarded as a power hardly of the second order"—

it happened not a day later, much less the following week. Unlike James, his son and heir Charles I was commendably unattached to "minions," though otherwise "crooked" and "despotic." Meanwhile two parties emerged, one disposed to order and the other to liberty. Both were essential to England's future greatness, especially when "they united their strength in a common cause." Charles provoked the friends of liberty and the Puritans to mount a "Revolution" intended to give "Parliament a supreme control over the executive administration." The king's loss of his throne and his head enabled Macaulay again to eulogize Oliver Cromwell: "such was his genius and resolution that he was able to overpower and crush everything that crossed his path, to make himself more absolute master of his country than any of her legitimate Kings had been, and to make his country more dreaded and respected than she had been during many generations under the rule of her legitimate kings."[16]

Macaulay understood what "absolute master of his country" implied for English liberty and meant what he wrote. The words signaled his preoccupation with the art—even the erotica—of power: "While he lived his power stood firm, as object of mingled aversion, admiration, and dread to his subjects. Few indeed loved his government; but those who hated it most hated it less than they feared it." Here Macaulay personified Machiavelli's dictum that for a prince "it is much safer to be feared than loved." Unfortunately for England, Oliver, powerful and progressive, died and was succeeded by a son who was merely nice. Soon the generals took charge and recalled Charles's namesake and heir. Macaulay went on to offer a counterfactual history of "the House of Cromwell" under whom there might have emerged "an order of things similar to that which was afterwards established under the House of Hanover" after 1714.[17]

The contingency of politics—the rule of fortune—was Machiavelli's insistent lesson, which Macaulay's experience richly confirmed. He nonetheless bracketed randomness and followed David Hume, who showed England "the remote, and commonly faint and disfigured originals of the most finished and most noble institutions, and . . . the great mixture of accident, which commonly concurs with a small ingredient of *wisdom* and foresight in erecting the complicated fabric of the most perfect government." Where Hume was unpersuasive, Macaulay won acceptance, in part because "the unplanned quality of the change in historical progress" had become a truism. If politics seemed to be contingent—no William III, no Glorious Revolution—progress appeared in retrospect to be virtually inevitable. Political advance occurred as the state responded to improvements in society. Sometimes Macaulay also echoed Hume's cultural and historical relativism, but his desire to acquire moral authority made him parade high dudgeon, even against the moralistic: "The Puritan hated bearbaiting, not because it gave pain to the bear, but because it gave pleasure to the spectators. Indeed, he generally contrived to enjoy the double pleasure of tormenting both spectators and bear." Macaulay's selective relativism let him ignore Hume's shrewd argument that because modern liberty is modern, the Stuarts could not be blamed for resisting it. Instead, with one eye cocked toward the present and the other straining toward the future, Macaulay followed Hallam in depicting English liberty as not ancient but "certainly not merely modern."[18]

At times the *History* resembles a kaleidoscope of stories. Narrating Charles II's twenty-five-year reign, the second chapter sets the tone for almost everything that follows. That charming and crafty rake triggered Macaulay's crowd-pleasing prudery, but he was a more complex and adroit ruler than the simple plotline of the *History*—retrograde Stuart despotism and ineptitude weakened England—allows. But a simple theme connects Macaulay's tales: the unparalleled greatness of England depended on the Revolution of 1688. Twenty years earlier he had hailed Cromwell as "the greatest Prince and Soldier of the Age." Now the shade of "the greatest prince that has ever ruled England," Oliver, loomed to rebuke his successor's toxic weakness: "his power was the terror of all the world"—evidence of the Chunzhi Emperor trembling in Beijing is sparse. Macaulay had already signaled to knowing readers the allegory underlying the contrast between Cromwell and Charles, along with much else in his book: "Thomas Hobes [*sic*] had, in language more precise and luminous than has ever been employed by any other metaphysical writer, maintained that the will of the prince was the standard of right and wrong."[19]

With rhetoric, flattery, moralism, and flashy stories, Macaulay sought to brand into simple readers' minds that they must obey the state because in England "the history of the government, and the history of the people" were "in inseparable conjunction and intermixture." He succeeded because he made the Revolution of 1688–89 seem at once national and transformative. In the wake of its centennial, Edmund Burke and Tom Paine had wrangled over the historical significance of William II, Stadholder of Holland, ousting his father-in-law James II. Burke had defended "the ancient organic, elastic constitution of England which the pragmatic Revolution of 1688 preserved," while Paine, champion of revolutionary America and France, had predicted that by 1888 "the Glorious Revolution of England so cried up by Burke . . . would be altogether forgotten." It was Macaulay's achievement to put that revolution "so firmly and so magisterially in the centre of our history—and indeed give it a new significance as the motor of economic progress."[20]

His third chapter is an original, brilliant, and tendentious effort to fabricate from vignettes and data a collage of English society barely touched by progress when James II became king in 1685. He found it "the most difficult part of my task." His research was creative and wide-ranging, but the chapter contains a hole that discloses both its purpose and the limits of his historical imagination and human sympathy. After 100 pages he wrote, "Nothing has as yet been said of the great body of the people, of those who held the ploughs, who tended the oxen, who toiled at the looms of Norwich and squared the Portland stone for Saint Paul's. Nor can very much be said . . . But it would be a great error to infer from the increase of complaint that there has been any increase in misery." Macaulay neither looked for nor presented detailed evidence to support his verdict, which was a reiteration of the chapter's drumbeat: you've never had it so good. As much as in his attacks on Southey and Sadler in 1830, he was debating the condition of contemporary England, engaging particularly the "those were the good old days" critique of the situation of workers, peasants, and the poor, who were "the great body of the people." In chapter three Macaulay insisted on progress as if it were "Holloway's Universal Family Ointment," a patent medicine of the time guaranteed to cure every complaint from nervousness to tumors: "We too shall, in our turn, be outstripped, and in our turn be envied." His pages offer no hint of the fraught interplay between economic progress and social dislocation that present-day historians find in the late seventeenth century. With the exception of a lament for "hundreds of excellent inns

... fallen into utter decay," the chapter is an exercise in disparagement of the past meant to impress on "the great body of the people" the manifest superiority of the present. His determination to tell a nationalistic story from the top down created another hole in the chapter. In the late seventeenth century even more than in his own time, local worthies and structures of authority had been pervasively strong. Devoted Londoner that he was, he barely nodded at them: "The example of London was followed by the provincial towns."[21]

The chapter is a tantalizing homage to the new kind of cultural and social history he had proposed to write twenty years earlier, but it stands alone. He never tackled the projected book-end chapter demonstrating that English "progress, having continued during many ages, became at length, about the middle of the eighteenth century, portentously rapid, and has proceeded during the nineteenth, with accelerated velocity. In consequence partly of our geographical and partly of our moral position, we have ... been exempt from evils which have elsewhere impeded the efforts and destroyed the fruits of industry." Put another way, "The history of England is emphatically the history of progress." But the chapter bristles with original ideas that he failed to develop and integrate into his story of high politics. A few seemed novel when they were rediscovered during the twentieth century. Thus, the German philosopher Jürgen Habermas has built a famous career on a theory about the appearance of the public sphere—"private people gathered together as a public and articulating the needs of society with the state"—in early-modern Europe, beginning with Britain. Macaulay sketched the theory—including the pivotal role of coffeehouses as meeting places.[22]

In chapter four the aggressively Catholic James finally accedes. Mostly about high politics, the first installment's remaining six chapters relate his malevolent and blundering attempts to tyrannize England to benefit his coreligionists: "That the King should wish to obtain for the Church to which he belonged a complete toleration was natural and right; nor is there any reason to doubt that, by a little patience, prudence, and justice such a toleration might have been obtained." Macaulay had reinterpreted the event whose unfolding he was narrating. When reviewing Hallam in 1828, he had sneered at what "has often been called, a glorious revolution. William, and William alone, derived glory from it. The transaction was, in almost every part, discreditable to England." William's indispensability was a constant for him, but seven years had transformed his view of the English role: "Thank God, our deliverers were men of a very different order . . . They were statesmen accustomed to the management of great affairs." Now he hewed to that line. Imbued with counterrevolutionary anxiety, his book includes a parable about how Whigs and Tories united to depose a tyrant and restrain "the mob of the capital." Far from the staunch Whig of legend, Macaulay wrote as "a partisan for consensus and civil peace" founded on respect for the state.[23]

Audiences and Voices

Into whose minds did he seek to brand his *History?* In 1850 about 31 percent of males and 46 percent of females in England and Wales could not sign their marriage registers. Some illiterates might listen to his book read aloud, but their attention was a collateral advantage. That literacy had grown steadily since 1750s and was nearly universal in 1900 gave his book a purchase on the future, particularly because literacy fed the vogue of respectability, which Macaulay insistently catechized. His book bristled with class consciousness. In both the present and the past, he identified the "nation" primarily with the respectable haves: "the majority of the upper and middle classes hastened to rally round the throne." His disdain for "the multitude" was massive and edgy—"Rabble," "Multitude," "Common people," "the vulgar"—equated with the "people"—"clowns," "Rustics," and "ignorant populace." Reading him perhaps flattered his respectable readers that they were superior, whatever their class. "The common people are sometimes inconstant; for they are human beings. But that they are inconstant as compared with educated classes, with aristocracies, or with princes, may be confidently denied . . . The charge which may with justice be brought against the common people is, not that they are inconstant, but that they almost invariably choose their favourite so ill that their constancy is a vice and not a virtue."[24]

Macaulay impressed on his readers the permanent connection between respectability and Englishness. Near the end of the first installment he fashioned a nightmarish story of London reverting almost to Hobbes's state of nature after James II fled the capital. Here Macaulay out-Burked Burke, who had stigmatized a revolutionary mob temporarily emancipated from the restraints of deference and religion as "a swinish multitude." Macaulay imagined a permanent underclass threatening respectability, property, and order and waiting to assault—"the human vermin."

Never within the memory of man, had there been so near an approach to entire concord among all intelligent Englishmen as at this conjuncture: and never had concord been more needed. Legitimate authority there was none. All those evil passions which it is the office of government to restrain, and which the best governments restrain but imperfectly, were on a sudden emancipated from control; the hatred of sect to sect, the hatred of nation to nation. [Respectability, the thin integument of civilization, had cracked]. On such occasions it will ever be found that the human vermin which, neglected by ministers of state and ministers of religion, barbarous in the midst of civilization, heathen in the midst of Christianity, burrows among all physical and all moral pollution, in the cellars and garrets of great cities, will at once rise into a terrible importance. So it was now in London. When the night, the longest night, as it chanced of the year, approached, forth came from the labyrinth of tippling houses and brothels in the Friars, thousands of housebreakers and highwaymen, cutpurses and ringdroppers [ingenious pickpockets]. With these mingled thousands of idle apprentices, who wished merely for the excitement of a riot. Even men of peaceable and honest habits were impelled by religious animosity to join the lawless part of the population. [Temporarily, the horror Macaulay warned against in the debates over parliamentary reform was realized, and many of those in-between united with the very poor.] ... First, the rabble fell on the Roman Catholic places of worship ... To the savage and ignorant populace the law of nations and the risk of bringing on their country the just vengeance of all Europe were as nothing. The houses of the Ambassadors were besieged ... It is honourable to the English character that, notwithstanding the aversion with which the Roman Catholic religion and the Irish race were then regarded ... no atrocious crime was perpetuated at this conjuncture.

Karl Marx once reported that bourgeois historians and economists had taught him "the historic development of this struggle of classes" and its "economic anatomy."[25] Insofar as Macaulay was representative of that tribe, Marx was not joking.

Macaulay's desire for big money moved him to write for audiences of markedly different interests and aptitudes. His book is an unfinished Fabergé, not the curate's egg, and its long popularity and survival depended on his literary genius. Appealing to naïfs and sophisticates alike, it gained a wide audience because it could engage readers wherever they picked it up or put it down. Beneath its verbal sheen complex purposes were at work. He understood the need to provide "the vulgar" with "visible symbols . . . imposing forms . . . mythological fables." Simple readers would read entertaining, moralistic, patriotic, and instructive stories and savor stock English characters, while the knowing and the clever would find embedded in them lessons about the frequent mercilessness of power. Deviously, ironically, and anxiously mingling uplift and subversion, Macaulay rebuked both stubborn clichés about the Victorians' complacency and our own confidence in our privileged disillusionment. Much noticed during his lifetime and then often studied, his book's style reveals something of its character. Macaulay preferred English words, mostly familiar and preferably with Anglo-Saxon roots, and usually shunned both imports and neologisms. But writing a best-seller required more than an easy vocabulary. To "arouse" and thus "inform" the naïve he relied on many of the techniques that he had mastered during decades of "speechifying": polarizing but also synthesizing antitheses, "insistent short sentences, either beginning with the same word . . . or cast in the same shape." As an astute present-day historian discerned, his "rage for anaphora"—the repeated use of a word or phrase to begin a sentence—was "borrowed from the rhetoric of the Bible and intensified for his own secular assignment."[26] It imparted a virtually religious aura to his book.

Vulgar and juvenile literates, however, were not his largest audience. He counted readers of novels, men as well as most women, among his preponderantly "dull readers," whose slowness required him regularly to "repeat myself"—a virtual license to skim. To entice them he plotted numerous melodramas featuring a variety of snarling villains and, devoted reader of Jane Austen though he was, women usually stereotyped

as either ladies or tarts. Thus, when "the wicked king" James II "determined to make his mistress countess of Dorchester in her own right,"
and the news spread, "the whole palace was in an uproar. The warm
blood of Italy boiled in the veins of the Queen [Mary of Modena]. Proud
of her youth and of her charms, of her high rank and her stainless chastity, she could not without agonies of grief and rage see herself deserted
and insulted for such a rival." The duty of inculcating respectability
caused Macaulay to hold his pen. For all that he admired *Tristram Shandy,*
a novel of superb bawdry, and relished the absurd, he honed the scrupulous diction proper to his notion of great historical writing and his prospective market's sensibility. Ostentatious tut-tutting while dishing out
mild titillation was a moralist's duty: "The King [Charles II] sate there
chatting and toying with three women, whose charms were the boast,
and whose vices were the disgrace, of three nations."[27]

Macaulay also spoke to serious readers who wanted "to draw from the
occurrences of former times general lessons of moral and political wisdom." Satisfying them depended on his ability to marshal and craft a
mass of details. Bacon, his ideal philosopher, had described what "Machiavel chose wisely and aptly for government: namely *discourse upon histories or examples.* For knowledge drawn freshly and in our view out of
particulars, knoweth the way best to particulars again. And it hath much
greater life for practice when the discourse attendeth upon the example,
than when the example attendeth upon the discourse." Convinced that
"history . . . is philosophy teaching by example," Macaulay brilliantly re-
juvenated the theory in *The History of England from the Accession of James
II.* He lavished care on crafting arresting stories that would grip his readers so that he could "brand" into their minds lessons in "that noble science of Politics." Informed by his respect for "Machiavel" as the modern
master of the "general maxims of statecraft," they offer a primer on
power. Narrating a botched effort to overthrow James II, Macaulay paraphrased and footnoted such a maxim:

> Experience has fully proved that in war every operation, from the
> greatest to the smallest, ought to be under the absolute direction of
> one mind, and that every subordinate agent, in his degree, ought to
> obey implicitly, strenuously, and with the show of cheerfulness, or-
> ders which he disapproves, or of which the reasons are kept secret

from him. Representative assemblies, public discussions, and all the other checks by which, in civil affairs, rulers are restrained from abusing power, are out of place in a camp. Machiavel justly imputed many of the disasters of Venice and Florence to the jealousy which led those republics to interfere with every act of their generals.

Immediately he resumed his story: "The Dutch practice of sending to an army deputies . . ."[28]

His maxims convey his almost "unfailing appreciation of political situations" as "abstract doctrines" to "the initiated." Because they were "general" or universal, they were timeless, and Macaulay depended on them to give his *History* a purchase on immortality. Their disillusioned and often cynical burden echoed his private voice. Thus, he noted that an acquaintance "was much affected & seemed grateful. But gratitude is the last thing that I expect from human beings." Two examples convey something of their tone and substance. Of religion, he wrote, "The general fate of sects is to obtain a high reputation for sanctity while they are oppressed, and to lose it as soon as they are powerful." And a few pages later he advised prospective rulers, "No man is fit to govern great societies who hesitates about disobliging the few who have access to him for the sake of the many whom he will never see." Abundant in the beginning, his insights thin out as the first installment unfolds.[29] Even when the subject is power, only so much can be said. *The Prince* is shorter than Macaulay's first chapter.

There are numerous obituaries of what he called the "art" of history. With characteristic learning and charm, Anthony Grafton recently delivered the most sophisticated of them. After correctly identifying the defect of the *ars historica*—"the professional deformations of the rhetorician"—and the necessary cure—kicking the 1,500-year habit of treating history "not as an independent discipline but as the empirical handmaiden of politics, a handy and endless cornucopia of examples to fit any theoretical need"—he described a long eighteenth-century detoxification. It permitted the scholarship of Leopold von Ranke "and other somewhat ungrateful heirs." Grafton's characterization of Ranke is just, but the death notice is premature. Until recently Ranke was misidentified as the first obituarist of the exemplar theory of history. No historical positivist, concerned like Thucydides with high politics, and publicly de-

ferring to Macaulay—"that great master of the art of descriptive history"—Ranke retailed a cliché about historical realism. His bow to the
History of England suggests that Macaulay's insistence on his own assidu-
ity and accuracy was read less as a rhetorician's shtick than as a scholar's
commitment. The confusion sustained his book's credibility and influence. Macaulay showed how to refashion *ars historica* into a modern historical narrative. Theodor Mommsen, the nineteenth century's greatest
historian of antiquity and the only professor of history awarded the No-
bel Prize in Literature, "was keen on Macaulay's *History of England,*"
which his publishers recommended as a model for his own *History of
Rome.* Like Macaulay, Mommsen "was driven by a message which makes
. . . [his book] a work out of whole cloth": present-minded and nation-
building.[30]

As much as people, books are judged by the company they keep.
Macaulay's modernization of the art of history took in part because
many of the "professional deformations of the rhetorician" continued to
mark even distinguished academic historians during the second half of
the twentieth century—and beyond. The continuing appeal of history
with a useful message owed something to the nineteenth-century rein-
vigoration of the classics as the foundation of elite male education. Outliving that curriculum, it owes even more to our abiding urge to find
in—or impose on—history order and meaning. By the late nineteenth
century the proliferation of historical data was subverting big stories and
easy generalizations about the past of nations, religions, and societies, as
well as sowing doubts about whether "objective" history could be written. Another episode of the Atlantic world's recurrent skeptical crisis, it
failed to instill a permanent "incredulity toward metanarratives" in either
historians or their readers, nor could it.[31] Even now, all of us live on the
stories we hear and tell about ourselves.

The Art of Invention

During the 1820s English historians were expected to produce more and
better evidence for their work. With help from two dead acquaintances
Macaulay complied. He mined French documents that Lord Holland
had reproduced in an appendix to Charles James Fox's fragmentary history of the reign of James II. More important were James Mackintosh's

forty volumes of research, including transcripts from foreign archives. They documented the years 1688–1702, which are the core of Macaulay's *History*. Without Mackintosh's unfinished, posthumously published *History of the Revolution in England in 1688,* Macaulay's book would be unrecognizable or perhaps nonexistent. Written after "several very attentive perusals," his careful review of Mackintosh enabled him to stake his claim on the whole period by outlining a narrative that creatively imitated the book and trashed the editor's effort to extend Mackintosh's text into 1689: "The Continuation which follows Sir James Mackintosh's Fragment is as offensive as the Memoir which precedes it." Rewriting the review for his collected essays, he confessed to attacking the man "with an asperity which neither literary defects nor speculative differences can justify." Perhaps the most vexing of those "differences" was the belief shared by Mackintosh and his editor that James II's design to impose a toleration that included his fellow Catholics, Quakers, and other Dissenters was more liberal than William III's Toleration Act, which excluded papists and Friends along with non-Christians. But more important than any disagreement was the dialectic of progress that Macaulay discovered in Mackintosh's pages. History moves by "actions and reactions," but the "recoil which regularly follows every advance" never prevails: "the great flood is steadily coming in." That Mackintosh's dialectic was becoming a transatlantic commonplace helped to prepare the way for the acceptance of Macaulay's *History*.[32]

Within weeks of returning to England in 1838, he secured "all Mackintosh's papers": "very valuable they seem to be." His engagement with Mackintosh deepened as he rushed to complete the first installment of his own book. By May 1848 he was "hard at work" on what promised "to be a source of wealth as well as of enjoyment." In early June he was still doing research and was fact-checking seven weeks later. By mid-August he was "working intensely," but still out of sequence and dining out four nights a week. On 1 September he signed a contract with his publisher, who suggested the misleading subtitle. Apprehensive about success during the last week of October, Macaulay put in almost twelve-hour days revising proofs to improve the style—his interpretations were lapidary. Facing the debut, he pronounced himself "pretty well satisfied."[33]

After nearly a decade he again kept a daily journal. It refutes G. O.

Trevelyan's description of his uncle as "never quite easy unless he completed . . . [his "task"] daily." His account of how Macaulay wrote is more credible. After conceiving a "story" in his head, he rapidly sketched "in the outlines under the genial and audacious impulse of a first conception"—inconsistently, he is also described as possessing "all the information relating to any particular episode"—onto big pieces of paper, which, after "a multitude of erasures" and interpolations, resembled "a chaos of hieroglyphics." He later added continuity between one big story and another. All the while, he slaved over details to make his book as readable as possible, in balance and in punctuation, "until every paragraph concluded with a telling sentence, and every sentence flowed like running water."[34] Crafting memorable rhetoric was laborious.

Throughout the *History* he quoted and paraphrased Mackintosh's book without citation, but he also contested, revised, and, more often, elaborated and embellished it.[35] Usually an advantage, Macaulay's almost photographic memory sometimes betrayed him into forgetting that the words in his mind were not his own. Mackintosh had clinically interrogated his sources. Macaulay was impressed, though not intimidated, by his success in extracting and condensing "the valuable and interesting part" from a "vast mass of intractable materials." Working from Mackintosh's evidence spared him "much of the labour which ordinary historians have to do." It also rendered him dependent on Mackintosh's interpretations and selectivity: "The judgment with which Sir James, in great masses of the rudest ore of history, selected what was valuable, and rejected what was worthless, can be fairly appreciated only by one who has toiled after him in the same mine." Although Macaulay both did and hired his own research, his metaphor was inapt and self-serving.[36] Not he but Mackintosh differentiated the "valuable" from the "worthless" in the sources. Never checking the transcripts against the originals, Macaulay stood at the pit head receiving and processing whatever Mackintosh had chosen to mine.

Dismissing Macaulay as an occasional plagiarist from Mackintosh distorts the intricate connection between their books. In his day historical literature was still viewed by some as a public resource, and borrowers who reinvented what they imitated were not quite plagiarists. For Macaulay, writing history was an exercise in the ancient and complex art of imitation, which was informed by "imagination" and hence inventive rather than merely replicative. Learning invention had been integral to his rhetorical education and all the well-crafted sermons he had heard as a boy. They aimed to achieve "scrupulous care in construction—UNITY in the design, PERSPECUITY in the arrangement, and SIMPLICITY in the diction." Thirteen years before the first installment of the *History* appeared, he understood that if he successfully invented—organized and crafted—material into persuasive or insinuating stories, his book would be popular and memorable: "The object of the historian's imitation is not within him; it is furnished from without . . . [from] a real model which he did not make, and which he cannot alter. Yet his is not a mere mechanical imitation. The triumph of his skill is to select such parts as may produce the effect of the whole, to bring out strongly all the characteristic features, and to throw the light and shade in such a manner as may heighten the effect." Macaulay remade Mackintosh's careful, chronological analysis into a drama rife with subplots. When read silently straight through, the *History* can appear serpentine, less fluent and more ornate than its model. But when read aloud—or better yet declaimed as he regularly did—it remains great fun in doses, exactly the rich and abundant "suet" he had missed when, devouring Mackintosh, he complained, "There is perhaps too much disquisition and too little narrative." But Mackintosh had also provided the remedy: "Sir James could tell a story . . . The most superficial reader must be charmed . . . by the liveliness of the narrative . . . A history of England, written throughout in this manner, would be the most fascinating book in the language. It would be more in request at the circulating libraries than the last novel."[37]

Crucially, Macaulay portrayed the accession of William and Mary as a transforming revolution actively supported by all patriotic Britons. His sixth chapter was "King James at Odds with England." Mackintosh, in contrast, had presented James's overthrow as primarily the decision of the English elites—"The nation trusted their natural leaders, who, perhaps, gave, more than they received, the impulse on this occasion." He titled his prerevolutionary eighth chapter "State of the Nation": "Remarkable Quiet.—Its Peculiar Causes." According to Macaulay, after William landed with his foreign army, "the English people [a few Devonian rustics] formed the most favourable opinion of a general and an army so attentive to the duties of religion." As he progressed through

Devonshire, "the acclamations redoubled when, attended by forty running footmen, the Prince himself appeared." Mackintosh's depiction of
the impetus and uncertain popularity of William's coup was more realistic. In the words of a standard recent history, "For day after day the overwhelming response to the invasion among the English was inaction. William hoped to attract Englishmen to his side, but his Declaration had no
immediately visible effect and few made the move."[38]

But Macaulay followed Mackintosh into libelous error by confusing
the Quaker leader William Penn with the unrelated George Penn(e),
who tried to extort a bribe to secure the release of young women imprisoned for sedition by James II: "Yet it should seem that a little of the
pertinacious scrupulosity which he had often shown about taking off his
hat would not have been altogether out of place on this occasion."
Macaulay remorselessly pilloried Penn's relations with James and refused
to retract his libel when confronted with persuasive contrary evidence:
"I leave the text and shall leave it exactly as it originally stood. (1857)."
He also cut a favorable reference to Penn in "Temple." The version in
his collected essays rebroadcast his endorsement of civilizing, imperial
slaughter, but it dropped his qualified praise for Penn as one of those
"honest men . . . who valued toleration so highly that they would willingly have seen it established even by the illegal exertion of the prerogative."[39]

His animus against Penn was more the result of political and religious
calculation than of antipathy. Once he determined to cast his *History* as
the epic of the whole people rallying to expel the tyrannical James in
favor of William and Mary, it was necessary to discredit Mackintosh's
theory that James had been more religiously tolerant than his son-in-law.
Not content with making the plausible case that James's policy was a
sham, Macaulay wrote as if Dissenters had overwhelmingly seen through
it in 1687–88: "The great body of Protestant Nonconformists firmly attached to civil liberty, and distrusting the promises of the King and of the
Jesuits, steadily refused to return thanks for a favour which . . . concealed
a snare." The contention required him to ignore available evidence of
considerable Dissenting support for James's Declarations of Indulgence,
especially in the provinces, and caused him to brand supporters whom
he could not ignore as men "corrupted by the court," especially the revered Penn, whom he once lauded as an "honest man": "the life which

... [Penn] had been leading during two years had not a little impaired his moral sensibility." Of the Quakers Macaulay owned in private, "I hate that sect. It is the dullest, vilest, most absurd of Christian sects—indeed I might say of all sects"—and he came to relish tormenting them: "I shall drive the Quakers mad." Like most such obsessions, Macaulay's hatred for the Quakers had deep roots. His editorial decision in the revised "Temple" to retain slaughter and excise Penn suggests that the pacifism of the "most absurd of sects" insulted the ethic of imperial power that he wanted to identify with England and its civil religion. One reference to Penn in the *History* may be telltale: "He will always be mentioned with honour as a founder of a colony, who did not, in his dealings with a savage people, abuse the strength derived from civilization."[40] Paying homage to Penn's humanity lent credibility to Macaulay's effort to discredit him for his dealings with James II.

Macaulay's Penn was a saint with clay feet—"his rectitude was not altogether proof against the temptations to which it was exposed"—a stock character like those Macaulay read in Tacitus, "unrivalled among historians" and almost unsurpassed "among dramatists and novelists" for his "delineation of character." He admired Tacitus on the Emperor Tiberius as a "miracle of art." It made "us intimately acquainted with a man singularly dark and inscrutable" by revealing "the specious qualities of the tyrant," "an Asiatic sultan," and "the most terrible of masters." Scholars continue to debate the accuracy and meaning of Tacitus' character of Tiberius. What matters for how Macaulay represented people is that he found the surreptitious depravity of "Tiberius" to be simple and appealing. Adam Smith believed that a sentimentalizing view of domestic life obtained in all wealthy and civilized societies, ancient as well as modern. Adapting Tacitus' technique to suit Victorian conventions enabled Macaulay to move his plot from one major public event to another by introducing human "passions and experiences": "William was not less fortunate in marriage than in friendship. Yet his marriage had not at first promised much domestic happiness." Macaulay used a scene from that marriage to introduce another of his principal sources, Gilbert Burnet, a Whiggish bishop whose *History of His Own Times* he mined to his own purposes. Then he returned to high politics: "A time had arrived at which it was important to the public safety that there should be entire concord between the Prince and Princess."[41]

Two ancient assumptions shaped the actors who populate Macaulay's *History:* their characters inform their destinies without quite determining them, and the circumstances and events of their lives shape them in ways that influence their actions and their fate. Tracing human action to an inner self is a postclassical notion related to the search for deep and particular motives and motivation. As innocent of such inner depth as Achilles, Macaulay's people sometimes change, but seldom very much. In addition, Macaulay, as much as Thucydides, lacked any sense "of the presence of evil as an active force in history." Hence his numerous villains tend to be figures of bathos more than of menace. Rebuked even by English Catholics, James II was an irresistible target, and Macaulay piled on him: "the excesses which filled such ['respectable'] men with horror were titles to the esteem of James." His portrayal of James's grandfather and namesake suggests that Macaulay's characters were not depictions of real people to be studied and evoked with insight born of shared humanity but instead his rhetorical creatures. To discredit James I as an effeminate coward and bungler who had harmed England, Macaulay, himself high-pitched and slightly lisping, prodigiously teary, and unskilled in arms, painted him as "stammering, slobbering, shedding unmanly tears, trembling at a drawn sword."[42]

More telling is how Macaulay invented the character of William III, greater than any of his contemporaries and a hero worthy of antiquity: "The place which . . . [he] occupies in the history of England and of mankind is so great that it may be desirable to portray with some minuteness the strong lineaments of his character." William was crucial for Macaulay's plot of the new England superseding the old. His story is a hand-me-down, which he first retold with dubious sincerity in the flush of his youthful classicism. Competing at Cambridge to win the ten-pound prize awarded annually for the best paean to William, he was twenty-one. The portrait he drew in the "Essay on the Life and Character of King William III" and much besides he elaborated and embellished in his great book. George Otto Trevelyan observed that "the characters of James, of Shaftesbury, of William himself; the Popish plot; the struggle over the Exclusion bill; the reaction from the Puritanic rigour into the licence of the Restoration, are drawn on the same lines and painted in the same colours as those with which the world is now familiar. The style only wants condensation, and a little of the humour which he had not yet learned to transfer from his conversation to his writings, in order to be worthy of his mature powers." Prefacing the piece was a Latin epigraph summarizing the vision of both his essay and his *History*. In the sixth book of the *Aeneid* the shade of the hero's father foretells the glory that will belong to his descendants:

> I know the Roman king.
> He shall to peaceful Rome new laws ordain,
> Call'd from his mean abode a scepter to sustain [*Missus in imperium magnum*].

Trevelyan declared it "the very appropriate motto."[43]

Decades later Macaulay, now more erudite and practiced in power, again cast William as the "lofty" savior whom with much rhetoric and little research he had confected for pocket money. His *History* perpetuates the prize essay's rhetorical purposes and limitations but without its undertone of sly self-mockery. In 1822 he was at the height of his dodgy radicalism and wrote with his tongue tilted toward his cheek. Chairing the prize committee was the Master of Trinity College, an unpopular clerical reactionary who had won the same award during Britain's war against revolutionary France. Macaulay knew his man and how to manipulate him for profit. In 1848 he still wrote for profit—potentially huge—but now in service of national uplift. He was disinclined to infuse his story with either irony or tragedy. It was Thucydides' skill in making "his narrative like a painting with events and people" that he emulated, not his evocation of human bleakness and futility. But irony cannot be indefinitely denied. In deploying the classical tools of rhetoric to airbrush and magnify William, Macaulay opted for the mythmaking of the *Lays of Ancient Rome* over the comparative realism of essays such as "Von Ranke." By propagating the Victorian fantasy of upbeat national rectitude, he built obsolescence into his *History*. A soldier died unblinking in the last days of World War I:

> My friend, you would not tell with such high zest
> To children ardent for some desperate glory,
> The old Lie; Dulce et Decorum est
> Pro patria mori.[44]

Wilfred Owen was not unique in either his death or his disillusionment.

The Message

One of Macaulay's best late twentieth-century readers discovered him converting "history into romance without violating any of the canons of truthfulness." In Macaulay's century the conventions of historical truthfulness could be generous. Abraham Lincoln reportedly said that "biographies as written are false and misleading," but the only source is his former law partner, a notoriously unreliable biographer. Whether or not the judgment was Lincoln's, George Otto Trevelyan's *Life and Letters* of his uncle confirms it. The book has been correctly described as "wholly unreliable in its transcription of documents" and "false again and again." Even greater leeway obtained among classical rhetoricians. To make a case they deployed an armory of figurative language and treated pleading as a professional obligation. What they said and wrote was neither meant nor taken as literal truth. By those standards, not just "and" and "the" but most of the words Macaulay wrote were truthful, including his vindication of William's superior liberality: "The opinion expressed by the Prince . . . respecting the disabilities to which Roman Catholics were subject was that of almost all the statesmen and philosophers who were then zealous for political and religious freedom . . . Such are the weighty arguments by which the conduct of the Prince of Orange towards the English Roman Catholics may be reconciled with the principles of religious liberty." As useful to Macaulay as rhetorical license was his Frederick the Great standard of truthful interpretation. Macaulay believed that history, and hence God, sided with big battalions, especially when they were English. Truthfulness therefore obliged him to affirm whatever appeared to serve his nation's interests.[45]

Identifying the magic whereby national histories offer "the powerless and disenfranchised a tremendous sense of entitlement and potential for the future," the historian Peter Mandler asserts that Macaulay's *History* was "only a halfway house between philosophic [enlightened] and nationalist history." His book was neither populist nor essentially racialist in its vision of Englishness. Mandler's high bar, however, excludes the robust, sometimes bellicose cultural and political nationalism that flourished throughout the Atlantic world during Macaulay's life. Antedating racialism and populism, it thrived into the twentieth century. It was the nationalism of Gerhard Ritter (1888–1967), professorial mandarin, admiring biographer of Frederick the Great, dedicated historian of the Prussian state and its officer class, antidemocratic but unwavering opponent of the Nazi regime, and cheerleader for Germany's annexation of Austria, but never a loud anti-Semite and one of the few plotters against Hitler in 1944 to emerge from prison alive.[46]

It was also the nationalism that Macaulay infused into his *History:* "Every yeoman from Kent to Northumberland viewed himself as one of a race born for victory and dominion, and looked down with scorn on the nation [France] before which his ancestors had trembled . . . In so splendid and imperial a manner did the English people, properly so called, first take place among the nations of the world." The political, cultural, and economic superiority of the "great English people" was the leitmotiv of Macaulay's story. Flattering stereotypes of Englishness color his depiction of the national character: "his stout English heart"; "the spirit of Englishmen, that sturdy spirit"; "his honest English spirit"; "the stern English nature, so little used to outward signs of emotion." He sometimes identified the national character with its "Protestant feeling," but he also knew that the race card trumped it: "No man of English blood then regarded the aboriginal Irish as his countrymen. They did not belong to our branch of the great human family. They were distinguished from us by more than one moral and intellectual peculiarity, which the difference of situation and of education, great as that difference was, did not seem to explain . . . The blood of the whole nation boiled at the thought."[47] If Macaulay's talk about competing nations' superiority, inferiority, and differing blood never quite congealed into an ideology asserting the existence of essential racial differences, in his pages Englishness made the English permanently better than the rest, particularly better than subject races.

Throughout the 1840s Macaulay relied on the imperialist rhetoric he carried home with him from India. In addition to giving Lord Palmerston the words he needed to sell his bellicose realpolitik, he anticipated Benjamin Disraeli's expansive approach in the Mediterranean and Asia during the 1870s: "Now that we have placed England at the head of the world, we may be easy about the rest. To dictate peace at once in the heart of Bactria, at the mouth of the Nile and in the Yellow Sea is something new." Macaulay scorned every premonition of liberal internationalism, and as famine depopulated Ireland he reiterated the occasional utility of civilizing slaughter in his book. Invoking metaphors of "blood" likeness and difference, he suggested that racial "enmity" sometimes warranted the extirpation of a backward race: "That cruel, but most complete and energetic system, by which Oliver had proposed to make the island thoroughly English was abandoned." Again echoing "Temple" several chapters later, he blamed James for Ireland's servitude after William's victory and associated the aftermath with Israel's divine mandate in Canaan. "The contest was terrible, but short. The weaker went down. His [the Irishman's] fate was cruel; and yet for the cruelty with which he was treated there was, not indeed a defence, but an excuse: for, though he suffered all that tyranny could inflict, he suffered nothing that he would not himself have inflicted. The effect of the insane attempt to subjugate England by means of Ireland was that the Irish became hewers of wood and drawers of water to the English."[48] There is no second-guessing an elect nation.

Macaulay knew that it is wise "to disguise strong acts under popular forms." Here as so often when his political lesson might seem too "cruel," he palliated it with doses of moral indignation and church-speak: "But, in the wicked court where the Hydes [James II's Tory, High Church brothers-in-law] had long been pushing their fortunes, such injuries were easily forgiven and forgotten, not from magnanimity or Christian charity, but from mere baseness and want of moral sensibility." Then he resumed making the case that the issue was "either the Irish or us" by alluding to rumors apparently spread by the sort of people whom he elsewhere dismissed as "the rabble": "It was well known that the extermination of the English colony in Ireland was the object on which" James's Irish Catholic lord deputy's "heart was set." Macaulay supplied no evidence. There is none. The deputy's "consistent objectives were to reverse the Act of Settlement so as to restore Catholics to their confiscated lands, to place the civil administration in Catholic hands, and to prevent any armed opposition to this by purging the army of protestants and by disarming the protestant militia"—revolution but not "extermination."[49]

During the 1880s a gimlet-eyed French nationalist insisted that "the essence of a nation is that all individuals have many things in common, and also that they have forgotten many things." Understanding that truth, Macaulay long benefited from it afterward. That the burden of his insistent rhetoric about race, subjugation, and civilizing slaughter continues to elude able and disinterested historians of various nationalities and religions—"to an Irish reader the bullying is merely amusing stage-Englishry"—testifies to the staying power of the humane portrait of him that his eminent nephew lovingly crafted and his still more eminent grandnephew preserved within living memory. Even more, it testifies that after World War II England had a fair claim to being, if no longer "top Nation," still a notably meritorious one. Its luster rubbed off on the reputation of more than one great Englishman: "What Macaulay did was to infuse the Liberal creed with the spacious and sanguine spirit of humanism and history." Above all, the commanding silence about Macaulay's imperial ethic of extermination testifies that generations of Americans and Europeans have ignored too much and forgotten even more, leaving a chapter in the moral history of the modern Atlantic world to be written.[50]

Edmund Burke had pioneered some of the counterrevolutionary and antidemocratic rhetoric that informs *The History of England*. Crucially, both he and Macaulay were silent about John Locke as a theoretician of the Glorious Revolution. Locke had believed in absolute natural rights; they did not. In the juvenile essay on William III, Macaulay had acknowledged Burke as "the most brilliant popular political writer of our country." On rereading most of Burke's works during his last decade, he wrote, perhaps with more conviction, "How admirable! The greatest man since Milton." Like other Whigs, Macaulay used Burke's notion of tradition selectively. Essential to it was a belief in deep-rooted and organically developing practices and institutions, but tradition also encompassed a perspective on nations and their history. To possess it was to be able to see the past come alive, neither lost nor imaginary but always beneath the surface of events.[51]

Macaulay's vision of the glorious English tradition enabled him to prophesy its future, which would be still greater so long as peaceful and gradual change prevailed. England was stable but dynamic because its government and its people were historically "in inseparable conjunction and intermixture." The state's legitimacy depended not on a social contract among mere individuals but on the whole people, who realized their collective identity through their nation and their government. As long ago as the thirteenth century, "the great English people was formed." Combining a plural noun and a singular verb was essential. It enjoyed the "best" medieval government, which alone in Europe endured and matured. Burke had declaimed to a similar end: "It is to be looked on with utter reverence . . . It is a partnership in all science; a partnership in all art; a partnership in every virtue and in all perfection. As the ends of such a partnership cannot be obtained in many generations, it becomes a partnership not only between those who are living, but between those who are living, those who are dead, and those who are yet to be born." In many of the stories Macaulay told he insinuated a more vivid sense of shared Englishness, as when he presented a few Devonian rustics as "the English people," forming "the most favourable opinion" of William's piety after he landed with his invading army. Apart from anaphora and hyperbole, synecdoche may be Macaulay's favorite trope. To "brand" his version of English nationality into his readers' minds, he artfully selected the parts he conflated with "the whole nation."[52]

There were, however, key differences between his nationalism and Burke's. Macaulay had no time for Burke's particularism, regionalism, or late anti-imperialism, his swooning over local magnates with ancient pedigrees, and his decrying the oppression of the Indians and Irish. For Macaulay, the civilizing imperative was integral to modern England's identity and power. It required establishing "the ascendancy which naturally and properly belongs to intellectual superiority," first over the domestic "mob" or "multitude," then over the Celtic fringes, and finally over a global empire, above all over India. In his story what seemed like chance fulfilled England's destiny as a nation and an empire, virtually the logic of God. Macaulay may have seemingly "banished the Empire to the margins" of his *History,* but only because he failed to reach the eighteenth century, his promised land. There he planned to make good on the imperial down payment of "Clive," "Hastings," and the rest.[53]

Macaulay also disagreed with Burke about the establishment's proper role. Both supported the union of church and state. Burke had seen it as the foundation of national identity and had championed laws penalizing Dissenters, but Macaulay championed including non-Anglicans to broaden the state's popular support. Like many believing Anglicans, he was a robust anticlerical who acquiesced in the church as the state's necessary tool. Apprehension about the Puseyites' assertive clericalism informed his portrait of one of their saints, Archbishop William Laud: "his understanding was narrow, and his commerce with the world had been small. He was by nature rash, irritable, quick to feel for his own dignity, slow to sympathize with the sufferings of others, and prone to the error, common in superstitious men, of mistaking his own peevish and malignant moods for emotions of pious zeal." Charles I's overweening ecclesiastical adviser "departed farthest from the principles of the Reformation," because he repudiated it as the watershed when politicians began to replace priests as England's guardians and to preside over its transformation into an increasingly modern because generically Protestant nation. In 1688–89 the relationship between religion and politics was at issue. Macaulay, however, inflated the ensuing partial religious pluralism into a theory about the ebbing of the establishment and its God before a "more secular outlook." At that point in his *History* politics, respectability, and language and literature more than Christianity started to define Englishness. It was another instance of Macaulay looking "at ancient transactions by the light of modern knowledge."[54]

In slighting the religious dimension of history, he also followed Thucydides. The Hellenist Peter Green, like Macaulay a sometime Craven Scholar at Trinity College, has wittily catalogued the tenets of "Thucydidean fundamentalism": "his obsession with eternal truths, his tendency to substitute dogmatic assertion for argument from evidence and to base universal generalizations on a minimum of parochial fact, his insistence on his own objectivity; all this fits the familiar profile of the *parti pris* fundamentalist with uncommon precision. But it also manages to avoid the normal fundamentalist's central tenet: religion. Or rather, it contrives to make a religion out of rationalism." On the subject of religion, a mixture of silence, deprecation, and ridicule leavened by insistent propriety and occasional unction informs *The History of England from the Accession of James II*. Within days of its publication, Macaulay noted in his journal: "It is odd that I have not yet seen a single line—encomiastic or vituperative—on the religious disquisitions which fill so many pages of the book, & which, I should have thought, must have excited the indignation of all sects, Papists, Churchmen, Puritans, & Quakers." He embedded many of his analyses in his stories, leaving his readers to discover England's precocious secularization. A few pages before reasserting the virtue of civilizing slaughter, he deprecated the moral authority of the Church of England: "It is an unquestionable and a most instructive fact that the years during which the political power of the Anglican hierarchy was in the zenith were precisely the years during which national virtue was at the lowest point." Under naughty Charles II the clergy, bent on "crushing the Puritans," winked at too many cakes, too much ale, and an appalling if titillating amount of promiscuity, upstairs and downstairs, not to mention political turpitude that encompassed treason.[55] At the apogee of their power they shrank from fulfilling their duty to uphold English respectability. By implication, the nation needed and deserved better.

More subtly, Macaulay also evacuated Providence from English history. Divines labeled the events of 1688–89 the "Glorious Revolution" to extol God as the deliverer of pulpit and throne. Bishop Burnet, whose *History* Macaulay reprocessed to his own secular purposes, perhaps coined the name. Believing that God controlled human affairs, Burnet remembered landing in England with William, who shared his belief: "I made what haste I could to the place where the prince was; who took me heartily by the hand, and asked me, if I would not now believe predestination. I told him, I would never forget the providence of God, which had appeared signally on this occasion. He was cheerfuller than ordinary." Macaulay retailed their conversation as a joke on Burnet. After turning his paraphrase of William's question into a direct quotation, Macaulay noted, "The reproof was so delicate that Burnet, whose perceptions were not very fine, did not perceive it," and then paraphrased Burnet's reply to William: "He answered with great fervour that he should never forget the signal manner in which Providence had favoured their undertaking." In a note Macaulay insisted that "nobody who compares Burnet's account of this conversation with Dartmouth's can doubt that I have correctly represented what passed," but provided no reference. Far from being a witness to that conversation, "Dartmouth" commented years afterward on Burnet's *History:* "a tory refutation of the period's most whiggish historian." A couple of hundred pages earlier Macaulay had belittled Dartmouth, defended Burnet against charges of inaccuracy ("altogether unjust"), and praised him because his "parts were quick."[56] Relying on dull readers' short memories, he knew that his inconsistencies need not damage their faith in his truthfulness.

That sleight of hand exemplifies Macaulay's "tendency to substitute dogmatic assertion for argument from evidence and . . . his insistence on his own objectivity." He was also making "a religion out of rationalism." Incredulous and present-minded, Macaulay imposed his vision of the mid-nineteenth century on William and Burnet. The story he told about "our Revolution" was mostly political: "a vindication of ancient rights" and the source "of every good law which had been passed during a hundred and sixty years, of every good law which may hereafter, in the course of ages, be found necessary to promote the public weal, and to satisfy the demands of public opinion." William for his part had declared that "above all" it was the danger to the Church of England that had provoked his invasion.[57]

After twitting the establishment's allergy to religious pluralism, Macaulay closed the first installment of his book with a doxology culminating in its hero: "our gratitude is due, under Him who raises and pulls down nations at his pleasure, to the Long Parliament, to the Convention, and to William of Orange." The peroration foreshadowed the rest of his history and his vision of the future. Along with most of his less cheeky expropriations from Christianity and its Bible to propagate secular English nationalism, it went undetected. When he was growing up in Clapham, tales of Noah's sons and all that had still helped to shape popular notions of British nationality. Insofar as Thomas Babington Macaulay correctly identified the "history of the national mind" with the history of the nation, he may still be England's most influential historian.[58] Who has done more to clarify and change its mind?

Previews

Macaulay's journals offer glimpses of him writing some of the stories that he told in volumes three and four of his *History*, as well as others that appeared in the posthumous fifth volume. Writing the book was the principal occupation of his last years. The process will be explored in that context, but the volumes themselves continue the themes and techniques of the first installment. Chapters eleven through fourteen almost cover 1689, and chapter fifteen launches his account of 1690 in England. Ireland and Scotland dominate the next chapter. Chapters sixteen and seventeen detail events principally of 1691. By the end of chapter eighteen 1692 has begun, and two more chapters take the story to Mary's death early in 1695. Chapter twenty-two, the last of the second installment, ends in 1697 with the celebration of the signing of the Treaty of Ryswick, which almost restored the status quo ante in Europe and beyond.

Instead of rethinking his book with a view to finishing it, he remained enmeshed in telling lively stories.

The later volumes also relied on the *ars historica* to create a modern nationalist history of England. Macaulay launched the second installment with a technique he had learned as a boy from Horace and revisited in Calcutta. Instead of recapitulating the first two volumes, he hurried "to the action" and snatched "the listener into the middle of things just as if it were already known": "The Revolution had been accomplished." It was an epic device as old as Homer's *Iliad* ("Sing, O goddess, the anger of Achilles son of Peleus, that brought countless ills upon the Achaeans") and as English as Milton's *Paradise Lost,* which opens in hell after the fall of Lucifer and the other rebellious angels. A couple of pages later Macaulay introduced King William III, no fallen angel but now trying to save an England threatened by a hellish darkness of its own. While "superficial observers" exulted, William anxiously and unhappily saw "that the difficulties of his task were only beginning. Already that dawn which had lately been so bright was overcast; and many signs portended a dark and stormy day." The Revolution that William and England had "accomplished" was unfinished. As long ago before the walls of Troy, battles and uncertainty lay ahead. For the benefit of sophisticated readers, he continued offering maxims, some of them adapted from the pages of Machiavelli: "what at one stage in the progress of society is pernicious may at another stage be indispensable."[59]

Starting *in medias res* allowed Macaulay to shunt between related episodes, looking backward as well as forward. Whereas the first installment of his *History* was mainly a present-minded exercise in searching for and often stigmatizing lost time, the second projected the future, when the nation and its Parliament would supersede the church and the court as the English race's center. It was, however, impossible to keep his hero at center stage as the presiding genius of that transformation. William III spoke "bad" English: "His accent was foreign: his diction was inelegant: and his vocabulary seems to have been no larger than was necessary for the transaction of business"—and trying to reproduce chunks of his guttural "taciturnity" risked turning "this great soldier and politician" into a figure of fun, "no better than a Low Dutch bear." Macaulay had to speak for and through the king, asserting the accuracy of his own paraphrases and projections by encasing them in quotation marks.[60]

What Macaulay foretold in his first installment now became an un-folding reality. He relied on English-speakers to show the nation quickly evolving into the great unifier of the people. His character of Bishop Thomas Ken, familiar in the nineteenth century through "his morning and evening hymns . . . still repeated daily in thousands of dwellings," captured the Revolution rendering the High Church obsolete. It is a brilliant performance. In chapter four Ken debuted "as a man of parts and learning, of quick sensibility and stainless virtue." Respecting him as a divine "zealous for the monarchy" and "no sycophant," the dying Charles II refused his ministry in favor of a stealthy conversion to Ca-tholicism. Later as a walk-on, Ken succored the first rebels against James II. His charity allowed Macaulay to introduce with unction one of the flaws that marked Ken as yesterday's man: "His intellect was indeed dark-ened by many superstitions and prejudices: but his moral character, when impartially reviewed, sustains a comparison with any in ecclesiastical his-tory, and seems to approach as near as human infirmity permits, to the ideal perfection of Christian virtue." Here Macaulay was using the rhe-torical technique of amplification to expand his description of Ken in order to diminish him and thereby refashion him as "a new reality." Two chapters later he recalled when Ken, chaplain to Princess Mary at The Hague, had discovered William's longtime mistress. Here Macaulay am-plified both to mitigate William's offense and to minimize "the excellent Ken, who was . . . so much incensed by . . . the wrongs [done to Mary] that he, with more zeal than discretion, threatened to reprimand her hus-band severely."[61] Ken thus stood exposed as both zealous and supersti-tious 135 pages before he and six other bishops became the heroes of the opposition to James II. In the spring of 1688 James imprisoned them on a charge of seditious libel for opposing his toleration decree. Generally hailed, their acquittal bled his credibility.

Summarizing evidence of the bishops' moral authority enabled Macaulay to subordinate the establishment to England: "Never had the Church been so dear to the nation as on the afternoon of that day." Twenty-seven pages later he interpreted their trial: "The prosecution of the Bishops is an event which stands by itself in our history. It was the first and the last occasion on which two feelings of tremendous potency, two feelings which have generally been opposed to each other, and ei-ther of which, when strongly excited to convulse the state, were united in perfect harmony. Those feelings were love of the Church and love of freedom. During many generations every violent outbreak of High Church feeling, with one exception, had been unfavourable to civil liberty; every violent outbreak of zeal for liberty, with one exception, had been unfavourable to the authority and influence of the prelacy and the priesthood." Ken's subsequent career proved that the modern church was both an expression of England's identity and unity and the habitual enemy of "civil liberty." Hesitantly, Ken declined to take the required oath of loyalty to the new regime and forfeited his see. Disdaining lesser clergymen who upheld the old order, Macaulay also emphasized Ken's reluctance and minimized his rejection of the new regime: "It is a curious fact that, of the seven nonjuring prelates, the only one whose name carries with it much weight was on the point of swearing, and was prevented from doing so, as he himself acknowledged, not by the force of reason, but by a morbid scrupulosity which he did not advise others to imitate." Ken had acknowledged no such thing. Macaulay went on to preview his life ending "in a happy and honoured old age," steady in his refusal "and yet constantly . . . more and more indulgent to those whose views of duty differed from his own."[62] The best of the old order cheerfully gave way to the new.

Macaulay never declared postrevolutionary England a secular nation, but his second installment ends with a giant ellipsis that insinuates as much. Evoking the state of the nation when peace returned in 1697, he omitted the security of the establishment, even of Protestantism. Instead of "love of the Church and love of freedom" as powerful, if usually "opposed," national "feelings" commingling in the Glorious Revolution, Macaulay depicted it as vindicating England's "liberty," reclaiming her "independence," and launching her progress: "The ploughmen, the shepherds, the miners of the Northumbrian coalpits, the artisans who toiled at the looms of Norwich and the anvils of Birmingham, felt the change, without understanding it; and the cheerful bustle in every seaport and every market town indicated, not obscurely, the commencement of a happier age." In 1828 he had insisted that the "reign of William the Third . . . was the Nadir of the national prosperity." A generation later he lacked any new economic data, especially about those lowly people. He needed, however, to bring down to earth a religious lesson he had learned in Clapham: "faith is the substance of things hoped for, the evidence of things not seen." Long after abandoning the hope of "a bet-ter *country,* that is an heavenly," he continued to believe that a nation's identity and well-being required a hopeful future. However little the En-glish people understood their unfolding progress in 1697—even in 1855—they must see that theirs was a "happier age" because after 1689 they were united with their government: "These all died in faith, not having received the promises, but having seen them afar off, and were persuaded of *them,* and embraced *them.*"[63]

In present-day America, the alluring power of the royal court in 1697 seems more alien than that of assertively politicized churches. Because monarchs then ruled as well as reigned, they remained the greatest sources of grace, favor, and power, which made the personal political and the political personal. To become a player required establishing and sus-taining access to the sovereign. From adolescence Hans Willem Bentinck was William of Orange's confidant. Following William to England, he served him loyally and mostly successfully and was richly rewarded with offices, titles, and estates. Bentinck "maintained a good relationship with Queen Mary and had married a lady-in-waiting of hers, Anne Villiers, sister of William's mistress Elizabeth . . . as a foreign favourite he started his career in England without any clientele, and was wholly dependent on the king's favour."[64] Both Charles II and James II had dispensed with favorites. Rootless in England, William revived the practice, which served to make his rule seem even more personal than theirs.

Macaulay's great theme was "the English revolution of the seventeenth century, that is to say, the transfer of the supreme control of the executive administration from the crown to the House of Commons." The revival of royal favorites undermined his story of the achievement of parliamen-tary supremacy and responsible government. There was, in any case, no denying the king's supreme authority, especially in "foreign affairs": "It was also fully expected that a prince of William's capacity and experi-ence would transact much important business without having recourse to any adviser." But advisers he had, informal and unelected, includ-ing his mistress, to whom "he still, in difficult conjunctures, frequently applied for advice and assistance," and Bentinck, "early pronounced . . . to be the best and truest servant that ever prince had the good fortune to possess, and continued through life to merit that honourable char-acter."[65]

Unable either to deny or to denounce William's court politics but eager to write off monarchical dominance, Macaulay needed to distract by creating a courtier worthy of sustained pillorying. With James and his entourage all exiled, dead, or reconciled to the new order, Macaulay turned on John Churchill. Under William III's sister-in-law and successor, Anne, he became the English generalissimo during most of the War of the Spanish Succession (1701–1713) and died the first duke of Marlborough. Sarah, his formidable wife, was Anne's longtime favorite. Macaulay, who learned from Henry Hallam how to blackguard Churchill, introduced him in the first installment as the brother of James's mistress and the kept lover of one of Charles II's concubines. But Macaulay painted him in contrasting colors—"handsome," "singularly winning," dignified, self-possessed, commanding "natural eloquence," with a "courage [that] was singularly cool and imperturbable, and "admirable judgment," which would make him a great commander. He was also greedy unto rapacity. When Churchill's troops were successful, Macaulay belittled them and by implication him: "The difference . . . between a regiment of the foot guards and a regiment of clowns just enrolled, though doubtless considerable, was by no means what it is now." Churchill darts in and out of these chapters, occasionally complimented but more often decried.[66]

Macaulay associated Churchill's personal immorality with the corruption of the establishment and the court: "He was bound to James, not only by the common obligations of allegiance, but by military honour, by personal gratitude, and, as appeared to superficial observers, by the strongest ties of interest. But Churchill himself was no superficial observer. He knew exactly what his interest really was." Foreseeing that James's design to purge Protestant officers from the army and replace them with Catholics would make popery the condition of royal favor, he prepared to forsake James.

> . . . it might seem that one who was not less distinguished by avarice and baseness than by capacity and valour was not likely to be shocked at the thought of hearing a mass. But so inconsistent is human nature that there are tender spots even in seared consciences. And thus this man, who had owed his rise to his sister's dishonour, who had been kept by the most profuse, imperious, and shameless

of harlots, and whose public life, to those who can look steadily through the dazzling blaze of genius and glory, will appear a prodigy of turpitude, believed implicitly in the religion which he had learned as a boy and shuddered at the thought of formally abjuring it . . . The earthly evil which he most dreaded was poverty. The one crime from which his heart recoiled was apostasy. And, if the designs of the court succeeded, he could not doubt that between poverty and apostasy he must soon make his choice. He therefore determined to cross those designs; and it soon appeared that there was no guilt and no disgrace which he was not ready to incur, in order to escape from the necessity of parting either with his places or with his religion.[67]

Almost droll, Macaulay's invective reiterated the church's inability to inspire either personal morality or national feeling.

Macaulay's character of Sarah Churchill supplemented that of her husband: "She was not yet what she became when one class of vices had been fully developed in her by prosperity, and another by adversity . . . that most odious and miserable of human beings an ancient crone at war with her whole kind." A footnote declared his self-evident authority: "It would be endless to recount all the books from which I have formed my estimate of the duchess's character. Her own letters, her own vindication, and the replies which it called forth, have been my chief materials." The future duke, and to a lesser extent his duchess, appeared regularly as the *History*'s first installment ended, notably as the "soul" of the "conspiracy" that undid James's will to resist his son-in-law's invasion. Losing the favor of William and Mary, they became less visible in volumes three and four: "In his behaviour on the field of battle malice itself could find little to censure: but there were other parts of his conduct which presented a fair mark for obloquy." Because Marlborough opened lines of communication with James II in December 1691 and may have confirmed details of the joint Dutch-British attack on France thirty months later, Macaulay indicted his as "the treason of a man of great genius and boundless ambition." Marlborough's purpose was to exploit English defeat in order to become the nation's inevitable general.[68]

The *History*'s fragmentary third installment was the product of illness and ennui. Containing only three chapters, the fifth volume narrates mostly domestic high politics and the lead-up to the War of the Spanish Succession, which began after Louis XIV violated his treaty undertakings by accepting the last Spanish Habsburg's bequest of his vast empire to a younger grandson and recognizing James II's son as king. The last chapter includes polished set pieces like James's death and the pirate Captain Kidd's adventures in the Indian Ocean and elsewhere, as well as a draft account of William III's fatal accident in March 1702. There is nothing about the earlier outbreak of the European war or other events of future consequence. Famously victorious, Marlborough would have occupied center stage had the *History* continued. Macaulay projected him as an inveterate courtier who finally grasped the main chance: "That very ambition, that very avarice, which had, in former times, impelled him to betray two masters, were now sufficient securities for his fidelity to the order of things established by the Bill of Rights. If that order of things could be maintained inviolate, he could scarcely fail to be, in a few years, the greatest and wealthiest subject in Europe."[69] Macaulay perhaps intended Marlborough's career as a fable personifying his book's theme: "The history of the government, and the history of the people, would be exhibited in that mode in which alone they can be exhibited justly, in inseparable conjunction and intermixture." If the secular nation garnered the loyalty of even that "prodigy of turpitude," need anyone be lost to England?

Macaulay's Plutarchan character of Marlborough seems over-the-top, indeed seemed so on publication to at least one close student of the evidence. But decades later it retained enough credibility to provoke the ornate and fulsome indignation of Marlborough's greatest descendant. In 1933 Winston Churchill published the first volume of *Marlborough: His Life and Times,* dedicated to "The Grenadier Guards Formerly 'the 1st Guards,'" in which the duke was commissioned and later commanded, and which showed Churchill "courtesies and kindness in the Great War." Almost five inches long, the index entry for "Macaulay, Lord" maps a detailed refutation: "It was reserved for Macaulay, writing in 1858 in the pristine vigour of Victorian propriety, to add lurid colour to this already sharply defined woodcut." Gently, Lewis Namier, an austere historian, tried to temper Churchill's obsession with Macaulay. It was unnecessary; royalties from the four volumes helped to restore Churchill's solvency.[70]

He was already campaigning against the British government's appeasement of Hitler.

While Churchill vindicated his ancestor, George Macaulay Trevelyan, Regius Professor of Modern History at Cambridge and Macaulay's grandnephew and "literary descendant," was covering the same ground in *England under Queen Anne*. It belonged to the Trevelyan family's project to put paid to Macaulay's *History of England from the Accession of James II* by extending it into the nineteenth century. Although Trevelyan reverently depicted Marlborough as the designated strategic heir of William III, he wrote with Macaulay in his rearview mirror. When Churchill's first volume appeared, he defended not his granduncle's portrayal of Marlborough but Macaulay's reputation against Churchill's charge that he lied: "ghastly mistakes, without being a 'liar.'" Earlier Trevelyan suggested that Macaulay intended to paint the conquering general differently: "He had blacked in the background, but did not live to put in the full-length figure of the victor of Blenheim in all his magnificent panoply." Politely noticing, Churchill remained unappeased. Trevelyan imagined that Macaulay meant to write a modern biography, though ineptly: "he was certainly not right on all the points of human character."[71] Neither he nor Churchill had received Macaulay's rhetorical education, and both failed to understand the nature of his character of Marlborough.

Although Macaulay built obsolescence into his *History,* he also endowed it with tenacity. All exquisite courtesy and mutual compliments, his grandnephew and Marlborough's remote descendant argued about a few pages in a huge old book because it still seemed to matter, and not only to them. Contemporaries at Harrow and sturdy British patriots, Churchill and Trevelyan respected each other as men and historians. Their shared sense of Englishness owed much to Macaulay and transcended family pride. Trevelyan "knew the *Lays of Ancient Rome* by heart (and have never forgotten them)." In boyhood Churchill memorized 1,000 lines of the *Lays* and always remembered "Horatius." His son insisted that "the stirring patriotism these verses evoked abided with him for ever and were the mainspring of his political conduct." Both wrote Macaulay's kind of history. It was mostly political, assertively nationalist, and meant to be widely read—"swinging narrative, careful study of the authorities, clear technical exposition, acute insight into several of the

principal characters, and an understanding of the conditions of the period so different from those of our own day"—but different only up to a
point. As a subaltern in India, Churchill studied "all Macaulay (12 vols)"
and became his greatest disciple. More than Trevelyan, Churchill adapted
Macaulay's style and some of his antique historical techniques. Ungently,
Namier rebuked him for painting "imaginary pictures of what *may* have
happened or what some people *must* have felt." Churchill repented: "a
weak indulgence on my part, but they sometimes make the ordinary
reader realize the position."[72]

Sharing religious unbelief with Macaulay, Churchill and Trevelyan remained occasionally and decorously conforming Anglicans. In Bangalore
Churchill read a now-forgotten book that consigned religion to the
dustbin of history. It "impressed me as being the crystallization of much
that I have for some time reluctantly believed . . . He may succeed in
proving Christianity false. He completely fails to show that it is wise or
expedient to say so. 'Toute verité n'est pas bonne à dire'—is the criticism
I have saddled his book with." For Churchill and Trevelyan, Britain—
what Macaulay called "England"—was a surrogate church, almost a surrogate deity. The archbishop of Canterbury whom Churchill appointed
remembered: "he had no very real religion but it was God as the God
with a special care for the values of the British people . . . it was utterly
right. But not at all linked on to the particular religion which bears the
name of the Christian faith."[73] Macaulay would have understood and
been glad. While that common faith in the nation retained the power to
assuage skepticism and inspire sacrifice, the importance of Macaulay's
History appeared self-evident. Now in most of the north Atlantic world it
all seems like antiquity.

[8]

THE LION

The History of England from the Accession of James II was an immediate triumph, whose success grew during Macaulay's lifetime and beyond. But acclaim and sales did not translate into contentment. Lionized and widely misunderstood on two continents as an embryonic political liberal, Macaulay was in fact poised almost to embody a stock figure of mid-nineteenth-century European literature: economic man, perhaps Silas Marner but as a respectable hedonist, never separated from his lucre, and set on pursuing love with something of the calculation that made him rich. At once self-aggrandizing and self-protective, Macaulay's sensibility also stymied progress on his book. He reckoned that he could never equal the success of the first volumes, and surpassing it seemed inconceivable. A more basic calculation enabled him to shake off his brief disorientation—a mixture of laughter and revulsion—at the sight of some of the human debris of the Irish famine during the summer of 1849: "what use is there in making oneself miserable."

Foreseeing none of that when the goddess success began blessing him, Macaulay relished her favor. As early as 9 December 1848, the first printing of 3,000 copies was nearly sold out. Over dinner that night Macaulay accepted "felicitations with great modesty and compliments." Three historians were among the admirers. On New Year's Day 1849 he told Hannah that his "success is beyond all precedent" and predicted, "I shall be a rich man if this mine bears working." Charles Dickens usually outsold Macaulay, but his novels were cheaper than the *History,* and his figures include sales of the magazines that serialized them. Volumes one and two of Macaulay's book went through thirteen printings, selling 36,570 copies in the United Kingdom by 1858, when a one-volume edition appeared. Another shrewd marketing strategy, the new format sold 34,949 copies by 1864. In 1876 total domestic sales of the book reached 140,000 copies. The demand was even larger in America, which rejected international copyright protection. By 4 April 1849 the authorized American edition had sold 40,000, with another 20,000 in four unauthorized editions. According to his New York publishers, by midsummer 200,000 copies would be gone. His gold mine yielded a bonanza. On 5 December 1849 he received his first year's royalty check from Longman: £5,500, with a purchasing power of £433,722 in 2007.[1]

Regardless of party or creed, Macaulay's compatriots learned to accept as their own his story about how England became modern. Puffing his book a few days before publication, the Peelite daily certified it as above partisanship: "four columns in my praise . . . a little too laudatory even for my self-love." An older historian professed shock—and perhaps implicit envy—at the merchandizing: "review a book before it had made its appearance? Why, I think that even managers of banks might take a lesson in jesuitry from book publishers." It was inevitable that John Wilson Croker, Macaulay's relentless enemy, would review the *History* in the *Quarterly Review.* The publisher warned Croker: "I have not the least desire in any respect to see Mr. Macaulay spared—but the book is so clever, so entertaining, and has taken such a hold on the public mind and affections, that a critic that would begin by abusing M. or showing signs of irritation against him, would run little chance of being read." As Croker dawdled, Macaulay tightened his "hold." Many reviews printed long block quotations, which enticed potential readers like present-day prepublication excerpting. Croker's essay proved to be long and feline: "one feels as if vibrating between facts that every one knows and consequences which nobody can believe." Besides correcting errors, he scored some direct hits, as when he noticed how often Macaulay paraphrased or quoted without attribution from Mackintosh's *History of the Revolution in England,* Macaulay's misrepresentation or overinterpretation of evidence, and his decision "to double-gild his idol" William III. But Croker finally subverted his own indictment. Affirming both that he was "as strongly convinced as Mr. Macaulay can be of the necessity of the Revolution of 1688" and that there was little new in the book effectively conceded that Macaulay had written a consensus history. Macaulay gave the review a

Thomas Babington Macaulay, by John Partridge (1849) (© National Portrait Gallery, London). "Sate two hours to Partridge . . . Still flattery—flattery—at least praise—vanitas vanitatum" (TBM, J1:515–16, 22.ii.49).

two-week run but primed the critic assigned his book for the *Edinburgh Review* with material "sufficient to smash twenty Crokers."[2]

More than politics, the *History*'s treatment of religion threatened its popular reception. Its handling of the establishment bothered Croker, but his was a minority opinion. Interpreting the erosion of the church's monopoly as an enduring political issue blinded him to how often Macaulay belittled or ridiculed its role in English history. A clergyman distantly related to Macaulay understood what his contempt for the mass of the clergy meant for their authority: "one of the lessons most earnestly inculcated on every girl of honourable family was to give no encouragement to a lover in orders, and that, if any young lady forgot this precept, she was almost as much disgraced as by an illicit amour." A searching correction of Macaulay's evidence failed either to change his mind ("silly book") or deter buyers. The continuing silence or cordiality of the "sects" that he twitted pleasantly surprised him—the Quakers inevitably remained a case apart. In a footnote the major Catholic reviewer noted Croker's "very damaging" criticism only to dismiss all objections to the book as "details": "we cordially agree with . . . [Macaulay] in almost all his general views of the history of the period." That complaisant Irish priest owed his job to the increased government aid for Maynooth, which Macaulay had urged at political risk to himself. Privately, a Catholic peer objected, but it mattered more for Macaulay's acceptance as a weighty Protestant voice that John Henry Newman, England's most notorious "pervert" to Catholicism, backhandedly accepted the *History*'s identification of Protestantism with progress. Croker's review passed into oblivion, and other *Quarterly* writers—including clergymen—began citing the book as authoritative. A Nonconformist journal gave him a "high eulogy": the "newspapers are full of me." Even a bishop's criticism was "civil clever & learned." Despite his "approbation" of most of the *History*, Macaulay jousted with him over particulars. Mocking him in private, Macaulay also adroitly played him: "We are the most courteous and affectionate of adversaries. You cannot think how different an opinion I entertain of him since he has taken to subscribing himself, 'with very high esteem.'" Approving bishops swamped grumbling about the *History*'s arch anticlericalism.[3]

Scattered evidence of how both his enemies and his admirers read the book confirms that it told a generally acceptable story. In late January 1849 John Stuart Mill, predictably captious, was "reading Macaulay's book": "it is in some respects better than I expected, & in some worse." He faulted it as an effort to ape "what people of genius do when they write history." More annoying was that "it will be & continue popular," because of its shallowness and tendency to play "to English conceit." Mill preferred reading French history. Our age has learned to revere Mill as a secular saint, but when his subject was Macaulay he routinely succumbed to power envy: "He is what all cockneys are, an intellectual dwarf, rounded off & stunted, full grown broad & short, without a germ or principle of further growth in his whole being." Nobody's candidate for any kind of sainthood, Thomas Carlyle damned the volumes as "the most popular history book ever written": "trivial." It was English, readable, and politically accommodating. Because Lord John Russell deemed it insufficiently Whiggish, both the duke of Wellington and Peel could praise it. Other sophisticated readers shared their appreciation of Macaulay's version of modern England. Born into the Monmouthshire gentry, the Prussian ambassador's wife was a cosmopolitan, religious, and well-connected bellwether. Frances Baroness Bunsen felt obliged to the book, "in truth of facts, in reality of character . . . for giving me *ten* reasons where I had *one* before, for holding opinions I have long held!" The *History*'s power to articulate and verify tacit knowledge ran downscale. A satirical journal reported that "gents at the Casino discuss the character of William of Orange" and imagined that "crossing-sweepers may soon be expected to differ on the true motives of Strafford." It was of greater moment that Macaulay received a "vote of thanks from the working people" in an industrial suburb of Manchester, "for the pleasure given them by my book which has been read to them on the Wednesdays of several months in the schoolhouse. I really prize this vote."[4]

Apparently having everything, Macaulay wanted more. His grudging acceptance of the Irish priest's endorsement of his *History* suggests a craving for universal adulation: "not unhandsome, nor, for Roman Catholics, unfair." He was allergic to criticism. Hearing of one longtime antagonist's hostility, he professed to "care little" but then went at her for thirty-two lines in his journal—he spent only fourteen summarizing the rest of that day. Self-protectively, he continued brooding over her. He also needed to demean another historian then sharing the spotlight. Beginning to sense that his own "book will live," he contrasted it with George Grote's vast, pathbreaking, and successful *History of Greece:* "Learned doubtless—but detestably written, affected & full of particularities." He fantasized about writing something in six months "which should blow Grote's work to atoms"—there is no evidence that Grote reciprocated Macaulay's explosive envy. For the most part there was unstinting approval. Dining out, he "talked with great success," perhaps "too much about my book," to please the other guests. But he also fretted about an inevitable "reaction." Telling himself that the "infinite flattery" was beginning "to pall lamentably," he nonetheless endured it. A year later it pleased him to hear that "the Queen was delighted with my book."[5]

When confronted with indisputable factual errors, he corrected them, but grudgingly and surreptitiously when they threatened his interpretation. There was no budging from his remorseless hostility to the Quakers or correcting his libel on William Penn. Macaulay turned a meeting with a delegation of aggrieved Friends into a publicity stunt. Preparing for a joust, he ridiculed the Quakers' "practices" to amuse some aristocratic ladies. Seconded by three of his friends, he routed the five protesting Friends—"every charge against Penn came out as clear as any case at the Old Bailey"—and "after their departure" mocked them. Macaulay remembered that the Quakers "complimented me on my courtesy and candour." In fact one of them described him as "extremely rude, treating the Friends with contempt." *Punch* obliged with a cartoon poem celebrating his victory. For years thereafter he dined out on the story. At Windsor Castle in 1851 he gave the queen "an account of it, which made her laugh most heartily": another royal endorsement.[6]

A few contemporaries recognized why Macaulay heaped "every vituperative epithet of the English language" on Penn and other seventeenth-century Quakers: they had "greatly accepted the freedom offered by" James II. Penn's early nineteenth-century biographer was instrumental in convincing other Anglicans of the righteousness of the Friends' opposition to slavery. Within months of the debut of the *History,* Thomas Clarkson's biography was republished with a critique of Macaulay's character of Penn. Zachary's habits of do-gooding and bad parenting had left his heir contemptuous of the whole tribe of philanthropists. In a railway carriage people once talked modern "cant": "not religious but Harriet Martineauish philanthropical and phrenological. I never heard such stuff." Personal animus merged with ideological antipathy to envenom Tom Macaulay against that energetic reformer: a "hideous woman,—if it

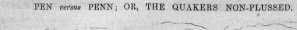

PEN *versus* PENN; OR, THE QUAKERS NON-PLUSSED.

MACAULAY wrote a book,
In which if once you look,
You 're fast, as with a hook, for volumes two, two, two ;
And this book shows WILLIAM PENN
Behaving, now and then,
Like something 'twixt a donkey and a "do," "do," "do."

The Pennsylvanian strand
PENN purchased out of hand,
When for toys and trash their land Red-men sold, sold, sold ;
Though the natives of the State
Have been avenged of late,
Since with Pennsylvanian bonds was bought our gold, gold, gold.

The Friends thought truth too bad
Of one who virtues had,
Such as wearing garments sad, and a broad brim, brim ;
And refusing, fair and flat,
To the king to doff his hat,
Tho' the king politely took off *his* to him, him, him.

Only worldly wits who scoff—
'Gainst such graces would set off,
That PENN of slaves made profit in sales, sales, sales ;
That he managed Court affairs,
And up and down back-stairs
That he carried heavy bribes and light tales, tales, tales.

Thus MACAULAY did arise,
Having not before his eyes
The grace in brims that lies, and in drab, drab, drab ;
And did wickedly declare,
That for nothing PENN did care,
So the Quakers got their share of the grab, grab, grab.

That his brims were so broad,
None could see him blush at fraud,
And that he who groaned and pshawed at a lace, lace, lace ;
For the Maids of Honour screwed
Their gold from those who sued
For themselves or guiltless children for grace, grace, grace.

So the Friends, extremely wroth
At this stain upon the cloth—
For MACAULAY pledged his troth to the fact, fact, fact—
They filled a Clarence cab
With valiant men in drab,
And off to the Albany packed, packed, packed.

The historian unscared,
Primed, loaded, and prepared,
Stood there with papers bared, and a grin, grin, grin ;
When, prepared his facts to floor,
They knocked at his door,
And were most politely asked to walk in, in, in.

Then their batteries they let fly,
But MACAULAY, in reply,
At their heads he did shy such a hail, hail, hail ;
From memory and from note,
Of reading and of rote,
There was nought he didn't quote, fresh or stale, stale, stale !

Not a single "thee" or "thou"
Could they put in, I vow,
But he counter'd, where and how they scarce knew, knew, knew ;
Till, faint and flabbergast,
They backed—backed—and at last
Unquakerishly fast down stairs they flew, flew, flew !

And, sad as their own drab,
Mounted ruefully their cab,
By the gift of the gab overborne, borne, borne ;
And, all Piccadilly thro',
In their faces plain to view,
Was "Lo! we went for wool and came back shorn, shorn, shorn."

Then, worthy Friends, take heed,
When next a truth you read,
Tho' unpleasant, 'tis agreed, to your pride, pride, pride ;
Don't suppose it can't be true,
Since it hits at one of *you*,
But vexation in humility pray hide, hide, hide.

CON. FOR CONVERTIBLES.—Why are SIR ROBERT PEEL and the bullionists eminent for philanthropy ?—Because they are distinguished as friends of their specie.

THE UNIVERSAL INSTRUCTOR.—A Book has been published with the title of *Who's Who in* 1849." If anybody wishes to know "What's What" during the same period, let him read *Punch.*

"PEN versus PENN," *Punch,* 17.ii.49. "I am to be honored by a visit from a deputation of Quakers who mean to give me a lecture . . . touching the character of William Penn. I . . . hope to reduce them to the state of a silent meeting" (TBM to Holland, 2.i.49, *L*5:6).

be not an insult to the sweet sex to call her so." Living to become one of his obituarists, Martineau dissected him as a soulless celebrity.[7]

The annoyances and pleasures of everyday life reveal some of his fragile humanity: a railway accident, delayed trains, "miserable" accommodations, stumbling and ripping his trousers, hurriedly breakfasting on coffee and buttered bread, failing to bring his spectacles to the British Museum and losing them to a pickpocket, regret at laughter missed, dainties from Fortnum and Mason, the frisson of gossip that made him feel concerned for its subject, forgetting to groom, and binge buying, especially books. He tirelessly loved London and for hours lost himself walking its streets, sometimes day after day. Despite his attentive family and heavy socializing, his celibacy created much solitude. He often dined alone over a novel at the Trafalgar Hotel in Greenwich. As he aged, memories of boyhood comforted him. Self-protectively, he more than ever clung to proprieties and routines. As his starchiness intensified, his compassion narrowed. Writing that the "modern fine gentleman" had "much in common with" Alcibiades was no compliment. Forgetting his earlier sardonic amusement at British prudery and sympathy for Byron's troubled childhood, Macaulay now condemned him as "a bad fellow, and horribly affected." He was as censorious of his own banker, a friend since Clapham who was determined to marry his deceased wife's sister: "how strange that such an instance of the tyranny of passion should be furnished by a man apparently so steady, grave, and decorous." Macaulay's own regrets, fears, and desires were seemly. Despite all his success, he often cried. Margaret's death haunted him, and his Edinburgh defeat in 1847 permanently grated. Concerned about his health, he worried that he was becoming "a regular valetudinarian"; he also briefly wondered whether acclaim might turn him into a fool. Although he fretted about his weight, his appetite could be uncontrollable. One night he took pills for distress. Feeling better the next evening, he sampled "some of the pâté de foie gras" that he planned to serve to guests: "I partly undid the good."[8]

Pilgrims from America

That tens of thousands of foreigners bought his book "pleased" and "puzzled" him. Its popularity abroad depended on England's reputation after counterrevolution triumphed on the Continent in 1849. Already the model of modern progress, Macaulay's nation became a redoubt of freedom and his "the voice whose tones would sustain the sinking spirits of the friends of constitutional liberty in Europe." In reality he was cheering on all the forces of continental reaction, including the pope. He imagined "the friends of order" as an international group. Although he sympathized with the defeated Hungarian rebels, he regarded the dissolution of the Austrian Empire as an unacceptable threat to the European balance of power. The brutal crushing of "the Red Party" in Paris delighted him. Visiting France in September 1849, he rejoiced that "the word republic is hardly uttered without a sneer." He supported Louis Napoleon Bonaparte's 1851 coup and championed him as Napoleon III: "The soldier is in France now what the priest was in Europe six centuries ago—he must govern, & ought to govern." The revolutions of 1848 left Macaulay contemptuous and fearful of "the rabble": "we are, I think, quite beyond the reach of infection now. The risk was something in 1848." More than ever, he respected domination as the precondition of civilization. In matters of property, "I am always for the man in possession." He explained to friends his "theory for being always in favor of dominant & successful races—Spaniards against Indians, Anglo-Saxons agst Spaniards, Russians agst Poles, Virginians agst negroes." For decades to come, many of his readers shared his apprehensions about threats to public authority and his deference to those possessing property or power.[9] Macaulay reassured them that England's history was at once a winner's tale and the story about the rise of modern liberty.

During his lifetime the first two volumes of the *History of England* were available in German, as well as "in the Polish, the Danish, the Swedish, the Italian, the French, the Dutch, the Spanish, the Hungarian, the Russian, [and] the Bohemian languages"—in some cases in rival versions. Continentals who read English preferred the original. An authorized version available in Germany and France "sold near ten thousand copies," and the reforming king of Portugal sent him "a most gracious" fan letter in English. Macaulay welcomed his unexpected European readership but relished and promoted the burgeoning American sales of his "insular" book, which even friendly "Scotch critics" found incomprehensibly Anglo-Saxon in spots. It confirmed his hunch that many influential northeasterners agreed that "the concord of the two great branches of the English race is of the highest importance to the happiness of both."[10] His steady American appeal made him loom larger at home into the twentieth century.

A few Americans pestered him with questions ranging from "the eternity of hell" to the meaning of "Truth" ("a great fool"). Unobtrusively, thousands of their compatriots also accepted Macaulay as an authority, "*the* English historian," at a time when "knowing about England seemed incumbent on every educated American." In the United States sales of his collected essays remained brisk, perhaps because reviewers, even when more disapproving than admiring, were confused about Macaulay's politics. By 1860 there were forty-six American editions, mostly pirated and cheap. Dressmakers, gas fitters, and pleasure-seeking readers who shared Zachary Macaulay's religious opposition to novel-reading found his son's *History* accessibly amusing. It also became appropriate reading for bright young people. In Boston, Oliver Wendell Holmes Jr. received volumes three and four just before his fifteenth birthday.[11]

Great fools and other ordinary Americans, Macaulay ignored, but he cultivated influential ones who crossed his path: "the Americans were particularly pleased, as I meant them to be." American culture was young and impressionable, and Anglophile New Englanders were crucial in shaping it. Visiting the mother country affected their sensibility and their speech. They or their children began to assimilate their inherited accent to "the language of the growing British Revised Standard." During Macaulay's lifetime many of them were learning to feel and think and talk in ways that helped to create a common Anglo-American culture that may also be called "Revised Standard." At a breakfast party on 13 July 1856 Macaulay strengthened one American's sense of belonging to that culture. Apart from a French prince, Richard and Annabella Milnes's guests were all English-speakers. They included three peers and a future peer, Elizabeth and Robert Browning, a future master of Trinity College, Florence Nightingale's mother and sister—Florence was returning from the Crimea—a popular novelist, the Boston politician and historian who owned the American counterpart to the *Edinburgh Review,* Lord John Russell's nephew, the Harvard professor who began the historical study of Spanish literature, and Nathaniel Hawthorne. The Americans were eager for Macaulay, "the lion": "He has been asked to meet us seven times, so that it has got to be a sort of joke."[12]

Arriving late, Hawthorne missed the introductions: "all through breakfast I had been more and more impressed by the aspect of one of the guests, sitting next to Milnes . . . There was a somewhat careless self-possession, large and broad enough to be called dignity; and the more I looked at him, the more I knew that he was somebody, and wondered who. He might have been a minister of state; only there is not one of them who has any right to such a face and presence. At last—I do not know how the conviction came—but I became aware that it was Macaulay . . . Well, I am glad to have seen him—a face fit for a scholar, a man of the world, a cultivated intelligence." Hawthorne viewed his hosts with a poor relation's emulous insecurity: "I liked greatly the manners of . . . all the people at this breakfast; and it was doubtless owing to their being all people either of high rank, or remarkable intellect, or both." When the senior English peer "made me precede him," Hawthorne felt "his sense of condescension"—the word was not yet a pejorative. Later that day he was inspired to visit the "State Paper office" to "ascertain the place, in England, whence the [Hawthorne] family emigrated."[13]

From afar Macaulay studied America. During a deadly meeting he "amused" himself by reading "Agricultural Reports from Michigan." A cyclorama of the Mississippi River interested him, as did "powerful passages" in a novel by Frances Trollope indicting American slavery. Economic calculation persuaded him that the Anglo-American connection would withstand frequent political tensions. A "benignant system of Free Trade" could bind America to England, just as his investments directed his attention there. He studied American reviews of his *History*. Predictably, critical ones, even in obscure journals, annoyed him, though he protested otherwise. He monitored the sales figures for his book: "the trade has been deluged with copies." Most of his American securities were similarly profitable. Macaulay understood American elites' sense of cultural inferiority, and his visceral Englishness sometimes turned xenophobic in the face of the vulgarity of ordinary Americans. Once while vacationing in France, he fell in with "dull bad company—Yankees smoking & spitting." Some of his kind of American, however, he regarded as honorary English gentlemen: "we Anglo-Saxons are not much given to expressing all that we feel. We leave that to the Celts, who generally overdo the matter as much at least as we underdo it. But when either the New Englander or the Old Englander really does pour his heart out, the effusion is not to be despised." Husbanding such sentiments, Macaulay routinely assumed that Americans were vulgar: "dull bad company." A young man appeared unannounced while he was hosting a breakfast party: "Though educated here at Cambridge he had the dullest nasal twang & all the manners of a thorough Jonathan [Yankee]." He was a grandson of the plutocrat John Jacob Astor and a foundation scholar of Trinity College. A proper introduction did not always appease Macaulay's hauteur. An accomplished and cultivated friend of a friend properly called to pay his respects: "He looked like a Spaniard & demeaned himself like a dissenting preacher."[14]

Macaulay's "fear of being mobbed" killed any thought of visiting the United States. As much as he despised American vulgarity and cultural leveling, he loathed American democracy and the prospect of its crossing the Atlantic. Late in life he "wrote an answer to a Yankee who is utterly unable to understand on what ground I can possibly dislike Jefferson's politics." His reply began with a straw man. He had never asserted "that the supreme authority in a state ought to be entrusted to the poorest and most ignorant part of society"—his youthful infatuation with "American institutions" did not go that far. It was inevitable "that institutions purely democratic must, sooner or later, destroy liberty, or civilization, or both." Democracy would either enable "the poor to plunder the rich, and civilization would perish," or trigger the defense of property by "a strong military government," thus destroying liberty. America's apparent exemption from that rule would end when it became "as thickly peopled as old England." England's order and prosperity depended on its powerful ruling class.

> Distress every where makes the labourer mutinous and discontented, and inclines him to listen with eagerness to agitators who tell him that it is a monstrous iniquity that one man should have a million while another cannot get a full meal. In bad years there is plenty of grumbling here, and sometimes a little rioting. But it matters little. For here the sufferers are not the rulers. The supreme power is in the hands of a class, numerous indeed, but select, of an educated class, of a class which is, and knows itself to be, deeply interested in the security of property and the maintenance of order. Accordingly, the malcontents are firmly, yet gently, restrained. The

bad time is got over without robbing the wealthy to relieve the indigent. The springs of national prosperity soon begin to flow again:
work is plentiful: wages rise; and all is tranquillity and cheerfulness. I
have seen England pass three or four times through such critical
seasons as I have described.

Ultimately, the hungry majority would finish American democracy: "a
multitude of people, none of whom has had more than half a breakfast
or expects more than half a dinner." But they could vote for their rulers,
and "you will act like people who should, in a year of scarcity, devour
all the seed corn, and thus make the next year, not of scarcity, but of
absolute famine. There will be, I fear, spoliation. The spoliation will increase the distress. The distress will produce fresh spoliation." He closed
by prophesying the victory of new "Huns and Vandals . . . engendered
within your own country by your own institutions."[15] "Huns and Vandals" was a euphemism for the people whom he called "human vermin"
elsewhere.

Macaulay's savaging of democracy in America was published after his
death. It provoked controversy there and had lasting implications elsewhere: for India and Ireland as well as England. Karl Marx had little to
teach him about class conflict, and Macaulay would have required no
instruction about what a twentieth-century Marxist called "hegemony."
The word epitomizes "supreme power . . . in the hands of a class, numerous indeed, but select, of an educated class." Macaulay commanded
the classical sources of the Marxist theory, and his up-to-date, take-no-
hostages version of Malthusianism provided the coercion that "an educated class" needed to dominate their inferiors." It inspired him to pul-
verize the Tory paternalist Michael Sadler and to greet the Irish famine
as a metaphorical godsend. Macaulay accepted the undemocratic implications of lethal dearth. But a boy who witnessed the 1943 famine in
British-ruled Bengal grew up to invert that lesson. Its three million victims taught Amartya Sen that "although by most indicators, from life
expectancy to literacy, Mao's China was ahead of Nehru's India, China
had had a catastrophic famine between 1958 and 1961 in which up to
30m people starved to death. There was no free press or alternative political parties to give early warning. In democratic India, free from the
Raj, this could not have happened."[16]

Macaulay enjoyed a huge transatlantic impact because he hid his distaste for most Americans and their institutions. Somehow, the implications of his ethical calculus were regularly overlooked. In 1857 Charles
Sumner, an abolitionist senator, sought him out in London. After dinner
Macaulay felt "great joy": "We had no talk about slavery." Sumner left
eager to enlist his support for emancipation in America: "If Macaulay
would do it, he might by one article do as much against slavery as his
father did in his whole life." Sumner's desire testified to the transforming
power of fame. When he had first met Macaulay nearly twenty years earlier, he marked him as "truly oppressive": "I have heard him called the
most remarkable person of his age; and again the most over-rated one."
The novelist Harriet Beecher Stowe also cultivated Macaulay, and he
flattered her. Before Sumner, she tried and failed to enlist Zachary's more
famous son in the cause of abolishing American slavery: "He who should
direct the feelings of England on this subject wisely and effectively might
do a work worthy of your father." To his considerable annoyance, Stowe
wrote about him as a trophy of her English tour. He once slyly mocked
her in company: "I'll give thee—Ah! Too charming maid; / I'll give thee
to the Devil." Macaulay continued to play Stowe. Years later he effused to
her: "I have just returned from Italy, where your fame seems to throw
that of all other writers into the shade." Concerns deeper than oppor-
tunism motivated his double-dealing. Five months after first flattering
her, he read *Uncle Tom's Cabin:* "cried a little." He thought it "the finest
work of the imagination that America has produced." But his reservation
about the novel was insurmountable: "as a political and moral work, I
entertain some doubts whether it may not do more harm than good."[17]

George Bernard Shaw once described England and America as "two
nations separated by a common language." True or not, Macaulay's distinction between "the imagination" on the one hand and the "political
and moral" on the other explains why he subordinated his private tears
to ensuring "the security of property and the maintenance of order." As
much as Zachary Macaulay, Stowe saw readers' weeping at Little Eva and
cursing of Simon Legree as politically legitimate expressions of their
moral imaginations. For Tom, however, the lodestar of public morality
was the calculating use of power to serve England's interests, the supremacy of his class, and international order. Zachary perhaps glimpsed the
ethical ocean separating him from his heir, but Tom commanded palpa-

ble moral authority in America because of the naïveté of Stowe, Sumner, and thousands of nameless readers.

Starting Over

Facing "two foolscap sheets on 1 February 1849," Macaulay ceremoniously began the next volumes of his *History.* He "wrote a little more" the next day before deciding that he needed to "fix on some subject to get it thoroughly up." He fancied that a week's work in London libraries would suffice. Although he lacked a plan for proceeding, he understood that he must hold his audience's attention. Surveying his *History's* triumphal debut, he reaffirmed his preference for the ancient over the modern masters: "I admire no historians much except Herodotus, Thucydides & Tacitus—Perhaps in his way—a very peculiar way—I might add Fra Paolo [Sarpi]. The modern writers who have most of the great qualities of the ancient masters of history are some memoir writers, St Simon, for example. There is good, no doubt, in Hume, Robertson, Voltaire, Gibbon. Yet it is not the thing. I have a conception of history more just, I am confident, than theirs."[18] High politics preoccupied his ancient masters, Saint-Simon wrote about Louis XIV's court, and Sarpi reveled in the folly and mischief of prelates during the Council of Trent. Macaulay shared their focus.

George Otto Trevelyan piously described his uncle at work on his *History* as "a labour of love." Macaulay could delight in polishing his prose, but he increasingly found writing a "task." Looking at those foolscap sheets, he ignored the obstacles that would keep him, first, from continuing his *History* and then from finishing it. He needed to supplement Mackintosh's research and develop a story line for a period about which he knew little. It was, moreover, impossible for him to cover the eighteenth century and sustain the attention he had lavished on James II's reign—an average of over 170 pages a year. To reach even the accession of George III in 1760 demanded the ruthless economy of his second chapter, which covers 1660 to 1685 in 380 pages: less than 15 pages a year. That pace would have permitted him to move forward but without telling "everything dramatically" and risking a smaller audience and reduced royalties. Dispatch, moreover, would have kept him from proving William III's indispensability and greatness in the history of England, where his "subsequent reputation has been patchy, but generally muted."[19] Macaulay's decision to portray the Glorious Revolution as both popular and inimitable required him to present William as almost omnipresent.

Other problems turned his great book into a huge fragment. Besides mastering new printed sources, he discovered that he had to learn how to use manuscripts. Disinclined to reconsider, revise, or retract, Macaulay also discovered little in the sources that intrigued him. It was more congenial—and potentially more profitable—to revisit his original triumph by repolishing it for a new edition and to bundle most of his essays into a collected edition. Doubts about his market nagged him: "I cannot expect to produce again an effect like that of my first two volumes." He worked around his schedule rather than creating a schedule that forced him to write. His nights were mostly his own. After multiplying distractions for months, he confessed to a habit long chided by his father: "I must not go on in this dawdling way." Diagnosis was easier than change, and he exaggerated his productivity to his family: "I am however daily employed in collecting materials, reading Dutch histories and French Gazettes, and making extracts from despatches and private letters which have never been published." As June 1849 ended, he congratulated himself for establishing a routine—"I mean to persevere"—but soon reverted to fitfulness. But there was no overcoming his impatient intelligence. Stupidity annoyed him, like drafts of cold air, and boredom was as insufferable. Fabricating entertainments about the rump of the seventeenth century required dull labor. From a distance the long eighteenth century that extended into his adulthood attracted and energized him.[20]

Seeing Ireland

Macaulay's ever more stunted human sympathies made him suspicious of honorary Englishmen. After the House of Lords refused to exempt the banker Lionel de Rothschild from swearing on the New Testament in order to remain in the Commons, Macaulay dined at his mansion. Days later he berated "these Jews & Philo Jews" for their reaction to the Lords' decision. Their "folly & insolence" threatened to turn him "into a persecutor. They are raising a senseless clamour against the House of Lords and trying to set up ye City of London as the legislature of the country. That is insupportable. And it is not a game wh[ich] will answer for their own ends." Belonging to a despised and landless people had taught Rothschild compassion toward the afflicted who were not his own. He helped to found the British Relief Association in 1846, contributed £1,000 to its aid to Irish peasants devastated by the famine, and was a principal in contracting for them a loan of £8 million. When Macaulay dined at Rothschild's house, such charity was unfashionable. In the Commons three months earlier, Peel had echoed Trevelyan's analysis of the famine as England's God-given opportunity to regenerate depopulated Ireland.[21]

Later that August Macaulay for perhaps the only time in his life felt the moral anxiety of belonging to a "dominant & successful" race. In India he had enveloped himself in a protective cocoon. A few days in Ireland confronted him with the human cost of empire. Imagining that the famine was over, he went to inspect the battlegrounds of the war between William and James. They would furnish his next installment with "lively and striking passages." He felt his "prospects brightening"—"the second part of my history will not be inferior to ye 1st"—but prepared for the excursion by returning to the history of the Roman Empire rather than to the seventeenth-century printed sources. Angrier than ever at the Irish, he was also "much depressed without reason." Crossing St. George's Channel, he put aside Jonathan Swift, a most ambivalent Irishman, in favor of still more Roman history: "was greatly amused & interested, more certainly than when I read . . . [it] in Calcutta." When light failed on board, he went "through Paradise Lost in my head." Satan's flight from Eden at the end of book four reminded him of Euripides, and he translated part of Milton's passage into Greek iambics, a rare exercise for him and a reminder of the learned intelligence that made him formidable and sometimes dangerous.[22]

For Macaulay Ireland's want highlighted England's abundance. There were some attractive spaces in Dublin, but many were shabby and some "detestable." The only people who impressed him were English or Anglo-Irish. On the first evening he read the Emperor Trajan's correspondence with the governor of a maladministered province. Trajan opposed both raising taxes to pay for public improvements and authorizing private associations in an area that was "the prey of factions." Macaulay thought that the emperor "made a most creditable figure." Dublin's "look

of beggary" was "frightful," but the heavy police presence and an interview with the viceroy reassured him. In the museum his memory flitted
back to India—"saw strange female figures, such as I have seen in Hindoo Temples"—but he relished trophies of the "contemptible abortion
of a rebellion" in 1848. Packed days left him short-tempered. Much "dis-
composed" by an impudent cabbie, he railed at "the scoundrel."[23]

Traveling in the countryside—Oscar Wilde's father was a companion—he first thought that it "looked like a flourishing part of England."
Then the train passed "some figures [obliterated] . . . swarthy, gaunt,
and dressed like scarecrows." His Irish companions reassured him that
such people "were generally not inhabitants of Dublin." As they neared
Drogheda, scenes worthy of "a thriving town in Lancashire" alternated
with "hovels" and "absolute pig styes." In his mind he began drafting his
story of William's victory over James at the Battle of the Boyne: "I got a
tolerable notion of the whole." He would publish it seven years later.
That night he dined in Dublin with Anglo-Irishmen, too many of them
journalists. They sang native songs for him, but their "brogue," "tone,"
"attitude and eye" he found "bordered on vulgarity." It "amused" him to
hear them called "the hope of Ireland." After an Irish scholar praised his
History "in terms which were too strong even for my self-esteem," he
went to bed content "that the popularity of my book will not be merely
ephemeral." On the morning train to Limerick, Macaulay found the
countryside "decidedly above my expectations" but the people "extremely shabby" by English standards. As dawn broke near Killarney, the
contrast between agricultural prosperity and human misery appeared
starker: "the beggary is worse than that of the worst governed parts of
the continent that I have ever seen." He could not "avoid seeing & almost touching" the "scarecrows." The town brought relief, and his horse-
manship drew a gratifying compliment. He had last trotted and cantered
in an Indian mango grove.[24]

Now the enveloping misery became inescapable—"'Give me a halfpenny' is the cry of the whole rising generation of Kerry"—and he also
passed through acres of farms "deserted by tenants running away to
America." Scenes of "wretchedness" jostled with the "handsome houses
of gentlemen, & fine woods & pleasure grounds." The human debris of
the famine briefly incarnated his "luminous and terrifying" but disembodied theory of quick, merciful, and civilizing "extirpation." From Cork

he recalled for Hannah some of what he saw and heard and felt: "the clothes of the people:—you never saw a beggar in such things. And the endless mendicant whine which follows you mile after mile,—the dozens of children who run after you in every village and up every hill crying 'Give me halfpenny—mother dead in workhouse—' Their strange appearance sometimes made me laugh, and I yet could hardly help crying. But what use is there in making oneself miserable." The distancing word "oneself" created even more space between him and the wretched people whose baying caused him to hesitate between laughter and tears. They were, he knew, helpless and hopeless.[25]

His next sentence to Lady Trevelyan contains a telling misquotation. Macaulay knew much of Shakespeare by heart and had once ranked *Macbeth* above *Hamlet*. The vision of an almost feral humanity reminded him of Lady Macbeth's words to her husband, frenzied after murdering King Duncan at her behest: "These things must not be thought on after this way. / So, it will make us mad." Shakespeare had written of suppressing not unthinkable "things" but unthinkable "deeds." That evening Macaulay also wrote to Ellis, again describing his reaction to the Irish "scarecrows," but now even more distantly: "I will have done. I cannot mend this state of things, and there is no use in breaking my heart about it. I am comforted by thinking that between the poorest English peasant and the Irish peasant there is ample room for ten or twelve well marked degrees of poverty." Macaulay knew both that poverty is relative and that the human misery facing him in Ireland exceeded anything India offered. When dealing with English subordinates, his ration of the "milk of human kindness" was slight. His longtime servant ("my man") accompanied him to Ireland, as usual taken for granted and nearly invisible. But there was no disregarding the revolutionary potential of hungry, indocile Englishmen. Every summer during his last decade, he monitored the harvest at home.[26]

In late August 1849 a hotel in Cork provided him with first-class refuge on the cheap from things and perhaps deeds that "must not be thought." Draining his wine, he fell asleep in his chair. The next day he began censoring his memory. He studied not the people who passed him in the streets but a "very imposing Doric" prison and a friend's prose, which suggested a puzzling Greek phrase. The profusion of images of the duke of Wellington and "more beyond all comparison of ye Queen &

Prince Albert" reassured him: "It seems that marvelous delusion [repealing the union with England] is over. For ever, I hope." Back in Dublin, he continued forgetting and anticipated seeing Ulster "more thriving still." The trip, he recorded, provided him with "a large share of images and thoughts" for his *History*. It owed little to conventional research. Having done no preparation for mining libraries, he found in them "very little to my purpose." But two days later he wandered with "sagacious incredulity" around Londonderry's walls, separating "legends" from "facts" about its siege in 1688–89 and forming a "picture of the whole in my mind." The story he would tell reflected both his powerful visual memory and his casual scholarship. They combined to suggest the Irish reality he had emphasized in volume two—"Hostility of Races; the aboriginal Peasantry." Macaulay helped bury the Whig practice of tracing Irish discontent more to history and environment than to "different national characters as strongly opposed as any two national characters in Europe": "the same line of demarcation which separated religions separated races."[27]

To prepare for Ireland, he had read imperial Roman history. Before the ensuing jaunt to France with Ellis, he turned to Balzac, the great realist novelist of its modern social classes, and inspected the first German translation of his *History*. Apart from a few hours in the National Archives in Paris spread over two days, the trip was a crowded and gourmandizing delight. Macaulay lived at the beginning of a debate over obesity that first stigmatized it and then classified it as a disease.[28]

Glimpsing human scarecrows failed to make him susceptible to the world of pain. Irish solecisms quickly obliterated Irish suffering. He dismissed Carlyle's "trash Latter-day something or other" *(Latter-day Pamphlets)*, which used the Irish famine to assail the economic dogmas that he and Trevelyan shared: "beneath criticism." Macaulay's indifference to politically harmless British dearth extended to the Scottish Highlands, which also starved during the 1840s. Months after writing off Carlyle, he replied to "My dear Cousin"—perhaps a Highlander—promising to send her appeal for aid to Trevelyan but cautioning:

> I shall be truly glad if your application succeeds. If not, you must remember that there is a wide difference between your position and that of the official men here. You are naturally and laudably

anxious for the welfare of the particular district where your lot has been cast. They have to take thought for a great empire, and to distribute the very scanty machinery which is at their command in such a manner as may on the whole effect the greatest quantity of good. It is impossible that, however faithfully, ably, and humanely they may discharge their duty, they should not often seem to people whose view is bounded by the limits of a single parish, very unjust and hard hearted.

Both his kin and the aboriginal Irish belonged to the Celtic, not the Saxon race, but the Irish, uniquely "among the nations of northern Europe" exhibiting many regressive Mediterranean characteristics, were ill-suited to benefit from England's civilizing and imperial mission. His *History* later insisted that it was otherwise with his fellow Highlanders. Despite their Celtic "blood" it "might safely have been predicted that, if ever an efficient police should make it impossible for the Highlander to avenge his wrongs by violence and to supply his wants by rapine, if ever his faculties should be developed by the civilizing influence of the Protestant religion and of the English language, if ever he should transfer to his country and to her lawful magistrates the affection and respect with which he had been taught to regard his own petty community and his own petty prince, the kingdom would obtain an immense accession of strength for all the purposes both of peace and of war." The Scots were, in other words, fit to be anglicized. In 1827, recovered from his flirtation with democracy but honoring his promise to his father, he had derided the notion that "Negroes" were innately inferior to Europeans.[29] Unlike "Temple," that essay he relegated to his anonymous and disowned juvenilia.

In the *History* Macaulay articulated what the English public mind was disposed to accept as facts about race, civilization, and the ethics of extirpation. Reviewing the recent demographic anguish of the Celtic fringe in 1851, one journalist invoked Macaulay's elegy of Cromwell's "iron rule" in Ireland, and hoped that the annual emigration of 250,000 Irish would continue. Another contributor to *The Economist* was Herbert Spencer, poised to command as the oracle of "Social Darwinism" before Charles Darwin. In 1852 Spencer formulated the concept of the "survival of the fittest" and coined the phrase twelve years later: "This survival of the fittest, which I have here sought to express in mechanical terms, is that which Mr. Darwin has called 'natural selection,' or the preservation of favoured races in the struggle for life." In 1871 Darwin ratified it as a law of nature: "Extinction follows chiefly from the competition of tribe with tribe, and race with race . . . When civilized nations come into contact with barbarians the struggle is short, except where a deadly climate gives its aid to the native race . . . The grade of their civilization seems to be a most important element in the success of competing nations."[30] Spencer became an anti-imperialist, and Darwin was a reliable Liberal except on Irish Home Rule. Their eminence contributed, however, to giving prejudices and policies that they abhorred "scientific" authority. Much that maimed the twentieth century derived from what Macaulay taught his contemporaries to see as reasonable.

Paterfamilias

Back home he "resolved that there shall be no day without a page or so" of writing and briefly fulfilled his resolution. He remained more attentive to his family than to his writing. They inspired in him and received in return lavish sentimentality: "What can be more delightful than the . . . family . . . perfect goodness & kindness & happiness. They are very affectionate in all their conduct to me; and I love them dearly." A verbal tic suggests why he enthused about "their mutual attachment." In his journal he routinely appended "God bless her [or him]" after speaking of one or another beloved Trevelyan, just as he sometimes greeted English success with "Thank God!" It was a residue of Clapham, where church, nation, and home had merged, and testified to his piety toward both his kin and his country. His exclamations perhaps warmed his gelid calculations. Their hollowness testifies to his abiding contempt for his father and his religion. Hannah understood something of the permanent damage that Tom had suffered at their father's hands. When he was powerful, rich, and famous, he recalled Zachary disparaging him in boyhood almost as vividly as he remembered having being scared long ago by a snake. Of his niece Baba, he told himself: "I respect her more, I am sure, than I ever respected my father—She is goodness, truth, nobleness personified."[31] She was then fifteen.

More than ever, Macaulay's family was an affective and economic pyramid. At the apex were the Trevelyans, whom he desired to "see ... every day"—a desire he almost fulfilled in London as he had in Calcutta. They, and above all Hannah, "were the lives on which my happiness depends." He cherished Baba and, to a lesser extent, George and doted on their baby sister, Alice. Their father, Charles, he liked, respected, and worked with, but his "society is not necessary to me." Tom's unfailing "delight" in his sister owed much to her unwavering care of him, but also to the knowledge that she understood him better than anyone else: "Nothing escapes her." When she contracted scarlet fever, which had killed the first Margaret, he "could do nothing but weep for half an hour." Three years later she endured a cancer scare, which she kept from him—the knowledge would "have nearly killed me." Posthumously he became for her "the light of our home, the most tender, loving, generous, unselfish of friends ... What a world of love he poured out upon me and mine!"[32]

Below the Trevelyans were his two unmarried sisters, Selina, a shadowy invalid, and Frances, the dependable family caregiver, whose household in Brighton he financed. Underneath them were his surviving brothers, John, a country parson, and Charles, a civil servant. Tom was friendly with both but close to neither. His brother Henry died in 1846, leaving a widow whom he detested. As head of his extended family, Tom was financially responsible for them. In the late winter of 1854 he exulted: "All my brothers and brothers in law are now comfortably quartered on the public, and I alone remain without a halfpenny of the Queen's money." His principle that public employment should depend solely on merit permitted energetic jobbery for himself and his nearest male relatives. It was his duty to support his unmarried sisters, and he expected no thanks from them. He made few demands on his brothers apart from fulfilling routine family duties. At the base of the pyramid were members of his extended family, many of whom asked for and often received Macaulay's patronage and largesse. His mother's brother James was a halfmad annoyance, to whom he sometimes succeeded in giving no "£."[33]

But his relations with the Trevelyans were also transactions, a reality that fed his insecurity: "They were all most affectionate to me. Much talk on business with H[annah]." He helped them financially, and in exchange they cared for him emotionally. Negotiating with Hannah about buying a carriage of his own, he insisted: "It is fair too that I should have some of the advantage of my own labours." Working to manage one another's reputations belonged to the family's public business. That enterprise was untroubled by his need to be reassured that they reciprocated what he felt toward them: "I seem to perceive that they love me more at G. C. [the Trevelyans' house]. God knows how truly I love them." For all his invocations of the deity and gift-giving at "G. C." that Christmas, he skipped church in favor of Cicero's great rebuke to superstition, *On Divination*. There were always presents for the children, but his gifts to them and their parents were seldom quite gratuitous. It hurt when Charles, after a long day's work, fell asleep while Tom declaimed from a draft chapter. Needing to entertain them and to have proof of their delight in him, he once put aside Hume and Plato to spend "an hour playing with dear Alice" and on another occasion concocted for all the children a yarn about "an embassy to America," including a visit to "the Indians,—how they gave me the name of the Great Wise Beaver."[34]

He was livelier than the dour Charles, who deferred to him and toward whom he acted like "a most kind brother." The brothers-in-law routinely discussed public business. Charles actively participated in finding government employment for the extended family. Tom regarded him affectionately but also protectively, like an apt pupil. At home Tom also practiced the art of insinuating religious doubt while feigning Christianity, designing for Charles a plan of reading that helped "to temper his evangelicalism . . . by reason and good sense." He knew Charles's habitually rash speech and action and was given to "advising & remonstrating" with him. Once Tom imparted to "him some hints about London life, & cautioned him not to walk late in the parks, or to talk to strangers, particularly soldiers, as his simple good nature sometimes inclines him to do." The boundaries that Tom recommended were a rare acknowledgment that London was a gamier place than his staid preaching and practice suggested.[35]

The details of Baba's life preoccupied him. Teasingly but firmly, he corrected her "orthography" and commended her reading of Gibbon: "Excellent sense she has." Uncle Tom also tried to make his morality her own. After she accompanied him to her first "antislavery meeting," they talked: "she despised the nonsense as much as I could wish." She grew up, however, to be the reverent biographer of her grandfather Zachary. Uncle Tom was more successful in teaching his ethics to Georgy, her brother. Hannah's annoyance at their uncle's subversion exposed a divide in their family. While at Harrow, Georgy mocked Harriet Beecher Stowe. In rebuke, his mother praised Mrs. Stowe: "a woman burning with a holy zeal for a cause which is really a very noble one . . . the opposite scale is the cause of the Evil One . . . it is particularly ungraceful in anyone of your grandfather's descendants to speak disrespectfully of any Antislavery exertions." Did Hannah recall that on April Fool's Day 1853 she received a letter from Tom describing "how Mrs. Beecher Stowe had come to my Chambers and invited herself to lunch tomorrow—how she had brought with her a parson—a man of colour—the Rev. Caesar Ugbark and his wife etc. etc?" The prank "took in several people." Uncle Tom regularly shared with Baba details of his prosperity and some of its fruit and exaggerated for her the depth of his compassion. There were, however, limits to his care for her. Relishing "the dear child's company," he avoided assuming even brief "responsibility" for her abroad.[36]

His feelings toward Margaret seemed transparent to him: "I love her as if she were my own daughter." She reminded him of the love of his life and aroused in him something of what he still felt for her namesake. He enjoyed reliving the past, and the company of "my dearest child" enabled him to revisit his cherished boyhood. Baba's approaching marriage caused him to relive a trauma and exposed the knottiness of his affection for her. Her fiancé was a slightly older widower, excellent in every way, and Uncle Tom pronounced himself pleased, "above all" by "the circumstance that the separation will hardly be a separation." He was determined "to do as much as her parents at least." If his desire even to outdo his sister and brother-in-law in outfitting their daughter expressed the primordial urge to turn affection into a commodity, it also captures the mixture of generosity, need, calculation, and control that can belong to giving. The £500 note he gave Baba was worth £36,961 in 2007: "Her gratitude & affection moved me to tears." In the weeks before her wedding day, he dwelt on his deep love for her.[37]

But as the event neared, his self-pity flared. He sympathized with Hannah's grief "from my soul. I know what it is—I suffered as much or more [when their sister married]. But nobody pitied me—but what a scar that wound has left unknown to anybody but myself." Revisiting the marriages of both Baba's namesake and her mother, he dreaded that she, too, "will be gone—The light of the house. The desire of my eyes. How I love her." Thomas Babington Macaulay was not Humbert Humbert, and

Baba was then older than Lolita. His effusion owed something to the Victorian taste for florid expressions of affection, especially toward children. On Valentine's Day 1849 he found her five-year-old sister Alice "absolutely irresistible." Although he permanently infantilized Margaret, he knew what "desire" meant. His long flirtation with her recapitulated his attentions a generation earlier, first to her aunt and then to her mother. It was erotic, but in Baba's case its effect and perhaps its intention were distancing rather than seductive: sexless intimacy. After her wedding, he read the same pages in a book that he had leafed through when sulking alone on her mother's "wedding day near 24 years ago." He treated it as a mere coincidence: "odd." The next day, feeling "a tending of blood to the head," he took a laxative. His knotty feelings toward Baba survived her marriage. She remained "my dear child," but one of her visits to Uncle Tom prompted him to test his memory by reciting "five or six hundred lines" of Catullus, whose poetry was not always erotic. Her patience with his needs seems to have been inexhaustible: "We looked over my accounts & I read her some of my old journals—So we spent two very pleasant hours."[38] Their ambiguous reciprocity ended with the grave. In his will, he left her £10,000, but her brother, not she, wrote his biography.

Macaulay's attentions to George, whose bequest was only £5,000, were less effusive but finally closer and posthumously more useful. As he expected, his nephew turned out to be "a considerable man": a politician, imperial administrator, and historian. In all these roles he was his uncle's primary heir, the conservator of his memory, and the father of another historian whose work recalls Macaulay's. At eleven Georgy showed promise of becoming "a very excellent scholar": "a good boy & very clever & industrious, but almost too eager about his studies." At twelve he wrote a "Melodrama of Hymen and Mars," which he and Baba performed to their uncle's delight. Undoubtedly innocuous, the skit is lost. What would Zachary have made of one of his grandchildren's playing a god of love? By such little steps families change their mores over generations. Baba acted in the playlet and acquired enviable German, but she learned neither Greek nor Latin. Those languages and the culture they informed belonged mostly to men. As a trustee of the British Museum, Macaulay "did the honors" by exhibiting a Greek manuscript to some visiting ladies, one of whom "showed herself a Hellenist,

& displayed her skill in distinguishing θ from o." On Christmas Day 1849 "dear Baba" read Sophocles but "in a vile prose translation." George thrived on doing what his sister was denied. Uncle Tom once "examined" him on a tragedy of Euripides: "he is not yet thirteen, and is as good a Greek scholar as I was at fourteen." Then he "read the first Canto of Dante with Baba": "She entered into it perfectly." Macaulay devoted hundreds of hours to his nephew's classical education. He encouraged Charles to read Greek with his son. Choosing the right public school for George mattered to his uncle, who was delighted at his admission to Harrow, more aristocratic than Eton and a conduit for Trinity College. Macaulay long planned for the boy to follow him there: "G is off for Cambridge this afternoon—God bless him!"[39]

Calculation entered into his dealings with George—he wanted an intellectual heir—but he gave the boy intense, encompassing, and shrewd care: "His natural feeling about me has done him some harm, with, I hope, some good." He had in mind particularly the youth's "neglect of mathematics"—a stubborn deficiency that he shared with his uncle. George always reciprocated: "All the little interviews that took place between us as master and pupil . . . are as fresh in my memory as if they had occurred last summer, instead of twenty years ago"; "he had very seldom occasion to give verbal expression to his disapprobation. His influence over us was so unbounded." G. M. Trevelyan, his father's biographer, recorded that Uncle Tom and the Trevelyan household essentially "fixed" how George's mind worked before he started school: "The likeness of his mind to Macaulay's is obvious; the one was moulded on the other." George understood that his own work ethic derived from the experience of his uncle's watching and often directing his own "classical reading." Uncle Tom's close and artful supervision "fixed" more than the boy's opinion of Harriet Beecher Stowe. He sent Georgy, then fourteen, "Hobbes's Thucydides, which I hope you will study, and compare carefully with the original. Your Mamma tells me that you have some scruple about using a translation. There can be no possible objection to your doing so . . . You will find Hobbes's English in some places as tough as the original or nearly so."[40]

Thomas Hobbes had read Thucydides as an ideological ancestor, who also saw power as the motive force of politics, democracy as absurdity, a strong state as the bulwark against anarchy, and nations locked in a "war of all against all." Directing George to master the Greek text through Hobbes's eyes might enable him to discover political reality as if on his own. Macaulay's admiration of Hobbes as a translator was specific. He dismissed his version of the *Iliad* as "detestable." A more accessible translation of *The History of the Peloponnesian War* existed, but the late, eminent, and Reverend Thomas Arnold had freighted his version with what Macaulay dismissed as his "crotchets about religion and politics." Arnold's Thucydides lost some of what he knew to be "really valuable in [Hobbes's] speculations": the "coldblooded and hardheaded" realism that he clothed in "language more precise and luminous than has ever been employed by any metaphysical writer." For Macaulay, it was wrong to be politically "sentimental and romantic."[41] Sympathy belonged at home.

George's parents were observant Anglicans, and Uncle Tom worked to dilute their influence on their son's religious beliefs. When George was fifteen, he recalled for the boy four lines in Greek from Aeschylus' *Prometheus Bound* ("nothing finer"): "Worship, adore, and fawn upon whoever is thy lord. But for Zeus I care less than naught. Let him do his will, let him hold his power for his little day—since not for long shall he bear sway over the gods." His avuncular insinuation about the limits of heavenly dominion took. George "from boyhood to old age, treated religion respectfully but shyly. Since he did not understand Christianity, he left it alone with little remark"; "He recognised it as a great fact in the history of England, and in human nature—at least in the nature of others." Uncle Tom, who treated it more tartly but also as inevitable, encouraged the boy's prudery, as if in compensation. It pleased him when George read a comedy by Aristophanes in an "expurgated" edition that cut a reference to "male whores": "it is not agreeable to read with a virtuous boy those unutterably beastly lines"—he had been examined and cross-examined about them at Cambridge. At Harrow on visitors' day together with "many great people," the boys "huzzaed him": "George was so much elated that he broke from the crowd, & ran to me." At fourteen the boy was junior and eager for recognition. Because Macaulay died before his nephew's mildest of undergraduate rebellions could break the spell, he commanded Georgy's devotion from the grave.[42]

[9]

BARON MACAULAY
OF ROTHLEY

A classical education integrated England's leaders intellectually, socially, and ethically. Guaranteeing that solidarity first for Georgy and his peers and then for their sons depended on perpetuating the ancients' hold over the best modern schools. The regime lasted as long as the classics belonged to the fabric of the everyday lives of such men. Macaulay's one close male friendship thrived on much Latin and even more Greek. Learned but self-effacing, Thomas Flower Ellis was a natural foil. Despite his serious churchmanship, they were compatible temperamentally and intellectually. Out of Parliament, Macaulay's long talkative dinners with that prodigious listener became more frequent. Dining richly—once on broiled mackerel, "a brace of young ducks—asparagus—plovers' eggs"— Macaulay deepened his knowledge of wines, and sometimes declaimed draft passages from his *History* like a British dessert. His dependence on Ellis' companionship grew, not least as an outlet for some of his venom. Macaulay once avowed "great obligations" to Ellis and attributed "to the kind severity of his criticism a large part of the literary success which I have obtained." He was once again unsuccessfully recommending Ellis for a government job. After Macaulay's death Ellis recalled "a friendship of more than thirty years, more affectionate and confidential than that of brothers, uninterrupted, to the best of my recollection and belief, by a single unkind word or thought."[1]

Their extroverted classicism endowed them with shared cultural assumptions that ran deeper than ideology. Their conversations sometimes became games of male one-upmanship. Ellis questioned Macaulay's assertion that Homer had mentioned an event similar to a recent flood in

Barcelona, only to be corrected a few days later with a four-line quotation embedded in an explanatory paragraph. It was not learning primarily for learning's sake. Their talk owed little to the footnotes steadily enveloping the pages of the editions where they engaged the ancients. Both Oxford and Cambridge men learned Greek, but the Cantabrigians, trained to read for language more than for wisdom, were less disposed to troll for useful analogies or lessons for living.[2] Assimilating them was another matter.

Social networks exercise a pervasive but understudied power. Recent research suggests that they help to spread even obesity by normalizing it. More obviously, various prestigious and often interconnected networks sustained the culture of modern English classicism. Worn as a badge of commanding intelligence, their arcane learning bolstered their claim to automatic deference as a secular priesthood. A few groups perpetuated themselves into the mid-twentieth century. Present at the creation of one of them, Macaulay instructed his readers to respect "that control to which it is the glory of free nations to submit themselves, the control of superior minds." Because lineage, wealth, and power remained connected in his England, some hereditary nobles were regarded as possessing such intellects, at least *honoris causa*. Certain that they deserved the best because of what they knew best, Macaulay's controllers routinely mingled their public and private concerns.[3]

A chance encounter captures their small and self-perpetuating world. While walking on 18 August 1854, Macaulay met Benjamin Jowett, then serving on his committee charged with framing competitive examinations for admission to the Indian Civil Service and a year away from appointment as Oxford's Regius Professor of Greek: "Chatted half an hour with him & his friend Temple." They discussed "the Epistles of St Paul, the early history of Christianity," including a book by the Prussian ambassador on another Greek text. A year later Jowett published an interpretation of Paul that drew accusations of heresy. He survived into the 1890s as master of Balliol College, childless but the mentor of many admiring and masterful protégés. By then Frederick Temple, also an educator and the target of heresy-hunters, was the archbishop of Canterbury. His son, William, took a double first in classics at Balliol, overcame doubts about his orthodoxy to be ordained, served as a don and a headmaster, and died as archbishop of Canterbury in 1944. Himself childless, "He was loyal above all to the legacy of his father."[4]

The modern culture of classicism transcended national and religious divisions. In August 1857 Georgy took a walking tour in the Tyrol, chaperoned by an Anglican cleric who became first headmaster of Harrow and later master of Trinity College, Cambridge. When Montagu Butler fell ill, they found refuge with a village priest. Lacking a common modern language, the men spoke Latin. Skilled at writing the language, Butler initially struggled to converse, "whereas our interlocutor rattled away without hesitating for a word, or fumbling over a sentence." Within a couple of days, the two older men were able to engage in "mild joking." Before they left, their Catholic host, learning that Butler would soon be ordained an Anglican priest, warmly blessed him. Two years later and half a world away in Springfield, Illinois, a distraught mother boarded her oldest son on an eastbound train. Because Robert Todd Lincoln's Greek and Latin were too feeble for admission to Harvard, he needed a year's prepping at an elite New England school to complete the academic rites that would certify him as a gentleman.[5] A generation later the log-cabin-born president's heir was ambassador to the Court of St. James.

Classically educated Englishmen were a diverse lot. Most of them probably forgot their early drills, and some permanently regretted them. Seeing Athens reminded the novelist W. M. Thackeray of years wasted at Charterhouse School: "I was made so miserable in youth by a classical education, that all connected with it is disagreeable in my eyes; and I have the same recollection of Greek in youth that I have of castor-oil." In contrast, Anthony Trollope also bypassed university but prized his Latin education because, more than his great novels, it marked him as a gentleman. During the mid-eighteenth century the classical emphasis shifted from Latin to Greek throughout Protestant Europe. Even before 1800 mastery of the language was conspicuous erudition. Latin remained "an orderly resource" for educated men, while Greek, not immediately useful, became prized for "its flexibility hinting at a freedom which was potentially dangerous." During the 1820s Greek manifested its radical potential in Macaulay and other young men moving in James Mill's orbit. George Grote's devotion to ancient democratic Athens remained as constant as his atheism and Philosophic Radicalism, but he was in the minority. More representative, Macaulay's mature classicism shadowed his belief in human progress and informed his support for the rights of "possession," not only of power and property but also of received knowledge and accepted meaning apart from religion. Orphaning "The London University," which urged dethroning the classics in the modern university, he now held mostly backward-looking opinions about higher education. Even his ambition to secularize the university shrank to urging that laymen be admitted to Oxbridge residential fellowships in order to encourage both better scholars and better priests.[6]

A Refuge from the Zealots' Blasts

With due allowance for hyperbole, classicism provided its adepts with a common faith. Herbert Spencer, an autodidact who became late nineteenth-century England's favorite philosopher, scorned it as vestigial barbarism. A lifetime of listening to better-educated men convinced him that "priests and people alike, while taking their nominal creed from the New Testament, take their real creed from Homer. Not Christ, but Achilles is their ideal." He intuited the spiritual hold that the classics exercised over other brainy members of the Athenaeum Club. The aura was tenacious. Edmund Burke, from whom Macaulay selectively learned much of his politics and apparently a sincere Christian, owed less to precepts drawn from the Bible or treatises of divinity than to a principled version of reason of state. Cicero appears in *Reflections on the Revolution in France;* Christ is absent. Burke's horror at the revolution caused him to split from his longtime ally, Charles James Fox, postreligious and even more profoundly classical.[7] Fox was buried in Westminster Abbey, with Lord Holland, Macaulay's early patron, as his principal mourner. He is immortalized there in a toga, reposing in the arms of Liberty, dressed as a Roman matron in a *palla.*

In the face of the insoluble skeptical crisis, nationalism clarified and broadened the appeal of the British state. Combining that devotion with classicism enabled many skeptics to find public meaning and private solace unavailable to them in Christianity. Skeptical and reluctantly but deeply a classicist, Alfred Tennyson in 1850 published *In Memoriam,* an elegy for Henry Hallam's older son, whom he loved:

> I stretch lame hands of faith, and grope,
>   and gather dust and chaff, and call
>   To what I feel is Lord of all,
> And faintly trust the larger hope.

And

> Who trusted God was love indeed
>   And love Creation's final law—
>   Tho' Nature, red in tooth and claw
> With ravine, shriek'd against his creed.[8]

The poem led Prince Albert to arrange Tennyson's appointment as poet laureate.

During the spring of 1859 rumors of a French invasion spread. Young patriots rushed to join the National Volunteer Association, whose patrons were Victoria and Albert. With unquestioning patriotism, Tennyson cheered them on with "Riflemen form!": "Form, be ready to do or die! / Form in Freedom's Name and the Queen's"—here not "faintly trust the larger hope" but fight and be prepared to kill and die for the nation's sake. At Cambridge George Trevelyan was "impatient to be a soldier," and Uncle Tom wanted "to provide him with his arms and uniform. He will soon, I hope, be able to pick off a French officer at the distance of a quarter of a mile." The same fervor marked the deluge of volunteers after England declared war on Germany in August 1914. A poet turned warrior, the "neo-pagan" Rupert Brooke, became the avatar of both Tennyson and Trevelyan and in death a propaganda asset:

> If I should die, think only this of me:
>   That there's some corner of a foreign field
> That is for ever England.

During World War I, 2.5 million Britons of every class, a quarter of all eligible men, volunteered for military service. Even after conscription was imposed in March 1916, volunteers for combat could have filled the ranks.[9] They lived and died in a vanished world of self-sacrificing nationalism.

A complex of evangelical energy, solid churchmanship, and genteel tolerance, the Anglican consensus of Zachary Macaulay's generation began to dissolve during the 1820s. In response to a wholesale flight from the center and a decline in forbearance, charges of heresy proliferated. Evangelical zeal could turn raw and aggressive. The religious histories of the families of Samuel Wilberforce and John Henry Newman illustrate the variety of mid-nineteenth-century Anglican experience. Catholicism and doubt became competing options. Only Samuel retained a faith like his father's, but he embellished it with some of the Tractarians' novelties. No Wilberforce or Newman joined the Reverend Baptist Noel, an earl's brother whose evangelical zeal led him to abandon Anglican orders and become a Baptist minister. He was among Macaulay's favorite butts: "I always hated confessors—protestant or Catholic." Anglican tempers rose, and by the 1850s two parties were facing and firing at each other. Personally religious, Macaulay's fan Frances Bunsen articulated a widespread anxiety: "Alas, between one religious party and another, people are screwing narrower and narrower, and darkening the light of Heaven more and more, Low Church almost as bad as the High—and where this practical Popery, though in name out of the Popedom, is to end, who can tell?"[10]

Sharing her anxiety but not her faith, Macaulay scorned the longing that caused many to discover intimations of divinity—or at least of the spiritual—in paranormal manifestations. Encouraged by the march of progress, they hoped to understand and perhaps control more of the mysteries that dogged their lives. Two days in May 1852 showed Macaulay that credulity alive in his own circle. On the eighteenth he accompanied his friend Lord Mahon "to a house on Gerard Street" to see a practitioner exhibit "his feats of phrenology & mesmerism or some such trash—I was half ashamed of going." They were joined by Bishop Samuel Wilberforce, himself a devotee, and his brother, an archdeacon and theologian already Rome-bound: "The fraud was absolutely transparent." The next day Bishop Wilberforce, the bishop of London, and Macaulay "got into a somewhat keen argument about clairvoyance. The 2 Bps lost their temper." Prince Albert, chancellor of the University of Cambridge and sometime president of the British Association for the Advancement of Science, succumbed to the vogue. Anxiously, he invited Britain's foremost phrenologist to Buckingham Palace to feel the bumps on the Prince of Wales's head. Macaulay minded that intelligent and respectable people patronized "spirit rappers & other such vagabonds." Long engagement with Lucretius and Malthus prepared him to understand natural selection as the mechanism of evolution. Backward-looking in so many ways, he did not blink when he looked into his acquaintance

Charles Darwin's new book, *On the Origin of Species by Means of Natural Selection, or the Preservation of Favoured Races in the Struggle for Life,* a month before he died.[11]

Macaulay's disillusioned support for the establishment separated him from a new breed of insistently sincere doubters. They started calling themselves agnostics in 1869. He remained an Anglican, irregularly observant but loyal in his fashion. As much as the legions of British youths who volunteered to serve in the Great War, he and his like-minded contemporaries belong to a lost world. When the Crimean War broke out in 1854, Queen Victoria declared 26 April a day of "Solemn Fast, Humiliation, and Prayer." Her former secretary at war's participation epitomized his Anglicanism. Recovering from a toothache and craving solid food, he cadged a dinner invitation on the twenty-sixth from Ellis, reminding him that "whatever is to be eaten on Wednesday must be laid in on Tuesday": shops would be closed on the fast day. Receiving the invitation, Macaulay winked: "I will fast with you to morrow." After publicly worshiping in St. Anne's Church, he dined privately with Ellis. Had Macaulay been charged with duplicity, he could have properly maintained that his wry words and sinuous behavior were consistent with his Anglican commitment. Unlike other religious societies, the establishment had been created, endowed, and privileged to serve the state. It was England's default religion, just as Presbyterianism was Scotland's. Therefore, in the case of abandoned children who "have no more religion than cats or dogs," he did "not see why the State, being *in loco parentis,* may not teach its own religion." The "religious education of the people" was its proper concern.[12]

But apostates and separatists were beyond the pale. Macaulay wanted to deny the totemic English Christian John Bunyan a monument in Westminster Abbey because he was a Baptist. It "is a religious edifice," and Bunyan was a man "who has publicly separated himself from the Church, who publicly denies the validity of the initiatory sacraments of the Church, who writes and preaches against the Church." Only in 1912 did Bunyan receive a monument there. As Macaulay knew, the adverb "publicly" defined formal apostasy in church law. Technically no apostate, Charles James Fox once told the House of Commons, "Religion was best understood when least talked of." He graced the Abbey in death because he was a major politician who never publicly abandoned the establishment. In religion Macaulay also acted on the principle, "Don't ask, don't tell." As he confided to his diary: "if a Deist thinks it justifiable & right to wear a cover, he acts most wisely if he wears the cover which is in fashion in his age & country." All classically educated men understood that the Roman virtue of *sinceritas* meant public integrity not personal sincerity. That the great Gothic mélange which is the Abbey houses the skeptic Fox's flamboyantly neopagan monument and long denied Bunyan even a plaque captures a style of secularization dominant in nations that have or once had state churches. Often more hollowed than hallowed, their visible forms now dwarf the marrow of belief.[13]

Despite Tom's revulsion at Zachary's monitory piety, he relished studying religion and theology. He fondly remembered the high, dry churchmen of his boyhood: "correctness of taste, decency but no enthusiasm." In contrast, the Puseyites, their unworthy successors, both aped Romish practices and revered episcopal more than governmental authority. Catholicism's increasing militancy similarly annoyed him. All such hot religion was fit for "the lower class" and "silly women." Visiting a newfangled evangelical church, Macaulay heard worshipers speaking "in the unknown tongue for the first time." Glossolalia raised in him "the strongest suspicions of deliberate hypocritical imposture." The spread of American revivalism to Britain also offended his sense of reason and decorum. After reading a popular do-it-yourself manual explaining the phenomenon, he sniffed: "strange fanaticism—the working up of religious fury reduced to a mere trick, almost mechanical—his divinity, I think, more than American, quite Pelagian,—that is, if logic can be applied to such chaotic nonsense." But when American fervor kept a proper distance from England, he could be judicious and farsighted. A "most wonderful history" of the Mormons convinced him that they "will do something considerable."[14]

Occasional churchgoing was necessary, though not always as pleasurable as in Cambridge: "The beauty of King's College Chapel of course produced its effect." In pious stately homes, he sometimes managed to avoid morning prayers by rising late. It was easier for him to disregard church in anonymous London. What he heard there could displease him: "I go seldom to church ... Prayers very ill read—Sermon m[o]st contemptible—The T[revelyan]s were all there—walked with them to their house, & then home." Attending services with his family united him with them and evoked happy memories of childhood. He also loved the Clapham parish church "for the sake of old times." Being seen when the archbishop of Canterbury preached advertised his own Anglicanism. At Easter 1849 he inaugurated what became an annual family pilgrimage to cathedral cities—monumental evidence of Christianity as "a great fact in the history of England, and in human nature." Bangor disturbed him as an architectural connoisseur and an English nationalist. Its cathedral was "the meanest edifice of its kind in the island," and he "was surprised to find everybody speaking Welsh & very few speaking pure English." Along with many others he left after the sermon on Sundays when the Eucharist was celebrated. After relocating to suburban Campden Hill in 1856, he would be seen more often in church. In his small, noticing community, he met neighbors and fellow parishioners like the duke and duchess of Argyll and welcomed the "extremely polite" rector's visits. Although for Macaulay Sunday churchgoing became "a habit which I have lately contracted" as his health, disposition, and the weather allowed, he suffered no late-onset piety. To analyze the preacher's illogic he reserved a seat for himself "in the front row of the gallery" facing the pulpit: "I went to Church yesterday to please my sisters: but I had better have stayed away."[15]

Macaulay's bipolar curiosity about religion enabled him to mediate doubt to faith for both nation and his family and undergirded his public authority. An ordinary day's reading included a life of Jabez Bunting—"Voltaire"—Bunting led England's Methodists for decades. His journal also shows him believing little or nothing while regularly acting religiously and talking and writing about religion. The effort mingled impersonation, memory, and curiosity. A series of deaths in the family into which his sister Margaret had married led him to ask, "Was ever such a curse on a home? It reminds me of the Greek stories. Alas, alas"—here no thought of Job's afflictions. Two days later he was in church "with Hannah & the girls." With his boyhood friend James Stephen, still possessing something of Clapham's faith, he "talked about providence &c an hour or more."[16]

He remained a Ciceronian, skeptical of all religious claims but certain that religion was inevitable and, when properly controlled, indispensable: "Religion has nothing to do with the order of the strata or the motions of the stars. But it has a great deal to do with the relations of men to each other & to God." Scorning fanatical enemies of religion as much as its enthusiasts, he remained ambivalent about it as a necessary but potentially dangerous reality. Though not "exactly" a "Voltairian," he dragged Ellis on a pilgrimage to Voltaire's Swiss chateau and kept in his study a statuette of Voltaire that Lady Holland had given him as a memento of her husband. But Macaulay came to cringe at Voltaire: "His hatred of Xtianity is positively a disease. A very little man—& he wd have been as mad as Don Quixote to try to eliminate it." Pleased that Baba read Gibbon, he was also surprised that *The Decline and Fall of the Roman Empire* endured, "though it is offensive to the religious feeling of the country, & really most unfair where religion is concerned." He now memorized great chunks of Lucretius: "somehow the philosophy strikes me as less absurd than I used to think it—I mean as compared with other atheistic systems." But Macaulay still resisted the stark implications of Lucretius' naturalistic vision of humanity and the cosmos: "all anointment for broken bones."[17]

Some of his reading reflected his desire to believe in more than "atoms and the void," if only his mind could accept what seemed to be unknowable. It also showed him identifying with his lineage as a skeptic. On summer holiday in 1853 he indulged himself in "the best Sherry," "good Champagne, Plato and Lucian." Macaulay's reaction to two of the dialogues in which Socrates prepares to swallow the hemlock captured his own settled disillusionment: "They are fine in parts. But the story about the oracle—the divine monitor—the dream . . . &c are absurd. I imagine that with all his skill in logomachy, he was a strange fanciful superstitious old fellow—Extreme credulity has often gone with extreme logical subtlety." The next day "with admiration & contempt mingled" he read the last of those dialogues, in which Socrates/Plato evoked the benign gods extending their care for just souls beyond death. The beauty of the *Phaedo* moved him to exclaim: "What writing!" But its talk of the hereafter caused him to quote the disillusioned motto of a great sixteenth-century skeptic: "But que sais-je?" As much as Lucian from the second century c.e., Montaigne seemed to him like-minded, in certain moods almost contemporary. Macaulay then returned to writing his old parliamentary speeches for publication.[18] Whether he remembered or invented his own words, they addressed not theological "logomachy" but the reality of England and its power.

Macaulay heard some nineteenth-century religious voices but on his own terms. Among them were Thomas Arnold—at least occasionally—and the Italian novelist Alessandro Manzoni. Critically for Macaulay's private comfort and public authority, the thin theology of Conyers Middleton, an eighteenth-century divine and freethinker, seemed prevalent: "Odd how times change—he would now be called a timid neologist" (a proponent of new theological ideas). Macaulay both practiced and preached a surrogate religion: a primness that rivaled his father's. In May 1852 he saw "Mr. Albert Smith's Ascent of Mont Blanc," a hit show in Piccadilly. Smith interspersed his monologue with patter songs, mimicry, and cockneyisms before reaching the top against a background of dramatic panoramas and dioramas. Though Macaulay scorned climbing as folly, he enjoyed the show—"The views of the mountain made me shudder"—until Smith suggested that reaching the summit moved him "to damn the view." Macaulay felt "rather scandalized": "A little decent respect to the religion of his country would have done no harm." Smith's "cursing and swearing" seemed insupportable. That he became a favorite of Queen Victoria and her starchier consort after a command performance suggests that Macaulay, along with many other post-Christian Victorians, was a prude without piety.[19]

Macaulay's community of classically minded Anglicans was compact and civilized. As early as 1842, Henry Hart Milman, a protégé of Peel and then the rector of the fashionable parish serving the Houses of Parliament, pointed educated men to the classics as a refuge from raging bigotry and superstition. Like Macaulay, Milman and George Grote belonged to The Club, dining regularly together in a tavern between Pall Mall and Piccadilly. Despite their theological and political differences, they mostly regarded the church as a source of comity and cooperated as if by instinct to protect their place in society. Though only approximate, the returns of England's first and last religious census seemed to reveal the establishment as shrinking into another voluntary organization. On Sunday, 30 March 1851, about 40 percent of the English population attended church; Macaulay was not among them: "walked—languidly and not much ...Voltaire." Baptized Anglicans greatly outnumbered the Dissenters, but the count showed that the two groups attended in roughly equal numbers. The number of Anglican worshipers rose after mid-century.[20] During the 1850s, however, both churchmen's authority over the public mind and their social status appeared to be declining, tendencies that Macaulay eagerly projected onto the late seventeenth century.

His circle of friendly clerics was decisive in advancing the hollowing-out that preserved the establishment on Macaulay's terms: a major agency of cultural Protestantism. Lecturing Dubliners on an ideal university in the mid-1850s, Newman defined a gentleman as "one who never inflicts pain." He meant to engrave "some of the lineaments of the ethical character, which the cultivated intellect will form, apart from religious principle." It sounds like a dogmatist's indictment of placatory religion. While still an Anglican, Newman had publicly associated Milman with heresy. Numerous and prominent gentlemen faced Newman across a divide. They were religious reconcilers and he an irreconcilable. The urge to find common ground in letters was venerable—Macaulay correctly identified it as a force mitigating seventeenth-century Europe's bloodthirsty religion. At the height of the Victorian "crisis of faith," the fracas over Darwinism complicated the older division. Religious reconcilers and irreconcilables sometimes changed places. After 1859 Bishop Wilberforce, guided by his friend the geologist Richard Owen, ruined his historical reputation by mocking human evolution, whereas Newman, though an implacable dogmatist, concluded that strict logic required him to "go whole hog with Darwin."[21]

Valuing consensus, many clerical gentlemen were susceptible to Macaulay's disenchanted and nationalist reading of modern English history. From Germany on New Year's Day 1849 Jowett wrote to the Reverend A. P. Stanley, once Dr. Arnold's favorite pupil and later his admiring biographer, praising the new *History of England* as the "best . . . since Gibbon." Stanley retained Arnold's faith in the pertinence of ancient history, his hope that the progressive education of the human race would culminate in "spiritual unity," and his love for England as both a "national personality" and a "perfect" civilization. To Stanley, it seemed to follow that an absolute theology was now impossible and that the true religion belonged to the future. He also scoured history books for evidence of "high moral tone" rather than of Providence directing human affairs. Holder of a first-class degree in classics from Oxford, he began a eulogistic review of the latest volumes of Grote's rationalist *History of Greece* in the *Quarterly Review* by alluding to the other great English historian of the day.[22] Writing within months of Croker's assault on the *History of England* and in deference to the polite fiction that the magazine spoke with one voice, Stanley did not name Macaulay. His greatness was already self-evident.

Although High Church bigots and evangelical enthusiasts alarmed divines like Milman, Jowett, and Stanley, they found congenial reasonable gentlemen of similar education and taste whose doubts were discreet. "Broad Church," the neologism applied to advocates of an inclusive and nondogmatic establishment, became the religious middle way that Baroness Bunsen desired. Jowett remembered first hearing the term in the late 1840s from a friend who had lost his faith, and Stanley first publicly announced in 1850 that the Church of England "is by the very conditions of its being, not High, or Low, but Broad." His definition suggested generous possibilities. In Grote's pages Stanley discovered "lessons of the truest Christian wisdom" and regarded Socrates' death as "an epoch in the history not only of Greece but of the world." Stanley's Socrates caused a revolution that "is still in operation in every part of the civilized world" and exemplified the union in a skeptical world of "religious belief" with "common sense and vigorous inquiry." He longed for Socrates to reappear and intervene "in a conversation, in a book, in a speech, in a sermon": "Differences, doubtless, would still remain, but they would be differences of serious and thinking men, not the watchwords of angry disputants." Stanley wanted to invest Socrates with an authority "not merely religious, but Christian," but Grote "rendered it all but impossible."[23] In the wake of a quarrel over how baptism made infants into Christians that riled theologians and raised the fundamental question of the church's relation to the state, Stanley fantasized about baptizing Socrates. Inevitably, the state prevailed.

For Stanley, "elasticity" identified the establishment. Invasive heresy-hunters confirmed a lesson that Stanley had learned from Arnold and Milman. He saw England as a virtual church: "his lifelong aim was to do something towards breaking the collision between the beliefs and doubts of the age, to bring out what is common, to overlook that which is peculiar." As dean of Westminster Abbey, Stanley expanded the church's elasticity. By making the Abbey "the place of interment for illustrious persons," he fulfilled Macaulay's vision of it as the nation's "great temple of silence and reconciliation"—at least for nominal Anglicans. Acting in 1871 on a petition from Grote's colleagues in The Club, the dean sanctioned his burial in the Abbey; John Stuart Mill reluctantly served as a

pallbearer. Four years later, Stanley authorized the burial in Grote's grave
of his lifelong friend and fellow ancient historian, Connop Thirlwall,
bishop of St. David's and, of course, an acquaintance of Macaulay. Non-
chalantly, the archbishop of Canterbury attended the interment of the
"great Bishop Thirlwall"; "six bishops carried the pall." That his remains
lie with Grote's under a Ciceronian epitaph proclaims the emollient
power of their shared classicism.[24]

By translating Plato from Grote's forbidding language and pervasive
skepticism into congenially spiritual English, Jowett recaptured Socrates
for religion. In Balliol College Chapel an alert undergraduate heard the
master preaching "Platonism flavoured with a little Christian charity."
Dean Stanley was not alone in welcoming the mix. From 1866, he invited Jowett to preach occasionally in the Abbey. He debuted before "a
vast congregation, chiefly of men," and Stanley judged the sermon "truly
characteristic and truly Christian." High Church divines shunned the
Abbey's pulpit. Once burned, Jowett was discreet about his beliefs and
his doubts. In his old age, someone asked him whether both "the Broad
Church clergy" and Marcus Aurelius, Stoic philosopher and the "Pope
of Paganism," dishonestly practiced "conformity" to a state religion in
which they disbelieved. "Jowett assented" but characterized the philosophical attempt "to spiritualise Paganism" as "the nobler course." The
questioner pressed on, asking whether ancient sages "might have thought,
as many Broad Churchmen now think, that a certain alloy of supernatu-
ralism is the only way in which spiritual truths can be made" palatable to
"the infirm digestions of the multitude." Jowett's reply was cagey: "I
think that in the present day a religion without miracles would suit many
people better than a religion with miracles." Years earlier Macaulay had
discerned what divines like Jowett were about. During his last months,
he read much eighteenth-century polemical theology, including books
by John Toland, a reviled freethinker when he died: "Very little in
them—Some of the points on which he was thought most heretical
would be frankly conceded by the most eminent divines of our time; &
others would be hardly considered as worth a contest." Satisfied at the
widespread diffusion of Toland's naturalism, he returned to a section of
his *History* that addressed a more immediate concern—"India Bill of
1698." Formerly he had questioned Toland's contemporary pertinence.[25]

Also part of Macaulay's world, Gladstone in the 1850s grasped classicism's seeping effect on the establishment. Just before the decade began, he had published an essay on the great Italian classical scholar and poet Giacomo Leopardi, who abandoned the hothouse Catholicism of his youth for a bleak and neopagan naturalism. There Gladstone asked whether Leopardi's life might provide a cautionary tale about the direction of England's "choicest youth [who] are trained almost from infancy to read and digest both the thoughts and diction of Latin and Greek authors." He demurred. At home "Christian studies" supplied a "powerful corrective" to classicism, and, unlike Catholic Italy, England fostered a "real and vital activity of the mind upon the subject matter of religion, as there is upon the subject matter of pagan learning." It was "the unquestionable fact that classical studies in this country are not found to have any sceptical tendency." For all the theological differences then separating Gladstone from Newman, both persuaded themselves "that the University of Oxford finds in Aristotle one of her most powerful engines of ethical, and indirectly of Christian, teaching." Gladstone, however, awoke to the drift of Grote's radical skepticism about the earliest Greek history, which made Homer's age "irrecoverable to the historian." Gladstone believed that to deny historical value to Greece's heroic poetry undermined the authority of the Hebrew Bible.[26]

He therefore labored in a vast and idiosyncratic book published in 1858 to prove that "the Homeric works still bore witness to a vanished world near the dawn of time." *Studies on Homer and the Homeric Age* made bold claims. Best exhibited in Homer, the Hellenic mind was "the original mould of the modern European civilization." Homer evoked the greatness that human cooperation could achieve: "He supplied a full account of 'religion, ethics. Policy, history, arts, manners.' His poems enable the reader to understand 'the whole range of our nature, and the entire circle of human action and experience' . . . in isolation from religious truth."[27] If Homer's epics anticipated Christian revelation, it followed that Christianity, not modern skepticism, was privileged to interpret them and the civilization they inspired. Theologically more encumbered than Jowett, Gladstone also strove to recapture classicism for the church.

After Calcutta, Macaulay sometimes entertained flights of classical fancy but without succumbing to antiquity's spell as in his youth. He looked into "Gladstone's book on Homer—some good things but far too much of it—and some twaddle." After reading the "three thick volumes," he recoiled: "Alas! Idle fancies—endless prolixity about trifles—not one deep or ingenious observation, moral, political, historical, or critical . . . Sometimes too strange ignorance." Although classical antiquity sustained both Gladstone and him, their disagreement cut deep religiously as well as historically. Macaulay refined and inculcated a widely appealing cultural Protestantism, while *Studies on Homer* showed Gladstone's continuing evolution from the "stern and unbending" churchmanship that Macaulay had begun softening twenty years earlier. The process ultimately brought not Gladstone's conversion to a light Anglicanism, but "the growth of a more latitudinarian element" in his theology: a kinder, gentler, and more accommodating Christianity.[28]

Respectability

The respectability that Macaulay so prized and cultivated in lieu of faith was hard-won. He once saw a "description of myself" that had migrated from a Scottish to a New York paper. It reads like a script for a John Cleese sketch. The details were recognizable: "short, stout, energetic . . . [with] a big round face, and large staring and very bright hazel eyes," with a "gait" that was "firm and decided with a touch of pomposity" and wielding his ever-present umbrella, which he "batters on the pavement with mighty thumps." If accurate, what followed qualifies Macaulay for membership in the thickly populated upper-middle ranks of eccentric eminent Victorians, or as the masterly publicist of his own ethereal genius, or both. Working his face, his eyes gleaming, and his lips muttering, he walked oblivious to gaping onlookers, some smiling, others respectful of the "unmistakable air of mental power and energy, approaching grandeur, about the man." The piece went on to show him giving still "freer vent to the mental impulses which appear to be continually working within him." Macaulay was dining alone "in the coffee room of the Trafalgar Hotel at Greenwich"—credible—muttering, fidgeting, and gesturing to illustrate "his mental dreamings," until he "seized a massive decanter, held it for a moment in the air, and dashed it down upon the table with such hearty good will, that the solid crystal flew about in fragments while the numerous parties dining round instinctively started up and stared at the curious iconoclast. Not a whit put out, . . . Macaulay . . . called loudly for his bill" and "strode out" with a flourish.[29]

Thomas Pinney, the scholar who knows him best, wondered whether the description "was totally untrue." Macaulay, who indignantly and properly denied a later American report "about my having destroyed my faculties with opium," summarized the article for Baba. He caviled at none of it up to the tale of the broken decanter: "I have no recollection of such an occurrence; but if it did take place, I do not think that it would have deprived me of my self possession. This is fame. This is the advantage of making a figure in the world." His careful phrasing sounds like a "no contest" plea in a criminal case. As a lawyer, Macaulay knew that it serves in some instances as an admission of guilt but is not technically an admission. He also sounded as if he had adjusted to the diminished privacy that is the price of fame and savored the possibilities "of making a figure in the world." Now his prestige and wealth occasionally permitted him to act as he pleased.[30]

Macaulay could publicly indulge his tics and idiosyncrasies because he knew that the public expected their geniuses to be edgy; but impropriety was another matter. Notoriously "mad, bad, and dangerous to know," Lord Byron had started the fashion in another age. Whatever Macaulay's eccentricities, he helped to teach his contemporaries to regard decorum as an ethical and political imperative minus the old Anglican consensus. In 1854 he went to Westminster Abbey for the funeral of one of Byron's poetic heirs, only to find himself "very coolly shut out" along with Disraeli and other notables. Annoyed, they indulged in "a good deal of talk not very appropriate"—a smart-alecky game of one-upmanship about the deceased's poems. Predictably, Macaulay prevailed and later demanded an apology from the deceased's executors, which he "received civilly, but very drily." Taken as a whole, the episode exhibits the style of high propriety and ready deference that he practiced, encouraged, and exploited.[31]

Anticipating the American jurist Potter Stewart on identifying pornography, Macaulay knew rudeness when he saw it. His standard for judging others' behavior was "my taste." In his mind the rules of decorum were clear and authoritative, and discreet hypocrisy provided an indispensable safety valve. Elaborate courtesy to women was imperative. Especially in their presence displays of coarseness "disgusted" him: "It was the tone of a man in a brothel among strumpets of a high class,—bordering on ribaldry—I saw that Mrs [Caroline] Norton was some-

times abashed—and it is not a little that abashes her." Parliamentary procedure showed how conventions maintained order in an increasingly
variegated society. His own rule was more demanding: "Perfect deport-
ment in a situation." Preserving and exchanging civility always mattered,
of course with members of the royal family but even with Thomas Carlyle: "Why not? Nothing is so easy as to be civil where you despise." In
the Commons Lord Palmerston once "lost his temper & good manners":
"disgusted me." Palmerston offered the best evidence that respectability
was "up for grabs" at the top as well as the bottom of society into the
1860s, but he was then a very old buck from Byron's generation—
"Womanizing, until desire outran performance, was only one of Palmerston's recreations." As much as any vigilant Victorian pater, Macaulay
monitored transgressions within his family. About the nephew who was
his namesake he was incurious, except for his transformation from an
"uncouth half savage urchin." Any display of gaucheness relieved him
from the obligation of reciprocal propriety. Aging intensified Macaulay's
respect for decorum, including the spirit that informed the Victorian
Sabbath. He grew scrupulous about others and himself. When Lord John
Russell asked about an edition of Fox's papers, he "recommended publication, but advised him to suppress some coarse words." In a great country house Macaulay once played "a game of chance ... I forget what it is
called—Dice—but very innocent."[32]

Like any other complex society, Macaulay's England respected codes
of honor and shame as well as of guilt. Many Britons could feel embarrassed at one transgression and self-accusing responsibility for another.
Equating calculation with rationality and deferring to the marketplace of
convention to fix value, Macaulay knew shame but seemed impervious
to guilt. He normally envisioned personal relations as transactions, the
exchange of services or the promise of service: "I was very civil—the
least I could be; for he had been very kind & useful." Unless his reputation was at stake, the impact of what he did—or failed to do—on other
people was of little moment to him. Knowing neither moral absolutes
nor a God to whom all people are equally accountable, he regarded others and himself as means rather than ends. Upholding honor intensified
his sensitivity to routine embarrassments and especially to the damage of
"disgrace" to both individuals and their families. Small gaffes like forgetting about an invitation made him feel "shame and vexation." When a

lapse offended strangers, he instinctively tried to avoid blaming himself. Eleven years afterward, he continued brooding over the ridicule he had provoked by puffing his appointment as secretary at war and a privy councilor by addressing a public letter "from Windsor Castle." For all his cosmopolitan eminence and *savoir-faire,* he could neither laugh it off nor accept responsibility: "Was ever man so persecuted for such a trifle? . . yet my life must be allowed to have been a very, very happy one, seeing that such a persecution was among my greatest misfortunes."[33]

As much as recent historians, Macaulay understood respectability as integral to how nineteenth-century Britons defined themselves. Respectability mattered before Macaulay and even more after him. The origin of the word suggests how it unified the nation's social classes by promoting both downscale uplift and upscale inhibition. "Respectability" was coined in 1785 by a parson who wrote self-help manuals. A tavernkeeper, his father "took care to educate his son as a gentleman." John Trusler's hard-won and elevating classical education taught him to embed his new word in the mores of a shame-and-honor society: "He is very sensible that there are in all classes of life, men of honour and respectability."[34] From the beginning, respectability provided an inclusive standard of conduct that deepened the attachment of a solidly commercial and religious people to a hierarchical order.

Respectability therefore linked classes without minimizing the differences among them. Bishop Wilberforce might thunder that it was not conversion to Christ, but other gentlemen venerated it as a surrogate religion. Macaulay, on his way to becoming both "Parvenu & Peer," became an even more discerning connoisseur of the theory and practice of status. He frequented Clubland: the Athenaeum, where the conspicuously and fashionably brainy mingled with pillars of society; Brooks's, Whiggish and aristocratic; the Reform; and the only The Club. There men gathered "who are not mere flatterers of the rabble." Lacking the vocabulary, Macaulay nevertheless understood some of the elementary forms of our sociological jargon. In his England, status remained ascribed as well as achieved. He and his upwardly mobile kind were gentlemen because of who they had become, but they remained parvenus because of their fathers. It belonged to the third generation to transcend their grandfathers. But even after Macaulay was ennobled, the aristocratic pleasure of displeasing eluded him. Entering the House of Lords one day,

he sputtered at the sight of a pierced peer: "I had never seen an Englishman of any rank, except that is on sailors, with earrings in my life."
More than a vulgarity, that hereditary nobleman's jewelry betrayed his
obligation to edify his inferiors. Macaulay's connoisseurship of social differences complicated his taxonomy of the economic classes. He retained
Aristotle's categories of the very rich, the very poor, and those in between, which had informed his case for the Reform Act. But socially
and politically he subdivided the lower orders into the docilely respectable—including the deserving poor—and the threatening "rabble" or
"mob."[35] His counterrevolutionary nightmare of the uprising of "human
vermin" lay dormant.

Macaulay's depiction of respectability as accessible even to the poor
was perhaps as important as his nationalism in converting working-class
journals "overwhelmingly" to "the Whig interpretation of history." Some
of their readers noticed and followed his gospel of propriety. They belonged to the "many" or the "multitude." They lacked the governing
capacity that was the burden and the privilege of the few. Those categories harkened back to the ancient distinction between the knowledgeable, who could rule, and the incorrigibly ignorant, perhaps respectable
or even hereditary gentlemen who were unfit for the kingdom and the
power.[36] It was unlikely that Macaulay's pierced peer read much Greek
and Latin.

Inveterately a noting, evaluating, and sometimes envious consumer,
Macaulay, as much as any present-day historian, also knew that access to
greater comfort and convenience was a mark of respectability. Sometimes he imagined what he would do with grandees' possessions—books
as well as palaces—if they were his. Buying a carriage was an epoch in
his life, fit for savoring and display: "I went to Ld John's [Russell], pleased
and proud . . . This is the first time that I ever had a carriage of my own
except in office."[37] "Carriage trade" was not coined until fifty years after
Macaulay's death, but even without the word he and his contemporaries
marked the prestige and independence that came with a brougham of
one's own.

Macaulay's position required him to behave generously toward his inferiors: "gave the men something to drink our health." Encouraging a
uniform spoken English was also a responsibility. The regional accent
that was not yet the received pronunciation of all the best English people

bespoke nationality even more than privilege. During a long walk he felt chest pains. A downpour forced him to take shelter in an alehouse, where he joined a group of hop-pickers: "I liked their looks, & thought their English remarkably good for their rank in life. It was in truth the Surrey English," which to his ears was as pure as the Italian of Tuscany. After ordering "a foaming pot" they could not pay: "it was but four pence half-penny. I laid the money down; & their delight & gratitude quite affected me." When two of their mates arrived, he ordered a round for them and left, "followed by more blessings than, I believe, were ever purchased for nine pence . . . I did my best to play the courteous host." Three years later receiving a peerage caused him to resolve to fulfill the elementary obligation of nobility: "I ought now to be courteous."[38] The parvenu in him inhibited noblesse oblige as well as aristocratic flamboyance.

Often teary or on the verge of tears, he prized good-heartedness and practiced charity widely and often. His easy sentimentality enabled him to accommodate some of the injury he incurred by living life mostly as a series of transactions. His dealings with his help seemingly caused no tension between his heart and his head. He pensioned off his weeping old servants ("I was moved") and noted that his "new servants [were] very attentive & respectful, quite satisfied apparently with their places." But his charities could vex him. With Christmas approaching, he again complained to himself about a plague of ingrates: "I can truly say that all the reward that I get for relieving the distressed is derived from my own feelings. I never in my life had reason to believe that my benefactions, often very large for my means, produced the smallest gratitude." Although such disinterestedness failed to compute, he continued giving money to complete strangers.[39]

Acquaintance or kinship elicited his charity, variously spontaneous, grudging, and in defiance of his maxim that "liberality" could be an unkindness. In January 1856 he sent money to a cousin, married to a dodgy clergyman but friendly with his sister Selina. By the end of the year she was "begging" him for another £100, and after Selina intervened he offered "to assist her at a proper time and to a reasonable extent." Thirteen months later he concluded that from "begging she has proceeded to something very like swindling" and "sent a resolute refusal." But two months before he died he sent her and her husband £10. Other poor relations proved to be better investments. With "much satisfaction," he laid out three guineas to a young first cousin for a library membership: "likely to get on & do credit to those who have helped him forward."[40] His instinct was shrewd. The youth became Sir Robert Hamilton, K.C.B., a distinguished colonial administrator.

Networking

Companionship sustained Macaulay's congenial and powerful circle. The glittering invitations that belonged to fame became less important to him. Riding the success of his *History*, he retained some appetite for talking with continental princesses. But he picked and chose invitations to suit himself. An unavoidable summons from Prince Albert to the palace "greatly vexed" him because it disrupted his own plans. To his "extreme astonishment" Albert offered him Cambridge's Regius Professorship of Modern History, which he declined on the spot. Surrendering his liberty for a paltry salary was no bargain. Instead of picking up his *History*, he celebrated his deliverance by reading novels. Before Macaulay turned fifty, he began to take a precociously geriatric pleasure in cultivating his habits and routines. Novelty came to bore or unsettle him, and he often declined invitations to occasions where foreigners would abound. French was the diplomatic language, and he felt uncomfortable speaking it "before men of eminence whom I do not know well." Age and illness would deepen his aversion to dining out, but a few dinners were irresistible. In 1857 he accepted an invitation from Lord Granville, the foreign minister. The other guests included George Grote, Leopold von Ranke, and Granville's stepson, who was on his way to becoming the hugely learned Lord Acton.[41]

Macaulay's perception of Englishness contracted along with his social life. Never generous, his terms for treating acceptable Jews as primarily English narrowed. During the summer before he saw Ireland, he wrote an ungrateful account of his dinner at the Rothschilds' mansion: "bad paintings." Anglicized and sophisticated as well as philanthropic, Lionel de Rothschild had assembled a famous collection of old masters. It was "the most stupid of stupid parties—half a dozen Jews of the family— some Jewesses—a diplomate [sic] or two ... I was wedged between a Jew from Naples & the envoy from Copenhagen, both talking broken English." Macaulay long remembered a blunder by his Neapolitan dinner partner ("my Jew"). Only the table impressed him. Dining with mostly "popish" peers bothered him less, but they were "rather dreary." Dull company they may have been, but in that house he was, exceptionally, an outsider inhibited by the rules of deference from outshining his betters and perhaps powerless to amuse them. Especially on unfamiliar ground he needed to entertain or to feel that others wanted him to entertain them: "fancied I talked too much. They seemed to want me to talk"; "I thought—perhaps wrongly—that I talked very successfully." But the passing of old political battles had harmonized Macaulay and Robert Peel years before Peel's fatal riding accident triggered national mourning in July 1850. Macaulay grieved long and publicly for him: "I have been more affected . . . than I could have believed."[42] Their visible amity helped to entrench his *History* as the consensus version, both in its conception and in its reception.

Neither of Macaulay's apartments in the Albany could accommodate formal dinners. Routinely hosting breakfast parties, a fashion "prevalent among literary men," he frequently accepted the hospitality of his guests. Beginning between 9:30 and 10:00 in the morning, they usually lasted into the early afternoon. His company often included women, and the fare suggests a present-day champagne brunch, though with more meat and fish than fruits and vegetables. The regulars around his table included Henry Hallam, Dean Milman, Bishop Wilberforce, Lord Mahon, the earl of Carlisle, and later the duke of Argyll. Sometimes there were guests like George Bancroft, the retiring American ambassador and its pioneer nationalist historian; or Peel's second son, recently returned as a Liberal M.P.[43]

Macaulay's dining room could sound like an echo chamber. The table talk is mostly irretrievable, though we can hear snatches of his, as well as that of some of the regulars and a few outsiders who wandered into their tight society. There men of the world felt free to become boys again: "Extremely agreeable, and would have been still more so but there was a tendency to talk very loud and all at once." Sometimes they indulged in buffoonery, as when Wilberforce delighted Macaulay by mimicking "the brogue of his Right Reverend Brother of Cashel" in Ireland. But the breakfasters relished antiquity and high politics: "Extremely pleasant—much Greek." Did Milman, toward whom Macaulay felt "a true good will," accept his "conjecture" about a passage of Juvenal? Had Peel's speech in the Commons the night before fulfilled its promise? A guest remembered bits of Macaulay's conversation, mingling disquisition, jousting, wit, gossip, and realpolitik: "The wines of ancient Gaul scarcely figure at all in the Latin classics . . . the desptaches [*sic*] of the Tuscan Envoy to the effect that the courtesies passing between Cromwell and the Grand Duke Ferdinand the Second took the characteristic form of presents of 'Elle' and Montepulciano . . . when you come to know him better you will find the monomania branching out into a polymania . . . There never was an act politically more necessary than that *coup d'état* [of Napoleon III]." Sometimes the breakfasters sharpened their claws. Wilberforce once characterized Lord Ashley, a pious evangelical and effective advocate of state intervention on behalf of workers, as a Pharisee. Macaulay thought that his lordship's antipopery showed a "strange wild vehemence."[44]

Command of both classical languages and proper etiquette demonstrated a man's *savoir-faire,* but erudite machismo prevailed over self-effacement. When Gladstone first invited Macaulay to one of his regular Thursday breakfasts, Macaulay acknowledged by inquiring about the meaning of a passage from Juvenal that Gladstone had quoted in his invitation. A joust over how to emend the text ensued. Meeting the novelist Thomas Love Peacock, Macaulay judged him "a clever fellow & a good scholar": "I am glad to have an opportunity of becoming better acquainted with him." The next day they "had out Aristophanes, Aeschylus, Sophocles, and several other old fellows, & tried out each other's strength pretty well. We are both strong enough in these matters for gentlemen." Benjamin Disraeli was no gentleman, and Macaulay sniffed at his incompetence in Greek. Given enough wine and a detested opponent, he was prompted to show that his was the greater classical erudition. He once argued across the table with Brougham ("a dirty lying scoundrel") about how to spell "Euripides." Macaulay weighed in "by quoting a couple of lines from Aristophanes": "I could have overwhelmed him with quotations." The thrill of winning helped to keep Macaulay rereading: "Plato's Euthydemus—very good,—but less so than it seemed to me thirty years ago . . . nevertheless very good"; "Plato's Symposium. What a mixture of disgust & admiration it excites"—for him, its homoeroticism compromised its eloquence. Sometimes he spoke to himself in Greek. His frequent walks enabled him to read the ancients and daydream: "After breakfast put Demosthenes in my pocket & took an immense walk—20 miles, I should think." When he failed to exercise, he felt it.[45]

Comfortably living much in his head, he neither sought nor welcomed challenging society. Agreeable and, even better, familiar voices were the thing. After derailing the Aborigines' Protection Society, he maintained friendly relations with the Buxtons, the Trevelyans' sometime neighbors. Encountering John Austin, once a taciturn and radical legal philosopher—"a Chartist or nearly so"—he found him now "wonderfully fluent & wonderfully conservative." Macaulay often socialized with the aristocrats whose ranks he eventually joined. After dinner the ladies "retired [and] we had some lively chat." The company of attractive or clever women pleased him. Though tamer than ever, his libido was alive, often amusing and sometimes anxious. At table he relished some "very agreeable women" as much as the good vintages. Facing an aging flirt, he imagined both of them younger and himself reciprocating: "before I had grey hair and she moustachios." At a duke's country house he watched "voluptuous" dancing and wondered whether "I am growing more licentious in my imagination as I grow old." That in his eyes "the gallopade" was "almost as expressive as the fandango" speaks volumes about the boundaries of his decorum.[46]

How did others see and hear Macaulay? Public acclaim and unrivaled success relieved the insecurity that drove him to perform and to try to outperform others. The urge, however, was permanent and occasionally insistent. Although the little boy who had delightedly preached standing on a chair to Hannah More's wondering farmhands survived in him, the repetitiveness of performance, the routine of applause, and the constraints of primness dampened his conversation as well as his writing. He once "dropped asleep while talking; & strangely I went on talking, & so coherently that E[llis] could perceive no difference." Carlyle etched him presiding over a breakfast party: "Niagara of eloquent commonplace talk . . . man cased in official mail of proof; stood my impatient fire-explosion with much patience, merely hissing a little steam up, and continued his Niagara—supply-and-demand, power ruinous to powerful himself, impossibility of govt. doing more than keep the peace, suicidal distraction of new French Republic &c, &c. Essentially irremediable commonplace nature of the man . . . A squat thickset, low-browed, short, and rather pot-bellied, grizzled little man of fifty: these be thy gods O Is-

rael!"[47] Carlyle's acid about the popular worship of Macaulay like some
"molten calf" suggests the resentment of an aspiring British idol shown
up as an also-ran.

Macaulay recorded his side of a couple of their rare encounters. He
avoided Carlyle at one dinner party, lest he be forced to "take him down."
At another they were "mutually civil, but with mutual repulsion. His
cant makes me sick": "Carlyle & I could not keep from exchanging
some thrusts. I thought I had greatly the advantage." But there was truth
in Carlyle's evocation of Macaulay discharging a "Niagara of eloquent
commonplace talk." A decade later John Lothrop Motley, a cosmopolitan
American, watched Macaulay perform at table and sent home a "photograph" that resembles Carlyle's etching. Macaulay's "general appearance
is singularly commonplace"; he suavely dominated the conversation, but
"there was nothing to excite very particular attention in its even flow."
The encounter left him imagining Macaulay and Carlyle facing off across
a table: "It would be like two locomotives, each with a long train, coming against each other at express speed." He captured the old rivals' shared
aggressiveness, but, underestimating Macaulay's ability to dominate, he
imagined that both would "be smashed into silence at the first collision."
Macaulay grew to like Motley "much," because "we agreed wonderfully
well" in hating both slavery and the abolitionists. Whatever Macaulay's
impact on his peers, he could always captivate young people. Over dinner a few weeks before he met Motley, a Trinity undergraduate reverently hung on his words. On the printed page they, too, appear commonplace.[48] Yet his glittering reputation as a conversationalist would
survive him.

Wealth

Wealth intensified Macaulay's preoccupation with money. He often
counted his, sought to increase it, and fretted about spending it. Both
his fortune and his expenses grew steadily. In 1852 his capital alone
amounted to £40,000 (a 2007 purchasing power of about £3.32 million), and four years later it increased to £60,000, apart from copyrights
worth "a good £15,000 more." A few weeks before he died he calculated
his net worth at approximately "eighty thousand pounds." The resworn
probate filed in August 1860 estimated his wealth "at under £70,000,"

but that sum excluded the value of his copyrights. In 2007 the purchasing power of his probated estate was about £4.7 million. And he spent more as he earned more. Between 1849 and 1854 he received royalties from volumes one and two of his *History* of "at least £18,000." Much more followed. In 1849 his royalties amounted to £5,500 and his estimated expenses to only £2,000; but the first flush of wealth left him anxious: "I am surprised at my own extravagance; the more so because I was not at all sensible that I was squandering." He proved to be thriftier than he feared: £175.1 "Rent/Albany dues"; £25.2 "Taxes & Rates; £365.3 "Weekly bills"; £365.4 "Pocket money"; £150.5 "Dress"; £100.6 "Wine"; £66.1 "Wages"; £250.8 "Sisters" (Selina and Frances); £75.9 "Regular subscriptions"; £75.10 "Miscellaneous Bills" = £1,698, "Exclusive of Treats, Travelling, & charities extraordinary." In 2007 his annual expenditures would have been £133,902. "Getting rich fast" required him to change how he felt and acted as a consumer: "I must cure myself of the bad habit of buying things without sufficient consideration." Outgrowing his scruples, he arranged in 1856 "that I shall henceforth have an income of 3000 a year" from his investments, in addition to "copyrights wh[ich] cannot be rated at less than 1500£ a year for a long-time to come." His projection was nearly accurate: in 1859 he took in over £5,000, with a 2007 purchasing power of £366,024.[49]

In his prosperity he imagined that he was almost self-made, an effort that required forgetting his father's connections' indispensable role in launching his career. It also required him to shrink his uncle Colin's largesse: "twenty-two years ago, I had just nothing when my debts were paid;—and all that I have with the exception of a small part left me by my uncle the Genl, had been made by myself, & made easily & honestly, by pursuits which were a pleasure to me, & without one insinuation from any slanderer that I was not ever liberal in all pecuniary dealings. E[llis] to dinner—I wish from my soul that he were as well off." And three years later Macaulay remembered, "Twenty five years ago I was worth exactly & literally nothing . . . My whole fortune—except about 8000£ from my uncle Colin is of my own acquisition. The "small part" amounted not to "8000£" but, as he had boasted to Ellis upon learning of his inheritance, £10,000: "the most important matter about which I had to write."[50] Our self-glorification feeds on and feeds our self-isolation.

Macaulay understood that his moneymaking colored his friendship with Ellis. Back from India for two decades and familiar with wealth, he faulted himself for bragging to Ellis about it "in a way which must have hurt him." Again wishing that his friend "were as well off," Macaulay insinuated that he could easily help him. An assertion of moral superiority accompanied the hint of charity. With a Latin tag, he "wrote to E— strongly—about the pusillanimity with wh. he seemed to sink down under what, after all, is no such ponderous load of misfortune." Annoyed when Ellis felt too strapped to travel with him to Italy, he lent him £600, which was repaid in December 1858. But Macaulay seemed oblivious to what his pounds-and-shillings criterion of success meant for his writing. He studied sales figures and projected his annual royalties—"I shall be rich"; "I am richer than ever"—and treated his "official and literary gains as capital," while sniffing at Thackeray for practicing "literature as a sort of trade." In rebuking another, he once more deceived himself: "Money is a good thing no doubt. But when a man has played a great part in life . . . it is not good that his mind should seem to be chiefly filled with thoughts about the number of dollars that he has got, and the number that he ought to have."[51]

Honors

Hankering for voices with an "unmistakable air of mental power and energy, approaching grandeur," Macaulay's contemporaries venerated sages. He both thrived on the cult and stimulated it. Because he wrote in the demotic, he is often omitted from lists of the usual suspects: Matthew Arnold, Thomas Carlyle, J. H. Newman, and John Ruskin. Macaulay's index of his own public standing was characteristically realistic. It pleased him to see himself often referred to in other people's books—"& always agreeably." By the winter of 1853 he was honored as an English sage in western and central Europe and beyond. To Ellis and with a tincture of self-mockery, he strutted some of the prizes that proved how widely and well his generation respected him:

T B Macaulay, FRS [Fellow of the Royal Society], MRIA [Member of the Royal Irish Academy], MP, late fellow of Trin Coll Cambridge, late Lord Rector of the University of Glasgow,

Knight of the Order of Merit of Prussia, Member of the Royal
Academies of Munich and Turin, Member of the Historical
Society of Utrecht, and,—die of envy—

Member of the French Institute
in the Department of Moral Science ! ! ![52]

More than any of his fellow sages, Macaulay, by helping to create the
conventional version of Englishness when England seemed to be the
exemplary modern nation, made himself iconic. Honoring him amounted
to honoring England. The risk was obvious: to win acceptance as a
prophet in one's own time is to court the neglect of posterity after it has
moved on.

He failed to remind Ellis that he, like Dr. Johnson, was also Professor
of Ancient Literature in the Royal Academy of Literature—"I value it
very little but I can hardly refuse it"—as well as a bencher of Lincoln's
Inn and a member of the Senate of London University. Other awards
followed, including an honorary Oxford doctorate. In late August 1857
he became the first English author to be ennobled for his services to literature: "a great day in my life"; "greatly surprised: but I did not hesitate
one moment." Writing to Hannah, he crossed out the "TBM" with
which he habitually closed:

I must sign by my title for the first time. I do assure you that I
often forget it hours together ... [His butler, however,] My Lords
me at every other word.

Ever yours,
Macaulay

Thereafter he never forgot his title when writing to her, but to him she
was always "Dearest Hannah," never Lady Trevelyan. As if to compensate
for being "a man of humble origin," he styled himself after the country
seat of his uncle by marriage Thomas Babington: "I determined to be
Baron Macaulay of Rothley": "I was born there. I have lived much there.
I am named from the family which long had the manor." Nobility also
meant free advertising. Sensing that the public greeted his peerage "with
more applause than any thing of the sort since Wellington was made a

Thomas Babington Macaulay, by Sir Francis Grant (1853) (© National Portrait Gallery, London). "At the Exhibition yesterday I thought my own portrait . . . by Grant excellent" (TBM, J8:51, 29.iv.54).

Duke," he anticipated a boost in the sales of a new edition of his *History.* But his title came at a price. He also told his journal that he endured the costly investiture ceremony—a "mummery" and "rather a tedious one" —for the sake of Hannah and her daughters.[53] Rome taught him that solemnity can cast a powerful spell, but in the back of his mind lingered both his father's contempt for such displays and his horror at paying for them.

Sometimes he merely accepted honors, scorning those who honored him or grumbling at the duties he incurred: "The thing must be done; & I shall be glad to get it over." Except when the subject was India, he tried to avoid sittings of the Lords: "To the H of L much against my will." But he embraced other dignities, some of which required considerable lifting. They usually enabled him to advance his project of shaping the memory of England's past according to his vision of its present and future. Sitting on the Committee for Inscriptions on Medals of the Great Exhibition of 1851 was ephemeral. Membership on the Fine Arts Commission for the new Houses of Parliament mattered. Advised by Macaulay, the painter charged with decorating the Commons corridor produced eight frescoes from seventeenth-century history. Three of his sketches bore inscriptions from *The History of England*. Two other posts gave Macaulay even more cultural power. A founding trustee of the National Portrait Gallery, he was charged with framing the principles for selecting "sitters" and artists. He succeeded in having "everything pretty much my own way" and counterattacked when he met opposition. The gallery now houses twenty-one portraits of him. Crucially, he served as a trustee of the British Museum during the last decade of his life. Although he groused about ill-run meetings and wrote letters during boring ones, he attended faithfully. The forty-eight trustees were an elite group: "Nearly all family and elected trustees were aristocrats, among them were several dukes, marquises and earls." An adept committeeman as well as a cultural icon, Macaulay more than held his own in guiding Britain's repository of memory during its years of imperial growth.[54]

Power

His ramifying power made him an attractive patron: "I have had to day a whole budget of letters asking for places." One transaction captures him at work manipulating a system that perpetuated continuity while celebrating change. Bishop Wilberforce's friend Richard Owen was England's most famous comparative anatomist and paleontologist—a word barely two years old when he visited an ailing Macaulay at home on 27 February 1856. Although they both belonged to The Club, they were bare acquaintances. It mattered, however, that they were each other's kind. Pinched, Owen asked about "the possibility of doing something for him in the [British] Museum." Macaulay "really felt for him—for the nation too which is disgraced by the distresses of a man so eminent." "Doing something" would require government money and reorganizing the museum's hierarchy. Like a real wizard effectively pulling levers behind an impenetrable curtain, Macaulay acted efficiently and almost surreptitiously. He promptly wrote to his old friend the chancellor of the Exchequer, on whom funding depended, and to Lord Stanhope—Mahon had inherited his earldom—a fellow trustee whom he hosted at breakfast that morning. Both the chancellor and Stanhope shared Macaulay's permanent devotion to the ancients. He told Stanhope that Owen's tears had moved him to tears. Macaulay's crying, however, was more national than personal: "I was touched by learning that a great natural philosopher, whose name is mentioned with honor at Petersburg, Florence, Philadelphia, should be growing old in distress and anxiety. What he asks would, in my judgment, be not merely a boon to himself, but a great public benefit." Macaulay asked Stanhope, if he agreed, to rally the archbishop of Canterbury, another trustee.[55]

A briefing followed, and Stanhope, now "zealous in the cause," enlisted the archbishop's support. The chancellor reacted favorably, but Macaulay left nothing to chance. On 29 February, he wrote on Owen's behalf to his old patron Lord Lansdowne, also a trustee. Tactfully conceding ignorance of Owen's "pursuits," Macaulay proposed the creation of "a whole department of Natural History, including geology, zoology, mineralogy, and botany," with Owen as "Superintendent" directly responsible to the principal librarian.[56] All classically educated alumni of the ancient universities with an instinctive preference for the established and familiar, Macaulay's collaborators were no more knowledgeable than he. None of them grasped the scientific turn against Owen's theory that the anatomical differences among organisms exhibited an underlying plan.

On 2 March the chancellor dropped by to report that the day before he had read Macaulay's letter "in the cabinet," where it "was generally approved." Feeling "great delight," Macaulay expected "that we shall be able to manage this matter at the Museum." Within two weeks Owen became the first superintendent of the British Museum's natural history units, a position that paid well but entailed little administration: "Thank God, Owen's business has been done." That success and the happy prospect of Gladstone's joining the trustees outlasted Macaulay's annoyance at a nameless "brazen fellow in Scotland": not one of his kind, but a twenty-three-year-old aspiring novelist who asked for fifty pounds to enable him to "come up & show me his M.S." For a few years, the appointment Macaulay engineered gave Owen a unique authority among England's scientists, but it fizzled long before his death in 1892. His vitriolic opposition to Charles Darwin's new biology undid it. Not all of Macaulay's negotiations were equally successful, but he always adroitly played the game.[57]

During his last months, he once more took stock of his life by computing his wealth and reflecting on his success. His accounting was meticulous, but neither his worth nor his achievements consoled him: "I shall be this Christmas richer than ever I was— ...Wealth—rank—fame —and yet I am very unhappy—more unhappy than I have been these many years. I am sick of life. I could wish to lie to sleep and never wake."[58] A decade earlier, Carlyle had heard him declare, "power ruinous to powerful himself." Then basking in international fame and savoring unrivaled royalties, Macaulay did not anticipate that his cliché about tragic self-destruction prefigured his own fate.

[10]

PROCRASTINATOR

For all Macaulay's ballyhooing of progress, he welcomed reassurance. Twenty-one years after declaring that the "history of England is emphatically the history of progress" and nineteen after identifying "Utility and Progress" as the national philosopher's "key" doctrine, he noted the "bustle & incessant progress which are characteristic of England." Though now more than a prophecy, progress was not yet the self-evident direction of British history. Macaulay therefore delighted in evidence of progress wherever he found it. When he visited Woburn Abbey in 1850, England was still more agrarian than industrial. At first regarding the duke of Bedford's elaborate agricultural improvements as a rich man's hobby, he admired "books, pictures & statues." Then he saw some of the duke's state-of-the art farming machinery: "I had no notion that such works were to be found in any purely agricultural district for the mere service of a great landed estate." Progress toward finishing the second installment of *The History of England* remained more elusive.[1]

Publicly he insisted that progress was encompassing. It flattered superficial readers to be told that, far from standing on the shoulders of giants, in their knowledge, prosperity, goodness, and prospects they dwarfed their ancestors. During the 1850s he pioneered in making belief in "perpetual progress" English public doctrine. On both the right and the left even Macaulay's enemies accepted it. By identifying Protestantism with progress, he baited Newman into denying that Catholicism "has professed or ought to have professed, directly to promote mere civilization": "Such is the philosophy and practice of the world;—now the Church looks and moves in a simply opposite direction." The pope later condemned the proposition that he "can and ought to, reconcile himself, and come to terms with progress, liberalism and modern civilization." But Newman, still very English though now Roman Catholic, saw "our civilization" as progressive, in contrast to China's "huge, stationary, unattractive, morose, civilization." During the 1850s parts of England still lethally refuted Macaulay's celebration of its material trajectory. In the slums of Manchester and Liverpool life expectancy was below the national average, a little over thirty, and comparable to that during the Black Death. Those realities galvanized some. Once merely a neologism, "socialism" became a political worry for him.[2] As much as Macaulay, the socialists believed in progress, but better distributed and sooner rather than later.

The "Great Exhibition of the Works of Industry of All Nations" vindicated Macaulay's vision of progress. When it opened in Hyde Park on 1 May 1851, May Day did not yet belong to the Left. Long in the making and planned by a committee of the great and the good—Prince Albert presided—the exhibition aimed "less to demonstrate Britain's industrial successes than to identify and rectify Britain's manufacturing deficiencies." But from the committee's first meeting a tension was present: "Nationalism and internationalism formed the two columns upon which the exhibition was built." Difficulties beset the project, but in the end it took less than six months to erect a translucent prefabricated structure of glass and wrought iron. Covering a space four times larger than St. Peter's, the Crystal Palace housed "more than 100,000 exhibits . . . from Britain, its colonies and dependencies, and numerous other countries." Displays from the empire filled the center. The exhibition became a test of whether nationalism and respectability could unite the classes and the masses. There were debates first about offering one-shilling tickets, and then about policing the "labouring classes" who bought them. Macaulay and Dickens agreed that such workers were respectable enough to attend "even on the opening day." Others wanted to segregate their queues, and the duke of Wellington urged mounting a force of 15,000 to guarantee public order on shilling days. In the event, holders of cheap tickets were admitted on 26 May.[3]

Reactions to the exhibition varied. It evoked pseudoreligious awe in the queen and many of her subjects. She imagined the palace as a temple housing "a peace Festival," which would inaugurate a new era—a panacea that the late twentieth century learned to call globalization—and "confessed to having felt more truly devotional than at any Church service." Victoria "God-blessed" both her husband "and my dear Country which has shown itself great today." Joining her on 1 May, Macaulay saw English nationalism as the exhibition's principal column. During the lead-up the realities of class proved to be inescapable. Scrounging for another ticket required that he "write to a Duke": "What a plague." He also heard that "the Socialists" were threatening to field "men of action" to disrupt the opening. His months in Rome had left him with a permanent conviction that in architecture size matters, a taste for monumental churches, and a heightened appreciation of the importance of rendering hierarchical order in material form. A peek at the Crystal Palace abuilding pleased him: "Certainly very magnificent and striking—It surpasses my expectations." Opening day evoked in him something like awe, but it was Roman: "a most gorgeous sight . . . I cannot think that the Caesars ever exhibited a more splendid spectacle—I was quite dazzled—I felt as I did on entering St Peter's." He appreciated the many attractive women, rated the national exhibits, and above all relished the crowd's decorum: "There is just as much chance of a revolution in England at present as of the falling of the moon."[4]

Until the exhibition closed on 11 October 1851, he frequented it, on May 8 for two hours: "A most splendid & spiriting sight it is. I admired particularly the English display of plate & jewellery up stairs." The spectacle did not always prompt him to write, but on 19 and 20 May it inspired him: "I never knew a sight which extorted from all ages & classes & nations such unanimous and genuine admiration. I felt a flow of eloquence or something like it come on me from the mere effect of the place, & I thought of some touches which will greatly improve my Steinkirk. Home wrote." Many of the exhibition's champions were free-trade utopians who regarded ditching tariffs as the precursor of universal prosperity and peace. Macaulay knew better. At Steinkirk in 1692 the French had defeated William IIII. Macaulay's later account dramatized his conviction that conflict and blood sacrifice undergirded the wealth of nations: "the ground where the conflict had raged was piled with corpses; and those who buried the slain remarked that almost all the wounds had been given in close fighting by the sword or the bayonet"; "The people lined the roads to see the princes and nobles who returned

THE POUND AND THE SHILLING.

"Whoever Thought of Meeting You Here?"

"The Pound and the Shilling," *Punch,* 14.vi.51. "There is just as much chance of a revolution in England at present as of the falling of the moon" (TBM, J4:75–76, 1.v.51).

from Steinkirk. The jewellers devised Steinkirk buckles: the perfumers sold Steinkirk powder. But the name of the field of battle was peculiarly given to a new species of collar"—the French flaunting their victory over England.[5]

Six days later he attended the first workers' day: "It seems to be the fate of this extraordinary show to confound all predictions favourable & unfavourable. Fewer people went to the shilling day than on any five shilling day." Tutored in nationalist rhetoric by Macaulay but lacking his appreciation of the power of respectability, Palmerston stayed away and thereafter attended only when "the number of working-class visitors was low." Macaulay, however, returned the next day "to see how the shilling crowd looked." Their numbers increased, their good order proved unfailing, and he kept coming, usually with Baba. He "could hardly help shedding tears" when they made their last visit: "The sight wonderfully grand & pleasing." Seeing the crowds "managed with perfect order" moved him: "it is associated in my mind with all that I love most." For him the exhibition became the outward and visible sign of England's inner strength and progress. He told Baba: "This will long be remembered as a singularly happy year, of peace, plenty, good feeling, innocent pleasure, national glory of the best and purest sort."[6]

Macaulay again correctly read the public mind that he was doing so much to shape. About revolution, he remained convinced that in 1848 "the risk was something." It lingered among the desperately poor who were effectively barred from the Great Exhibition. On 25 June 1855, Marx, for whom the wish was routinely father to the prophecy, witnessed Chartist demonstrators forcing aristocrats and other toffs out of their carriages and putting them to flight: "We . . . do not think we are exaggerating in saying that the English Revolution began yesterday in Hyde Park." Complaining that the press mostly ignored the riot, he failed to grasp that in England and elsewhere the appeal of nationalism and respectability would eclipse that of forging a shared working-class consciousness. The cannier prophet, Macaulay continued writing his *History* as a prophylactic against another but inglorious English revolution. Marx despised him as a "Scotch sycophant and fine talker," who "falsified English history in the interest of the Whigs and the bourgeoisie."[7] But who read Marx?

Evading "History"

Macaulay had once walked in the country for "at least twelve miles without stopping," only to be felled by a sore heel "eight miles from home." A passing carriage had rescued him. There was no vehicle to deliver him from the overreach of his *History*. Although he did not quite waste the three years after its debut, he failed either to settle on a goal or to devise a plan for proceeding. His struggle was poignant. Within weeks his preliminary agenda left him struggling to keep at his "task": "no great stomach to my work"; "not in the vein." He tried to convince himself that avoiding the task would invigorate him. When 1850 began, he was working "doggedly . . . but not, I am afraid, to much purpose." Two days later he faced reality: "Still this strange difficulty about working—I have all my life been subject to it; & I hardly know whether it be not better to yield for a time." After a walk, he again tried to write: "no great value." Uncertain about "how all this will succeed," he shrunk his ambition and proposed to finish "the only readable history of Wm the Third's reign." Working hard on a few pages and seeking perfection, he failed "to please myself." A month into 1850 he was still wrestling with chapter eleven, which would begin the next volume: "Little done & that little ill as usual." He feared that "this history of Wm III will be a failure. If so, I will not publish it." Casanova's *Memoirs* provided diversion: "Extremely licentious—not genuine I am sure." Despite "a sad disinclination to work," he hoped that his chronic insecurity would once again make him productive and successful. Still delaying, he counted the books in his library and anticipated death: "Odd how indifferent I have become to the fear of death—And yet I enjoy my life greatly." A few weeks later he was writing steadily—"enough to fill seven or eight printed pages"—but again without a fixed schedule.[8]

He trapped himself on an erratic emotional treadmill. At the start of 1851, he imagined that he "might be out in 1852" if he kept writing "at this pace." Two months later he tried to rationalize his slow pace: "Had no heart to write. I am too self indulgent in that matter, it may be. Yet I attribute much of the success which I had to my habit of writing only when I am in the humour, & of stopping as soon as thoughts & words cease to flow. There are therefore few lees in my wine—It is all the cream

of the bottle." As always, he found distractions: Plato's *Symposium,* the
Dutch translation of volumes one and two of the *History,* and a royalty
check from Germany. As 1851 wore on, he seemed to be barely trying:
"It is a strange morbid inactivity to wh. I have all my life long been occasionally subject. I will wait a day or two." October found him resolving
"to begin & work straight on from the first page to the death of [Queen]
Mary." But he continued to jump from chapter to chapter, fussing over
episodes or characters that interested him rather than working "straight
on." Days of renewed confidence came and went: "Home—wrote—I
feel despondency creeping in me again. But I must persevere." A friendly
inquiry about his delay led him to bluster: "I do not think that I can
justly be accused of tardiness, at least by comparison with other historians . . . I have to turn over thousands of pages of manuscript, French,
Dutch and Spanish as well as English. I have been once to the Archives at
Paris, and I must go again. I have visited . . . and I shall probably visit
Steenkirk, Landen and Namur. [Thomas Pinney notes: 'He did not.'] If
in five or six years I can produce a tolerable history of William's reign I
shall think that I have done my duty." In his journal he fretted. Looking
forward to 1852, he committed himself to "a year of real hard work" after holidaying in stately homes. Back in London, he lavished irreplaceable time on a paper about the authorship of political tracts that appeared
generations after William III's death. His heart and mind still belonged in
the eighteenth century. Refusing a cabinet post in January 1852 energized him, but the mood again passed.[9]

In addition to his habit of "strange morbid inactivity," uncertain health
left him unable to understand the evidence of his own body and thinking about death. The book he chose to write increasingly bored him intellectually, even as he continued savoring his royalties. Now his concern
was "the all-important one of making meaning pellucid." He congratulated himself for being almost uniquely a "popular writer" who worked
at it. The others preyed on readers who "give credit for profundity to
whatever is obscure, and call all that is perspicuous shallow." Procrastinat-
ing, he looked for vindication from a remote posterity: "But corrag-
gio—and think of A.D. 2850. Where will your Carlyles and Emersons be
then? But Herodotus will still be read with delight. We must do our best
to be read too."[10]

Almost a generation earlier, Macaulay had found in Herodotus "the

faults of a simple and imaginative mind." "The father of history" had
written childishly for "a nation susceptible, curious, lively, insatiably de-
sirous of novelty and excitement; for a nation . . . in which philosophy
was still in its infancy." He also wrote primarily for the many, probably
"not to be read, but to be heard." A critic "of a cold and skeptical nature"
would have arisen and "asked for authorities," but that was not the pellucid Herodotus' way: "As was the historian, such were the auditors,—
inquisitive, credulous, easily moved by religious awe or patriotic enthusiasm." In contrast, the grave Thucydides scorned gossip, anecdote, and
flashiness and wrote "weighty, condensed, antithetical, and not infrequently confused" Greek. Even so, Macaulay admired him as the master
of "the art of producing an effect on the imagination, by skilful selection
and disposition."[11]

He continued to regard Herodotus, Thucydides, and Tacitus as the
greatest of the ancients, but Herodotus was the exemplar of the second
installment of his own *History.* It was an effortful choice. Like Herodotus,
Macaulay felt his patriotism deeply but more realistically than enthusias-
tically, and he understood that the English nation was also attracted by
"whatever gave a stronger air of reality to a narrative so well calculated
to inflame the passions, and to flatter national pride." But as much as
Thucydides, Macaulay was "distinguished by . . . practical sagacity . . . insight into motives [and] . . . skill in devising means for the attainment of
. . . [his] ends." He admired Herodotus' ability to dramatize events rather
than his sympathetic effort to understand the histories of alien peoples
and regimes. The sustained and subtle analysis that Macaulay valued in "a
really philosophical historian" is less prominent in the third and fourth
volumes of *The History of England,* where he works close to the ground,
massing details into appealing stories. The labor subverted his principle
that the interpretation trumped the details.[12]

Even if his new volumes failed to meet his public's "highly raised expectations," he meant them to swamp any imaginable competitor. The
ancient historians suggested to him a fetching way of trying to make
dead voices speak: "The substitute which I supply for the orations of the
ancient historians seems to me likely to amuse." Thucydides had explained the technique: "With reference to the speeches in this history,
some were delivered before the war began, others while it was going on;
some I heard myself, others I got from various quarters; it was in all cases

difficult to carry them word for word in one's memory, so my habit has been to make the speakers say what was in my opinion demanded of them by the various occasions, of course adhering as closely as possible to the general sense of what they really said . . . Such were the words of the Corcyræans. After they had finished, the Corinthians spoke as follows." Advocating a new kind of history a generation earlier, before he rediscovered the ancients onboard the *Asia,* Macaulay had scorned the technique. But now, near the beginning of volume three, he imagined the collective voices of the parties after the accession of William and Mary: "Many lords and gentlemen, who had, in December taken arms for the Prince of Orange and a Free Parliament, muttered, two months later, that they had been drawn in . . . Thus the Tories, as a body, were forced to admit, very unwillingly . . . The Whigs loved William indeed: but they loved him not as a King, but as a party leader . . . Such were the difficulties by which, at the moment of his elevation, he found himself beset." In a footnote he asserted his ability to intuit the thoughts of the long-dead: "Here, and in many other places, I abstain from citing authorities, because my authorities are too numerous to cite. My notions of the temper and relative position of political and religious parties in the reign of William the Third, have derived, not from any single work, but from thousands of forgotten tracts, sermons, and satires: in fact from a whole literature which is mouldering in old libraries." As a young man, he had absolved Herodotus for "putting speeches of his own into the mouths of his characters," because it was consistent with his method: "The conventional probability of his drama is preserved from the beginning to the end. The deliberate orations and the familiar dialogues are in strict keeping with each other." At the same time he had faulted Thucydides for resorting to that "usage": "Invention is shocking where truth is in such close juxtaposition with it."[13] Now Macaulay also wanted to preserve "the conventional probability of his drama."

Rhetoric is even more the lifeblood of the second installment of the *History of England* than of the first. Chapter eleven opens with an "exordium," the rousing attention-getter that every polished classical oration required. The sonorous and improbable result perhaps strengthens the case for Oscar Wilde's dictum that the truth is "rarely pure and never simple." An excerpt captures something of the mingled power and weakness of his exordium. "The Revolution had been accomplished. The decrees of the Convention were everywhere received with submission. London, true during fifty eventful years to the cause of civil freedom and of the reformed religion, was foremost in professing loyalty to the new Sovereigns . . . All the steeples from the Abbey to the Tower sent forth a joyous din. The proclamation was repeated, with sound of trumpet, in front of the Royal Exchange, amidst the shouts of citizens." He closed the passage by echoing an enthronement psalm acclaiming the Universal King: "God is gone up with a shout, the Lord with the sound of a trumpet. / Sing praises to God, sing praises: sing praises unto our King, sing praises." The rule of William and Mary was legitimate, and, by implication, the state was godlike in its sovereignty. Two pages later Macaulay began to qualify his assertion that the new monarchs had been "everywhere received with submission": "It was observed that two important classes took little or no part in the festivities by which, all over England, the inauguration of the new government was celebrated. Very seldom could either a priest or a soldier be seen in the assemblages which gathered round the market crosses where the King and Queen were proclaimed."[14]

On the next page he introduced William III's vulnerability, but as a "reaction" rather than as a besetting condition. It was impossible to portray William as an invader leading a coup d'état, lest 1688–89 seem not the origin of the modern nation but merely another wrangle. On Macaulay's showing, the "discontent" of priests and soldiers spread like some virulent airborne infection: "The enthusiasm with which men of all classes had welcomed William to London at Christmas had greatly abated before the close of February." His airbrushing of the debut of the Glorious Revolution illustrates how an ancient rhetorical education equipped advocates to make the most persuasive case. In that school eloquence outweighed not only consistency but also evidence. It was a classical lesson taught by Tacitus. At twenty-seven Macaulay had censured his "style" as "peculiarly unfit for historical composition."[15] Although Macaulay changed his mind about rhetorical history, he always maintained that historical truth was more than a collection of facts, necessarily selective, and never objective.

The toil of educating and pandering to "the multitude" burdened his intelligence. He once observed that amusement was "the highest of all recommendations" in a book. But the amusement he derived from his

favorites was cerebral, often lucid but too sustainedly and overtly disillusioned to be salable to a huge market of "dull" readers: "Hume's
Dialogues on Natural Religion—His best work, I think—very able . . .
Pascal should have answered him." Among Hume's elegantly incredulous works were *The Enquiry Concerning Human Understanding*—"generally assenting, & always admiring"—and "The Essay on Miracles"
—"certainly most sound." Writing a best-seller demanded trading in
flashiness and cheering, not in enigmas and doubts. Moreover, he was, as
he knew, more disposed to "raillery" than to unction. For a sister he once
described a mossback chairing the British Museum trustees as looking
"very fat and red, and in the highest state of Protestant zeal." Macaulay
therefore muted and disguised his natural voice. Although his *History*
increasingly bored his intelligence, it also gave him a dangerous license.
Both rhetoric and popularity were consistent with handling historical evidence like a lawyer's brief. Macaulay's favorite modern historian, Paolo Sarpi—"Excellent"—was an antipapal Venetian whom he
regarded as "'A Protestant in a friar's frock.'" The epithet reflected his
appreciation of Fra Sarpi's artful way with religion—he has been read as
cryptically "irreligious." Macaulay, however, ignored Ranke's accusation
that "it is obvious that Sarpi does not adhere with strict truth to the facts
laid before him."[16]

Macaulay's intensifying priggishness enabled his courtship of big royalties and stunted his writing. Bishop Wilberforce once related that his
father, while an unconverted Cambridge undergraduate, drank "tea every evening at a brothel," though not "for any licentious purpose." The
verbal indiscretion of both Wilberforces shocked Macaulay. His pseudo-
Christian voice he could turn on or off, but starchiness now became
him. It heightened the tension between the book he was writing and the
book he aspired to bequeath. Propriety kept him from admitting to himself that a classic demanded greater subtlety than an amusing best-seller.
Dr. Johnson had captured the motivation of naturally indolent authors
such as Macaulay and himself: "No man but a blockhead ever wrote,
except for money." Macaulay relished the "strangely prosperous career"
that depended on entertaining a wider audience than Johnson had imagined. Innocent of both Johnson's unsparing self-knowledge and his contempt for appearances, Macaulay invested himself with "the sensibility of
artists." Thus in one breath he could insist that he was not "tied to time

... do not write for money" and that he aimed "at interesting and pleasing readers whom ordinary histories repel." The tension was permanent. Despite the sustained impersonation required to subdue his "cold and skeptical" intelligence and produce a blockbuster, he clung to the belief that he, as much as Thucydides, was creating a thing for the ages.[17] Writing with an abridged imagination and a distorted voice, Macaulay avoided the heights and the depths of human experience. The result is a *History* with too much rah-rah and too little irony, pity, and awe.

After reading to Ellis his account of the Battle of Steinkirk, which killed or wounded more than 16,000 men, he again inconsistently congratulated himself: "Surely there are not many books more amusing than this will be, considering that it is not meant for a book of mere amusement." Glanced at from above, Steinkirk's gore barely touches Macaulay's pages: "Five fine regiments were entirely cut to pieces. No part of this devoted band would have escaped but for the courage and conduct of Auverquerque, who came to the rescue in the moment of extremity with two fresh battalions." The count of Nassau and William's cousin, Auverquerque is a walk-on in the *History,* but the common soldiers, once dutifully "cut to pieces," vanish from its pages. In contrast, a younger Russian contemporary of Macaulay discovered humanity in a war zone and memorably evoked both the cruelty and moral illumination that can coexist there. Even in an age of industrialized battle and an old translation, Leo Tolstoy's words are compelling:

> The Frenchman, probably an officer from his uniform, sat crouched upon his grey horse, and urging it on with his sword. In another instant Rostov's horse dashed up against the grey horse's hindquarters, almost knocking it over, and at the same second Rostov, not knowing why he did so, raised his sword, and aimed a blow at the Frenchman.
>
> The instant he did this all Rostov's eagerness suddenly vanished. The officer fell to the ground, not so much from the sword cut, for it had only just grazed his arm above the elbow, as from fright and the shock to his horse. As Rostov pulled his horse in, his eyes sought his foe to see what sort of man he had vanquished ... Rostov galloped back with the rest, conscious of some disagreeable sensation, a kind of ache at his heart. A glimpse of something vague and con-

fused, of which he could not get a clear view, seemed to have come to him with the capture of that French officer and the blow he had dealt him.

Tolstoy believed that "it is on this capacity of man to receive another man's expression of feeling and experience those feelings himself, that the activity of art is based."[18] Edmund Burke had believed much the same about the moral imagination.

The same capacity informs great historical writing. Although Macaulay emoted lavishly in private, his descriptions of what he felt tend to be either banal or visceral. He seldom interrogated, elaborated, and generalized from his own emotions and was therefore mostly blind to others' expressions of theirs. The sometime secretary at war found it tedious to write about "military details." Because ruthlessness, like heroism, requires the ability to ignore the blood, he casually discussed and urged death even on a huge scale. Except when he read while being shaved, his own blood was never at risk. Impatiently and from above, he mentioned soldiers' being "cut to pieces" on a battlefield and promptly forgot them. For him, they were abstractions—"military details"—not people. Deprived of the compassion necessary to see in them human strength and anguish—the sanguinary drumroll of the *Lays of Ancient Rome* speaks for itself—he was powerless to evoke what a great poet killed in battle later called "War and the pity of War."[19]

Macaulay could brilliantly disentangle complexities, but the second installment of his *History* offers few of the penetrating analyses that distinguish his best essays. A detailed account of the recoinage of 1696–1699, which aimed to stabilize the value of English money by standardizing its bullion content, pleased him: "no writer has made that subject more amusing." It also illustrates his scope and limits as an historian. Covering twenty-one pages, the episode occupies four times the space he devoted to the epochal creation of the Bank of England. Without acknowledgment Macaulay retold another author's story—his source would return the favor in a later edition of his book. Besides magnifying the recoinage, Macaulay also simplified and distorted its significance. The practice of clipping coins and thereby "paring down money" was epidemic during the 1690s and occasioned the act of January 1695/6, which decreed "that the various species of clipped money should cease to pass current in turn, leaving no clipped coin in circulation after 4 May." Locke is crucial in the *History*'s version, but too simply, as a present-day scholar has noted: "In place of the co-operation of Locke and Newton with Somers and Montague, so lauded by Macaulay, there emerges the far more interesting spectacle of Locke's involvement in conflict within the ministry and of rivalry between Locke and Newton as to who should be the principal adviser over recoinage." Macaulay also accepted Locke's arguable theory that the value of coins depended on their bullion content. Macaulay consulted the economist David Ricardo's major disciple to locate a pamphlet published during the run-up to the recoinage but seemingly never read Ricardo, who as early as 1816 had undermined Locke's bullionism.[20]

Abundant published and unpublished evidence was available to Macaulay, but he neither explained the context of the epidemic of clipping—"the disruption of a relatively primitive and vulnerable economy through war"—nor dwelt on its disastrous aftermath: "a further deterioration in monetary conditions leading to the virtual collapse of public credit in the summer of 1696 . . . At home those worst affected by the crisis were the poor." Rather, his short account of the unintended consequences of the recoinage was predictably sweet: "On the following Monday began a cruel agony of a few months, which was destined to be succeeded by many years of almost unbroken prosperity." It was a variation on his theme whenever the poor intruded on his *History:* "The bad time is got over without robbing the wealthy to relieve the indigent." In his pages the recoinage was not the "largely wasted" effort that later economic historians would discover. Learnedly tentative in their generalizations, they suggest that real wages generally slumped in most years until about 1709. Macaulay not only failed to situate the economic dislocation that attended the recoinage in the context of war; he also ignored the ultimate irony of the Glorious Revolution. John Brewer, a distinguished historian who can be fairly numbered among his great-great-grand-pupils, has analyzed the upshot of a regime change meant to preserve the church and liberty. It occasioned years of ultimately successful but costly warfare and the unprecedented growth of the powers and reach of the state: increasingly a "fiscal-military" regime that paradoxically secured and menaced English liberty.[21]

For Macaulay, perfecting a best-selling style was imperative: "The great object is that after all this trouble, [the words] . . . may sound as if they had been spoken off, & may seem to flow as easily as table talk—We shall see." Trying to impose credible fluency on the stammering past also inhibited the analyst in him. Sometimes he overvalued his earlier achievement, but he could also depreciate it. In late 1850 he reread a hundred pages of volume two: "did not much like it." Increasingly, he believed that his power to move readers would give his *History* purchase on immortality, but not all their emotions were equal. He welcomed Dickens' turn against "that odious mawkish sentimentality which he formerly patronized"—it informed Josiah Bounderby's soulless prosperity as much as Little Nell's wretched death—but relished some books that gave him a good cry. Walking in the countryside and rereading the *Iliad* through for the first time since India, he "was at last forced to turn into a by path, lest the parties of walkers should see me blubbering for imaginary beings, the creations of a ballad-maker who has been dead two thousand seven hundred years. What is the power and glory of Caesar and Alexander to that?" Like the *Iliad,* the *Odyssey* was cathartic of violence. Macaulay sniffed at its last two books, "But the opening of the twenty second book is one of the grandest things in poetry":

> Now shrugging off his rags the wiliest fighter of the islands
> leapt and stood on the broad door sill, his own bow in his hand.
> He poured out at his feet a rain of arrows from the quiver and
>   spoke to the crowd:
> "So much for that. Your clean-cut game is over."[22]

Macaulay's greatest achievements heightened both his desire for more and his self-doubt. Disappointed with *David Copperfield,* he worried that he, like Dickens, was becoming "a mine worked out." The next day news of additional royalties persuaded him that he was finding his stride and could now write a daily quota of pages. Almost nineteen months later he was still magnifying his past success and downplaying his prospects: "the second part will interest and amuse readers. The success of the 1st part I can hardly hope to see,—Indeed I have seen nothing like it in my life & yet I remember the greatest triumphs of Scott & Byron." Accepting that he could not have everything eluded him. The applause was too loud and sustained—sometimes almost worshipful—to foster realism about his book. One reader was making it "into a catechism." The bishop of Litchfield's "high compliments" mattered more because "in my young days he was an object of my admiration on account of the singular beauty of his Latin verses."[23]

The presence of radicals in London kept alive the menace of 1848. Macaulay could refuse to receive an exiled Italian revolutionary, but there was no escaping an acquaintance over dinner: "I found her a raving red republican—communist—God knows what." Danger from religionists, raving and otherwise, seemed more immediate. Because the Tractarians' clericalism made them widely hated, Macaulay's anticlericalism helped to solidify his hold on the public mind. His animus against "Bishops in general" was impersonal. His mitered fans included his friend Bishop Wilberforce, who wanted to believe that he was really a Christian: "Walked home with Macaulay, trying to get him more on religion— 'God' and causality." Their chat was necessarily inconclusive, but in the end he was persuaded of Macaulay's good faith by "how he used those wonderful faculties. His purity, affection, and manifest increase of seriousness; attention to worship, etc." It also mattered that "at the Club, and at our Club-bish breakfasts," he regaled his companions with "those marvelous torrents of information."[24]

But Macaulay's Erastianism continued to offend Bishop Wilberforce. The *History* reaffirmed that the Reformation had made English bishops agents of the state. Privately, he sought to disabuse Wilberforce of the notion that Parliament was no longer qualified to legislate for the church and that it was therefore necessary to revive the convocations, two clerical assemblies moribund since 1717. His friend was not persuaded. The meetings were revived, but Parliament remained in control. In the second installment Macaulay again depicted the history of England's "ecclesiastical polity" as an aspect of its "secular history." His intended audience included "young fellows [who] waste all their time on Puseyite trash," ignoring their country's literature and history: "The announcement that a Convocation was to sit for the purpose of deliberating on a plan of comprehension [of all Protestants] roused all the strongest passions of the priest who had just complied with the law, and was ill satisfied or half satisfied with himself for complying. He had an opportunity of contributing to defeat a favourite scheme of that government." Writing about the powers of convocation as a matter of living politics, Macaulay reread much Voltaire and too much of St. Augustine with predictable results: "vile taste—vile Latin—abundance of nonsense and cant resembling that of our lowest field preachers, but here & there passages indicating great force of mind." A walk with Baba brought home the menace: "talk about the dignity of the clerical character—Dear child—she has so much leaning toward the Puseyite superstitions—But she is the best of human beings."[25]

In politics as well as religion Macaulay continued to purpose a consensus history: "I shall not be thought partial to the Whigs." He emphatically wrote about his nation, and the other parts of Britain mattered to him only insofar as they troubled England. Docile Wales he almost ignored—only three passing references. But seventeenth-century Scotland and Ireland were troublesome and hence inescapable. Planning to devote a chapter to each early in volume three, he concurrently wrote his thirteenth and eighteenth. The more tractable since 1745, Scotland appeared to make the easier subject. New evidence only confirmed his interpretations and enabled him to see more clearly how to plot the story. The writing, however, proved burdensome. Macaulay concentrated on retelling the massacre of thirty-eight members of the clan Macdonald, former partisans of James II/VII, at Glencoe on 13 February 1692—dozens more died of exposure after the troops whom they were hosting burned their village. Because of the machinations of the secretary of state for Scotland, who wanted to eradicate them, the Highlanders failed to swear allegiance to William by the appointed day. The butchery continued to shadow Macaulay's hero: "the crime which has cast a dark shade over his glory."[26]

In 1695 a governmental inquiry implicated the secretary, but at one remove by portraying him as the dupe of a nobleman from a rival clan: the unmoved mover of the slaughter. There were thus two degrees of separation between the massacre and William, who pardoned the secretary after relieving him of office. Macaulay rebuffed additional evidence. When a descendant of the official villain offered him pertinent documents, "I told him in the plainest words that I had formed an unfavourable opinion of his ancestor's character, that I must speak the truth, and that I should not at all complain if, after hearing this, he thought fit to deny me access to the family papers." Holding a less solipsistic notion of "truth," the descendant sent the manuscripts to Macaulay. They under-

mined his brief for the secretary of state's defense. He never acknowledged them, and they had no effect on his single-minded version of
truth-telling. Macaulay's original research consisted in visiting Glencoe
to absorb the atmosphere: "In the Gaelic tongue Glencoe signifies the
Glen of Weeping; and in truth that pass is the most dreary and melancholy of all the Scottish passes, the very Valley of the Shadow of Death."
Even his dull readers could recognize two allusions. Psalm twenty-three
was helpful in vindicating a state action that defied conventional morality: "Yea, though I walk through the valley of the shadow of death, I will
fear no evil: for thou art with me; thy rod and thy staff they comfort
me." There was also a contemporary resonance. To vast acclaim, Tennyson
evoked a mixed band of English, Scottish, and Irish troops' apparently
futile heroism during the Crimean War, a slaughter redeemed by allied
victory over Russia:

> Forward, the Light Brigade!
> "Charge for the guns!" he said:
> Into the valley of Death
> Rode the six hundred.

In reality, Glencoe signified and signifies "Valley of the Coe," a stream
that passes through it.[27] Macaulay's wordplay allowed him to portray
Glencoe as both a natural killing field and the prelude to the progress
that would follow Scotland's union with England in 1707 and the solution of the Highlander problem a generation later.

Intermittently over two years Macaulay reworked his account of the
massacre, finally wrestling with a draft for almost three weeks in 1851.
Then he moved on to research another topic: "I think that those ab-
stracts of parliamentary debates will be a new & striking feature in my
book." His version of Glencoe illustrates his ability to transform a brief
into a story. Because the implicit lesson he derived from "Temple" would
be stern, his task was delicate: "it is in truth more merciful to extirpate a
hundred thousand human beings at once . . . than to misgovern millions
through a long succession of generations." Relying on allusion, insinuation, and obfuscation, Macaulay narrated Glencoe as a botched episode
in the continuing battle between civilization and savagery: the secretary
was "able, eloquent and accomplished." It was otherwise with the official

villain: "In his castle among the hills . . . [he] had learned the barbarian pride and ferocity of a Highland chief." The secretary "seems to have proposed to himself a truly great and good end, the pacification and civilisation of the Highlands. He was, by the acknowledgement of those who hated him, a man of large views. He justly thought it monstrous that a third part of Scotland should be in a state scarcely less savage than New Guinea . . . His object was no less than a complete dissolution and reconstruction of society in the Highlands, such a dissolution and reconstruction as, two generations later, followed the battle of Culloden." That civilizing mission might reasonably demand calculated slaughter, which was always not mere killing: the "statesman . . . had planned it with consummate ability," but the troops "committed the error of dispatching their hosts with firearms instead of using cold steel." Years earlier Macaulay had stopped decrying the "merciless severity" of the duke of Cumberland—"The Butcher"—victor of Culloden, the last battle fought on the British mainland, and architect of the ensuing ruthlessness that integrated the Highlands socially, economically, and politically into the English system: "With courage, he had the virtues which are akin to courage."[28] Macaulay was invoking the authority of Homer's ancient ethic. Brave Odysseus "poured out at his feet a rain of arrows from the quiver and spoke to the crowd: / 'So much for that. Your clean-cut game is over.'"

A printed document that could not be ignored undermined Macaulay's effort to absolve William from complicity in the massacre. The king had signed an "order, directed to the Commander of the Forces in Scotland": "As for Mac Ian of Glencoe and that tribe, if they can be well distinguished from the other Highlanders, it will be proper, for the vindication of public justice, to extirpate that set of thieves." Macaulay's effort to exonerate the king was lawyerlike: Can we be sure that William read the document? If so, the "words naturally bear a sense perfectly innocent, and would, but for the horrible event which followed have been universally understood in that sense. Governments are duty-bound 'to extirpate gangs of thieves,' to round them up and ground them down if they resisted." Unlike with "Temple," his casuistry was noticed. When questioned, he clung to his definition of "to extirpate": William III "would naturally have thought that it had not what you call 'a remorseless and annihilating meaning attached to it.'" That had been exactly Macaulay's definition of "extirpate" in 1838: "The words, 'extirpation,'

and 'eradication,' were often in the mouths of the English back settlers
. . . cruel words, yet in their cruelty, containing more mercy than much
softer expressions . . . it is in truth more merciful to extirpate a hundred
thousand human beings at once." It was also what the seventeenth century meant by extirpating people. The available evidence indicates that
the secretary for Scotland instigated the massacre and that William III
was complicit.[29]

Writing a few weeks after visiting Ireland in 1849, Macaulay found
the first pages he wrote about it "strangely interesting." The character of
dominant castes made "a grand subject." Narrating "military details" now
engaged him. Two episodes in the war between William and James for
control of the other island were paramount: the Battle of the Boyne,
which vanquished James; and the siege of Londonderry (Derry). Between 18 April and 1 August 1689 James's forces encircled the northern
port and barricaded egress to the mouth of the River Foyle and the sea.
The siege fills twenty-seven pages. Extensive quotation captures his eulogy (*eulogia* or *benedictio*) to Ireland's "dominant caste" in what he and
they cherished as their finest hour.

And now Londonderry was left destitute of all military and . . . civil
government. No man in the town had a right to command any
other: the defences were weak: the provisions were scanty: an incensed tyrant and a great army were at the gates. But within was
that which has often, in the desperate extremities, retrieved the
fallen fortunes of nations. Betrayed, deserted, disorganized, unpro-
vided with resources, begirt with enemies, the noble city was still
no easy conquest. Whatever an engineer might think of the strength
of the ramparts, all that was most intelligent, most courageous, most
highspirited among the Englishry of Leinster and of Northern Ulster was crowded behind them. The number of men capable of
bearing arms within the walls was seven thousand; and the whole
world could not have furnished seven thousand men better qualified to meet a terrible emergency with clear judgement, dauntless
valour, and stubborn patience. They were all zealous Protestants; and
the Protestantism of the majority was tinged with Puritanism. They
had much in common with that sober, resolute, and Godfearing
class out of which Cromwell had formed his unconquerable army

... The English inhabitants of Ireland were an aristocratic caste, which had been enabled, by superior civilisation, by close union, by sleepless vigilance, by cool intrepidity, to keep in subjection a numerous and hostile population. Almost every one of them had been in some measure trained both to military and to political functions ... they spoke English with remarkable purity and correctness, and ... they were, both as militiamen and as jurymen, superior to their kindred in the mother country.[30]

These pages engaged him perhaps more than anything else in the second installment. In volume one he had decried Ireland as "cursed by the domination of race over race, and of religion over religion." Now along with Scotland, Ireland exemplified the inevitable march and costs of civilization. Traces of his emotions as he wrote survive. When he returned from Ireland in 1849, Hannah thought he was "such a hot Orangeman, that he says if he had stayed in Ireland he should have joined an Orange Lodge ... and says he cannot trust himself to write the siege of Derry as yet he feels so excited." Founded in 1795, the lodge took the name of William III's dynasty to declare its loyalty to the crown and Protestantism and its antipathy to Irish Catholics. The "Historic Siege of Londonderry" is the core of its foundation narrative. Macaulay calmed down, but resonances of the siege endured. Later in the autumn of 1849 he discovered "great merit as an artist" in an anti–Irish Catholic author. After weekending as the guest of Lord Lansdowne, owner of 162,000 statute acres in Ireland, he was annoyed to discover that a page from his "narrative of the siege of Londonderry was missing." Rewriting it and confident of the superiority of the "new performance," Macaulay anticipated his birthday by celebrating with Lady Trevelyan and her "dear girls" over "lobster curry; a wild duck, scalloped oysters; tarts, grapes; & champagne." He liked his "Irish part," and so did Ellis, to whom he declaimed it a month later. "Hannah cried" when Tom finally read it to her.[31]

The Orange Order website endorses Macaulay's story of Londonderry's "defiance, solidarity, sacrifice, deliverance" and remains alert to "the unchanging threat to their faith and liberties posed by the Catholic majority in Ireland." But the memory of the siege was fluid. In the eighteenth century it first separated Presbyterian Dissenters from the Anglican establishment, and Catholics united with Protestants to celebrate its centennial. The fracturing of Irish politics during the late 1790s erased that harmony. In Macaulay's day Catholics formed the majority of the population of Derry—their usage—and the city was becoming religiously segregated. His story "strengthened the emotional and historical links between Great Britain and the Protestants of Ulster, achieving a massive public relations *coup* for the loyalist cause."[32]

In some moods, Macaulay imagined himself writing dispassionately—almost: "I have little hope of being able to tell the story of the Irish wars in such a manner as to satisfy the bigots of any party. But I do not think that I shall be accused by any candid man of injustice towards the defenders of Londonderry." In the end, his prejudices, rhetorical technique, and desire for royalties prevailed over his intelligence. The brilliant insight that he routinely stifled informs his analysis of the public memory of the siege. What begins with effusion ends in illumination: "Five generations have since passed away; and still the wall of Londonderry is to the Protestants of Ulster what the trophy of Marathon was to the Athenians," namely the principal relic of the victory that won their freedom. After detailing the official pieties associated with the event and the site, he considered how collective memories are fashioned to create and sustain the identity of a "people." He also tallied the political costs of the memory-making of "dominant castes":

It is impossible not to respect the sentiment which indicates itself by these tokens. It is a sentiment which belongs to the higher and purer part of human nature and which adds not a little to the strength of states. A people which takes no pride in the noble achievements of remote ancestors will never achieve any thing worthy to be remembered with pride by remote descendants. Yet it is impossible for the moralist or the statesman to look with unmixed complacency on the solemnities with which Londonderry commemorates her deliverance, and on the honours which she pays to those who saved her. Unhappily the animosities of her brave champions have descended with their glory. The faults which are ordinarily found in dominant castes and dominant sects have not seldom shown themselves without disguise at her festivities; and even the expressions of pious gratitude which have resounded from her pulpits have too often mingled with words of wrath and defiance.

Unlike the flashy purple patches to which he devoted painstaking labor, those sentences are original and profound.[33] They anticipate the present-day study of the history of memory.

Macaulay's description of himself as mastering "a whole literature which is mouldering in old libraries" was braggadocio. His research continued to be a gentleman scholar's desultory reconnoitering, not Gibbon's bibliophagy or Ranke's grubbing in archives. Besides Mackintosh's cache of transcribed documents, his investigations depended on the resources of the British Museum, Oxford, and congenial country houses. Sometimes he worked long and hard, taking notes after he had developed a "feel" for an episode or a character. When he formed his template, he searched quickly, confidently, and purposefully for evidence: "740 . . . pages in 2 hours or little more. I found scarcely anything." He was looking for "the secrets." His research usually confirmed his interpretation, and he easily became bored. Although he greeted the appearance of one "most curious" new document with "great delight," it engaged him less than berating a defunct literary rival. On a day of weak resolve he spent more time reading his old journal entries than working in the museum. When a duke sent him "15 folios" of family papers, he merely "looked through a couple of volumes." By late 1850, collecting sources from the late eighteenth century seemed pointless: "nor do I at all expect that I shall live long enough to tell the story of the events of 1794."[34]

Three years after *The History of England* triumphantly debuted, its future was uncertain not least because of Macaulay's inefficiency. His intense visual imagination slowed him. To make events like the massacre and the siege come alive, he had to visualize them. Seeing Glencoe and Derry inspired the words he needed to enable readers not just to hear but virtually to see what he described. His mind's eye could stimulate, even excite his writing. It also caused him to dwell on disconnected sections and to put off composing the necessary filler. Writing as the spirit moved him, neither linearly nor topically, was a further drag. Recall that he imagined the siege of Londonderry (spring and summer 1689) and the Battle of the Boyne (July 1690) as a diptych after visiting the sites. In the *History*, the siege appears in chapter twelve and the battle four chapters later, separated by almost three hundred pages. Instead of moving on to other Irish topics, he wrote a section on English religious quarrels, which he finally embedded in chapter eleven. Routinely taking up and

putting down and zigzagging may have eased his boredom, but it resulted in time-consuming discontinuity. Thriving on encouragement, he
read many pages aloud—another source of delay. Once, Ellis "did not
seem to like . . . [a section,] which much vexed me, though I am not very
partial to it. It is a good thing to find sincerity. I shall try the Trevelyans."
He failed to record his listeners' advice. Other sources of delay lay outside his control. Often hieroglyphic, his handwriting was deteriorating
into illegibility. The sharp-eyed if erratic amanuensis who transcribed
the first installment left England, and no suitable replacement was at
hand.[35] All of this was troublesome. Another predicament became lethal.

[11]

PRAECEPTOR
GENTIS ANGLORUM

In 1850, as Macaulay was becoming an iconic teacher of his fellow Britons and his gospel of utility and progress public doctrine, his health began to fail. Illness would shadow the rest of his life. He continued walking long, hard, and sometimes painfully, aiming to establish a routine
of sixteen or seventeen miles a day. Invincibly confident and practicing
medicine like his cherished ancients, his doctors at their best did him
no good. Macaulay's record of his sufferings at their hands recalls Fanny
Burney's account of her mastectomy with only a wine cordial for an an-
esthetic and belies his cheery voice. John Bright, his longtime physician,
"was an accomplished Greek and Latin scholar, distinguished more for
this by some colleagues and obituarists than for his contributions to
medicine." In April 1850 Bright fashionably diagnosed "latent gout" and
prescribed what amounted to a placebo. Its effect soon waned, leaving
Macaulay "tortured by rheumatic pains." The juju of Bright and most of
his colleagues fed on their patients' credulous helplessness. Macaulay was
not alone in acquiescing to them. With "spirits . . . a little low from pain,
solitude, & other causes," he sought comfort in his books. For the first
time since sailing from India, he reread *Clarissa,* an eighteenth-century
novel, artful but also moralistic, snobbish, and perhaps sadomasochistic:
"I nearly cried my eyes out." When his pain intensified, Bright called,
first to reassure him and then to pronounce "me recovered & said that he
should discontinue his visits." Macaulay's body refuted the verdict. To
distract himself he shopped and visited the zoo two days in a row, staring
at a hippopotamus as if in self-reproach: "the ugliest, most unwieldy of
beasts—type of sloth & gluttony." Six weeks after Bright's pronounce-
ment, Macaulay, feeling himself again, took an enormous walk "under a

hot sun." Exercise helped him to control his weight—always worrisome—but it could neither motivate him to write nor cure him.[1]

On his fiftieth birthday he described himself as almost contented: "Good spirits—tolerable health—domestic affections—easy fortune—liberality—leisure—fame beyond that of almost any living writer—Some things I regret. But on the whole, who is better off—?" His "familiar symptoms" reappeared in January 1851, and within a month he first complained of "palpitation of heart, or something or other." Sometimes he endured a "miserable night—painful difficulty of breathing." Macaulay and his contemporaries attributed many of their illnesses to the weather and the atmosphere. Until 1854 the cholera plaguing London was blamed on foul air rather than on a waterborne bacterium. Anxious and ignorant, Macaulay traced his cardiopulmonary symptoms to "a cold which will . . . be completely removed by fine weather." He lacked the benefits of medical specialization and standards of medical competence. When his self-diagnosis failed, he accepted his dentist's verdict: "rheumatism." Turning fifty-one, he slighted the evidence of his own body to accentuate the positive: "A happy life—May it only continue to be as happy."[2]

Surviving toughened Macaulay's generation whatever their class. During 1852 he endured two heart attacks—at least one massive. Racked by pain, he soldiered on in deference to Dr. Bright. Reading letters over breakfast on 30 June, he "felt a certain disagreeable physical excitement." Throughout the day he was "unstrung.—a weight at my heart, and an indescribable anxiety." He attributed it all to "advancing life" and carried on. After two walks he "came back refreshed." During the next three days he was uncomplaining. Then during the night of 3–4 July his chest "plagued" him. Bad London air made him "quite asthmatic." He medicated himself with "a mustard poultice & . . . rhubarb," savoured his recent effortless reelection to Parliament for Edinburgh, and followed other returns. Almost two weeks after first feeling "a weight at my heart," Macaulay finally summoned Bright. The best that money could buy, his care was virtually lethal. Bright and Prince Albert's doctor, an old friend who happened by, agreed "that it is all bile." Their remedy was to purge him with "enough calomel to poison a gun elephant." It was mercury chloride, a toxic that stopped being prescribed as a purgative only after Macaulay's death: "Bright's pills disordered me much." On 14 July he went to take the sea air in Clifton: "I was a good deal shaken by the journey. However, I walked out, though feebly." Following a day of near-prostration, he forced himself: "The air, I hope, is beginning to show its work."[3]

Back in London, he suffered another heart attack on the twenty-second but now accurately diagnosed himself: "The circulation deranged —something with the heart. I felt a load on my breast." Instead of resting, he went to the Trevelyans: "I was much unstrung, and could hardly help shedding tears of mere weakness: but I did help it." Even so, it was two days more before Macaulay summoned the hapless Bright, who finally performed "a very long and close examination with the help of a mysterious looking tube"—"a stethoscope, I think they call it." Invented in France in 1816, the device entered the English lexicon four years later. Did Macaulay first see one only in 1852? The stethoscope was accurate but Bright incorrigible. Forgetting about bile, he pronounced his patient's heart "deranged,—not dangerously" and ordered him back to Clifton for a couple of months' rest. Later that day Macaulay "walked a little" and dined with his family. He found that "a quarter of an hour, during which I am forced to lean on a stick, is as much as I can bear" and worried lest "my faculties" were diminishing. He was relieved to "find no want of my usual vivacity in conversation." Leaving London with Hannah on 3 August, he was able to eat "a lunch—the first time for six months." To lure Ellis to Clifton he promised "a dozen of special sherry, half a dozen of special Hock, and a tureen of turtle soup." Hannah was an instinctive diagnostician: "'Such gluttons men are!'"[4]

Classical medicine also reigned in the provinces. A doctor in Clifton—"cautious in diagnosis, vigorous in treatment"—"must have quoted Horace and Virgil six times at least apropos of his medical inquiries": "a very clever man, a little of a coxcomb, but . . . not the worse physician for that." Reading "a great quantity of execrably bad Latin" and having just survived a semiliterate druggist's bungling, Macaulay was not about to stop identifying classicism with competence. The clever physician kept "the stethoscope ten minutes at my breast in different positions," declared that "I had no internal malady except a deficiency of tone," and prescribed a diet rich in protein and animal fat washed down with "very liberal" quantities of wine, but abstinence from "green vegetables and fruit tarts": "I want only strengthening medicines and a nutritious diet." Macaulay soon did "ample justice to the turtle and Champagne." His body sent an ominous message: "Very poorly—One of my worst days—

Thought that I should faint." By 8 September, however, he could walk "a good three hours & a half": "I felt quite strong & alert." He remained overweight—187 pounds three months after the attacks. He was slightly below the average height of contemporary British men—less than five feet seven inches—and his Body Mass Index was then at least 30.2. Twenty-five is now identified as the upper healthy limit, and he would regain the weight he lost to illness.[5]

Macaulay remained a credulously docile patient rather than the paragon of afflicted but optimistic self-mastery described by G. O. Trevelyan. Despite his damaged cardiopulmonary system, he continued dosing himself with the poisonous calomel. In his suffering, he struggled to fulfill his resolution to be thankful for all he enjoyed. Many heart attack victims feel "the indescribable anxiety" and depression that Macaulay endured during the summer of 1852, particularly if, like him, they are already depressives. He recorded some of his own earlier bouts, manifested internally as "desponding" or socially as aggression. Seven months before his first attack after again pillorying the Quakers—"I hardly know why"—he read an erotically fraught tale in German. Though disapproving, he found it affecting, "in an odd morbid way like a very vivid, very wild & very disagreeable dream." Before the summer of 1852 spells of depression came and went: "I am very little haunted by the devils; and when I am, my reason makes a gallant fight." Five days later he was "in low spirits about my history." Then "the devils" returned: "I feel desponding—But I have often felt so." Illness made them familiars, sometimes causing him to "wish it were over." Anxiety attacks also haunted his efforts to persuade himself that all was well: "I am fifty two—well, happy, rich, & honoured—I ought to be content." The Trevelyans—above all Hannah—softened his loneliness, which, together with his illness, constricted his world and accelerated his sense of aging. Hopeful intimations of progress were also consoling. A few months before his attacks, he saw Regent Street illuminated at night. It seemed "probable" that a century later "in 1952 every street in London" would be thus "lighted up."[6]

Finishing History

Macaulay struggled to write his book ("a fair quantity"), but now as if under sentence of death: "I should be glad to finish W[illia]m before I go—But this is like the old excuses that were made to Charon—Then again to the Augustan History." His dense sentence hints at the tension between classical disillusionment and the modern will to believe that both informed and subverted his story of utilitarian England's emphatic progress. In Greek myth Charon ferried the dead across the River Styx to Hades. Beloved by Macaulay and other skeptical moderns, Lucian's *Dialogues of the Dead* mocked various eminent ancients trying to talk their way out of the voyage. As David Hume lay dying, he read the *Dialogues:* "'I could not well imagine,' said he, 'what excuse I could make to Charon in order to obtain a little delay. I have done every thing of consequence which I ever meant to do . . .' He then diverted himself with inventing several jocular excuses, which he might make to Charon." Serenely skeptical, Hume accepted that his game was over, much as he believed "that when the arts and sciences come to perfection in any state, from that moment they naturally, or rather necessarily decline, and seldom or never revive in that nation, where they formerly flourished." Personally, Macaulay wanted a happy ending. Politically, it was imperative to tell a story of England's continual uplift rather than of its rise and inevitable decline. Contemplating death, he found distraction in the *Augustan History,* an amusing set of biographies of Roman emperors, some of them imaginary. Feeling "much better" the next day, he translated "into English some bits" of the book for his sister and his niece, "to their great amusement." He knew how to plot an amusing historical romance, but he also needed to believe that his progressive story of England was true rather than a case of making "fiction look like truth."[7] He still wanted it all.

The prospect of death—feared or wished for—failed to turn Macaulay into a single-minded author. Recovering in Clifton, he claimed that he was more than halfway toward reaching his goal: 1702. Continuing to work as the spirit moved him and then backing-and-forthing, he puttered with a dramatic story that his sister would insert in the final chapter of his posthumous last volume. He reported that it "goes on slowly." As always, there were too many diversions and distractions. Recuperating, he deserved his repeated visits to the zoo. Sitting again as an M.P. for Edinburgh was sweet revenge that made few demands on his time, but it was time that he lacked. His work on the committee to set admissions standards for the Indian Civil Service was more intense. Even the

Trevelyans, his mainstays, were sometimes labor-intensive. An "idle report" that Charles would be offered the governorship of Madras vexed him: "it would be madness in him to go." Renewing his acquaintance with Charles Austin, the muse of his radical youth, proved to be more pleasant. At Cambridge they had relished Socrates' debunking skepticism. Now Macaulay did "not wonder that they poisoned him." Ailing, he was averse to risk, incurious, backward-looking, and ever more determined to uphold the order of things.[8]

Piqued vanity moved him to write but not his *History*. In January 1853 piratical Americans published a collection of his speeches. Complying with British copyright laws, Henry Vizetelly ("that vagabond") secured the rights to the uncorrected, often sloppy transcripts of his parliamentary speeches in *Hansard*. Macaulay was determined to control the remembrance of his own words. That working up his speeches must further delay the next installment of his book was incidental. His edition would remind the public that both he and his book were progressing and enable him to exact a delicious revenge: "I found that people really wished to have the speeches . . . By the bye I learned yesterday that Mr. Vizitelly [*sic*] was hard run for money the other day, and hanged himself, but was cut down." The fantasy recurred:

> But the rope broke; and down he fell;
> And his guts burst out of his belly:
> So did this second Judas die
> The pirate Vizitelly.

When Macaulay started in July, he imagined that he would be done after working a few hours daily while vacationing. In the event, he finished in mid-October, corrected proofs a month later, and published in early December. His prodigious memory was not infallible, and he failed to calculate that "many . . . must be rewritten.[9]

Reconstructing—or composing—his old speeches, he delighted in reliving past triumphs. The project owed something to the technique of "putting speeches of his own into the mouths of his characters" that he adapted from the ancient historians. Asserting his "perfect ingenuousness," he admitted that the "substance" of most of "the speeches which I really made" was the product of correcting Vizetelly according to his recollection of what he had said years before. Indignation colored the introduction: "I cannot permit myself to be exhibited, in this ridiculous and degrading manner, for the profit of an unprincipled man." Yet Macaulay regretted harkening back to an era in politics less quiet than the "times in which we are so happy as to live." Ruing his own sharp words, he extolled Peel for "the moderation, the disinterested patriotism, which he invariably showed during the last and best years of his life." Macaulay both stated how things finally stood between them and showed who he had become and how he wanted to be remembered.[10]

As 1853 wound down, he projected that "a year of hard work will do the whole. Then I am a free man, & probably a rich man." Reputation, money, and the quality of his prose rather than fascination with his *History* kept him going. On New Year's Day 1854 he was working on chapter nineteen, which dealt with European high politics: "I toiled on it some hours, and now & then felt dispirited. But we must be resolute & work doggedly as Johnson said. Read some of his life with great delight." A few days later he "meditated a new arrangement for my history. Arrangement & transition are arts which I value much, but which I do not flatter myself that I have attained. However something may be done— Read a good deal of what I have written—Tolerable." When he wrote from memory, he was assiduous. He told himself that he must assemble "a great collection of facts fit for my purpose," but research remained unappetizing. In Paris that autumn he "made a good day's work" of "six or seven folios of records" in the War Department archives. Returning the next day, he wrapped up his work "early." The knowledge that he would "never go down the Loire again" made touring more urgent.[11]

Into mid-1854 his writing mostly repeated the cycle of discouragement, boredom, and delay. Then he "definitively and deliberately . . . [braced himself] to the work of completing" the second installment. To concentrate his diminished energy, he suspended journalizing for eight months on 2 March 1855. Traces of his immersion in his project include a letter misdated as 1689. It began to seem realistic to anticipate publishing before Christmas. In July he showed chapter eleven to the publisher and his wife: "they are in ecstasies, and certain that it will succeed. I accept the omen: for there are many Longmans and Mrs. Longmans in the world." Macaulay's reckoning was eloquent about both the intended audience of his *History* and the strain of sustained writing down to appeal to it. He complained about the off-putting morals of his period, but his hyperbolic phrase "such a dreary, monotonous spectacle of depravity" suggests that boredom more than epidemic naughtiness—his stomach remained strong—made his book enervating: "However, I have now got through the worst part of my task. If I should live seven or eight years longer, and should retain my faculties, I may hope to bring my narrative down to the accession of the House of Hanover. There I shall stop. In this way only I can now hope to be of use to my country."[12]

August saw him revising and trying to pull together "scattered scrawls." Awaiting the revised proofs, he rewarded himself by reading eighteenth-century books and his preferred ancient exemplar: "Began Herodotus with great delight; read Clio [book one]"; "Read my book—Herodotus." Briefly, his old vigor seemed to return: "Is this a constitutional renovation?" On 24 November he read the proofs: "Not ill pleased on the whole." But revisiting "two very much better historians than myself Herodotus and Thucydides" renewed his anxiety: "people expect so much that the seventh book of Thucydides would hardly content them." His "devils" also reappeared: "Anxious & sometimes low—yet on the whole I bear up. Odd that I should care so very little about the money—though it is full as much as I made by banishing myself for four & a half of the best years of my life to India." Homebound for days at a time with winter setting in, he felt "much easier about my book" despite the gloom outdoors.[13]

He aimed to finish on 11 November and publish on 10 December. Although delivery was a few days late, Longman's efficient pre-Christmas merchandising worked. The first run was 25,000 copies at thirty-six shillings for the two volumes, which were projected to sell out by 1 January 1856. On Saturday, 15 December, bookstores with orders of more than 1,000 sets were stocked, and lesser consignees received their allotments the following Monday. Boosted by the appearance of the latest volumes, the first installment once again made an attractive gift, and it sold briskly. Mudie's Subscription Library was Netflix for an era of readers. Normally stocking 150–2,000 copies of new books, it advertised 2,500 copies of the second installment of the *History,* 1,500 more than its nearest competitor. The subscribers were solidly middle class, able to pay a guinea for an annual membership. Macaulay knew his market and shrewdly helped to manage it. When the first printing ran low, Longman wanted to produce 5,000 more copies. He "insisted" on printing only 2,000 in January, and the run lasted until October. Mostly imprisoned in his sickroom, he received both news of another triumph and a visiting official seeking his advice "about the diplomatic examinations."[14]

Jackpot

On publication his fear that the second installment would disappoint vanished. He already commanded deference worthy of a national monument, and the new volumes increased it. As much as anyone, Macaulay was now the teacher of his nation. Unlikely articles in improbable journals cited him as an authority. Even his critics accepted that he set the terms of debates. As the long wait for new volumes ended, a staunchly Protestant magazine republished one of his old poems in the hope of capturing some of his fame. More than free advertising, the reprint testified to the success of his effort to redefine English patriotism by emphasizing the nation over its God, who makes only a cameo appearance as a shadowy helpmate. Readers of the new volumes welcomed them as no less nationalistic their predecessors. Baroness Bunsen found "in broad light and shade the curious characteristics of John Bull!": "a delightful event in life." The secular continuity of modern English politics that Macaulay revealed seemed undeniable to her. One of his acquaintances who understood reason of state but read little identified the *History*'s audience among people of his class: "the best ethical study for forming the mind and character of a young man, for it is replete with maxims of the highest practical value." Reprising his earlier objection to its Englishness, John Stuart Mill carped: "This disregard of consistency & probability spoils the book even as a work of art." But it belonged to an old and admiring friend to judge how Macaulay's decision to dilate on William III bedeviled the reading as well as the writing of the volumes: "too long, and it is overdone with details." That said, "All the part about Ireland is excellent. He is particularly strong upon ecclesiastical and controversial questions of all sorts."[15]

Public carping was mostly restricted to fringe groups, like "Papists & ye High Presbyterians," and Quakers: "Fortunately their attacks are even more stupid than scurrilous." A Presbyterian journal called on him to write a Christian history, and "the Glencoe Highlanders . . . burned me in effigy" because of his treatment of their ancestors' massacre. Representative of mainstream opinion was his sister Fanny's report of a sermon eulogizing him and his book. In response Tom proposed "a thanksgiving day for my book, and a service prepared by the Archbishop." Flattery evoked his usual profession of Olympian detachment. *The Times* bestowed "three columns of small cavils & a few sentences of the most highflown praises—It matters little—Straw." But ever attentive to the marketplace, he studied his reviews, predictably correcting occasional solecisms without changing a word about anything of importance. Some hostile comments that left him defensive marred the joy of converting one prominent critic. Macaulay depicted himself as uniquely alert to his own defects: "praise & blame—like other writers I swallow the praise & think the blame absurd—But in truth I do think that the faultfinding is generally unreasonable, though the book is, no doubt faulty enough. It is well for its reputation that I do not review it, as I could review it."[16]

The new installment received a review that was perhaps worthy of him. His reaction, if any, is unrecorded. Poised to become famous as a political and economic analyst, Walter Bagehot anonymously vivisected the *History*. After praising it as a "marvelous book," he anticipated the judgments of many of its later critics. Macaulay's style was as "brilliant" as his human sympathies were limited and his theology and philosophy superficial: "The history of the English Revolution is the very history for a person of this character. It is eminently an unimpassioned movement." Macaulay's rhetorical fireworks exploded on a flat surface: "the poetic mind cannot bear the weight of its narrations and the dullness of its events." His "curious" talent of dressing the "dry and dull transactions" of government with "the charm of fancy" enabled him to attract both the intellectually curious and amusement-seekers. Crowd-pleasing, however, required him to reduce human behavior "to formulae or principles," which resulted in "a diorama of political pictures." Sacrificing human depth exacted a heavy toll: "It is too omniscient. Everything is too plain. All is clear; nothing doubtful." Macaulay's attention to "a hundred details" saved him from serial inaccuracy, but he confused amassing minutiae with proof. Did Bagehot, himself so charmingly disillusioned, grasp that Macaulay was a skeptic impersonating a dogmatist? In any case, he discerned that the *History* would never be finished, because it was too small a stage for Macaulay's "great powers": "The one thing which detracts from the pleasure of reading these volumes is the doubt whether they should have been written." Trenchant as well as readable, Bagehot now has more pages in print than Macaulay.[17]

He appreciated the superiority of the new journal in which Bagehot published, but the review damaged neither his reputation nor his sales. Six German translations of the second installment were scheduled to appear almost simultaneously. A "very laudatory" German review persuaded him that "the judgment of foreigners . . . [is] a more sure prognostic of what the judgment of posterity is likely to be than the judgment of my own countrymen." And his royalties grew. In March 1856 Longman deposited in his bank a check for £20,000—with a purchasing power of £1.297 million in 2007: a "transaction . . . quite unparalleled in the history of the book trade." A few days later, he heard of a forthcoming hostile review but comforted himself: "I am pleased to be rich."[18]

"Equipoise"

Long before Henry Kissinger, Macaulay understood that "power is the ultimate aphrodisiac." Out of office and a rich historian, he remained a connoisseur of its erotic, mostly as a graying eminence except on all aspects of the "Indian question." A breathless summary will explain why Macaulay found the stimulus gratifying during his last years. The period 1850–1870 became "an era of comparatively good feelings . . . in which a cross-class political consensus did in fact emerge." The political classes saw good government as both cheap and "disinterested," spending too little to fuel the "corruption" that enriched some individuals and families at the expense of the nation. Their goals included prosperity, sound money, tight budgetary control, voluntarism, and deference to the initiatives of local government and private associations. For the state to be accepted as impartial, the regime of aristocratic privilege had to be replaced by merit—or at least its appearance. Equipoise resulted from the great fear of the nonevent of 1848, which cemented a "new solidarity of property, now uniting sometime Radicals with sometime Tories." Meanwhile the consolidation of an inclusive "English" national identity diffused interclass tensions: the "English values" card. Into the 1860s, however, politics were fluid. Although byzantine flirtations sometimes turned into dead ends, at least one became a serious courtship. As early as June 1849 Macaulay had correctly discerned that the Peelites were "drawing nearer to the [Whig] govt. & further from ye Protectionists."[19]

In the Commons those "Liberal Conservatives" dwindled to no more than forty after Peel's death. They were, however, the self-promoting elite of the old Tory party, and as late as 1851 their votes—mostly as back-benchers—were required to form even a minority government. The "traditionary" Tories had one experienced and well-regarded leader, the future earl of Derby. Macaulay thought him an "able" man and occasionally breakfasted with him. In the Commons the gap on the Tory front bench was increasingly filled by Benjamin Disraeli, the target of Macaulay's demeaning and borderline anti-Semitic scorn: "spiteful, false, and a mountebank." During the 1850s the Tories cobbled together two short-lived minority governments, first in 1852 for less than ten months and then from February 1858 to June 1859. After 1849 Lord John Russell's government—virtually a Whig cousinhood—lurched but managed to stumble on until 1852. Macaulay treated him respectfully, sometimes cordially, but was clear about his limitations and blunders. When the pope restored a regular Catholic hierarchy in England, its new chief announced with inflammatory pomposity the return of "Catholic England to its orbit in the ecclesiastical firmament." In the face of surging anti-Catholicism, Russell introduced legislation to penalize any Roman Catholic bishop who assumed a title derived from a place in the United Kingdom. He was less annoyed by "Papal Aggression" than by the Tractarians, whom he, along with many other Anglicans, regarded as crypto-Catholics. Russell's aim was to needle them—but indirectly—while trolling for no-popery voters. A close student but no friend of Rome, Macaulay watched his former chief's antics with his customary shrewdness and phlegm.[20]

Russell was yesterday's and, finally and briefly, tomorrow's man. His government almost collapsed in February 1851—the Peelites saved it—and though a member of most subsequent cabinets he became premier again only after Palmerston died in 1865. For all that political enthusiasm was alien to Macaulay, he professed to admire "Pam" and perhaps agreed with him more often than with any other living politician. It was his single-minded defense of England's interests that first attracted Macaulay

and survived every disappointment with him. In 1850 Palmerston provoked a crisis by deciding to blockade Athens to force the Greek government to overcompensate a moneylender who claimed British nationality and British protection after an anti-Semitic mob destroyed his
house. Macaulay rallied to Pam while privately deprecating his lack of
nuance and discretion. When the old Peelites maneuvered his censure by
the House of Lords, Macaulay marked his nearly five-hour self-defense
in the Commons. Palmerston adapted from Macaulay the famous lines
in his *"Civis Romanus sum"* speech declaring England to be the new
Rome. Palmerston's vigorous rejection there of any double-edged class
warfare was at least as appealing as his paraphrase. England was "a nation
in which every class of society accepts with cheerfulness the lot which
Providence has assigned to it, while at the same time every individual of
each class is constantly striving to raise himself in the social scale—not
by injustice and wrong, not by violence and illegality, but by persevering
good conduct, and by the steady and energetic exertion of the moral and
intellectual faculties with which his Creator has endowed him." The
"public mind" that Pam was helping to articulate and Macaulay to form
consisted of "the educated middle classes in whose (commercial) interests . . . [Palmerston's] foreign policy was regularly directed," men self-
consciously if diversely Protestant.[21]

The Radicals rallied to the government to defang the censure, a sign
of their movement under Pam's guidance away from internationalism.
After the repeal of the Corn Laws, free trade enabled a worldwide British mercantile presence for which investors wanted protection. The
Union Jack followed the factors. Palmerston's triumph made him seem
—perhaps feel—almost indispensable to the Russell government, and he
characteristically overreached. When Louis Napoleon Bonaparte made
himself dictator in France, Palmerston endorsed the coup to the French
ambassador. Also supporting the new regime, Macaulay faulted both Palmerston's indiscretion and Russell's weakness on national defense. Palmerston's colleagues were weary of him. A frayed cabinet usually agreed
over foreign policy but squabbled in pursuit of tactical advantages. Perhaps angling for the Whig-Peelite coalition that Pam opposed, Russell
secured his dismissal as foreign minister on 19 December 1851 to howls
of protest from the press. From the outside Palmerston resurrected the

old Whig dispute between those who looked back to Pitt the Younger's activist European policy and those who hewed to Fox's noninterventionism. It was a clever ploy. Working with protectionist and some Tory-leaning Peelites, he succeeded in bringing down Russell's government in February 1852. When a stopgap Tory government ended with 1852, Macaulay concluded that there was no possibility "of a union of ye Liberals": "an irreducible difference, particularly the vital question of national defence."[22]

He was again an M.P. Palmerston's ouster left him judiciously sympathetic: "It was high time. Yet I could not help being sorry—A clever, daring, indefatigable, high spirited man—but too fond of conflict & of hazard, and ready to sacrifice everything for victory when once he was in the ring." The impending cabinet shuffle reawakened Macaulay's appetite for the game. With Russell courting him, he became practiced in saying no. In early 1851 he declined the offer of a pocket borough and four months later the proposal that he "come again into parliament as an independent member—I was resolute." The prime minister's scheme indicates how far Macaulay had migrated from Whig partisanship. On 18 January 1852 Russell invited him to 10 Downing Street to discuss joining the government. He approached the meeting "anxious," wanting to refuse but finding it difficult to do so "face to face." But refuse he did. He was no debater, and now "my literary habits and literary reputation had made it impossible." Moreover, he "did not wish to be forced to take part" in a personal dispute with Palmerston and was uneasy about Russell's talk of widening the franchise. Russell acquiesced, and Macaulay left "rejoicing in my own freedom, but not quite easy about the public." But the prospect of being returned for Edinburgh by virtual acclamation proved to be irresistible. His defeat in 1847 remained "one of the calamities which cut deep," leaving "a permanent scar." Hearing talk of a movement to reelect him, he professed to be "quite indifferent": "I should like the *amende*—I should dislike the trouble." His protests reflected the strength of the temptation, and the Trevelyans were soon working with some leading Edinburghians to repair their city's affront to his "honour." On 13 July 1852 he was returned on his own terms: "No town had sinned more deeply than Edinburgh. I am therefore glad that Edinburgh has repented signally, and has, after the good old forms of

Kirk discipline, had the courage to appear on the cutty stool."[23] Even post-Freudians must pause at his arcane reference to a form of public shaming reserved for repentant adulterers and fornicators.

Past Master

G. O. Trevelyan remembered his uncle's reelection for Edinburgh as occasioning national celebration. When Albert Smith, the music-hall star whom Macaulay scorned as vulgar, worked the election into a patter song, Trevelyan heard "prolonged and repeated cheering" from an audience that he reckoned to "have been at least three-fourths Tory." Macaulay's frail health led him to defer his victory speech in Edinburgh until 2 November. He cast it as a panoramic assessment, but like many aging men he enjoyed looking backward. Successive paragraphs honoring Peel and evoking the pan-European specter of 1848 reflected both his hope for a Whig-Peelite fusion and his preoccupation with lost time. As much as hyperbole, a visceral fear of revolution leavened his "haranguing": "I did for one moment doubt whether the course of mankind was not to be turned back, and whether we were not doomed to pass in our generation from the civilisation of the nineteenth century to the barbarism of the fifth." The revolutionaries were "a race of Huns fiercer than those who marched under Attila, and Vandals more bent on destruction than those who followed Genseric." Defeated five years earlier partly because of his support for increased government aid to the Catholic seminary at Maynooth, he included a pope-baiting aside for the benefit of his Presbyterian electors still resentful of Papal Aggression. In a reprise of the hymn of national praise and thanksgiving that climaxed the first installment of his *History,* he coupled Russell's contribution to the 1832 Reform Act and Peel's to ending the Corn Laws to vindicate the British constitution's self-improving genius. Consolidating their achievements might entail redistributing seats more equitably and extending "the franchise, further than I admit I once thought would be safe or practicable." Macaulay ended, however, with vague uplift. After denouncing socialism and the "other 'isms' for which the plain English word is 'robbery,'" he prophesied "that good times are coming for the labouring-classes of this country," but without promising to work for their enfranchisement.[24]

The government that emerged combined Whigs, sundry Radicals, and

Peelites. Although the "Liberal-Conservatives" were reduced to about thirty M.P.'s, they took as many seats in the cabinet as the Whigs. Among them was Lord Aberdeen, the prime minister. Russell, viewing himself as the rightful premier, led the House of Commons and played musical chairs in and out of the cabinet, while Palmerston served as home secretary. On 2 June 1853 Macaulay announced that he united "in myself the character of Liberal and Conservative." It was a signal of his commitment to the Aberdeen experiment and even more a token of his drift to the right. As Britain waged another war against the "Caffres" in South Africa, his nephew heard him say, "You call me a Liberal, but I don't know that in these days I deserve the name . . . I am in favour of war, hanging, and Church Establishments." His vision of order admitted at least one loophole: "opium might well be put into the list of articles which are to be imported duty-free"—he was advising Gladstone, the chancellor of the Exchequer and an addict's brother.[25]

Macaulay's social opinions were generally more severe. If he did not look for socialists under beds, he saw socialism lurking in Dickens' novels, with their melodramatic appeals to a basic standard of human community and equality against the appearance "that the rich were getting richer at a faster rate than the poor, and that inequalities were increasing." Deviating from the theology of classical economics only to support the Ten Hours Act, which limited the working hours of women and adolescents in textile mills, Macaulay disdained sentimentalism as much as "cant": "Finished Bleak House—much moved by it—But it is a most exaggerated picture of life and manners." Rereading *Hard Times* a year later, he discovered "socialism—The evils which he attacks he caricatures grossly & with little humour." Unlike those Whigs who looked back to Charles James Fox for inspiration, Macaulay separated the middle and working classes, to the disadvantage of the latter. He objected to Russell's project for parliamentary reform because it would empower the poor and ignorant, all of them potentially "robbers" bent on pillaging men of property and intelligence. Palmerston shared his suspicions, but Macaulay promised to remain loyal to his former chief despite their disagreement: "I will not vote against Ld J [Russell] in his extremity."[26] Events reprieved him.

Even on the back benches, Macaulay counted. When Palmerston effused about him in Glasgow, he noticed with becoming modesty. Had

Britain in concert with France not been moving toward war to prop up the Ottoman Empire against Russia, the political shoving match between Pam and Russell would have been droll. Although the home secretary and the M.P. for Edinburgh agreed that firmer diplomacy could have averted the Crimean War, as the conflict neared both welcomed it. Palmerston fanned the flames at the time and later hid evidence of his participation in the decisions that turned a quagmire into a stalemate. The triumph of his *"Civis Romanus sum"* speech proved that he could persuade the urban poor that the Englishness which made them superior to other peoples outweighed their material disadvantages. About such demagogy Macaulay was ambivalent—or self-deceiving. A couple of weeks before the declaration of war against Russia, he professed to be "disgusted" by Palmerston's bluster. But he also welcomed the conflict for preventing further reforms. As he later generalized, "foreign troubles always act on our domestic troubles as a blister acts on an inflammation of the chest." Here as elsewhere, his political judgment was shrewder than his choice of nostrums. The regnant doctrine of cheap government and low taxes limited social spending, but waging war was expensive. In trying to finance it, Gladstone precipitated one of the government's rare internal squabbles over fiscal policy. He proposed raising the income tax to a new high rather than increasing the national debt. Instinctively favoring guns and butter, Macaulay disagreed but continued to admire him as "a good & an able man."[27]

Macaulay's monarchism was always calculating rather than visceral. The state incarnated as the nation mattered to him. Revering the "state-nation," not the nation-state, he spoke and wrote to mobilize the "national, ethnocultural group" he called England "to act on behalf of the State . . . [which] can thus can call on the revenues of all society, and on the human talent of all persons." His state did "not exist to serve or take direction from the nation," namely the whole British people. Hence he valued reasonable wars for providing the common enemies that helped to promote national solidarity and strategic alliances. Properly skeptical when the press reported the fall of the great port of Sevastopol—"too glorious . . . to be all true"—he thought that the success of Anglo-French arms could prove mutually useful: "the war, which has not yet been national in France, will become so, and . . . consequently, neither the death of the Emperor nor any revolution which may follow, will easily dissolve the present alliance between us."[28]

A second-generation nationalist with a folkish sense of the "British race," Trevelyan remembered that his uncle "viewed with great and increasing satisfaction the eagerness of his fellow-countrymen to make all the sacrifices which the war demanded. He was fond of reminding himself and others that the prosperity and independence of England had not been bought for nothing, and could be retained only so long as we were willing to pay the price." An old-fashioned state-nationalist, Macaulay was also the more scrupulous grammarian, respectful of the difference between the first person singular on the one hand and both the first and third persons plural on the other. He knew that there was no "we" making the "sacrifices" in the Crimea: "I am well pleased on the whole. It is impossible not to regret so many brave men and to feel for the distress of so many families. But it is a great thing that, after the longest peace ever known, our army should be in a higher state of efficiency than at the end of the last war." The blundering course of battle refuted him. Two months later events seemed "blacker and blacker." Unlike the Indian empire, the fate of those "brave men"—indeed the course of battle itself—became something to be ignored whenever possible: "A friend of ours said not long ago that my chambers were the only place where a man could pass a quarter of an hour in company without hearing the Crimea mentioned." Macaulay's insouciance is a reminder that it took the twentieth century's serial carnage to persuade most of the noncombatants who rule at least to pay lip service to the fact that even necessary warfare is regrettable.[29]

Acting as the "titular member" for Edinburgh from the beginning, he treated the Commons' routine business as an imposition: "I never go down to the House except in case of life & death. The late hours and the bad air would kill me in a week, if I attended as I used to do seven years ago." He persuaded himself that he stayed on because the electors wanted to make amends for using "me unjustly in 1847"—as if his continued presence in Westminster removed not his but their shame. During the almost forty-one months that he was again an M.P. he spoke three times, all in June and July 1853. His only major address was the second—inevitably on India. He debuted successfully opposing a bill to change a rule of the House.[30] What he said on 2 June 1853 is now of less interest than how he said it and its reception. They open a window onto a scarcely imaginable world in which a great orator possessed something of the glamor of a rock star: Mick Jagger on yet another farewell tour, but quoting Latin tags.

Trevelyan abridged a voluminous newspaper account of his uncle's reception and performance:

> the position of Mr. Macaulay in Great Britain was measured in a great way. On a Wednesday the house, and the Committees, are sitting at once . . . More doors open; more Members rush out; Members are tearing past you, from all points, but in one direction . . . Why, what's the matter? Matter? Macaulay is up. It was an announcement that one had not heard for years; and the passing of the word had emptied the committee rooms, as, of old, it emptied the clubs . . . The old voice, the old manner, and the old style;— glorious speaking! Well prepared, carefully elaborated, confessedly essayish; but spoken with perfect art, and consummate management; the grand conversation of a man of the world, confiding his learning, his recollections, and his logic, to a party of gentlemen, and just raising his voice enough to be heard through the room . . . Mr. Macaulay had rushed through the oration of forty minutes with masterly vigour; but the doubts about his health, which arise when you meet him in the street,—when you take advantage of his sphinx-like reverie . . . to study the sickly face,—would be confirmed by a close inspection on Wednesday. The great orator was trembling when he sat down; the excitement of a triumph overcame him.

For Macaulay, it was a "day of painful anxiety, and great success. I thought that I should fail; and, though no failure can now destroy my reputation . . . it would have mortified me deeply." Unseen in the gallery, Hannah and Baba watched and listened. His third speech addressed a Scots concern. After drafting a bill in consultation with Presbyterian civic leaders and negotiating the details with Lord Aberdeen, he briefly spoke on behalf of the majority of his constituents who favored abolishing the annual tax on all Edinburgh's rate-payers to support the Kirk's ministers.[31]

Sectarian fury continued to annoy him. Always skeptical of "the multitude's" capacity to live docilely out of their individual moral resources and grown suspicious of expansive autonomy, Macaulay desired to invest the government with the responsibility of providing "education for the people of every religious persuasion. My wish would be to see a national system of secular education established, and to leave the religious education of the young to their own parents and pastors. The state of public feeling in England has hitherto made such an arrangement impossible." Both publicly and privately, he was resolute in his commitment to projects of cultural and political secularization. As a realist, however, he understood that the religious neutrality obtaining in British India was impossible at home. While supporting the establishment, he sought to divest it of functions and revenues that now should be the government's and rejected residues of its bygone monopoly. Thus he favored making Oxbridge and the Scots universities more religiously inclusive. Other proposals to "reform" the ancient universities now affronted him.[32]

By 1856 Macaulay felt detached from daily politics: "I live much in the past; and I am therefore less violently excited than my neighbours about the present." When he retired from Parliament on 31 January, the masterfully immobile Palmerston was prime minister. Apart from the Tory interlude in 1858–1859, he held office until his death in 1865. Though subject to criticism, he remained Macaulay's man and patron. Like Palmerston, Macaulay believed that to "innovate for innovation's sake . . . [was] a thing always disliked in England." In diplomacy he remained a cool realist, scornful of crusades and cold toward causes unless they advanced England's interests. Pam courted liberal opinion by selectively cheering on the continental revolutionaries of 1848 and promoting a "moral nationalism" that would suppress the international slave trade. Zachary's more famous son was more even-handed: "I hate slavery from the bottom of my soul, and yet I am made sick by the cant and the silly mock reasons of the Abolitionists." No more solicitous of underdogs at home, Lord Macaulay resolutely blamed Lord John Russell for talking "Jacobite jargon" by "canting about the poor hardworking honest man who ought to be enfranchised." Even respectable enfranchised workingmen needed oversight. Despite Macaulay's support for the secret ballot, he knew that his servant would "vote for the Whig candidate" in an election.[33]

Entering the House of Lords at the end of 1857 threatened to revive the tug between the literary life and the political—his perennial "Cicero problem"—until his physical frailty prevented it. Routinely deferring to Palmerston, the author of his peerage, he dreamed of making speeches that he could not deliver. But he still read public opinion, recalculated his own opinions, and sometimes reversed himself. He saw the dawn of the most curious of Victorian political agitations. Decades later W. S. Gilbert joshed about it: "He shall prick that annual blister,/ Marriage with deceased wife's sister." That a boyhood friend from Clapham went abroad to marry his former sister-in-law at first scandalized Macaulay, but he reversed himself because the Dissenters championed eliminating the ban. It was, however, a whitecap on a mostly placid sea. After the 1859 general election, he saw politics as very good: "they are all for neutrality, but for armed neutrality. They are all for reform, but for moderate reform. They are all for free trade . . . The Jew question has been disposed of. The India question has been disposed of. There remain only questions of detail, which may easily be compromised, and questions of a personal kind, which ought to be compromised."[34]

Indian Agendas

More than anything else, the ramifications of the "India question" engaged Macaulay politically after he returned home in 1838. His efforts were long disappointing. Out of Parliament in 1850 he supported legislation that placed "British-born subjects under the criminal jurisdiction of the ordinary courts—courts which were often presided over by Indian judges." The "domiciled British" who opposed the bill were perhaps intellectual and moral ciphers, but they mattered politically. Their agitation led the East India Company's directors to suspend the act. When it was reintroduced a generation later, the opposition remained formidable: another symptom of the fate of the vast ambitions to anglicize the Indian elites that Macaulay began to pare down while exiled in Calcutta. In 1852 he caught himself stereotyping "the Rajah of Coorg— all the vices of an Oriental despot written on his face—or was it imagination?" His penal code languished. In 1852 one old India hand anonymously derided it as utopian. A year later Karl Marx summarized "the adventures of that yet unborn code" for American readers. It was sent to the various local authorities in India, which sent it back to Calcutta, from which it was sent to England, to be again returned from England to India. In India, Mr. Macaulay having been replaced as legislative counsel . . . the code was totally altered, and on this plea the Governor-General, not being then of opinion "that delay is a source of weakness and danger," sent it back to England, and from England it was returned to the Governor-General, with authority to pass the code in whatever shape he thought best. But now . . . the Governor-General thought best to submit the code to a third English lawyer, and to a lawyer who knew nothing about the habits and customs of the Hindoos, reserving himself the right of afterward rejecting a code concocted by wholly incompetent authority.[35]

But in 1854 the Commission on the Laws of India—Ellis was a member—prompted a committee of the Indian Legislative Council to recommend adopting the code. Macaulay became wistful: "Had this justice been done sixteen years ago, I should probably have given much more attention to legislation and much less to literature than I have done. I do not know that I should have been either happier or more useful than I have been." A few months later he warned Ellis against a scheme before the law commissioners to vet and select judges: "you are going to introduce frightful jobbing and corruption into the Indian administration." Although an article in *The Times* insisted that his "wonderful" code deserved a better fate, it continued to languish. The eulogist was Sir Charles Wood, president of the Board of Control of the East India Company. A patron of Trevelyan, he sat with Ellis on the law commission and spearheaded the India Act of 1853, which led to the creation of the Indian Civil Service Commission, chaired by Macaulay. The members belonged to Britain's small and intersecting "political circles." Enacted with revisions in 1860, Macaulay's great code finally received full "justice" and binding effect in 1862, a year after the Criminal Law Consolidation and Amendment Acts enabled the "humanisation"—the systematizing and relaxing but also the secularizing—of British penal law necessary to make it compatible with Macaulay's Benthamite design.[36]

Returning to Parliament enabled him to help shape the terms of the

Company's new charter in 1853. He served on the Select Committee on
the Indian Territories: "I find that India occupies the thoughts of people
more than I had expected. The nation generally is indifferent; and I do
not suppose that a single election will turn on any Indian question. But
in the political circles there is a good deal of stir and a wish to do something without any clear notion either of what now exists or of what is
wanted." He promoted the Raj's continuing evolution into a formal empire. An activist secretary of state for India, Wood clung to "liberal imperialism," aiming to prepare the Indians for self-rule in some remote future. Against the Tories and along with Macaulay and Trevelyan, he
opposed turning complete responsibility for governing the subcontinent
over to Whitehall. The East India Company served as a check on the ignorance of elected M.P.'s and a generally "indifferent" nation.[37] Realizing
most of their objectives, the revised charter provided for imperial consolidation under the aegis of the Company, which lost its commercial
side but gained administrative power. It also mandated replacing patronage appointments in the Indian Civil Service with selection through examinations that were presumed to be objective because they were uniform and competitive. Therefore the East India Company's college—
top-heavy with Orientalists—would remain but with a less distinctive
curriculum.

In the Commons Macaulay endorsed Wood's bill as a provisional measure, which left "us free agents to effect future improvements." Invoking
his experience in Calcutta, he insisted that "India is, and must be, governed in India." He envisioned a despotic government not of specialists
but of meritocrats serving under a succession of competent governors-
general. A bravura display of erudition adorned his speech: a 1771 newspaper clipping, the Mahrattan word for blackmail, a Calcuttan oral tradition about Clive, and a private comment of Lord William Bentinck.
Macaulay reminded the House of his proposal twenty years earlier that
"all admissions to the civil service, shall be distributed among young
men by competition in those studies ... which constitute a liberal education." He then parried his foe Lord Ellenborough's charge that a deep
classical education rendered young men "utterly unfit for the contests of
active life." After citing the learning shared by Gladstone, Lord Derby's
father, and several eminent India hands, above all of Warren Hastings—
the "ablest man who ever governed India"—Macaulay extolled a Latin

poem that had won Ellenborough a Cambridge gold medal: "men, who distinguish themselves in their youth above their contemporaries, almost always keep to the end of their lives the start which they have gained." The anecdotes personalized Macaulay's conviction that a classical education endowed the "political circles" with shared cultural assumptions. However loud, their occasional disagreements were likely to remain in the family. Broken "down in health, uncontrollably nervous, and unable to control his voice," he could not complete his speech: "the great effort was frigidly talked about and cruelly criticized." But he "succeeded better than I had expected" and was listened to abroad. The *New York Times* summarized his message: "Utility of Classical Studies: Another Speech by Macaulay."[38]

India: Who Is to Be Master?

A classical manifesto that colored the selection of India's rulers for almost a century followed the Government of India Act of 1853. Joining Macaulay, Trevelyan, Jowett, and Gladstone in shaping it was Stafford Northcote, a Balliol man who had taken a first-class degree in classics and a third in mathematics before serving as Gladstone's awestruck private secretary. They planned the institutions that sustained the elite educational consensus into the twentieth century. Their shared classicism accommodated somewhat different but finally convergent goals. Macaulay's interest was imperial: ensuring that India was governed by a like-minded elite—a cadre of liberally educated and class-conscious Englishmen posted abroad—rather than by the Company's Anglo-Indians, prone first to go half-native and then to retire home as déclassé aliens. Always earnestly striving, Trevelyan craved administrative reform. By the end of 1848 he was looking to improve the quality of British civil servants by changing the method of recruiting and appointing them. Jowett fretted over the future of Oxford—even of Cambridge—seeking to transform the universities from ecclesiastical into national institutions. Unless Oxbridge defined a "manifest utilitarian purpose" for itself, he feared, it would become "a German or a London University." Preventing such an academic revolution depended on guaranteeing suitable employment for able classically educated graduates not attracted to the professions. Above all, Gladstone wanted to solidify the governing caste: "one of the great recommendations of the change in my eyes would be its tendency to strengthen and multiply the ties between the higher classes and the possession of administrative power." Northcote shared his chief's wish to ensure solidarity at the top, though he phrased it less baldly: "there is no kind of education, so likely to make a man a gentleman, to fit him to play his part among other gentlemen & to furnish him forth for the world, as that of an English university." Despite their differences, the five promoted the vogue of introducing or strengthening examinations for admission to privileged institutions. Empowering merit to trump jobbery was the purport of the Oxford University Act of 1854, which Gladstone pushed; a parallel act for Cambridge followed two years later. From the academy the vogue spread to the civil service, with Trevelyan taking the lead and Jowett, a fervent convert to the Raj, serving as both his adjunct and his occasional muse.[39]

The day before yesterday some impersonal theories, variously good, bad, and indifferent and not all French, purported to explain the mechanisms by which authority is established and perpetuated in complex societies. More down-to-earth, the details of Trevelyan, Jowett, Macaulay, Gladstone, and Northcote at work reforming the civil service illustrate how one English political circle negotiated change in order to ensure continuity. In November 1848 Trevelyan, just knighted for his achievement during the Irish famine, was charged with investigating the Treasury. He proceeded to trigger a domino effect. After remaking that department, he turned his attention to the Colonial Office. Within a year he proposed restructuring the entire civil service: clerks would be divided between the "superior," charged with administration and policy, and the "inferior," mere copyists and filers. They should be appointed on the basis of their success in specialized competitive examinations—recruiting by testing general knowledge came later. The novelist Anthony Trollope, a Post Office bureaucrat, satirized Trevelyan as Sir Gregory Hardlines: "Great ideas opened themselves on his mind as he walked to and from his office daily. What if he could become the parent of a totally different order of things! What if the Civil Service, through his instrumentality, should become the nucleus of the best intellectual diligence in the country, instead of being a byeword for sloth and ignorance! Mr. Hardlines meditated deeply on this, and, as he did so, it became observed on all sides that he was an altered man."[40] Thus Trevelyan consolidated his ascendancy in Whitehall.

In December 1852 Gladstone appointed Northcote to serve with Trevelyan on a committee investigating yet another ministry. Their report stipulated that successful candidates for clerkships should be eighteen to twenty-five years of age, in good health, of certified character, and supervised as probationers for a year before receiving permanent status: all prerequisites of Trevelyan's new order. The following summer Northcote, also sitting on the commission of inquiry into Oxford, and Trevelyan investigated five more departments and reached similar conclusions. By mid–October 1853, after reviewing additional departments, he was drafting *The Report on the Organisation of the Permanent Civil Service, together with a Letter from the Rev. B. Jowett:* the "Northcote-Trevelyan Report." Submitted to the cabinet on 23 November 1853, its stated aim—to create a civil service of "permanent officers . . . able to advise, assist, and to some extent to influence those who are from time to time set above them"—inspired "Sir Gregory's" rapture of bureaucratic ascendancy. On 26 January 1854 the cabinet voted "that a Bill be prepared providing for admission to the Civil Service by free competition"—it was Northcote's idea—and the queen ordered the report's publication. Within the cabinet the Peelites and a former Radical were supportive, but not the Whig grandees. For Macaulay, the "civil service plan" was Trevelyan's cause, and at Brooks's, the Whig Valhalla, he "found everybody open-mouthed . . . against Trevelyan's plans about the Civil Service. He has been too sanguine . . . The time will come, but it is not come yet. I am afraid that he will be much mortified."[41] As usual, Macaulay's political antennae were accurately tuned. The project had to be launched not by statute but by executive decree, and Trevelyan's bureaucratic utopia came into being only after World War I.

John Stuart Mill denigrated Jowett as a "great auxiliary of Trevelyan," but the *"Letter from the Rev. B. Jowett"* that graced the Northcote-Trevelyan Report hints at his real status. Linking the report and the committee on the Indian bureaucracy, Jowett left his fingerprints on the overhaul of both the home and Indian services. He successfully lobbied to amend the original India Bill, which had in effect reauthorized the monopoly of the East India Company College at Haileybury, to permit the competitive examination of other candidates. An alumnus of Haileybury, Trevelyan endorsed it as providing "a very satisfactory system of special [professional, including 'Oriental'] instruction for the Indian Civil Service." While converting Trevelyan, Jowett enlisted Gladstone, M.P. for Oxford and, as chancellor of the Exchequer, Trevelyan's chief: "I cannot conceive a greater boon which could be conferred on the University than a share in the Indian appointments." He also lobbied Wood, an Oxford double-first in classics and mathematics, and courted the bill's shepherd in the House of Lords. Trevelyan became an enthusiastic convert to "the quite irrelevant educational twist" to benefit "our two great Universities, & especially Oxford, *in relation* with the active life of the country." Jowett and a former Cambridge don revised his project for a new administrative order: "from August 1853, the initiative in the movement for civil service reform [in India] passed increasingly into the hands of Jowett and Trevelyan. They steadily transformed the case for opening the appointments to general competition, into one for effectively closing them to all but the products of the universities, and in which no provision could be made for Haileybury." The cultural assumptions and goals of the five principals had so converged that they were parroting one another.[42]

Trevelyan advised Wood on the composition of the committee charged with drafting a plan to appoint Indian bureaucrats on the basis of competitive examinations. Constituted in March 1854 and charged with reporting before the end of the year, it was a clubby group of five. Macaulay chaired, seconded by two of his political friends, the principal of Haileybury, who was no Orientalist, and Jowett. Before meeting with Wood to discuss "the Competition," Macaulay read an "account of the system of Chinese Examinations."[43] It was seemingly his sole engagement with an Asian civilization during his chairmanship. China's impact on the report is irrecoverable, but the similarities between its imperial bureaucracy and what Macaulay's committee proposed are obvious. Selected by rigorous competitive examinations that equated a particular kind of learning with merit, the mandarins were men of letters become bureaucrats. The Chinese tests' classical bias efficiently limited the pool of viable applicants to young men with the means, leisure, and aptitude for such studies. Guaranteed both prestige and security, the mandarins shared a mindset and an esprit de corps.

An assertive chair as skilled in manipulation as in phrasemaking, Macaulay informed Wood: "As to instructions,—it seems to me that had better not limit us. Refer the Act to us; and request us to suggest what we think the best mode of carrying it into execution." He was already managing the politics of the report's reception and lobbying Haileybury out of existence. During the deliberations Jowett was "constantly" at Trevelyan's house, often when Macaulay visited. He came to find Jowett "rather a bore," and Jowett reciprocated: "a fine old fellow . . . excellent at monologue, with a most sincere and genuine pleasure in hearing himself talk. In power of mind he is very inferior to Gladstone." Their backbiting did not disrupt the committee's work. Appointing himself the draftsman, Macaulay looked to "finish it in a week." Five days on, he felt "rather fagged," but almost on schedule he read his draft to Trevelyan, who "seemed much pleased." It caused Macaulay "great trouble" and was "much longer" than he planned. After the committee vetted it, he continued tinkering. He also began to sell its recommendations and intensified his management of its reception—efforts that continued into 1855. In November Wood pronounced himself "satisfied," but Macaulay, ever anxious, expected that the plan "will be violently abused." There could be no relaxing. During a long discussion with the Company's Board of Control, which had frustrated his 1833 scheme for remaking the Indian bureaucracy, "I carried most points my way."[44]

Just after Christmas *The Times* published the report along with a supportive leader—Trevelyan was practiced in managing the editor—and in January 1855, "my plan is adopted almost to the letter." But the "almost" left Macaulay "vexed." It remained to ensure the social cohesion that would make the members of the Indian Civil Service a self-conscious and self-confident ruling caste. Unlike the domestic bureaucracy, the Company's existing cadres were manifestly efficient. But appointment as a cadet depended on "an act of patronage by a Director" of the Company, and "the Directors' nets could catch some poor and ill-favoured fish." Because of the social and educational deficiencies of many who attended Haileybury, students there had to be made "more like English gentlemen," which required "a general enlargement of knowledge and elevation of intellectual character." Macaulay insisted on privileging Oxbridge graduates. Lowering the eligible age for examination to twenty-two "will tell greatly against Oxford and Cambridge, which, much as they need reform, are still the first schools in the empire, and in favour of the London University, the Scotch Universities, and the Queen's Colleges in Ireland." His bow to reforming the ancient universities was a feint. Improbable petitioners sent him "the most delicious letters" that vindicated his biases: "The best is that of a clerk in a confectioner's house in Limerick who begs that I 'will send him a prospectus informing him in what he is capable of undergoing an examination, for admission into the above Service.'" Oxbridge prevailed. Although the report was "wonderfully well received, on the whole," it remained to manage the closing of Haileybury. Working primarily with Trevelyan and Jowett, he would succeed in 1857. An even more complex goal required that Macaulay continue playing the politics of "the Civil Exams."[45]

Masterful but now little known, his "Report on the Indian Civil Service" captures many of the cultural and social assumptions of England's rulers when their nation's power was becoming unrivaled.[46] Candidates for admission to the Indian bureaucracy must be proficient in "those branches of knowledge to which it is desirable that the English gentlemen who remain at home should pay some attention." Here Macaulay's habitual synecdoche for all the subjects of the United Kingdom of Great Britain and Ireland speaks volumes. Certified as possessors of the requisite intelligence and become probationers, they could acquire whatever local knowledge they needed to govern later, even on-site: "It therefore seems to us quite clear that those vernacular Indian languages which are of no value, except for the purpose of communicating with natives of India, ought not to be subjects of examination." Hesitantly, he allowed that "the Sanscrit and the Arabic" were "by no means without intrinsic value in the eye both of philologists and of men of taste." Each would be graded at half the value of Greek and Latin. More than knowledge of European antiquity was desired of the candidates, but the classical sections would count for 19 percent of a hypothetical perfect score, 1 percent less than mathematics.

A classical education in the public schools that prepped boys for the ancient universities was an insufficient cause for admission as probationers, but it was a necessary cause, unless an examinee somehow managed to excel in "chymystry," German, French, and Italian. The desired knowledge was that of a university honors graduate—preferably from Oxford or Cambridge. Proper to a man of letters, it amounted to an abridgment of the secular canon that helped to sustain Macaulay spiritually: "Foremost" were England's language, history, and literature: "knowledge of our poets, wits, and philosophers." Such learning also certified an examinee's probity. When the committee was formed, Jowett declared on the basis of abundant "University experience . . . that in more than nineteen cases out of twenty, men of attainments are also men of character."[47] The report embellished his faux-statistical insistence on the nexus of breeding, success, and honor:

> it is not among young men superior to their fellows in science and literature that scandalous immorality is generally found to prevail. It is notoriously not once in 20 years that a student who has attained high academical distinction is expelled from Oxford or Cambridge. Indeed, early superiority in science and literature generally indicates the existence of some qualities which are securities against vice,—industry, self-denial, a taste for pleasures not sensual, a laudable desire of honourable distinction, a still more laudable desire to obtain the approbation of friends and relations. We therefore believe that the intellectual test which is about to be established, will be found in practice to be also the best moral test that can be devised.

Because social cohesion was paramount, the report discovered ethical import even in a quirk of English classical education of which Macaulay personally disapproved.

> It would be grossly unjust . . . to the great academical institutions of England, not to allow skill in Greek and Latin versification to have a considerable share in determining the issue of the competition . . . the youth who does best what all the ablest and most ambitious youths about him are trying to do well, will generally prove a superior man; nor can we doubt that an accomplishment by which Fox and Canning, Grenville and Wellesley . . . first distinguished themselves above their fellows, indicates powers of mind, which, properly trained and directed, may do great service to the State. On the other hand, we must remember that in the north of this island the art of

metrical composition in the ancient languages is very little cultivated . . . We have . . . an anxious desire to deal fairly by all parts of
the united kingdom, and by all places of liberal education.

Skill in classical versification provided no sure moral prophylaxis. Already "a classical scholar of note" at Eton by fourteen, Charles James Fox
was "taken to Paris by his father . . . given a substantial amount of money
with which to gamble[,] and the ever-indulgent father arranged for him
to lose his virginity." Lifelong and famous, Fox's genial debauchery did
not keep him from doing "great service to the State," which Macaulay's
moral calculus reckoned as covering far more of "the multitude of sins"
than charity.[48]

Specialized South Asian and other practical studies dominated the
curriculum at Haileybury. When it was founded in 1805, responsible
voices throughout the north Atlantic world had questioned the utility of
the classical monopoly on the education of privileged males. As late as
1826, Macaulay had briefly joined their chorus. In an encounter after the
Indian Civil Service report was filed, he silenced it. At his invitation
Max Müller, a famous Sanskritist, visited to discuss the contents of the
examination. Müller came primed "with facts and arguments in support
of the necessity of Oriental studies." Professing to know "nothing of Indian languages and literatures," Macaulay asked "a number of questions."
Before he could answer one of them, Macaulay began relating the history of his "Minute on Indian Education." For a futile hour Müller tried
"to put in a single word"; then Macaulay thanked "me for the useful information I had given him, and I went back to Oxford a sadder and I
hope a wiser man." In contrast, Macaulay's classical education of two
generations of Trevelyan men amounted to a sustained if unequal dialogue. In April 1858 Charles, who in Calcutta had refreshed his Greek
under his guidance, called with the good news "that the Indian Civil
Service Examinations are transferred to the department of the Civil Service Commissioners." After he left Macaulay detected a syllabic error in
his Latin verses. Later in the day he delighted in both correcting a line in
a Greek tragedy and receiving a letter from George Trevelyan, then at
Cambridge preparing to become "second in merit order on the list of
candidates for the classical tripos." Georgy would go on to serve as his
father's private secretary in Madras.[49]

As that appointment suggests, the process of first determining merit by academic examination and then placing and promoting an applicant according to his merit guaranteed no objectivity. The Northcote-Trevelyan regime was neither the result nor the cause of some noiseless circulation of elites. Instead, it extended and formalized how "the existing network of patrons and sponsors" worked to ensure that promising new men helped to lead society instead of becoming alienated subversives. Intelligent "jobbery" had done as much. In January 1830, two years before the word was coined, Lord Lansdowne had offered Macaulay a seat for a pocket borough. They were strangers, but the patron knew Macaulay's father and his successes at Cambridge and in print, as well as his best friend. Such patronage survived under merit. While the committee was deliberating, Macaulay's younger brother Charles was appointed by Gladstone as secretary to a Treasury board at the behest of Charles Trevelyan, the department's senior bureaucrat. Breathing public-spiritedness, Trevelyan thanked Gladstone: "I do not yield to my Brother-in-law in the feelings of gratitude expressed by him . . . for although I am well aware that you had no personal motive in making the appointment, perfect rectitude and justice and a conscientious following out of the dictates of duty are not so common qualities as not to be regarded by me with a feeling which can only be described by *respect* and *gratitude*. I confidently predict that you will be better served than any Minister has ever been."[50]

Disdainful of cant, Tom wrote: "All my brothers and brothers in law are now comfortably quartered on the public, and I alone remain without a halfpenny of the Queen's money." He regarded Trevelyan as both an incorrigible naïf and "almost a monomaniac" about the possibility of achieving total reform. During the late 1920s Humphrey Trevelyan, fresh from a triumph in Cambridge's classical tripos, was advised by his second cousin, George Macaulay Trevelyan, to "go to India" like Charles Trevelyan: "I had had no thought of an Indian career, but replied immediately that I would go, and went." His education made the examination seem like second nature. Humphrey Trevelyan's distinguished career vindicated the Macaulay commission's notion of meritocracy. It marginally broadened access to higher government posts, but it also reinforced the hold of inequality by making it seem rational and inevitable rather than partly the result of a good legacy and good luck. Macaulay's belief that permanent intellectual distinctions outweighed nurture in deciding who should govern would enjoy a long if chequered future.[51]

He prevailed in India, though not automatically or exactly as he had imagined. The first recruits to the new bureaucracy were overwhelmingly the university men—and especially the Oxbridge alumni—whom he sought. In 1855–1859 graduates made up 96 percent of the total and those of the ancient universities 57 percent, but by 1878–1882 the respective percentages had fallen to 18 and 4. The shift was the result of aspirants'—mostly public school graduates—bypassing university in favor of crammers—in the United States they are now called "review services." Their trainers prepared them only for subjects on the set examinations. That most of the new recruits were apparently upper middle class was insufficient. As early as 1864, Wood "added more marks for Greek and Latin by way of giving . . . ['University men who are gentlemen'] a turn." He confided to Trevelyan, "It is difficult to say this in public, for I should have half a dozen wild Irishmen on my shoulders and as many middle class examination students, but that makes all the more reason for not giving in to anything which might lead to similar results." The House of Commons heard a kinder story. "Our object is to go into the world and get well educated men wherever they are to be found, no matter where or in what manner their education has been acquired. We wish to obtain the best cultivated young men . . . without requiring that that knowledge should have been imparted at a commercial school, a university, or any other particular establishment." A turnaround took time, creativity, and much revision of Macaulay's original plan, but among the 1892–1896 cohort 93 percent were university men, and 52 percent of them were from Oxbridge. In 1893 the indefatigable Jowett died after twenty-three years as master of Balliol College, where his genius for spotting and nurturing imperial talent had flourished: "he did govern India through three successive viceroys, Lansdowne, Elgin, and Curzon, and the scores of probationers or future members of the Indian Civil Service whom he attracted to the college."[52]

Indirectly, Macaulay made another contribution to expanding the South Asian job market on which British classicism thrived for generations. When Wood drafted his 1854 dispatch projecting a comprehensive educational system for India, Trevelyan advised him. Wood was realizing a suggestion that Macaulay had made in the 1830s. An Indian Educational Service parallel to the civil service was created, with the right kind of Englishmen populating its higher ranks: "second class honours in classics," Merton College, Oxford; "brilliant classics scholar from Emmanuel College, Cambridge"; "third class honours in classics" from Corpus Christi College, Cambridge; and "a fourth class in *Litterae Humaniores* from Worcester College, Oxford" but the son of a retired colonel of the Indian Army and "in the fullest sense of the word a gentleman." Neither last nor least among them was "a First in *Litterae Humaniores*" from Christ Church, Oxford, where he had notably fenced and boxed. In Bihar he went on to edit Macaulay's "Milton" for the "British Classics for India" series. The classical presence in both services weakened as curricula expanded and diversified, but the examination system endured, producing a sometimes hereditary caste of a couple of thousand all-rounders governing and instructing one-fifth of the human race: "force-fed with classics and mathematics from early childhood," often "celibate until middle age," but well paid, secure, powerful, and effective. Coined in the mid-eighteenth century to designate the Chinese bureaucracy, the English word "mandarinate" by 1884 also meant any dominant group.[53]

A mild irony shadowed Macaulay's success in overseeing the classical redesign of the Raj's civil service. No muscular post-Christian, he failed to see an innovation in university life that outlived the ancients' hold. An aptitude for sports was also coming to identify a gentleman. Within a few years of his death, the bias was enshrined in an official report on the major public schools: their alumni should be distinguished by "their capacity to govern others and control themselves, their aptitude for combining freedom with order, their love of healthy sports and exercise." Did Macaulay ever hear Georgy's undergraduate "Trinity Boat Song," which hailed merit as a brew of Englishness, manliness, and superiority measurable by "skill and brawn" as well as by brains?

> Drink to the men who, so trusty and strong,
> 'Midst the danger and treachery pulled her along,
> As Englishmen should, to the head of the river!
> Drink to our boat, and three beauty cheers give her![54]

Nearly a century after the ancient universities ceased to require Greek for admission and almost fifty years after they dispensed with the Latin requirement, their annual boat race is a profitable televised event.

India Rising and Subjugated

Until 1857 Macaulay regarded the people of India as docile subjects fit for social experimentation. Then the revolt of tens of thousands of them enraged him. During Lord Dalhousie's governor-generalship (1848–1856), annexation and conquest "equivalent to annexing an Austria each year" expanded the scope of the Company's direct rule and accelerated its evolution into the subcontinent's effective government. Dalhousie favored the interests of peasants at the expense of their landlords. The Great Game was in progress. To block Russian expansion in Central Asia, Britain sought to create a buffer of client states on India's North West Frontier. On 1 November 1856 Lord Canning, Dalhousie's successor, declared war on Persia after it invaded Afghanistan. Victory was quick and decisive, but Canning faced peril. To offset the British forces' overextension, the terms of service of the Company's army of Bengali sepoys were altered to permit their redeployment. Some Hindus regarded sea travel as impious, and rumors spread that the fat of pigs and cattle greased the cartridges that the troops had to bite open in order to load their new rifles. Feeling defiled and betrayed, both Hindu and Muslim sepoys began to fear that forced Christianization would follow. As 1857 began, the Company ruled "about 63 percent of the territory and 78 percent of the population" of India, and further expansion seemed inexorable. In early May scattered refractoriness among the sepoys turned into revolt. One garrison murdered its officers, captured Delhi, killed the European inhabitants, and proclaimed the shadowy Mughal king the emperor of India. Within weeks, the bulk of the Bengal army, together with troops and civilians in the northern states, were rebelling.[55]

Blindsided, Canning acted decisively. Most of the Indian Army held fast, but on 15 July 1857 at Cawnpore (now Kanpur), about 250 miles southeast of Delhi, sepoys wielding meat-axes slaughtered more than 100 women and children. The atrocity and rumors of mass rape enraged the English community. Already unpopular among expatriates, especially Calcuttans like those who had pestered Macaulay during the 1830s, Canning eventually rejected the indiscriminate and gory vengeance that many craved. On 31 July, with the outcome still uncertain, he acted to curtail vigilante "special committees." The order was dubbed the "Clemency Resolution," and he was soon mocked as "Clemency Canning."

Loyal troops recaptured Delhi, but guerrilla warfare continued for months after Lucknow in Oudh fell on 5 March 1858. With victory certain, Canning issued a proclamation confiscating almost all the land in Oudh. The effort to break the local landlords' power provoked Ellenborough, Macaulay's old antagonist in everything Indian, now reinstalled as president of the Board of Control. On 2 August the Tory government enacted a bill turning over the Company's political power to the governor-general, transformed into a viceroy accountable to a new secretary of state for India with cabinet rank. Canning shifted his support from peasants to traditional elites, restoring their estates and reducing most villagers to tenants at will. Thereafter it was British policy "to enlist on our side, and to employ in our service, those natives who have, from their birth or their position, a natural influence in the country." As secretary of state, in 1857 Charles Wood founded three universities in India to educate "those natives."[56] Two of Macaulay's Indian legacies, promoting the Western-style education of an indigenous elite and, eventually, the penal code, were the only parts of the old "liberal" imperialist agenda that survived the rebels' defeat.

In late June 1857 Macaulay rejoiced in the centennial celebration of Clive's victory at Plassey and his role in popularizing it: "What a century." Three days later he heard of the capture of Delhi: "Horrible news from India—Massacre of Europeans at Delhi. Mutiny—I have no apprehensions for our Indian Empire—But this is a frightful event." His interest in the details of the Crimean War had been conventionally if intermittently patriotic, but he was "painfully anxious for India news." The deteriorating situation insulted his sense of Englishness: "More barbarities—there must be a terrible retribution"; "the national character has come out nobly." The revolt "affected my spirits more than any public events in the whole course of my life." Briefly, he felt "half ashamed at the craving for vengeance which I feel. I could be very cruel just now, if I had the power." Toward the insurgents he uniquely felt "real vindictive hatred," and he emulously imagined a "monstrous" passage in Livy: "Fulvius put to death the whole Capuan Senate in the Second Punic War." They were scourged and then beheaded. Imagining the mass slaughter of the insurgents "and all the accursed rabble of the bazaar" brought to mind a variation on the imperial question that he, just back from India, had first publicly raised in "Temple": "Is this wrong? Is not the severity which springs from a great sensibility to human suffering a better thing than the lenity wh. springs from indifference to human suffering? The question may be argued long on both sides." From sources on the scene Trevelyan learned that reports of atrocities against the English were over-blown: "Trevelyan came—We talked about India, of course." Macaulay's habitual calculation eventually cooled his bloodlust. Viscerally, Palmer-ston urged razing Delhi after its recapture. Macaulay counted the over-throw of the Mughals as a victory in what he imagined as a clash of civi-lizations: "glorious to the nation . . . which will resound through all Christendom and Islam. What an exploit for this little handful of En-glishmen in the heart of Asia to have performed."[57]

He was even more exquisitely calculating about collective hatred: "And these feelings are not mine alone—Is it possible that a year passed under the influence of such feelings should not have some effect on the national character." He thought it would be "a very good thing," because "effeminate mawkish philanthropy . . . will lose all its influence . . . The nerves of our mind will be braced." In passing, he derided two do-gooders agitating to improve the lot of England's poor. But he also reck-oned that acting out of "real vindictive hatred" could deform "the na-tional character": "But shall we not hold human life generally cheaper than we have done. Having brought ourselves to exult in the misery of the guilty, shall we not feel less sympathy for the sufferings of the inno-cent. For in a sense no doubt humanity to these hell hounds would be cruelty; and in exacting a horrendous retribution we are doing our duty & performing an act of mercy. So is Calcraft [the veteran public execu-tioner] when he hangs a murderer. Yet the habit of hanging murderers is found to injure the character." Then Macaulay stopped: "I do not know how I wandered into these speculations—Rain—Rain with wind from the East."[58]

In victory his realism prevailed, but events vindicated his intuition about the impact of collective hatred on the "national character." At first Canning's reluctant policy of pacification made him "very angry." Then a "very manly & judicious speech" in the House of Lords by Canning's closest friend proved that those who mocked him as "Clemency" were guilty, "God knows, of calumny." Macaulay's misgivings about excessive mercy persisted, but he also recognized that some expressions of "real vindictive hatred" would be politically intolerable. When Ellenborough

JUSTICE.

"Justice," *Punch,* 12.ix.57. "In exacting a horrendous retribution we are doing our duty & performing an act of mercy" (TBM, J11:178–179, 19.ix.57).

urged "that all the mutineers whose lives are spared should be made eu-
nuchs," he allowed that in theory "the thing might do well enough. But
the utter impossibility of proposing such a thing in any English assembly
ought to have been obvious to an English statesman." It was characteristic of Macaulay coolly to weigh the possibility of mass castration before rejecting it. For him horrific violence—even wholesale torture and
slaughter—could be a legitimate extension of calculating politics in some
circumstances, but it was intolerable when done out of mere rage. The
suppression of the rebellion was, in any case, undiscriminating in its brutality. Martin Farquhar Tupper, its unofficial laureate—"a likable figure,
courageous in adversity, generous, firm in his Christian faith"—urged:

> England, now avenge their wrongs by vengeance deep and dire,
> Cut out their canker with the sword, and burn it out with fire;
> Destroy those traitor regions, hang every pariah hound,
> And hunt them down to death, in all hills and cities 'round.

A bellwether of national sentiment devoid of Macaulay's cool rationality,
Charles Dickens was more succinct. He wished that he could "do my
utmost to exterminate the Race upon whom the stain of the late cruelties rested."[59] The lessons of "Temple" and the *Lays of Ancient Rome* were
becoming English common sense.

Constantly and articulately involved in Indian affairs, Macaulay continued advising cabinet members. As a result of the happy news that
Victoria would take "on herself the government of India," the British
stopped annexing territory within India, and loyal princes kept their
thrones for the duration of the Raj. Between 1861 and 1901, moreover,
imperial expansion vindicated Macaulay's judgment that England would
come to hold "human life generally cheaper than we have done." During
that long generation the British Empire grew from 8.5 million to 11.9
million square miles. The *Lays of Ancient Rome* fostered and benefited
from the imperial vogue. At the end of 1842 Macaulay reckoned "a clear
profit" of £140 on the first edition "a great success." In 1850 the *Lays*
were still a modestly selling amusement. In late 1857 he estimated that
the *Lays* would earn him "near 6000£," with a 2007 purchasing power
of £398,460. The impulse that began making them England's ersatz national epic also strengthened the identification of England's Christianiz-

ing and civilizing missions, first in India and then worldwide. Macaulay was determined to spread English civilization, not Christianity. On the Day of National Humiliation proclaimed to atone for the sins that had triggered the Indian uprising, he fumed at a "detestable" sermon urging the government to promote converting the subcontinent. It would trigger "the rebellion of the whole nation."[60]

Always politically more realistic than John Mill, Macaulay grasped that the uprising doomed the East India Company and meant consolidating direct rule from Westminster. Popular support for the change was useful, but he rallied Whig M.P.'s against Disraeli's "insane" bill to give the electorate a direct voice in the council governing the subcontinent. Peeking into the House of Commons, he spied Disraeli wrangling with a Radical M.P.: "Odd that they should both be of Jew blood." Disraeli's sparring partner was a generation ahead of him in assimilation. But although Macaulay sometimes saw race as a collective, inheritable, and essentially immutable quality, memories of his father's African associations kept him from quite embracing white supremacy. Long after Macaulay's death, Gladstone reminisced: "The repulsion thus inspired by the typical negro is commonly described as physical and as irremediable . . . Macaulay has said in conversation that . . . there was much exaggeration in this and kindred statements; he found it hard to reconcile them with the very close personal relation which not infrequently subsists between individuals of the two races." As with so much else, his personal muddle about race epitomized his time and place. The English public mind achieved more discriminating clarity only after he died.[61]

Glimpsing the Promised Land

While avoiding the *History* Macaulay contributed five long characters to the *Encyclopaedia Britannica*. It was a wistful, laborious, and gratuitous exercise, which he justified as another merchandising device to keep his name alive until he finished his book.[62] The essays provided a diversion from William III's tedious reign, with John Bunyan back to the turbulent decades before 1688 and forward into the eighteenth century with Francis Atterbury, Oliver Goldsmith, Samuel Johnson, and William Pitt the Younger. That century remained Macaulay's Promised Land, which he, like Moses, could only glimpse with longing from a distant vantage.

More importantly, the essays diffused his story of England's growth into a modern because increasingly secular nation.

Both "Atterbury," finished in late March 1853, and "Bunyan," completed nine months later, were assaults on the Puseyites. Atterbury, who had died in 1732, was a famous High Church preacher, Jacobite, and champion of the clergy's privileges and power against the crown's authority: a proto-Puseyite. In writing to oppose the agitation to revive the inert convocations, where Atterbury had once dazzled, Macaulay aimed to vindicate the establishment's dependence on the state. Though an opportunistic primitive of uncertain faith, Atterbury had possessed an eloquence that enabled him to ascend to "the front rank of the high-churchmen" and command the admiration of "the great body of the clergy."[63]

By implication the Puseyites, his spiritual descendants, adhered to a dogmatic and ritualistic Anglicanism as hollow and outmoded as his. In 1854 as in 1831, Macaulay depicted Bunyan as a recovering lunatic: "Years elapsed . . . before his nerves, which had been so perilously over-strained, recovered their tone." However distempered, his plain faith rebuked the Puseyites' turgid formalism: "Those, he said with much point, who have most of the spirit of prayer are all to be found in gaol; and those who have most zeal for the form of prayer are all to be found in the alehouse." Macaulay pointed to the canonization of *The Pilgrim's Progress* as a rare example of "the educated minority's" accommodating itself to the tastes and instincts "of the middle and lower classes." To vindicate Bunyan's allegory as an English classic, Macaulay denounced as "the most extraordinary of all the acts of Vandalism" a recent "Tractarian" effort "to transform" it into a book "for the use of the children of the English church."[64]

Two years later, in "Goldsmith" and "Johnson," Macaulay continued scouting the superstitious past to boost the reasonable but embattled present. Goldsmith's biography, moreover, enabled Macaulay to introduce race into his antithesis between the modern and the primitive. Although Goldsmith was the son of a Church of Ireland parson, Macaulay depicted him not as a major British author but as a stage Irishman: a natural entertainer, ignorant, feckless, and comedic. Goldsmith's Irishness informed "The Deserted Village," his most famous poem. The happy village was "true English," and its decayed counterpart "is an Irish village":

"the felicity and the misery which Goldsmith has brought close together belong to different countries and to two different stages in the progress of society." For all Goldsmith's insistence that he was "inveighing against the increase of our luxuries," Macaulay's racialist interpretation remained current into the early twentieth century.[65]

His second assault on Johnson's legacy was less brutal than its predecessor but scarcely a "compassionate diagnosis of the man." His insistence on identifying religious seriousness with primitiveness required him to patronize both Johnson's beliefs and his achievement. Despite sharing many of his now unfashionable classical assumptions about literature, Macaulay traced his Christianity to retrograde politics and personal weirdness. Johnson's faith could not console him because it "partook of" the besetting problem of "his own character." His manners were "almost savage," and his Toryism was absurd. Risking a boomerang effect, Macaulay, himself so often torpid, ridiculed Johnson's fruitless resort to "prayer and sacrament" for relief from bouts of "strange impotence." Macaulay continued to find Johnson's spontaneous charity as incomprehensible as his religion. Progress, he was certain, had been no kinder to Johnson's writings than to his faith. They were mostly obsolete, but because of Boswell's great biography he survived as "a great and good man." "Johnson" pleased him, and the *Encyclopaedia Britannica* embalmed it until 1965.[66] Unlike Macaulay's thousands of pages, Johnson's complete works exist in a modern edition, and many of his books are available in competing paperbacks.

Filling fifty-six closely printed pages, "Pitt" was a sketch for Macaulay's vast unwritten history of late eighteenth-century politics. While writing, he complained: "interminable"; "Nothing ever cost me more." But he kept at it with a persistence that the *History* no longer inspired. Finishing a draft, he read "old newspapers" and an ancient book on India. Almost nine months after beginning, he sent off the highly polished article in August 1858, returning the next day to his *History* after "a long interval." More than most pages in the book's later volumes, the essay instructs and sparkles. Pitt the Younger belonged to a vanished world. His parents soused him with port at fourteen to make him grow—unthinkable in "an abstemious age." But his politics had anticipated the present. Receiving the thorough classical education that equipped him to gain oratorical ascendancy in the House of Commons, the dominant arm of

government, he early realized his promise. Macaulay blamed him for in-
dulging George III's whims, but by instinct and conviction Pitt was a
great Whig peacetime premier whose misfortune it was after 1792 to
lead an unnatural wartime coalition heavy with Tory reactionaries.[67]

Macaulay rescued Pitt from his Tory hijackers, much as he saved
Bunyan from the Tractarians. As always, England's survival was his over-
arching good. In the wake of 1848 Macaulay's view of the French Revolution had darkened. He now painted its leaders as "inflamed by a fanaticism resembling that of the Musulmans who, with the Koran in one
hand and the sword in the other, went forth, conquering and converting." Even more dangerous, Napoleon had sought "nothing less than the
dominion of the whole civilised world." Pitt's error was not to "have
proclaimed a Holy War for religion, morality, property, order, public law,
and . . . thus opposed to the Jacobins an energy equal to their own." Naïvely, he had sought "a middle path." But Macaulay celebrated Pitt as
"preeminently qualified, intellectually and morally" to lead "the government of a prosperous and tranquil country." Because that was the state of
England in 1859 as well as in 1789, Macaulay acknowledged Pitt's "successors": Canning, whom he championed on the eve of entering politics,
had been Pitt's "favourite disciple"; and Peel, an author of England's current equipoise, carried on Pitt's legacy. Informed readers knew that foremost among living Pittites was Palmerston, who had launched "his career
as a supporter of William Pitt the younger" and, though no friend of
Canning, served in his cabinet and thereafter adhered to his policies. Tom
Macaulay cherished elements of Zachary's politics decades after jettison-
ing his religion.[68]

Suburbanite

Macaulay's wealth finally suburbanized him. When his health and the
weather allowed, he continued moving selectively in society. The Trevelyans' house provided an occasional gathering place for old India hands.
In mid-April 1856 he was the dinner guest of the soon-to-be speaker
of the Commons, along with a duke and a duchess, the Gladstones, the
American ambassador, Britain's leading railway engineer, and a prominent Australian politician. On that occasion he reverted to emulously
grading his hosts' possessions: "A fine house—The dining room painted

with frescoes—Bad art—but good upholstery." He was already looking forward to leasing a house of his own, which would enable him to realize some of his decorating fantasies and resume hosting dinner parties. Holly Lodge was situated on two acres on fashionable Campden Hill in Kensington—"my little paradise of shrubs and turf"—about twenty minutes by coach from Hyde Park Corner. Leaving the Albany after fifteen years led to predictable frets and extraordinary expenses: "upholsterers, linendrapers, silversmiths and dealers in China." Shortly after relocating, he calculated that his living costs for the year, apart from a continental holiday, would be £2,850—with a purchasing power of £184,884 in 2007. His multiplying possessions required the protection of "a dog, or rather a bitch, a little, sharp, yelping terrier."[69]

During his three and a half years at Holly Lodge it gradually became a plush infirmary. The day before becoming "master of my new house" he read Cicero, a ritual he repeated on his first full day of residence. He was asserting his basic allegiance and, hence, his continuity as a man. Only after his volumes were "in order" did he move in. Approached through "an ante-chamber lined with books," his library was a "quiet, sober, unpretending room," where he read and wrote with an engraving of John Milton overhead. Eighteen months before the move Macaulay's collection amounted to more than eight thousand volumes, and it grew to fill his new space. A few months before he died, his library was in "chaos," and he summoned his butler and footman "and went vigorously to work"—they, not he. More than ever, he depended on his servants, whom he treated as extensions of himself: "William ill, to my great vexation"; "Wrote to H[annah] begging her to bring her man." Increased comfort and service marked his status: "a new carriage," a "new butler—a good cook—two horses instead of one." Zachary's old servants, William Williams and Elizabeth, his wife, accompanied him to Holly Lodge until they were pensioned off in 1858. His regular staff then consisted of four people known only by their functions, plus uncounted maids. Continuing the habit of effacing the servants that he had learned in India and paying them quarterly, he saw himself as "a good master." Insofar as his health allowed, he entertained sumptuously but remained newly and nervously rich. Serving "the very best" wine to his dinner guests caused him to fret over the bills. But his ability to speak the languages of both ends of his audience helped to sustain his public authority. Even before moving into Holly Lodge, its lawn preoccupied him, and his subsequent fixation on the "execrable dandelions" linked him to his middle-class origins and readers. At the same time his growing friendship with the duke and duchess of Argyll, his next-door neighbors, bespoke his ascent into the aristocracy. Apart from the Argylls, Macaulay's inner circle remained closed. Often able only to receive, he minded the "loneliness" of his "confinement." While spending more on his household, he continued to accumulate money, but now "for the sake of others"—principally the Trevelyans.[70] He was endowing a family enterprise that thrived for more than a century.

[12]

A BROKEN HEART

Medical ignorance plagued Macaulay to death's door. Still treating his condition as respiratory rather than cardiovascular, he often used "blisters, to relieve my chest." The medical theory was classical and the practice sadistic. "Hippocrates"—a school not a person—taught that four humors compose the human body and that many diseases result from their imbalance. Macaulay's chest was burned—by hot plasters, acid, or a heated glass—and a blister formed to draw the "putrid or peccant humors" to the surface of his body. The pain apparently briefly distracted him from his damaged heart, and he persisted with the torture. As the spring of 1856 began, he foresaw his medical future: "always valetudinarian—but never positively ill." Later, looking to summer, he tried to come to terms with his mortality: "I do not at all expect to live 15 years more. If I do I cannot hope that they will be so happy as the last 15." His toughness sustained him. As late as 1857, he thought nothing of walking miles around Greenwich Hospital and then to Trafalgar Square. No longer a social lion, he enjoyed the company of a few eminent foreigners whom he found congenial and comprehensible. The author of *Carmen* "talked English well," but Alexis de Tocqueville, despite his stay in America, "has no English": "I got on pretty fairly in French. The party was agreeable."[1]

Fame neither enhanced his self-knowledge nor appeased his need to reassure himself. On his fifty-seventh birthday he took stock: "My health is not good. But I suffer little: my head is clear: my heart is warm: my fortune is easy: I receive numerous marks of the good opinion of the public—a large public, including the educated men both of the old & the new world." Almost to the end he rode a roller coaster, down with depression one month but up with cheer the next: "the last scene of the play was approaching"; "I am better. My health is certainly better than it was three years ago." For the first time in years he slept well. Even so, a semi-invalid's normal frets now bothered him: "some mental decay"; "bad weather, and that when increasingly important to me to have good weather." Seven months earlier he had briefly entertained the notion that the weather might not control his chest pains.[2]

The triumph of the second installment of his book exorcized none of the specters that had bedeviled its production: "impotence"—uncertainty and ennui. On 8 April 1856 he looked into materials for volume five: "It is good to break the ice." Three days later he "wrote a little." Then the temptation to go backward overcame him. He decided to re-polish the second installment—"Corrected some fifty pages of my 4th vol."—and could not stop tinkering with the first volumes, which continued to sell by the thousand. His frailty further weakened his resolve: "Not quite well, & felt no inclination to work." As Macaulay continued detailing his hero's reign but without imposing schedules or deadlines, he found the eighteenth century irresistible. By May he was already "reading many pamphlets of Q Anne's time" as well as writing "Johnson." For more than two years he avoided doing necessary research on the late 1690s. Despite boredom with his "task," he sometimes wrote in spurts but could not sustain them.[3]

Toward the end of January 1858, he hoped to "get Chap xxiii into a corrected shape." It was to open his fifth volume. More than two years had elapsed since the publication of chapter twenty-two: "I find it difficult to settle to any work—This is an old malady of mine; & it has not prevented me from doing a good deal in the course of my life. Of late I have felt this impotence more than usual. The chief reason I believe is the great doubt which I feel whether I shall live long enough to finish another volume of my book. I ought to work harder for India for ye H[ouse] of L[ords]. But to that sort of work I always had repugnance except when necessity brought it close to me." Notwithstanding his "repugnance," India preoccupied him during 1858. With an eye on the consolidation of the Raj, he wrote about the origins of the War of the Spanish Succession, which began vivisecting Spain's global empire. He passed days doing nothing and more doing virtually anything except working on his book: "Chatted . . . about Miss [Jane] Austen. If I could get materials I really would write a short life of that wonderful woman." The next day he "wrote a little & read two books of Propertius"—a Roman elegiac poet—but wrote nothing the following day. Whether classical or modern, most of his reading continued to be more sophisticated than the best-seller he was loath to finish. He envisioned securing his legacy, perhaps by preparing a collected edition of his works.[4]

Meanwhile, he continued oscillating between insecurity and exaltation. The winter blues brought self-reproach: "I can truly say that I never read again the most popular passages of my own works without painfully feeling how far my execution has fallen short of the standard which is in my mind." But readying himself for dinner at Buckingham Palace as spring approached, he insisted that "in my inmost heart I do not acknowledge myself inferior to any historian except Herodotus and Thucydides." Whether down or up, he needed both to believe that his was a "careful and profound study of history" and to use his royalty checks to gauge his historical achievement: "have made more thousands by literature than he [Southey] made hundreds." Macaulay's habit of turning other writers into competitors, depreciating their work, and magnifying his own sometimes blinded him to popular taste: "The Micawber scenes in Dav[id] Cop[perfield]—The only good things in a very poor book." Dickens' novel was then receiving a favorable second look. But Macaulay's belief in the English political consensus remained accurate and his determination to give the nation a consensus history fixed. Over dinner with a friendly Tory M.P.'s wife he envisioned confluence: "For there really are scarcely any public questions left on which the [Tory] Ministers differ from the Whigs; & if personal resentments can be quieted, there may now be a general fusion of parties." Even so, he was taken aback by his old antagonist Ellenborough "expressing all that I thought": "A mad world!" Detached from daily political machinations, and often living in his own past—including the happily distant culture wars of his youth—Macaulay rejoiced in the nation's rallying around the political language of economic rationality: self-interest and utility, held together by nationalism and glossed with heavy sentimentality.[5]

Realities occasionally troubled his celebration of secular progress. The *History*'s suave manipulation of popular antipopery made him seem a Protestant oracle. Nicknamed "Trash'em" for his assaults on Catholicism, the Reverend Tresham Danes Gregg sought Macaulay's imprimatur for a polemic: "And that he should imagine that I am likely to value a man highly for bellowing on a platform about the man of sin and scarlet whore!" If archaisms sometimes marred his England, the signs of its future could also elude him. Mystified by the tactics that were helping to form the Liberal party, he was displeased to learn that the Radicals were likely to be included. He failed to appreciate that Palmerston, by borrowing his words, had cast a nationalist spell on them. With little to show for 1858 except "Pitt," he resolved to correct "the dawdling habits that are growing on me": "Wrote vigorously." A week later he was "tolerably satisfied" with his new pace and looked forward to publishing another volume before Christmas 1860.[6]

He kept working uneasily on his book, even after the narrow capacity for human sympathy that informed it began to kill him. On 6 January 1859 Trevelyan announced that he was disposed to accept the governorship of Madras, "leaving H[annah] to keep house here": "If she were to go I should die of a broken heart, I think. But, if she is to stay, the question is very different . . . The question seems, in some sense, balanced. I think that he will decide for going." Most of the next two lines in his journal are effaced, but Macaulay's reasoning is clear and true to form. Hannah's care for him during his heart attacks sealed his dependence on her. He, however, no more understood her needs than in 1834 when he dragooned her into sailing to Calcutta. In 1859 her distress complicated his reckoning: "Everything must be done to prevent him from going. With her or without her, it is madness, destruction, misery." Tom was predicting his likely fate, not Hannah's or her husband's. Two days of anger, worry, and petulance followed. When Trevelyan accepted the appointment, Macaulay fumed: "All is over—go he will—A madman. I can hardly command my indignation. Yet what good can I do by suppressing" the appointment? The thought had crossed his mind, but India was central to the family business. Within seven months one of their nephews would join Trevelyan there. Briefly recovering himself, Macaulay evaluated the governorship as "a mere pecuniary scheme": "I must admit the thing may answer." But his emotions trumped the Trevelyans' rational choices. Unlike when Baba's marriage impended, his loss was undeniable. Weepy, he continued raging against Trevelyan: "He cannot get India out of his head. To be governor there was his earliest day dream;

& he must indulge his fancy at whatever cost"—namely the cost to Macaulay.[7]

The Sensibility of Power

His indifference to his family's ambitions, desires, and well-being captures his emotional consciousness. Neither a psychiatrist nor a psychologist, I am unwilling to inflict incompetent theories on someone long dead. Thomas Babington Macaulay understood my subject: his sensibility.[8] Lifelong patterns in his interactions and words—mostly to himself —reveal him as a powerful and ultimately tragic man. His stunted emotional consciousness caused him to live barely attentive to and mostly unconcerned about the people and places in front of him, while his masterful intelligence empowered him to interpret and help shape the English public mind during his nation's century. Macaulay's sensibility also made his life a tragedy. Blind to the humanity he shared even with the unseen thousands whom he recommended killing, he lived as if riveted to a mirror, contemplating himself hopelessly, and finally alone.

Clapham left him with limited ears and literal eyes. His artistic tastes marked him as an Englishman of his time and class. Music escaped him: "I am not very sensible to such impressions." Italy first taught him to appreciate sculpture and painting, but he could see beauty in them only when they reflected the reality visible to his bounded imagination. Admiring a picture by Edwin Landseer at an exhibition, he failed to detect subtlety underneath its literal surface—perhaps the glint in a dog's eyes. Similarly, he dismissed one of J. W. M. Turner's visionary sea pieces as a "miserable daub." It was otherwise with one of his "realistic" historical paintings: "noble." Baffled by symbol and metaphor, Macaulay saw almost nothing to prize in the works of contemporaries such as Dickens and Thackeray: "It is odd that the last twenty five years which have witnessed the greatest progress ever made in physical science, the greatest victories ever achieved by man over matter, should have produced hardly a column that will be remembered in 1900." He consigned Herman Melville to oblivion: "Began a queer book called The Whale . . . Absurd—yet better than I had expected from a glance which I gave to a thing of his called Mardi wh. seemed to me a bad imitation of the worst part of Rabelais." That Macaulay identified a source of *Mardi* was characteristically learned, but a century later what he judged "queer" in *Moby Dick* many found revelatory of their world so grudging of certitude. Macaulay handled Melville more gently than other contemporaries whom later readers found prophetic: of Walt Whitman, "Looked at Leaves of Grass again—What madness!"; of Charles Baudelaire's *Flowers of Evil,* preoccupied with Eros and Thanatos, "crazy ribaldry & blasphemy."[9] He would not—perhaps could not—try to surrender himself to the canvas, sculpture, or book before him and even briefly entertain the unexpected.

Demanding an effort to understand and care for other people on their own terms, love is a more ruthless discipline of self-surrender than connoisseurship. The experience of power and the lure of popularity taught Macaulay to avoid the tactics of Victorian literary "storm-troopers," who, often frustrated in their desire for domination, published not merely to win but to "massacre." But his private voice could be cruel. That he, so memorably articulate, delighted in repartee needs no explanation. Verbal sparring was safer than dueling, but much that he confided to his journal and to Ellis bludgeoned rather than cut. Increasingly taking himself at least as seriously as his public did, he constrained the self-mockery that can foster self-knowledge. But he often verbally pummeled other people: "What a mania—& her what an object—ugly, sickly, bad hearted, indelicate, stupid, ill educated." Complete strangers were also fair game. Receiving an "absurd letter" from "a vulgar, conceited fool," he resolved "to keep my temper with him." Macaulay turned demeaning at least one minor annoyance into a verbal blood sport: "the last fortnight of this eminent person's life has done more for his renown than the preceding seventy seven years. His fame has gone out into all lands." Macaulay's biblical allusion underscored his butt's absurdity. His dehumanization of "that wretch Bruce," whose offense was tediousness, continued posthumously: "just while we were laughing at him, and you were begging me to point him out. So goes on the Tragi Comedy of the world. I cannot think without tenderness and self reproach of the decent looking spruce old twaddle who is now lying no more. He has left bores enough behind him to keep up the breed." Macaulay was even more unsparing of a cousin who died "in a strange sudden way. She had a brute of a husband and he had a jade of a wife—He used to beat her; & she richly deserved it."[10] Battery was alien to Macaulay's ordinary experience. Here his voice sounds cruel but formulaic. It is powerless to convey either the woman's agony—terrified screams, spilled blood, blackened eyes, and broken bones—or the cuckold's blind rage. He knew the words but could not imagine the people of whom he wrote.

That disembodied fluency also informed his representations of historical characters, even of King William III, the hero whom he labored to resuscitate. Macaulay's ancient masters taught him how to overlook physical details in order to penetrate the depths of human character:

> He was now in his thirty-seventh year. But both in body and in mind he was older than other men of the same age . . . his features were such as no artist could fail to seize and such as, once seen, could never be forgotten. His name at once calls up before us a slender and feeble frame, a lofty and ample forehead, a nose curved like the beak of an eagle, an eye rivaling that of an eagle in brightness and keenness, a thoughtful somewhat sullen brow, a firm and somewhat peevish mouth, a cheek pale, thin, and deeply furrowed by sickness and by care. That pensive, severe, and solemn aspect could scarcely have belonged to a happy or goodhumored man. But it indicates in a manner not to be mistaken capacity equal to the most arduous enterprises, and fortitude not to be shaken by reverses or dangers.

Macaulay's profusion may or may not succeed in evoking William's character, but it misses obvious features of his body. He was not quite five feet six inches tall, and his hands and feet resembled a child's. His hair was brown and thick, and his portraits show brown eyes. After 1675 his cheeks were pockmarked, and his cough was constant and deep.[11]

When trying to describe other people, Macaulay could fix on a detail and turn it into an epithet—"venerable white headed"—or an epitome. Once at a dinner party he noticed a man and "envied his eminently fine face & his youth" but then "pitied him from my heart. Poor creature. He could not walk." Establishing his inferiority, his disability swamped Macaulay's envious first impression. But Macaulay knew his own face, and, more than most of us, he cringed at images of it: "Then came Fry, bringing me a hideous photograph of myself, ugly beyond all names of ugliness, & begging me to go again to have this delicious likeness re-touched. I was thoroughly provoked & gave him a piece of my mind." When the Trevelyans "laughed at it," he was mollified. Of an earlier da-guerreotype, he wrote, "Very like, I doubt not, but with the usual faults" of such likenesses. But five months later he rejected it as a "hideous . . . caricature" and demanded that an engraving of it be dropped from the American edition of his *History:* "I look sensual, impudent, and sulky at once." His publisher's London representative was perplexed: "it seemed to us to be an excellent likeness, though perhaps it had somewhat too stern a look." The only portrait he deemed "excellent," one of his broth-ers thought "not at all like Tom either in feature or expression." When Macaulay liked what he saw in images of himself, he avoided physical detail and discerned characteristics: "It is the face of a man of consider-able mental powers, great boldness, and frankness, and a quick relish for pleasure . . . I am quite content to have such a physiognomy." Despite his sensitivity about how painters and daguerreotypists represented him, his grooming was stubbornly haphazard: "My hair cut—A prodigious thing —It had not been cut for six months."[12]

Macaulay's inattention to human bodies parallels his aptitude for quick judgments based on superficial impressions. Confronted with the unfa-miliar, he tended to react out of prejudice. During April 1856 two prom-inent foreigners crossed his path: "the American minister—a venerable white headed old gentleman" and "Cavour the Sardinian minister, a very inferior person." George Dallas was a patrician, perhaps more at home in London than in Washington. Camillo Cavour, the prime minister of Piedmont-Sardinia, was then becoming the principal architect of the Italian state. When he visited Macaulay, he was campaigning to win En-glish support for expelling the Austrians from Italy. With Macaulay, first impressions often became lasting judgments unless he took umbrage. Two months later he downgraded Dallas for objecting to the exclusion of an improperly dressed "Yankee" from a royal levee: "I had hoped . . . that D was a man of good sense & good feeling. I am sorry to be unde-ceived." Then he went into free fall: "Dallas—a dirty dog!"[13]

Macaulay's disdain for Cavour, who, it is said, accomplished "in a short life span of fifty-one years more than any other European statesmen did in that era," owed something to his avoidance of the diplomatic circuit and his increasing aversion to strangers. But it also illustrates a lifelong habit. Because he craved insularity and shunned depths and variety both in human relations and in ideas, he engaged narrowly while avoiding and excluding widely. At twenty-five the American novelist Norman Mailer published a best-seller that became a classic and found that "it's not automatic or easy afterward to look upon other people with a simple interest, because generally they're more interested in us than we are in them." Put another way, "Individuals primed with power anchor too heavily on their vantage points and demonstrate reduced accuracy when assessing the emotions and thoughts of others."[14]

Success quickly constricted Macaulay's vantage point. When the abolitionist patriarch William Wilberforce died on 29 July 1833, Macaulay was enjoying fame, tasting power, and anticipating wealth. Three letters he wrote over the next two days exhibit the limits of his compassion. On the thirtieth he commiserated with his father: "I know how acutely you will feel this event . . . Even I, who have known so much less of him, cannot but be greatly affected at the loss of so great a man and so affectionate a friend." Later that day he wrote to an associate in Leeds expressing even more affection for Wilberforce but without mentioning any sense of "loss": "He was a very kind friend to me, and I loved him much." Writing to Hannah ("My love") the next day, "T B M" described his dear "friend" as

a man with a ruined fortune, a weak spine, a worn out stomach, a vixen wife and a reprobate son . . . I was truly fond of him—that is "je l'aimais comme l'on aime." And how is that? How very little one human being generally cares for another! How very little the world misses any body! . . . I thought as I walked back from Cadogan place [after viewing Wilberforce's corpse] . . . that our own selfishness when others are taken away ought to teach us how little others will suffer at losing us. I thought that, if I were to die to morrow, not one of the fine people whom I dine with every week will take . . . less on Saturday at the table to which I was invited to meet them, or will smile less gaily at the ladies over the Champagne. And I am quite even with them . . . There are not ten people in the world whose deaths would spoil my dinner. But there are one or two whose deaths would break my heart. The more I see of the world,—the more numerous my acquaintance becomes, the narrower and more exclusive my affection grows, the more I cling to my darling sisters, and to one or two old tried friends of my more quiet days.

He had confided the same bleak view of human relations to Margaret before he was thirty and she broke his heart by marrying. But as if shunning the human toll of his emotional exclusivity, he inserted an elevating biblical allusion for Hannah's benefit: "But why should I go preaching to you out of Ecclesiastes?": "Vanity of vanities, saith the preacher: all is vanity."[15] Tom's sermon would prove to be prophetic.

His inward-turning "affection" was at least as precocious as his literacy, his articulateness, and his memory. Before he was six, he had been sent to a neighborhood school. Memories of his reaction lasted within his family: "no one ever crept more unwillingly to school." "His reluctance to leave home had more than one side to it. Not only did his heart stay behind, but the regular lessons of the class took him away from occupations which in his eyes were infinitely more delightful and important; for these were probably the years of his greatest literary activity." Compelled by his father to leave Clapham for boarding school at twelve, he delighted in excluding his schoolmates from his room and felt "ever more gloomy" than he could remember.[16] By then, Zachary was blunderingly and remorselessly forming his heir to see human relations as primarily the realm of "selfishness," spells of mutual indifference punctuated by battles between competing wills to power: "I was truly fond of him—that is 'je l'aimais comme l'on aime.'"

When Tom Macaulay became famous, wealthy, and powerful, he could fail to recognize familiar faces. Persons and things that repelled or inconvenienced him he learned to will away: "Nothing can reconcile me to the daily sight of squalidity and want." In January 1852 he heard that an old friend was dying: "yet why poor? She has lived near 90 years—I do not wish so long a life for myself or for any body else. Wrote invitations for my Trinity dinner." He arrogated to himself the prerogative of denying another the longevity he rejected for himself. Macaulay's Englishness also blinkered his view of human experience and history. By his early twenties, he treated insular congenial or useful forms and customs as if they were universal verities and rules. Like most of our habits, his incuriosity only deepened with age. He turned against Dallas after he defended a countryman "who came in a costume evidently intended as an affront to the Queen—frock coat, yellow waistcoat, & black stock. Everybody—English or foreign—was disgusted by the fellow's impertinence & vulgarity"—everybody except Dallas.[17] It did not occur to Macaulay to ask the former vice president of the United States what his countrymen could properly wear to a White House reception.

Understood by Macaulay's family, his limited "vision and sympathy" and stunted "principle of self-knowledge" help to explain much in him that seems incomplete, puzzling, and disturbing. He enjoyed flashes of insight into himself, some of them brutally accurate. Inhibiting his ability to see either himself or others in depth, his penchant for snap judgments thwarted disciplined self-examination and fostered an outsize capacity for self-deception. It also kept him from fully developing and consistently applying his formidably analytic intelligence. Apart from "Ranke" nothing he wrote aimed to see the past as the "foreign country" it must remain. Rarely finding himself in error, he resisted correction: "I leave the text, and shall leave it exactly as it stood." The prodigy's routine of judging himself and others on the basis of appearances and performance lasted a lifetime: "These third rate & fourth rate Lombard towns seem to me very superior to towns of the corresponding rank in the other countries with which I am acquainted." The uncertain stiffness of his own upper lip failed to move him to commiserate with Ellis in his discouragement. Instead, Macaulay wrapped up platitudes with a classical tag and invoked a deity in whom he disbelieved: "But, for God's sake, do not make the evil ten times as great as it is by moping and pining and eating your heart."[18]

Fear of shame governed his conduct without tempering his judgments. His extrospective moral imagination both sprang from and reinforced his limited self-knowledge. Hearing praise from a cousin—"more than I have deserved of him, I am afraid"—reminded him to "repair past neglect": "I am quite ashamed"; "I am ashamed of myself." Condemnation came easily to him: "I gave him a good lecture. I hope that he will be the better for it. He seemed to be a little moved." Neither did the "moral defects" of the dead escape censure. He arraigned the formidable Richard Bentley for "his arrogance, his boundless confidence in himself, & disdain of everybody else," heedless of the irony that he faulted Bentley for "defects" that they shared. Macaulay's ethical standards were mid-nineteenth-century English respectability and calculations of gain and loss, personal as well as public. In strict logic, his skepticism provided him with no basis for judging anybody, much less a reason that anyone should accept his authority to judge. Awaiting the end failed to inspire any reflective summing-up: "As to me, I begin to put done to life. Death is daily—hourly in my thoughts, and gives me no uneasiness. Kind letter from Ld Lansdowne asking me to Bowood. But I dare not go. This day to be sure is delicious." He was one of those skeptics who, having decided that certainty is impossible, shun probing questions, both theoretical and concrete, and cling to life's surfaces. His flow of words scotched the philosophical urge to analyze and systematize. He was convinced of "the utter worthlessness" of studying logic. An encyclopedia article on metaphysics vexed him. He would rather have written an ephemeral comic ballad "than all the volumes of Fichte, Kant, Schelling, & Hegel together."[19] Struggling to answer questions that he refused to ask, those impenetrable Germans merely wasted his time.

A childlike hedonism—"a quick relish for pleasure"—informed Macaulay's way of life, and economic rationality shaped his mind. Whether craving things or persons, his sensibility caused him to operate to maximize pleasure and profit and minimize pain and loss. In 1849, however, he denounced the muse of the utilitarianism that guided both his policies and his life. "Trash—by a trashy man and about a trashy man—How Bentham ever imposed on me at all I cannot now understand; and yet he imposed on me less than on any other person, I think, who entered life at the same time with me and in the same circumstances. The truest words that he uttered are those which he used . . . to repeat in old age: 'An old old driveller am I, Which nobody nobody can deny.' I only wish that I had spared James Mill more and used the whipcord more unsparingly against old Jeremy." Four years later Macaulay praised him in the House of Commons: "Of Mr Bentham's moral and political speculations, I entertain, I must own, a very mean opinion: but I hold him in high esteem as a jurist." The "political speculations" that Macaulay scorned were perhaps the democratic ones which Bentham embraced late in life. But what in the moral theory of "old Jeremy" affronted him, who consistently, perhaps instinctively, found pleasure the only good and pain the only evil? Perhaps it was that Bentham, neither a nationalist nor an imperialist, coined the word "international" and pointed toward what was later called "liberal internationalism."[20]

Despite Macaulay's professed "mean opinion," his sensibility left him with no alternative to the ways of utility and the means of calculation. He finally revered Bentham as "a dead lion." Macaulay reread John Locke's books with a view to discussing them in the *History,* but the doctrine of natural rights, including that of revolution, persuaded him, firmly Hobbist and a convert to counterrevolution, to give Locke a slight nod as an enemy of "tyranny and persecution" and a polite bow as the precursor of the "illustrious" Adam Smith. Locke's *Essay Concerning Human Understanding* proved no more acceptable. Macaulay wanted to include "a short neat character of L[ocke]'s great book," but then he discovered an "error which pervades" it: confounding "mere words" with ideas.[21] By instinct and hence in philosophy, Macaulay believed that only particulars were real and all abstractions "mere words." The philosophy became the formidably imaginative, bookish, and articulate little boy and the intimidating and often intimidated child who grew up to be a masterful "haranguer": a rhetorician whose powerful words could conjure a plausible reality.

For all that Macaulay embodied the stereotype of Economic Man, savoring and celebrating the growth of consumption, his easy sentimentality betrayed his insatiable neediness. A depressed skeptic who was often nervous in the midst of towering success, he wanted to feel more than he could. Waiting for the end, he traced his weeping to habitual anxiety: "I have shed no tears during some days. Though with me tears wait only leave to flow." They served to mask and mitigate the ruthlessness with which he regarded the world. Notwithstanding everything his experience and intelligence taught him about the human "Tragi Comedy," more than most of us he never outgrew the need to believe in the possibility of a secure happiness. The disjunction between his knowledge and his desire guaranteed frustration. Reacting to Dante, he defined what he wanted from life: "reading the Purgatorio with exceeding delight. There is a sweet happy tranquillity about that poem wh. I find nowhere else. The Inferno is all darkness & misery. The enjoyments of Paradiso are unintelligible. But a state of suffering yet of hope and love furnishes abundance of the most soothing and winning imagery." Finding heaven "unintelligible" but "hope and love" indispensable, he was sustained by the prospect of progress: "I so much feebler and more broken—Yet it is pleasant to think that though we pass away, the world goes on improving—Home by omnibus—Wrote."[22] Willed rather than an expression of instinctive hopefulness, Macaulay's emphatic optimism was vulnerable. The fear of dissolution that almost undid him in Calcutta remained until the day he died. Lacking the conviction that human existence is ultimately mysterious, he could not reconcile his besetting sadness with the hopeful story he needed to believe about England and himself.

Macaulay had his fair share of banality, but he was no monster. Habitual conformity to propriety and physical vulnerability regulated his conduct, and his easy anger seldom caused him to harm other people: "I think prompt payment a moral duty"; "I am therefore a very opulent man, and well able to help others, which I will do as opportunities offer." What, then, rendered him blind to both Hannah's "agony" when he dragged her to India and her refusal to lose her husband to India? Why did he regard the subcontinent's culture and people with sovereign contempt, brush off starving Scottish Highlanders—perhaps including his kin—fail to imagine the past and its people deeply and sympathetically, and identify civilizing "eradication" as an occasionally merciful imperial policy? Why, after learning of his peerage during the Indian revolt, did he fix "the poor women at Delhi & Cawnpoor [all strangers to him] . . . more in my thoughts than my coronet"?[23] What connected his formidably articulate intelligence, his huge memory, his stunted introspection and empathy, and his rich imagination?

In 1857 the rebellious Indians seemed to reveal to Macaulay something of the paradox of his sensibility: "But it is painful to be so revengeful as I feel myself . . . I, who cannot bear to see a beast or bird in pain; could look on without winking while Nana Sahib underwent all the tortures of [François] Ravaillac." Lodged in his memory, that seventeenth-century French regicide "before being drawn and quartered . . . was scalded with burning sulphur, molten lead and boiling oil and resin, his flesh then being torn by pincers. Then his arms and legs were attached to horses which pulled in opposite directions . . . 'the animal was full of vigour and pulled away a thigh.' After an hour and a half of this horrendous cruelty, Ravaillac died." A process of association and reassociation governed Macaulay's imagination. Here he associated words he read in some book with condign revenge on perfidy, retained the association, and reassociated it with punishing an Indian rebel's villainy. Ravaillac's tortures were even more alien to his experience than wife-beating. Innocent of the smell of burning human flesh and the sight of it vivisected, he bloodlessly repeated "mere words." But the compelling diction of other stories made them real in his visual imagination. A newspaper account of the "suicide of a poor girl . . . quite broke my heart": "I cannot get it out of my thoughts, or help crying when I think of it."[24]

Accounts of women dying young, as Margaret had unforgettably, did not exhaust Macaulay's capacity to enliven abstractions that stirred him. From childhood he lived mostly within his own mind, which he stocked with abundant fuel for the powerful but selective engine of his imagination. Regulating his input of external reality enabled him to see and feel some virtual realities he stored there, even as he ignored perceptible realities or reduced them to abstractions. For him, England and its empire were palpable, like the images conjured by the words on the pages of Thucydides that he bled over in Calcutta. The faceless Englishwomen killed by the Indian rebels embodied the empire imperiled, just as the faceless Indians whose torture he fantasized embodied its peril. For Macaulay, affliction was a virtual reality whose details he could either fixate on or block out, rather like an aggressive adolescent male selectively obsessing over violent video games.[25]

Macaulay, however, imagined himself as peculiarly sensitive, unable to "bear to have constantly before my eyes the spectacle of great misery and degradation." He joined the Humane Society because "it is a good Society, & I am not unwilling to subscribe." Far from flinching at animals' pain, he succeeded in ignoring it all around him. Human pain was as easily ignored. After visiting the necropolis that a royal had created for sixty-four dogs, he told himself: "Humanity to the inferior animals I feel and practice I hope, as much as any man. But seriously to make friends of dogs is not my taste. I can understand however that even a sensible man may have a fondness for a dog. But sixty four dogs. Why it is hardly conceivable that there should be any warm affection in my heart for 64 human beings." A quarter of a century before he had been more discriminating: "There are not ten people in the world whose deaths would spoil my dinner." Hence Macaulay could ignore the human misery that made his beloved London the "capital of poverty," much as he ignored the fetid

Thames: "There are great complaints of the stench of the river: but I didn't perceive any stench at all." The destitute in their plight deserved private charity but also public discipline and the threat of condign punishment. He therefore rejoiced at the impact of the Indian rebellion on "all the philanthropic cant of Peace Societies, and Aborigines Protection Societies, and Societies for the Reformation of Criminals": "silenced."[26]

In 1847 a bare acquaintance coined the word "self-absorbed." Fifteen years later someone whom Macaulay had known since college introduced "self-absorption" in a sentence that evokes his sensibility: "self-absorption which the habit of reverie had fostered." It was a habit that the daydreaming boy who built castles in his mind carried into manhood: "I find that I dream away a good deal of time now—not more perhaps than formerly: but formerly I dreamed my daydreams chiefly while walking. Now I dream sitting or standing by my fire . . . that strange habit,—a good habit, in some respects." "Self-absorbed" also captures the preoccupied adult, whether bloodily riveted to a Greek text while being shaved or approving a laudatory author: "He has merit—and particularly the merit of being very civil to me." Here Macaulay managed a degree of saving irony about his self-regard. Absent such irony, he could linger in admiration or apprehension at his own works. After reading with satisfaction a French critic's appreciation of his writing, he "looked at some of my speeches, & liked them." His pleasure on that occasion reflected his most basic fascination. Rereading his journals in 1856 reminded him that "no kind of reading is so delightful, so fascinating, as this minute history of a man's self."[27]

During the nineteenth century the English language grew in response to the expansion of the individual's capacity, potential, and desires. In addition to "self-absorbed" and "self-absorption," Macaulay could have heard a multitude of other new "self" words, ranging from "self-abandonment" (1818) and "self-adjustment" (1849) to "self-supporting" (1829) and "self-sustaining" (1844). Their invention reflected the accelerating change in the way English-speakers—and many others in the Atlantic world—talked, thought, and felt about themselves. Attention to the self is nothing new. Some of Macaulay's esteemed ancients explored it with sophistication. Beyond their ken, however, were the expanded range of opportunities for individuals and the increased popularity of "self-observation," a word that Macaulay's frequent critic John Stuart

Mill coined in 1829: "the knowledge of supersensual things, of man's mental and moral nature, where the appeal is to consciousness and self-observation."[28]

Macaulay grew skeptical of the trend. He disapproved of neologisms if existing words made them "not wanted." Even more, he disapproved of Mill's mature project of articulating the political and social implications of modern "individualism"—a noun coined in 1827. Macaulay's rejection of *On Liberty* (1859) was a tribute both to his greatest debt to the classics and to the three regulators of his self-absorption: his family, his reputation, and his nation. A complex and disputed little book, it seems to forecast how most of us—admittedly or not—want to live now. We want to be and to express ourselves. Mill envisioned a social order that promoted maximum individuality, at least for some. One of his key terms was "self-regarding" actions: "the part of a person's life which concerns only himself." Because expanding their range advanced human progress, the capacity of institutions—principally churches—and customs to interfere with the private sphere must be curtailed.[29]

Fearfully upholding public order and the proprieties that undergirded it, Macaulay scored Mill for "recommending eccentricity as a thing almost good in itself . . . He is really crying Fire in Noah's flood." Macaulay's inhibited individualism now seems alien. The transformation of ancient skepticism into modern agnosticism eleven years after his death was inevitable—eventually, the burden of doubleness become duplicity must be collectively insupportable—but it marks a break between his world and ours. He would be buried as he wished, in a religious ceremony in "a religious edifice," believing not in God (or the gods) but in what Cicero had taught him as a young man about the state's proper demands on its subjects' allegiance: "the first question that we ask is, do the gods exist or do they not?" "It is difficult to deny their existence." "No doubt it would be [difficult] if the question were to be asked in a public assembly, but in private conversation and in a company like the present it is perfectly easy. This being so, I, who am a high priest . . . hold it to be a duty most solemnly to maintain the rights and doctrines of the established religion." Despite John Stuart Mill's deep classicism, he never doubted that England had outgrown that inhibition.[30]

Macaulay scanned *On Liberty* as the champion of a subservient establishment and as a fair-weather churchgoer in a face-to-face parish. He knew that the self-interest of states, including England, required them to privilege and control national churches. By then he also questioned whether he could even be called a liberal. Although attempts "to define liberalism are not likely to meet with success," of the making of definitions there is virtually no end. Insofar as Macaulay was a loud prophet of human progress and urged his vision with an unshakable confidence in his own rectitude and an outsize sentimentality, he perhaps enjoys a place in the history of a certain kind of "liberal" sensibility or "imagination." As an ensemble, however, his opinions defy more precise labels such as "negative" and "positive" liberalism.[31] Though he abhorred the state's assuming responsibility for the economic well-being of its subjects, his judgment on Mill's book shows him prepared to have it intervene to stanch the "Noah's flood" of unruly "eccentricity."

Abroad Macaulay's self-absorption became almost consuming. There was no renewing the susceptibility to the unexpected that briefly charged his 1839 sojourn in Italy. Between 20 August and 26 September 1856, he and Ellis toured on the Continent, mostly in northern Italy. In 1857 and again in 1858 they made shorter late-summer trips to France. Macaulay's recorded perceptions often sound narrow and flat. He enjoyed revisiting places and noted the scenery, weather, creature comforts, and his health. On some days Ellis seems to have disappeared in front of him. When other English travelers crossed his path, he usually noticed them, for better or worse. He remembered one "who stuck to us like a burr," as well as "a Serjeant Ballantyne," whom he and Ellis met "at the station on the frontier between France & Belgium" in August 1858: "The first person who My Lorded me." Foreigners usually entered his memory—perhaps his attention—if they were factotums doing something unexpectedly to help or disturb him, or if they attracted him. On the deck of a boat he studied "a remarkably handsome & graceful Italian family." His interest was wistfully erotic: "The eldest daughter, a girl of twenty, eminently beautiful, with the sweetest voice & pronunciation, & with the semblance at least of vivacity & good temper. I never saw a damsel with whom I could so easily have excused a young fellow for falling in love at first sight."[32] He failed to describe the features that made her seem "eminently beautiful."

Two weeks later on a train to Genoa he noticed "a good looking & engaging girl named Giuseppa" traveling with her mother, an anonymous "Italian lady." Again attracted, Macaulay fantasized "an adventure that I have had in the railway carriage—the lovely Giuseppa—handsome Englishman." What made her beautiful to him is almost as elusive as his fantasy of handsomeness, but she became alive in his mind. Macaulay's imagination could make fictional people seem real as easily as it effaced real people. Reading Alessandro Manzoni's *The Betrothed* on a train to Paris moved him to "many tears": "The scene between the Archbishop and Don Abbondio is one of the noblest that I know." Returning to Genoa after eighteen years, he found it "very much more prosperous & busy": "Alone in Italy this place reminds me of the bustle & incessant progress which are characteristic of England. A new Genoa is springing from the decay of the old Genoa."[33] He failed to speculate about the connection between the city's renewed prosperity and its political union with Piedmont, or to reconsider having marked Cavour, its prime minister, "a very inferior person" five months earlier.

Macaulay's minute record of his only trip to Venice captures his inability to entertain the unexpected even as it enveloped him. He saw the city's phantasmagoric treasures not as things of exotic beauty that, by challenging him to learn more, could deepen his understanding and delight, but as a source of private amusement to be taken on his own terms. There was no question of trying to engage the Venetians' humanity. What he saw "seemed strange to me beyond all words," although he was certain that he "had been prepared for what I was to see as a man could be. I had heard about Venice ever since I was a child. I had also been familiar with the best Canalettis [*sic*] and Stanfields." The critic John Ruskin shared Macaulay's admiration of the masterly realism of Clarkson Stanfield's landscapes. But a sympathetic imagination moved Ruskin to try to penetrate Venice's strangeness, much as he championed Turner's "daubs." A few years before Macaulay visited the city, Ruskin had discovered in its art the record of a community in which the hope of divinity suffused civic life. Without reading much, Macaulay despised "Ruskinism" as one of those "noxious isms." Ruskin purpled his account of his first reaction to St. Mark's, but his words manage to evoke something of its majesty: "their figures indistinct among the gleaming of the golden ground through the leaves beside them, interrupted and dim, like the morning light as it faded back among the branches of Eden, when first its gates were angel-guarded long ago."[34]

Though obviously once powerful, Macaulay's Venice was unfathomable, repetitive, and even kitschy: "St Mark's Church very strange. I do not know how it fascinated me. I do not think it—nobody can think it—beautiful—Yet I never was more entertained by any building. I never saw a building, except St Peter's, where I could be content to pass so many hours looking about me. There is something in the very badness of the rhyming monkish hexameters, in the queer designs & bad drawing of the pictures, which has an attraction." Venice's other churches abound in Old Masters in which Ruskin had discerned the fusion of the civic and the divine. To Macaulay they were mostly "the eternal recurrence of the same subjects" or a "jumble." The profusion of murals and frescoes in the Doge's palace "shocks and disgusts me." He never asked—much less tried to imagine—what Venice could mean on its own terms. Two years later in France his reaction was similar. Rereading Plautus' comedies in Latin stimulated him more than most of what lay before his eyes: "I like him better this time of reading than ever before." But Avignon and the countryside of Provence seemed merely "bare and dirty."[35] Not just the painterly eyes of Cézanne and Van Gogh, but hordes of us ordinary tourists have seen more there.

Macaulay's devouring self-absorption also shaped his relations with his supposed friends and immediate family. In the end, he felt "warm affection in my heart" for fewer than "ten people." Preparing to become a suburbanite in 1856, he took stock of his years in the Albany: "I have lost nothing that was very near to my heart while I was here—kind friends have died, but they were not part of my daily comforts. H[annah], B[aba], A[lice], G[eorge]—all well and good and happy." Uniquely, four Trevelyans were then fully real to him because they comforted him "daily"— Ellis, too, if somewhat less frequently. Excerpting the diary entry, "G" piously redacted "comforts" as "circle." Macaulay's visit to France two years later was a farewell tour. He sought no new acquaintances and mainly reviewed familiar places. Sick, old beyond his years, and increasingly living in the past, he suffered chest pains and read "a few sonnets of Petrarch," which "awakened old feelings, & drew . . . tears." One of them he remembered repeating a generation earlier in India, "when I lost M & H at once"—Margaret to death and Hannah to Charles Trevelyan. Three days later he learned of another sister's death. A single woman who had endured mysterious invalidism in frumpish gentility, Selina was fifty-six.

Tom, who had paid her bills, confided his reaction to the news to his journal: "I was surprised into much emotion; but I soon recovered. It is a most happy deliverance from suffering which had lasted during more than thirty years. She died cheerful, even happy, as was to be expected from the piety and virtue of her life. It would be hypocrisy in me to pretend to be deeply distressed by the loss of one whom I seldom saw more than twice or thrice a year, & who was then generally too infirm for long continued conversation. Yet there were early recollections which moved me much."[36]

On the manuscript page, G. O. Trevelyan bracketed the words between "It would be hypocrisy" and "Yet" to prompt himself not to quote them in his uncle's biography. Tom continued: "I shall . . . do my duty by S's memory & by Fanny [their sister and Selina's caregiver]—I wrote to approve of all that H[annah] has done & to take all charges connected with the funeral on myself—I shall do much more than this—But that must wait till I return." On 2 September, while he and Ellis continued touring, he found himself "thinking of S . . . But it is all for the best." Selina then disappeared from his journal until he received a letter from Fanny: "told her my intentions about S's property." Offering no condolence to Fanny on her loss, "Macaulay," as the new peer signed off, replied by discussing the details of his financial "duty." As for "S" herself: "I was very anxious to know whether she had received the few lines which I wrote to her just before I set out; and I was much gratified by learning from you that they gave her pleasure." Because Selina had struck her brother as torpid during their occasional encounters, she was not fully real to him. By implication, had she been more responsive to him, they might have met more often, and he could have felt more distress at her "loss." His conflicting assertions that hers was a "suffering which had lasted during more than thirty years" and that "she died cheerful, even happy" are suggestive. How could he know? Powerless to empathize with his sister, he was alert to what propriety required of him in regard to her: "my duty." In the year-end reckoning for 1858, Tom calculated: "The loss of S can scarcely be considered as a drawback."[37] The word "self-involved" was coined five years before "self-absorbed."

Macaulay's dismissal of his harmless dead sister was not isolated. For a couple of decades Henry Hallam belonged to his regular circle. In 1854 he suffered a stroke that permanently invalided him. He wrote indecipherable letters to Macaulay, which "cruelly embarrassed" their recipient. Exceptionally, Macaulay sometimes visited him: "A duty—Alas! No pleasure now!" When Hallam died four years later, Macaulay informed Ellis: "Poor Hallam. To be sure he died to me some years ago. I then missed him much and often. Now the loss is hardly felt. I am inclined to think that there is scarcely any separation—even of those separations which break hearts and cause suicides, which might not be made endurable by gradual weaning. In the course of that weaning, there will be much suffering; but it will, at no moment, be very acute."[38]

His sister Margaret, however, remained unforgettable: "parts of the poem beginning 'Siqua recordanti,' affect me more than I can explain. They always move me to tears. They did so in India twenty three years ago when first I became intimate with Catullus":

If a man can take any pleasure in recalling the thought of kindness done, when he thinks that he has been a true friend, and that he has not broken sacred faith, nor in any compact has used the majesty of the gods in order to deceive men, then there are many joys in a long life for you, Catullus, earned from this thankless love.

Apart from Hannah and perhaps her daughter, the other Margaret, Thomas Babington Macaulay could accommodate any human loss: "Poor Hallam. To be sure he died to me some years ago." His naked self-absorption was finally inescapable. He perhaps cherished Hannah and Baba because, uniquely, they made him feel not only loved and loving but also lovable. As he faced losing his sister to India in 1859, he told himself: "This calamity has brought out H's affection for me with much effusion. [Effaced]—But to what purpose? I have what I most prized—But I have it only to lose it—My dear B is left to me. God bless her." Weightier than his formulaic piety, his choice of a pronoun to describe why he "prized" Hannah—"what" not "whom"—captures both the apex of his calculation and the nadir of his power. During the years when he frequented the British Museum as a reader and a trustee, he was unaware of Karl Marx toiling in the Reading Room. Read neither as an economist nor as a prophet but as a mordant satirist of the bourgeois experience, Marx diagnosed the pathos that imbues all Macaulay's "Wealth—rank—fame—success": "This is the relationship of the worker

MAULL & POLYBLANK   LONDON

Thomas Babington Macaulay, Baron Macaulay, by Maull & Pollybank (1856) (© National Portrait Gallery, London). "A hideous photograph of myself, ugly beyond all names of ugliness" (TBM, J9:207, 21.iv.56).

to his own activity as something alien and not belonging to him, activity as suffering (passivity), strength as powerlessness, creation as emasculation, the *personal* physical and mental energy of the worker, his personal life (for what is life but activity?), as an activity which is directed against himself, independent of him and not belonging to him. This is *self-alienation.*"[39]

Taedium Vitae

Although Macaulay sometimes mustered saving irony about himself during his final years, it eluded him that Hannah and he were now reenacting an old melodrama but with their roles reversed. Twenty-five years earlier, when he had compelled her to accompany him to India, he, blind to her desolation, had imagined that "dear Nancy has behaved like an angel." In 1859 their intimacy was still all about him, though now he felt desolated. Premonitions of death troubled him. When he learned that Trevelyan expected his family to join him, he knew that their loss would be "a cruel wrench to me" but hoped that "I may be dead before then." On 1 May Hannah told him that she and her younger daughter would leave in November 1860 and suggested that he divide every year between London and Madras: "this would only make the pain, which must be borne, more severe. I can hardly look at little Alice without tears." Hannah worried that without her shrewd and steadying presence the governorship would fuel Charles's megalomania, and Tom began cautioning him by return mail.[40]

Then Hannah wrote that she would be joining Charles not in November but in February 1860. That night Macaulay felt "the blow dreadfully," and morning brought "many tears." Unable to write, he tried to distract himself by reading, but "I wish I were dead." G. O. Trevelyan airbrushed his uncle's despair into implacable stoicism: "he summoned all his resources in order to meet it with firmness and resignation." Macaulay's dying was more complex. Privately, the family admitted the toll on him. Tom told himself that "work is the best resource." With varying success he tried, but other distractions "from thinking of what would make me miserable"—losing Hannah—were necessary. Playing "calculations"—a counting game that tested his classical erudition—provided amusement but no relief: "I could have cried for vexation." Lacking sure affections deprived him of any reason to live: "I cannot bear to think that people make sacrifices on my account . . . I am too much inclined to doubt of the affection of those who are dearest to me; and yet to receive proofs of affection which cost them anything is painful to me, & almost irritating." The gifts with which he sought to connect with Hannah continued: "H really very poorly—took her . . . [home] through heavy snow—gave her £100. We were both much affected." Her presence was the one desire of his life: "A diploma from the Imperial Academy of Sciences at Petersburg—How little I care for such things." A year earlier he had finished the complicated business of arranging his estate: "gave H[annah] a copy of the will & told her the contents." Even contemplating his wealth no longer comforted him: "I am sick of life . . . I must drive these thoughts away by writing—Wrote."[41] Using work as a therapy was another enduring legacy of Clapham.

Routines anesthetized his last months. Although his socializing contracted even further, he was no recluse. Mordant flashes relieved the *taedium vitae:* "After dinner came the circle, the short conversations tête-à-tête with Her Majesty, everything else that makes the Palace the dullest house in London." The Trevelyans continued to anchor him. Being with Hannah, her daughters, and step-granddaughters reassured him that "the connection between goodness & happiness so obvious." When Baba asked him to stand godfather to her firstborn, he promised: "I shall love him dearly for the sake of his mama." At least one useful piece of networking was left to him. He decided to cultivate the elder son of a life-long friend, and Fitzjames Stephen, then a rising literary journalist, posthumously repaid his kind attention. More than ever, eighteenth-century literature brought relief. Knowing that he would never write his favorite century's history but also half-denying it, he vented his anger in his journal and the margins of books: "that dunce"; "stuff." The besetting symptoms plagued his effort to get on with his *History.* Suffering from low-level "apprehension," he fretted about "my literary fame" and "the spite of small writers" inflicting "wounds that fester." He also continued to dismiss his critics and their criticism. Even now, research could puzzle him. His writing remained undisciplined: the old pattern of backing-and-forthing and filling-in rather than working from an outline according to a schedule. On 9 June 1859 he "finished" chapter twenty-three "for the present": a small success that made him buoyant. If he could be done with William III, and "if I live," he looked forward to Anne's reign and hence read about it. There may have been a belated change in his attitude toward the book. A few days before receiving Hannah's wrenching letter, he recorded, "I begin to take to my work."[42] Almost twenty-four years had passed since he projected *The History of England.*

Now working almost steadily, he suffered acute chest pains during the night of 11–12 December. On the fourteenth he saw his way clear to finishing off William III: "I shall have little else left—And as to money & fame—What are they to me?" His cardiovascular system was failing. On the fifteenth he had "no heart to work"—he suffered an undiagnosed attack that evening—and the sixteenth seemed to him "one of the least agreeable days of my life." The next day he broke off writing, relived his 1852 heart attacks, "and read German, Latin, and English." Medicine again betrayed him. Feeling the too-familiar symptoms, he summoned a physician, who reported that "there is no organic affection [disease] of the heart—but that the heart is weak." On 18 December he wrote "all day" but felt abandoned: "People are dying to right & left—I shall not be missed." He took consolation from Lucretius: "It is a great thing to be emancipated from the fear of death." Neither the specialists nor his family expected him to die soon. Feeling as if he had aged twenty years in five days—"dull, torpid, weak, languid—often dropping asleep" —he remained depressed and self-pitying but was less tearful. Past looking for relief in quinine or a warm climate, he also dropped his *History.* On the morning of the twenty-third, as he left the water closet, part of the bedroom ceiling collapsed "just where my head had been." He remembered a line from the Burial Service in the Prayer Book: "In the midst of life [we are in death]."[43]

On Christmas Day Hannah found him uncommunicative and drowsy, so morose that "I rather avoided being long with him." He seemed improved on Boxing Day, and she returned home. On the twenty-eighth he could barely sign a letter enclosing a £25 donation to a poor clergyman. When George came, he found his uncle "in a languid and drowsy reverie" and again tearful. Alarmed at the apparent destruction of "his self-command," George went to fetch his mother, but before they left for Holly Lodge one of Macaulay's servants came to hasten them. Housemaids met them, lamenting Macaulay's death. George reported that he died in the presence of his butler, "without pain; without any formal

"Funeral of Thomas Babington Macaulay," by George Scharf (© National Portrait Gallery, London). "The last earthly honors were yesterday paid to the remains of the great man who has just gone from among us" (*New York Times*, 30.i.60, p. 1).

farewell; preceding to the grave all whom he loved; and leaving behind him a great and honourable name, and the memory of a life every action of which was as clear and transparent as one of his own sentences." He airbrushed how Macaulay had imagined his ideal death: "For my part, I feel that I should die best in the situation of Charles the First or Lewis the Sixteenth or Montrose. I mean quite alone—surrounded by enemies and nobody that I cared for near me. The parting is the dreadful thing." His models avoided leave-taking, but they also died heroically, fortified by their enemies' taunts. In any case, the accuracy of Trevelyan's account of Macaulay's death may be of a piece with his eulogy on his "transparent" life. Evidence exists that after suffering a final massive heart attack, he lingered long enough for a physician to come and watch him die.[44] In any case, history mocked his longed-for death. Officially censured for indiscretion, Charles Trevelyan would be recalled to England in the late spring of 1860.

The funeral of Thomas Babington Lord Macaulay had the polish he desired: a service in Westminster Abbey followed by internment there close to the feet of Addison's statue, within three yards of Johnson. Along with three peers, a bishop, four current or former cabinet members, and the speaker of the Commons, Dean Milman was a pallbearer. A noble friend recorded the event: "The pall-bearers met in the Jerusalem Chamber. The last time I had been there on a like errand was at Canning's funeral. The whole service and ceremony were in the highest degree solemn and impressive. All befitted the man and the occasion." He was already transmigrating into a national monument: "HIS BODY IS BURIED IN PEACE, BUT HIS NAME LIVETH FOR EVERMORE."[45]

ENVOI

Immortal

Macaulay's posthumous reputation encapsulates a chapter in the moral history of the modern world. After overseeing his funeral on 9 January 1860, Dean Milman composed a long memoir lauding him, inter alia, for never having written against "the loftiest principles of . . . rational religion" and for "Temple": "full, instructive, and amusing." The Trevelyans printed it as an imprimatur in *The History of England* until George Otto Trevelyan launched his double-decker biography in 1876. Within months of Macaulay's death, a self-taught Scots philosopher published a shrewd analysis of his religious doubleness and its effect on his identity and career. The piece was nearly stillborn. A national icon by 1868, Macaulay was an inviting target only for contrarians. A close friend of John Stuart Mill politely located him "among the imitators of Aristotle's 'caution'" about religion. In reviewing Trevelyan's biography, Gladstone observed the rule *de mortuis nil nisi bonum* but pointed in the same direction: "there are passages which suggest a doubt whether he had completely wrought the Christian dogma, with all its lessons and all its consolations, into the texture of his mind." It was not the imperial calculus of "Temple" but the revelation of Macaulay's private contempt for St. Augustine that set Gladstone on his trail. Gladstone had belonged to the Aborigines Protection Society, and in 1876 he agitated against Ottoman massacres of Bulgarian Christians. His involvement was, however, reactive, the agita-

tion barely survived the year, and he extolled Macaulay's personal morality: "singularly free of vices."[1] In Europe and America the public mind
was learning to accept the mass slaughter of uncivilized peoples as a regrettable law of history and perhaps of biology rather than as a cycle of
horrific choices.

Out of office and anxious about money, Gladstone grabbed writing
commissions. While reviewing Trevelyan's book, he was also working on
an article defining every religious position in "Christendom" from ultra-
montane Catholicism to atheism—a very Gladstonian project. Without
allowing for the constructive aspect of ancient skepticism, he may have
penetrated Macaulay's reserve and discerned in him "secularism glori-
fied." Ordinary secularists refused to "assert anything" and instead devoted themselves to "the purposes, the enjoyments, and the needs . . . [of]
the world of sight and experience." Equally skeptical and materialistic,
the adherents of "a revived Paganism" played a double game. Though
personally emancipated from religion, they upheld it in order to impose
"the restraint of terror upon the lower passions of the vulgar." But Gladstone failed to tag Macaulay with those opinions, enabling him to remain
a fount of much of the common sense—or "prejudices"—that guided
his modern, culturally Protestant, materialist, imperial, and nondemo-
cratic nation. F. D. Maurice, the astute pioneer of Christian socialism,
defined what kept Macaulay powerful after death: he combined that
"knowledge of the past and sympathy with the present which enabled
him to exhibit the middle-class movement in its most agreeable, historical, reasonable form, to bring the old aristocratical Whiggism into conformity with it, to hold it forth as the great protection against the perils
which might be threatening from any other quarter."[2]

Although Trevelyan carefully depicted his uncle as a Whig rather than
as a mid-century liberal, the temptation to fold Macaulay into an evolving "Liberal creed" and an expanding "vision of an educated democracy"
often proved irresistible. The interpretation required portraying Gladstone as Macaulay's ideological heir, just as he became G. O. Trevelyan's
party leader. Gladstone, unable to separate his politics from his humanity,
knew better. The politician of the next generation whom Macaulay most
closely resembled was a great Tory prime minister, Robert Arthur Talbot
Gascoyne-Cecil, third marquess of Salisbury: a formidable public intellectual, truculent class warrior, devout Christian, and political amoralist,

who at his peak was internationally hailed as "the most experienced of living travelers in the path of imperialism." In both theory and practice, Lord Salisbury was "too utilitarian, too lacking in reverence for authority, prescription, and tradition, too cynical and pessimistic" to be a typical Tory. He offered a "Toryism for the clever man": "a clear, hard, logical creed, realistic and sceptical, seeking an argumentative basis for resistance to radical change not in the sentimental or mystical idealization but in the rational justification of the existing order." He enjoyed reading Macaulay's "picturesque narrative of events."[3]

That Salisbury read him with amusement requires no explanation. But what accounts for Macaulay's persistently large working-class readership? In 1906 five Labour party M.P.'s voted him their favorite author, one more than the Fabian Socialists Beatrice and Sidney Webb. They had probably read not his *History* but his essays, which were canonized during the 1880s in a widely referenced list of the "100 Best Books" under "Miscellaneous Works." Workers read him according to their own lights. One who was born in 1879 and became a Communist militant found it seemingly incongruous that "Macaulay as much as anybody . . . gave me a push-off on the road from the conventional conception of history as a superficial chronicle-narrative to the wider philosophical conception of history as an all-embracing world-process as understood by Marx." Marx the class warrior, however, can be read as the anti-Macaulay. Probably more representative was a jailed World War I draft resister who studied Macaulay's style.[4]

A couple of generations of advanced writers sought to put Macaulay behind them. Leslie Stephen, a self-consciously modern and gloomy agnostic who in boyhood knew Macaulay, had shrewd insights: "we cannot avoid tracing certain peculiarities of . . . [his] career to his having been condemned from an early age to habitual reticence upon the deepest of all subjects of thought": religion. But mostly he disparaged Macaulay: "a curious defect of analytical power," "crude empiricism," "purple patches," "the prince of Philistines," "malice of prepense," and "brutal insularity." Silent about "Temple," he wanted to dethrone "the prophet of Whiggism to his generation," who "for the ordinary reader" was "one of the two authorities for English history, the other being Shakespeare." But he finally conceded the inevitable with a sneer: "So long as Englishmen are what they are—and they don't seem to change as rapidly as might be wished—they will turn to Macaulay's pages to gain a vivid impression of our greatest achievements during an important period." The cultural conservatism that separated "the working classes from the professional avant-garde" worked to prolong Macaulay's cultural authority, while "a classic Everyman's Library culture" kept it alive in British suburbia. In 1924 Virginia Woolf, Stephen's even more self-consciously modern daughter, sought to bury Macaulay but with some regret at "a body, a sweep, a richness" in his essays, "which show that his age was behind him."[5] Her perception that neither she nor any of her generation of writers could command such widespread regard was more accurate than her obituary of Macaulay's authority. It was down but not yet out.

During the early twentieth century the reputation that Macaulay had cultivated in America still thrived there despite his published horror of democracy. G. O. Trevelyan, like his uncle, assiduously collected a certain kind of American. Henry James was an annual guest at one of his country houses. The continuing applause of the elite in the New World buoyed Macaulay's reputation in the Old. Three of Trevelyan's American "friends"—the president, the secretary of state, and the future chairman of the Senate Foreign Relations Committee—joined in honoring him with "a silver loving cup" upon the publication of a volume of his *American Revolution*. An anonymous New York reviewer was less impressed with the project: "THE AMERICAN REVOLUTION; Sir George Trevelyan's History Continues in Drum and Trumpet Style—Delightfully Written Narrative, by a Man of Letters. ORIGINAL SOURCES NEGLECTED." Because President Theodore Roosevelt also wrote history that disdained grubbing in archives and celebrated national power, Macaulay loomed large in his twenty-year epistolary friendship with Trevelyan. Their letters capture the Indian summer of Macaulay's American appeal. A keen imperialist and Anglophile, Roosevelt played to his friend's family devotion and embraced him as an ally against "scientific historians": "I have been waging war with their kind (pedants) on this side of the water for a number of years. We have a preposterous little historical organization which, when I was just out of Harvard and very ignorant I joined . . . A thousand of them would not in the aggregate begin to add to the wisdom of mankind what another Macaulay, should one arise, would add."[6]

The president respected his friend's intense classicism but from afar: "I never got so that reading any Greek or Latin author in the original rep-

"Heirs": Sir George Otto Trevelyan, O.M. (1838–1928), and President Theodore Roosevelt (1858–1919), Welcombe, Stratford-upon-Avon, 1910 (Photograph by Andrew McGregor; at Wallington, Northumberland, © The National Trust).

resented to me anything other except dreary labor." Twelve years after
Roosevelt graduated, Harvard "for the time" admitted pupils with no
knowledge of Greek, but only under "very stringent conditions." A cultural benchmark in American history, it was the beginning of the end
first of Greek and then of Latin as an elite educational credential. Meanwhile, classical "pedants" were "moving Greece farther away from us
rather than bringing it closer." A similar "optical effect" was dimming the
luster of ancient Rome. After World War I the "Dream Time" vision of
Greek that Macaulay had taught Trevelyan lingered here and there in
Britain, but it ended at Wallington, one of his country homes, when he
died at ninety in 1928. A granddaughter born in 1915 remembers, "We
didn't read those books in my day."[7]

During the 1904 presidential campaign Roosevelt reread *The History
of England* as Macaulay intended for sophisticates: as the work of "a great
philosophical historian." In *The Winning of the West,* Roosevelt wrote the
kind of history he preached, "constructing the frontier as a site of origins
of the American race, whose manhood and national worth were proven
by their ability to stamp out completely savage races." As president, he
formally declared the end to the Philippine insurgency on Independence
Day 1902. Twenty-six of the thirty American generals who served there
were veterans of the Indian wars. Integral to their strategy was concen-
trating the population of an area after confiscating or destroying their
possessions and means of subsistence. Tens of thousands of Filipinos and
Filipinas died in concentration camps "from a combination of disease,
malnutrition, poor sanitation, and other health problems." The British
were then waging a similar but less deadly counterinsurgency in South
Africa. After leaving the White House, Roosevelt undertook a long trip
to the other side of "the water" in the course of which he would be
Trevelyan's houseguest. While on safari in "Kenia BEA," Roosevelt announced that he was rereading Macaulay's "Frederic the Great." He applauded its Anglocentrism as evidence of a moral sensitivity lacking in
Carlyle's worshipful biography, so popular in Germany: "The porters are
just bringing in to camp the skin and tusks of a bull elephant I killed
three days ago, and Kermit [his son] got another yesterday. We have killed
17 lions between us." Next door in German East Africa (present-day
mainland Tanzania, Burundi, and Rwanda) the suppression of the Maji-
Maji revolt had recently killed "an estimated 200,000 to 300,000" in-

digenous people. On the other side of the continent in what is now Namibia, the Germans had also quelled "Hottentot uprisings" by extirpating tens of thousands of Hereros and Namas. Although those feats of imperial genocide evaded the infamy that forced the closing of the for-profit killing fields of Belgium's King Leopold in his "Congo Free State," they were remembered and later imitated by Nazi Germany.[8]

Defeated for reelection in 1912, Roosevelt made do with the presidency of that "preposterous little historical organization." He lectured other members of the American Historical Association on "History as Literature" and recommended to them Macaulay, "read by countless thousands to whom otherwise history would be a sealed book." Roosevelt soon produced his biography of "the greatest soldier-statesman of the seventeenth century." On page one he declared the verdict on Cromwell of "Macaulay, with his eminently sane and wholesome spirit," to be "in all essentials accurate."[9] Two historians from Columbia University served as president of the association just before and after Roosevelt. In 1921 a man of letters presided over the American Historical Association for the last time. Jean Jules Jusserand was honored as France's ambassador to Washington during World War I, which killed 1.385 million of his countrymen and 947,000 of their British allies. That carnage engendered a certain incredulity toward Macaulay's narrative of progressive national greatness.

By 1937 the relative decline of Britain, the triumph of academic history, the dethronement of the classics in elite schools and colleges, and self-assertive democracy had sapped his transatlantic appeal. With so many suffering privation for so long, his cheery insistence that God-given economic laws almost inevitably yielded prosperity seemed incredible even in America, whose wartime casualties had been comparatively light and postwar prosperity bewitching. Speaking before an audience in Virginia's southwestern mountain country in the eighth year of the Great Depression, President Franklin D. Roosevelt, a convert to anti-imperialism, jeered at Macaulay's eighty-year-old denunciation of American democracy: "For here [in England] the sufferers are not the rulers." Then, with a dismissive archaism, he turned on his own political enemies: "Almost, methinks, I am reading not from Macaulay but from a resolution of the United States Chamber of Commerce, the Liberty League, the National Association of Manufacturers or the editorials written at the behest of certain well known newspaper proprietors." While Macaulay's antidemocratic class warfare dated him in the United States, scholars there continued to ignore the lethal calculus of "Temple."[10]

The slow death of Macaulay's England was also dissipating his spell at home. Democracy arrived in Britain before it surrendered its empire. All adult British subjects gained the right to vote only in 1928, but class distinctions continued to be tangible and fraught. World War I's "dynamic of destruction" made for useful wartime Allied propaganda but left the doctrine of sovereign immunity in possession—not least in the United States—and revealed to too few exercising power the insatiability of total war, much less the vulnerability of shared humanity.[11] In 1920 Longmans, Green republished the popular edition of Macaulay's *Collected Essays* in London, New York, Calcutta, Bombay, and Madras. "Temple," with its commendation of civilizing mass slaughter, still seemed as unobjectionable as when Dean Milman had pronounced it "charming."

M. K. Gandhi was then leading a campaign of nonviolent resistance to the Raj in reaction to the massacre the year before of hundreds of unarmed men, women, and children by troops under British command at Amritsar (now Jallianwala Bagh) in the Punjab. When Britain recognized the Irish Free State in 1921, Gandhi's campaign was foundering. In the House of Commons the colonial secretary denounced the massacre by invoking Macaulay: "'The most frightful of all spectacles [is] the strength of civilisation without its mercy.'" Rather, Winston Churchill insisted, England's "reign in India, or anywhere else . . . has never stood on the basis of physical force alone, and it would be fatal to the British Empire if we were to try to base ourselves only upon it. The British way of doing things . . . has always meant and implied close and effectual cooperation with the people. In every part of the British Empire that has been our aim." Despite the qualifiers "alone" and "only," and unlike Macaulay, Churchill was disingenuous about the moral burden of empire. Two years before he had championed the tactics that Britain used to quell the Iraqi insurgency: "a combination of aerial bombardment and punitive village-burning expeditions. Indeed, they even contemplated using mustard gas too, though supplies proved unavailable."[12]

Across the political spectrum devotees of human progress still rejected the scruples about slaughter that Thomas Carlyle had scorned as a "rose-water plan of Surgery." Tellingly, he became a magnet for disparate

twentieth-century revolutionaries. What would he have made of the Nazis' embrace of him as a "'Nordic thinker' . . . indeed as the 'first National
Socialist'" or of the very 1970s American academic effort to read him as
a proto-Maoist? With or without Carlyle's encouragement, bloodlust still
imbued the sensibility of power, and the insoluble skeptical crisis lured
many intelligent persons to glimpse in one or another murderous ideology "a vision of the Kingdom of God on earth." Nobelist, radical, and
charmer, Bernard Shaw was emphatic: "Do not do unto others as you
would that they should do unto you. Their tastes may not be the same . . .
The golden rule is that there are no golden rules." Not incipient senility
but frustrated optimism about the human capacity to direct and accelerate progress led him to embrace the higher mercy of apparent cruelty in
terms that looked backward to Macaulay and forward to mid-century
French academic Stalinism. After visiting Moscow in 1931, Shaw insisted with a straight face, "Our question is not to kill or not to kill, but
to select the right people to kill." Shaw admired Joseph Stalin above all,
but not to the exclusion of Benito Mussolini and Adolf Hitler. Elsewhere, death waited on events. During 1943 between 1.5 and 3 million
Bengalis perished because, like the Irish a century earlier, they could not
afford to buy food. Despite the famine Churchill remembered and perhaps half-believed: "No great portion of the world population was so
effectively protected from the horrors and perils of the World War as
were the peoples of Hindustan. They were carried through the struggle
on the shoulders of our small island. British Government officials in India were wont to consider it a point of honour to champion the particular interests of India against those of Great Britain whenever a divergence
occurred."[13]

The following year the word "genocide" was invented to define the
Nazis' extirpation strategy for dealing with the Jews and other "inferior"
groups. For the first time since the mid-nineteenth century talk of a universal human ethic and universal human rights spread. Deeds continued
to belie the rhetoric. When the Germans surrendered, rioting nationalists
at Sétif in Algeria killed "at least twenty-one" Europeans. The French
army responded with overwhelming force, and thousands of Algerians
perished. A V-E Day protest against French rule in Damascus, Syria, was
similarly beaten down, and "in 1947 there was an even greater bloodbath
against proindependence protests in Madagascar." In that year the Raj

ended, and in 1948 the United Nations issued a Universal Declaration
of Human Rights. Between 1952 and 1960, however, the authorities in
what Theodore Roosevelt knew as "Kenia BEA" pitilessly, inventively,
and relentlessly deployed terror to suppress an insurrection. Aware of the
tactics, Prime Minister Churchill gave a blank check to the general in
charge of the counterinsurgency. Tens of thousands died in "detention
camps" without occasioning much fuss.[14] By 1971 the British and other
empires had shriveled, and the sentimentalized politics of "eradication"
and "extirpation" increasingly seemed obsolete or at least embarrassing.
Tragedy, however, still bedevils all power that rests on violence or the
threat of violence.

More prudent than Carlyle in life, Macaulay has been more kindly
remembered by history. Five of his other legacies endure. At home his
style of secularization continues to inform the English civil religion.
Membership in the Church of England declined by half between 1960
and 1985, and the British national habit is now to believe "without belonging." Even so, Macaulay's preference for belonging without believing lingers. Early in the twenty-first century some vestiges confounded a
Jewish American scholar holding a visiting fellowship at an Oxford college. In the senior common room over the third port the young man
next to her confided that he was gay, prompting her to "blurt, 'I'm Jewish,'" and to feel "as exposed as if I had come out." For three weeks
she had not "felt safe" to disclose her "identity": "I feign familiarity with
the many details of Christian practice that govern daily life at Oxford
colleges." Accustomed to the American style of secularization that com-
bines widespread public effacement of religion and lavish personal fervor, she failed to comprehend that British secularization has involved a
hollowing-out which discards the religious substance while preserving
many of its forms. The Cambridge philosopher J. M. E. McTaggart, a
grandson of Macaulay's friend Ellis, was a juvenile agnostic who matured
into atheism. Like George Macaulay Trevelyan, he belonged to the Society of Heretics. McTaggart "developed a disbeliever's attachment to
Church," stationing "himself outside Great St Mary's to record and complain of the ecclesiastical irregularities he observed there." Even in Cambridge, he was a notable eccentric, but his friend G. M. Trevelyan, virtually a national monument, while master of Trinity College "habitually
attended Chapel on Sunday evenings, and once, in 1945, he preached . . .

on 'Religion and Poetry.'"[15] Intoning *Benedictus benedicat* as a postprandial grace does not require believing a word of it.

Two of Macaulay's Indian legacies are obvious: the endurance of his penal code as the subcontinent's shared law and of English as its shared language. The third is exemplified in the parallel lives of Jawaharlal Nehru (1889–1964), the political leader of Indian nationalism, first prime minister of the independent state, and progenitor of South Asia's premier dynasty; and his older contemporary, Sir Charles Philips Trevelyan (1870–1958), G. O.'s firstborn, the third baronet, and the last lord of Wallington. They proved the success of Macaulay's much-deprecated project of forming "a class who may be interpreters between us and the millions whom we govern; a class of persons, Indian in blood and colour, but English in taste, in opinions, in morals, and in intellect . . . fit vehicles for conveying knowledge to the great mass of the population."[16] Hereditary politicians, both Nehru and Trevelyan were formed by wealth and ease at Harrow and Trinity College, Cambridge. Neither was a brilliant student, but their status left them with immense—perhaps inordinate—self-confidence. Both were English gentlemen in their bearing, disposed to pontificating, and oblivious to irony. Both were viscerally secular and essentially uncomprehending of religious belief and believers. Both rejected Victorianism in their private lives. Both conceived of themselves as idealists and progressives and looked to Soviet dirigisme, though without Stalinism, for "scientific" solutions to mid-twentieth-century economic and social problems. Both lacked an appetite for heavy administrative detail. Both now seem almost as distant as Macaulay. There was, however, an essential difference between them. Trevelyan lacked the will to power. Though sometimes vague and even self-deluding, Nehru possessed one and knew how to realize it. Macaulay writing in his *History of England* voice would have rued that unintended consequence of his project to create a "new class" of Indian aristocrats. Writing in his "Ranke" voice, he might have appreciated the irony.

No politician, G. M. Trevelyan possessed a robust will to cultural power and was decisive for the endurance of Macaulay's fifth legacy. A professor as well as a best-seller, Trevelyan perpetuated Macaulay's style of history into the second half of the twentieth century by helping to transform it from a family into an academic enterprise. Published in 1944, his *English Social History: A Survey of Six Centuries from Chaucer to Queen Victoria* sold nearly 400,000 copies in Britain alone within seven years. Although he ranged from the fourteenth to the twentieth century, his major scholarly achievement in three big volumes informed by much archive-grubbing extended his granduncle's *History* to 1714—G. O.'s *American Revolution* began in 1766. Stylistically, *England in the Reign of Queen Anne* is "the most beautiful" of his books.[17]

At twenty-six Trevelyan heard Cambridge's Regius Professor of Modern History denounce the old "politico-ethical theory of history" and declare that history must now be studied "as a science not as a branch of literature"; his predecessor but one had dismissed Macaulay to Trevelyan's face as "a charlatan." The following year Trevelyan replied with a manifesto that was later recast as "Clio, A Muse"; Theodore Roosevelt became an immediate admirer. Trevelyan's argument was twofold: until "quite recent times . . . historical writing was not merely the mutual conversations of scholars with one another, but was the means of spreading far and wide throughout all the reading classes a love and knowledge of history, an elevated and critical patriotism and certain qualities of mind and heart"; and narrative was "the essence of history."[18]

Insisting that "Macaulay's History has no equal and ought to be carefully studied by every one who intends to write" a narrative, Trevelyan became the keeper of the flame. But after a couple of years on the Italian front during World War I, he increasingly dwelt in an emotional world more like Thucydides' than that which his great-uncle had trumpeted. It was marked by "an inherent sadness that sprang from his sense of the tragic plight of humanity and the inevitable isolation of the individual in Time." Trevelyan wrote the article in *The Times* commemorating the hundredth anniversary of Macaulay's death and misled a subsequent Regius Professor about the contents of Macaulay's closely watched papers. Trevelyan's fear was of "those Bloomsbury people laughing at my great-uncle" fixated on Margaret and Hannah. An ascetic, he was blind to the ethical implications of Macaulay's religious doubleness and political amorality. As a young man Trevelyan accepted democracy as "my religion, whereby I live and move and have my being," but throughout his life "he remained equivocal and uncertain about the British Empire, which he always thought a . . . formidable instrument of aggression and domination."[19] Despite Trevelyan's embrace of democracy and ambivalence about imperialism, he apparently failed to grasp the meaning and

"Heirs": George Macaulay Trevelyan, O.M. (1876–1962), by Francis Dodd (© National Portrait Gallery, London).

consequences of "Temple." He stands as a silent witness to the hold of the modern belief that civilizing slaughter, however undesirable or unpleasant, is inevitable.

At thirty-five he was grooming Theodore Macaulay Trevelyan, his middle child, as his intellectual heir. In mid-April 1911 the boy died at four, and his father "was never quite the same." As a young man, Trevelyan held a Trinity fellowship, but he became an academic only upon assuming the Regius professorship in 1928. For six years he attracted no research students. Then a twenty-three-year-old "from an almost unknown and certainly despised University College" who admired his "volumes on Queen Anne's reign" approached him. "Frozen by nerves," J. H. Plumb waited to speak until he was spoken to. Finally, the equally embarrassed Trevelyan asked what his topic was; the reply: "Elections to the House of Commons in the Reign of William III." For ten minutes Plumb explained his research agenda and was then told, "Good. Quite good. Good," and invited to report back at the end of term unless problems arose. They became friends, and Plumb practiced and championed Trevelyan's kind of history "at the nadir of his reputation": "to tell for his time the story of great events and to reach through these events to human character—its heroism, its endurance, its follies and its weaknesses. He was searching like a poet for human truth in time and attempting to make us feel it." Plumb refined a version of Macaulay's voice that could appeal to democratic and postimperial sensibilities. Leading Sir John to publish and lecture far afield, dedication to "the social function of history" proved to be profitable. In 2001 the son of "a shoe clicker in a boot and shoe factory" left an estate of £1.375 million.[20]

During the late spring of 1980, while Plumb lamented the eclipse of Trevelyan's reputation, a necessary reaction against the long "massive condescension" of historians toward the marginalized majority was already a couple of decades old. Groundbreaking work on the history of race, gender and sexuality, and class was enriching and complicating our view of the past. But as early as 1979 Lawrence Stone, one of the most creative and prolific of the latest wave of new historians, predicted "the revival of narrative."[21] Some of the younger scholars whom Plumb mentored have helped to vindicate that intuition, among them John Brewer, David Cannadine, Linda Colley, Niall Ferguson, Geoffrey Parker, the late Roy Porter, David Reynolds, and Simon Schama.

"Heirs": Sir John Harold Plumb (1911–2001), by Bernard Lee ("Bern") Schwartz (© National Portrait Gallery, London).

Plumb taught his students the lessons of "scientific" history: analyzing historical problems, digging in archives, and avoiding anachronism and boosterism. They learned as well that when Trevelyan had invoked the Muse of History at the start of the twentieth century, the weight of knowledge was collapsing broad-gauge stories about the past, frustrating credible replacements, and choking academic prose. Plumb therefore insisted that "reaching a wide public is the most exacting challenge you can have as a scholar, without compromising the truth or the complexities of what you want to say."[22] When Thomas Babington Macaulay put his mind to it, he could make the heady allure of power all too accessible to "a wide public."

ABBREVIATIONS

AT	Alice Trevelyan
BL	British Library
C & P	Thomas Babington Macaulay, *Selected Writings,* ed. John Clive and Thomas Pinney (Chicago: University of Chicago Press, 1972)
CET	Charles Edward Trevelyan
ER	*Edinburgh Review*
FM	Frances (Fanny) Macaulay
GOT	George Otto Trevelyan
HMT	Hannah Macaulay Trevelyan
HOE	[Thomas Babington] *Macaulay's History of England from the Accession of James II,* 4 vols. (London: Dent/Everyman's Library, 1906)
J	Thomas Babington Macaulay, Manuscript Journals, 11 vols., Trinity College, Cambridge, Library
JC	John Clive, *Macaulay: The Shaping of the Historian* (New York: Knopf, 1973)
L	Thomas Pinney, ed., *The Letters of Thomas Babington Macaulay,* 6 vols. (Cambridge: Cambridge University Press, 1974–1981)
LLLM	George Otto Trevelyan, *The Life and Letters of Lord Macaulay,* 2 vols. (1876; reprint, London: Oxford University Press/Humphrey Milford, 1932)
MMC	Margaret Macaulay Cropper
MT	Margaret Trevelyan
ODNB	H. C. G. Matthew and Brian Harrison, eds., *Oxford Dictionary of National Biography: in Association with the British Academy: From the Earliest Times to the Year 2000,* 60 vols. (Oxford: Oxford University Press, 2004)

OED	*The Compact Edition of the Oxford English Dictionary, Complete Text Produced Micrographically* (Glasgow and New York: Oxford University Press, 1971)
SM	Selina Macaulay (sister)
SMM	Selina Mills Macaulay (mother)
TBM	Thomas Babington Macaulay
TCL	Trinity College, Cambridge, Library
TFE	Thomas Flower Ellis
TLB	Trevelyan Letter Book, Robinson Library, University of Newcastle upon Tyne
TLS	*Times Literary Supplement*
Vizetelly	Thomas Babington Macaulay, *Speeches, Parliamentary and Miscellaneous,* 2 vols. (London: Henry Vizetelly, 1853)
WLM	[Hannah] Lady Trevelyan, ed., *The Works of Lord Macaulay Complete,* 8 vols. (London, 1866)
ZM	Zachary Macaulay

NOTES

Throughout the notes, semicolons distinguish multiple sources quoted or referenced within a single sentence, and periods demarcate sources in successive sentences. I cite titles by TBM as they are given in "A List of Macaulay's Published Writings," in Pinney, *L*6:289–302 ("Pinney, *L*" refers to the research and comments of Thomas Pinney). All works unattributed in the notes are by TBM.

Introduction

1. J1, front endpaper.

2. J9:22, 6.i.56; cf. 11:191, 9.x.57. J1:554–555, 27.iii.49; cf. 11:575, 9.x.59. J11:550, 17.viii.59; 2:76, 28.vii.49. *The Journals of Thomas Babington Macaulay,* ed. William Thomas, 5 vols. (London: Pickering & Chatto, 2008), 1:xiv, xx–xxi. The volumes were published while the manuscript of my book was under review. The references in these notes follow the manuscript volumes and folios and include the dates of TBM's entries, which are also found in the printed edition.

3. Max Weber, "Politics as a Vocation," in *From Max Weber: Essays in Sociology,* trans. and ed. H. H. Gerth and C. Wright Mills (New York: Oxford University Press, 1958), 125–126. Richard Holbrooke, "The Doves Were Right," *New York Times Book Review,* 28.xi.2008, available at http://www.nytimes.com/2008/11/30/books/review/Holbrooke-t.html.

4. Aristotle, *Poetics* 1452a, 1453a (= chaps. 9, 12), in S. H. Butcher, *Aristotle's Theory of Poetry and Fine Arts with a Critical Text and Translation of the Poetics,* 2d ed. (London, 1898), 39, 45.

5. To MMC, 26.xi.32, *L*2:203.

6. [MMC], "Recollections of a Sister of T. B. Macaulay" (1864), reprinted in J. B. Macaulay, *Memoirs of the Clan "Aulay" with Recent Notes of Interest* (Carmarthen, 1881), 246. "Parliamentary Reform" (2.iii.31), *WLM* 8:12. To TFE, 8.ii.35, *L*3:129.

7. "Sir William Temple," *WLM* 6:264. E.g., Jane Millgate, *Macaulay* (London: Routledge & Kegan Paul, 1973), 79–92.

8. "Edinburgh Election" (29.v.39), *WLM* 8:156.

9. Carlyle, journal (7.iii.48), in *The Collected Letters of Thomas and Jane Welsh Carlyle,* ed. Clyde deL. Ryals and Kenneth J. Fielding, 36 vols. to date (Durham: Duke University Press, 1970–), 22:265–266n1.

1. Heir

1. ZM, quoted in [Margaret Trevelyan Holland], Viscountess Knutsford, *Life and Letters of Zachary Macaulay* (London: Arnold, 1900), 3 (cf. 171), 4–5.

2. Richard H. Popkin, *A History of Scepticism from Erasmus to Descartes* (New York: Humanities Press, [1964]). R. A. Watson and J. E. Force, eds., *The Sceptical Mode in Western Philosophy: Essays in Honor of Richard H. Popkin* (Dordrecht: Martinus Nijhoff, 1988); and Richard H. Popkin, "Scepticism and Anti-Scepticism in the Latter Part of the Eighteenth Century" and "New View on the Role of Scepticism in the Enlightenment," in *Scepticism in the Enlightenment,* ed. Richard H. Popkin, Ezequiel de Olaso, and Giorgio Tonelli (Dordrecht: Kluwer, 1997), 17–34, 157–172; Michael N. Forster, *Hegel and Skepticism* (Cambridge, Mass.: Harvard University Press, 1989), 170–180; and Frederick C. Beiser, *German Idealism: The Struggle against Subjectivism, 1781–1801* (Cambridge, Mass.: Harvard University Press, 2002). Nicola Karras at www.nazg.com/iqrai, a reference I owe to the kindness of John Van Engen.

3. Giambattista Vico, *The New Science of Giambattista Vico,* trans. Thomas Goddard Bergin and Max Harold Frisch (Ithaca: Cornell University Press, 1984), para. 1106. Benedict [*sic*] de Spinoza, *The Ethics,* in *The Chief Works,* ed. and trans. R. H. M. Elwes, 2 vols. (reprint; New York: Dover, 1951), 2:58 and 55 (= Pt. 1, Prop. XV and Note).

4. Knutsford, *Life,* 8, 10, 9–10; cf. Virgil, *Aeneid* 10:467.

5. Knutsford, *Life,* 11. Naomi Tadmor, *Family and Friends in Eighteenth-Century England: Household, Kinship, and Patronage* (Cambridge: Cambridge University Press, 2001), 144. To TFE, 25.vii.–12.viii.36, *L*3:182. Knutsford, *Life,* 232–234. Ian Bradley, *The Call to Seriousness: The Evangelical Impact on the Victorians* (New York: Macmillan, 1976); Seymour Drescher, *Capitalism and Antislavery: British Mobilization in Comparative Perspective* (New York: Oxford University Press, 1987), 50–134; and Paul Michael Kielstra, *The Politics of Slave Trade Suppression in Britain and France, 1814–1818* (Houndsmills: Macmillan, 2000), 7–15.

6. Knutsford, *Life,* 171, 271. Pinney, *L*1:xxv–xxvi; cf. *LLLM* 1:24–25. *LLLM* 1:25–26. Knutsford, *Life,* 279.

7. Catherine Morris Cox, assisted by Lela O. Gillian, Ruth Haines Livesay, and Lewis M. Terman, *The Early Mental Traits of Three Hundred Geniuses,* Genetic Studies

of Genius, vol. 2 (Stanford: Stanford University Press, 1926), xix, 690, and 149. *LLLM* 1:55–56; to SMM, 25.iii.21; *L*1:155. Pinney, *L*1:xxvi–xxviii.

8. Kielstra, *Politics,* 44 and passim. Knutsford, *Life,* 226, 227, 363, and 261n1. Seymour Drescher, "Whose Abolition? Popular Pressure and the Ending of the British Slave Trade," *Past & Present* 143 (1994): 163–165; idem, *The Mighty Experiment: Free Labor versus Slavery in British Emancipation* (New York: Oxford University Press, 2002), 48–54, 232–237; and J. R. Ward, *British West Indian Slavery, 1750–1834* (Oxford: Clarendon Press, 1988), 56–57, 261–272. ZM to TBM, 28.ii.14, Macaulay MSS., TCL, 0.15.72.

9. To FM, 10.vii.44, *L*4:207. Elisabeth Jay, *The Religion of the Heart: Anglican Evangelicalism and the Nineteenth-Century Novel* (Oxford: Clarendon Press, 1979), 16–30; Boyd Hilton, *The Age of Atonement: The Influence of Evangelicalism on Social and Economic Thought, 1785–1865* (Oxford: Clarendon Press, 1992), 3–35; and Frank M. Turner, *John Henry Newman: The Challenge to Evangelical Religion* (New Haven: Yale University Press, 2002), 24–64.

10. To FM, 10.vii.44, *L*4:207.

11. Daniel Wilson, "Recollections of the Reverend Charles Simeon, by the Right Reverend Daniel Wilson," in *Memoirs of the Life of the Rev. Charles Simeon, M.A.,* ed. William Carus and Chas. P. McIlvaine (New York, 1852), 488, 490.

12. Ibid., 490. ZM to SMM, 7.vi.23, Macaulay MSS., TCL 0.15.73-24.

13. J. W. Cunningham, *The Velvet Cushion,* 10th ed. (London, 1816), 17. Charles Smyth, *Simeon and Church Order: A Study of the Origins of the Evangelical Revival in Cambridge in the Eighteenth Century* (Cambridge: Cambridge University Press, 1940), 201–312. A. W. Brown, *Recollections of the Conversation Parties of the Rev. Charles Simeon* (1863), as quoted in Jay, *Religion of the Heart,* 43. James Stephen, in Robert Isaac Wilberforce and Samuel Wilberforce, *The Life of William Wilberforce,* 2d ed., 5 vols. (London, 1839), 3:390–391.

14. William Wilberforce, *A Practical View of the Prevailing Religious System of Professed Christians, in the Higher and Middle Classes in This Country, Contrasted with Real Christianity* (London, 1797), 296, 411–412.

15. David W. Bebbington, *Evangelicalism in Modern Britain: A History from the 1730s to the 1980s* (London: Unwin, Hyman, 1989), 81. Grayson Carter, *Anglican Evangelicals: Protestant Secessions from the "Via Media," c. 1800–1850* (Oxford: Oxford University Press, 2001), 1–57. Wilson, "Recollections," 490. Carter, *Anglican Evangelicals,* 156.

16. John Gascoigne, *Cambridge in the Age of the Enlightenment: Science, Religion and Politics from the Restoration to the French Revolution* (Cambridge: Cambridge University Press, 1989), 237–270. Wilson, "Recollections," 488. ZM, quoted in Knutsford, *Life,* 411.

17. Wilson, "Recollections," 488. For antecedents in antiquity, Terry Owen,

"Macaulay's Secondhand Theory of Poetry," *South Atlantic Quarterly* 72 (1973): 280–294; for Bacon, Karl R. Wallace, *Francis Bacon on Communication and Rhetoric, or: The Art of Applying Reason to Imagination for the Better Moving of the Will* (Chapel Hill: University of North Carolina Press, 1943), 27–50; Robert M. Schuler, *Francis Bacon and Scientific Poetry,* Transactions of the American Philosophical Society, vol. 82, pt. 2 (Philadelphia, 1992), 11–24. Francis Bacon, *The Advancement of Learning,* in *Advancement of Learning and Novum Organum,* rev. ed. (New York: P. F. Collier & Son, 1900), 45–46, 63 (= bk. 2:1 and 13); cf. James Stephen, "William Wilberforce," reprinted "with some additions" in *Essays in Ecclesiastical Biography,* new ed. (London, 1875), 501–502.

18. ZM, quoted in Knutsford, *Life,* 112, 335, 178–179, and 155–156.

19. Ibid., 114, 155–156. Stephen [Woolf] to Dickinson, 24.viii.[06], in *The Letters of Virginia Woolf,* ed. Nigel Nicolson and Joanne Trautmann, vol. 1 (New York: Harcourt Brace Jovanovich, 1975), 235.

20. Knutsford, *Life,* 262, 263. Hilton, *Age of Atonement,* 4, 6–7, and 36–70. A. M. C. Waterman, *Revolution, Economics, and Religion: Christian Political Economy, 1798–1833* (Cambridge: Cambridge University Press, 1991), 15–112, 135, 145, and 154.

21. Jay, *Religion of the Heart,* 132–148. Lawrence Stone, *The Family, Sex, and Marriage in England, 1500–1800* (New York: Harper and Row, 1977); cf. Tadmor, *Family and Friends,* 1–17; Keith Wrightson, "The Family in Early-Modern England: Continuity and Change," in *Hanoverian Britain and Empire: Essays in Memory of Philip Lawson,* ed. Stephen Taylor, Richard Connors, and Clyve Jones (Woodbridge: Boydell Press, 1998), 1–22; and Leonore Davidoff and Catherine Hall, *Family Fortunes,* rev. ed. (London: Routledge, 2002), 193–316. ZM to Babington, 27.xii.33, Babington Papers, TCL, box 27, no. 290. Knutsford, *Life,* 331.

22. Knutsford, *Life,* 365, 318. HMT, quoted in *LLLM* 1:119.

23. ZM to TBM, 1807, Macaulay MSS., TCL, 0.15.72. Knutsford, *Life,* 271 and 364–365.

24. *LLLM* 1:24.

25. *LLLM* 1:25, 27. [MMC], "Recollections of a Sister of T. B. Macaulay" (1864), reprinted in J. B. Macaulay, *Memoirs of the Clan "Aulay" with Recent Notes of Interest* (Carmarthen, 1881), 189–190. *LLLM* 1:27. To SMM, 3.ii.13, *L*1:14. ZM to TBM, 5.iv.13, Macaulay MSS., TCL, 0.15.72. More to ZM, 7.viii.12, in *Letters of Hannah More to Zachary Macaulay, Esq. Containing Notices of Lord Macaulay,* ed. Arthur Roberts (New York, 1860), 45. *OED,* s.v. "Loner," available at http://oed.com; cf. Sula Wolff, *Loners: The Life Path of Unusual Children* (London: Routledge, 1995).

26. To K. Macaulay, 4.iv.07, *L*1:5 and n10. "Samuel Johnson" (1831), *WLM* 5:507. Walter J. Ong, "Latin Language Study as a Renaissance Puberty Rite," *Studies in Philology* 56 (1959): 103–124; Sheldon Rothblatt, *Tradition and Change in English*

Liberal Education: An Essay in History and Culture (London: Faber and Faber, 1976); Christopher Stray, "The Smell of Latin Grammar: Contrary Imaginings in English Classrooms," *Bulletin of the John Rylands Library* 76 (1994): 201–220; and idem, *Classics Transformed: Schools, Universities, and Society in England, 1830–1860* (Oxford: Clarendon Press, 1998), 1–116.

27. Benjamin Rush, *Thoughts upon the Mode of Education Proper in a Republic* (Philadelphia, 1786); cf. Edward Duce, "Condorcet on Education," *British Journal of Educational Studies* 19 (1971): 280–282; [Sidney Smyth], "Edgeworth's Essays on Professional Education," *ER* 29 (1809): 40–53; [Edward Copleston], *A Reply to the Calumnies of the Edinburgh Review against Oxford. Containing an Account of the Studies Pursued in that University* (Oxford, 1810); [Sidney Smyth], "Response to a Reply to the Calumnies of the Edinburgh Review against Oxford," *ER* 31 (1810): 158–187; [Edward Copleston], *A Second Reply to the Edinburgh Review* (Oxford, 1810); and [Edward Copleston], *A Third Reply to the Edinburgh Review* (Oxford, 1811). To HMT, 22.vii.33, *L*2:275–276.

28. ZM to TBM, 2.iii.13, Macaulay MSS., TCL, 0.15.72. SMM to TBM, 6.ii.13, ibid., 0.15.72. ZM to TBM, 5.iv.13, ibid., 0.15.72. ZM to TBM, 26.ix.13, ibid., 0.15.72. To ZM, 23.iii.13 and 8.v.13, *L*1:23, 31. To ZM, 10.iv.15, and to SMM, 17.iv.15, *L*1:60–61.

29. George A. Kennedy, *A New History of Classical Rhetoric* (Princeton: Princeton University Press, 1994), xi. To SMM, 6.ii.13, [21?iv.16], and 9.ix.16, *L*1:15–16, 76–77, and 81. To SMM, 8.iii.13, 30.iii.i3, 19.iv.13, and 14.xi.14, *L*1:21, 24, 26, and 54–55; to ZM, 23.iii.13 and 14.v.16, *L*1:23, 77. To ZM, 26.ii.13, *L*1:18 and n2; and to SMM, 8.iii.13 and 17.iii.13, *L*1:21, 22.

30. To SMM, 30.iii.15 and 12.iv.15, *L*1:24, 25–26. To SMM, 17.iii.13, *L*1:22. To SMM, 17.v.13, *L*1:32. To SMM, 30.iii.13, *L*1:24. To ZM, 26.iv.13, and to SMM, 20. iv.13, *L*1:29, 28.

31. To SMM, 12.viii.13, *L*1:32–33. Knutsford, *Life,* 307–308. To SMM, 9.ix.13 and 15.ix.13, *L*1:35, 37.

32. JC, 252. ZM to More, 24.i.14, *L*1:40n3; to SMM, 11.iv.14, *L*1:42. To ZM, 13.vii.14, and to SM and J. Macaulay, 23.x.15, *L*1:49, 68. To SMM, 31.i.15, *L*1:57. To SMM, 26.x.14, *L*1:52. E.g., to SMM, 17.iv.15, *L*1:60–61.

33. More to ZM, 2.ii.15, in Roberts, *More Letters,* 73–74. To More, 16.i.15, *L*1:56. To SMM, [21?iv.16], *L*1:77. "Observations on Novel Reading," *Christian Observer* 15 (1816): 784–787; "To the Editor," ibid., 16 (1816): 23–31. JC, 33; cf. *LLLM* 1:56–57. To ZM, 18.iv.18, *L*1:97, quoting Cicero, *Epistles to His Friends* 2.15.

34. To More, 11.xi.16, *L*1:83. To SMM, 26.x.14, *L*1:53. To ZM, 24.x.17, *L*1:88; cf. to ZM, [20?x.17], *L*1:87–88. To SMM, 9.xii.16, *L*1:85–86; cf. to ZM, 20?x.17, *L*1:87–88.

35. To ZM, 18.iv.18, *L*1:97; to ZM, [10?xi.17], *L*1:91. To ZM, 28.xi.17, *L*1:92.

36. To SMM, 26.x.14 and 17.iv.15, *L*1:53, 61; to ZM, 14.v.16, *L*1:77–78; and to More, 11.xi.16, *L*1:83. To ZM and SMM, [4?iii.16], *L*1:73. To ZM, 14.v.16, *L*1:78–79.

37. *LLLM* 2:371–373, 1:50. MMC, "Recollections," 209. Jonathan D. Spence, *The Memory Palace of Matteo Ricci* (New York: Penguin, 1985), 1–23; cf. Frances A. Yates, *The Art of Memory* (Chicago: University of Chicago Press, 2001), 1–26.

38. Michelle Zerba, "The Frauds of Humanism: Cicero, Machiavelli, and the Rhetoric of Imposture," *Rhetorica* 22 (2004): 215–240. To ZM, 18.iv.18, *L*1:97.

39. "Conquest of Ireland," Macaulay MSS., TCL, 0.15.69, nos. 9 and 10. "Essay on Patriotism" (ca. 1814), ibid., 0.15.69, no. 6. "Hymn" (1814?), ibid., 0.15.69, no. 11. To ZM, 28.xi.17, *L*1:92–96. To ZM, 18.iv.18, *L*1:98.

40. Knutsford, *Life,* 347. To SMM, 25.iii.21, *L*1:155; cf. MMC, "Recollections," 207. JC, 31–33, 59–60. Gertrude Himmelfarb, "A Genealogy of Morals from Clapham to Bloomsbury," in *Marriage and Morals among the Victorians and Other Essays* (New York: Vintage Books, 1987), 23.

41. To H. Macaulay, 12.ix.21, *L*1:165. To ZM, 23.x.18, *L*1:101–102. To More, 11.xi.18, *L*1:106. To ZM, 16.xi.18, *L*1:108. To SMM, 30.xi.18, *L*1:110. To ZM, [22].i.19 and 5.ii.19, *L*1:115, 119.

42. Pinney, *L*1:114n4; to ZM, [22.i.19], *L*1:115–116; to SMM, 29–30.i.19, *L*1:117; to ZM, 12.iii.19 and 13.i.21, *L*1:126, 151. To ZM, [27?x.20] and 13.i.21, *L*1:147, 151. *LLLM,* 1:77. To SMM, [24.ii.19], *L*1:122–123. To ZM, 12.iii.19, 1:126 and n4.

43. To ZM, 8.ix.21, *L*1:163.

44. To ZM, 3.xi.19, *L*1:136–137. To ZM, [19?].viii.20, *L*1:145–146. To SMM, 16.ii.22, *L*1:171.

45. James Hankins, *Plato in the Italian Renaissance,* 2 vols. (Leiden: Brill, 1991), 1:25. Christopher Stray, "Curriculum and Style in the Collegiate University: Classics in Nineteenth-Century Oxbridge," *History of Universities* 16 (2000): 186–190. *Statutes and Ordinances of the University of Cambridge* (Cambridge: Cambridge University Press, 2004), Statute E, c.VII. J11:222, 2.xii.57; to ZM, 6.iii.21, *L*1:154. *LLLM* 1:78; cf. Pinney, *L*1:168n1 and 169n1.

46. Pinney, *L*1:171–172n5, 173n4. *LLLM,* 1:78–80. To ZM, 26.vii.22, *L*1:175. To ZM, 2.viii.22, *L*1:177. *LLLM* 1:77.

47. *LLLM,* 1:63. To ZM, 4.i.23, *L*1:183–184; cf. n3; *LLLM,* 1:74–76; Pinney, *L*1:190n3; JC, 48–50. Henry C. J. Clements, *Lord Macaulay, His Life and Writings* (London, 1860), 24–27.

48. To ZM, [10?xi.17], *L*1:91–92. "Dante," *WLM* 7:609. To ZM, 15.iii.23, *L*1:185; "Dante," 617. "On the Athenian Orators," *WLM* 7:660, 664, 671. Ibid., 668.

49. John Moultrie, "The Dream of Life," in *The Dream of Life: Lays of the English Church and Other Poems* (London, 1843), 88–89. Charles Knight, *Passages of a Working*

Life: During Half a Century with a Prelude of Early Reminiscences, 3 vols. (Shannon: Irish University Press, 1971), 1:299–300, 307–308, 314, 317, and 331. "Fragments of a Roman Tale" and "On West Indian Slavery," *Knight's Quarterly Magazine* 1 (1823): 33–34, 85–94.

50. William R. McKelvy, *The English Cult of Literature: Devoted Readers, 1774–1880* (Charlottesville: University of Virginia Press, 2007), 156–159; cf. Judges 11:29–40. ZM to More, quoted in Knutsford, *Life,* 349. To ZM, [ix.19], *L*1:132–134.

51. *OED,* s.v. "Utilitarian." William Paley, *The Principles of Moral and Political Philosophy* (1785) (New York: Garland, 1978), 61. Latham Wainewright, *The Literary and Scientific Pursuits Which Are Encouraged and Enforced in the University of Cambridge, Briefly Described and Vindicated* (London, 1815), 61, 60, 63, and 68. Rose, quoted in David A. Valone, "Hugh James Rose's Anglican Critique of Cambridge: Science, Antirationalism, and Coleridgean Idealism in Late Georgian England," *Albion* 33 (2001): 218. *OED,* s.v. "Utilitarianism."

52. James E. Crimmins, "Bentham's Political Radicalism Reexamined," *Journal of the History of Ideas* 55 (1994): 278–281. [James Mill], "Works of Plato," *ER* 14 (1809): 127–211; H. O. Pappé, "The English Utilitarians and Athenian Democracy," in *Classical Influences on Western Thought,* A.D. 1650–1870, ed. R. R. Bolgar (Cambridge: Cambridge University Press, 1979), 296–301; Mariangela Ripoli, "The Return of James Mill," *Utilitas* 10 (1998): 105–121; M. F. Burnyeat, "What Was 'The Common Arrangement'? An Inquiry into John Stuart Mill's Boyhood Reading of Plato" and "James Mill on Thomas Taylor's Plato: Introduction," *Apeiron* 34 (2001): 51–89 and 101–110; and, more generally, Kyriacos Demetriou, "The Development of Platonic Studies in Britain and the Role of the Utilitarians," *Utilitas* 8 (1996): 15–37.

53. Lionel A. Tollemache, "Mr. Charles Austin," *Fortnightly Review,* n.s., 99 (1875): 322; cf. Jack Stillinger, ed., *The Early Draft of John Stuart Mill's "Autobiography"* (Urbana: University of Illinois Press, 1961), 82. ZM to SM, 18.x.18, in R. J. Bufano, "Macaulay's Arrival at Cambridge," *Notes and Queries* 20 (1973): 58. *LLLM* 1:71–72, 73. Tollemache, "Mr. Charles Austin," 326, 333 and n2, 329, 328n1, and 334. Mark Francis, "The Nineteenth Century Theory of Sovereignty and Thomas Hobbes," *History of Political Thought* 1 (1980): 519.

54. Charles Austin, *The Argument for the Genuineness of the Sacred Volume, as Generally Received by Christians, Stated and Explained* (Cambridge, 1823), 2n. Tollemache, "Mr. Charles Austin," 332.

55. To ZM, 5.i.20, *L*1:139. "Oh Rosamond," as quoted in McKelvy, *English Cult,* 160. ZM to SMM, 7.vi.23, Macaulay MSS., TCL, 0.15.73-13.

56. Pinney, *L*1:188n1. To ZM, [7?vi.23], *L*1:187–189. To Knight, 20.vi.23, *L*1:189.

57. To ZM, 2.ii.22, *L*1:168–169. Pinney, *L*1:162n2.

58. To ZM, 15.iii.23, *L*1:186. *LLLM* 1:118, 117. *The Times* quoted in Pinney, *L*1:192n3. To ZM, 31.xii.23, *L*1:192–195; to *The Times,* [31.xii.23], *L*1:195–196. To Napier, 19.viii.30, *L*1:281–282 and nn2–6.

59. McKelvy, *English Cult,* 162. "Scenes from 'Athenian Revels,'" *WLM* 7:582–583, 585, and 586; ZM to SMM, 7.vi.23, Macaulay MSS., TCL, 0.15.73-13. "Scenes," 587; to TFE, 8.ii.35, *L*3:130.

60. "Scenes," 598, 599. To More, 11.xi.16, *L*1:83; cf. to TFE, 30.xii.35, *L*3:160; and *LLLM* 2:422n1.

61. To Haywood, 21.xi.48, *L*4:381–382. *OED,* s.v. "Acatalepsy." Cicero, *On Academic Scepticism [Academica],* trans. and ed. Charles Brittain (Indianapolis: Hackett, 2006), 106–107. G. M. Trevelyan, *Sir George Otto Trevelyan: A Memoir* (London: Longmans, 1932), 15; cf. JC, 489.

62. To Milman, 29.xii.55, *L*5:484; cf. *LLLM* 2:422 and to TFE, 29.xii.58, *L*6:182. Leonard Nordenfelt, "The Stoic Conception of Mental Disorder," *Philosophy, Psychiatry, & Psychology* 4 (1997): 286. To ZM, [17.viii.23], *L*1:191.

63. Cicero, *De Finibus* 2.76; 3.29, 35, 64, 67, 68, 46, 60; 4.26b–29a, 3–5a, 19–20, 36, 40–42, 43, 11–12, 13, 19–20, 35; cf. 2.104–108 and 5.49. *LLLM* 2:387. Cicero, *De Finibus* 5.76. *LLLM* 2:423–424; cf. to TFE, 8.ii.35, *L*3:129.

64. "Dante," 608. Cicero, *De Natura Deorum* 3.66–71a; cf. 3.79–85, 43–52.

65. Edward Gibbon, *The Decline and Fall of the Roman Empire,* ed. Oliphant Smeaton, 3 vols. (New York: Modern Library, n.d.), 1:27n6 and 25.

66. Francis Oakley, *Kingship: The Politics of Enchantment* (Malden, Mass.: Blackwell, 2006), 49–50. *OED,* s.v. "Nationalism." Gibbon to Sheffield, 31.v.91, in *The Autobiography of Edward Gibbon* (London: Oxford University Press, n.d.), 258.

67. "Dante," 602, 607–608, 609–610, 611, 612–613, and 615.

68. Ibid., 615–616. To SMM, 26.x.14, *L*1:53.

69. To ZM, 1 and 3.x.24, *L*1:200 and n2, 201. *LLLM* 1:117.

70. To SMM, [23.viii.24], *L*1:200. To ZM, 30.iii.26, *L*1:209.

71. To TFE, 22.xii.43, *L*4:169. "On Mitford's History of Greece," *WLM* 7:696.

72. "Mitford's History," 702, 703.

73. Ibid., 702, 703. To TFE, 8.ii.35, *L*3:129.

2. Star

1. *LLLM* 1:72. *OED,* s.vv. "Secularism" and "Secular." J2:119, 21.x.49.

2. "Abolition of Slavery," in Vizetelly, 2:285. Pinney, *L*1:202n1. *LLLM* 1:105. Pinney, *L*1:203n2; and Jane Millgate, "Father and Son: Macaulay's *Edinburgh* Debut," *Review of English Studies,* n.s., 21 (1970): 159–167.

3. Benedetto Fontana, *Hegemony and Power: On the Relation between Gramsci and Machiavelli* (Minneapolis: University of Minnesota Press, 1993), 18. E.g., "Warren Hastings," *WLM* 6:609. "On the Royal Society of Literature," *WLM* 7:576.

4. "Royal Society," 575–578; cf. J11:218–220, 29.xi.57; "Sir James Mackintosh," *WLM* 6:79. E.g., "Machiavelli," *WLM* 5:50; R. K. Webb, "A Crisis of Authority: Early Nineteenth-Century British Thought," *Albion* 24 (1992): 3–4. George Levine, ed., *The Emergence of Victorian Consciousness: The Spirit of the Age* (New York: Free Press, 1967), captures the range of possibilities. F. Rosen, *Bentham, Byron, and Greece: Constitutionalism, Nationalism, and Early Liberal Political Thought* (Oxford: Clarendon Press, 1992), 125–243; cf. Robert M. Ryan, *The Romantic Reformation: Religious Politics in English Literature, 1789–1824* (Cambridge: Cambridge University Press, 1997), 1–42, 119–151; and Philip Connell, *Romanticism, Economics and the Question of "Culture"* (Oxford: Oxford University Press, 2001). Chester W. New, *The Life of Henry Brougham to 1830* (Oxford: Clarendon Press, 1961), 154, 304. Alexis de Tocqueville, *Journeys to England and Ireland,* trans. George Lawrence and J. P. Mayer, ed. J. P. Mayer (New Haven: Yale University Press, 1958), 87.

5. Pinney, *L*1:211n1. J. G. A. Pocock, "The Varieties of Whiggism from Exclusion to Reform: A History of Ideology and Discourse," in *Virtue, Commerce, and History: Essays on Political Thought and History, Chiefly in the Eighteenth Century* (Cambridge: Cambridge University Press, 1985), 274–310, is magisterial; and Joseph Hamburger, *Macaulay and the Whig Tradition* (Chicago: University of Chicago Press, 1976), indispensable. Lytton Strachey and Roger Fulford, eds., *The Greville Memoirs, 1814–1860,* 8 vols. (London: Macmillan, 1938), 4:77. To Napier, 27.xi.30, *L*1:313. To Rawson, 2.ix.31, *L*2:92–93; F. W. Arnold, *Public Life of Lord Macaulay* (London, 1863), 116–117. "Defense of the Ministry" (29.i.40), *WLM* 8:162. To Russell, 23. iv.48, *L*4:363–364. "To Edinburgh Electors" (2.xi.52), *WLM* 8:428. "Parliamentary Reform" (19.iii.32), in Vizetelly, 1:90. "On Mitford's History of Greece," *WLM* 7:687–688; cf. "Mill's Essay on Government," *WLM* 5:270. Patrick Brantlinger, *The Spirit of Reform: British Literature and Politics, 1832–1867* (Cambridge, Mass.: Harvard University Press, 1977), 18.

6. Adapting the formulation of Peter Mandler, *Aristocratic Government in the Age of Reform: Whigs and Liberals, 1830–1852* (Oxford: Clarendon Press, 1990), 6. Joanne Shattock, *Politics and Reviewers: The "Edinburgh" and the "Quarterly" in the Early Victorian Age* (Leicester: Leicester University Press, 1989), is standard; cf. William St. Clair, *The Reading Nation in the Romantic Period* (Cambridge: Cambridge University Press, 2004), 573; and Michael J. Turner, "Radical Opinion in an Age of Reform: Thomas Perronet Thompson and the *Westminster Review,*" *History* 86 (2001): 20–21. *LLLM* 1:109.

7. Pieter Geyl, "Macaulay in His Essays," in *Debates with Historians* (Groningen: J. B. Wolters, 1955), 29. Ken Wheatley, "Paranoid Politics: The *Quarterly* and *Edinburgh* Reviews," *Prose Studies* 15 (1992): 337.

8. J2:217, 28.i.50. *LLLM* 1:110; William A. Davis Jr., "'This Is My Theory': Macaulay on Periodical Style," *Victorian Periodicals Review* 20 (1987): 12–20.

9. "The West Indies," *ER* 51 (1825): 465, 473, and 475; cf. Thomas Hobbes,

The Elements of Law Natural and Politic, ed. Ferdinand Tonnies (New York: Cambridge University Press, 1969), 34–35 (pt. 1, chap. 8).

10. *LLLM* 1:109. Preface to *WLM* 5:xii; to Napier, 24.vi.42, *L*4:40–41. Michael Fry, in *ODNB,* s.v. "Jeffrey, Francis, Lord Jeffrey"; "Milton," *WLM* 5:3. To Napier, 25.i.30, *L*1:262. Martin J. Svaglic, "Classical Rhetoric and Victorian Prose," in *The Art of Victorian Prose,* ed. George Levine and William Madden (New York: Oxford University Press, 1968), 268–288.

11. Sidney Lee, rev. Penelope Hicks, in *ODNB,* s.v. "Walker, William Sidney"; to Wilberforce, 9.iv.56, *L*6:34 and n1.

12. "Milton," 4, 14, 5. J3:3 and 6, 30.vii.50, 14.viii.50. Terry Otten, "Macaulay's Critical Theory of Imagination and Reason," *Journal of Aesthetics and Art Criticism* 28 (1969): 33–43; idem, "Macaulay's Secondhand Theory of Poetry," *South Atlantic Quarterly* 72 (1973): 280–294; J. C. L. Simonde de Sismondi, *Historical View of the Literature of Southern Europe,* trans. Thomas Roscoe, 4th ed., 2 vols. (London, 1888), 1:27–29; cf. Thomas Love Peacock, *The Four Ages of Poetry* (1820), in *Works of Thomas Love Peacock,* ed. H. F. B. Brett-Smith and C. E. Jones, 10 vols. (London: Constable, 1934), 8:15–17. "Milton," 16, 3.

13. "Milton," 17, 16.

14. Stephen to Napier, 9.v.38, in *Selection from the Correspondence of the Late Macvey Napier, Esq.,* ed. Macvey Napier (London, 1879), 253. "Dante," *WLM* 7:602, 610; "Milton," 18–19, 10–12. [MMC], "Recollections of a Sister of T. B. Macaulay" (1864), reprinted in J. B. Macaulay, *Memoirs of the Clan "Aulay" with Recent Notes of Interest* (Carmarthen, 1881), 201n1; "Milton," 10, 11, 2, 9–12, and 19–20.

15. "Milton," 39, 38, 40, 41, 42, 43, 23, and 33–35; cf. to ZM, 5.x.22, *L*1:180.

16. MMC, "Recollections," 190. William R. McKelvy, *The English Cult of Literature: Devoted Readers, 1774–1880* (Charlottesville: University of Virginia Press, 2007), 135; "A Moral Estimate of Milton's Paradise Lost," *Christian Observer* 22 (1822): 211–218, 278–284. "Sacred Poetry," *Quarterly Review* 32 (1825): 228–230. McKelvy, *English Cult,* 138. [Henry Hart Milman], "Milton—*On Christian Doctrine,*" *Quarterly Review* 32 (1825): 442–457; cf. Kathleen McSwain, "Milton in 1825," *Milton Quarterly* 22 (1988): 44–50. Henry Hart Milman, *History of Latin Christianity; Including That of the Popes to the Pontificate of Nicolas V,* 2d ed., 6 vols. (London, 1857), 6:365–366.

17. James G. Nelson, *The Sublime Puritan: Milton and the Victorians* (Madison: University of Wisconsin Press, 1963), 77–78; Joseph Anthony Wittreich Jr., ed., *The Romantics on Milton: Formal Essays and Critical Asides* (Cleveland: Press of Case Western Reserve University, 1970), 5–7; and Lucy Newlyn, *Paradise Lost and the Romantic Reader* (Oxford: Clarendon Press, 1993), 1–2, 6–7, 30–33, and 42. H. H. Gerth and C. Wright Mills, eds., *From Max Weber: Essays in Sociology,* (New York: Oxford University Press, 1958), 51–55. "Dame Cicely Saunders the Founder of the Modern Hospice Movement Who Set the Highest Standards in Care for the Dying,"

The Times, 15.vii.05, available at http://www.timesonline.co.uk/tol/comment/ obituaries/article544059.ece; and Wolfgang Saxon, "Cicely Saunders Dies at 87; Reshaped End-of-Life Care," *New York Times,* 31.vii.05, available at http://www .nytimes.com/2005/07/31/obituaries/31saunders.html.

18. Richard Brent, *Liberal Anglican Politics: Whiggery, Religion, and Reform, 1830– 1841* (Oxford: Clarendon Press, 1987), 117–118; Leslie Mitchell, *The Whig World, 1760–1837* (London: Humbledon and London, 2005), 117. John Christian Laursen, *The Politics of Skepticism in the Ancients, Montaigne, Hume and Kant* (Leiden: Brill, 1992), 63. Edith J. Morley, ed., *Henry Crabb Robinson on Books and Their Writers,* 3 vols (London: Dent, 1938), 1:341. Hamburger, *Macaulay and Whig Tradition,* 150–151; idem, *Intellectuals in Politics: John Stuart Mill and the Philosophic Radicals* (New Haven: Yale University Press, 1965), 27; cf. John Stuart Mill, *Autobiography* (New York: New American Library, 1964), 102–103. Hamburger, *Intellectuals in Politics,* 18, 22. [Charles Austin], "Greek Courts of Justice," *Westminster Review* 7 (1826–27): 266–267. "On the Athenian Orators," *WLM* 7:664.

19. Pinney, *L*1:208n1. To H. Macaulay, 15.iii.27, *L*1:217. J11:233, 30.xii.57. J10:143, 20.ix.56; to ZM, 19.i.28, *L*1:231–232. Ellis quoted in Pinney, *L*1:218n2. To HMT, 20.iii.27, *L*1:219–220. J3:69a, 1.vii.50.

20. Pinney, *L*1:xix; cf. Biancamaria Fontana, *Rethinking the Politics of Commercial Society: The "Edinburgh Review," 1802–1832* (Cambridge: Cambridge University Press, 1985), esp. 147–180; and P. R. Ghosh, "Macaulay and the Heritage of the Enlightenment," *English Historical Review* 112 (1997): 358–395. Nigel Harte, *The University of London, 1836–1986: An Illustrated History* (London: Athlone Press, 1986), 61–62, 64. [Margaret Trevelyan Holland], Viscountess Knutsford, *Life and Letters of Zachary Macaulay* (London: Arnold, 1900), 434–436.

21. "The London University," in C & P, 14, 15, 23, 4–5, and 8. Aristotle, *Politics* 4.xi.1295b; cf. "London University," 23, 6, and 7.

22. "London University," 5–10, 11–14, 32, 17, 16, 17, and 19.

23. Ibid., 20, 22, and 23.

24. Ibid., 24–26, 29, and 31.

25. Ibid., 26, 29, and 31.

26. Hamburger, *Macaulay and Whig Tradition,* 180. William R. Thayer, "Machiavelli's Prince," *International Journal of Ethics* 2 (1892): 483; cf. Felix Raab, *The English Face of Machiavelli: A Changing Interpretation, 1500–1700* (London: Routledge & K. Paul, 1964); and Albert O. Hirschman, *The Passions and the Interests: Political Arguments for Capitalism before Its Triumph* (Princeton: Princeton University Press, 1997), 33–50. Aspects of that political language are examined in J. C. D. Clark, *English Society, 1688–1832: Religion, Ideology, and Politics during the Ancien Regime,* 2d ed. (Cambridge: Cambridge University Press, 2000); Joanna Innes, "Politics and Morals: The Reformation of Manners Movement in Later Eighteenth-Century England," in *The Transformation of Political Culture: England and Germany in the Late Eighteenth Century,*

ed. Eckhart Hellmuth (Oxford: Oxford University Press, 1990), 57–118; James J. Sack, *From Jacobite to Conservative: Reaction and Orthodoxy in Britain, c. 1760–1832* (Cambridge: Cambridge University Press, 1993), 156–216; M. J. D. Roberts, *Making English Morals: Voluntary Association and Moral Reform in England, 1787–1886* (Cambridge: Cambridge University Press, 2004), 17–192; Ben Wilson, *The Making of Victorian Values: Decency and Dissent in Britain, 1789–1837* (New York: Penguin, 2007). "Social and Industrial Capacities of Negroes," *ER* 45 (1827): 413, 421.

27. To TFE, 18.xii.37, *L*3:238. To Hobhouse, 12.vii.43, *L*4:130–131.

28. "Machiavelli," 46–48, 64.

29. "Machiavelli," 79, 75, and 76. "Hallam's Constitutional History," *WLM* 5:164.

30. A. Aspinall, *The Formation of Canning's Ministry from February to August 1827* (London: Royal Historical Society, 1937), xxv–liii; cf. Wendy Hinde, *George Canning* (Oxford: Blackwell, 1989), 432–461; and William Anthony Hay, *The Whig Revival, 1808–1830* (London: Palgrave/Macmillan, 2005), 137–173. J9:259–260, 14.v.56.

31. Derek Beales, in *ODNB,* s.v. "Canning, George." Patrick C. Lipscomb, "Party Politics, 1801–1802: George Canning and the Trinidad Question," *Historical Journal* 12 (1969): 448; to ZM, 5.x.22, *L*1:179.

32. "The Present Administration," *ER* 56 (1827): 245, 247, 253, and 255.

33. Ibid., 256, 260, 262, and 261. To ZM, 8.viii.27, *L*1:224; [Henry Brougham], "State of Parties," *ER* 46 (1827): 415, 431. To ZM, 8.viii.27, *L*1:224; "Present Administration," 257. Mandler, *Aristocratic Government,* 124 and n4. [W. H. L. Bulwer], "Lord Melbourne," *ER* 89 (1849): 271.

34. Mandler, *Aristocratic Government,* 124n1. To [AT], [14?]9.59, *L*6:237. To ZM, 19.i.28, *L*1:230 and n3. To ZM, 8.iv.28, *L*1:234.

35. "Dryden," *WLM* 5:83, 104, 121, 99; and "Machiavelli," 81.

36. "History," *WLM* 5:133, 161, and 122.

37. Ibid., 123–124, 128–131, 133, and 155.

38. Ibid., 134, 135–138, 140, and 155.

39. Ibid., 140–144.

40. Ibid., 145–146; "Hallam," 217; "History," 122, 146, and 148–151.

41. "History," 151–152, 154–155, 158, 156, and 160. [Francis Jeffrey], "Millar's View of English Government," *ER* 3 (1803): 161; cf. 157–158, 160, and 173–181.

42. J. P. Kenyon, *The History Men: The Historical Profession in England since the Renaissance* (Pittsburgh: University of Pittsburgh Press, 1984), 79. David M. Fahey, "Henry Hallam—A Conservative as Whig Historian," *Historian* 28 (1966): 625–647; and Timothy Lang, *The Victorians and the Stuart Heritage: Interpretations of a Discordant Past* (Cambridge: Cambridge University Press, 1995), 23–52. "Hallam," 164, 162, 164, 169, 171–177, 192, 195, 225, 178, 218, 187, 205, 217, 211, and 214.

43. "Hallam," 220–226, 227, 229, 231, and 235–237.

44. Brent, *Liberal Anglican Politics,* 49. "Hallam," 236–238. Boyd Hilton, *A Mad, Bad, and Dangerous People? England, 1783–1846* (Oxford: Clarendon Press, 2006), 411.

45. Pinney, *L*1:252–253n5. A. Aspinall, "The Reporting and Publishing of the House of Commons' Debates, 1771–1834," in *Essays Presented to Sir Lewis Namier,* ed. Richard Pares and A. J. P. Taylor (London: Macmillan, 1956), 227. Joanne Shattock, "Politics and Literature: Macaulay, Brougham, and the *Edinburgh Review* under Napier," *Yearbook of English Studies* 16 (1986): 37; cf. Pinney, *L*1:253–254n2.

46. E.g., Jack Lively and John Rees, eds., introduction to *Utilitarian Logic and Politics: James Mill's "Essay on Government," Macaulay's Critique and the Ensuing Debate* (Oxford: Clarendon Press, 1978); and William Thomas, *The Philosophic Radicals: Nine Studies in Theory and Practice, 1817–1841* (Oxford: Clarendon Press, 1979), 134–143. William Thomas, "James Mill's Politics: The 'Essay on Government' and the Movement for Reform," *Historical Journal* 12 (1969): 249. To Stephen, 21.i.34, *L*3:16; MCC, "Recollections," 222. George L. Nesbitt, *Benthamite Reviewing: The First Twelve Years of the Westminster Review* (New York: Columbia University Press, 1934), 36, 41, and 130–144.

47. "Mill on Government," 240, 239. Terence Ball, ed., introduction to *James Mill: Political Writings* (Cambridge: Cambridge University Press, 1992), xxvii. F. Rosen, *Jeremy Bentham and Representative Democracy: A Study of the "Constitutional Code"* (Oxford: Clarendon Press, 1983), 169, 179; "Mill on Government," 239.

48. "Mill on Government," 242, 255, 246, 252, 241, 262, 251–252, 260, 261, 263, and 264–265.

49. T. Perronet Thompson, "'The Greatest Happiness' Principle," in *Exercises, Political and Others,* 6 vols. (London, 1842), 1:125. "Westminster Reviewer's Defence of Mill," *WLM* 5:272–273, 300, 274, 282–283, 292, 294, 298, and 299.

50. "Westminster Reviewer's Defence," 300. T. Perronet Thompson, "Edinburgh Review and the 'Greatest-Happiness Principle,'" in *Exercises,* 1:180. "Utilitarian Theory of Government," *WLM* 5:301–302, 328, 303, and 327.

51. Nesbitt, *Benthamite Reviewing,* 143. John Stuart Mill, preface to James Mill, *Analysis of the Phenomena of the Human Mind,* ed. Alexander Bain, Andrew Findlater, and George Grote, 2 vols. (London, 1869), 1:xvii. Mill, *Autobiography,* 121–122. Strachey and Fulford, *Greville Memoirs,* 3:280 (9.ii.36). To Whewell, 15.v.46, *L*4:298.

52. Smith to Murray, 4.xii.29, in *The Letters of Sydney Smith,* ed. Nowell C. Smith, 2 vols. (Oxford: Clarendon Press, 1953), 1:512. Donald Winch, *Riches and Poverty: An Intellectual History of Political Economy in Britain, 1750–1834* (Cambridge: Cambridge University Press, 1996), 246; Thomas Robert Malthus, *An Essay on the Principle of Population,* ed. Anthony Flew (Harmondsworth: Penguin, 1970), 200. David Eastwood, "Robert Southey and the Intellectual Origins of Romantic Conservatism," *English Historical Review* 104 (1989): 324–325; Winch, *Riches and Poverty,*

288–323; W. A. Speck, *Robert Southey: Entire Man of Letters* (New Haven: Yale University Press, 2006), 189–207. To Napier, 15.xii.29, *L*1:258.

53. "Southey's *Colloquies on Society*," *WLM* 5:330–331; to Napier, 18.iv.42, *L*4:27–28. "Southey's *Colloquies*," 330–332, 335.

54. "Southey's *Colloquies*," 331. Edmund Burke, *Reflections on the Revolution in France*, ed. Frank M. Turner (New Haven: Yale University Press, 2003), 66. E.g., to HMT, 10.viii.57, *L*6:103.

55. Southey as quoted in W. A. Speck, "Robert Southey, Lord Macaulay and the Standard of Living Controversy," *History* (2001): 473–474. "Southey's *Colloquies*," 357–358, 349–351.

56. "Southey's *Colloquies*," 342, 348. Perry Miller, *The Life of the Mind in America from the Revolution to the Civil War* (New York: Harcourt, Brace, and World, 1965), 295–306. "Southey's *Colloquies*," 359, 363.

57. "Southey's *Colloquies*," 362, 365, and 366–368.

58. Robert Dingley, in *ODNB*, s.v. "Montgomery [formerly Gomery], Robert." "Mr. Robert Montgomery," *WLM* 5:372, 380. J2:278, 2.iv.50; cf. to TFE, 4.iii.54 and [ii?54?], *L*5:387–388, *L*6:269–270.

59. Harold A. Boner, *Hungry Generations: The Nineteenth-Century Case against Malthusianism* (New York: King's Crown Press, 1955), 117–119; cf. Kim Lawes, *Paternalism and Politics: The Revival of Paternalism in Early Nineteenth-Century Britain* (New York: St. Martin's Press, 2000), 97–184. Michael Thomas Sadler, *The Law of Population: A Treatise, in Six Books, in Disproof of the Superfecundity of Human Beings, and Developing the Real Principle of Their Increase,* 2 vols. (London, 1830). "Sadler's Law of Population," *WLM* 5:421, 424–425, 430, and 429. Michael Thomas Sadler, *A Refutation of an Article in the Edinburgh Review (No CII.)* (London, 1830), 471. "Sadler's Law," 473, 475. To Napier, 25.xii.30, *L*1:315.

60. Henry Hunt quoted in Hilton, *Mad, Bad, and Dangerous,* 432n236. To MT, 7.viii.59, *L*6:232. To TFE, 10.ii.30, 1:263–264 and n2.

61. To ZM, 10.ii.30, *L*1:265–266; Frances Hawes, *Henry Brougham* (London: Jonathan Cape, 1957), 198–199. *LLLM* 1:173. To Napier, 17.xii.30, *L*1:314 and n5. To HMT, 15.ix.31, *L*2:101–102 and nn4 and 1. To TFE, 24.viii.47, *L*4:352.

62. Clark, *English Society,* 548. Mandler, *Aristocratic Government,* 125; generally, Ian Newbould, *Whiggery and Reform, 1830–41: The Politics of Government* (Stanford: Stanford University Press, 1990), 40–151.

63. Hilton, *Mad, Bad, and Dangerous,* 416. *Napoleon and the Restoration of the Bourbons,* ed. Joseph Hamburger (New York: Columbia University Press, 1977), 2–5, 43.

64. Ian R. Christie, *British 'Non-elite' MPs, 1715–1820* (Oxford: Clarendon Press, 1995), 4; cf. Gerrit P. Judd IV, *Members of Parliament, 1734–1832* (New Haven: Yale University Press, 1955), 40–41. J1:534, 12.iii.49; "William Pitt," *WLM* 7:378. "Athenian Orators," 668. To Whewell, 5.ii.31, *L*1:318. To HMT, 17.vi.33, *L*2:258. To HMT, 23.vii.31, *L*2:74–75.

65. To Napier, 25.i.30, *L*1:262. "Disabilities of the Jews" (5.iv.30), in Vizetelly, 1:3, 4. To ——, [8.iv.30], *L*1:272; Geoffrey Alderman, in *ODNB,* s.v. "Goldsmit, Sir Isaac Lyon, first baronet."

66. "Corn Laws" (2.xii.45), *WLM* 8:353. Israel Finestein, "A Modern Examination of Macaulay's Case for the Civil Emancipation," *Transactions, Jewish Historical Society of England* 28 (1981–82): 39–59; cf. Todd M. Endelman, *The Jews of Britain, 1656–2000* (Berkeley: University of California Press, 2002), 110–112, 150–151. To HMT, 8.vi.31, *L*2:36. To HMT, 10.vi.31, *L*2:39. To Napier, 17.xii.30, *L*1:314; "On Jews Declaration Bill" (31.iii.41), in Vizetelly, 1:320–324.

67. L. G. Mitchell, "Foxite Politics and the Great Reform Bill," *English Historical Review* 108 (1993): 338–364. E. A. Smith, in *ODNB,* s.v. "Grey, Charles, second Earl Grey." Hilton, *Mad, Bad, and Dangerous,* 420–438, which I follow, is trenchant.

68. Michael Brock, *The Great Reform Act* (London: Hutchinson, 1973), 295, 312–313, and 320. Hilton, *Mad, Bad, and Dangerous,* 435.

69. Hilton, *Mad, Bad, and Dangerous,* 424. JC, 160. To Napier, 27.xi.30, *L*1:313 and n1. "On West India Petition" (13.xii.30), in Vizetelly 1:10. "On West Indian Slavery," *Knight's Quarterly Magazine* 1 (1823): 93. Joseph Hamburger, *James Mill and the Art of Revolution* (New Haven: Yale University Press, 1963), 48–111.

70. MMC and SM, quoted in Pinney, *L*2:5n2. "Parliamentary Reform" (2.iii.31), *WLM* 8:12; cf. Hilton, *Mad, Bad, and Dangerous,* 431–432. "Parliamentary Reform," 13, 15; and Ball, *James Mill: Political Writings,* 41–42.

71. "Parliamentary Reform," 17–18 and 23–24. MMC to Thatcher, 30.ix.31, quoted in Pinney, *L*2:99n1.

72. J. L. Adolphus, quoted in Pinney, *L*2:5n2. Strachey and Fulford, *Greville Memoirs,* 2:124 (3.iii.31). To TFE, 7.iii.31, *L*2:5.

73. G. H. Francis, *Orators of the Age* (London, 1847), 92–93; cf. "Parliamentary Reform" (20.ix.31), *WLM* 8:42; Brock, *Great Reform Act;* 319, and Hilton, *Mad, Bad, and Dangerous,* 432–433. Dror Wahrman, *Imagining the Middle Class: The Political Representation of Class in Britain, c. 1780–1840* (Cambridge: Cambridge University Press, 1995), 356–357. Ellis Wasson, *Born to Rule: British Political Elites* (Thrupp: Phoenix, 2000), 159–169.

74. "Athenian Orators," 666. G. M. Young, "Macaulay," in *Victorian Essays,* ed. W. D. Handcock (London: Oxford University Press, 1962), 39. J3:134, 12.i.51. Margaret Wood, "Lord Macaulay, Parliamentary Speaker: His Leading Ideas," *Quarterly Journal of Speech* 44 (1958): 377. Lord Ellenborough's diary, 28.ii.33, in *Three Early Nineteenth Century Diaries,* ed. A. Aspinall (London: Williams and Norgate, 1952), 311.

75. "The Earl of Chatham," *WLM* 6:50. E. J. Littleton's diary, 6.vii.31, in Aspinall, *Three Diaries,* 100.

76. "Chatham," 49. William Thomas, *The Quarrel of Macaulay and Croker: Politics*

and History in the Age of Reform (Oxford: Oxford University Press, 2000), 9–12 and passim. Littleton diary, 17 and 18.xii.31, in Aspinall, *Three Diaries,* 171, 172.

77. Littleton diary, 11.x.31 and 22.iii.32, in Aspinall, *Three Diaries,* 150, 213; cf. to HMT and MMC, 21.vii.32, *L*2:156. Strachey and Fulford, *Greville Memoirs,* 2:203 (24.ix.31). Lionel A. Tollemache, *Gladstone's Boswell: Late Victorian Conversations,* ed. Asa Briggs (Sussex: Harvester Press, 1984), 126.

78. Holland to Moore 16.vii.24, in *Journal of Thomas Moore,* ed. Wilfred S. Dowden, 6 vols. (Newark: University of Delaware Press, 1983–1991), 2:751. "Moore's Life of Lord Byron," *WLM* 5:390–392.

79. "Moore's Life of Byron," 394–396, 418. To HMT, 10.vi.31, *L*2:38. To HMT, 25.vi.31, *L*2:54. J2:206, 15.i.50.

80. *OED,* s.v. "Conservative." To HMT, 5.viii.31, *L*2:84; "Samuel Johnson" (1831), *WLM* 5:505, 507. To Napier, 19.i. 32, *L*2:111–112 and n6. "Athenian Orators," 665. "Johnson," 533; cf. "Mitford's History," 146.

81. "Johnson," 528–529 and 526–527. "History," 149–150; cf. "Mitford's History," 695; and to ZM, [10?.xi.17], *L*1:92. "Johnson," 530, 538. Nicholas Hudson, *Samuel Johnson and the Making of Modern England* (Cambridge: Cambridge University Press, 2003), 3.

82. "John Bunyan," *WLM* 5:445, 450, 451, 453, and 456. C. Stephen Finley, "Bunyan among the Victorians: Macaulay, Froude, and Ruskin, *Journal of Literature and Theology* 3 (1989): 78.

83. To HMT, 14.vi.31, *L*2:44. "John Hampden," *WLM* 5:539–586; to Napier, 9.i.32, *L*2:110. To Napier, 19.i.32, *L*2:111. "Burleigh and His Times," *WLM* 5:604–605, 608–609. To Napier, 3 and 18.iv.32, *L*2:119, 121. To HMT and MMC, 2.vii.32, *L*2:144–145; Lang, *Victorians,* 53–92.

84. "Mirabeau," *WLM* 5:613, 617–618, and 624–625.

85. To HMT, 25.ix.32, *L*2:195. "Mirabeau," 619.

86. To Napier, 5.ix.32, *L*2:190. To Napier, 12.xi.32, *L*2:201; and to MMC, 11.i.33, 2:223. "War of the Succession in Spain," *WLM* 5:677, 684. To HMT, 9. [x].33 and 14.x.33, *L*2:315, 317. To Napier, 15.xi.33, *L*2:335. "Horace Walpole," *WLM* 6:17–35; cf. Herbert Butterfield, *George III and the Historians,* rev. ed. (London: Collins, 1959), 90–91. "War of the Succession," 679.

87. To Napier, 14.x.33, *L*2:316. To Napier, 13 and 18.i.34, *L*3:12, 14. "Chatham," 68, 63, and 73. "Machiavelli," 75.

88. Pinney, *L*1:273n1 and 2:14n2 (quoting FM) and 2:17n1.

89. Pinney, *L*1:xi–xii. Alan Richardson, "Rethinking Romantic Incest: Human Universals, Literary Representation, and the Biology of Mind," *New Literary History* 31 (2000): 553–572.

90. To HMT, 13.vii.31, *L*2:69.

91. To MMC, 6.viii.31, *L*2:85–86. To HMT, 3.vi.31, *L*2:28–29; cf. to MMC, [9].x.30, *L*1:308.

92. To MMC, 18.viii.32, *L*2:184. To MMC, 26.xi.32, *L*2:203.

93. J. P. T. Bury, ed., *Romilly's Cambridge Diary, 1832–42* (Cambridge: Cambridge University Press, 1967), 20. Strachey and Fulford, *Greville Memoirs,* 2:249 (6.ii.32). MMC, "Recollections," 212, 213.

94. MMC, "Recollections," 189, 240, and 194; Pinney, *L*1:xxviii. MMC, "Recollections," 190, 238, 215, 209, and 237.

95. MMC, "Recollections," 215, 236, 194, 202, and 207.

96. Ibid., 213, 247, 187, and 211. "Hallam," 165. MMC, "Recollections," 208, 197.

97. MMC, "Recollections," 235; 237 (emphasis added); cf. 245, 209, and 246. Plato, *Republic* 1.338–339; *Phaedrus* 261–263c, 266c–267b, 269e–270a, 271a. Mark Francis, "The Nineteenth Century Theory of Sovereignty and Thomas Hobbes," *History of Political Thought* 1 (1980): 521–525.

98. Hilton, *Mad, Bad, and Dangerous,* 494–495. "Repeal of the Union with Ireland" (6.ii.33), *WLM* 8:97–98. J. Graham as quoted in Hilton, *Mad, Bad, and Dangerous,* 495. Strachey and Fulford, *Greville Memoirs,* 2:363 (27.ii.33). "Disturbances in Ireland" (28.ii.33), in Vizetelly, 1:139–140 and 148.

99. MMC, "Recollections," 222. Abraham D. Kriegel, ed., *The Holland House Diaries, 1831–1840: The Diary of Henry Richard Vassall Fox, Third Lord Holland, with Extracts from the Diary of Dr. John Allen* (London: Routledge & Kegan Paul, 1977), 106. Pinney, *L*2:122n2; cf. to MMC, 8.xii.32, *L*2:209; and MMC, "Recollections," 216, 217. To HMT and MMC, 21.vi.32, *L*2:136.

100. To Rawson, 2.ix.31, *L*2:92–93 and n1; and to HMT, 3.ix.31, *L*2:94. To HMT and MMC, 10.vi.32, *L*2:129.

101. To HMT and MMC, 18.vi.32, *L*2:129–130 and nn1 and 2. D. Fraser, "The Fruits of Reform; Leeds Politics in the Eighteen-Thirties," *Northern History* 7 (1972): 90, 92. Mandler, *Aristocratic Government,* 146.

102. To Lees, [2].viii.32, *L*2:163. JC, 221, 227–228, and 224. *LLLM* 1:260–261.

103. R. J. Morris, *Class, Sect and Party: The Making of the British Middle Class, Leeds, 1820–1850* (Manchester: Manchester University Press, 1990), 128; to MMC, 11 and 21.i.33, *L*2:223, 225. To HMT, 14.x.33, *L*2:317. Morris, *Class, Sect and Party,* 129.

3. Legislator

1. To HMT, 1.xii.32, *L*2:207. To HMT, 29.viii.31, *L*2:91. To HMT, 16.vii.33, *L*2:271 and n1. To HMT, 11.vii.33, *L*2:268–269.

2. To HMT, 11 and 4.vii.33, *L*2:268, 266–267 and n2. "On Slavery in the Colonies" (24.v.32) and "The Abolition of Slavery" (24.vii.33), in Vizetelly, 1:115, 203. Richard A. Gaunt, ed., *Unrepentant Tory: Political Selections from the Diaries of the Fourth Duke of Newcastle-under-Lyne, 1827–38* (Woodbridge: Parliamentary History Yearbook Trust/Boydell Press, 2006), 215 (11.v.33). C. H. Philips, *The East India Com-*

pany 1784–1834, rev. ed. (New York: Barnes and Noble, 1961), 276. H. V. Bowen, *The Business of Empire: The East India Company and Imperial Britain, 1756–1833* (Cambridge: Cambridge University Press, 2006), 296. P. J. Marshall, *Problems of Empire: Britain and India, 1757–1813* (London: Routledge, 1968), 19; Bowen, *Business of Empire,* 5; Auber to Bentinck, 11.iv.29, quoted in ibid., 203.

3. To HMT, 1.xi.33, *L*2:329. *Parliamentary Papers* 11 (1831–32): 44–51. Boyd Hilton, *A Mad, Bad, and Dangerous People? England, 1783–1846* (Oxford: Clarendon Press, 2006), 568.

4. Philips, *East India Company,* 294. "Government of India," *WLM* 8:112–113, 119, and 120.

5. William Thomas, *The Quarrel of Macaulay and Croker: Politics and History in the Age of Reform* (Oxford: Oxford University Press, 2000), 149–150; cf. Javeed Majeed, *Ungoverned Imaginings: James Mill's "The History of British India" and Orientalism* (Oxford: Clarendon Press, 1992), 123–150; and Duncan Forbes, "James Mill and India," *Cambridge Journal* 5 (1951–1954): 19–33. "Government of India," 126.

6. "Government of India," 131–133. Philips, *East India Company,* 296–297.

7. "Government of India," 140, 142. *Parliamentary Debates,* Commons, 5th ser., 439:2441 ff. (10.vii.1947).

8. Gal. 4:4. To HMT, 20.vi.31, *L*2:47. To HMT, 21.v.33, *L*2:242. Adam D. Galinsky, Joe C. Magee, M. Ena Inesi, and Deborah H. Gruenfeld, "Power and Perspectives Not Taken," *Psychological Science* 17 (2006): 1068; e.g., to HMT, 21.v.33, *L*2:242.

9. "Government of India," 129, 137, 139, and 121. To MMC, 17.vii.33, *L*2:272.

10. To HMT, 24.vi.33, *L*2:261. To HMT, 17.viii.33, *L*2:299–301. To Lansdowne, 5.xii.33, *L*2:354. To Stephen, 21.i.34, *L*3:16. To HMT, 1.xi.33 and 21.xii.33, *L*2:329 and 365. [J. A. Roebuck], "Mr. Macauley [*sic*], a Legislator for the Hindoos," *Tait's Edinburgh Magazine* 4 (January 1834): 488.

11. Minute of B. Peacock (3.xi.59), in Courtenay Ilbert, *The Government of India: Being a Digest of the Statute law Relating Thereto with Historical Introduction and Illustrative Documents,* 3d ed. (Oxford: Clarendon Press, 1915), 83n1. To Lansdowne, 5.xii.33, *L*2:354; and to Spring-Rice, 8.ii.36, *L*3:170. F. W. Arnold, *The Public Life of Lord Macaulay* (London, 1863), 184. To HMT, 22.xi.33, *L*2:340.

12. [MMC], "Recollections of a Sister of T. B. Macaulay" (1864), reprinted in J. B. Macaulay, *Memoirs of the Clan "Aulay" with Recent Notes of Interest* (Carmarthen, 1881), 216. To MMC, 26.xi.32, *L*2:203; cf. Prov. 14:10. To HMT, 1.i.34, *L*3:5. To HMT, 17.viii.33, *L*2:300–301. To HMT, 21.viii.33, *L*2:303–304 and n1. To HMT, 2.i.34, *L*3:5–7.

13. To HMT, 2.i.34, *L*3:6–7. To HMT, 31.xii.33, *L*2:372. To MMC, 2.i.34, *L*3:8.

14. *LLLM* 1:326–327.

15. To Berry, 15.ii.34, *L*3:24. To TFE, 28.xi.34, *L*2:345–346. To HMT, 4.i.34, *L*3:9.

16. Adolphus to Milman (1861), quoted in *L*3:14n1. To MMC, 16.ii.34, *L*3:25. HMT to MMC, 16.ii.34, and C. Macaulay, 7.viii.73, quoted in *L*3:25n4.

17. To ZM, 22.ii.34, *L*3:26. HMT to MMC, 16.ii.34, quoted in *L*3:25n4. To MMC, 15.vi.34, *L*3:34.

18. To MMC, 15.vi.34, *L*3:32–40. To ZM, 22.ii.34, *L*3:27. Pinney, *L*3:210n4. To MMC, 15.vi.34, *L*3:37.

19. To TFE, 28 and 30.xi.33, *L*2:345–346 and 346–347; cf. to TFE, 1.vii.34, *L*3:59–64.

20. C. H. Dharker, ed., *Lord Macaulay's Legislative Minutes* (London: Geoffrey Cumberlege/Oxford University Press, 1946), 140; "Dispatch Accompanying the Government of India Act, 1833," in Courtenay Ilbert, *The Government of India: Being a Digest of the Statute Law Relating Thereto with Historical Introduction and Illustrative Documents* (Oxford, 1898), 492–532. To MMC, 15.vi.34, *L*3:35. Ilbert, *Government of India,* 3d ed., 89; to MMC, 15.vi.34, *L*3:38.

21. To MMC, 27.vi.34, *L*3:42, 54, 57 and n1. Paul B. Courtright, *Gaṇeśa: Lord of Obstacles, Lord of Beginnings* (New York: Oxford University Press, 1985). To MMC, 27.vi.34, *L*3:55.

22. To MMC, 15.vi.34, *L*3:40, 38, and 39. To MMC, 10.x.34, *L*3:89.

23. To MMC, 27.vi.34, *L*3:53. To MMC, 10.viii.34, *L*3:68–69; cf. "Gladstone on Church and State," *WLM* 6:371–372.

24. To MMC, 3.x.34, *L*3:77. Hazel M. Griffin, "Thomas Babington Macaulay and the Anglicist-Orientalist Controversy in Indian Education, 1833–37" (Ph.D. diss., University of Pennsylvania, 1972), 81n113. To SM and FM, 28.xi.36, *L*3:198. Blair B. Kling, *Partner in Empire: Dwarkanath Tagore and the Age of Enterprise in Eastern India* (Berkeley: University of California Press, 1976), 158–159. To [Humphreys, iv?56], *L*6:38. Kling, *Partner in Empire,* 10–11. C. A. Bayly, *Empire and Information: Intelligence Gathering and Social Communication in India, 1780–1870* (Cambridge: Cambridge University Press, 1999), 218–219; to TFE, 30.v.36, *L*3:176.

25. Dharker, *Legislative Minutes* (3.x.36), 190.

26. To MMC, 17.x.34, *L*3:93. To MMC, 3.x.34, *L*3:86. Balachandra Rajan, *Under Western Eyes: India from Milton to Macaulay* (Durham: Duke University Press, 1999), 7.

27. To MMC, 3.x.34, *L*3:79, 80, and 82–83. Lytton Strachey and Roger Fulford, eds., The *Greville Memoirs,* 7 vols. (London: Macmillan, 1938), 5:135 (16.x.43); Mark Noll, *America's God: From Jonathan Edwards to Abraham Lincoln* (Oxford: Oxford University Press, 2002), 148–149.

28. Conflation of to MMC, 27.vi.34, and TFE, 1.vii.34, *L*3:58 and 60. To MMC, 3.x.34, *L*3:83, 79.

29. To MMC, 6.vii.34, *L*3:66, 65. To MMC, 10.viii.34, *L*3:71. To SM and FM, 10.viii.34, *L*3:72; to MMC, 10.viii.34, *L*3:72. To MMC, 8.x.34, *L*3:89. E.g., to MMC, 15.vi.34, *L*3:40. To MMC, 10.viii.34, *L*3:72.

30. Douglas M. Peters, in *ODNB*, s.v. "Bentinck, Lord William Henry Cavendish (known as Lord William Bentinck)." Bentinck, quoted in *The Correspondence of Lord William Cavendish Bentinck, Governor General of India, 1828–1835*, ed. C. H. Philips, 2 vols. (Oxford: Oxford University Press, 1977), 1:xv. Whittingham to Bentinck, 16.vi.34, ibid., 2:1309.

31. Bentinck to Metcalfe, 31.vii.34, in Philips, *Correspondence of Bentinck*, 2:1337–38. The literature on the language controversy is enormous. The fullest study remains Griffin, "Macaulay and the Controversy," vastly informed by evidence from India. See also Percival Spear, "Bentinck and Education," *Cambridge Historical Journal* 6 (1938): 78–101; David Kopf, *British Orientalism and the Bengal Renaissance: The Dynamics of Indian Modernization, 1773–1835* (Berkeley: University of California Press, 1969), 215–272; Gerald and Natalie Robinson Sirkin, "The Battle of Indian Education: Macaulay's Opening Salvo," *Victorian Studies* 14 (1971): 407–428; JC, 342–426; Bernard S. Cohen, "The Command of Language and the Language of Command," *Subaltern Studies* 4 (1985): 276–329; Gauri Viswanathan, *Masks of Conquest: Literary Study and British Rule in India* (New York: Columbia University Press, 1989), 30–44; Suresh Chandra Ghosh, "Bentinck, Macaulay and the Introduction of English Education in India," *History of Education* 24 (1995): 17–24; Rajan, *Under Western Eyes*, 174–197; Lynn Zastoupil and Martin Moir, eds., *The Great Indian Education Debate: Documents Relating to the Orientalist-Anglicist Controversy, 1781–1843* (London: Curzon, 1999), 1–72; Katherine Prior, Lance Brennan, and Robin Hines, "Bad Language: The Role of English, Persian and Other Esoteric Tongues in the Dismissal of Sir Edward Colebrook as Resident in Delhi in 1829," *Modern Asian Studies* 35 (2001): 75–112; Stephen Evans, "Macaulay's Minute Revisited: Colonial Language Policy in Nineteenth-Century India," *Journal of Multilingual and Multicultural Development* 23 (2002): 260–281; and G. J.V. Prasad, "A Minute Stretching into Centuries: Macaulay, English, and India," *Nineteenth-Century Prose* 33 (2006): 175–196. Spear, "Bentinck and Education," 82. Pinney, *L*3:381n3; and to Hallam, 28.x.42, *L*4:66.

32. To MMC, 7.xii.34, *L*:3:102–103 and n1. To the Governor-General in Council, 1.vi.35, and to [Sutherland, v?35?], 3:144–145. K. A. Ballhatchet, "The Home Government and Bentinck's Educational Policy," *Cambridge Historical Journal* 10 (1951): 225–226. M. A. Laird, *Missionaries and Education in Bengal, 1793–1837* (Oxford: Clarendon Press, 1972), 94–95.

33. To MMC, 8.x.34, *L*3:89. To MMC, 17.x.34, *L*3:90–97. To SM and FM, 10.viii.34, *L*3:73.

34. Joseph Schumpeter, *Imperialism and Social Class: Two Essays*, trans. Heinz

Norden (New York: World/Meridian, 1955), 61–98, 129–134; cf. David Cannadine, *Ornamentalism: How the British Saw Their Empire* (Oxford: Oxford University Press, 2001). P. J. Marshall, "British Society in India under the East India Company," *Modern Asian Studies* 31 (1997): 102. To SM and FM, 19.x.34, *L*3:97; and to MMC, 17.x.34, *L*3:90–91. To MMC, 3.x.34, *L*3:87. To MMC, 27.vi.34, *L*3:56.

35. To MMC, 7.xii.34, *L*3:100–101. CET, in Messrs. Trevelyan, J. Prinsep, and Tytler et al., *The Application of the Roman Alphabet to All the Oriental Languages; Contained in a Series of Papers* (Calcutta, 1834), 9; CET to TBM, 30.ix.34, Trevelyan Letter Books, 19(3), Robinson Library, University of Newcastle upon Tyne; and A. D. Webb, "Charles Edward Trevelyan in India: A Study of the Channels of Influence Employed by a Covenanted Civil Servant in the Translation of Personal Ideas into Official Policy," *South Asia* 6 (1983): 15–33. To MMC, 7.xii.34, *L*3:102, 103, 104, and 106.

36. To MMC, 7.xii.34, *L*3:104, 106, and 105. To MMC, 24.xii.34, *L*3:115. *A Supplement to the Oxford English Dictionary,* s.v. "Emotional." To MMC, 7.xii.34, *L*3:106, 104; cf. to MMC, 26.xi.32, *L*2:203–204.

37. To TFE, 15.xii.34, *L*3:110–111.

38. Ibid., 111. To MMC, 24.xii.34, *L*3:115. To TFE, 15.xii.34, *L*3:112.

39. To TFE, 15.xii.34, *L*3:113, 110.

40. Ibid., 111; to Lansdowne, 27.xii.34, *L*3:118. To TFE, 30.xi.33 and 15.xii.34, *L*2:347, 3:113. Henry David Thoreau, *Walden; or, Life in Woods,* in *Walden and Other Writings,* ed. Brooks Atkinson (New York: Random House/Modern Library, 1950), 91–92.

41. To TFE, 15.xii.34, *L*3:111. To MMC, 24.xii.34, *L*3:114; Mark 14:34. To MMC, 24.xii.34, *L*3:115–116.

42. To MMC, 24.xii.34, *L*3:114; and to SM and FM, 26.xii.34, *L*3:117. HMT quoted in Pinney, *L*3:116n1.

43. To MMC, 24.xii.34, *L*3:116. To Napier, 10.xii.34, *L*3:107 and n2; and "Sir James Mackintosh," *WLM* 6:76n; cf. ibid., 83–84; cf. "Sir James Mackintosh's *History of the Revolution,*" *ER* 61 (1835): 272–273. "Mackintosh," 78–79, 84, 85, and 96–97.

44. "Mackintosh," 100, 104, 95–96, 104, and 129.

45. Ibid., 97, 90.

46. Ibid., 130–132, 82–83.

47. Ibid., 95, 97. To MMC, 7.xii.34, *L*3:105.

48. James Mill, *The History of British India,* ed. William Thomas (Chicago: University of Chicago Press, 1975), 224. "Mackintosh," 90.

49. To MMC, 17.x.34, *L*3:94–95. To Lansdowne, 27.xii.34, *L*3:119; to SM and FM, 26.xii.34, *L*3:117. To Lansdowne, 27.xii.34, *L*3:118. To TFE, 15.ix.38, *L*3:256;

cf. J8:7, 29.i.54. J10:206–207, 29.viii.58. V. Menon, J. M. Boyett-Anderson, A. F. Schatzberg, and A. L. Reiss, "Relating Semantic and Episodic Memory Systems," *Brain Research Cognitive Brain Research* 13:2 (2002): 261–265.

50. HMT quoted in Pinney, *L3*:129n1. To ZM, 2.v.36, *L3*:172; and to TFE, 30.v.36, *L3*:176. Griffin, "Macaulay and the Controversy," 356, 372n69. HMT quoted in Pinney, *L3*:116n1. To TFE, 29.v.35, *L3*:141. J11:253–254, 10.ii.58; cf. *LLLM* 2:444.

51. To TFE, 8.ii.35, *L3*:131, 129, and 130. Euripides, *Hippolytus* 255–258, in Euripides, *Medea, Hippolytus, Electra, Helen,* trans. James Morwood (Oxford: Clarendon Press, 1997), 46. Edith Hall in ibid., xix, quoting F. I. Zeitlin, "The Power of Aphrodite: Eros and the Boundaries of the Self in Euripides' *Hippolytus,*" in *Playing the Other: Gender and Society in Classical Greek Literature* (Chicago, 1996), 223. To TFE, 8.ii.35, *L3*:130.

52. To TFE, 8.ii.35, *L3*:129, 132. Ruth Padel, *Whom Gods Destroy: Elements of Greek and Tragic Madness* (Princeton: Princeton University Press, 1995), 238. William V. Harris, *Restraining Rage: The Ideology of Anger Control in Classical Antiquity* (Cambridge, Mass.: Harvard University Press, 2001), 68, 358. Alfred North Whitehead, *Religion in the Making* (New York: Macmillan, 1926), 16–17. *LLLM* 1:359n1; to Moultrie, 11.ii.35, *L6*:281; to Sharp, 11.ii.35, *L3*:137; to ZM, 24.x.17, *L1*:89; cf. Thomas Dixon, *From Passions to Emotions: The Creation of a Secular Psychological Category* (Cambridge: Cambridge University Press, 2003), 109–112.

53. John Henry Newman, "Literature: A Lecture in the School of Philosophy and Letters," in *The Idea of a University Defined and Illustrated,* ed. Martin J. Svaglic (Notre Dame: University of Notre Dame Press, 1982), 221; cf. Martin B. Keller, James P. McCullough, Daniel N. Klein, and Bruce Arrow, "A Comparison of Nefazodone, the Cognitive Behavioral Analysis System of Psychotherapy, and Their Combination for the Treatment of Chronic Depression," *New England Journal of Medicine* 342:20 (2000): 1462–70. To TFE, 8.ii.35, *L3*:129, 132. To TFE, 30.xii.35, *L3*:160. Pinney, *L1*:122n4. Pinney, *L3*:155n5; and to TFE, 30.xii.35, *L3*:158. To TFE, 30.xii.35, *L3*:160; and to SM and FM, 1.i.36, *L3*:162. To TFE, 18.xii.37, *L3*:235. To TFE, 23.x.37, *L3*:226–229.

54. To SM and FM, 1.i.36, *L3*:162. To TFE, 30.v.36, *L3*:177.

55. Hesiod, *Theogony* 98–103, quoted in to TFE, 8.ii.35, *L3*:129 and n2.

56. *LLLM* 2:449 and n1. To SM and FM, 1.i.36, 9.v.36, 5.x.36, and 28.xi.36, *L3*:162, 173, 191–192, and 197–198. To Spring-Rice, 8.ii.36, *L3*:170. To TFE, 30. xi.36, *L3*:199. To TFE, 8.iii.37, *L3*:210.

57. To TFE, 30.v.36, *L3*:177. *LLLM* 2:448–449. To TFE, 29.v.35 and 30.v.36, *L3*:140, 177; to Mahon, [1.xii.48], *L4*:383. To TFE, 8.ii.35, *L3*:129; Lucretius, *De Rerum Natura* 1.66. To ZM, 2.v.36 and 12.x.36, *L3*:171–172, 192–193; to SM and

FM, 1.i.36 and 5.x.36, *L*3:161–162, 191–192; to C. Macaulay, 5.xii.36, *L*3:203–205. Paul Ricoeur, *The Symbolism of Evil,* trans. Emerson Buchanan (Boston: Beacon, 1969), 347–351. To TFE, 30.xii.35, 30.v.36, and 18.xii.37, *L*3:160, 178, and 237.

58. *LLLM* 2:423. William Chislett Jr., "Macaulay's Classical Reading," *Classical Journal* 11 (1915): 142–150; and Wynne Williams, "Reading Greek like a Man of the World: Macaulay and the Classical Languages," *Greece & Rome* 40 (1993): 201–216. Hugh Sykes Davies, "Macaulay's *Marginalia* to Lucretius," in Lucretius, *De Rerum Natura,* trans. R. C. Trevelyan (Cambridge: Cambridge University Press, 1937), 281, 284. "Lord Bacon," *WLM* 6:136–137.

59. *OED,* s.v. "Spiritual." To Chappell, 24.viii.57, *L*6:108. "History," *WLM* 5:131.

60. "History," 133. To TFE, 8.ii.35, *L*3:130. To TFE, 27.ii.35, *L*3:137. To TFE, 25.viii.35, 30.xii.35, and 30.v.36, *L*3:154, 159, and 177–178; to Mahon, 31.xii.36, *L*3:207. To TFE, 25.viii.35, *L*3:152. To SM and FM, 9.v.36, *L*3:174; *Thucydidis de Bello Peloponnesiaco. Libri octo* (Oxford, 1696), Wallington Library (Northumberland), new shelflist 3710, comments at 12, 14–15, 40, 72–73. For Herodotus and Tacitus, to TFE, 18.xii.37, *L*3:237; for Plutarch, to TFE, 30.v.36, *L*3:177; and for Livy, to TFE, 29.v.35, *L*3:142; cf. Donald R. Kelley, *Frontiers of History: Historical Inquiry in the Twentieth Century* (New Haven: Yale University Press, 2006), 1.

61. To Lansdowne, 27.xii.34, *L*3:118–119; to Bentinck, [xii.34] and 7.ii.3[5], *L*3:120, 125–126; to Tytler, 28.i.35, *L*3:122–123; and to James Mill, 24.viii.35, *L*3:148–149. J. F. Hilliker, "Lord William Bentinck's Resolution of 1835 on Indian Education: A Rejected Draft," *Journal of the Royal Asiatic Society* 1 (1981): 40–45. "Minute on Indian Education," in C & P, 241.

62. "Minute on Indian Education," 246–247; and CET, *On the Education of the People of India* (London, 1838), 93; cf. Robert E. Frykenberg, "Macaulay's Minute and the Myth of English as a 'Colonialist' Imposition upon India: A Reappraisal with Special Reference to South India," *Journal of the Royal Asiatic Society* 2 (1988): 314. Griffin, "Macaulay and the Controversy," 77–80; "Epitaph on Henry Martyn" (1812), *WLM* 8:543. Spear, "Bentinck and Education," 84. "Minute on Indian Education," 239.

63. Rowan Strong, *Anglicanism and the British Empire, c. 1700–1850* (Oxford: Oxford University Press, 2007), 118–197. Homi K. Bhabha, *The Location of Culture* (London: Routledge, 1994), 86–87; Thomas R. Trautmann, *Aryans and British India* (Berkeley: University of California Press, 1997), 99–130; Jeffrey Cox, *Imperial Fault Lines: Christianity and Colonial Power in India, 1818–1940* (Stanford: Stanford University Press, 2002), 12, 39–40; Brian K. Pennington, *Was Hinduism Invented? Britons, Indians, and the Colonial Construction* (Oxford: Oxford University Press, 2005), 182–183; and Nicholas B. Dirks, *The Scandal of Empire: India and the Creation of Imperial*

Britain (Cambridge, Mass.: Belknap Press of Harvard University Press, 2006), 285–312. "Minute on Indian Education," 246 and 242–243; cf. to Tytler, 28.i.35, *L*3:122, and "Barère," *WLM* 7:194. "Minute on Indian Education," 242.

64. "Minute on Indian Education," 241. J11:226, 11.xii.57. Sabine MacCormack, "'The Discourse of My Life': Peru's Greatest Historian Reflects on Culture and Language," 18; I am grateful to Professor MacCormack for letting me read her unpublished paper. To Mill, 24.viii.35, *L*3:150.

65. To ZM, 12.x.36, *L*3:193. "Minute on Indian Education," 249. Ainslee Thomas Embree, *Charles Grant and British Rule in India* (New York: Columbia University Press, 1962), 286.

66. Edward W. Said, *Orientalism* (New York: Vintage Books, 1979), 196. Richard Fynes, "Sir William Jones and the Classical Tradition," in *Sir William Jones 1746–1794: A Commemoration,* ed. Alexander Murray (Oxford: Oxford University Press, 1998), 623–624. To TFE, 8.ii.35, *L*3:129. To Spring-Rice, 8.ii.36, *L*3:169; to SM and FM, 5.x.36, *L*3:191; and to C. Macaulay, 5.xii.36, *L*3:203.

67. "History," 149–150. To HMT, 22.vii.33, *L*2:275–276; *The Christianity of Stoicism: or, Selections from Arrian's Discourses of Epictetus, Translated by Mrs. Carter* (Carmarthen, 1822). To Napier, 1.i.[36], *L*3:163; cf. to TFE, 30.xi.36, *L*3:199–200. Thomas R. Metcalf, *Ideologies of the Raj* (Cambridge: Cambridge University Press, 1994), 34; Saree Makdisi, *Romantic Imperialism: Universal Empire and the Culture of Modernity* (Cambridge: Cambridge University Press, 1998), 116–119. "Lord Clive," *WLM* 6:405–406, 411; cf. "Warren Hastings," *WLM* 6:555–556.

68. "Draft of Governor-General's Resolution on Education," [ii?35], *L*3:138–139; "Minute on Indian Education," 250. H. T. Prinsep, diary (ca. 1835), quoted in *Selections from Educational Records, 1781–1839,* ed. Henry Sharp (Calcutta: Superintendent, Government Printing in India, 1920), 134. "Official Resolution," quoted in Griffin, "Macaulay and the Controversy," 411 n39. Ballhatchet, "Home Government," 225–226; to Hobhouse, 17.iv.37, *L*3:213–214. To Spring-Rice, 8.ii.36, *L*3:169. To Lansdowne, 22.viii.36, *L*3:189.

69. Pinney, *L*3:126n2; H. Woodrow, ed., *Macaulay's Minutes on Education in India. Written in the Years 1835, 1836, and 1837* (Calcutta, 1862), 66–67. Ballhatchet, "Home Government," 228. T. W. Clark, "The Languages of Calcutta, 1760–1840," *Bulletin of the School of Oriental and African Studies* 20 (1957): 167–187; Bayly, *Empire and Information,* 260, 298. Amy Waldman, "In India, a New Heyday for English (the Language)," *New York Times,* 14.xii.03, sec. 4, p. 5.

70. Ramachandra Guha, "Macaulay's Minute Revisited," *Hindu Magazine,* 24.ii.2007, available at http://www.hinduonnet.com/thehindu/mag/2007/02/04/stories/2007020400030300.htm.

71. James Mill to Brougham, 27.viii.34, quoted in Alexander Bain, *James Mill: A Biography* (London, 1882), 374–375. To the Governor-General in Council, 1.vi.35,

*L*3:145 and n2. *LLLM* 1:381. To TFE, 3.vi.35, *L*3:146. To Mill, 24.viii.35, *L*3:146 and n3, 148. The locus classicus is Eric Stokes, *The English Utilitarians and India* (Oxford: Clarendon Press, 1959), 219–240, 261–262; JC, 326–341 and 427–472, is standard; see also David Skuy, "Macaulay and the Indian Penal Code of 1862: The Myth of the Inherent Superiority and Modernity of the English Legal System Compared to India's Legal System in the Nineteenth Century," *Modern Asian Studies* 32 (1998): 513–557.

72. Dharker, *Legislative Minutes,* 180. "Introductory Report upon the Indian Penal Code," *WLM* 7:416; and Radhika Singha, *A Despotism of Law: Crime and Justice in Early Colonial India* (Delhi: Oxford University Press, 1998), 298. "Introductory Report upon Penal Code," 423. Kalyan Raman, "Utilitarianism and the Criminal Law in Colonial India: A Study of the Practical Limits of Utilitarian Jurisprudence," *Modern Asian Studies* 28 (1994): 778, 779. Dharker, *Legislative Minutes,* 130–131, 219. Singha, *Despotism of Law,* 299.

73. "Introductory Report upon Penal Code," 415; to Lansdowne, 22.viii.36, *L*3:186; to Napier, 29.viii.36, *L*3:189. To TFE, 8.iii.37, *L*3:210; Pinney, *L*3:213n3. To [Governor-General in Council], 1.v.37, *L*3:214. To TFE, 17.xii.37, *L*3:237–238.

74. John Stuart Mill, "Penal Code for India" (viii.38), in *Writings on India,* ed. J. M. Robson, Martin Moir, and Zawahir Moir, vol. 30 of *The Collected Works of John Stuart Mill,* ed. J. M. Robson (Toronto: University of Toronto Press, 1990), 20. "Penal Code Prepared by the Indian Law Commissioners," *Parliamentary Papers, 1837–38,* 41:90: 22, 23, 24–25, and 70–71.

75. To ZM, 12.x.36, *L*3:193. Mill, "Penal Code for India," 22. Jerome Taylor, "Gay Activists in India Want British Apology for Sex Law," *The Independent,* 16. viii.08, available at http://www.independent.co.uk/news/world/asia/gay-activists-in-india-want-british-apology-for-sex-law-898979.html.

76. "Introductory Report upon Penal Code," 518. Baron de Montesquieu, *Spirit of the Laws,* in *The Portable Enlightenment Reader,* ed. Isaac Kramnick (New York: Penguin, 1995), 520–521 (bk. XII, sec. V). "Penal Code Prepared," 53. A. D. Harvey, *Sex in Georgian England: Attitudes and Prejudices from the 1720s to the 1820s* (New York: St Martin's Press, 1994), 123, 125–126.

77. To Hobhouse, 6.i.36, *L*3:165. "Government of India," 139. J. Fitzjames Stephen, "Laws of England as to the Expression of Religious Opinion," *Contemporary Review* 25 (1878): 448–475; John V. Orth, "'Casting the Priests Out of the Temple': John Austin and the Relation between Law and Religion," in *The Weightier Matters of the Law: Essays on Law and Religion,* ed. John Witte Jr. and Frank S. Alexander (Atlanta: Scholar's Press, 1988), 229–249. Guha, "Macaulay's Minute." Martin J. Weiner, *Reconstructing the Criminal: Culture, Law, and Policy in England, 1830–1914* (Cambridge: Cambridge University Press, 1990), 61.

78. Skuy, "Macaulay and Penal Code of 1862," 539. To Lansdowne, 22.viii.36,

*L*3:184–186 and n4; *LLLM* 1:360–362. Dharker, *Legislative Minutes,* 183–197. "Inscription," *WLM* 8:589. J4:15, 10.iii.51; Robert Fagles, quoted in Charles McGrath, "Translating Virgil's Epic Poem of Empire," *New York Times,* 30.x.2006, available at http://www.nytimes.com/2006/10/30/books/30fagl.html.

79. To TFE, 25.vii.36–12.viii.36, *L*3:180–183. Bernard Semmel, "T. B. Macaulay, 'The Active and Contemplative Lives,'" in *The Victorian Experience: The Prose Writers,* ed. Richard A. Levine (Athens: Ohio University Press, 1982), 22–46. To TFE, 30. xii.35, *L*3:158–159.

80. To TFE, 30.xi.36 and 30.v.36, *L*3:199, 177, and 174. To ZM, 30.xi.36, *L*3:198–199. To TFE, 30.xii.35, *L*3:158; to SM and FM, 9.v.36, *L*3:173–174; and to ZM, 30.xi.36, *L*3:198. To SM and FM, 5.x.36, *L*3:191–192; and to TFE, 30.v.36, *L*3:179. J2:192, 30.xii.49.

81. To SM and FM, 11.ix.37, *L*3:222. To C. Macaulay, 5.xii.36, *L*3:203. To Empson, 19.vi.37, *L*3:219. To C. Macaulay, 5.xii.36, *L*3:203–204.

82. To Mahon, 31.xii.36, *L*3:208; to Empson, 19.vi.37, *L*3:219; and to Drummond, 20.ix.37, *L*3:225. To Empson, 19.vi.37, *L*3:218–219. J10:230, 4.ix.58. To Cropper, 5.xi.37, *L*3:232; to SM and FM, 13.xii.37, *L*3:234.

4. Sinister Prophet

1. To Lansdowne, 22.viii.36, *L*3:187. To Spring-Rice, 8.ii.36, *L*3:167–169. To Lansdowne, 22.viii.36, *L*3:188. To Mahon, 31.xii.36, *L*3:208; and to Empson, 19. vi.37, *L*3:219. Boyd Hilton, *A Mad, Bad, and Dangerous People? England, 1783–1846* (Oxford: Clarendon Press, 2006), 496–499.

2. To Napier, 1.i.36, *L*3:163; to TFE, 25.vii–12.viii.36, *L*3:181–182; and to Napier, 26.xi.36, *L*3:194. To Napier, 29.viii.36, *L*3:190. Marginal comments transcribed by GOT in Plato, *Euthyphro,* in *Platonis dialogi Graece et Latine,* 10 vols. (Berlin, 1816–1817), Wallington Library (Northumberland), new shelflist no. 3387, at 1:360, from *Divini Platonis opera omnia quae exstant* (Frankfurt, 1602), Wallington new shelflist no. 3361. Plato, *Phaedo,* in *Divini Platonis,* at 44; cf. "Theaetētus," in *Platonis dialogi,* at 267–268. Plato, *Phaedo,* in *Platonis dialogi,* vol. 2, pt. 3, 128, 22.v.37.

3. Plato, *Euthyphro,* in *Divini Platonis,* at 4. Dates transcribed by GOT in *Aeschinis Orationes* (Leipzig, 1908), title page, Wallington new shelflist no. 3361; to TFE, 25.vii–12.viii.36, *L*3:180; Cicero, *De Oratore* 1.34.151, in *M. Tullii Ciceronis opera,* 13 vols. (London, 1831), at 2:880, Wallington new shelflist no. 3382 (transcribed by GOT); cf. to TFE, 18.xii.37, *L*3:237. To James Mill, 24.viii.35, *L*3:150. To ZM, 12.x.36, *L*3:193; TBM, *Critical and Historical Essays,* 2 vols. (London, 1843), 1:viii. To ZM, 30.xi.36, *L*3:198–199; and to TFE, 15.xii.34, *L*3:110–113.

4. "Lord Bacon," *WLM* 6:136–137. To TFE, 8.ii.35, *L*3:129; cf. to Sharp, 27.ii.35, *L*3:136–137.

5. Richard Yeo, "An Idol of the Market-place: Baconianism in Nineteenth-Century Britain," *History of Science* 23 (1985): 257–285. "Bacon," 202, 206. Ibid., 237; cf. Brian Vickers, "Bacon and Rhetoric," in *The Cambridge Companion to Bacon,* ed. Markku Peltonen (Cambridge: Cambridge University Press, 1996), 200–231. J1:414, 21.xi.48. "Sir James Mackintosh," *WLM* 6:95; Paolo Rossi, "Bacon's Idea of Science," in Peltonen, *Cambridge Companion to Bacon,* 42.

6. To Napier, 30.viii.36, *L3*:190. To Napier, 26.xi.36, *L3*:194. To Napier, 1.i.[36] and [26.xi.36], *L3*:163, 194, 195–196; to SM and FM, 13.xii.37, *L3*:234; and "Bacon," 242–243.

7. "Bacon," 175–176, 182, and 185. James E. Crimmins, "Bentham and Hobbes: An Issue of Influence," *Journal of the History of Ideas* 63 (2002): 677–696; Jeffrey R. Collins, *The Allegiance of Thomas Hobbes* (Oxford: Oxford University Press, 2005), 32–33.

8. "List of Books, The Library of the Right Honourable T. B. Macaulay. November 1852," Wallington. To Napier, 20.x.43, *L4*:159. *HOE* 1:135 = chap. 2.

9. To Stephen, 26.xii.48, *L4*:392–393; cf. to McLaren, 30.i.41, *L3*:364–365. *HOE* 1:135–136 = chap. 2. "Samuel Johnson" (1831), *WLM* 5:498–538; cf. "Samuel Johnson" (1856), *WLM* 7:324–356; "Samuel Johnson" (1831), 132. James Henry Monk, *The Life of Richard Bentley, D.D.,* 2 vols. (London, 1833), at 1:41, Macaulay 218, TCL. *LLLM* 1:260–261.

10. "Warren Hastings," *WLM* 6:611. Transcription of marginalia to Friedrich Melchior Grimm, *Correspondance littéraire, philosophique et critique,* 17 vols. (Paris, 1812–1814), at 1, pt. 2:260, in Macaulay MSS., TCL, 0.15.73, fols. 64–68. Grimm, *Correspondance,* at 4, pt. 4.1:266; cf. to HMT, 2.viii.33, *L2*:288; and to Napier, 13. ii.34, *L3*:22.

11. To ZM, 18.iv.18, *L1*:97; to TFE, 30.xi.36, *L3*:202; cf. his marginal comments printed in *LLLM* 2:434–440. Plato, *Politeia,* in *Platonis dialogi,* at 3, pt. 1:106. Plato, *Republic* 3.389c–d, trans. Paul Shorey, in *The Collected Dialogues of Plato Including the Letters,* ed. Edith Hamilton and Huntington Cairns (New York: Pantheon, 1961), 634. Angus Ross, in *ODNB,* s.v. "Arbuthnot [Arbuthnott], John."

12. Paraphrasing Hannah Arendt, "The Public and the Private Realm," in *The Portable Hannah Arendt,* ed. Peter Baehr (New York: Penguin, 2000), 570. To TFE, 25.vii.36 *L3*:180. To SMM, 17.iv.15, *L1*:61. To TFE, 25.vii.36, *L3*:181, 180. The character of Livia, Tiberius' mother, in *Annals* 5.1 is the starting point of Bacon's "Of Simulation and Dissimulation"; cf. "History," *WLM* 5:144. Macaulay was "deep in the Annals" while working on "Bacon" and went "again through Tacitus" eighteen months later (to TFE, 30.v.36 and 18.xii.37, *L3*:178, 237). Edwin B. Benjamin, "Bacon and Tacitus," *Classical Philology* 60 (1965): 104–105; cf. Markku Peltonen, "Ciceronian Humanism and Tacitean Neostoicism—Replacement or Transformation? The Case of Francis Bacon's Moral and Civil Philosophy," *European Legacy* 1 (1996):

220–226; see also Peter Burke, "Tacitism, Skepticism, and Reason of State," in *Cambridge History of Political Thought, 1450–1700,* ed. J. H. Burns with Mark Goldie (Cambridge: Cambridge University Press, 1991), 479–498; and Howard K. Weinbrot, "Politics, Taste and National Identity: Some Uses of Tacitism in Eighteenth-Century Britain, in *Tacitus and the Tacitean Tradition,"* ed. T. J. Luce and A. J. Woodman (Princeton: Princeton University Press, 1993), 168–184. "Bacon," 224, 237.

13. Francis Bacon, "Of Simulation and Dissimulation," in *The Works of Francis Bacon, Baron of Verulam, Viscount St. Albans, and Lord High Chancellor of England,* new ed., 10 vols. (London, 1826), 2:255. The quotations from the essay in this and the following paragraphs are found on 255–257.

14. Ian Box, "Bacon's Essays," *History of Political Thought* 3 (1982): 39–41, discussing the interpretation of Stanley Fish in *Self-Consuming Artifacts: The Experiences of Seventeenth-Century Literature* (Berkeley: University of California Press, 1972).

15. "The London University," in C & P, 26. To Randall, 23.v.57, *L*6:94. "Hallam's Constitutional History," *WLM* 5:164–165. "Bacon," 242–243.

16. "Bacon," 243.

17. F. W. Arnold, *The Public Life of Lord Macaulay* (London, 1863), 184. "Hallam," 162. Marginalia to Bacon's *Works,* 2:255, "agst 1st line of Essay II," TCL, 0.15.73, fols. 36–41a (transcribed by Viscount Knutsford). To TFE, 8.ii.35, *L*3:129, quoting Lucretius, *De Rerum Natura* 1.66. Hugh Sykes Davies, "Macaulay's *Marginalia* to Lucretius," in Lucretius, *De Rerum Natura,* trans. R. C. Trevelyan (Cambridge: Cambridge University Press, 1937), 279. *LLLM* 2:443–444.

18. Francis Bacon, "Of Death," in *The Essayes or Counsels, Civill and Morall,* ed. Michael Kiernan (Cambridge, Mass.: Harvard University Press, 1985), 9. Marginalia to Bacon's Works, 2:255, "agst 1st line of Essay II," TCL, 0.15.73, fols. 36–41a. Bacon, "Of Atheisme," in Kiernan, *Essayes or Counsels,* 52. Marginalia to Bacon's Works, "agst line 8 from bottom," TCL, 0.15.73, fols. 36–41a. Bacon, "Atheisme," 51. Marginalia to Bacon's Works, 2:255, "agst line 'Epicurus,'" TCL, 0.15.73, fols. 36–41a.

19. "John Dryden," *WLM* 5:97. *Encyclopaedia Britannica,* quoted in W. R. Johnson, *Lucretius and the Modern World* (London: Duckworth, 2000), 103. Frank M. Turner, "Ancient Materialism and Modern Science: Lucretius among the Victorians," in *Contesting Cultural Authority: Essays in Victorian Intellectual Life* (Cambridge: Cambridge University Press, 1993), 262–283.

20. "Bacon," 209, quoting Lucretius, *De Rerum Natura* 6.9–10.

21. "Bacon," 209, quoting Lucretius, *De Rerum Natura* 3.2–3. Abraham Cowley, "To the Royal Society," lines 37–40; and Lucretius, *De Rerum Natura* 1.66; cf. Anthony Szynkarak, "Bodies and Boundaries: Thinking with Lucretius from Cowley to Thompson," *Cambridge Quarterly* 27 (1998): 317–318. Lucretius, *De Rerum Natura* 3.2–3, 13–43, and 964–971.

22. To TFE, 18.xii.37 and 25.viii.35, *L*3:237, 153. Plutarch, "Alcibiades," in *The Lives of the Noble Grecians and Romans,* trans. John Dryden and Arthur Hugh Clough (New York: Modern Library, n.d.), 234. "Bacon," 139; to HMT, 5.x.46, *L*4:314. Notably by James Spedding, *Evenings with a Reviewer or Macaulay and Bacon,* 2 vols. (London, 1881); e.g., Nieves Mathews, *Francis Bacon: The History of a Character Assassination* (New Haven: Yale University Press, 1996).

23. "Bacon," 163, 165–166, and 186; cf. Col. 3:2.

24. "Bacon," 202, 203, and 220–221.

25. Ibid., 163–164, 194–195, 143, and 142; Kris E. Lane, *Pillaging the Empire: Piracy in the Americas, 1500–1750* (Armonk, N.Y.: M. E. Sharpe, 1998), 3–61. "Bacon," 194.

26. "Bacon," 137–138, 163, 165–166, and 186; cf. Col. 3:2 and, inter alia, Ps. 11:4, 90:3, 107:8, and 115:16. To HMT, 30.v.31, *L*2:22; cf. E. E. Kellett, "Macaulay and the Authorized Version," *London Quarterly Review* 148 (1927): 196–208.

27. Quoted in *LLLM* 2:430. "Bacon," 140, 143, 144, 148–149, 183–184, 187, and 143. To TFE, 25.vii–12.viii.36, *L*3:183–184. To TFE, 25.viii.35, *L*3:153; cf. *LLLM* 2:446.

28. Marginal comment on Plato's *Callicles,* dated 1 May 1837, quoted in *LLLM* 2:437. To Napier, 29.viii.36, *L*3:189–190; [CET], "The Thugs; or, Secret Murderers of India," *ER* 64 (1837): 357–395. C. H. Dharker, ed., *Lord Macaulay's Legislative Minutes* (London: Geoffrey Cumberlege/Oxford University Press, 1946), no. 26 [19. vi.37], 247; Radhika Singha, "'Providential' Circumstances: The Thuggee Campaign of the 1830s and Legal Innovation," *Modern Asian Studies* 27 (1993): 107. "Government of India," *WLM* 8:114–115, 122.

29. For Robinson's *History of the Reign of the Emperor Charles V, with a View of the Progress of Society in Europe, from the Subversion of the Roman Empire to the Beginning of the Sixteenth Century,* see J. G. A. Pocock, *Barbarism and Religion,* vol. 2: *Narratives of Civil Government* (Cambridge: Cambridge University Press, 1999), 275–299; cf. to SMM, 12.ii.13, *L*1:17. "Bacon," 139–140.

30. "Bacon," 140, 142.

31. S. J. Barnett, *Idol Temples and Crafty Priests: The Origins of Enlightenment Anticlericalism* (New York: St. Martin's Press, 1999); and Hugh McLeon, "Varieties of Anticlericalism in Later Victorian and Edwardian England," in *Anticlericalism in Britain, c. 1500–1914,* ed. Nigel Ashton and Matthew Cragoe (Stroud: Sutton, 2000), 198–220. "Bacon," 147, 167, and 195–196.

32. "Bacon," 141, 140, 153, 167, 141–143 (cf. Matt. 16:3), 153, and 154.

33. "Bacon," 145–146, 240–241; cf. 183–185 and 200–201. To Napier, 5.xi.41, *L*4:15. "Bacon," 169.

34. To TFE, 3.vii, 25.viii, 30.xii.35, and 25.vii–12.viii.36, *L*3:146, 153, 159, and

181. Plato, *De Legibus*, in *Divini Platonis*, at 769 and 879. Plato, *Politeia*, in *Platonis dialogi*, at 164. Plato, *Republic* 8.549b, and *Laws* 12.965. *Politeia*, in *Platonis dialogi*, at 425 and 516.

35. To Napier, 26.xi.36, *L*3:194. "Bacon," 204. To Napier, 1.i.35, *L*3:163. To Napier, 26.xi.36, *L*3:194. Marginalia to Bacon's *Works*, 2:122, 267, and 283, TCL, 0.15.73, fols. 36–41a.

36. "Bacon," 227–233, 204, 144, 175, and 193. James E. Crimmins, introduction to *Utilitarians and Religion* (Bristol: Thoemmes Press, 1998), 3–25; cf. David Spadafora, *The Idea of Progress in Eighteenth-Century Britain* (New Haven: Yale University Press, 1990), 213–415. "Bacon," 203–204; cf. 146.

37. "Bacon," 206. To TFE, 30.xii.35, 25.vii–12.viii.36, and 8.iii.37, *L*3:159, 181, and 210–211. Aristotle, *Metaphysics* 983a24–990a32; W. D. Ross's translation of 988b24–26 in *The Basic Works of Aristotle*, ed. Richard McKeon (New York: Random House, 1941), 703.

38. "Bacon," 221. "On Mitford's History of Greece," *WLM* 7:683–703; cf. TFE, 15.xii.34 and 8.ii.35, *L*3:111, 131. William Mitford, *The History of Greece*, 8 vols. (Boston, 1823), 3:170, 171–172, and 174.

39. "Bacon," 206; William Paley, *The Principles of Moral and Political Philosophy* (1785) (New York: Garland, 1978), 35–45. To TFE, 29.v.35, *L*3:141. Owen Chadwick, "Gibbon and the Church Historians," in *Edward Gibbon and the Decline and Fall of the Roman Empire, Daedalus* 105:3 (1976): 113–115; "Bacon," 209; cf. 212–220.

40. Quoted in Pinney, *L*1:xxiii. To TFE, 30.v.36, *L*3:178; to HMT, 4.i.34, *L*3:9; to TFE, 1.vii.34, *L*3:62; and to Empson, 19.vi.37, *L*3:220. Macaulay quotes Gibbon in "Bacon," 211, from *The Decline and Fall of the Roman Empire*, 3 vols. (New York: Modern Library, n.d.), 3:722, and builds on Gibbon, *Decline and Fall*, 3:712–726 (= chap. 45). "Bacon," 210–212, 237.

41. To More, 11.xi.16, *L*1:83; cf. "Bacon," 137. "Bacon," 211–220.

42. As quoted in G. M. Trevelyan, *Sir George Otto Trevelyan: A Memoir* (London: Longmans, Green, 1932), 15; cf. *LLLM* 2:385–386n1; and "Bacon," 138. "Bacon," 217 (cf. Matt. 5:45), 218–219.

43. "Bacon," 220. Gibbon, *Decline and Fall*, 2:440, 442. Adam Smith, *An Inquiry into the Nature and Causes of the Wealth of Nations*, ed. Edwin Cannan (New York: Modern Library, 1937), 625. *OED*, s.v. "Consumer."

44. "Bacon," 220–221, 235, and 239–240. Marginalia to Bacon's *Works*, at 2:122, TCL, 0.15.73, fols. 36–41a.

45. "Sadler's Law of Population," *WLM* 5:430; cf. E. A. Wrigley, "The Classical Economists, the Stationary State, and the Industrial Revolution," in *Was the Industrial Revolution Necessary?*, ed. Graham Snooks (London: Routledge, 1994), 27–42; and generally N. R. C. Crafts, *British Economic Growth during the Industrial Revolution* (Oxford University Press, 1985). Simon Szreter and Graham Mooney, "Urbaniza-

tion, Mortality, and the Standard of Living Debate: New Estimates of the Expectation of Life at Birth in Nineteenth-Century British Cities," *Economic History Review*
51 (1998): 84–112. To TFE, 30.xii.35 and 18.xii.37, *L*3:159–160, 237. To Lansdowne,
22.viii.36, *L*3:184.

46. "Bacon," 222–223, 221, 222, and 224; cf. Matt. 7:16 and Luke 6:44; "Bacon,"
223.

47. "Bacon," 223; Lucretius, *De Rerum Natura* 2.1–19. "Bacon," 224.

48. "Mill's Essay on Government," *WLM* 5:258–259; cf. "History," 148, 149–
151. To Napier, 1.i.35, *L*3:163; "Minute on Indian Education," in C & P, 244; cf.
"Bacon," 209–210. Conflates *HOE* 4:377(= chap. 23) and "Minute on Indian Education," 243.

49. "Bacon," 224 (cf. James 2:18), 226.

50. "Bacon," 235, 227, 243, 238–239, and 242; R. DeWitt Mallary, "Macaulay's
Use of Scripture in His Essays," *Old Testament Student* 7 (1888): 248.

51. "Bacon," 241. To TFE, 30.xii.35, *L*3:158. "Bacon," 242.

52. "Bacon," 206. Paul Ricoeur, *Time and Narrative,* vol. 3, trans. Kathleen
Blamey and David Pellauer (Chicago: University of Chicago Press, 1988), 180–181.
Cowley, "To The Royal Society," lines 93–100; cf. Deut. 34:1–4 and Lucretius, *De
Rerum Natura* 1.66 and 3.2–3. "Bacon," 243–244.

53. To Napier, 11.xii.36 and 15.vi.37, *L*3:205, 216; and "Bacon," 239. To SM
and FM, 13.xii.37, *L*3:234. Yeo, "Idol of the Market-place," 271–272.

54. [Philip Pusey], "Plato, Bacon, and Bentham," *Quarterly Review* 61 (1838):
476–485, 505–506. Christian Baron Bunsen, quoted by F. M. L. Thompson, in
ODNB, s.v. "Pusey, Philip." Pusey, "Plato, Bacon," 462–463, 504, 465, 485, 487–488,
491–492, 493, 497, and 502–503.

55. Pusey, "Plato, Bacon," 501, 503, 500–501, and 505–506.

56. To [HMT, 8.xi.38], *L*3:263. Theodore Dwight Bozeman, *Protestants in an
Age of Science: The Baconian Ideal and Antebellum American Religious Thought* (Chapel
Hill: University of North Carolina Press, 1977), 26.

57. To TFE, 25.vii–12.viii and 30.xi.36, *L*3:183 and n3, 201–202; and to Napier
15.vi.37, *L*3:217. Joseph M. Levine, *The Battle of the Books: History and Literature in
the Augustan Age* (Ithaca: Cornell University Press, 1991), 13–84. "Sir William Temple," *WLM* 6:319, 322.

58. To TFE, 18.xii.37, *L*3:236–237. To SM and FM, 13.xii.37, *L*3:235.

59. To TFE, 18.xii.37, *L*3:236. To Napier, 15.xi.37, *L*3:216–217. "Temple," 325;
cf. Bernard Semmel, "T. B. Macaulay: The Active and Contemplative Lives," in *The
Victorian Experience: The Prose Writers,* ed. Richard A. Levine (Athens: Ohio University Press, 1982), 22–46. Joanne Shattock, "Politics and Literature: Macaulay,
Brougham, and the *Edinburgh Review* under Napier," *Yearbook of English Studies* 16
(1986): 46–50. To Napier, [28.xi.36], *L*3:196. To Lansdowne, 19.xii.38, *L*3:268; to

Austin [early 1840?], *L*3:325–26; [to Hettner], 13.iii.56, *L*6:27; and to TFE, 17.i.59, *L*6:191. John Brewer, *The Pleasures of the Imagination: English Culture in the Eighteenth Century* (New York: Farrar Straus Giroux, 1997), 169–171. Pinney, *L*3:243n1. E.g., to FM, 20.vi.42, *L*4:38. John Tosh, *A Man's Place: Masculinity and the Middle-Class Home in Victorian England* (New Haven: Yale University Press, 1999), 6–7.

60. JC, 499. To Napier, 20.vii.38, *L*3:251; cf. Pinney, *L*3:341n2. To Empson, 19.vi.37, *L*3:219; cf. to FM, 10.vii.44, *L*4:207. HMT to SM and FM, 6.vi.38, in [Margaret Trevelyan Holland] Viscountess Knutsford, *Life and Letters of Zachary Macaulay* (London, 1900), 488; J. R. Oldfield, in *ODNB,* s.v. "Macaulay, Zachary." *LLLM* 1:432. [To Weekes], 10.iii.43, *L*4:112.

61. Thomas Fowell Buxton, *Memoirs of Sir Thomas Fowell Buxton, Baronet. With Selections from His Correspondence,* ed. Charles Buxton (London, 1848), 222. Patricia M. Pugh, ed., *Calendar of the Papers of Sir Thomas Fowell Buxton, 1786–1846* (London: List and Index Society, 1980), 111, summarizing a note by Sarah Buxton. Buxton, *Memoirs,* 124. Philip to Buxton, 16.vii.28, ibid., 210, 211.

62. Quoted in Buxton, *Memoirs,* 330. Buxton to ZM, x.35, ibid., 367. Benjamin Madley, "From Terror to Genocide: Britain's Tasmanian Penal Colonies and Australia's History Wars," *Journal of British History* 47 (2008): 77–106. Matt. 7:12; cf. Ludwik Sternbach, "Similar Thoughts in the Mahābhārata, the Literature of 'Greater India' and in the Christian Gospels," *Journal of the American Oriental Society* 91 (1971): 438–442. D. A. Brading, *The First America: The Spanish Monarchy, Creole Patriots, and the Liberal State, 1492–1867* (Cambridge: Cambridge University Press, 1991), 80–99.

63. *Report from the Select Committee on Aborigines (British Settlements)* (London, 1836), ii, 13, 368, 454, 455, and 780–781. Buxton to ZM, 6.ix.36, in Buxton, *Memoirs,* 382.

64. *Report from the Select Committee on Aborigines (British Settlements)* (London, 1837), 2. Richard Brent, *Liberal Anglican Politics: Whiggery, Religion, and Reform, 1830–1841* (Oxford: Clarendon Press, 1987), 274. *Report on Aborigines* (1837), 8. Ronald Rainger, "Philanthropy and Science in the 1830s: The British and Foreign Aborigines' Protection Society," *Man,* n.s., 15 (1980): 707. *Report on Aborigines* (1837), 200. Buxton to Gurney, 30.vii.37, in Buxton, *Memoirs,* 422. *Report of the Parliamentary Select Committee on Aboriginal Tribes (British Settlements). Reprinted, with Comments, by "The Aborigines Protection Society."* (London, 1837), v, x, xii. Ibid., xi. Buxton to Gurney and Johnson to Gurney, 17.v.38, in Pugh, *Calendar of Papers of Buxton,* 118. *Report . . . Reprinted,* vi.

65. To HMT, 25.vii.33, *L*2:278; to Napier, 31.x.[32], *L*3:200; to ——, 1.i.32, *L*2:221 and n2; Pinney, *L*2:237n1; to ZM, 9.vii.33 and 27.vii.33, *L*2:267–268, 279. To HMT, 21.v.33, *L*2:242 and n1. To Napier, 2.xi.33, *L*2:333. To HMT, 28.v.33, *L*2:246.

66. To Napier, 14.vi.38, *L*3:243. To Napier, 8.x.38, *L*3:258–259. Brewer, *Pleasures of Imagination,* 427–489. To TFE, 15.xii.34, *L*3:111.

67. "Government of India," *WLM,* 8:120; "Mackintosh," 94–95; to Empson, 19.vi.39, *L*3:219. "Lord Clive," *WLM* 6:411.

68. To HMT, 28.v.33, *L*2:246. "Irish Coercion Bill," in Vizetelly, 1:149. To TFE, 25.vii–12.viii.36, *L*3:182; and to Lansdowne, 22.viii.36, *L*3:186–187. To Drummond, 20.ix.37, *L*3:224–225; cf. to HMT, 29.xii.38, *L*3:271. To Napier, 20.vii.38, *L*3:251–252. To MMC, 3.x.34, *L*3:87. To TFE, 8.ii.35, *L*3:129. To Empson, 19.vi.37, *L*3:219. To TFE, 23.x.37, *L*3:226–229.

69. To Napier, 12.ix.38, *L*3:253–254 and 253n3. To SM, 15.x.39, *L*3:305. To Cropper, 20.vi.42, *L*4:39. To TFE, [17.iv.47], *L*4:334 and n4. Claude Rawson, *God, Gulliver, and Genocide: Barbarism and the European Imagination, 1492–1945* (Oxford: Oxford University Press, 2001), 115, 138–139.

70. Paul W. Schroeder, *The Transformation of European Politics, 1763–1848* (Oxford: Oxford University Press, 1994), 440–441; idem, "Napoleon's Foreign Policy: A Criminal Enterprise," in *Systems, Stability, and Statecraft: Essays on the International History of Modern Europe,* ed. Robert Jervis, David Wetzel, and Jack S. Levy (New York: Palgrave/Macmillan, 2004), 2–36; and David Bell, *The First Total War: Napoleon's Europe and the Birth of Warfare as We Know It* (New York: Houghton Mifflin, 2007). Pieter Geyl, *Napoleon For and Against,* trans. Olive Renier (New Haven: Yale University Press, 1964), 8–9. "Hallam," 210–211; cf. Joseph Hamburger, ed., *Napoleon and the Restoration of the Bourbons* (New York: Columbia University Press, 1977), esp. 52–66; to Napier, 14.x.40, *L*3:340. [Archibald Primrose] Lord Roseberry, *Napoleon: The Last Phase* (New York: Harper, 1901), 247. Patrick Brantlinger, *Dark Vanishings: Discourse on the Extinction of Primitive Races, 1800–1930* (Ithaca: Cornell University Press, 2003).

71. To HMT, 9.x.44, *L*4:217; and "Temple," 263. Andrew Ross, *John Philip (1775–1851): Missions, Race and Politics in South Africa* (Aberdeen: Aberdeen University Press, 1986), 77–115. John L. O'Sullivan, "The Great Nation of Futurity," *United States Democratic Review* 6 (1839): 426–430. Roy Harvey Pearce, *Savagism and Civilization: A Study of the Indian and the American Mind,* rev. ed. (Baltimore: Johns Hopkins Press, 1965), 53–134 (I owe this reference to the kindness of Margaret Abruzzo); and Anthony F. C. Wallace, *Jefferson and the Indians: The Tragic Fate of the First Americans* (Cambridge, Mass.: Belknap Press of Harvard University Press, 1999), 168–169, 226, 273–275, 326–329, and 336–338. Robert V. Rimini, *Andrew Jackson and His Indian Wars* (New York: Viking, 2001), 269, 90.

72. To TFE, 1.vii.34 and 18.xii.37, *L*3:62, 237. To C. Macaulay, 5.xii.36, *L*3:203; Krister Stendahl, "The Apostle Paul and the Introspective Conscience of the West," in *Paul among Jews and Gentiles* (Philadelphia: Fortress Press, 1976), 78–96; James Morrison, *A Companion to Homer's Odyssey* (Westport, Conn.: Greenwood Press,

2003), 184. To TFE, 25.vii–12.viii.36, *L*3:181. "Clive," 423, 431. Machiavelli to Soderini, ca. 15.ix.1506, in [Niccolò] Machiavelli, *The Prince,* trans. Russell Price, ed. Quentin Skinner and Russell Price (Cambridge: Cambridge University Press, 1988), 99.

73. To TFE, 18.xii.37, *L*3:238. Edward B. Pusey, "What Is Puseyism?" (1840), in *The Mind of the Oxford Movement,* ed. Owen Chadwick (Stanford: Stanford University Press, 1961), 51. Peter Benedict Nockles, *The Oxford Movement in Context: Anglican High Churchmanship, 1760–1857* (Cambridge: Cambridge University Press, 1994), 270–306.

74. L. Perry Curtis Jr., *Anglo-Saxons and Celts: A Study of Anti-Irish Prejudice in Victorian England* (Bridgeport, Conn.: Conference on British Studies, 1968), 14, 100–107; G. K. Peatling, "The Whiteness of Ireland under and after the Union," *Journal of British Studies* 44 (2005): 115–133; cf. L. Perry Curtis Jr., John Belchem, David A. Wilson, and G. K. Peatling, "Roundtable," ibid., 134–166. To Empson, 19.vi.37, *L*3:218; cf. [Thomas Robert Malthus], "Newneham and Others on the State of Ireland," *ER* 12 (1808): 336–355. Virginia Crossman, *Politics, Law and Order in Nineteenth-Century Ireland* (London: Gill and Macmillan, 1996), 66–75; and K. Theodore Hoppen, *Ireland since 1800: Conflict and Conformity,* 2d ed. (London: Longman, 1999), 36–58.

75. Jane Millgate, "Macaulay at Work: An Example of His Use of His Sources," *Transactions of the Cambridge Bibliographical Society* 5 (1970): 90–98; cf. A. N. L. Munby, *Macaulay's Library* (Glasgow: Jackson, Son, 1966), 23–25. To Napier, 12.ix.38, *L*3:256. To TFE, 15.ix.38, *L*3:257; to Napier, 12.ix.38, *L*3:256. To Napier, 20.vii.38, *L*3:252–253.

76. To Napier, 12.ix.38, *L*3:255. "Temple," 246, 247, and 249–250.

77. "Temple," 251, 252, and 254; cf. Matt. 16:3 and Gen. 49:4.

78. "Temple," 255–262, 263. J. D. Davies, in *ODNB,* s.v. "Temple, Sir William (baronet)." Charles Carlton, "Civilians," in *The Civil Wars: A Military History of England, Scotland, and Ireland 1635–1660* (New York: Oxford University Press, 2002), 278. Robert Dunlop, rev. Sean Kelsey, in *ODNB,* s.v. "Temple, Sir John (1699–1677)."

79. John Temple, *The Irish Rebellion,* quoted in Willy Maley, *Salvaging Spenser: Colonialism, Culture, and Identity* (New York: St. Martin's Press, 1997), 129. Deanna Rankin, *Between Spenser and Swift: English Writing in Seventeenth-Century Ireland* (Cambridge: Cambridge University Press, 2005), 39. Edmund Spenser, *A View of the Present State of Ireland,* in *Spenser's Prose Works,* ed. Rudolf Gottfried (Baltimore: Johns Hopkins Press, 1949), 148. John Milton, *Observations upon the Articles of Peace with the Irish Rebels,* ed. William Haller, in *The Works of John Milton,* ed. Frank Allen Patterson, vol. 6 (New York: Columbia University Press, 1932), 245. Joad Raymond, "Complications of Interest: Milton, Scotland, Ireland, and National Identity in 1649," *Review*

of English Studies 55 (2004): 315–345. Oliver Cromwell, letter of 17.ix.1649, quoted in J. G. Simms, "Cromwell at Drogheda, 1649," *Irish Sword* 2 (1974): 219. Milton, quoted in Maley, *Salvaging Spenser,* 128–129. Edward [Hyde], Earl of Clarendon, *The History of the Rebellion and Civil Wars in England Begun in the Year 1641,* ed. W. Dunn Macray, 6 vols. (Oxford, 1888), 5:102–103, 214–217, and 264–265 and 6:2–5; Simms, "Cromwell at Drogheda," 212–221; and Micheál Ó Siochrú, "Atrocity, Codes of Conduct and the Irish in the British Civil Wars," *Past & Present* 195 (2007): 55–86.

80. John Morrill, "The English Revolution," in *Three Nations—a Common History? England, Scotland, Ireland and British History, c. 1600–1920,* ed. Ronald G. Asch (Bochum: Brockmeyer, 1993), 106. Raymond Gillespie, "Temple's Fate: Reading the Irish Rebellion in Late Seventeenth-Century Ireland," in *British Interventions in Early Modern Ireland,* ed. Ciaran Brady and Jane Ohlmeyer (Cambridge: Cambridge University Press, 2005), 333.

81. Margaret T. Hodgen, *Early Anthropology in the Sixteenth and Seventeenth Centuries* (Philadelphia: University of Pennsylvania Press, 1971), 364–365. Geoffrey Plank, *Rebellion and Savagery: The Jacobite Rising of 1745 and the British Empire* (Philadelphia: University of Pennsylvania Press, 2006), 22, 92. Bruce Lenman, *The Jacobite Risings in Britain, 1689–1746* (Aberdeen: Scottish Cultural Press, 1980), 262–291. Idem, *Britain's Colonial Wars, 1688–1783* (Harlow, Essex: Longman, 2001), 242–245; cf. P. J. Marshall, *The Making and Unmaking of Empires: Britain, India, and America, c. 1750–1783* (New York: Oxford University Press, 2005), 5.

82. Niccolò Machiavelli, *Discourses on the First Ten Books of Titus Livius,* trans. Christian E. Detmold, in *The Prince and the Discourses* (New York: Modern Library, 1950), 288 (= 2:3). Idem, *The Prince,* 18. Russell Price, in *The Prince,* 107, s.v. *occasione.* Machiavelli, *The Prince,* 66.

83. "Temple," 262. Machiavelli, *Discourses,* 153–155 (= 1:13). D. N. Hempton, "Bickersteth, Bishop of Ripon: The Episcopate of a Mid-Victorian Evangelical," in *Religion in Victorian Britain,* vol. 4: *Interpretations,* ed. Gerald Parsons (Manchester: Manchester University Press, 1988), 54–55; Baruch J. Schwartz, "Reexamining the Fate of the 'Canaanites' in the Torah Traditions," in *Sefer Moshe: The Moshe Weinfeld Jubilee Volume: Studies in the Bible and the Ancient Near East, Qumran, and Post-Biblical Judaism,* ed. Chaim Cohen, Avi Hurvitz, and Shalom M. Paul (Winona Lake, Ind.: Eisenbrauns, 2004), 152, which I owe to the kindness of Gary Anderson. Henry Hart Milman, *The History of the Jews* (1830), 2 vols., 2d ed. (London, [1863]), 1:190, 22–23.

84. "Temple," 262–263.

85. Ibid., 263.

86. Ibid., 263–264. To Napier, 19.x.42, *L*4:61. Knutsford, *Zachary Macaulay,* 467.

87. "Temple," 264, 263.

88. David P. Jordan, "The Robespierre Problem," in *Robespierre,* ed. Colin Haydon and William Doyle (Cambridge: Cambridge University Press, 1999), 27–32. Thomas Peregrine Courtenay, *Memoirs of the Life, Work, and Correspondence of Sir William Temple, Bart.,* 2 vols. (London, 1836), 1:2, 22–24, and 381–385. "Temple," 264.

89. "Temple," 317, 319. To Napier, 26.vi.38, *L*3:245; to Napier, 20.iii.39, *L*3:282; cf. "Clive," 381–382.

90. Jennifer Pitts, *A Turn to Empire: The Rise of Liberal Imperialism in Britain and France* (Princeton: Princeton University Press, 2005), 168. Melvin Richter, "Tocqueville in Algeria," *Review of Politics* 25 (1963): 365. Jefferson to Humboldt, 6.xii.13, quoted in Ben Kiernan, *Blood and Soil: A World History of Genocide and Extermination from Sparta to Darfur* (New Haven: Yale University Press, 2007), 329. Robert J. Miller, *Native America Discovered and Conquered: Thomas Jefferson, Lewis and Clark, and Manifest Destiny* (Westport, Conn.: Greenwood Press, 2006), 93.

91. "Mirabeau," *WLM* 5:613–614, 615–616, 617, 615–616, and 620, paraphrasing Eccles. 3:3a.

92. Nicholas Phillipson, "Providence and Progress: An Introduction to the Historical Thought of William Robertson," in *William Robertson and the Expansion of Empire,* ed. Stewart J. Brown (Cambridge: Cambridge University Press, 1997), 55–73; Daniele Francesconi, "William Robertson on Historical Causation and Unintended Consequences," *Storia della Storiografia* 36 (1999): 55–80; and Jeffrey Smitten, "Impartiality in Robertson's *History of America,*" *Eighteenth-Century Studies* 19 (1985): 56–77. William Robertson, *The History of the Discovery and Settlement of America* (New York, 1837), 347, 386.

93. Jeremy Bentham, *The Commonplace Book,* in *The Works of Jeremy Bentham,* ed. John Bowring, 11 vols. (London, 1843), 10:142. Frances Hutcheson, *Inquiry into the Original of Our Ideas of Beauty and Virtue* (1726), (New York: Garland, 1971), bk. 2, 3, 8. "Bacon," 242.

94. An enormous literature grows; the starting points are assembled in Thomas Bender, ed., *The Antislavery Debate: Capitalism and Abolitionism as a Problem in Historical Interpretation* (Berkeley: University of California Press, 1992). [Anon.], "An Account of His Life and Writings," in Robertson, *History of America,* xxii. *OED,* s.v. "Eradication." "Delayed and Denied," *The Economist,* 15.x.2008, available at www.economist.com/world/asia/displaystory.cfm?story_id=12411498.

95. "Temple," 316. Samuel Johnson, *Taxation No Tyranny,* in *Political Writings,* ed. Donald J. Greene, in *Works of Samuel Johnson,* vol. 10 (New Haven: Yale University Press, 1977), 419; this paragraph summarizes and quotes from 419–422.

96. As quoted in Edmund Burke, *On Empire, Liberty, and Reform: Speeches and Letters,* ed. David Bromwich (New Haven: Yale University Press, 2000), 14. To MMC, 27.vi.34, *L*3:41; cf. to Napier, 11.i.4[1], *L*3:361.

97. James J. Sheehan, *Where Have All the Soldiers Gone? The Transformation of Modern Europe* (Boston: Houghton Mifflin, 2008), 46. To TFE, 15.ix.38, *L*3:258. "Mirabeau," 634. [Francis Jeffrey], review of *Life and Voyages of Columbus* by Washington Irving (ix.28), in *Contributions to the Edinburgh Review,* 4 vols. in 1 (Boston, 1856), 271.

98. "Minute on Indian Education," in C & P, 241. Joseph Conrad, *Heart of Darkness,* ed. Robert Kimbrough (New York: Norton, 1963), 51. Sheehan, *Where Have All the Soldiers Gone?,* 47. To TFE, 18.xii.37, *L*3:235, 238.

99. Geoffrey Carnall, "Robertson and Contemporary Images of India," in Brown, *Robertson and Expansion of Empire,* 211–214, 226. Prasannan Parthasarathi, "Rethinking Wages and Competitiveness in the Eighteenth Century: Britain and South India," *Past & Present* 158 (1998): 79–109. Kenneth Pomeranz, *The Great Divergence: China, Europe, and the Making of the Modern World Economy* (Princeton: Princeton University Press, 2000), 207–208, 274–279; cf. David S. Landes, *The Wealth and Poverty of Nations: Why Some Are So Rich and Some So Poor* (New York: Norton, 1998), 165, 538n27. To MMC, 3.x.34, *L*3:87; and Pinney, *L*3:129n1. Rudyard Kipling, "The Ballad of East and West."

100. Richard Ely, "From Sect to Church: Sir James Stephen's Theology of Empire," *Journal of Religious History* 19 (1995): 75–91; cf. H. R. Fox-Bourne, *The Aborigines Protection Society: Chapters in Its History* (London, 1899); Raymond Cooke McIntyre, "British Evangelicals, Native Peoples, and the Concept of Empire, 1837–1852" (Ph.D. diss., University of Oregon, 1963), 46–47; Amalie M. Kass and Edward H. Kass, *Perfecting the World: The Life and Times of Dr. Thomas Hodgkin, 1798–1866* (Boston: Harcourt Brace Jovanovich, 1988), 257–272, 373–386, 455–456, and 571n30; Charles Swaisland, "The Aborigines Protection Society, 1837–1909," in *After Slavery: Emancipation and Its Discontents,* ed. Howard Temperley (London: Frank Cass, 2000), 265–280. Gary J. Bass, *Freedom's Battle: The Origins of Humanitarian Intervention* (New York: Knopf, 2008). Buxton to Hodgkin, 4.vii.40, in Pugh, *Calendar of Papers of Buxton,* 184; Innes to Buxton, [15.xii.40], ibid., 201. Buxton to Wilkin, 23.xii.42, ibid., 246. Howard Temperley, *White Dreams, Black Africa: The Antislavery Expedition to the Niger, 1841–1842* (New Haven: Yale University Press, 1991), xiii. Patrick Brantlinger, *Rule of Darkness: British Literature and Imperialism, 1830–1914* (Ithaca: Cornell University Press, 1988), 178. Uday Singh Mehta, *Liberalism and Empire: A Study in Nineteenth-Century Liberal Thought* (Chicago: University of Chicago Press, 1999), 77–114; cf. Sankar Muthu, *Enlightenment against Empire* (Princeton: Princeton University Press, 2003), 259–284.

101. Buxton to TBM, 5.iv.41, in Pugh, *Calendar of Papers of Buxton,* 212. Alexis de Tocqueville, *Democracy in America,* trans. Henry Reeve, Francis Bowen, and Phillips Bradley, 2 vols. (New York: Random House/Vintage, 1954), 1:354. *The Second Annual Report of the Aborigines Protection Society* (London, 1839), 26. Herbert S. Klein,

The Atlantic Slave Trade (Cambridge: Cambridge University Press, 1999), 188–190. Blair Worden, *Roundhead Reputations: The English Civil Wars and the Passions of Posterity* (London: Allen Lane/Penguin, 2001), 215–250. Fred Kaplan, in *ODNB*, s.v. "Carlyle, Thomas (1795–1881)." Thomas Carlyle, *Oliver Cromwell's Letters and Speeches with Elucidations,* 3 vols. in 1 (1845), (London, 1893), 2:45.

102. Joseph Chamberlain, *Mr. Chamberlain's Speeches,* ed. Charles W. Boyd (London: Constable, 1914), 2. Leo Tolstoy, *Anna Karenin,* trans. Rosemary Edmonds, rev. ed. (London: Penguin, 1978), 727. James Joyce, *Portrait of the Artist as a Young Man* (New York: Huebsch, 1916), 181.

5. Statesman

1. To Napier, 4.xi.38, *L*3:262. J1:1, 11, and 13; 20, 23, and 24.x.38. J1:4, 21.x.38.

2. J1:13, 25.x.38 (Job 3:3). J1:17, 26.x.38. J1:20, 26.x.38. J1:20–23, 27.x.38.

3. John Pemble, *The Mediterranean Passion: Victorians and Edwardians in the South* (Oxford: Clarendon Press, 1987), 15–39. J1:25, 28.x.38. J1:31–32, 28.x.38. J1:24–32, 28.x.38. J1:33–38, 28–30.x.38.

4. To HMT, 30.x.38, *L*3:260–261; J1:39–42, 30.x.38. J1:38–39, 30.x.38. To HMT, 30.x.38, *L*3:261; J1:42–50, 31.x.38. J1:19, 26.x.38. J1:50–60, 1 and 2.xi.38.

5. J1:60–62, 2.xi.38. J1:67, 3.xi.38. J1:68, 3.xi.38. J1:77, 5.xi.38. J11:602, 10.xii.59. To Napier, 4.xi.38, *L*3:262. Depressives are susceptible to migraines, just as migraine-sufferers are often depressed. Lewis Wolpert, *Malignant Sadness: The Anatomy of Depression* (New York: Free Press, 1999), 61; www.neuropsychiatryreviews. com/sep02/npr_sep02_migdepres.html, which reports on Dr. Naomi Breslau's 2002 clinical study at Henry Ford Hospital, Detroit.

6. To [HMT, 8.xi.38], *L*3:263. Graziella Magherini, *La sindrome de Stendhal* (Florence: Ponte alle Grazie, 1989), 49–74.

7. J1:54, 1.xi.38; J1:63, 3.xi.38. J1:71–72, 5.xi.38. J1:72, 5.xi.38; J1:73–74, 5.xi.38.

8. J1:76–78, 5.xi.38. J1:78–79, 6.xi.38. J1:80, 6.xi.38. J1:83, 6.xi.38.

9. J1:85–87, 7.xi.38. V. E. Chandler, in *ODNB*, s.v. "Fox, Henry Edward, fourth Baron Holland." Idem, in *ODNB*, s.v. "Fox, Caroline." J1:87, 90–91, 7–9.xi.38. J1:96, 10.xi.38. J1:98, 10.xi.38. J1:102, 13.xi.38; J1:105, 14.xi.38.

10. J1:93–95, 10.xi.38. Smith to Grey, 15.xi.38, and x.39, in *Selected Letters of Sydney Smith,* ed. Nowell C. Smith (London: Geoffrey Cumberlege/Oxford University Press, 1956), 258, 266–267. To HMT, 14–15.xi.38, *L*3:264–265. To Lansdowne, 19.xii.38, 3:266–267.

11. J1:101, 104, 13 and 14.xi.38. J1:105, 14.xi.38. J1:109–110, 15.xi.38. J1:259–260, 22.xii.38.

12. J1:110–111, 15.xi.38. J1:112–114, 15.xi.38.

13. J1:115–117, 16.xi.38. J1:118, 16.xi.38. J1:120–121, 17.xi.38. J1:122, 18.xi.38. J1:124–126, 18.xi.38. J1:133–137, 20.xi.38. J1:143, 21.xi.38; cf. J1:130, 141–143, 20 and 21.xi.38. J1:145, 148, 22.xi.38.

14. J1:156–157, 25.xi.38. J1:176, 28.xi.38. J1:178, 28.xi.38. To Lansdowne, 19.xii.38, *L3*:267. J1:191, 1.xii.38.

15. J1:151, 23.xi.38. J1:153, 24.xi.38. J1:168, 26.xi.38; cf. J1:189, 1.xii.38. J1:251, 21.xii.38. J1:173, 27.xi.38. J1:172, 27.xi.38. J1:186, 30.xi.38; J1:184, 29.xi.38.

16. J1:193, 2.xii.38. J1:169, 26.xi.38. J1:199, 2.xii.38. J1:202, 2.xii.38. J1:217, 6.xii.38. J1:247, 16.xii.38; J1:218, 6.xii.38. J1:221, 7.xii.38; J1:223, 8.xii.38.

17. J1:249–250, 18.xii.38. J1:243–244, 14.xii.38; J1:245, 15.xii.38. J1:245, 16.xii.38. J1:261, 22.xii.38. J1:248–249, 18.xii.38. To Lansdowne, 19.xii.38, *L3*:267–268; cf. J1:282, 27.xii.38.

18. J1:263–264, 24.xii.38. J1:265–270, 25.xii.38; cf. Richard J. Grace, "Macaulay, Mummery, and Mystery: Christmas, 1838, at Rome," *Catholic Historical Review* 74 (1988): 558–570.

19. J1:271, 25.xii.38. *LLLM* 2:21–22. To SM, 23.i.40, *L3*:317; and Stuart to Napier, 28.i.40, summarized in Pinney, 3:317n2.

20. J1:272, 26.xii.38. J1:275, 26.xii.38. J1:276, 26.xii.38. J1:277, 26.xii.38.

21. J1:282, 27.xii.38. J1:286–287, 29.xii.38. J1:288, 292, 30 and 31.xii.38.

22. J1:296–297, 298–300, and 309, 2 and 7.i.39. J1:304, 5.i.39. J1:309, 7.i.39. J1:302, 4.i.39. J1:301A–B, 3.i.39; J1:302–303, 305–306, 319, and 335, 4, 6, 10, and 17.i.39.

23. J1:333, 16.i.39. J1:336, 18.i.39. J1:336, 350, 18 and 29.i.39. J1:302, 318–319, 331, and 332, 6, 10, 14, and 15.i.39; J1:324–325, 11.i.39. J1:321, 323, 326, and 330–331, 10, 11, 12, and 14.i.39.

24. J1:329, 333, and 336, 13, 16, and 18.i.39. J1:344–345, 25.i.39. J1:348, 27.i.39. J1:355, 2.ii.39. J1:351, 30.i.39. J1:352–353, 31.i.39.

25. J1:362, 10.ii.39. J1:364–365, 11 and 13.ii.39. J1:367, 13–14.ii.39. J1:374–375, 16.iii.39. J1:371, 26.ii.39; to Napier, 26.ii.39, *L3*:277. J1:372, 6.iii.39. J1:373, 10 and 11.iii.39. J1:380, 3–9.iv.39; J1:381, 12.iv.39.

26. J1:374–377, 14–15 and 17–23.iii.39. J1:379, 382, 2 and 13.iv.39. E.g., J1:360–367, 7–13.ii.39. J1:381, 11.iv.39. J1:381–382, 12.iv.39. J1:384–385, 23.iv.39. J1:372, 5.iii.39. Richard Davenport-Hines, in *ODNB, s.v.* "Milnes, Richard Monckton."

27. Boyd Hilton, *A Mad, Bad, and Dangerous People? England, 1783–1846* (Oxford: Clarendon Press, 2006), 501. J1:386, 7.v.39. J1:363, 387, 10.ii and 10.v.39. J1:386–88A, 7 and 12–15.v.39.

28. "Election" (25.ix.39), *WLM* 8:151. To HMT, 29.v.39, *L3*:290 and n1. "Election," 151. Ibid., 158. Ibid., 155. "The Earl of Chatham," *WLM* 7:204–205. To Baines, 4.vi.39, *L3*:291; and to Black, 15.v.39, *L3*:287.

29. To TFE, [9.ii.39], *L3*:275. J1:321, 10.i.39. Major studies include David Beb-

bington, *The Mind of Gladstone: Religion, Homer, and Politics* (Oxford: Oxford University Press, 2004), 43–76—the quoted matter appears on 55–56; Perry Butler, *Gladstone: Church, State, and Tractarianism: A Study of His Religious Ideas and Attitudes, 1809–1859* (Oxford: Oxford University Press, 1982), 77–92; and above all Richard J. Helmstadter, "Conscience and Politics: Gladstone's First Book," in *The Gladstonian Turn of Mind: Essays Presented to J. B. Conacher,* ed. Bruce L. Kinzer (Toronto: University of Toronto Press, 1985), 3–42.

30. J1:378, 29–31.iii.39. To Napier, 26.ii.39, *L*3:277. "Gladstone on Church and State," *WLM* 6:328–329. To Black, 20.x.40, *L*3:346. Stewart J. Brown, *The National Churches of England, Ireland, and Scotland 1801–1846* (New York: Oxford University Press, 2001), is a masterly study of the context. W. E. Gladstone, "A Chapter of Autobiography," in *Gleanings of Past Years,* 7 vols. (London, 1879), 7:144.

31. "Gladstone," 326–329, 330–331. John Kenyon, "Gladstone and the Anglican High Churchmen, 1845–52," in Kinzer, *Gladstonian Turn of Mind,* 47. "Gladstone," 331–334.

32. "Gladstone," 333–338, 340–341, 343, 343–344, and 345.

33. Ibid., 345. John Keble, review of W. E. Gladstone, *The State in Its Relations with the Church, British Critic* (October 1838): 369, 386, as quoted in Helmstadter, "Conscience and Politics," 33. "Gladstone," 353–357.

34. Ibid., 361–362, 366–367, and 370. Ibid., 371–372.

35. Ibid., 372–373; for Warburton, see Robert E. Sullivan, "The Transformation of Anglican Political Theology, c. 1716–1760," in *Politics, Politeness, and Patriotism,* ed. Gordon J. Schochet with Patricia Tatspaugh and Carol Brobeck (Washington, D.C.: Folger Institute/Folger Shakespeare Library, 1993), 55–57. "Gladstone," 374–376.

36. "Gladstone," 377–379.

37. J1:384, 22.iv.39. M. R. D. Foot and H. C. G. Matthew, eds., *The Gladstone Diaries, with Cabinet Minutes and Prime-Ministerial Correspondence,* 14 vols. (Oxford: Clarendon Press, 1968–1994), 2:592 (9–10.iv.39); Gladstone to TBM, 10.iv.39, as quoted in *LLLM* 2:4–5. To Gladstone, 11.iv.39, *L*3:283–284; Foot and Matthew, *Gladstone Diaries,* 2:593 (15.iv.39). Ibid., 380 (9.ii.39); Boyd Hilton, "Peel: A Reappraisal," *Historical Journal* 22 (1979): 609. Gladstone, "Chapter of Autobiography," 115. To Napier, 13.xi.40, *L*3:344.

38. Frank M. Turner, *John Henry Newman: The Challenge to Evangelical Religion* (New Haven: Yale University Press, 2002), 331–333, 358–403, and 465–467. John Henry Newman, *The Tamworth Reading Room,* in *Newman Prose and Poetry,* ed. Geoffrey Tillotson (Cambridge, Mass.: Harvard University Press, 1970), 76. J1:379, 2. iv.39. G. I. T. Machin, *Politics and the Churches in Great Britain, 1832 to 1868* (Oxford: Clarendon Press, 1977), 173.

39. To Austin, [early 1840?], *L*3:325–326 and nn 5, 3; and to Napier, 12.vi.40,

*L*3:325; cf. J1:372, 6.iii.39. To Napier, 17.ix.40, *L*3:336. Leopold von Ranke, preface to *Histories of the Latin and Germanic Nations from 1494–1514,* in *The Varieties of History from Voltaire to the Present,* ed. Fritz Stern (Cleveland: World/Meridian Books, 1956), 57. Idem, *History of the Popes, Their Church and State,* rev. ed., trans. E. Fowler. 3 vols. (New York: Collier, 1901), 1:xxii.

40. To Napier, 14.x.40, *L*3:340 and n1; D. G. Paz, *Popular Anti-Catholicism in Mid-Victorian England* (Stanford: Stanford University Press, 1992), 18–19, 299–302; Michael Wheeler, *The Old Enemies: Catholic and Protestant in Nineteenth-Century English Culture* (Cambridge: Cambridge University Press, 2006), 9–37, 95–96. "Von Ranke," *WLM* 6:455. Edward Gibbon, *Autobiography* (London: Oxford University Press, n.d.), 160.

41. "Von Ranke," 6:464, 470, 472, 482, 456–460, 470–471, 462, and 461.

42. Thomas Hobbes, *Leviathan: or the Matter, Forme and Power of a Commonwealth Eccesiasticall and Civil,* ed. Michael Oakeshott (New York: Collier, 1962), 500, 502. "Von Ranke," 460, 476.

43. "Von Ranke," 462–464, 467, 473, and 474.

44. Ibid., 477–479, 481–482. Max Weber, *The Protestant Ethic and the Spirit of Capitalism,* trans. Talcott Parsons (New York: Scribner's, 1958), 175 and 280n96.

45. "Von Ranke," 483–484, 487. "Barère," *WLM* 7:175. "Hallam's Constitutional History," *WLM* 5:226. *OED,* s.v. "Nationalism."

46. J1:389–390, 5[?].vi.40. J1:406, 11.vi.40; and to Napier, 20.ix.39, *L*3:299. Ian Newbould, *Whiggery and Reform, 1830–41: The Politics of Government* (Stanford: Stanford University Press, 1990), 242–321.

47. To SM, 23.i.40, *L*3:317. To Napier, 12.vi.40, *L*3:326. To Millar, 1.x.39, *L*3:302. To Electors, 1.x.39, *L*3:303–304. *The Times,* 8.x.39, quoted in Pinney, *L*3:310n4; to Napier, 15.i.40, *L*3:315. To Bacon, 8.ii.40, *L*3:319 and n2.

48. J1:388, 388a, 15.v.39; John Cam Hobhouse, quoted in Pinney, *L*3:302n4. J1:391A, 7 and 8.vi.40; cf. to TFE, 14.iii.40, *L*3:321; and to Hill, 12.viii.40, *L*3:331–335. J1:391A, 9.vi.39. To Bird, 18.xi.40, *L*3:345. To SM, 25.ix.39, 3:301. G. M. Young, ed., *Macaulay: Prose and Poetry* (Cambridge, Mass.: Harvard University Press, 1952), 804; J1:392–406, 10–11.vi.40.

49. To Napier, 13.xi.40, *L*3:344 and n2; and to FM, 28.vi.41, *L*3:379. To McLaren, 30.i.41, *L*3:364–365.

50. To Napier, 28, 8.xii.40, *L*3:360 and 353–354; and to Palmerston, [7?xii.40], *L*3:352. To Ebrington, 6.i.4[1], *L*3:360. To McLaren, 8.v.41, *L*3:373.

51. To FM, 1.vii.41, *L*3:380. Hilton, *Mad, Bad, and Dangerous,* 506. To Napier, 27.vii.41, *L*3:385. To TFE, 12.vii.41, *L*3:382 and n2; and to Napier, 10.viii.39, *L*3:297. To Adolphus, 4.xi.41, *L*4:14. J1:388, 13.v.39.

52. To Black, 14.vii.41, *L*3:384. To Napier, 30.x.41, *L*4:12. To Napier, 3.ix.41, *L*4:5. To Everett, 8.iii.49, *L*5:33.

53. J1:389, 5.vi.40; "Election," 156. "Ballot" (18.vi.39), in Vizetelly, 1:209, 213, 222, 216, and 219–220.

54. G. H. Francis, *Orators of the Age* (New York, 1847), 64–65, 68, 72, 74–75, and 76–79.

55. "The Ministry" (29.i.40), *WLM* 8:161, 168, 175, and 168–169. "Privileges" (6.iii.40), in Vizetelly, 1:252. "Jews' Declaration Bill" (31.iii.41), in Vizetelly, 1:320–321. "Sugar Duties" (11.v.41), in Vizetelly, 1:330–331. J1:388, 391A, 11.v.39 and 8. vi.40; cf. to HMT, 20.iii.39, *L*3:281.

56. "Copyright" (5.ii.41), *WLM* 8:196, 197, and 198–199.

57. Ibid., 204–205. To Napier, 7.iv.42, *L*4:25 and n1. "Copyright" (6.iv.42), *WLM* 8:212–215. [George Nathaniel] Earl Curzon of Kedleston, *Modern Parliamentary Eloquence* (London: Macmillan, 1913), 22; to Talfourd, 30.iv.42, *L*4:33. William St. Clair, *The Reading Nation in the Romantic Period* (Cambridge: Cambridge University Press, 2004), 128.

58. Heera Chung, "From a Protectionist Party to a Church Party, 1846–48: Identity Crisis of the Conservative Party and the Jew Bill of 1847," *Albion* 36 (2004): 256–278. "Dissenters' Chapels" (6.vi.44), *WLM* 8:272, 282–283. "Theological Tests" (9.vii.45), *WLM* 8:335, 336, 338–339, and 346–347.

59. To Napier, 23.ii.42, *L*4:22; and to McLaren, 4.i.43, *L*4:91. To McLaren, 13.iv.42, *L*4:26. To McLaren, 29.i.42, *L*4:21. To Napier, 28.ii.42, *L*4:22; "The Gates of Somnauth" (9.iii.43), *WLM* 8:242; to McLaren, 13.iv.42, *L*4:26. "Income Tax" (11.iv.42), in Vizetelly, 1:376–387. To McLaren, 4.i.43, *L*4:91; and to Black, 22.ii.43, *L*4:100.

60. To FM, 7.v.42, *L*4:34–35. Hilton, *Mad, Bad and Dangerous,* 612. "The People's Charter" (3.v.42), *WLM* 8:219–220.

61. "People's Charter," 220, 223, 221, 222, 224, and 225. To Secretary of the Committee, 16.ii.[46], *L*4:293. Niall Ferguson, *The Pity of War: Explaining World War I* (New York: Basic Books, 1999), 29.

62. "Ten Hours Bill" (22.v.46), *WLM* 8:361; cf. 375, 367, 360, and 373. "Education" (18.iv.47), *WLM* 8:387, 396, 388, 390, 373, 387, 393, 394, 398–399, and 403–404. Will R. Jordan, "Religion in the Public Sphere: A Reconsideration of David Hume and Religious Establishment," *Review of Politics* 64 (2002): 687–713.

63. To Napier, 14.x.40, *L*3:340. To Napier, 29.x.40, *L*3:342. Jeremy Collier, *A Short View of the Immorality and Profaneness of the English Stage* (London, 1698), 1. To Napier, 26.xi.40 and 11.i.4[1], *L*3:348, 361. "Leigh Hunt," *WLM* 6:493.

64. To H. Macaulay, 6.v.42, *L*4:34. To Hunt, 6 and 24.iii.41, *L*3:365–366, 367–368. To Hunt, 29.x.41, *L*4:10–11; and to Napier, 30.x.41, *L*4:12–13; e.g., to Napier, 25.iv.42 and 19.x.42, *L*4:30, 61–62. Francis Jeffrey, quoted in Pinney, *L*4:34n2.

65. "Madame D'Arblay," *WLM* 7:46–47, 2–3.

66. "The Life and Writings of Addison," *WLM* 7:53; to Napier, 6.ii.43, *L*4:98.

To Napier, 6.ii.43, *L4*:98; cf. to Napier, 18.iv.42, *L4*:27; and Carey McIntosh, *The Evolution of English Prose, 1700–1800: Style, Politeness, and Print Culture* (Cambridge: Cambridge University Press, 1998), 94–97. "Addison," 53, 63, 95, 100–101, 105, 92, and 120–121. Bonamy Dobrée, *Essays in Biography* (London: Oxford University Press, 1925), 210–334.

67. J1:391, 7.vi.40. "Barère," 202, 144–146 (Luke 22:53), 160, 161, 162, 171–172, and 203, riffing on Phil. 4:8.

68. To FM, 14.vi.42, *L4*:37; and to Napier, 4.x.41, *L4*:7. "Warren Hastings," *WLM* 6:643; cf. "Chatham," 278–279. To Napier, 4.v.41, *L3*:372; and to Lady Holland, 18.v.[41], *L3*:374. "Lord Holland," *WLM* 6:533, 540.

6. Empire Builder

1. To Napier, 13.xi.40, *L3*:344; "Lord Clive," *WLM* 6:382, 442, 413, and 381; cf. Uma Satyavolu Rau, "The National/Imperial Subject in T. B. Macaulay's Historiography," *Nineteenth-Century Contexts* 23 (2001): 89–119.

2. "Clive," 410–411, 382, 406, 405, 407, and 411.

3. "Clive," 418–419; cf. 447, 452–453, 415, and 416. Robert Travers, "Ideology and British Expansion in Bengal," *Journal of Imperial and Commonwealth History* 33 (2005): 7–27. "Warren Hastings," *WLM* 6:582–584, 591, and 611–612; cf. Max Boot, *War Made New: Technology, Warfare, and the Course of History, 1500 to Today* (New York: Gotham, 2006), 77–80, 89–102. "Clive," 416. To FM, 18.xi.54, *L5*:429; and to Russell, 6.iv.58, 6:146–147. To Napier, 14.i.40, *L3*:315; "Hastings," 545.

4. Glenn Melancon, *Britain's China Policy and the Opium Crisis: Balancing Drugs, Violence, and National Honour* (Burlington, Vt.: Ashgate, 2003), 105–107. "War with China" (7.iv.40), *WLM* 8:188, 190, 191, and 193. *Hansard,* 3d ser., 53 (1840): 719 = "War with China," 193.

5. "War with China," 193, 194. To Napier, 8.iv.40, *L3*:324. Herbert C. F. Bell, *Lord Palmerston,* 2 vols. (London: Longmans, Green, 1936), 1:275–277. *Hansard,* 3d ser., 112 (1850): 444; cf. Acts 22:25–29. *A Supplement to the Oxford English Dictionary,* ed. R. W. Burchfield, 4 vols. (Oxford: Clarendon Press, 1987), s.v. "Gunboat."

6. To Napier, 13.xi.40 and 25.i.41, *L3*:344, 363. To Napier, 27.vii.41 and 3.ix.41, *L3*:385 and 4:5. To Napier, 11.i.40, *L3*:362. To Napier, 20.ix.41 and 18.iv.42, *L4*:6, 29.

7. To Napier, 24.i.42, *L4*:21. To Napier, 30.iii.41, *L3*:369; cf. to Napier, 8 and 18.iv.42, *L4*:25–26, 27–29. To Napier, 24.vi.42 and 3.xii.42, *L4*:40–41, 79. To Napier, 12.xii.42, *L4*:82; and Pinney, *L4*:96n3. *LLLM* 2:71–72.

8. To Napier, 14.i.40 and 11.i.4[1], *L3*:315, 362. Brougham, quoted in John Morley, "Macaulay," *Critical Miscellanies,* rev. ed. (London: Macmillan, 1923), 421–422. "Hastings," 543, 644, and 543–544. Owen Dudley Edwards, "Macaulay's Warren

Hastings," in *The Impeachment of Warren Hastings: Papers from a Bicentenary Commemoration,* ed. Geoffrey Carnal and Colin Nicholson (Edinburgh: Edinburgh University Press, 1989), 109–144; cf. Thomas J. Gillcrist, "The Macaulay Nobody Reads: Second Thoughts and 'Warren Hastings,'" *Nineteenth-Century Prose* 31 (2004): 1–27.

9. "Hastings," 545, 548, 558, 549, and 595. Thomas Hobbes, *Leviathan: or the Matter, Forme and Power of a Commonwealth Eccesiasticall and Civil,* ed. Michael Oakeshott (New York: Collier, 1962), 132. "Hastings," 554–555.

10. "Hastings," 556, 571, 578, 562–563, 571, and 599; Robert Knox, *The Races of Man: A Fragment* (Philadelphia, 1850), 216. To Palmerston, 27.viii.42, *L*4:50–51 and n4.

11. "Hastings," 577, 578, 580, 582, 591–592, 596, 597 (cf. 603), 604–605, and 607. To Napier, 11.i.40, *L*3:361. "Hastings," 606–614.

12. "Hastings," 615, 616, and 620. Edmund Burke, "Speech in Opening the Impeachment of Warren Hastings, Esq., Fourth Day" (18.ii.1788), in Edmund Burke, *On Empire, Liberty, and Reform: Speeches and Letters,* ed. David Bromwich (New Haven: Yale University Press, 2000), 398. "Hastings," 625–626.

13. "Hastings," 629, 631, 634, 636, 638, and 644.

14. To Ebrington, 12.i.41, *L*3:362. To Napier, 24.i.42, *L*4:21. Mukhtar Ali Isani, "Some Sources for Poe's 'Tale of the Ragged Mountains,'" *Poe Studies* 5 (1972): 38–40. "Hastings," 440. P. J. Marshall, "The Making of an Imperial Icon: The Case of Warren Hastings," *Journal of Commonwealth and Imperial History* 27 (1999): 1–2.

15. To Napier, 1.xii.41, *L*4:18; cf. "Hastings," 582. To Napier, 24.i.42, *L*4:21. To Napier, 23, 28.ii.42, *L*4:22. "Frederic the Great," *WLM* 6:660, 692–693; cf. Timothy C. F. Stunt, "Thomas Babington Macaulay and Frederick the Great," *Historical Journal* 23 (1980): 939–947.

16. "Frederic," 702–703. To Napier, 1.iv.42, *L*4:24. To Napier, 8.iv.42, *L*4:26. "Barère," *WLM* 7:162. To FM, 1.xii.52, *L*5:298; and to Tauchnitz, 1.viii.57, *L*6:100.

17. "The Earl of Chatham," *WLM* 7:223. "William Pitt," *WLM* 6:73, 64. "Chatham," 204, 222; cf. "Pitt," 74. "Chatham," 262–263.

18. Herbert Butterfield, *George III and the Historians,* rev. ed. (London: Collins, 1957), 89–92, 231–32. "Chatham," 223. "Pitt," 73, 64. "Chatham," 204, 222; cf. "Pitt," 74. "Chatham," 227, 205. "Pitt," 75; and "Chatham," 257–258. "Chatham," 255. P. R. Ghosh, "Macaulay and the Heritage of the Enlightenment," *English Historical Review* 112 (1997): 358–395. "Chatham," 233–234.

19. To Hallam, 28.x.42, *L*4:66; cf. to TFE, 12.vii.41, *L*3:381–382 and 381n3. T. P. Wiseman, *Historiography and Imagination: Eight Essays on Roman Culture* (Exeter: University of Exeter Press, 1994), 12. Recent studies of the *Lays* include K. R. Prowse, "Livy and Macaulay," in *Livy,* ed. T. A. Dorey (London: Routledge & K. Paul, 1971), 159–176. Donald J. Gray, "Macaulay's *Lays of Rome* and the Publication of

Nineteenth-Century Poetry," in *Victorian Literature and Society,* ed. James R. Kincaid and Albert J. Kuhn (Columbus: Ohio State University Press, 1984), 74–93; Owen Dudley Edwards, *Macaulay* (New York: St. Martin's Press, 1988), 54–82; Catherine Edwards, "Translating Empire? Macaulay's Rome," in *Roman Presences: Receptions of Rome in European Culture, 1789–1945,* ed. Catherine Edwards (Cambridge: Cambridge University Press, 1999), 70–87; and William McKelvy, "Primitive Ballads, Modern Criticism, Ancient Skepticism: Macaulay's *Lays of Ancient Rome," Victorian Literature and Culture* 28 (2000): 287–309, which is penetrating on the *Lays* and much else. To Napier, 14.vii.42, *L4*:44; cf. Arnaldo Momigliano, "Perizonius, Niebuhr and the Character of Early Roman Tradition," *Journal of Roman Studies* 47 (1957): 104–114. GOT, *Marginal Notes by Lord Macaulay* (London: Longmans, Green, 1907), 38. To TFE, 22.viii.42 and [viii?42], *L4*:48–49, 52. *LLLM* 2:44. To TFE, 12. vii.41, *L3*:382.

20. "Preface" to *Lays of Ancient Rome, WLM* 8:461. To TFE, 14.ix.42, *L4*:56.

21. "Horatius," *WLM* 8:464, 463, 464, 474, and 473.

22. "The Battle of the Lake Regillus," *WLM* 8:485–486, 488–489, 504, 501, and 507. McKelvy, "Primitive Ballads," 299–302, caught it. Anglican divines regularly identified Castor and Pollux with modern papist idolatry. Conyers Middleton used them to help make the case for severing the apostolic from the post-apostolic church.

23. "Virginia," *WLM* 8:514. To Napier, 5.xi.41, *L4*:15. "Virginia," 517, 520, 522, and 523. To FM, 29.x.42, *L4*:68.

24. "The Prophecy of Capys," *WLM* 8:530. Horace, *Epode* 9; Virgil, *Aeneid* 6.851–853 (the Dryden translation). "Prophecy of Capys," 537.

25. Pinney, *L4*:53n1. To Napier, 19.x.42 and 16.xi.42, *L4*:62, 69. Archie Burnett, "A Clough Poem—by Macaulay," *Notes and Queries* 37 (1990): 32–33. John Stuart Mill, "Macaulay's Lays of Ancient Rome" (1843), in *Autobiography and Literary Essays,* ed. John M. Robson and Jack Stillinger, vol. 1 of *Collected Works,* ed. J. M. Robson (Toronto: University of Toronto Press, 1981), 523–532. Stephen to Napier, 26.xii.42, in *Selection from the Correspondence of Macvey Napier,* ed. Macvey Napier (London, 1879), 415. Pinney, *L5*:vii. *LLLM* 2:69. To FM, 29.x.42, *L4*:68. Krishan Kumar, *The Making of English National Identity* (Cambridge: Cambridge University Press, 2003), 195–225. Anthony Pagden, *Lords of All the World: Ideologies of Empire in Spain, Britain, and France, c. 1500–c. 1800* (New Haven: Yale University Press, 1995), 8. R. C. Jebb, *Macaulay: A Lecture Delivered at Cambridge* (Cambridge: Cambridge University Press, 1900), 46; *The Lays of Ancient Rome and Other Poems,* ed. J. H. Flather (Cambridge, 1899), v.

26. Mahon to Peel, 26.xii.47, in *Were Human Sacrifices in Use among the Romans? Correspondence on the Question between Mr. Macaulay, Sir Robert Peel, and Lord Mahon*

(London, 1860), 13. To Mahon, 15.xii.47, *L*4:357. A. M. Eckstein, "Human Sacrifice and Fear of Military Disaster in Republican Rome," *American Journal of Ancient History* 7 (1982): 69–95.

27. "The Gates of Somnauth" (9.iii.43), *WLM* 8:231, 242, 231–233, and 236–237.

28. To McLaren, 8.v.41, *L*3:373. "Sugar Duties" (26.ii.45), *WLM,* 8:296, 301–302, and 297. "Madame D'Arblay," *WLM* 7:47. "Sugar Duties," 300, 286. Seymour Drescher, *The Mighty Experiment: Free Labor versus Slavery in British Emancipation* (Oxford: Oxford University Press, 2002), 179–230. "Sugar Duties," 291–294; cf. Frank Tannenbaum, *Slave and Citizen: The Negro in the Americas* (New York: Knopf, 1947 [1946]).

29. "Edinburgh Election" (29.v.39), *WLM* 8:156. "Maynooth" (14.iv.45), *WLM* 8:311, 314, 315. J1:319–320, [?10.i.39.] "Maynooth," 314. To Longman, 16.iv.45, *L*4:251. "Maynooth," 314. To Forrest, 30.iv.45, *L*4:254 and nn2, 3.

30. "Maynooth," 309, 310. "Church of Ireland" (23.iv.45), *WLM* 8:317, 321, and 324.

31. "Sugar Duties," 297. "The State of Ireland" (19.ii.44), *WLM* 8:248, 249. Disraeli, in *Hansard,* 3d ser., 72 (1844): 1171. Robert Blake, *Disraeli* (New York: St. Martin's Press, 1967), 646.

32. Jane Millgate, "History and Politics: Macaulay and Ireland," *University of Toronto Quarterly* 42 (1973): 110–121, offers a different interpretation. G. R. Searle, *Morality and the Market in Victorian Britain* (Oxford: Clarendon Press, 1998), 31.

33. Boyd Hilton, *A Mad, Bad, and Dangerous People? England, 1783–1846* (Oxford: Clarendon Press, 2006), 551–558. To HMT, 11.xii.45, *L*4:270–271. "Corn Laws" (2.xii.45), *WLM* 8:359, 349–350, and 356–358. To Napier, 19.i.46, *L*4:287. Hilton, *Mad, Bad, and Dangerous,* 508–513.

34. Edward Hughes, "Sir Charles Trevelyan and Civil Service Reform, 1853–5," *English Historical Review* 64 (1949): 53. Cecil Woodham Smith, *The Great Hunger* (New York: Harper and Row, 1962), 105. E.g., E. A. J. Johnson, review of *The Great Hunger* by Cecil Woodham Smith, *Journal of Economic History* 24 (1964): 120–121. James Donnelly, *The Great Irish Potato Famine* (Phoenix Mill: Sutton, 2001). Pinney, *L*4:328n2; Boyd Hilton, "Peel, Potatoes, and Providence," *Political Studies* 49 (2001): 106–109.

35. CET to Lansdowne, 22.vi.48, TLB 21:282. CET to Superior of Presentation Convent, 18.ix.48, TLB 22:241.

36. [CET], "The Irish Crisis," *ER* 87 (1848): 230, 320.

37. Peter Gray, *Famine, Land and Politics: British Government and Irish Society, 1843–50* (Dublin: Irish Academic Press, 1999), 331. CET to Longman, 5.vi.48, TLB 19:165. Robin Haines, *Charles Trevelyan and the Great Irish Famine* (Dublin: Four

Courts Press, 2004), 52. CET to Empson, 22.iv.48, TLB 21:18; Haines, *Charles Treve-lyan and Irish Famine,* 410.

38. "People's Charter" (3.v.42), *WLM* 8:224. To HMT, 3.ii.47, *L4*:328–329. John Stuart Mill, *England and Ireland* (London, 1868), 22.

39. Francis Jeffrey, quoted in Haines, *Charles Trevelyan and Irish Famine,* 236; [Nassau Senior], "Proposals for Extending the Irish Poor Law," *ER* 84 (1846): 267–314. To TFE, 3.iii.47, *L4*:331. To TFE, 15.iii.47, *L4*:332.

40. CET to TBM, 21.viii.49, quoted in Haines, *Charles Trevelyan and Irish Fam-ine,* 527. *HOE* 2:485 = chap. 12.

41. To HMT, 30.vii.47, *L4*:341; cf. n1; to Macfarlan, 22.xii.45, *L4*:280–281; and to Napier, 10.i.46, *L4*:285. To HMT, 9.vii.46, *L4*:301–302 and nn1, 2. To MT, 21. viii.47, *L4*:351. *LLLM* 2:118–119. Cockburn, quoted in *LLLM* 2:124.

42. *LLLM* 2:127–129. To FM, 28.vi.41, *L3*:379. "Lines Written on the Night of the 30th July, 1847," *WLM* 8:601, 602. To HMT, 30.vii.47, *L4*:341. To FM, 6.viii.47, *L4*:348; and to Denison, 6.viii.47, *L4*:347.

43. To TFE, 11.xi.47, *L4*:355. To Russell, 23.iv.48, *L4*:362–364. To Wood, 1.v.48, *L4*:364. CET to TBM, 5.iv.48, TLB 20:267.

44. To Holland, 3.v.39, *L3*:286. To Napier, 20.vii.38, *L3*:252; and to TFE, 12.vii.41, *L3*:382. To Mahon, 21.i[42], *L4*:20 and n1. To Napier, 1.xii.41 and 6.xii.44, *L4*:17–18, 226. To Russell, [ii.42?], *L4*:23.

45. "D'Arblay," 46–50. To Napier, 5.xi.41, *L4*:15.; Edward Gibbon, *Autobiogra-phy* (London: Oxford University Press, n.d.), 180. "Barère," 176. To Napier, 25.iv.44, *L4*:30. "D'Arblay," 40, 43. "Barère," 166. "The Life and Writings of Addison," *WLM* 7:112; and "Barère," 124. To TFE, 22.viii.48, *L4*:372.

7. The Last Ancient Historian

1. *HOE* 1:1, 2, 1 = chap. 1. J. G. A. Pocock, *Barbarism and Religion,* 4 vols. to date (Cambridge: Cambridge University Press, 1999—), 2:199–200. Virgil, *Aeneid* 1.1, 10 (Dryden translation).

2. "Warren Hastings," *WLM* 6:611; cf. Clifford Ando, *Imperial Ideology and Pro-vincial Loyalty in the Roman Empire* (Berkeley: University of California Press, 2000), 73–130. Anthony Grafton, *The Footnote: A Curious History* (Cambridge, Mass.: Har-vard University Press, 1999), 24; *HOE* 1:3n★ = chap. 1. Grafton, *Footnote,* 224, 97–104. Charles Firth, *A Commentary on Macaulay's History of England* (London: Mac-millan, 1938), 54–80. John Clive, "The Most Disgusting of Pronouns," in *Not by Fact Alone: Essays on the Writing and Reading of History* (Boston: Houghton Mifflin, 1991), 27–28.

3. To ZM, [10.xi.17], *L1*:91, 92; to Sharp, 11.ii.35, *L3*:137.

4. To TFE, 15.xii.34, *L*3:111. "History," *WLM* 5:150. Erich Auerbach, *Mimesis: The Representation of Reality in Western Literature,* trans. Willard Trask (Garden City, N.Y.: Doubleday/Anchor, 1957), 41, 40. "History," 156. *HOE* 1:145 = chap. 2. *HOE* 1:309 = chap. 3; cf. *HOE* 2:347 = chap. 10; *HOE* 4:244–245 = chap. 22; etc. Thomas P. Culviner, "The Style of Change: Historical Attitudes in the Prose of Scott, Carlyle, Macaulay, and Thackeray" (Ph.D. diss., University of Wisconsin–Madison, 1984).

5. "History," 136, 141. TBM's transcribed notes to F. M. Grimm, *Correspondance littéraire, philosophique et critique,* 17 vols. (Paris, 1812–1814), in Macaulay MSS., TCL, 0.15.73, fols. 64–68, n.d. To C. Macaulay, 5.xii.36, *L*3:203–205. Augustine, *City of God* 4.4. To TFE, 25.viii.35, *L*3:154. *HOE* 1:1 = chap. 1. To ——, 25.iii.49, *L*5:39; and to Everett, 7.v.49, *L*5:52.

6. Hugh Trevor-Roper, introduction to TBM, *The History of England* (Harmondsworth: Penguin, 1979), 39. Douglas Martin, "Arthur Schlesinger, Historian of Power, Dies at 89," *New York Times,* 1.iii.2007, A1. *HOE* 4:366–371 = chap. 23; *HOE* 1:223, 238, 255–258 = chap. 3; *HOE* 2:238–240 = chap. 9.

7. Ronald Weber, "Singer and Seer: Macaulay on the Historian as Poet," *Papers on Language and Literature* 3 (1967): 219. Olive Anderson, "The Political Uses of History in Mid Nineteenth-Century England," *Past & Present* 36 (1967): 89; Carl E. Schorske, *Thinking with History: Explorations in the Passage to Modernism* (Princeton: Princeton University Press, 1999), 4. "History," 122. Patrick Parrinder, *Nation and Novel: The English Novel from Its Origins to the Present Day* (Oxford: Oxford University Press, 2006), 82–212.

8. "History," 122–123, 158, 160, 154, and 158.

9. "Hallam's Constitutional History," *WLM* 5:164, 217, 163–164, 221, and 225. "Mill's Essay on Government," *WLM* 5:270. *HOE* 2:374, 376 = chap. 10; *HOE* 2:444–245 = chap. 11; cf. "History," 131; John Burrow, in Stefan Collini, Donald Winch, and John Burrow, *That Noble Science of Politics: A Study in Nineteenth-Century Intellectual History* (Cambridge: Cambridge University Press, 1983), 183–206.

10. "History," 131. "Sir James Mackintosh," *WLM* 6:97; cf. *HOE* 2:153 = chap. 8; cf. Thucydides, *Peloponnesian War* 7.29.

11. "History," 129–130. *Pace* Bonnie G. Smith, *The Gender of History: Men, Women, and Historical Practice* (Cambridge, Mass.: Harvard University Press, 1998), 9, 70–112. H. R. Trevor-Roper, *The Romantic Movement and the Study of History* (London: Athlone Press, 1969), 20–21; Pinney, *L*6:455–456, s.v. "Scott, Sir Walter"; Cicero, *On Invention* 1.19. Sheldon Rothblatt, *Tradition and Change in English Liberal Education: An Essay in History and Culture* (London: Faber and Faber, 1976), 48. To SMM, 8.vii.12, *L*1:8–14. To TFE, 15.xii.34 and 8.iii.37, *L*3:111–112, 210–211.

12. *HOE* 1:415 = chap. 5; and John Burrow, *A Liberal Descent: Victorian Historians and the English Past* (Cambridge: Cambridge University Press, 1981), 65. J1:441,

15.xii.48. J1:429–430, 431, 3 and 4.xii.48; J1:410–415, 19–22.xi.48; J1:419, 421, and 422, 24, 25, and 27.xi.48.

13. *HOE* 1:113 = chap. 2. Burrow, *Liberal Descent,* 44–45.

14. W. C. Sellar and R. J. Yeatman, "Compulsory Preface," in *1066 and All That: A Memorable History of England, Comprising All the Parts You Can Remember, Including 103 Good Things, 5 Bad Kings and 2 Genuine Dates* (1930) (Stroud: Alan Sutton, 1993), xv. *HOE* 1:6, 7, 14, 15, 19 = chap. 1. Edmund Burke, *Reflections on the Revolution in France,* ed. Frank M. Turner (New Haven: Yale University Press, 2003), 19, 73, 14–15. *HOE* 1:2 = chap. 1.

15. *HOE* 1:5, 31–32, 33–45, and 44–48 = chap. 1.

16. *HOE* 1:52, 55–56, 63, 76, 81, 84, 97, and 88–105 = chap. 1.

17. *HOE* 1:105. Niccolò Machiavelli, *The Prince,* trans. Russell Price, ed. Quentin Skinner and Russell Price (Cambridge: Cambridge University Press, 1988), 59; "Machiavelli," *WLM* 5:76. *HOE* 1:106–107 = chap. 1.

18. David Hume, *The History of England,* vol. 2, chap. 28, in *David Hume: Philosophical Historian,* ed. David Fate Norton and Richard H. Popkin (Indianapolis: Bobbs-Merrill, 1965), 150; Philip Hicks, *Neoclassical History and English Culture: From Clarendon to Hume* (New York: St. Martin's Press, 1996), 193. P. B. M. Blass, *Continuity and Anachronism: Parliamentary and Constitutional Development in Whig Historiography and in the Anti-Whig Reaction between 1890 and 1930* (The Hague: Nijhoff, 1978), 22. *HOE* 1:121 = chap. 2. Burrow, *Liberal Descent,* 25–34.

19. "On the Reform Bill" (16.xii.31), *Hansard,* 3d ser., 9:390–392. "Hallam," 215; *HOE* 1:117, 144, and 135 = chap. 2.

20. H. R. Trevor-Roper, "Epilogue: The Glorious Revolution," in *The Anglo-Dutch Moment: Essays on the Glorious Revolution and Its World Impact,* ed. Jonathan I. Israel (Cambridge: Cambridge University Press, 1991), 482–483.

21. To TFE, 22.viii.48, *L*4:372. Julian Hoppit, *A Land of Liberty: England, 1689–1727* (Oxford: Clarendon Press, 2000), 9. *HOE* 1:311, 321, and 290 = chap. 3. *HOE* 2:382 = chap. 11; *HOE* 1:269 = chap. 3; cf. *HOE* 1:251–255 = chap. 3 and *HOE* 1:471–472 = chap. 5.

22. *HOE* 1:210 = chap. 3. "Mackintosh," 95. Jürgen Habermas, *The Structural Transformation of the Public Sphere: An Inquiry into a Category of Bourgeois Society* (1962), trans. Thomas Burger and Frederick Lawrence (Cambridge, Mass.: MIT Press, 1991), 157, 57–66; *HOE* 1:290–295 = chap. 3.

23. *HOE* 1:505 = chap. 6. "Hallam," 227. "Mackintosh," 123. *HOE* 2:362 = chap. 10. T. W. Heyck, *The Transformation of Intellectual Life in Victorian England* (New York: St. Martin's Press, 1982), 124; cf. Joseph Hamburger, *Macaulay and the Whig Tradition* (Chicago: University of Chicago Press, 1976), x.

24. Harvey J. Graff, *The Legacies of Literacy: Continuities and Contradictions in Western Culture and Society* (Bloomington: Indiana University Press, 1987), 314, 334–335;

and W. B. Stephens, "Literacy in England, Scotland, and Wales, 1500–1900," *History of Education Quarterly* 30 (1990): 555. E.g., *HOE* 1:479 = chap. 5; *HOE* 1:558 = chap. 6. *HOE* 1:198 = chap. 2; cf. *HOE* 1:440 = chap. 5. *HOE* 1:164 = chap. 2; *HOE* 1:576 = chap. 6; *HOE* 1:187, 189, and 195 = chap. 2; *HOE* 1:431, 440 = chap. 5; *HOE* 1:322 = chap. 4; *HOE* 1:431 and 472, 460, and 476 = chap. 5; *HOE* 1:507, 532, and 576 = chap. 6. *HOE* 2:6, 7 = chap. 7; and *HOE* 1:473, 474 = chap. 5.

25. Burke, *Reflections,* 68. *HOE* 2:297–298, 303 = chap. 10. Marx to Weydemeyer, 5.iii.52, in *The Letters of Karl Marx,* trans. and ed. Saul K. Padover (Englewood Cliffs, N.J.: Prentice-Hall, 1979), 81.

26. "Hallam," 164. Studies of his prose abound, including "Literary Style," *Fraser's Magazine* 55 (1857): 258; William Minto, *A Manual of English Prose Literature Biographical and Critical,* 3d ed. (Boston: Ginn, 1901), 77–130; William Strunk Jr., *Macaulay's and Carlyle's Essays on Samuel Johnson* (New York, 1896), 11–53; J. Cotter Morison, *Macaulay* (New York: Harper, 1902); Richard C. Jebb, *Macaulay* (Cambridge: University Press, 1900); Clive, "Macaulay's Historical Imagination" (1960), in *Not by Fact,* 66–73; William A. Madden, "Macaulay's Style," in *The Art of Victorian Prose,* ed. George Levine and William Madden (New York: Oxford University Press, 1968), 127–153; Jane Millgate, *Macaulay* (London: Routledge & Kegan Paul, 1973), 116–181; Margaret Cruikshank, *Thomas Babington Macaulay* (Boston: Twayne, 1978), 115–121; Sheridan W. Gilley, "Macaulay as Historian," *Australian Journal of Politics and History* 29 (1983): 328–343; Bruce A. Castner, "A Computer-Assisted Analysis of Thomas Babington Macaulay's Prose" (Ph.D. diss., University of South Carolina, 1984); Rosemary Jann, *The Art and Science of Victorian History* (Columbus: Ohio State University Press, 1985), 66–104; and Edward Adams, "Macaulay's *History of England* and the Dilemmas of Liberal Epic," *Nineteenth-Century Prose* 33 (2006): 149–174. Peter Gay, *Style in History* (New York: McGraw-Hill, 1974), 108–110.

27. J1:443, 16.xii.48. *HOE* 1:496 = chap. 5; *HOE* 1:554 = chap. 6. To Napier, 28.xi.36, *L3*:197; to Bulwer-Lytton, 30.xii.48, *L4*:393–394. *HOE* 1:322 = chap. 4.

28. "Hallam," 162. Bacon, quoted in George H. Nadel, "Philosophy of History before Historicism," in *Studies in the Philosophy of History: Selected Essays from "History and Theory,"* ed. George H. Nadel (New York: Harper and Row/Harper Torchbooks, 1965), 69. To Hobhouse, 12.vii.43, *L4*:130–131; *HOE* 1:129 = chap. 2; *HOE* 1:406 = chap. 5.

29. "Hallam," 164. J1:446, 21.xii.48. *HOE* 1:124, 127 = chap. 2; e.g., *HOE* 1:122, 130, 134, 135, 137, 138, 141, 150, 155, and 189 = chap. 2; *HOE* 1:321–22 = chap. 4. *HOE* 4:420, 443, and 474 = chap. 5; *HOE* 1:576 = chap. 6.

30. "History," 161. Anthony Grafton, *What Was History? The Art of History in Early Modern Europe* (Cambridge: Cambridge University Press, 2007), 189–254, 9, 222, 48–49, and 190–191. George G. Iggers and James M. Powell, eds., *Leopold von Ranke and the Shaping of the Historical Discipline* (Syracuse: Syracuse University Press,

1990); Leopold von Ranke, *A History of England Principally in the Seventeenth Century,* 6 vols. (Oxford, 1875), 6:144. E.g., *HOE* 1:243n★, 211 = chap. 3. Thomas Wiedemann, "Mommsen, Denmark and England," available at http://www.dur.ac .uk/Classics/histos/1997/wiedemann.html. G. H. Mueller, "Weber and Mommsen: Non-Marxist Materialism," *British Journal of Sociology* 37 (1986): 4; cf. Anthony Grafton, "Roman Monument," *History Today* 56 (2006): 48–50.

31. David Hackett Fischer, *Historians' Fallacies: Toward a Logic of Historical Thought* (New York: Harper & Row/Harper Torchbooks, 1970), 135–140, 263–281, and 315; cf. the theory and practice of another Craven Scholar at Trinity College turned historian, E. H. Carr, *What Is History?* (London: Macmillan, 1961) and *A History of Soviet Russia,* 14 vols. (London: Macmillan, 1950–1978). Annette Wittkau-Horgy, *Historismus: Zur Geschichte des Begriffs und des Problems* (Göttingen: Vandenhoeck & Ruprecht, 1992), 57–125. Peter Novick, *That Noble Dream: The "Objectivity Question" and the American Historical Profession* (Cambridge: Cambridge University Press, 1988), 281–411. Jean-François Lyotard, *The Postmodern Condition: A Report on Knowledge,* trans. Geoff Bennington and Brian Massume (Minneapolis: University of Minnesota Press, 1984), xxiv.

32. Blass, *Continuity and Anachronism,* 76. Firth, *Commentary,* 57, 58–59. "Sir James Mackintosh's History of the Revolution," *ER* 61 (1835): 271. "Mackintosh," 76n★. Ibid., 97. Ralph Waldo Emerson, "The Conservative" (9.xii.41), in Ralph Waldo Emerson, *Essays and Lectures,* ed. Joel Porte (New York: Literary Classics of the United States, 1983), 171–172.

33. To Napier, 20.vii.38, *L*3:252. To SM, 9.v.48, *L*4:365. To Whewell, 6.vi.48, *L*4:367; to TFE, 27.vii.48, *L*4:371. To TFE, 22.viii.48, *L*4:372; J1:407a, 18.xi.48. Pinney, *L*4:365n2; to Longman, 22.vi.48, *L*4:369. To HMT, 24.x.48, *L*4:377. J1:407A, 18.xi.48.

34. *LLLM* 2:163–168; cf. BL Add. MSS. 24094, the only extant part of the draft (chap. 25).

35. James Mackintosh, *History of the Revolution in England in 1688. Comprising a View of the Reign of James II from His Accession, to the Enterprise of the Prince of Orange* (London, 1834), 5 (*HOE* 1:185–186); 7 (*HOE* 1:191); 8 (*HOE* 1:182–184); 11 (*HOE* 1:191–192, 337–339); 15–16 (*HOE* 1:477–478); 18 (*HOE* 1:479, 481, and 482); 21 (*HOE* 1:482–483); 29 (*HOE* 1:462); 32 (*HOE* 1:492—with reference to the "Mackintosh Collection"); 34 (*HOE* 1:490); 37 (*HOE* 1:510–511); 45 (*HOE* 1:525); 46 (*HOE* 1:527–528); 51 (*HOE* 1:535–537, 541); 52 (*HOE* 1:552–557); 52–56 (1:552–557); 59 (1:564); 66 (1:561); 67–68 (1:570); 73–75 (*HOE* 2:78–81); 77 (*HOE* 1:577–578); 79 (*HOE* 1:578–582); 82 (*HOE* 1:567); 83 (*HOE* 2:28); 85 (*HOE* 1:559–560); 94 (*HOE* 1:612–618); 97 (*HOE* 1:614–615, 582–584); 99 (*HOE* 1:584); 101 (*HOE* 1:585); 103 (*HOE* 1:588); 104 (*HOE* 1:590–591); 105 (*HOE* 1:589–590); 113 (*HOE* 1:604–605); 114 (*HOE* 1:596–601); 120 (*HOE* 1:608); 123

(*HOE* 1:618–622); 131 (*HOE* 1:621); 133 (*HOE* 1:565); 135 (*HOE* 1:565; 2:86, 101–102); 136 (*HOE* 1:566–567); 138–139 (*HOE* 2:90–91); 145–154 (*HOE* 1:567–621, 2:38–58); 162–163 (*HOE* 2:49–51); 167–171 (*HOE* 1:378–382); 172–173 (*HOE* 1:486–497, 2:51–52); 178–179 (*HOE* 2:82–83); 181–196 (*HOE* 2:116–225); 202–205 (*HOE* 2:112–115); 222 (*HOE* 2:39–41, 56–57); 227 (*HOE* 1:541); 231–238 (*HOE* 1:541–547); 239–241 (*HOE* 2:137–138 and n; 242 (*HOE* 2:138); 246 (*HOE* 2:140); 249 (*HOE* 2:142–143); 252–257 (*HOE* 2:143–149); 261–262 (*HOE* 2:157–158); 265 (*HOE* 1:259); 266–279 (*HOE* 2:159–175); 280–284 (*HOE* 2:151–154); 285–286 (*HOE* 2:153, 195, and 194); 293–301 (*HOE* 2:199–202, 177–181); 303 (*HOE* 1:621, 163); 321–322 (*HOE* 1:164–165); 329 (*HOE* 1:20–21); 335 (*HOE* 1:172–173); 340–342 (*HOE* 1:172–177); 343 (*HOE* 1:20–21); 348 (*HOE* 1:209, 348 and 2:22); 350–351 (*HOE* 1:405–406) = chaps. 2, 4–9, etc.

36. "Mackintosh," 82. Firth, *Commentary,* 59; *HOE* 1:294 = chap. 3. [To Disbrowe], 27.x.47, *L*4:354.

37. Tilar J. Mazzeo, *Plagiarism and Literary Property in the Romantic Period* (Philadelphia: University of Pennsylvania Press, 2006), 84–85. "Mackintosh," 83; cf. John Muckelbauer, "Imitation and Invention in Antiquity: An Historical-Theoretical Revision," *Rhetorica* 21 (2003): 61–88. Arthur Pollard and Michael Hennell, eds., *Charles Simeon (1759–1836)* (London, 1959), quoted in Madden, "Macaulay's Style," 135. "Mackintosh," 82–83.

38. *HOE* 1:502–503 = chap. 6; cf. Mackintosh, *History of Revolution in 1688,* 215. *HOE* 2:244, 246 = chap. 9. Hoppit, *Land of Liberty,* 17; cf. Tim Harris, *Revolution: The Great Crisis of the British Monarchy, 1685–1720* (London: Penguin, 2007), 303–304.

39. *HOE* 1:492 = chap. 5; Firth, *Commentary,* 269–273. *HOE* in *WLM* 1:512n = chap. 5. "The Life and Writings of Sir William Temple," *ER* 68 (1838): 129–130, 165; cf. "Sir William Temple," *WLM* 6:262–264, 301.

40. *HOE* 2:48 = chap. 7; cf. 2:139–140 = chap. 8. Scott Sowerby, "James II's Revolution: The Politics of Religious Toleration in England, 1685–1689" (Ph.D. diss., Harvard University, 2006); and Sowerby to Sullivan, e-mail, 1.ii.2007, information that I gratefully acknowledge; *HOE* 2:48 = chap. 7. J3:152, 28.i.51; J3:152, 29.i.51. *HOE* 1:381 = chap. 4.

41. *HOE* 1:381 = chap. 4; "History," 143, 144; to TFE, 25.vii–12.viii.36, *L*3:180–181. Mark Phillips, "Macaulay, Scott, and the Literary Challenge to Historiography," *Journal of the History of Ideas* 50 (1989): 117–133. Mark Salber Phillips, *Society and Sentiment: Genres of Historical Writing in Britain, 1740–1820* (Princeton: Princeton University Press, 2000), 85–87. *HOE* 2:9, 15 = chap. 7; Firth, *Commentary,* 67.

42. Charles Taylor, *Sources of the Self: The Making of the Modern Identity* (Cambridge, Mass.: Harvard University Press, 1989), 115–142. Perez Zagorin, *Thucydides: An Introduction for the Common Reader* (Princeton: Princeton University Press, 2005), 145–146. John Lingard, *The History of England from the First Invasion by the Romans to*

the Accession of William and May in 1688, vol. 10 (Edinburgh: John Grant, 1902), 117–228; *HOE* 1:341 = chap. 4. *HOE* 1:56 = chap. 1.

43. *HOE* 2:1 = chap. 7. In A. N. L. Munby, "Germ of a History: Twenty-three Quarto Pages of a Macaulay Cambridge Prize Essay," *TLS,* 1.v.1969, 468–469. *LLLM* 1:79; Virgil, *Aeneid* 6.809–812 (Dryden translation).

44. To ZM, 21.xi.20, *L*1:150 and 151n6; to TFE, 15.xii.34, *L*3:112. Plutarch, *De Gloria Atheniensium* 1.347; I owe the reference and its translation to the kindness of Scott Moringiello. Wilfred Owen, "Dulce et Decorum Est," lines 25–28.

45. George E. Levine, *The Boundaries of Fiction: Carlyle, Macaulay, Newman* (Princeton: Princeton University Press, 1968), 158. William H. Herndon and Jesse W. Weik, *Herndon's Lincoln,* ed. Douglas L. Wilson and Rodney O. Davis (Urbana: University of Illinois Press/Knox College Lincoln Studies Center, 2006), 264–265n+ and 445n18; Owen Dudley Edwards, *Macaulay* (New York: St. Martin's Press, 1988), 173. *HOE* 2:56, 60 = chap. 1. "Frederic the Great," *WLM* 6:658, 705.

46. Peter Mandler, *History and National Life* (London: Profile, 2002), 22, 33; cf. ibid., 32, 35, and 38. Peter Paret, introduction to Gerhard Ritter, *Frederick the Great: A Historical Profile,* 3d ed., trans. Peter Paret (Berkeley: University of California Press, 1968), vii–xiii; Klaus Schwabe and Rolf Reichardt, *Gerhard Ritter: Ein politischer Historiker in seinen Briefen* (Boppard am Rhein: Harold Boldt, 1984), 709, 772–774.

47. *HOE* 1:14–15 = chap. 1. *HOE* 2:51 = chap. 7; *HOE* 2:107, 130, and 168 = chap. 8. *HOE* 2: 191, 199–200 = chap. 9; cf. *HOE* 1:49–51 = chap. 1.

48. To Ebrington, 12.i.41, *L*3:362; and "Warren Hastings," *WLM* 6:549, 555–556. Jonathan Parry, *The Politics of Patriotism: English Liberalism, National Identity and Europe, 1830–1886* (Cambridge: Cambridge University Press, 2006) 145–175, 199–201, 235, and 324–324. *HOE* 1:49 = chap. 1; *HOE* 1:140, 141 = chap. 2; *HOE* 1:604 = chap. 6; cf. Josh. 9:18, 21.

49. *HOE* 1:55 = chap. 1. *HOE* 1:608 = chap. 6, cf. "Temple," 264; *HOE* 1:618 = chap. 6. Piers Wauchope, in *ODNB,* s.v. "Talbot, Richard, first earl of Tyrconnell and Jacobite Duke of Tyrconnell"; cf. Firth, *Commentary,* 210; and Harris, *Revolution,* 126–138.

50. Ernest Renan, "What Is a Nation?" in *Nation and Narration,* ed. Homi K. Bhabha (London: Routledge, 1990), 11. "History," 157–158; and *HOE* 1:3 = chap. 1. Edwards, *Macaulay,* 174; cf. ibid., 31, 115–116, and 125; Burrow, *Liberal Descent,* 71–72; Peter Mandler, "'Race' and 'Nation' in Mid-Victorian Thought," in *History, Religion, Culture: British Intellectual History 1750–1950,* ed. Stefan Collini, Richard Whatmore, and Brian Young (Cambridge: Cambridge University Press, 2000), 224–244. JC, 497. Jonathan Glover, *Humanity: A Moral History of the Twentieth Century* (New Haven: Yale University Press, 2000); and Hannah Arendt, *The Origins of Totalitarianism* (San Diego: Harcourt Brace Jovanovich, 1968), 123–304, constitute a down payment.

51. J. G. A. Pocock, "The Varieties of Whiggism from Exclusion to Reform," in

Virtue, Commerce, and History: Essays on Political Thought and History, Chiefly in the Eighteenth Century (Cambridge: Cambridge University Press, 1985), 302. Munby, "Germ of a History," 469. J6:24, 22.i.[53]. Mark Salber Phillips, "Historical Distance and the Historiography of Eighteenth-Century Britain," in Collini, Whatmore, and Young, *History, Religion, and Culture,* 44.

52. *HOE* 1:19 = chap. 1. *HOE* 1:13, 22, and 19 = chap. 1. "History," 158; Burke, *Reflections,* 82. *HOE* 2:244 = chap. 9; *HOE* 1:111 = chap. 1.

53. Lord [John E. D.] Acton, *Lectures on Modern History* (London: Collins/Fontana, 1960), 220; A[lfred]. B. C. Cobban, "Edmund Burke and the Origins of the Theory of Nationality," *Cambridge Historical Journal* 4 (1926): 36–47; Tom Furniss, "Cementing the Nation: Burke's *Reflections* on Nationalism and National Identity," in *Edmund Burke's Reflections on the Revolution in France: New Interdisciplinary Essays,* ed. John Whale (Manchester: Manchester University Press, 2000), 115–144. Jürgen Osterhammel, "Nation und Zivilisation in der britischen Historiographie von Hume zur Macaulay," *Historische Zeitschrift* 254 (1992): 281–340; *HOE* 1:17, 26, and 35 = chap. 1; cf. *HOE* 1:601 = chap. 6. *HOE* 1:116–117 = chap. 2. Catherine Hall, "At Home with History: Macaulay and the History of England," in *At Home with the Empire: Metropolitan Culture and the Imperial World,* ed. Catherine Hall and Sonya O. Rose (Cambridge: Cambridge University Press, 2006), 32–52, quotation at 34; I owe this reference to an anonymous reader for Harvard University Press.

54. Norman Ravitch, "Far Short of Bigotry: Edmund Burke on Church Establishments and Confessional States," *Journal of Church and State* 37 (1995): 365–383. S. J. Barnett, *The Enlightenment and Religion: The Myths of Modernity* (Manchester: Manchester University Press, 2003), 50. *HOE* 1:66 = chap. 1. Hoppit, *Land of Liberty,* 207–241. "Mackintosh," 94.

55. Simon Hornblower, "The Religious Dimension to the Peloponnesian War, or What Thucydides Does Not Tell Us," *Harvard Studies in Classical Philology* 94 (1992): 169–197. Peter Green, "A Triumph for Herodotus," *TLS,* 3.x.2003, 3. J1:439, 12.xii.48; cf. Timothy Lang, *The Victorians and the Stuart Heritage: Interpretations of a Discordant Past* (Cambridge: Cambridge University Press, 1995), 53–92. *HOE* 1:136 = chap. 2.

56. James R. Hertzler, "Who Dubbed It 'The Glorious Revolution'?" *Albion* 19 (1987): 579–585. Gilbert Burnet, *History of His Own Times,* ed. Martin Joseph Routh (1833), 6 vols. (Hildesheim: Georg Olms, 1969), 1:91 (*HOE* 1:66–67); 145–149 (*HOE* 1:88–105); 168 (*HOE* 1:126–129); 175 (*HOE* 1:160); 183 (*HOE* 1:160); 184 (*HOE* 1:135); 185 (*HOE* 1:136–138, 161); 341 (*HOE* 1:135); 342 (*HOE* 1:248–249, 349); 492 (*HOE* 1:183); 582 (*HOE* 2:1–23); and 2:18 (*HOE* 1:185–186) = chaps. 1–2. Burnet, *History of His Own Times,* 3:327–328; Stuart Handley, in *ODNB,* s.v. "Legge, William, first earl of Dartmouth (1672–1750)"; *HOE* 2:242–243 and n★ = chap. 9; *HOE* 2:12n+, 11 = chap. 7.

57. *HOE* 2:378 = chap. 10; [William II/III], "William's Declaration 1688," in *The Eighteenth-Century Constitution, 1688–1815,* ed. E. N. Williams (Cambridge: Cambridge University Press, 1960), 10–11.

58. *HOE* 2:379, 381 = chap. 10. E.g., *HOE* 1:117, 124, 139–140, and 160 = chap. 2; *HOE* 1:354, 362, and 363 = chap. 4; *HOE* 1:415, 416, 474, and 498–499 = chap. 5. Colin Kidd, *British Identities before Nationalism: Ethnicity and Nationhood in the Atlantic World, 1600–1800* (Cambridge: Cambridge University Press, 1999); "Mackintosh," 97.

59. Horace, *Ars Poetica* 147–148; cf. to SMM, 8.vii.12, *L*1:10; and to TFE, 15.xii.34, *L*3:110–112. *HOE* 2:381 = chap. 11. Homer, *Iliad* 1.1 (Samuel Butler translation). *HOE* 2:383 = chap. 11. *HOE* 2:415 = chap. 11; cf. Machiavelli, *Prince,* 48–51.

60. *HOE* 2:419 = chap. 11; cf. Edwards, *Macaulay,* 131–132; and Firth, *Commentary,* 334–367.

61. *HOE* 1:326 = chap. 4; *HOE* 1:467–468, 478, and 495 = chap. 5. Richard A. Lanham, *A Handbook of Rhetorical Terms,* 2d ed. (Berkeley: University of California Press, 1991), 8–9. *HOE* 2:10 = chap. 7.

62. *HOE* 2:145 = chap. 8; cf. Harris, *Revolution,* 258–269; *HOE* 2:172–173 = chap. 8. *HOE* 3:58–59 and nn★ = chap. 14. *HOE* 3:296 = chap. 17.

63. *HOE* 4:323 = chap. 22. "Hallam," 229. Heb. 11:1, 16, and 13; TBM's transcribed notes to Grimm, *Correspondance littéraire,* in Macaulay MSS., TCL, 0.15.73, fols. 64–68.

64. David Onnekink, "'Mynheer Benting now rules over us': the 1st Earl of Portland and the Re-emergence of the English Favourite, 1689–99," *English Historical Review* 121 (2006): 699.

65. *HOE* 2:379 = chap. 10. *HOE* 4:42–114 = chap. 20; *HOE* 2:391 = chap. 11. *HOE* 4:71 = chap. 20; *HOE* 2:9 = chap. 7.

66. J. R. Jones, *Marlborough* (Cambridge: Cambridge University Press, 1993), 2; cf. "Hallam," 228–229. *HOE* 1:346–347 = chap. 4; *HOE* 1:460 = chap. 5; cf. *HOE* 1:458–459n+, 487 = chap. 5; and *HOE* 1:531 = chap. 6.

67. *HOE* 2:70–71 = chap. 7; cf. Jones, *Marlborough,* 28–29, 31–32.

68. *HOE* 2:72, 73n★ = chap. 7. E.g., *HOE* 2:74 = chap. 7; *HOE* 2:211, 254, 257, 265–270, and 273 = chap. 9. *HOE* 3:46 = chap. 14; *HOE* 3:147, 167 = chap. 15; *HOE* 3:216, 227–230 = chap. 16; *HOE* 3:385–386, 457–458 = chap. 18; *HOE* 3:488–489, 497–498, and 525 = chap. 19; *HOE* 4:74 = chap. 20; *HOE* 4:139–141 = chap. 21; *HOE* 4:256–258, 284 = chap. 22. *HOE* 3:306, 309–314 = chap. 17; *HOE* 3:388, 390–395 = chap.18; *HOE* 4:98–99, 101–102 = chap. 20; and *HOE* in *WLM* 4:100n★; cf. Jones, *Marlborough,* 48–52.

69. *HOE* 4:526–534, 497–502, and 538–542 = chap. 25. *HOE* 4:410 = chap. 23; cf. *HOE* 4:447 = chap. 24; *HOE* 4:505 and 523 = chap. 25.

70. Jones, *Marlborough*, 2–3; cf. John Paget, *The New "Examen" or an Inquiry into the Evidence Relating to Certain Passages in Lord Macaulay's History* (Edinburgh, 1861), 1–58, which first appeared in *Blackwood's Magazine*, June 1859, as "Lord Macaulay and the Duke of Marlborough." Winston S. Churchill, *Marlborough: His Life and Times*, vol. 1 (London: Harrap, 1933), 597 and 64. Namier to Churchill, 14.ii.1934, in Martin Gilbert, *Winston S. Churchill*, vol. 5: *1922–1939. The Prophet of Truth* (Boston: Houghton Mifflin, 1977), 501 and 785n1.

71. George Macaulay Trevelyan, *England under Queen Anne: Blenheim* (London: Longman's, Green, 1930), 143–144, 115–116. Trevelyan to *TLS*, 19.x.1933, reprinted in George Macaulay Trevelyan, *England under Queen Anne: The Peace and the Protestant Succession* (London: Longmans, Green, 1934), xi–xiii; Trevelyan, *England under Queen Anne: Blenheim*, 178; and Churchill, *Marlborough*, 144–145.

72. G. M. Trevelyan, *An Autobiography & Other Essays* (London: Longmans, Green, 1949), 49, 3. Randolph S. Churchill, *Winston S. Churchill*, vol. 1: *Youth, 1874–1900* (Boston: Houghton Mifflin, 1966), 107–108. Trevelyan, *England under Queen Anne: Peace*, xi; Churchill to Lady Randolph, 31.iii.97, in Churchill, *Winston S. Churchill*, 1:321; Namier to Churchill, 14.ii.1934, and Churchill to Namier, 18. ii.1934, in Gilbert, Winston S. *Churchill*, 5:501, 502.

73. Trevelyan, *Autobiography*, 22. Churchill to Lady Randolph, 14.i.97, in Churchill, *Winston S. Churchill*, 1:308; (William) Winwood Reade, *The Martyrdom of Man* (N.p., 1872). Geoffrey Fisher, quoted in Edward Carpenter, *Archbishop Fisher—His Life and Times* (Norwich: Canterbury Press, 1991), 441.

8. The Lion

1. [Charles Greville], *The Greville Diary*, ed. Philip Whitwell Wilson, 2 vols. (London: Heinemann, 1927), 2:162. To HMT, 1.i.49, *L*5:5; J1:455, 1.i.49; cf. J1:463, 11.i.49. Edgar Johnson, *Charles Dickens: His Tragedy and Triumph*, rev. ed. (New York: Viking Press, 1977), 251. *LLLM* 2:316; Pinney, *L*5:414n3. *LLLM* 2:173. J2:162, 5. xii.49.

2. *Morning Chronicle*, 30.xi.48, 5–6; J1:425, 30.xi.48. Lingard to ——, in Martin Haile and Edwin Bonney, *Life and Letters of John Lingard, 1771–1851* (London: Herbert and Daniel, [1911]), 342. Murray to Croker, 2.ii.49, quoted in Myron F. Brightfield, *John Wilson Croker* (Berkeley: University of California Press, 1940), 373. [Anon.], "Macaulay's History of England," *Chamber's Edinburgh Journal* 261 (xii.48): 425–428; and [C. W. Russell], "Macaulay's History of England," *Dublin Review* 26 (1849): 398–400. [John Wilson Croker], "Mr. Macaulay's *History of England*," *Quarterly Review* 84 (1848–49): 555, 549, 551–552, and 604–625. To Westwood, 11.iv.49, *L*5:44; J1:566, 574–576, 7 and 14.iv.49; J1:587, 24.iv.49; cf. [James Moncrieff], "Macaulay's *History of England*," *ER* 90 (1849): 249–292; and J2:54–55, 5.vii.49.

3. Churchill Babington, *Mr. Macaulay's Character of the Clergy in the Latter Part of the Seventeenth Century Considered* (Cambridge, 1849); *HOE* 1:246 = chap. 3. J2:26, 9.vi.49. Russell, "Macaulay's History," 397n, 439. J1:494, 7.ii.49. J3:50, 12.ix.50. [Francis Head], "Valentine's Day at the Post Office," *Quarterly Review* 87 (1850): 100; [M. J. Higgins], "Reports on the Finance and Commerce of the Island of Ceylon," *Quarterly Review* 88 (1850): 105; [James Craigie Robertson], "The Life of Thomas Ken, D.D.," *Quarterly Review* 89 (1851): 281, 286, 287, and 303. J1:470–471, 472, 22 and 23.i.49. J1:469, 18.i.49. To Philpotts, 8.i.49, *L*5:11–14. To TFE, 10.i.49, *L*5:15; cf. to Philpotts, 22.i.49, *L*5:18–23. Edward Charles Harington, *Reformers of the Anglican Church, and Mr. Macaulay's History of England* (London: 1849), went through a second edition in 1850.

4. Mill to Taylor, 27.i[49], in *The Later Letters of John Stuart Mill, 1849–73,* ed. Francis E. Mineka and Dwight N. Lindley, vol. 14, pt. 1 of *The Collected Works* (Toronto: University of Toronto Press, 1972), 5–6. Mill to Taylor, 16.ii[55], ibid., 332. Journal, 26.iv.49, as quoted in *The Collected Letters of Thomas and Jane Welsh Carlyle,* ed. Clyde deL. Ryals and Kenneth J. Fielding, 36 vols. to date (Durham: Duke University Press, 1970–), 24:30n7; cf. T. Carlyle to Emerson, 19.iv.49, ibid., 29–30. To Russell, 3.i.49, *L*5:6; J1:487, 509, 2 and 16.ii.49. Bunsen to Mother, 15.ii.49, in Augustus J. C. Hare, *The Life and Letters of Frances Baroness Bunsen,* 2 vols. (New York, 1879), 2:126; cf. Edith J. Morley, ed., *Henry Crabb Robinson on Books and Their Writers,* 3 vols. (London: Dent, 1938), 2:686–687 (entries for 17, 21, 22, and 25.i.49). [Anon.], "Macaulay's England Dramatised," *Man in the Moon* (May 1849): 249. J2:6, 7.v.49.

5. J2:47, 30.vi.49. J1:501–503, 13.ii.49; cf. J1:510–512, 17.ii.49; J1:517, 23.ii.49. J1:480, 27.i.49. J1:473–474, 23.i.49. J1:500, 12.ii.49. J1:463, 11.i.49. J1:515, 21.ii.49. J1:516, 22.ii.49. J2:240, 23.ii.50.

6. To Holmes, 22.vi.49, *L*5:60; cf. to Adolphus and Denison, 5.i.49, *L*5:10 and n2. J1:488–489, 2.ii.49. J1:491–492, 5.ii.49. Allan C. Thomas, "William Penn, Macaulay, and 'Punch,'" *Bulletin of the Friends Historical Society* 7 (1916): 94. J3:141, 15.i.51.

7. John Paget, *An Inquiry into the Evidence Relating to the Charges Brought by Lord Macaulay against William Penn* (Edinburgh, 1858), 33. Thomas Clarkson, *Memoirs of the Private and Public Life of William Penn,* ed. W. E. Forster (London, 1849). J3:142, 16.i.51. J4:158, 3.vii.51; cf. to Napier, 3.i.43, *L*4:90. Harriet Martineau, "Thomas Babington Macaulay" (1859), in *Biographical Sketches* (London, 1869), 102–112.

8. J2:3, 5.v.49; J2:4, 6.v.49; J2:5, 7.v.49; J2:65; 18.vii.49; J2:309, 5.v.50; J3:134, 12.i.51; J4:41, 30.iii.51; J4:139, 15.vi.51; J4:148, 26.vi.51; William J. Thoms, "Gossip of an Old Bookworm," *Nineteenth-Century* 10 (1881): 65. J2:61–63, 13–15.vii.49. J2:56, 8.vii.49. J2:75, 26.vii.49. J2:76, 28.vii.49. J2:53, 4.vii.49; cf. J3:32, 33, 12 and 15.ix.50. J1:466, 13.i.49. J2:63–64, 16.vii.49; cf. "Moore's Life of Lord Byron," *WLM* 5:390–391. J1:558, 30.iii.49. J1:562, 7.iv.49. J3:29, 9.ix.50; J3:80, 21.xi.50;

J2:209, 18.i.50. J1:460, 458, 9 and 5.i.49; cf. J1:456–460, 1–9.i.49; J1:506, 14.ii.49; J2:11, 36–37, 51–52, and 65–66, 17.v.49, 23.vi.49, and 18.vii.49. J1:506, 514, 16 and 20.ii.49.

9. To Everett, 7.v.49, L5:52. Adam Black, as quoted in *LLLM* 2:240. J2:7, 54, 9.v.49 and 4.vii.49. J2:31, 16.vi.49. J3:31a, 25.viii.49. To MT, 26.ix.49, L5:75. To FM, 11.ix.49, L5:72; cf. J2:95, 10.ix.49. J4:320–321, 2.xii.51; cf. J4:319–321, 3 and 4.xii.[51]; to SM, 5.iv.53, L5:323–324; and J11:323–324, 28.v.[58]. J4:320–321, 2.xii.51. J3:51a, 20.vi.50. J6:128, 9.viii.53. Diary of seventh earl of Carlisle, 17.iii.49, quoted in Joseph Hamburger, *Macaulay and the Whig Tradition* (Chicago: University of Chicago Press, 1976), 235n22. Richard Price, *British Society, 1680–1880: Dynamism, Containment, and Change* (New York: Cambridge University Press, 1999), 299.

10. *LLLM* 2:317. To TFE, 19.vii.56, L6:49; J9:45, 25.i.56. To Everett, 7.v.49 and 8.iii.49, L5:52, 33; cf. to Bigelow, [11.]x.52, L5:287.

11. J11:583, 29.x.59; J6:155, 29.x.53. David Lee Lundberg, "Thomas Macaulay and American Victorian Culture, 1840–1910" (Ph.D. diss., University of California at Berkeley, 1975), ii–iii. I owe access to this dissertation to the kindness of John Connelly. Lundberg, "Macaulay and American Victorian Culture," 139, 77–78. Everett to Milman, 21.v.49, in Arthur Milman, *Henry Hart Milman, D.D.: Dean of St. Paul's: A Biographical Sketch* (New York, 1900), 161–162; Lundberg, "Macaulay and American Victorian Culture," 246. Holmes's copy inscribed on the front endpaper is in the Houghton Library, Harvard University, ★EC8 M1196 849hb v.3-4.

12. J11:534, 23.vii.59; J11:514, 16.vii.59, cf. J11:10, 604, 15.vi.56 and 15.xii.59. Charlton Laird, *Language in America* (New York: World, 1970), 199, i.e., the accent shared by President Franklin Delano Roosevelt, a Hudson Valley squire, and, improbably, Cardinal William Henry O'Connell of Boston, a millhand's son. Ticknor to Prescott, 17.vii.56, in *Life, Letters, and Journals of George Ticknor,* ed. Anna Ticknor, 2d ed., 2 vols. (London, 1876), 2:323.

13. Entry of 13.vii.56, in Nathaniel Hawthorne, *The English Notebooks, 1856–1860,* ed. Thomas Woodson and Bill Ellis, in *The Centenary Edition of the Works of Nathaniel Hawthorne,* vol. 22 (Columbus: Ohio State University Press, 1997), 82. Ibid., 83.

14. J11:86, 14.ii.57. J1:487, 1.ii.49. "Edinburgh Election" (2.xi.52), in Vizetelly, 2:391; J2:39, 27.vi.49; J2:66, 18.vii.49; J2:77, 30.vii.49. J2:18, 29.v.49; J3:96, 9.xii.50; J11:23, 19.vii.56. J11:604–605, 15.xii.59. J8:120–121, 17.ix.54. J2:6, 7.v.49; J1:483, 29.i.49; to Everett, 7.v.49, L5:52; J2:6, 8.v.49. J2:346, 19.vi.50; Pinney, L5:394n3. J2:354, 15.vii.50.

15. J3:54, 18.x.50. J1:483, 27.i.49. J11:122–123, 23.v.57. To Randall, 23.v.57, L6:94–96; cf. "Edinburgh Election," 379.

16. H. M. Lydenberg, "What Did Macaulay Say about America?" *Bulletin of the New York Public Library* 9 (1925): 459–481. Benedetto Fontana, "The Democratic

Philosopher: Rhetoric as Hegemony in Gramsci," *Italian Culture* 23 (2005): 110. "Food for Thought—The Guardian Profile: Amartya Sen," *The Guardian,* 31.iii.01, available at http://www.guardian.co.uk/saturday_review/story/0,3605,465796,00. html; cf. James Vernon, *Hunger: A Modern History* (Cambridge, Mass.: Belknap Press of Harvard University Press, 2007), 17–80.

17. J11:144, 11.vii.57. Sumner to Argyll, quoted in Lundberg, "Macaulay and American Victorian Culture," 76. To Stowe, 20.v.52, *L*5:230. Sumner to Hilliard, 16.ii.39, in E. L. Pierce, *Memoirs and Letters of Charles Sumner,* 4 vols. (Boston, 1877–1893), 2:65. Harriet Beecher Stowe, introduction to *Uncle Tom's Cabin,* new ed. (Boston, 1887), xviii. To FM, 1.xii.52, *L*5:298; cf. J6:68, 6.v.53. To TFE, 21.iii.53, *L*5:321–322 and n1. To Stowe, [23?].x.56, *L*6:63. To TFE, 5.x.52, *L*5:286.

18. J1:486, 1.ii.49. J1:487–488, 2.ii.49. J2:167–168, 7.xii.49.

19. *LLLM* 2:165. E.g., J2:110–113, 9–13.x.49. J2:7–8, 9.v.49. Tony Claydon, in *ODNB,* s.v. "William III and II."

20. J1:467–468, 16.i.49; J1:492–493, 6.ii.49; J1:495, 8.ii.49; J1:496, 8.ii.49; J1:508–510, 16.ii.49; J1:510–532, 17.ii–11.iii.49; J1:499, 11.ii.49; J2:11, 18.v.49; J2:47, 30.vi.49; J2:38, 26.vi.49; J2:45–46, 29.vi.49. J2:36, 23.vi.49. J1:490, 4.ii.49; J2:59–60, 121, 11.vii.49 and 23.x.49; to Longman, 16.vi.49, *L*5:59 and n4. J2:7–8, 9.v.49. J1:556, 28.iii.49. J2:15, 26.v.49. J1:552, 23–24.iii.49; J1:555–556, 28.iii.49. J2:12, 19.v.49; J2:12, 20.v.49; J2:13, 21.v.49; J2:13, 22.v.49; J2:32–33, 19.vi.49; J2:8, 10.v.49; J2:9–10, 15.v.49; J2:10, 16.v.49; J2:11, 17.v.49; J2:14, 23.v.49; J2:15, 16, 27 and 28.v.49; J2:23–24, 7.vi.49; J2:26–27, 9 and 10.vi.49; J2:36–37, 23–24.vi.49; J3:49A, 3.ix.49; J2:2, [4].v.49. To SM, 16.vi.49, *L*5:59. J2: 49–52, 1–3.vii.49. J2:67, 19.vii.49; J2:59, 11.vii.49; J2:73–74, 24.vii.49; J2:101, 26.ix.49. J2:21, 4.vi.49. J2:28, 12.vi.49. J2:1, [4].v.49; J2:29, 14.vi.49; J2:49, 1.vii.49; J2:15–16, 26 and 28.v.49; J2:16–18, 29.v.49.

21. J2:92–93, 14.viii.49. J2:46, 29.vi.49. J3:144, 167, 16.i.51 and 14.ii.51. Victor Gray and Melanie Aspey, *ODNB,* s.v. "Rothschild, Lionel Nathan de." Robert Peel, "Poor Laws (Ireland)—Rate in Aid Bill" (1849), in *The Speeches of the Late Right Honourable Sir Robert Peel, Bart.,* 4 vols. (London, 1853), 4:804.

22. J2:77, 30.vii.49; GOT's account in *LLLM* 2:201–202n2 illustrates his ability to elide, conflate, and invent evidence. J2:80, 2.viii.49. J2:82, 4.viii.49; J2:84, 6. viii.49. J1:464–466, 13.i.49; cf. J2:85–87, 6, 7, and 8.viii.49. J2:83, 4.viii.49; J2:90–91, 12.viii.49. J2:93, 15.viii.49; J3:1A, 16.viii.49. J3:2A, 16.viii.49. J3:3A, 16.viii.49, cf. cover page to J3.

23. Pliny, *Letters* 10.25 ff.; I owe this reference to the kindness of Sabine Mac-Cormack. J3:4A–7A, 17.viii.49. J3:7A–11A, 18.viii.49. J3:13A–15A, 20.viii.49.

24. J3:15A–21A, 21.viii.49; cf. *HOE* 3:191–198 = chap. 16. J3:21A–22A, 22.viii.49. J3:23A–27A, 23.viii.49. J3:27A–30A, 24.viii.49.

25. J3:30A, 25.viii.49. To HMT, 26.viii.49, *L*5:67.

26. *Macbeth,* act II, scene 2. To HMT, 26.viii.49, *L*5:67. To TFE, 26.viii.49, *L*5:69. J3:42A–44A, 31.viii.49. E.g., J2:358–359, 22.vii.50. E.g., J8:92, 2.viii.54; J11:157, 353, 357, and 358, 31.vii.57 and 2, 9, and 12.viii.58.

27. J3:30A–31A, 25.viii.49. To TFE, 26.viii.49, *L*5:69; J3:32A–35A, 26.viii.49. J3:35A–37A, 27.viii.49. J3:37A–39A, 28.viii.49. J3:40A–41A, 29.viii.49. J3:42A–44A, 31.viii.49; to TFE, 2.ix.49, *L*5:71. J3:44A–48A, 1.ix.49. *HOE* 1:xvi = "Contents"; and 1:597 = chap. 6; Roberto Romani, *National Character and Public Spirit in Britain and France, 1750–1914* (Cambridge: Cambridge University Press, 2002), 225–227, who first recognized the moral originality of "Temple."

28. J3:40A–41A, 29.viii.49. J3:50A, 4.ix.49; to TFE, 2.ix.49, *L*5:69–71. J3:96 and 94–95, 13–14, 20, and 7[*sic*].ix.49. Sander L. Gilman, "Obesity and Diet in the Nineteenth Century: Framing Verdi and Boito's Healthy Falstaff," *University of Toronto Quarterly* 74 (2005): 759–767.

29. J2:279–280, 4.iv.50. J3:59A, 26.vi.50. To "Cousin," 9.xii.50, *L*:5:140–141. *HOE* 1:49, 98 = chap. 1, *HOE* 2:614–615 = chap. 13. "Social and Industrial Capacities of Negroes," *ER* 45 (1827): 383–423.

30. [W. R. Greg], "Highland Destitution and Irish Emigration," *Quarterly Review* 90 (1851): 196–197. Herbert Spencer, *Principles of Biology,* 2 vols. (London, 1864), 1:444; cf. idem, "A Theory of Population Deduced from the General Law of Animal Fertility," *Westminster Review,* n.s., 1 (1852): 501. Charles Darwin, *The Descent of Man, and Selection, in Relation to Sex,* in *The Works of Charles Darwin,* 29 vols., ed. Paul H. Barrett and R. B. Freeman (London: William Pickering, 1986–1990), 21:188–189.

31. J2:97, 18.ix.49. J11:232, 27.xii.57; cf. J2.34, 20.vi.49. J4:251, 19.ix.51. J11:322, 25.v.58; J9:83, 11.ii.56. HMT, "Reminiscences," 16–17, TCL. J2:53, 3.vii.49; J4:257, 21.ix.51. J4:135–136, 12.vi.51.

32. To C. Macaulay, 3.iii.49, *L*5:29–30. J1:521, 2.iii.49. J3:178, 22.ii.51. J11:413, 6.i.59. J11:78, 29.i.57; J11:470, 13.iv.59. J8:7, 28.i.54. J11:82, 4.ii.57. *LLLM* 2:400.

33. To TFE, 4.iii.54, *L*5:387; to SM, 24.iii.54, *L*5:392; J2:1, [4].v.49; to FM, 5.v.49, *L*5:51; to J. Macaulay, 4.v.49, *L*5:50; to SM, 4.v.49, *L*5:51; to TFE, 10.v.49, *L*5:55; J2:255, 12.iii.50; J3:7, 15.viii.50. To FM, 5.v.49, *L*5:51; and to [HMT?], [7.v.49], *L*5:52. J4:182, 24.vii.51.

34. J11:365, 15.ix.58. J4:182, 23.vii.51. J3:50, 12.x.50; cf. to HMT, 9.x.50, *L*5:127. J11:420, 16.i.59. J11:407, 25.xii.58. J8:108, 1.ix.54; J3:44, 3.x.50. J2:310, 7.v.50; J4.60, 18.iv.51.

35. George Macaulay Trevelyan, *Sir George Otto Trevelyan: A Memoir* (London: Longmans, Green: 1932), 45. J1:476, 24.i.49; J2:2, [4].v.49; J2:2, 5.v.49; J2:7, 9.v.49; J2:19–20, 1.vi.49; J2:27, 10.vi.49; J2:78–79, 1.viii.49. Humphrey Trevelyan, *The India We Left: Charles Trevelyan, 1826–65; Humphrey Trevelyan, 1929–47* (London: Macmillan, 1972), 58. Trevelyan, *Trevelyan,* 7. J11:505, 8.vi.59; J11:184, 26.ix.57. J2:34, 1.vi.49. Roy Porter and Lesley Hall, *The Facts of Life: The Creation of Sexual*

Knowledge in Britain, 1650–1950 (New Haven: Yale University Press, 1995), 132–154.

36. To MT, 18.ix.51, *L*:5:195; J6:150, 20.x.53. J4:181, 22.vii.51. Quoted in Trevelyan, *Trevelyan,* 36. J6:55–56, 31.iii.53 and 3.iv.53. To MT, 1.x.53, *L*5:358; J4:240, 6.ix.51; cf. to MT, 9.ix.51, *L*5:187–188. J9:165–166, 29.iii.56.

37. J2:49, 30.vi.49; to MT, 24.v.49, *L*5:55–57. J1:477, 25.i.49. To HMT, 15.viii.52, *L*5:271; J5:99, 9.viii.52. J11:321, 25.v.58. J11:375, 12.x.58. J11:380, 381, 24 and 25.x.58.

38. J11:386, 12.xi.58. J11:383, 2.xi.58. J11:22, 17.vii.56. J1:504, 14.ii.49; J3:19, 1.ix.50. J11:536, 565, 26.vii.59 and 20.ix.59. J11:391, 25.xi.58. J11:391, 26.xi.58. J11:393, 29.xi.58. J11:487, 4.v.59.

39. J11:393, 29.xi.58. J1:478, 25.i.49; J2:72, 22.vii.49. J2:211–211A, 21.i.50. J5:18, 13.iii.52. J8:19, 21.ii.54. J2:186, 25.xii.49. J4:48, 7.iv.51. E.g., J3:124, 1.i.51; cf. J3:135, 13.i.51; J3:156, 1.ii.51; J4:188, 31.vii.51; to TFE, 22.iii.54, *L*5:391; to TFE, 20.ix.54, *L*5:421–422; to TFE, 29.iii.52, *L*5:228. J11:39, 50, 16 and 21.viii.56. J4:63, 179; 20.iv.51 and 20.vii.51; Edward A. Allen, "Public School Elites in Early Victorian England: The Boys at Harrow and Merchant Taylor Schools from 1825 to 1850," *Journal of British Studies* 21 (1982): 87–117. J11:239, 13.i.58; J2:277, 1.iv.50.

40. To TFE, 1.iv.59, *L*6:206; cf. to SM, 23.xii.54, *L*5:434; J11:80, 31.i.57; cf. J11:369, 29.ix.58. *LLLM* 2:347, 344. Trevelyan, *Trevelyan,* 17, 151. *LLLM* 2:346. To GOT, 13.x.52, *L*5:287.

41. Richard Schlatter, ed., *Hobbes's Thucydides* (New Brunswick, N.J.: Rutgers University Press, 1975), xviii–xix, xxii–xxiii, and 10–27; Clifford W. Brown, "Thucydides, Hobbes and the Linear Causal Perspective," *History of Political Thought* 10 (1989): 215–256; Thomas Hobbes, *De Cive* (Whitefish, Mont.: Kessinger, 2004), 18 = chap. 1.xiii. J5:55, 31.v.52. Thomas Arnold, "Preface to the Third Volume of the Edition of Thucydides," in *The Miscellaneous Works of Thomas Arnold, D.D.,* ed. Arthur Penrhyn Stanley (London, 1845), 392–399; to FM, 22.xii.52, *L*5:304. Conflates *HOE* 1:135 = chap. 2 and 4:201 = chap. 21.

42. To GOT, 1.viii.53, *L*5:345. Trevelyan, *Trevelyan,* 15–16. To TFE, 14.viii.54, *L*5:415 and nn5, 6. J5:61, 24.vi.52. Trevelyan, *Trevelyan,* 39.

9. Baron Macaulay of Rothley

1. To HMT, 12.x.42, *L*4:59; to Hallam, 28.x.42, *L*4:66. To TFE, 4.viii.53, *L*5:347; Pinney, *L*1:xxii–xxiii; J2:6, 8.v.49; J2:9, 15.v.49; J2:16, 28.v.49; J2:29, 14. vi.49; J2:33, 19.vi.49. J2:14, 22.v.49; cf. J1:478, 25.i.49; J2:35, 22.vi.49; J2:309, 6.v.50. To TFE, twice on 20.vii.53, *L*5:342–343; J4:247, 11.ix.51; to TFE, 12 and 21.ix.51, *L*5:190, 196. J11:404, 20.xii.58. To Wood, 23.xi.51, *L*5:206–207. J4:314–315, 23. xi.51; to TFE, [23.xi.51], *L*5:207–208. TFE to CET, 20.ii.60, in Pinney, *L*1:xxiii.

2. To TFE, 19.iv.58, *L*6:150; and 9.iii.50, *L*5:100. J2:10, 22, 8.v.49 and 5.vi.49; to TFE, 9.vii.49, *L*5:62. To TFE, 22.xi.50, *L*5:135. To TFE, 9.iii.50 and 22.xi.50, *L*5:100, 135; to Gladstone, 7, 9.vi.51, *L*5:166–167.

3. Nicholas Christakis and James Fowler, "The Spread of Obesity in a Large Social Network over 32 Years," *New England Journal of Medicine* 357 (2007): 370–379. Thorstein Veblen, *The Theory of the Leisure Class* (Oxford: Oxford University Press, 2007), 237–238. *HOE* 4:412 = chap. 24. J5:45, 15.v.52.

4. J8:100–101, 18.viii.54. Adrian Hastings, in *ODNB,* s.v. "Temple, William (1881–1944)."

5. Françoise Waquet, *Latin or the Empire of a Sign from the Sixteenth to the Twentieth Century,* trans. John Howe (London: Verso, 2001), tells part of the story. G. M. Trevelyan, *Sir George Otto Trevelyan: A Memoir* (London: Longmans, 1932), 25–27. John S. Goff, *Robert Todd Lincoln: A Man in His Own Right* (Norman: University of Oklahoma Press, 1968), 22–27; and Justin G. Turner and Linda Levitt Turner, *Mary Todd Lincoln: Her Life and Letters* (New York: Knopf, 1972), 58.

6. M. A. Titmarsh [W. M. Thackeray], *Notes of a Journey from Cornhill to Grand Cairo* (New York, 1848), 39. F. P. Jones, "Anthony Trollope and the Classics," *Classical Quarterly* 37 (1944): 227–231. Christopher A. Stray, "Culture and Discipline: Classics and Society in Victorian England," *International Journal of the Classical Tradition* 3 (1996): 79. "Inaugural Address as Lord Rector, University of Glasgow" (1849), *WLM* 8:406–413; and to TFE, 22.iii.54, *L*5:391. To Whewell, 27.ii.54, *L*5:385.

7. Herbert Spencer, *An Autobiography,* 2 vols. (New York: D. Appleton, 1904), 2:516–518. To Caszelles, 6.xii.96, in David Duncan, *The Life and Letters of Herbert Spencer,* 2 vols. (New York: D. Appleton, 1908), 2:122; I owe this reference to the kindness of Jim Turner. David Armitage, "Edmund Burke and Reason of State," *Journal of the History of Ideas* 61 (2000): 617–634. Edmund Burke, *Reflections on the Revolution in France,* ed. Frank M. Turner (New Haven: Yale University Press, 2003), 77, 83, 117, 130–131, 145, 163, 183, and 194. M. L. Clarke, "Charles James Fox and the Classics," *Greece & Rome* 9 (1940): 81–87.

8. John Talbot, "Tennyson's Alcaics: Greek and Latin Prosody and the Invention of English Meters," *Studies in Philology* 101 (2004): 204n18. Alfred Tennyson, *In Memoriam,* lines 157–160, 173–176.

9. F. A. Simpson, "England and the Italian War of 1859," *Historical Journal* 5 (1962): 111–121 ("In Memoriam G[eorge]. M[acaulay]. T[revelyan]."). Alfred Tennyson, "The War" (1859), lines 22–23. To CET, 16.v.59, *L*6:214 and n1. Rupert Brooke, "The Soldier" (1914), lines 1–3. Niall Ferguson, *The Pity of War: Explaining World War I* (New York: Basic Books, 1999), 198.

10. David Newsome, *The Wilberforces and Henry Manning: The Parting of Friends* (Cambridge, Mass.: Belknap Press of Harvard University Press, 1966); and Frank M. Turner, *John Henry Newman: The Challenge to Evangelical Religion* (New Haven: Yale

University Press, 2002). To HMT, 1.vi.33, *L2*:247. Bunsen to Mother, 3.ii.49, in Augustus J. C. Hare, *The Life and Letters of Frances Baroness Bunsen,* 2 vols. (New York, 1879), 2:127.

11. J4:180, 22.vii.[51]; J5:161, 2.xi.[52]; J11:89, 22.ii.[57]; J11:115–116, 11.v.[57]; to FM, 17.i.54, *L5*:377. Roger Cooter, *The Cultural Meaning of Popular Science: Phrenology and the Organization of Consent in Nineteenth-Century Britain* (Cambridge: Cambridge University Press, 1984), 101–200; Alison Winter, *Mesmerized: Powers of the Mind in Victorian England* (Chicago: University of Chicago Press, 1998), 1–108; and Mioara Deacc, "Mirror of the World or Submerged Unconscious? Hallucinations and the Victorians" (Ph.D. diss., University of Notre Dame, 2005). J5:48–49, 18.v.52. J5:50, 19.v.52. Christopher Hibbert, *Queen Victoria: A Personal History* (New York: Basic Books, 2000), 187. J11:401, 16.xii.58; J4:91–92, 13.v.51. Frank M. Turner, "Ancient Materialism and Modern Science: Lucretius among the Victorians," in *Contesting Cultural Authority: Essays in Victorian Intellectual Life* (Cambridge: Cambridge University Press, 1993), 268. J11:21, 16.vii.56; J11:595, 26.xi.59.

12. [Thomas Huxley], "Agnosticism" (1889), in *Agnosticism: Contemporary Reponses to Spencer and Huxley,* ed. Andrew Pyle (Bristol: Thoemes Press, 1995), 149–152; Bernard Lightman, *The Origins of Agnosticism: Victorian Unbelief and the Limits of Knowledge* (Baltimore: Johns Hopkins University Press, 1987); Frank M. Turner, "Shifting Boundaries," in *Contesting Cultural Authority,* 3–100. To TFE, 24 and 25. iv.54, *L5*:395–396; J8:50, 26.iv.54. To Murray, 21.vii.18[54], *L5*:411. J3:36, 22.ix.50.

13. To FM, 14.x.54, *L5*:426. John Russell, ed., *Memorials and Correspondence of Charles James Fox,* 4 vols. (London, 1853–1857), 1:71. J1:475–476, 23.i.49; cf. J2:9, 15.v.49; J2:29, 13.vi.49. Hugh McLeod, introduction to *The Decline of Christendom in Western Europe, 1750–2000,* ed. Hugh McLeod and Werner Ustoff (Cambridge: Cambridge University Press, 2003), 15–18; Eva M. Hamberg, "Christendom in Decline: The Swedish Case," ibid., 47–62; David Hempton, "Established Churches and the Growth of Religious Pluralism: A Case Study of Christianisation and Secularisation in England since 1700," ibid., 81–98; and Sheridan Gilley, "Catholicism in Ireland," ibid., 108–110.

14. J3:60a, 27.vi.50. J11:226, 10.xii 57; J6:116, 19.vii.53; J11:427, 29.i.59. To Mrs. Milman, 23.i.49, *L5*:23; J1:484, 30.i.49; to FM, 21.vii.51, *L5*:171; J3:64, 30.x.50; J2:14, 22.v.49, J1:465, 13.i.49. To Adolphus, 8.xi.[50], *L5*:130. J11:388, 19.xi.58. J8:57, 14.v.54. J2:34, 20.vi.49; J2:81, 3.viii.49. J4:179, 19.vii.51.

15. J2:4–5, 7.v.49. J2:137, 177, 4.xi.49 and 20.xii.49. J8:106, 27.viii.54; J2:21, 3.vi.49. J2:56, 8.vii.49. J1:490, 4.ii.49. J5:146, 10.x.52. J1:562, 5.iv.49. J1:564, 6. iv.49. J2:132, 4.xi.49. J9:240–241, 4.v.56. J9:247, 8.v.56. J6:96, 19.vi.53; cf. J11:512, 12.vi.59. J9:255, 11.v.56; to TFE, 8.x.57, *L6*:124.

16. J11:503, 2.vi.59. J11:458–459, 27.iii.59. J2:36, 22.vi.49. J2:37, 24.vi.49. J4:311, 17.xi.51.

17. J1:512, 17.ii.49; cf. J5:175, 68, 21.xi.52 and 25.vi.52; J11:407, 24.xii.58. J3:159, 3.ii.51. J7:64, 10.ix.53; to ——, [xi?40], L3:349. J11:392, 26.xi.[58]. J3:48, 9.x.50. J11:274, 13.iii.58. J11:276, 16.iii.58.

18. To TFE, 20.vii.53, L5:343. J6:124, 2.viii.53. J6:124–125, 3.viii.53.

19. J3:124, 141, 2 and 15.i.51; cf. Arthur Penrhyn Stanley, *The Life and Correspondence of Thomas Arnold, D.D.* (London, 1846), 95; *LLLM* 2:335. J11:389, 22. xi.58. J3:95, 6.xii.50. To HMT, 18.vi.44, L4:196. J5:42, 11.v.52. Peter H. Hansen, in *ODNB*, s.v. "Smith, Albert"; Michael Mason, *The Making of Victorian Sexual Attitudes* (Oxford: Oxford University Press, 1994), 117–166.

20. [H. H. Milman], *"Arundines Cami,"* Quarterly Review 69 (1842): 440–471. J11:487, 3.v.59. J4:40–41, 30.iii.51. Mason, *Making of Victorian Sexual Attitudes,* 44–45, 47.

21. John Henry Newman, *The Idea of a University: Defined and Illustrated,* ed. Martin J. Svaglic (Notre Dame: University of Notre Dame Press, 1982), 159–160. F. M. Turner, *Newman,* 498–499. J11:578–79, 17.x.59. J. V. Jensen, "Return to the Wilberforce Huxley Debate," *British Journal for the History of Science* 21 (1988): 161–179; J. H. Newman, *The Philosophical Notebook of John Henry Newman,* ed. Edward Sillem, 2 vols. (New York: Humanities Press, 1969–70), 2:158.

22. Jowett to Stanley, 1.i.49, in *Letters of Benjamin Jowett,* ed. Evelyn Abbott and Lewis Campbell (London, 1899), 162. Thomas Arnold, quoted in Duncan Forbes, *The Liberal Anglican Idea of History* (Cambridge: Cambridge University Press, 1952), 115, 85, 51, and 50. Ibid., 110; [A. P. Stanley], "Grote's History of Greece," *Quarterly Review* 86 (1849–50): 394, 386.

23. *OED,* s.v. "Broad Church." Stanley, "Grote's History," 395; [A. P. Stanley,] "Socrates," *Quarterly Review* 88 (1850–51): 42. Ibid., 61, 66, and 62.

24. Arthur Penrhyn Stanley, *Essays Chiefly on Questions of Church and State from 1850 to 1870* (London, 1870). Rowland E. Prothero, *Life and Letters of Dean Stanley* (London: Nelson, 1909), 254. Rowland E. Prothero and G. G. Bradley, *The Life and Correspondence of Arthur Penrhyn Stanley Late Dean of Westminster,* 2d ed., 2 vols. (London, 1893), 2:320–321; "Hastings," *WLM* 6:643. Elizabeth Flagg Dow, "George Grote, Historian of Greece," *Classical Journal* 51 (1956): 219; Alexander Bain, *John Stuart Mill. A Criticism: with Personal Recollections* (London, 1882), 133. J11:456, 22. iii.59. John Connop Thirlwall Jr., *Connop Thirlwall: Historian and Theologian* (London: Society for Promoting Christian Knowledge, 1936), 265–266.

25. Malcolm Schofield, *Plato: Political Philosophy* (Oxford: Oxford University Press, 2006), 136–193. Henry Scott Holland, quoted in Peter Hinchliff, *Benjamin Jowett and the Christian Religion* (Oxford: Clarendon Press, 1987), 116. Prothero and Bradley, *Life and Correspondence of Stanley,* 289. Prothero, *Life and Letters of Stanley,* 364. Benjamin Jowett, quoted in Lionel A. Tollemache, *Gladstone's Boswell: Late Victo-*

rian Conversations, ed. Asa Briggs (Sussex: Harvester Press, 1984), 191–192. J11:492, 13.v.59. J9:144, 12.iii.56.

26. [W. E. Gladstone], "Giacomo Leopardi," *Quarterly Review* 86 (1849–50): 331. Ibid.; Newman, *Idea of a University,* 76, 82, and 354. D. W. Bebbington, *The Mind of Gladstone: Religion, Homer, and Politics* (Oxford: Oxford University Press, 2004), 146–147.

27. Gladstone, quoted in Bebbington, *Mind of Gladstone,* 148; see generally 143–216.

28. J11:290–291, 12.iv.58. J11:295–296, 17.iv.58. "Gladstone," *WLM* 6:326. Bebbington, *Mind of Gladstone,* 132.

29. New York *Albion,* 6.ix.51, 430, in Pinney, *L*5:202n2.

30. Pinney, *L*5:203n. J6:144, 11.x.53; to ——, 14.x.53, *L*5:360–361. To MT, 11.x.51, *L*5:203. I am grateful to Cathy Kaveny for explaining the *nolo contendere* plea. E.g., J4:264, 26.ix.51.

31. To FM, 4.vii.44, *L*4:202 and n3.

32. J2:61, 12.vii.49. J4:68, 23.iv.51. J4:348, 31.xii.51. J3:180–181, 23.ii.51. To FM, 24.iii.51, *L*5:156–157. J11:390, 25.xi.58. J4:100, 21.v.51; J4:156, 1.vii.51; J4:126, 10.vi.51. J8:29, 13.iii.54. Lynda Nead, *Victorian Babylon: People, Streets, and Images in Nineteenth-Century London* (New Haven: Yale University Press, 2000), 128; David Steele, in *ODNB,* s.v. "Temple, Henry John, third Viscount Palmerston." J2:61, 12.vii.49. J2:190, 29.xii.49. J11:258, 15.ii.58. J3:181, 24.ii.51. J4:324, 4.xii.51. J4:334, 18.xii.51.

33. J9:247, 8.v.56. J4:54, 13.iv.51. J4:87, 9.v.51. J4:92, 14.v.51. J4:124–125, 8.vi.51. To Electors of Edinburgh, 1.x.39, *L*3:303–304. J3:135, 13.i.51.

34. The enormous literature includes Peter Bailey, "'Will the Real Banks Please Stand Up?' Towards a Role Analysis of Mid-Victorian Working-Class Respectability," *Journal of Social History* 12 (1979): 336–353; F. M. L. Thompson, *The Rise of Respectable Society: A Social History of Victorian Britain* (Cambridge, Mass.: Harvard University Press, 1988); Michael Winstanley, "Oldham Radicalism and the Origins of Popular Liberalism, 1830–1852," *Historical Journal* 36 (1993): 619–643; Marjorie Morgan, *Manners, Morals, and Class in England, 1774–1858* (New York: St. Martin's Press, 1994); Simon Cordery, "Friendly Societies and the Discourse of Respectability in Britain, 1828–1875," *Journal of British Studies* 34 (1995): 35–58; Anna Clark, *The Struggle for Breeches: Gender and the Making of the British Working Class* (Berkeley: University of California Press, 1995); David Gadian, "Radicalism and Liberalism in Oldham: A Study of Conflict, Continuity and Change in Popular Politics, 1830–52," *Social History* 21 (1996): 265–280; Paul Langford, "The Uses of Eighteenth-Century Politeness," *Transactions of the Royal Historical Society,* 6th ser., 12 (2002): 311–331; and Robert B. Shoemaker, *The London Mob: Violence and Disorder in Eighteenth-Century*

England (London: Hambledon and London, 2004), 111–152. *OED,* s.v. "Respectability" (quoting John Trusler); Emma Major, in *ODNB,* s.v. "Trusler, John."

35. Standish Meacham, *Lord Bishop: The Life of Samuel Wilberforce, 1805–1873* (Cambridge, Mass.: Harvard University Press, 1970), 104. J2:223–224, 3.ii.50. J4:101, 22.v.51; J9:120, 1.iii.56; J11:416, 8.i.59. To TFE, 4.iii.53, *L5*:315. J11:328, 8.vi.58. *HOE* 2:297–298, 303 = chap. 10.

36. Patrick Joyce, *Visions of the People: Industrial England and the Question of Class, 1848–1914* (Cambridge: Cambridge University Press, 1991), 179, 206–208. Plato[?], *Letters* 7.341e; cf. Matt. 22:14.

37. J2:26, 9.vi.49; J2:40, 27.vi.49; J2:139, 5.xi.49; Woodruff D. Smith, *Consumption and the Making of Respectability, 1600–1800* (New York: Routledge, 2002), summarizes a vast literature. J4:175–176, 18.vii.51; J2:177–178, 20.xii.49. J3:143, 16.i.51.

38. J4:238, 4.ix.51. J8:124, 22.ix.54. J11:196, 20.x.57.

39. J9:234, 1.v.56; J9:258, 14.v.56. J11:262, 20.ii.58; J11:210, 9.xi.57. J11:371, 372, 2 and 4.x.58. J11:228, 17.xii.57; cf. J2:58, 10.vii.49; J3:121, 31.xii.50; J3:51, 14.x.50.

40. J2:80, 2.viii.49; J2:356, 17.vii.50. To SM, 5.xii.56, *L6*:69–70; to SM, 24.x.50, *L5*:128; J9:47–48, 26.i.56. J11:62, 25.xi.56; to SM, 5.xii.56, *L6*:69–70. To FM, 22.i.58, *L6*:138; J11:241, 18.i.58. J11:577, 14.x.59. J11:244, 24.i.58.

41. J1:469, 19.i.49. J3:34A–35A, 26.viii.49. J2:48, 30.vi.49. J2:49–50, 1.vii.49. J2:51, 2.vii.49. J5:9, 16.ii.52. J11:80, 4.i.57.

42. J2:40–41, 27.vi.49. J2:44, 28.vi.49. J1:495, 7.ii.49; cf. J1:518–519, 24.ii.49. J2:14, 23.v.49; J4:151, 28.vi.51. J2:250, 6.iii.50; J2:335, 7.vi.50. J3:72A–73A, 4.vii.50; J3:71A, 3.vii.50; J2:348, 8.vii.50; J4:234, 1.ix.51.

43. J11:377, 16.x.58. Pinney, *L4*:14–15n2. J2:6, 8.v.49; J2:2, 5.v.49.

44. Seventh earl of Carlisle diary (1848), quoted in A. R. Ashwell and R. G. Wilberforce, *Life of the Right Reverend Samuel Wilberforce, D.D.,* abr. ed. (New York, 1883), 179. J2:6, 8.v.49; J2:12, 20.v.49. J1:499, 11.ii.49; cf. J3:173, 20.ii.51; A. R. Ashwell and R. G. Wilberforce, *Life of the Right Reverend Samuel Wilberforce, D.D.,* 3 vols. (London, 1880–1882), 2:244 (diary for 22.v.54). J2:148, 14.xi.49; J2:7, 8.v.49. James Montgomery Stuart, *Reminiscences and Essays* (London, 1884), 25, 27, 32, and 43. J2:327, 28.v.50. J4:3, 1.iii.51.

45. To Gladstone, 7 and 9.vi.51, *L5*:166–167. J4:344, 30.xii.51. J4:346, 31.xii.51. J4:338, 24.xii.51. J1:507–508, 15.ii.49. J4:6, 3.iii.51; J4:9, 5.iii.51. J2:7, 9.v.49. J4:249, 16.ix.51; J4:220, 25.viii.51; J4:184, 26.xii.51; J4:200, 10.viii.51; to TFE, 17. ix.51, *L5*:193; J1:506, 14.ii.49; J2:2, [4].v.49; J2:11, 17.v.49.

46. J2:33, 20.vi.49; J4:334, 18.xii.51; J8:105, 26.viii.54. J8:106, 26.viii.54. J4:236, 3–4.ix.51. J4:128, 10.vi.51. J4:172, 17.vii.51. J2:250, 6.iii.50. J3:110–11, 23.xii.50.

47. J11:364, 25.viii.58. J11:179, 20.ix.57. Thomas Carlyle, journal, 7.iii.48, in *The Collected Letters of Thomas and Jane Welsh Carlyle,* ed. Clyde deL. Ryals and Kenneth J. Fielding, 36 vols. to date (Durham: Duke University Press, 1970–), 22:265–266n1; cf. Exod. 32:4.

48. J2:268, 21.iii.50. J4:330, 17.xii.51. Motley to M. Motley, 30.v.58, in *The Correspondence of John Lothrop Motley,* ed. George William Curtis, 3 vols. (New York: 1900), 1:302–304. J11:342, 8.vii.58. Henry S. J. D. Raikes, *The Life and Letters of Henry Cecil Raikes* (London, 1898), 22.

49. E.g., J1:501, 13.ii.49; J1:554, 27.iii.49; J2:55, 6.vii.49; J2:160, 2.xii.49; J2:163, 5.xii.49; J2:184–185, 24.xii.49; J2:202–203, 11.i.50; J3:62, 29.x.50; J9:148, 14.iii.56; *LLLM* 2:337–338. J6:14, 22.xii.52; J9:116, 29.ii.56. J11:599–600, 3.xii.59. CGPLA Eng. & Wales, as cited by William Thomas in *OBNB,* s.v. "Macaulay, Thomas." Pinney, *L5*:viii. J2:164–165, 6.xii.49. J6:134, 24.viii.53; cf. J5:93, 4.viii.52. J9:140–141, 149, 11 and 15.iii.56. J11:526, 8.vii.59.

50. J9:116–17, 29.ii.56. J11:599–600, 3.xii.59. To TFE, 25.vii–12.viii.36, *L3*:182.

51. J9:101–102, 21.ii.56. J9:116–117, 29.ii.56; to TFE, 11.iii.56, *L6*:25. J9:150, 16.iii.56; to TFE, 16.iii.56, *L6*:27–28. J11:16, 30.vi.56. J2:346–347, 354, 6 and 15.vii.50; J2:303, 27.iv.50; J4:180, 22.vii.51. J11:403, 19.xii.58.

52. Gavin Budge, "Rethinking the Victorian Sage: Nineteenth-Century Prose and Scottish Common Sense Philosophy," *Literary Compass* 2 (2005): 1–11. J9:218, 25.iv.56. To TFE, [3.ii.53], *L5*:309; cf. to TFE, 16.viii.53, *L5*:350.

53. J2:201, 10.i.50; to FM, 2.iii.50, *L5*:96–97; J1:214, 25.i.50; J2:284, 10.iv.50. J11:168, 28.viii.57; to SM and FM, 29.viii.57, *L6*:113. To HMT, 14.ix.57, *L6*:115. To HMT, 26.iii.58, *L6*:146. J11:169, 170, 28 and 29.viii.57. J11:177, 19.ix.57. J11:222, 3.xii.57.

54. J1:543–544, 546, and 549–550; 21–22.iii.49; J11:288, 7.iv.58. J11:325, 31.v.58. J2:351, 10.vii.50. To Ward, 12.viii.51, *L5*:175–176 and 175n4. To Stanhope, 16 and 25.ii.57, *L6*:78; J11:87–88, 16.ii.57; J11:150–151, 22.vii.57. J1:508, 16.ii.49. To FM, 30.xi.50, *L5*:137 and n3. Nicolaas A. Rupke, *Richard Owen: Victorian Naturalist* (New Haven: Yale University Press, 1994), 44. John Mack, *The Museum of the Mind: Art and Memory in World Cultures* (London: British Museum, 2003).

55. To MT, 1.x.53, *L5*:357. To Lewis, 27.ii.56, *L6*:20. J9:111–113, 27.ii.56. To Stanhope, 27.ii.56, *L6*:19–20.

56. To Stanhope, 29.ii.56, *L6*:21; and to Lansdowne, 29.ii.56, *L6*:22. J9:114–115, 29.ii.56. To Lansdowne, 29.ii.56, *L6*:21–22.

57. J9:121–122, 2.iii.56; to Stanhope, 3.iii.56, *L6*:23. J9:119, 1.iii.56. J9:147, 14.iii.56. [Richard Owen], "Darwin on the Origin of Species," *ER* 111 (1860): 487–532; cf. Rupke, *Richard Owen,* 284–316; and Janet Brown, *Charles Darwin: The Power*

of Place (Princeton: Princeton University Press, 2003), 99–230, 337–350, and 495–497. To Palmerston, 2.xii.59, *L*6:257–259; J11:599, 2.xii.59.

58. J11:599–600, 3.xii.59.

10. Procrastinator

1. "Sir James Mackintosh," *WLM* 6:95; "Lord Bacon," *WLM* 6:204; J10:128, 16.ix.56; cf. J2:30, 16.vi.49. J3:56A, 25.vi.50. J3:105, 23[*sic*].xii.50. J3:108, 23.xii.50.

2. [William Whewell], "On Mr. Macaulay's Praise of Superficial Knowledge," *Fraser's Magazine* 40 (1849): 171–175. John E. E. Dalberg-Acton, "Review of Philip's *History of Progress in Great Britain*" (1858), in *Selected Writings of Lord Acton,* ed. J. Rufus Fears, 3 vols. (Indianapolis: Liberty Classics, 1985–1988), 2:32. John Henry Newman, *Lectures on Certain Difficulties Felt by Anglicans* (London, 1850), 195–201. Pius IX, "Syllabus of Errors," in *Enchiridion Symbolorum,* ed. Henry Denzinger and Adolf Schönmetzer, 36th ed. (Freiburg im Breisgau: Herder, 1965), no. 2980. John Henry Newman, *The Idea of a University: Defined and Illustrated,* ed. Martin J. Svaglic (Notre Dame: University of Notre Dame Press, 1982), 189. Simon Szreter and Graham Mooney, "Urbanization, Mortality, and the Standard of Living Debate: New Estimates of the Expectation of Life at Birth in Nineteenth-Century British Cities," *Economic History Review* 51 (1998): 84–112. J3:4, 30.vii.50.

3. The paragraph quotes Jeffrey A. Auerbach, *The Great Exhibition of 1851: A Nation on Display* (New Haven: Yale University Press, 1999), 31, 10, 159, 33–81, 91, 100, 144, and 147.

4. Christopher Hibbert, ed., *Queen Victoria in Her Letters and Journals* (New York: Viking, 1985), 84 (entry of 1.v.51); and Elizabeth Longford, *Queen Victoria: Born to Succeed* (New York: Harper & Row, 1965), 224. J4:67, 22.iv.51. J4:70, 26.iv.51. J3:5A, 17.viii.49; J4:269, 1.xi.51; J4:226, 29.viii.51; and "Warren Hastings," *WLM* 6:629–630. J3:146, 19.i.51; cf. J3:156, 1.ii.51. J4:76, 1.v.51; this account summarizes and paraphrases J4:74–78, 1.v.51.

5. J4:84, 8.v.51. J4:95–96, 98, 19, 20, and 21.v.51; cf. J4:80, 4.v.51. *HOE* 3:478, 479; the whole account is in *HOE* 3:474–480 = chap. 19.

6. J4:105, 26.v.51. Auerbach, *Great Exhibition,* 158. J4:106, 27.v.51. J4:112, 31.v.51; J4:123, 7.vi.51; J4:144, 20.vi.51; J4:154, 30.vi.51; J4:158, 2.vii.51, with Baba "as usual"; J4:181, 22.vii.51. J4:274, 4.x.51. J4:278, 9.x.51. To MT, 14.x.51, *L*5:204.

7. Auerbach, *Great Exhibition,* 179–189. J4:318–319, 2.xii.[51]. Auerbach, *Great Exhibition,* 146. Karl Marx in *Neue Oder-Zeitung,* 28.vi.55, at http://www.marxists.org/archive/marx/works/1855/06/25.htm. Roman Szporluk, *Communism and Nationalism: Karl Marx versus Friedrich List* (New York: Oxford University Press,

1988), 1–96, 152–240. Karl Marx, *Capital,* trans. Samuel Moore and Edward Aveling (New York: Modern Library, n.d.), 300n1.

8. J4:205, 14.viii.51. J2:97, 18.ix.49; J2:110–113, 9–13.x.49. J2:114, 14.x.49. J2:193–194, 1.i.50. J2:196, 3.i.50. J2:198, 5.i.50. J2:227, 7.ii.50. J2:226–227, 6 and 9.ii.50. J2:229, 12.ii.50. J2:230, 13.ii.50. J2:239, 22.ii.50. J2:254–255, 11.iii.50.

9. J3:123, 1.i.51. J4:10–13, 6, 7, and 8.iii.51. J3:30–31, 10.ix.50; J4:116–117, 2.vi.51. J4:23, 18.iii.51; cf. J4:162, 7.vii.51; J4:164, 8.vii.51. J4:273, 3.x.51. J4:277, 7.x.51 = *HOE* chap. 11; J4:284, 15.x.51 = *HOE* chap. 13; J4:290, 22.x.51 = *HOE* chap. 14; J4:294, 28.x.51 = *HOE* chap. 14; J4:313, 21.xi.51 = *HOE* chap. 14; J4:322, 3.xii.51 = *HOE* chap. 11; J4:328, 12.xii.51 = *HOE* chap. 15. J4:289, 20.x.51. To Wood, 25.xi.51, *L*5:208–209 and n1. J4:316, 25 and 27.xi.51. J4:340, 26.xii.51. To Murray, 3.i.52, *L*5:215–216; cf. J4:351, 2.i.52. E.g., J4:366, 26.i.52.

10. J3:120, 30.xii.50; and J2:264, 19.iii.50; cf. J2:98–99, 20 and 21.ix.49; J2:98, 101, 21 and 26.ix.49; J2:115–116, 16.x.49; J2:170, 12–13.xii.49; J2:198–199, 6.i.50; J2:257–258, 13.iii.50. J2:209, 18.i.50; cf. J2:167–168, 7.xii.49.

11. "History," *WLM* 5:124, 125, 133, and 131.

12. J2:167, 7.xii.49. "History," 126 and 130–132.

13. J2:161, 3.xii.49. J2:167–168, 7.xii.49; J3:24–25, 5.ix.50; J3:87, 29.xi.50; J3:96, 10.xii.50. Thucydides, *The Peloponnesian War,* trans. Richard Crawley (New York: Modern Library, 1951), 14, 24 (1.22 and 36). "History," 130. *HOE* 2:386, 388, 389 = chap. 11. *HOE* 2:389. "History," 130, 131.

14. J2:228, 8.ii.50; cf. J8:159, 31.xii.54. *HOE* 2:381 = chap. 11. Ps. 47:5–6. *HOE* 2:383.

15. *HOE* 2:384 = chap. 11. Tacitus, *Dialogue on Oratory* 30–38. "History," 143.

16. J2:218, 28.i.50. J2:311–312, 8.v.50; J2:285, 11.iv.50; cf. J2:293–294, 16.iv.50; J9:96–103, 18–22.ii.56 (Lucian—often); J3:52a, 21.vi.50 (Cervantes). J3:121, 30. xii.50. To FM, 30.xi.50, *L*5:137. J3:23–33, 37–39, 3–13 and 23–27.ix.50; J3:27, 9. ix.50; J3:39–40, 28.ix.50. David Wootton, *Paolo Sarpi: Between Renaissance and Enlightenment* (Cambridge: Cambridge University Press, 1983), 36. Leopold von Ranke, *History of the Popes: Their Church and State,* trans. E. Fowler, rev. ed., 3 vols. (New York: Collier, 1901), 3:324.

17. J1:461, 10.i.49. 2:318, 16.v.50. James Boswell, *The Life of Samuel Johnson, L.L.D.* (Edinburgh, 1873), 292. J2:240–241, 23 and 24.ii.50; J2:246–247, 1.iii.50; J3:2, 28.vii.50; J6:182, 1.i.54; J8:13–14, 6.ii.54. J2:103, 29.ix.49. J2:123–126, 25.x.49. J2:255, 11.iii.50. "History," 129–130.

18. J4:170, 15.vii.51. *HOE* 3:478 = chap. 19. Leo Tolstoy, *War and Peace,* trans. Constance Garnett (New York: Modern Library, n.d.), 610–611. Idem, *What Is Art?* in *What Is Art? and Essays on Art,* trans. Aylmer Maude (New York: Oxford University Press, 1962), 121.

19. J11:171, 29.viii.57. Wilfred Owen, *Poems* (Kila, Mont.: Kessinger, 2004), 2.

20. J4:146, 23.vi.51. *HOE* 4:90–95 = chap. 20; cf. *HOE* 4:181–201 = chap. 21. Borislav Knezevic, *Figures of Finance Capital in the Age of Dickens* (New York: Routledge, 2003), 75–86. *HOE* 4:182; Patrick Hyde Kelly, "General Introduction," in John Locke, *On Money,* ed. Patrick Hyde Kelly, 2 vols. (Oxford: Clarendon Press, 1991), 1:32. Ibid., 23–24. To McCulloch, 21.iii.52, *L*5:223–224. David Ricardo, "Proposals for an Economical and Secure Currency," in *Pamphlets and Papers 1815–1823,* vol. 4 of *The Works and Correspondence of David Ricardo,* ed. Piero Sraffa and M. H. Dobb (Indianapolis: Liberty Fund, 2004), 62–65.

21. Kelly, "Introduction," 39, 64, and 65. *HOE* 4:238 = chap. 22. To Randall, 23.v.57, *L*6:95. Kelly, "Introduction," 66; and Ming-Hsun Li, *The Great Recoinage of 1696 to 1699* (London: Weidenfeld and Nicolson, 1963), 143–150. M. J. Daunton, *Progress and Poverty: An Economic and Social History of Britain, 1700–1850* (Oxford: Oxford University Press, 1995), 434. John Brewer, *The Sinews of Power: War, Money and the English State, 1688–1783* (New York: Knopf, 1989), xviii–xix.

22. J3:2, 28.vii.50; cf. J3:51A, 20.vi.50. J3:80, 21.xi.50. J3:66, 31.x.50. To MT, 19.viii.51, *L*5:178; cf. J4:123, 7.vi.51; J4:211, 213, 17 and 19.viii.51. J4:217, 22. viii.51; Homer, *The Odyssey,* trans. Robert Fitzgerald (Garden City, N.Y.: Doubleday/Anchor, 1963), 409 (22.1–4).

23. J2:104, 1.x.49. J2:105, 2.x.49. J4:66, 22.iv.51. J2:127, 27.x.49. J2:131, 2.xi.49.

24. J4:300, 1.xi.51; J4:302, 8.xi.51. To FM, 21.vii.51, and to ——, 28.vii.51, *L*5:172. Samuel Wilberforce, diary, 20.v.54, quoted in A. R. Ashwell and R. G. Wilberforce, *Life of Samuel Wilberforce,* 3 vols. (London, 1880–1883), 2:244. A. R. Ashwell and R. G. Wilberforce, *Life of Samuel Wilberforce,* abr. ed. (London, 1883), 304.

25. *HOE* 1:36–45 = chap. 1. To Wilberforce, 3.i.49, *L*5:7–8; and to Milnes, 20.xi.52, *L*5:297. Standish Meacham, *Lord Bishop: The Life of Samuel Wilberforce, 1805–1873* (Cambridge, Mass.: Harvard University Press, 1970), 237. *HOE* 1:38 = chap. 1. J4:231, 30.viii.51; *HOE* 3:76 = chap. 14. J3:126, 5.i.51. J3:166–167, 12–14. ii.51; J3:163–165, 9–10.ii.51. J3:165, 11.ii.51.

26. J2:161, 2.xii.49; J4:322, 3.xii.51. *HOE* 1:93, 237, and 445 = chaps. 1, 3, and 5. J2:171, 14.xii.49; J8:146, 3.xi.54; J2:174, 17.xii.49; J2:188, 27.xii.49. *HOE* 3:430 = chap. 18.

27. To Burton, 26.ii.53, *L*5:314. Paul Hopkins, *Glencoe and the End of the Highland War* (Edinburgh: John Donald, 1986), 4. J3:63A, 29.vi.50; to Wood, 25.xi.51, *L*5:208; *HOE* 3:410 = chap. 18. Ps. 23. Alfred Tennyson, "The Charge of the Light Brigade," lines 5–9. Andrew Lang, quoted in Charles Firth, *A Commentary on Macaulay's History of England* (London: Macmillan, 1938), 52.

28. J2:193, 31.xii.49; J4:27, 21.iii.51; J4:29–52 passim, 23.iii–11.iv.51. J4:53,

12.iv.51. "Sir William Temple," *WLM* 6:264. *HOE* 3:408, 409, 417 = chap. 18. *HOE* 3:425, 426 = chap. 18. "Lord Clive" (1840), *WLM* 6:427; "The Earl of Chatham" (1844), *WLM* 7:249.

29. *HOE* 3:420, 421 = chap. 18. To Kent, 24.iii.58, *L*6:145. "Temple," 263–264. *OED,* s.v. "Extirpate." Hopkins, *Glencoe,* 489–492.

30. J2:102, 28.ix.49. J2:107, 3.x.49; J2:111–112, 10.x.49. *HOE* 2:488–491, 522–523, and 553–563 = chap. 12. *HOE* 2:526.

31. *HOE* 1:2 = chap. 1. *HOE* 2:485 = chap. 12. HMT to Inglis, [x?].49, in Pinney, *L*5:74n1. J2:174, 16.xii.49. J2:121, 24.x.49; Tyler Anbinder, "From Famine to Five Points: Lord Lansdowne's Irish Tenants Encounter North America's Most Notorious Slum," *American Historical Review* 107 (2002): 354. J2:122, 24.x.49. J2:154, 155, 23 and 25.xi.49. J2:163, 5.xii.49; cf. Ian McBride, *The Siege of Derry in Ulster Protestant Mythology* (Dublin: Four Courts Press, 1997), 10, 12.

32. "The Historic Siege of Londonderry. The following account is taken for the most part from Macaulay's *History of England,*" available at www.orangenet.org /londonderry/siege%20of%20londonderry.htm - 30k." McBride, *Siege of Derry,* 25, 33, 45–46, and 59.

33. To ——, 3.xii.53, *L*5:368. *HOE* 2:562–563 = chap. 12. J2:123–126, 24.x.49.

34. *HOE* 2:389 = chap. 11. "Ranke," *WLM* 6:454. To Vreede, 3.ix.51, *L*5:186. J3:57–58, 23.x.50; to TFE, 4.x.54, *L*5:422–423; J2:182, 22.xii.49. J3:54A[1], 23. vi.50. J5:52, 25.v.52. J2:102, 28.ix.49. J3:54, 19.x.50; J2:348–350, 8 and 9.vii.50. J2:346–347, 6 and 7.vii.50. To ——, 12.x.50, *L*5:132.

35. J3:57A, 25.vi.50; J3:63A–64A, 29.vi.50; J2:308, 3.v.50. J3:2, 29.vii.50. J2:329, 29.v.50; J2:332, 1.vi.50; J2:337, 11.vi.50; *HOE* 2:563, 3:184. To FM, 23.xi.50, *L*5:137; *HOE* 2:433–467 = chap. 11. J4:52, 11.iv.51. J3:35, 20.ix.50. J. K. Laughton, rev. Elizabeth Baigent, in *ODNB,* s.v. "Snow, William Parker (1817–1895)"; J8:140, 19.x.54.

11. Praeceptor Gentis Anglorum

1. J2:256, 269–274, 13 and 23–28.iii.50; J2:274–275, 277, 29–30.iii.50 and 1.iv.50. J5:454, 16.v.52. Jonathan Andrews, in *ODNB,* s.v. "Bright, John (1780/81–1870)." J2:279, 4.iv.50. J2:280–281, 285, 5 and 8.iv.50. J2:285, 11.iv.50. J2:285, 287–288, and 294, 11–12 and 17.iv.50. J2:290, 13–14.iv.50. J2:292, 299, 15 and 22.iv.50. J2:301, 304, 25 and 29.iv.50. J2:307, 334, 3 and 5–6.v.50. J2:333, 2.vi.50. J4:107, 28.v.51.

2. J3:58–59, 25.x.50. J3:146, 18.i.51; J3:172, 19.ii.51. J4:24, 20.iii.51; J4:62, 20.iv.51. J3:51, 88, 13.x.50 and 1.xii.50. To TFE, 14.viii.54, *L*5:415; to SM, 28.iv.51, *L*5:160. J4:287, 16.x.51. J4:261–262, 291, 23.ix.51 and 25.x.51.

3. J5:72, 30.vi.52. J5:73, 75, and 80, 4, 6, and 10–11.vii.52. J5:76, 78, 7 and 8.vii.52. J5:81, 12.vii.52. To HMT, 13.vii[52], L5:245. J5:81, 13.vii.52. J5:82, 14. vii.52. J5:82, 15–16.vii.52.

4. J5:86, 22.vii.52. To Craig, 24.vii.52, L5:257; J5:87, 22.vii.52. To TFE, 24.vii.52, L5:258. J5:87, 24.vii.52. To Craig, 27.vii.52, L5:259; J5:89, 27.vii.52. J5:92, 3.viii.52; to TFE, [3.viii.52], L5:262. To TFE, [3.viii.52], L5:262.

5. Roger Hutchins in ODNB, s.v. "Symonds, John Addington primus." To HMT, 15.viii.52, L5:270. To FM, 16.vii.52, L5:251; to Mahon, 23.viii.52, L5:274; and to Russell, 31.viii.52, L5:278. To HMT, 15.viii.52, L5:270–271; and to FM, 15. viii.52, L5:272. To HMT, 27.viii.52, L5:276. J5:99, 100, 8 and 10.viii.52. J5:125–126, 8.ix.52. J5:138, 28.ix.52. Richard Steckel, "New Light on the 'Dark Ages': The Remarkably Tall Stature of Northern European Men during the Medieval Era," Social Science History 28 (2004): 215. See http://www.halls.md /ideal-weight/body.htm. To TFE, 22.iii.54, L5:391.

6. LLLM 2:247–248. J8:54, 6.v.54. J5:101, 11.viii.52. T. P. Guck, M. G. Kavan, G. N. Elsasser, and E. J. Barone, "Assessment and Treatment of Depression Following Myocardial Infarction," American Family Physician 64 (15.viii.2001), 641–648, 651–652. J3:153, 29.i.51. J4:82, 5.v.51. J4:88, 10.v.51. J4:90, 13.v.51. J5:134, 22.ix.52; J8:25, 3.iii.54. J8:53, 2.v.54; cf. J8:60, 74, 21.v.54 and 26.vi.54. J5:160, 2.xi.52. J5:153, 25.x.52. J11:606–607, 18–19 and 21.xii.59; cf. Louise C. Hawkley and John T. Cacioppo, "Aging and Loneliness: Downhill Quickly?" Current Directions in Psychological Science 16 (2007): 187–191. J5:44, 14.v.52.

7. J5:107, 17.viii.52. Smith to Strahan, 9.xi.1776, in The Essential Adam Smith, ed. Robert L. Heilbroner and Laurence J. Malone (New York: Norton, 1987), 329–330. David Hume, "Of the Rise and Progress of the Arts and Sciences" (1742), in Writings on Economics, ed. Eugene Rotwein (Madison: University of Wisconsin Press, 1955), 135. J5:108, 17.viii.52. J9:69, 5.ii.56.

8. To FM, 6.ix.52, L5:279 and n3. To TFE, 6.ix.52, L5:280. J6:163, 15.xi.53. J6:180, 27.xii.53. J6:113, 16.vii.53. J6:163, 15.xi.53; to Everett, 30.v.54, L5:400; J8:144, 26.x.54.

9. J6:105, 6.vii.53. J6:127, 151, 7.viii.53 and 21.x.53. To TFE, 11.vii.53, 4 and 16.viii.53, L5:339, 347–348, 350. To De Morgan, 14.x.53, L5:360; to Mahon, 15. xi.53, L5:365; and to TFE, 15.xii.53, L5:371. To TFE, 11.vii.53, L5:339.

10. To TFE, 4.viii.53, L5:347; cf. J6:139, 143, 27.ix.53 and 8.x.53. Speeches on Politics and Literature by Lord Macaulay (London: Dent, 1909), xvii–xx.

11. J6:168, 26.xi.53; cf. J6:177, 14 and 16.x.53; J6:179, 19.xii.53; J6:181, 31.xii.53. J6:182, 1.i.54. J6:182, 5.i.54. J8:99, 103, and 105, 17 and 23–26.viii.54; J8:107, 27.viii.54; J8:108, 31.viii.54; J8:110, 4.ix.54; J8:111, 5.ix.54; J8:110, 4.ix.54; J8:126, 26.ix.54; J8:144, 25.x.54. J5:16, 7.iii.52. J8:69, 14.vi.54. J8:119, 15–16.ix.54. J8:117, 12.ix.54.

12. *LLLM* 2:365. To Merewether, 23.vi.1689[55], *L*5:458 and n2. To SM, 24.vi.55, *L*5:458–459. To TFE, 19.vii.55, *L*5:463. To Wood, 26.xii.55, *L*5:482–483.

13. To TFE, 16.viii.55, and to FM, 22.viii.55, *L*5:465; to SM, 27.ix.55, *L*5:467. J8:169, 16.xi.55; J8:164, 6.xi.55; J8:176, 26.xi.55; cf. J8:172, 178, 21 and 30.xi.55. J8:170, 18.xi.55. J8:175, 24.xi.55. To Everett, 29.xi.55, *L*5:475. J8:177, 29.xi.55; cf. J8:176, 28.xi.55. J8:179, 3.xii.55. J8:182, 9.xii.55.

14. To TFE, 27.x.55, *L*5:469. J8:172, 22.xi.55. To FM, 19.x.55, *L*5:469; cf. to HMT, 5.x.55, *L*5:467. J8:174, 22.xi.55. To FM, 19.xii.55, *L*5:479–480. Advertisement in the *National Review* 4 (1856): 04. J8:187, 17.xii.55; and Pinney, *L*5:478n4. J8:184, 186, and 188, 13, 17, and 19.xii.55.

15. JCR, "Noctes Ambrosianae," *Fraser's Magazine* 52 (1855): 363; cf. [J. M. Kemble], "Macaulay's History of England," ibid., 53 (1856): 147–166. [Andrew Wynter], "Télégraphe Electrique," *Quarterly Review* 95 (1854): 133. [John Forster], "Life and Writings of Addison," *Quarterly Review* 96 (1855): 509–568; cf. [Robert Gascoyne-Cecil], "Lord Stanhope's *Life of Pitt*," ibid., 109 (1861): 531–565, and 111 (1862): 516–561. "Invincible Armada," *Home Friend* 2 (1854): 454–455 = "The Armada," *WLM* 8:587–588. Bunsen to Wynn, 30.vi.56, and Bunsen to Bunsen, 22. iv.56, in Augustus J. C. Hare, *The Life and Letters of Frances Baroness Bunsen*, 2 vols. (London, 1879) 2:207, 203; cf. Bunsen to Vernet, 12.i.60, ibid., 254. [Charles Greville], *The Greville Diary*, ed. Philip Whitwell Wilson, 2 vols. (London: Heinemann, 1927), 2:166 (2.i.60). Mill to Hardy, 29.ix.56, in *Later Letters of John Stuart Mill, 1848–1873*, ed. Francis Mineka and Dwight Lindley, vol. 15 of John M. Robson, ed., *The Collected Works of John Stuart Mill* (Toronto: University of Toronto Press, 1972), 511. Lewis to Head, 28.i.56, in *Letters of Sir George Cornewall Lewis*, ed. Gilbert Frankland Lewis (London, 1870), 310.

16. J9:115, 28.ii.56; J9:180–181, 3.iv.56. "Macaulay as a Historian," *Scottish Review* 4 (1856): 133–144. J9:118, 1.iii.56; cf. J9:123, 4.iii.56. To FM, 1.i.56, *L*6:5. J9:26, 11.i.56. To Palmerston, 2.xii.59, *L*6:258; and J11:600, 3.xii.59. J11:269–270, 4.iii.58; J9:161, 26.iii.56; Pinney, *L*6:31n2. J9:57–58, 59, 30.i.56 and 1.ii.56; J9:162, 26.iii.56; J11:76, 15.i.57; J9:200–201, 17.iv.56. J9:173–174, 31.iii.56; cf. J9:175, 179–180, 1 and 3.iv.56; J9:190, 11.iv.56; J9:210, 22.iv.56.

17. [Walter Bagehot], "Mr. Macaulay," *National Review* 4 (1856): 357, 368, 371, 374–375, 374, 377, 382, 381, 383, 384, 385–386, and 386.

18. J11:350, 26.vii.58. J9:186, 7.iv.56. J9:90, 14.ii.56. J9:124, 4.iii.56; J9:131, 7.iii.56; to Thornton, 7.iii.56, *L*6:24. To TFE, 11.iii.56, *L*6:25. J9:148–149, 15.iii.56. J11:238, 11.i.58.

19. Henry Kissinger, as quoted in Bryce Nelson, "How Does Power Affect the Powerful?" *New York Times*, 9.xi.82, available at http://www.nytimes.com /1982/11/09/science. Philip Harling, "Equipoise Regained? Recent Trends in British Political History, 1790–1867," *Journal of Modern History* 75 (2003): 900–901; cf.

W. L. Burn, *The Age of Equipoise: A Study of the Mid-Victorian Generation* (New York: Norton, 1964); and Martin Hewitt, ed., *An Age of Equipoise: Reassessing Mid-Victorian Britain* (Burlington, Vt.: Ashgate, 2000). Peter Mandler, *Aristocratic Government in the Age of Reform: Whigs and Liberals, 1830–1852* (Oxford: Clarendon Press, 1990), 282, 253. David Brown, *Palmerston and the Politics of Foreign Policy, 1846–55* (Manchester: Manchester University Press, 2002), 42. This section also draws on K. Theodore Hoppen, *The Mid-Victorian Generation, 1846–1886* (Oxford: Clarendon Press, 1998), 127–274. J2:32, 19.vi.49.

20. Norman Gash, *Sir Robert Peel: The Life of Sir Robert Peel after 1830* (Totowa, N.J.: Rowman and Littlefield, [1972]), 667, 686. To CET, 2.iii.50, *L*5:97–98; cf. J4:92, 21.vi.52. J5:177, 25.xi.52. To Russell, 21.iii.51, *L*5:154; cf. to FM 15.xi.50, 5:132–133. Saho Matsumoto-Best, *Britain and the Papacy in the Age of Revolution, 1846–1851* (Rochester, N.Y.: Royal Historical Society, 2003), 161–162. To FM, 24.iii.51, *L*5:156–157.

21. J1:489–490, 3.ii.49. J2:251, 7.iii.50; cf. J3:78, 18.xi.50. Palmerston quoted in Anthony E. M. Ashley, *The Life of Henry John Temple, Viscount Palmerston, 1846–1865,* vol. 1 (London, 1876), 222. David Brown, "The Power of Public Opinion: Palmerston and the Crisis of December 1851," *Parliamentary History* 20 (2001): 349, 353.

22. Brown, "Power of Public Opinion," 333, 339–345. To Mahon, 3.xii.51, *L*5:210; to SM, 13.xii.51, *L*5:211; to FM, 20.i.52, *L*5:217–218. J4:362, 19.i.52. Brown, "Power of Public Opinion," 338, 344–348, and 351. Mandler, *Aristocratic Government,* 273. Brown, *Palmerston,* 135. J5:180, 1.xii.52.

23. J4:337, 24.xii.51. J4:339, 25.xii.51. J3:183, 26.ii.51; J4:120, 4.vi.51. J4:359–360, 18.i.52. J4:360–362, 19.i.52. J4:159, 3.vii.51. J5:53, 27.v.52. J5:59, 61, 9 and 12.vi.52; to HMT, 27.v.52, *L*5:231–232 and 231n3; to Black, 30.vi.52, *L*5:240; to TFE, 10.vii.52, *L*5:244; to Mahon, 17.vii.52, *L*5:254. To ——, [22?vi.52], *L*5:237; cf. to Black, 23.vi.52, *L*5:239; to Craig, 8.vii.52, *L*5:242; to Rutherford, 15.vii.52, *L*5:248–249.

24. *LLLM* 2:245–246. "Edinburgh Election" (2.xi.52), in Vizetelly, 2:379, 381, and 389.

25. "Exclusion of Judges" (1.vi.53), in Vizetelly, 2:255. TBM quoted in *LLLM* 2:142. To Gladstone, 27.v.53, *L*5:332.

26. M. J. Daunton, *Progress and Poverty: An Economic and Social History of Britain, 1700–1850* (Oxford: Oxford University Press, 1995), 439; cf. Jeffrey G. Williamson, "British Inequality during the Industrial Revolution: Accounting for the Kuznets Curve," in *Income Inequality in Historical Perspective,* ed. Y. S. Brenner, Hartmut Kaelbe, and Mark Thomas (Cambridge: Cambridge University Press/Editions de la Maison des Sciences de l'Homme, 1991), 57–75. J6:148, 16.x.53. J8:98, 13.viii.54. Mandler, *Aristocratic Government,* 254. Brown, "Power of Public Opinion," 350. J8:23, 28.ii.54.

27. To FM 4.x.53, *L5*:358 and n3. Brown, *Palmerston,* 157; to SM, 29.ix.53, *L5*:357. Brown, *Palmerston,* 213–215. J8:29, 13.iii.54. To TFE, 13.ii.54, *L5*:381; to TFE, 19.iii.59, *L6*:201. Mandler, *Aristocratic Government,* 253. J8:27, 8.iii.54.

28. J11:27, 26.vii.56; J9:54, 29.i.56. Philip Bobbitt, *The Shield of Achilles: War, Peace, and the Course of History* (New York: Random House/Anchor, 2003), 146; cf. Mary Poovey, *Making a Social Body: British Cultural Formation, 1830–1864* (Chicago: University of Chicago Press, 1995), 25–54. To TFE, 4.x.54, *L5*:423.

29. *LLLM* 2:299; e.g., GOT, *The American Revolution,* new ed., 2 vols. (New York: Longmans, Green, 1908), 2:3–4, 19, 96, 102, 138, 166, and 197. To FM, 18. xi.54, *L5*:429. To Black, 25.i.55, *L5*:441. To Everett, 29.xi.55, *L5*:476; cf. J4:173, 17.vii.51.

30. J8:63, 1.vi.53. To Everett, 30.v.54, *L5*:400; to Black, 25.i.55, *L5*:441. "Exclusion of Judges," in Vizetelly, 2:243–255; to TFE, 29.iv.53, *L5*:328.

31. *LLLM* 2:265–266. J6:78, 1.vi.53. To McLaren, 17.iii.53, *L5*:319–320. "On Scottish Annuity Tax" (19.vii.53), *Hansard,* 3d ser., 129 (1853): 451–460.

32. J6:115–116, 19.vii.53; J8:80, 9.vii.54; to Stevenson, 10.vii.54, *L5*:408. To Black, 20.i.54, *L5*:379; cf. to Everett, 7.v.49, 5:53–54. E.g., to Belper, 29.vi.58, 6:157. J8:35, 28.iii.54; cf. to Lee, 16.vii.53, *L5*:341.

33. To Everett, 29.xi.55, *L5*:476; cf. to Black, 25.i.55 and 18.x.55, *L5*:441, 468; and to Electors of Edinburgh, 19.i.56, *L6*:9. To TFE, 8.iv.57, *L6*:87–88; J11:262–263, 22.i.58; to FM, 15.xi.59, *L6*:252–253. J9:81, 9.ii.56. To TFE, 2.iii.57, *L6*:79; cf. J11:481–482, 490, 27.iv.59 and 9.v.59. J11:342, 8.vii.[58]. J11:444, 1.iii.59; cf. to TFE, 24.iii.59, *L6*:202. J11:101, 1.iv.57.

34. J11:262, 20.ii.58; cf. to TFE, 25.vi.58, *L6*:156; and to Black, 6.x.59, *L6*:240. J11:453, 455–456, 9 and 22.iii.59. To CET, 16.v.59, *L6*:213–214.

35. J2:242–243, 25.ii.50. Katherine Prior, in *ODNB,* s.v. "Bethune, John Elliot Drinkwater." J5:46, 17.v.52. [Henry Ellis], "British Colonial Library—East India Company's Possessions," *Quarterly Review* 92 (1852): 62. Karl Marx, "Sir Charles Wood's East India Reforms," *New York Daily Tribune,* 22.vi.53, available at http://www.marxists.org/archive/marx/works/1853/06/22.htm.

36. To HMT, 4.x.54, *L5*:424 and n3. To TFE, 3.xii.54, *L5*:432. To TFE, 24.iii.56, *L6*:31 and nn2 and 3; J9:158, 24.iii.56. A. V. Dicey, *Lectures on the Relation between Law and Public Opinion in England during the Nineteenth Century* (London: Macmillan, 1905), 29; Rupert Cross, "The Reports of the Criminal Law Commissioners (1833–1849) and the Abortive Bills of 1853," in *Reshaping the Criminal Law: Essays in Honour of Glanville Williams,* ed. P. R. Glazebrook (London: Stevens, 1978), 10; David Skuy, "Macaulay and the Indian Penal Code of 1862: The Myth of the Superiority and Modernity of the English Legal System Compared with India's Legal System in the Nineteenth Century," *Modern Asian Studies* 32 (1998): 543–544.

37. To TFE, 4.iii.53, *L*5:315–316. R. J. Moore, *Sir Charles Wood's Indian Policy, 1853–1866* (Manchester: Manchester University Press, 1966). To HMT, 8.iv.53, *L*5:325; *Parliamentary Papers, 1852–3,* 27:214–226.

38. "The Government of India" (24.vi.53), in Vizetelly, 2:257, 260–261, 262–264, 265–266, and 267–269. Pinney, *L*5:336n4. J6:98, 24.vi.53. *New York Times,* 13.vii.53, 3.

39. Jennifer Hart, "Sir Charles Trevelyan at the Treasury," *English Historical Review* 75 (1960): 107. Jowett to Palmer, xi.47, in Evelyn Abbott and Lewis Campbell, *The Life and Letters of Benjamin Jowett,* 3d ed., 2 vols. (London, 1897), 1:190; and Jowett to Gladstone, 26.vii.53, in R. J. Moore, "The Abolition of the Indian Civil Service and the Closure of Haileybury College," *Historical Journal* 7 (1964): 250. That article along with Edward Hughes, "Sir Charles Trevelyan and Civil Service Reform," *English Historical Review* 64 (1949): 53–88 and 206–234; J. M. Compton, "Open Competition and the Indian Civil Service, 1854–1876," ibid., 83 (1968): 265–284; C. J. Dewey, "The Education of a Ruling Caste: The Indian Civil Service in the Era of Competitive Examination," ibid., 88 (1973): 262–285; and John Greenaway, "Celebrating Northcote/Trevelyan: Dispelling the Myths," *Public Policy and Administration* 19 (2004): 1–14, inform this section. Gladstone to Russell, 20.i.54, in John Morley, *The Life of William Ewart Gladstone,* 3 vols. (New York: Macmillan, 1903), 1:649. Memorandum from CET to Gladstone, 20.i.54, in Hughes, "Trevelyan and Civil Service Reform," 73. Abbott and Campbell, *Life and Letters of Jowett,* 1:184–185.

40. Anthony Trollope, *The Three Clerks* (Whitefish, Mont.: Kessenger, 2004), 57.

41. [Stafford H. Northcote and CET], *Report on the Organisation of the Permanent Civil Service, together with a Letter from the Rev. B. Jowett* (London, 1854), 3. Cabinet resolution quoted in Hughes, "Trevelyan and Civil Service Reform," 62. J8:22, 25. ii.54; J8:26, 4.iii.54.

42. Mill to Mill, 11.iv[54], in Mineka and Lindley, *The Later Letters of John Stuart Mill, 1848–1873,* vol. 14 of Robson, *The Collected Works of John Stuart Mill* (Toronto: University of Toronto Press, 1972), 203. Testimony of 28.vi.53, quoted in Moore, "Abolition of Indian Civil Service," 249. Jowett quoted in Abbott and Campbell, *Life and Letters of Jowett,* 1:185. Hughes, "Trevelyan and Civil Service Reform," 62. Moore, "Abolition of Indian Civil Service," 253. Ibid., 254; cf. Hughes, "Trevelyan and Civil Service Reform," 73n1; and Dewey, "Education of a Ruling Caste," 265, 270.

43. J6:159, 163, 6 and 15.xi.53.

44. To Wood, 17.iii.54, *L*5:389. J8:34, 36, 27 and 28.iii.54; J8:71, 16.vi.54. Abbott and Campbell, *Life and Letters of Jowett,* 1:197. J11:182, 23.ix.57. Jowett, quoted in [W. S. Sichel], review of *The Life and Letters of Benjamin Jowett,* by Lewis Campbell and Evelyn Abbott, *Quarterly Review* 185 (1897): 353. J8:40–41, 5.iv.54; J8:43–44,

10–11.iv.54; J8:54, 6.v.54; J8:70–71, 16.vi.54. J8:76, 1.vii.54. To TFE, 6.vii.54, L5:406; J8:80, 82, 9 and 11.vii.54. To TFE, 11.vii.54, L5:409. To TFE, 14.vii.54, L5:411; to C. Macaulay, 23.viii.54, L5:417. J8:85, 22.vii.54; J8:97, 11.viii.54; J8:148, 12.xi.54. To Wood, 27.xi.54, L5:431. *LLLM* 2:270. J8:155, 17.xii.54.

45. To TFE, 9.i.55, L5:436. P. J. Marshall, "British Society in India under the East India Company, *Modern Asian Studies* 31 (1997): 98–99. To Wood, 19.i.55, L5:438. To TFE, 22.iii.54, L5:391; J8:35, 27.iii.54; to Pleydell-Bouverie, 10.vii.55, L5:462 and n3; J9:77, 9.ii.56; R. E. Goodhart, "Fragments of Mr. Gladstone's Conversation," *Nineteenth Century and After* 50 (1901): 593. To TFE, 23.i.55, L5:440. To Wood, 19.i.55; and to TFE, 23.i.55, L5:439, 440. To Wood, 6.ii.55, L5:442–443. Humphrey Trevelyan, *The India We Left: Charles Trevelyan, 1826–65 / Humphrey Trevelyan, 1929–1947* (London: Macmillan, 1972), 60; to ——, 16.iv.56, L6:35 and n3. J9:216–217, 25.iv.56.

46. *The Times* (London), 27.xii.54, 7, which is quoted in this and the next two paragraphs, = "Report on the Indian Civil Service," xi.54, *Parliamentary Papers, 1854–5,* 40:112–120.

47. Jowett to CET, i.54, in *The Letters of Benjamin Jowett . . . Master of Balliol College,* ed. Evelyn Abbott and Lewis Campbell (London, 1899), 47, 44.

48. L. G. Mitchell, in *ODNB,* s.v. "Fox, Charles James." 1 Peter 4:8.

49. F. Max Müller, *Auld Land Syne* [1st ser.] (New York: Scribner's, 1907), 184–186; I owe this reference to the kindness of Jim Turner. J11:299, 25.iv.58. J11:300, 25.iv.58; cf. J9:154, 21.iii.56; J9:182, 4.iv.56.

50. Sheldon Rothblatt, *The Modern University and Its Discontents: The Fate of Newman's Legacies in Britain and America* (Cambridge: Cambridge University Press, 1997), 153, 157. CET to Gladstone, 3.iii.54, quoted in Hughes, "Trevelyan and Civil Service Reform," 215.

51. To TFE, 4.iii.54, L5:387; cf. to Broughton, 5.v.57, L6:90 and n4; J11:118, 12.v.57. J11:257, 14.ii.58. H. Trevelyan, *The India We Left,* 10. J9:29–35, 15–16.i.56.

52. Wood to CET, 9.xii.64, quoted in Compton, "Open Competition," 271. Wood, *Hansard,* 3d ser., 179 (1865): 418, quoted in ibid. Dewey, "Education of a Ruling Caste," 276. Peter Hinchliff and John Prest, in *ODNB,* s.v. "Jowett, Benjamin."

53. H. Trevelyan, *The India We Left,* 59–60. Clive Whitehead, *Colonial Educators: The British Indian and Colonial Education Service, 1858–1983* (London: Tauris, 2003), 5; cf. "Minute on Indian Education," in C & P, 248–250; and "Government of India" (10.vii.33), *WLM* 8:140–142. Whitehead, *Colonial Educators,* 14, 16, and 31. H. R. James, *Macaulay's Essay on Milton* (N.p., 1900). Clive Dewey, *Anglo-Indian Attitudes: The Mind of the Indian Civil Service* (London: Hambledon Press, 1993), 3, 6, and 5. *OED,* s.v. "Mandarinate."

54. J11:380, 25.x.58. Clarendon Commission Report (1864), quoted in Comp-

ton, "Open Competition," 269. GOT, quoted in Paul R. Deslandes, *Oxbridge Men: British Masculinity and the Undergraduate Experience, 1850–1920* (Bloomington: Indiana University Press, 2005), 166.

55. Michael H. Fisher, ed., introduction to *The Politics of the British Annexation of India, 1757–1857* (Delhi: Oxford University Press, 1993), 22, 24, and passim.

56. J11:161, 9.viii.57; J11:159, 1.viii.57; J11:161, 11.viii.57; J11:162, 12.viii.57. Wood, quoted in Thomas R. Metcalf, *The Aftermath of Revolt: India, 1857–1870* (Princeton: Princeton University Press, 1964), 172.

57. J11:135–146, 24–30.vi.57 and 1–13.vii.57. J11:137, 27.vi.57. J11:169, 29.viii.57; and J8:131, 8.x.54; e.g., J11:138, 29.vi.57; J11:143–145, 10 and 11. vii.57; J11:156, 29.vii.57; J11:162, 12.viii.57; J11:163–164, 16 and 18.viii.57; J11:168, 27.viii.57; J11:175–177, 17–19.ix.57; J111:186–187, 28, 29, and 30. ix.57; J11:227, 12.ix.57. J11:163, 14 and 15.viii.57. J11:301-302, 1.v.58; J11:199, 25.x.57. J11:166, 23.viii.57. J11:177, 19.ix.57. Livy, *History of Rome* 26.16. J11:199, 25.x.57. H. Trevelyan, *The India We Left,* 67; J11:195, 19.x.57. J11:200, 27.x.57.

58. J11:178–179, 19.ix.57.

59. J11:203, 29.x.57. J11:207, 5.xi.57; cf. J11:256, 258, 13 and 15.xii.58; and to Russell, 6 and 9.iv.58, *L6*:146–147, 148–149. J11:305, 6.v.58. J11:209–210, 8.xi.57. Martin Farquhar Tupper, quoted in Sashi Bhushan Chauduri, *English Historical Writing on the Indian Mutiny, 1857–1859* (Calcutta: World Press, 1979), 259; Robert Dingley, in *ODNB,* s.v. "Tupper, Martin Farquhar." Dickens, quoted in Lawrence James, *Raj: The Making and Unmaking of British India* (New York: St. Martin's Press, 1998), 283.

60. J11:243, 22.i.58; J11:500, 30.v.59. J11:386, 12.xi.58. *Manchester Guardian,* 9.iii.1906, available at http://century.guardian.co.uk/1899–1909/Story/0,126377,00 .html. To TFE and to Napier, 3.xii.42, *L4*:78, 79. J3:29, 9.ix.50. J11:211, 11.xi.57. J11:307, 29.iv.58. J11:189–190, 7.x.57.

61. Alexander Bain, *John Stuart Mill* (London, 1882), 95–96. J11:282–283, 27–28.iii.58. J11:276, 16.iii.58. Helen Davies, in *ODNB,* s.v. "Bernal, Ralph." To Palmerston, 2.xii.59, *L6*:258; Gladstone, quoted in Lionel A. Tollemache, *Gladstone's Boswell: Late Victorian Conversations,* ed. Asa Briggs (Sussex: Harvester Press, 1984), 24. Catherine Hall, "The Nation Within and Without," in *Class, Race, Gender, and the Reform Bill of 1867,* ed. Catherine Hall, Keith McClelland, and Jane Rendell (Cambridge: Cambridge University Press, 2000), 190–192, 197.

62. J11:448, 7.iii.59.

63. "Francis Atterbury," *WLM* 7:284–285, 286, 288, and 290.

64. "John Bunyan," *WLM* 7:301, 303, and 309; Eleanor A. Towle, *John Mason Neale: A Memoir* (London: Longmans, Green, 1906), 255.

65. "Oliver Goldsmith," *WLM* 7:310–311, 312–313, 319, 321, and 318. Oliver Goldsmith, "Dedication," in *The Deserted Village* (New York: Harper & Brothers, 1902), xxii; cf. Austin Dobson, introduction to ibid., vii.

66. David Fong, "Macaulay and Johnson," *University of Toronto Quarterly* 40 (1970): 37, 38–39. "Samuel Johnson," *WLM* 7:326–327, 330, 331, 342–343, 348–349, 354, 338, 339, 353, 356, and 346. J11:31, 9.viii.56; Margaret Cruikshank, *Thomas Babington Macaulay* (Boston: Twayne, 1978), 95.

67. J11:348, 25.vii.58. J11:355, 6.viii.58. J11:357, 9.viii.58. J11:357, 10.viii.58. "William Pitt," *WLM* 7:359, 375, 378–381, 382, 397–398, 389–391, and 405–406.

68. "Pitt," 393, 400, 394, 412, 401, and 377. David Steele, in *ODNB,* s.v. "Temple, Henry John, third Viscount Palmerston."

69. J9:183–184, 6.iv.56. J9:198–199, 15.iv.56; J9:227, 29 and 30.iv.56. To Everett, 25.ii.56, *L6*:18; J11:297, 21.iv.58. J9:108–109, 25.ii.56; to TFE, 11.iii.56, *L6*:25. J9:89, 14.ii.56. To TFE, 29.iii.56, *L6*:31.

70. J2:33, 19.vi.49. J9:160–161, 25–26.iii.56; J9:218, 26.iv.56. James Montgomery Stuart, *Reminiscences and Essays* (London, 1884), 20–21. J8:134, 10.x.54. J11:516, 20.vi.59. J9:152, 19 and 20.iii.56. J11:266, 26.ii.58. J11:370, 2.x.58. Pinney, *L6*:vii. J4:208, 15.viii.51; J11:457, 26.iii.59. J11:73, 1.i.57. To Whewell, 1.ii.56, *L6*:12. To A [1858?], *L6*:272; J11:362, 20.viii.58. J9:242, 5.v.56. J9:246, 7.v.56. J11:256, 12.ii.58. J11:238, 10.i.58.

12. A Broken Heart

1. To Black, 25.i.55, *L5*:441. John Duffy, *From Humors to Medical Science: A History of American Medicine,* 2d ed. (Champaign: University of Illinois Press, 1993), 14. J9:164, 28.iii.56. J9:232, 1.v.56. J11:133, 20.vi.57. J11:136, 24–25.vi.57.

2. J11:198, 25.x.57. J11:336, 24.vi.58; cf. J11:344, 16.vii.58. J11:271–272, 9.iii.58. J11:180, 20.ix.57; cf. J11:194, 16.x.57; J11:373, 5.x.58. J11:280, 20.iii.58.

3. J9:188, 8.iv.56. J9:191, 11.iv.56. J9:233, 1.v.56; J11:105, 14.iv.57; J9:221–222, 28.iv.56. J9:256–257, 12–13.v.56. J9:267, 18.v.56. J11:361, 17.viii.58; cf. J11:360, 15.viii.58; J11:361, 17.viii.58; and J11:377, 16.x.58. J11:220, 30.xi.57 and 1.xii.57.

4. J11:243, 22.i.58. J11:251–252, 7.ii.58; J11:255, 11.ii.58. J11:296, 18.iv.58. J11:400, 14 and 15.xii.58; *HOE* 4:390–410 = chap. 23. J11:267, 27.ii.58. J11:267, 28.ii.58; J11:268, 1.iii.58. J9:38, 18.i.56. J11:97, 17 and 18.iii.57. J11:163, 14.viii.57; J11:180–181, 21.ix.57; and J11:202, 28.x.57. J11:187, 1.x.57; J11:214, 20.xi.57. J11:363, 23.viii.58.

5. J11:247–248, 29.i.58. J11:279, 20.iii.58. J11:227, 12.xii.57; J11:247, 29.i.58. J11:268, 28.ii.58. J11:279–280, 20.iii.58. J11:506, 8.vi.59. J11:346–347, 18.vii.58; J11:218–219, 29.xi.57.

6. Desmond Bowen, in *ODNB*, s.v. "Gregg, Tresham Danes"; J11:293, 15.iv.58. J11:503, 505, 1 and 7.vi.59. J11:406, 407, 23 and 25.xii.58. J11:409, 30.xii.58.

7. J11:535, 26.vii.59. J11:413, 6.i.59. J5:94, 4.viii.52. J11:414, 7.i.59. J11:415–416, 8.i.59. J11:557, 28.viii.59. J11:417, 9.i.59. J11:354, 4.viii.58. J11:434, 10.ii.59; cf. J11:421, 19.i.59; J11:481–482, 27.iv.59.

8. Daniel Wickberg, "What Is the History of Sensibilities? On Cultural Histories, Old and New," *American Historical Review* 112 (2007): 661–684, is richly suggestive.

9. To SM, 30.viii.51, *L5*:184; cf. J2:8, 9.v.49. J2:1, [4].v.49; cf. J4:126–127, 10.vi.51. J6:106, 7.vii.53. To TFE, 9.iii.50, *L5*:99; cf. J11:296, 17.iv.58. J9:201, 205, 17 and 20.iv.56. J11:70, 23.xii.56; J11:167, 27.viii.57.

10. Walter E. Houghton, *The Victorian Frame of Mind, 1830–1870* (New Haven: Yale University Press, 1957), 210. J9:177, 178, 1 and 2.iv.56. To MT, 24.v.49, *L5*:55–56; cf. Thackeray to Brookfield, 13.ix.49, in *Letters and Private Papers of William Makepeace* Thackeray, ed. Gordon N. Ray, 4 vols. (Cambridge, Mass.: Harvard University Press, 1946), 2:593. J3:169, 15.ii.51. J11:292, 14.iv.58; cf. J1:538, 18.iii.49; J2:10–11, 17.v.49; J2:39, 27.vi.49; J3:168, 15.ii.51; cf. 1 Chron. 14:17. To TFE, 8 and 6.ix.52, *L5*:281, 280; to FM, 15.viii.52, *L5*:272. J9:176, 1.iv.56; cf. J2:12, 20.v.49; J9:224, 28.iv.56.

11. I owe this point to the kindness of Sabine MacCormack; *HOE* 2:1 = chap. 7. The description of William conflates Maurice Ashley, *The Glorious Revolution of 1688* (London: Hodder and Stoughton, 1966), 12; and Marion E. Grew, *William Bentinck and William III (Prince of Orange); the Life of Bentinck, Earl of Portland, from the Welbeck Correspondence* (London: Murray, 1924), 54–55.

12. J9:199, 15.iv.56. J11:299, 24.iv.58. J9:207, 21.iv.56; to [Fry], 3.iv.56, *L6*:33 and n1. J9:208, 21.iv.56. J1:430, 4.xii.48. To ——, 30.v.49, *L5*:57; and to MT, 24.v.49, *L5*:56. Pinney, *L5*:56n4. J8:51, 29.iv.54; C. Macaulay to Booth, 9.vii.79, in Pinney, *L5*:327n1. J2:238, 22.ii.50. J11:85, 11.ii.57.

13. J9:199, 206, 15 and 21.iv.56; William Thomas, ed., *The Journals of Thomas Babington Macaulay,* 5 vols. (London: Pickering & Chatto, 2008), 4:278, transcribes "inferior" as "superior." [Camillo Benso Cavour], *Cavour e l'Inghilterra: Carteggio con V. E. d'Azeglio,* 2 vols. in 3, vol. 2: *I conflitti diplomatici del 1856–61,* pt. 1 (Bologna: Zanichelli, [1933]), 1–4. J11:14, 25.vi.56. J11:350, 27.vii.58.

14. Charles E. Delzell, review of *Cavour,* by Denis Mack Smith, *American Historical Review* 91 (1986): 144. Mailer quoted in Michiko Kakutani, "Mailer Made America His Subject," *New York Times,* National Edition, 10.xi.07, 31. Adam D. Galinsky, Joe C. Magee, M. Ena Inesi, and Deborah H. Gruenfeld, "Power and Perspectives Not Taken," *Psychological Science* 17 (2006): 1068.

15. To ZM, 30.vii.33, *L2*:284. To [Baines], 30.vii.33, *L2*:285. To HMT, 31.vii.33, *L2*:286–287; Eccles. 12:8.

16. *LLLM* 1:27. To SMM, 3.ii.13, *L*1:14–15.

17. To MT, 10.viii.51, *L*5:173; J11:507, 8.vi.59. To FM, 4.vi.52, *L*5:232–233. J3:64–65, 22.i.52. J11:14, 25.vi.56.

18. George Macaulay Trevelyan, *Sir George Otto Trevelyan, A Memoir* (London: Longmans, Green, 1932), 151. J8:142, 23.x.54. To HMT, 22.vii.33, *L*2:275–276; cf. J11:481–482, 27.iv.59. To FM, 14.iv.51, *L*5:158; J4:55, 14.iv.51; J11:50, 22.x.56; to TFE, 28.x.56, *L*6:64–65; to FM, 25.viii.57, *L*6:109. J10:19–20, 28.viii.56. To TFE, 16.iii.56.

19. J11:310, 11.v.58; J2:295, 17.iv.50; to Mahon, 14.v.51, *L*5:162. J11:236, 6.i.58. J9:169–170, 30.iii.56. J11:73, 1.i.57. J11:215, 20.xi.57. J11:213, 13.xi.[57].

20. John Stuart Mill, "On the Definition of 'Political Economy' and on the Method of Investigation Proper to It" (1836), in *Essays on Some Unsettled Questions of Political Economy,* 2d ed. (Kitchener, Ont.: Batoche Books, 2000), 97. J2:119, 21.x.[49]. "Exclusion of Judges" (1.vi.53), in *Miscellaneous Writings and Speeches of Lord Macaulay* (London, 1889), 770. *OED,* s.v. "International"; Stanley Hoffman, "The Crisis of Liberal Internationalism," *Foreign Policy,* no. 98 (Spring 1995): 160–161.

21. J11:28, 27.vii.[56]; J11:99, 27.iii.[57]. J2:216, 27.i.50; cf. *HOE* 1:409, 507 = chaps. 5 and 6; *HOE* 4:189–190 = chap. 21. J4:130, 11.vi.51; J4:142–143, 18.vi.51.

22. J4:110, 28.v.51. J11:607, 21.xii.59. J11:489–490, 8.v.59. J11:560, 3.ix.59.

23. J11:236, 5.i.58; J9:125, 4.iii.56. J11:169, 28.viii.57.

24. J11:177–178, 19.ix.57. To Napier, 12.vi.40, *L*3:326; Alistair Horne, *La Belle France: A Short History* (New York: Knopf, 2005), 121. To TFE, 15.xii.34, *L*3:112. J11:296, 17.iv.58; cf. to MT, 19.viii.51, *L*5:178.

25. James Montgomery Stuart, *Reminiscences and Essays* (London, 1884), 22–23; Craig A. Anderson and Karen E. Dill, "Video Games and Aggressive Thoughts, Feelings, and Behavior in the Laboratory and in Life," *Journal of Personality and Social Psychology* 78 (2000): 772–790.

26. J11:272, 273, 11 and 13.iii.58; cf. James Turner, *Reckoning with the Beast: Animals, Pain, and Humanity in the Victorian Mind* (Baltimore: Johns Hopkins University Press, 1980). J11:24–25, 22.vii.56. Gertrude Himmelfarb, *The Idea of Poverty: England in the Early Industrial Age* (New York: Random House/Vintage Books, 1985), 311–312; and J11:507, 8.vi.59. To HMT, 10.viii.57, *L*6:103.

27. "Self-absorbed" came from Arthur Helps; cf. to Palmerston, 2.xii.59, *L*6:257. *OED,* s.v. "Self. 3a (compounds in which *self* is adverbial)," quoting Edward Bulwer Lytton. J11:88, 17.ii.57. J11:225–226, 9.xii.57. J11:262, 19.ii.58. J11:269, 2.iii.58. J9:22, 7.i.56.

28. Martin Raymond, *Naturalization of the Soul: Self and Personal Identity in the Eighteenth Century* (London: Routledge, 2000); cf. Dror Wahrman, *The Making of the Modern Self: Identity and Culture in Eighteenth-Century England* (New Haven: Yale

University Press, 2004). Richard Sorabji, *Self: Ancient and Modern Thoughts about Individuality, Life, and Death* (Chicago: University of Chicago Press, 2006). J. S. Mill, quoted in *A Supplement to the Oxford English Dictionary,* ed. R. W. Burchfield, 4 vols. (Oxford: Clarendon Press, 1972), s.v. "Self-observation."

29. To Napier, 18.iv.42, *L*4:28–29. E.g., Joseph Hamburger, *John Stuart Mill on Liberty and Control* (Princeton: Princeton University Press, 1999). John Stuart Mill, *On Liberty,* in *The English Philosophers from Bacon to Mill,* ed. Edwin A. Burtt (New York: Modern Library/Random House, 1939), 1011, 1004.

30. J11:432, 8.ii.59. Cicero, *De natura deorum,* trans. H. Rackham, Loeb Classical Library (Cambridge, Mass.: Harvard University Press, 1933), 59, 61 (1.22). John M. Robson, ed., *Journals and Debating Speeches, Part 1,* vol. 26 of *The Collected Works of John Stuart Mill,* ed. John M. Robson (Toronto: University of Toronto Press, 1988), 418–427; cf. John Stuart Mill, "Utility of Religion," in *Three Essays on Religion* (New York, 1874), 95–99.

31. E.g., J9:255, 11.v.56; J11:137, 29.vi.57; J11:144, 12.vii.57. To Craig, 24.xi.43, *L*4:161. Lionel Trilling, *The Liberal Imagination: Essays on Literature and Society,* uniform ed. (Oxford: Oxford University Press, 1981), 93. Isaiah Berlin, "Two Concepts of Liberty," in *Liberty: Incorporating Four Essays on Liberty,* ed. Henry Hardy (Oxford: Oxford University Press, 2002), 166–216.

32. J10:1–14, 20–26.viii.56. J10:60–63, 5.ix.56; J10:189–192, 13.ix.57; J10:204–251, 28.viii–13.ix.58. E.g., J10:50, 65–67, 3 and 6.ix.56; J10:137–138, 20.ix.56. J10:186, 9.ix.57; J10:202–203, 27.viii.58. To HMT, 26.viii.49, *L*5:67. J10:41, 1.ix.56.

33. J10:122, 15.ix.56. To HMT, 16.ix.56, *L*6:63. J10:151–152, 24.ix.56. J10:127, 16.ix.56.

34. J10:68–69, 6.ix.56. John Ruskin, *Modern Painters,* vol. 4: *Of Mountain Beauty* (Chestnut Hill, Mass.: Adamant Media, 2000), 59 and n2. John Ruskin, *The Stones of Venice,* vol. 1: *The Foundation,* in *Works,* ed. E. T. Cook and Alexander Wedderburn, 39 vols. (London: George Allen/Longmans Green, 1904), 9:348. To TFE, 1.iv.59, *L*6:206.

35. J10:72–73, 7.ix.56. E.g., Ruskin, *Stones of Venice,* vol. 2: *The Sea-Stories,* in *Works,* 10:145. J10:92–93, 10.ix.56. J10:106–107, 12.ix.56. J10:206, 29.viii.58; cf. J10:204, 210–211, 28 and 31.viii.58; J10:231, 235, 240, 250–259, 5, 7, 9, and 11. ix.58. J10:222, 228–229, 2 and 4.ix.58.

36. J9:231–232, 1.v.56. *LLLM* 2:322. J10:205–207, 29.viii.58. J10:216–217, 1.ix.58.

37. J9:176–177, 1.iv.56. J10:217–218, 1.ix.58; cf. J11:367, 20.ix.58. J10:221, 2.ix.58. J10:238, 8.ix.58. To FM, 8.ix.58, *L*6:168–169. J11:411, 1.i.59.

38. Pinney, *L*1:244n1. To TFE, 6.vii.54, *L*5:406. J9:242, 4.v.56. To TFE, 25.i.59, *L*6:191.

39. J11:253–254, 10.ii.58. Catullus, "Miser Catulle" 76.1–6, trans. Francis Warre Cornish, in *Catullus, Tibullus, and Pervigilium Veneris,* ed. G. P. Gould, 2d ed. Loeb Classical Library (Cambridge, Mass.: Harvard University Press, 1988), 155. J11:599–600, 3.xii.59. Karl Marx, *Early Writings,* ed. and trans. T. B. Bottomore (New York: McGraw-Hill, 1964), 126.

40. J11:261, 19.ii.58. To MMC, 16.ii.34, *L*3:25 and nn 2 and 4. J11:429, 435, 1 and 15.ii.59. J11:466, 6.iv.59. J11:485, 1.v.59. Humphrey Trevelyan, *The India We Left: Charles Trevelyan, 1826–65/Humphrey Trevelyan, 1929–1947* (London: Macmillan, 1972), 75; J11:519, 26.vi.59.

41. J11:577–578, 15 and 16.x.59. *LLLM* 2:395; cf. *LLLM* 2:399. Trevelyan, *Trevelyan,* 45. J11:581, 25.x.59. J11:586, 5.xi.59. J11:594, 22.xi.59. J11:590, 12.xi.59; cf. J11:596, 26.xi.59. J11:599, 2.xii.59. J11:600, 3.xii.59. J11:598, 30.xi.59. J11:382, 28.x.58; cf. J11:365, 15.ix.58; J11:366, 18.ix.58; J11:367, 20.ix.58. J11:600, 3.xii.59.

42. J11:471, 13.iv.59. J11:472, 15.iv.59. J11:575, 9.x.59. J11:565, 18 and 21.ix.59; J11:593, 19.xi.59. J11:468, 469, 10 and 12.iv.59; J11:488, 6.v.59. Macaulay's annotated copy of John Nichols, *Literary Anecdotes of the Eighteenth Century,* 6 vols. (London, 1812), "Notes have been rewritten in ink by his sister [Hannah] after his death": TCL Macaulay 220–228; the quoted comments are in vol. 2 (TCL Macaulay 221) at 222 and 277. He started reading volume one on 17.x.59 and finished the last volume on 21.xii.59; cf. J11:581, 583, 25 and 29.x.59; J11:585, 2 and 3.xi.59; and J11:599, 1.xii.59. J11:448, 7.iii.59. J11:411, 2.i.59; cf. J11:215–216, 22.xi.57. J11:558, 1.ix.59; cf. J11:235, 2.i.58. J11:477, 19.iv.59; cf. J11:163, 16.viii.57; and J11:577, 13.x.59. J11:509, 9.vi.59. J11:513, 13–14.vi.59. J11:576, 11.x.59.

43. J11:595, 24.xi.59; J11:603–604, 11–12.xii.59. J11:604, 14.xii.59. J11:604–605, 15–16.xii.59; to TFE, 17.xii.59, *L*6:260. J11:606, 18.xii.59. J11:606, 19.xii.59. J11:607, 21.xii.59; *LLLM* 2:399. J11:606–607, 18–19 and 21.xii.59. J11:608, 23. xii.59.

44. HMT quoted in *LLLM* 2:399–400. To TFE, 13.xii.52, *L*5:301–302; cf. J9:213, 22.iv.56. Randolph J. Bufano, "New Information on Macaulay's Death," *Notes and Queries* 216 (1971): 417–418.

45. Milman to Ticknor, 10.i.60, in Arthur Milman, *Henry Hart Milman, D.D., Dean of St. Paul's* (London, 1900), 199–200. Earl of Carlisle and epitaph quoted in *LLLM* 2:400–401.

Envoi

1. Milman to Ticknor, 10.i.60, in Arthur Milman, *Henry Hart Milman, D.D., Dean of St. Paul's: A Biographical Sketch* (New York: 1900), 199; H. H. Milman, "A Memoir of Lord Macaulay," in *The History of England from the Accession of James II,* ed.

Lady Trevelyan, 5 vols. (Boston, 1880), 5:xxi, xxvii. James Hutchison Stirling, "Lord Macaulay" (April 1860), in *Jerrold, Tennyson and Macaulay with Other Critical Essays* (Edinburgh, 1868), 119–141. E.g., Abraham Hayward, "Works of Lord Macaulay," *Quarterly Review* 124 (1868): 287. Alexander Bain, "Religious Tests and Subscriptions," in *Practical Essays* (Freeport, N.Y.: Books for Libraries Press, [1972]), 274. W. E. Gladstone, "Macaulay" (1876), in *Gleanings of Past Years,* 7 vols. (New York, [1878]), 3:284–286, 273; cf. H. C. G. Matthew, *Gladstone, 1809–1898* (New York: Oxford University Press, 1997), 267, 282–294.

2. W. E. Gladstone, "The Courses of Religious Thought," in *Gleanings,* 3:128–131; cf. 123. Acton to M. Gladstone, 1.ix.83, in *Selected Writings of Lord Acton,* ed. J. Rufus Fears, 3 vols. (Indianapolis: Liberty Fund, 1985–1988), 3:641–642. F. D. Maurice, "Macaulay," *Macmillan's Magazine* 1 (1860): 241–242.

3. JC, 497; cf. J. W. Burrow, *Whigs and Liberals: Continuity and Change in English Political Thought* (Oxford: Clarendon Press, 1988), 13. Gladstone, "Macaulay," 286. Peter Marsh, "Lord Salisbury and the Ottoman Massacres," *Journal of British Studies* 11 (1972): 63–83; [anon.], "Lord Salisbury on Our Imperialism," *New York Times,* 11. xi.98, 6. Paul Smith, ed., *Lord Salisbury on Politics: A Selection from His Articles in the Quarterly Review, 1860–1883* (Cambridge: Cambridge University Press, 1972), 3. Gwendolen Cecil, "Lord Cecil in Private Life" (1911), in *Salisbury: The Man and His Politics,* ed. Lord [Robert] Blake and Hugh Cecil (New York: St. Martin's Press, 1987), 38.

4. Jonathan Rose, *The Intellectual Life of the British Working Classes* (New Haven: Yale University Press, 2001), 42, 129–130, and 51.

5. Leslie Stephen, "Macaulay," in *Hours in a Library,* new ed., 3 vols. (London, 1892), 2:344, 352, 353, 354, 355, 365, 375, 363, 368, and 371–372. Rose, *Intellectual Life,* 442–443, 447–448. Virginia Woolf, "Character in Fiction," in *The Essays of Virginia Woolf,* ed. Andrew McNeillie, 3 vols. (San Diego: Harcourt Brace Jovanovich, 1988), 3:435.

6. GOT to Roosevelt, 10.ii.1904, in Joseph Bucklin Bishop, *Theodore Roosevelt and His Time Shown in His Own Letters,* 2 vols. (New York: Scribner's, 1920), 2:142 and 166. *New York Times Review of Books,* 23.xi.1907, BR741. Roosevelt to GOT, 23.i.1904, in Bishop, *Theodore Roosevelt,* 1:139–141.

7. Roosevelt to GOT, xi.08, quoted in Laura Trevelyan, *A Very British Family: The Trevelyans and Their World* (London: Tauris, 2006), 96. James Jay Greenough, "The Present Requirements of Admission to Harvard College," *Atlantic Monthly* 69 (May 1892): 671. Pierre Vidal-Naquet, *The Black Hunter: Forms of Thought and Forms of Society in the Greek World,* trans. Andrew Szegedy-Maszak (Baltimore: Johns Hopkins University Press, 1986), 252. Aldo Schiavone, *The End of the Past: Ancient Rome and the Modern West,* trans. Margery J. Schneider (Cambridge, Mass.: Harvard University

Press, 2000), 204–205. Peter Brown, *A Life of Learning* (New York: American Council of Learned Societies, 2003), 4. Patricia Trevelyan on seeing Macaulay's Greek Thucydides, to the author, Wallington, 23.iv.2007.

8. Roosevelt to GOT, 24.xi.1904, in Bishop, *Theodore Roosevelt,* 144. Gail Bederman, *Manliness and Civilization: A Cultural History of Gender and Race in the United States, 1880–1917* (Chicago: University of Chicago Press, 1996), 178. Max Boot, *Savage Wars of Peace: Small Wars and the Rise of American Power* (New York: Basic Books, 2002), 111, 107–108. Roosevelt to GOT, 10.ix.1909, in Bishop, *Theodore Roosevelt,* 173–174. Isabel V. Hull, "Military Culture and the Production of 'Final Solutions': The Example of Wilhelmine Germany," in *The Specter of Genocide: Mass Murder in Historical Perspective,* ed. Robert Gillately and Ben Kiernan (Cambridge: Cambridge University Press, 2003), 141–162, quoted at 161. Benjamin Madley, "From Africa to Auschwitz: How German South West Africa Inculcated Ideas and Methods Adopted and Developed by the Nazis in Eastern Europe," *European History Quarterly* 35 (2005): 429–464.

9. Theodore Roosevelt, "History as Literature," *American Historical Review* 18 (1913): 474. Idem, *Oliver Cromwell* (New York: Scribner's, 1913), 1.

10. To Randall, 23.v.57, *L*6:95. Foster Rhea Dulles and Gerald E. Ridinger, "The Anti-Colonial Policies of Franklin D. Roosevelt," *Political Science Quarterly* 70 (1955): 1–18; cf. Andrew Crawley, *Somoza and Roosevelt: Good Neighbour Diplomacy in Nicaragua, 1933–1945* (Oxford: Oxford University Press, 2007), 38–71, 153n113. "Macaulay at Roanoke," *Time,* 30.viii.1937, available at http://www.time.com/time /magazine/article/0,9171,930931–2,00.html. Clara Marburg Kirk, *Sir William Temple; A Seventeenth Century "libertin"* (New Haven: Yale University Press, 1932), xv; cf. Homer E. Woodbridge, *Sir William Temple: The Man and His Work* (New York: Modern Language Association, 1940), x–xi, 23, 30, 54, 120, 138, 141, 205–206, 311–313, and 314n23.

11. Alan Kramer, *Dynamic of Destruction: Culture and Mass Killing in the First World War* (Oxford: Oxford University Press, 2007); Binoy Kampmark, "Sacred Sovereigns and Punishable War Crimes: The Ambivalence of the Wilson Administration towards a Trial of Kaiser Wilhelm II," *Australian Journal of Politics and History* 53 (2007): 519–537.

12. William Manchester, *The Last Lion: William Spencer Churchill, Visions of Glory, 1874–1932* (Boston: Little Brown, 1983), 694. Niall Ferguson, *The War of the World: Twentieth-Century Conflict and the Descent of the West* (New York: Penguin, 2006), 420.

13. Peter Zenzinger, "Reputation: Thomas Carlyle's Reputation in Germany," in *The Carlyle Encyclopedia,* ed. Mark Cumming (Madison, N.J.: Fairleigh Dickinson

University Press, 2004), 394; Philip Rosenberg, *The Seventh Hero: Thomas Carlyle and the Theory of Radical Activism* (Cambridge, Mass.: Harvard University Press, 1974). Richard H. Crossman, in *The God That Failed,* ed. Crossman (New York: Columbia University Press, 2001), 3. George Bernard Shaw, *Man and Superman: A Comedy and a Philosophy* (New York: Brentano's, 1905), 227. Maurice Merleau-Ponty, *Humanisme et terreur: Essai sur le problème communiste* (Paris: Gallimard, 1947), 153. Michael Holroyd, *Bernard Shaw,* vol. 3: *The Lure of Fantasy* (New York: Random House, 1991), 253. Amartya Sen, *Poverty and Famines: An Essay on Entitlement and Deprivation* (Oxford: Oxford University Press, 1981), 58–59, 70–78. Winston S. Churchill, *The Second World War,* vol. 4: *The Hinge of Fate* (New York: Bantam Books, 1962), 177.

14. Omer Bartov, "Seeking the Roots of Modern Genocide: On the Macro- and Microhistory of Mass Murder," in Gillately and Kiernan, *Specter of Genocide,* 75–96. John Talbott, *The War without a Name: "France in Algeria," 1954–1962* (New York: Knopf, 1980), 22; I am grateful to Bill Ewald for alerting me to the Sétif massacre. Todd Shepard, *The Invention of Decolonization: The Algerian War and the Remaking of France* (Ithaca: Cornell University Press, 2006), 57. Caroline Elkins, *Imperial Reckoning: The Untold Story of Britain's Gulag in Kenya* (New York: Holt, 2005), 233–275, 53, and 304–306.

15. Grace Davie, *Religion in Britain: Believing without Belonging* (Oxford: Blackwell, 1994), 53. Gail A. Hornstein, "The Risks of Silence, or How I Went to England and Disappeared in Plain Sight," *Chronicle of Higher Education,* 15.xi.2002, B13. William C. Lubenow, *The Cambridge Apostles, 1820–1914: Liberalism, Imagination, and Friendship in British Intellectual and Professional Life* (Cambridge: Cambridge University Press, 1998), 400–401. Mary Moorman, *George Macaulay Trevelyan* (London: Hamish Hamilton, 1980), 232.

16. A. J. A. Morris, in *ODNB,* s.v. "Trevelyan, Sir Charles Philips"; and, more revealingly, L. Trevelyan, *A Very British Family,* 102–145; S. Gopal, in *ODNB,* s.v. "Nehru, Jawaharlal"; and Judith M. Brown, *Nehru: A Political Life* (New Haven: Yale University Press, 2003). "Minute on Indian Education," C & P, 249.

17. Moorman, *George Macaulay Trevelyan,* 233. David Cannadine, *G. M. Trevelyan: A Life in History* (New York: Norton, 1992), 28. J. H. Plumb, "G. M. Trevelyan," in *Men and Places* (London: Cresset, 1983), 245.

18. J. B. Bury, "History as a Science" (1902), in *The Varieties of History from Voltaire to the Present,* ed. Fritz Stern (Cleveland: World/Meridian, 1956), 215, 221; L. Trevelyan, *A Very British Family,* 157. George Macaulay Trevelyan, "The Latest View of History," *Independent Review* 1 (1903): 395–414; Bishop, *Theodore Roosevelt,* 2:139. George Macaulay Trevelyan, "Clio, A Muse," in *Clio, A Muse, and Other Essays Literary and Pedestrian* (London: Longman's, Green, 1913), 55, 14.

19. G. M. Trevelyan, "Clio," 41. J. H. Plumb, "The Road to Professional History," in *The Making of an Historian: The Collected Essays,* vol. 1 (Athens: University of Geor-

gia Press, 1988), 8. Cannadine, *G. M. Trevelyan,* 17, 45; David Knowles, *Lord Macaulay, 1800–1859* (Cambridge: Cambridge University Press, 1960), 4–5. G. M. Trevelyan, quoted in JC, 498. G. M. Trevelyan, quoted in Joseph M. Hernon Jr., "The Last Whig Historian and Consensus History: George Macaulay Trevelyan, 1876–1962," *American Historical Review* 81 (1976): 69; Cannadine, *G. M. Trevelyan,* 92.

20. L. Trevelyan, *A Very British Family,* 164, 169. Plumb, "Road to Professional History," 5. Idem, "The True Voice of Clio," in *The Making of an Historian,* 203–204. John Cannon, in *ODNB,* s.v. "Plumb, Sir John Harold [Jack]."

21. Lawrence Stone, "The Revival of Narrative: Reflections on a New Old History," *Past & Present,* no. 85 (1979): 3–24.

22. Simon Schama, quoted in Janet Tassel, "The Global Empire of Niall Ferguson: Doing History on a Sweeping Scale," *Harvard Magazine,* v.2007, available at http://harvardmagazine.com/2007/05/p2-the-global-empire-of-nia.html.

ACKNOWLEDGMENTS

My greatest debt is to Tom Pinney, whose exquisite edition of *The Letters of Thomas Babington Macaulay* (1974–1981) is the most important twentieth-century scholarship on Macaulay. But it runs deeper and wider than those six volumes. After reading and commenting on a proposal for this book, he gave me his photocopies of the complete eleven volumes of Macaulay's manuscript journal, which informs most of these pages.

Trying to write a book on how postreligious modern elites have derived spiritual meaning from the classics, I backed into *Macaulay: The Tragedy of Power* in May 2002. Over a beer Ciaran Brady, visiting from Trinity College, Dublin, challenged me to include a "flesh and blood" case study. Sensing that he was right, I blurted out, "I know something about Macaulay, who knew a lot about the classics." What was then a nodding acquaintance with his classicism I owe to John Clive, who directed my doctoral dissertation and was thereafter generous to me. I remain fondly grateful to him.

I am also obliged to Provost Thomas G. Burish of the University of Notre Dame and to President Nathan O. Hatch, his predecessor, for giving me the time I needed to write a long book. Mark W. Roche, then my dean, made available a helpful research grant; and John T. McGreevy, then my chair, gave crucial encouragement during a trying period. My other obligations are numerous but less easily summarized. Kathleen McDermott provided encouragement, support, and patience, as well as an acute editorial eye. For subsequent assistance I am grateful to Susan Abel, Kate Brick, and Ann Hawthorne. Cynthia Landeen accomplished the daunt-ing task of indexing the book. After reading the penultimate version, Professor Frank M. Turner made numerous shrewd and learned suggestions. The comments—and especially the caveats—of an anonymous reader of that version were also helpful. My friends and colleagues Sabine MacCormack and John Van Engen lavished learning, keenness, and time they could not afford on an earlier draft. In addition to giving wise advice about reorganizing it, Sabine corrected many classical howlers. Brad Gregory, Barbara Hanhrahan, Mark Noll, Matt Storin, Tom Slaughter, and Jim Turner, also friends and colleagues, read and improved drafts of various parts. In Macaulay's Cambridge David Thompson, Richard Rex, and the members of their seminar commented on a protosummary of the book and helped me to see that I was writing a chapter in the moral history of the modern world as much as the history of a single life. Kerrie McCaw has been Job-like in resourcefully coping with my technological and other ineptitudes. Near the end the efficient resourcefulness of Michele Fujawa and Sue Kobek was indispensable. At various stages Margaret Abruzzo, Heath Carter, Paul Cruikshank, Andrew Hansen, John McCormack, Nathaniel Peters, and Andrew Sullivan provided invaluable research and editorial assistance. From John Meier's erudite table talk I learned much about both the unbridgeable distance that separates us from the ancients and the reasons for their staying power. My debts to the learning of many others punctuate my notes. The remaining errors are my own.

In Cambridge the hospitable companionship of Rosemary and Nick Boyle and their family made my stay a memorable pleasure. At Wallington, the Trevelyans' country house in Northumberland, Lloyd Langley and Felicity Stimpson were as generously accommodating as they are efficient.

The kind professionalism of the interlibrary loan staff of the Hesburgh Library at Notre Dame was indispensable throughout. I am also obliged to the libraries and librarians of Trinity College, Cambridge, the University of Newcastle upon Tyne, and Stanford University, as well as to the British Library's microfilm copy service. Perhaps more controversially, Google Book Search has solved more problems than I care to remember.

I wish to thank the Master and Fellows of Trinity College, Cambridge, for permission to quote from Macaulay's manuscript journals and to reproduce the excellent photograph of Macaulay's statue in the antechapel taken by Jonathan Smith, the college archivist, and expedited by Joanna Bell, the sublibrarian. I also wish to thank the trustees of the National Trust, the National Portrait Gallery, and the Trevelyan family papers for permission to reproduce or quote from materials in their possession.

The dedication inadequately expresses my gratitude to those whose graced care helps to sustain me.

INDEX

tionary and antidemocratic rhetoric, 301; rhetorical, 384, 397

History of England from the Accession of James II (TBM), techniques: anaphora, 287, 302; synecdoche, 302; *media res*, 306; amplification, 307; authority as self-evident, 311, 384, 398; exordium, 384–385

History of England from the Accession of James II (TBM), writing: beginning, 6, 71, 270–271; research for, 190, 219, 270, 274, 283, 292, 329–330, 334, 382, 393, 398, 406, 446; preparation, 190–191, 213, 214, 239–240, 332; obstacles to completing, 230, 270, 329–330, 381–382, 386, 398–399, 403–404, 406–407, 439, 446, 469; references used in, 273, 290–295, 384; finishing, 376; TBM's intelligence bored by, 385–389, 398–399; inspiration for, 398; motivation for, 406

history of memory, 397–398

"History" (TBM), 68, 273

Hitler, Adolf, 481

Hobbes, Thomas, 214; TBM and, 38, 155–157, 223, 282, 285, 341–342; James Mill's teaching of, 39; philosophy of power, 39, 101, 246; paraphrased without reference by TBM, 55; on might makes right concept, 101; satirizing the papacy, 227–228; on Thucydides, 341–342

Hobbism, 38, 156

Holbrooke, Richard, 4

Holland, 3rd baron, 89, 93, 104, 241, 290, 346

Holland, 4th baron, 209, 210

Holland, Elizabeth, Lady, 113, 127, 241, 352

Holland, Mrs. Henry Thurston (second wife). *See* Trevelyan, Margaret (niece), and TBM

Holland House, 93, 98

Holly Lodge, 442–444

Holocaust, 481

Homer: TBM and, 31, 32, 189, 346, 390; Dante's writing influenced by, 47; CET studies with TBM, 129; Ellis studies with TBM, 343–344; Gladstone on, 357

Homer, works of: *Odyssey*, 189, 390; *The Iliad*, 252, 306, 390

homosexuality/homosexuals, 148–149, 482

honors and prizes: Craven Scholarship, 31; English verse medal competition, 31; Latin composition declamation prize, 31; William III eulogy prize, 34, 296–297, 301; income from, 34, 296–297, 301, 372; fellowship, 48, 49; list of, 370–371; expenses of, 372–373; peerage ceremony, 372; scorn for, 373

Horace, 11, 29, 211, 212, 256, 306

"Horace Walpole" (TBM), 94

"Horatius" (*Lays of Ancient Rome*) (TBM), 252, 313

Houses of Parliament. *See* Parliament

human rights, 144–145, 457, 481–482

Hume, David: TBM and, 26, 279, 281–282, 386; origin and causes of religious conviction, 39, 45; on education of the multitude, 238; prose style, 272; reading *Dialogues of the Dead* while dying, 404

Hume, David, works: *The Enquiry Concerning Human Understanding*, 386; "The Essay on Miracles," 386

Hunt, Leigh, 238–239

Hyder Ali, 242–243

illness, TBM's: heart condition, 8, 175, 363, 400–403, 445, 446, 470; eye inflammation, 92; on leaving for India, 115; fever in India, 151; headaches, 208, 210, 211, 212, 231; worry about, 322; emotions effect on, 340; toothache, 349; gout diagnosed, 400; as a patient, 400; distractions from, 400, 404, 470; enduring, 400–401; rheumatism diagnosed, 401;

Austen, 287; while dining, 322; an ordinary day's variety, 351; as distraction from writing, 381–382; during illness, 400, 470

reading for amusement: popular novels, 2–3, 9, 25–26, 39, 325, 364, 400; at Trinity College, 31, 32–33, 43; aesthetics in, 33; on voyage to India, 114–117; on America, 325

reading the classics: for pleasure, 27, 31, 114–116, 406; regimen in India, 45, 130, 138, 171, 181, 277; annihilating time and distance, 138, 139, 154–155; solace and amusement from, 138, 139, 154–155, 164, 169; stimulus to creativity, 155

realism, TBM's: political, 59, 234, 275, 439; brutality of, 234; in rhetoric of, 248; informs policies for Ireland, 260; regarding his own public standing, 370–371

reason: Cicero on, 45; TBM on the progress of, 56–57; history's location in, 68; ancients vs. moderns and, 70; argument distinguished from by TBM, 76; progress from imagination to, 178; women associated with the irrational, 178; human irrationality in will to believe, 227; revivalism offends TBM's sense of, 350

Recoinage Act, 388–389

Reform Act of 1832, 53–54, 66, 72–75, 83–87, 93, 233, 269–270, 362, 414–415

Reform Club, 361

relationships: TBM's view of, 5, 20, 360; power and control as inexorable in, 21; at school, 24–25; persuasion and intimidation used in, 30, 100; with women, 38, 95, 97; need to dominate in, 38, 97, 368; capacity for human affection and sympathy in, 97–98; networking and, 364–368; shunned depths and variety in, 452–454; self-absorption shapes, 464–466. See also friendships; patronage; individual family members

religion: TBM's subversion of, 3; as philanthropy by other means, 13, 31, 55; imagination and, 17, 57, 59; in antiquity, 45–46; education without, 60–62, 235–236, 238; TBM uses to propagate secular nationalism, 165–166, 305; social necessity of, 224; imperviousness of TBM to charms and logic of, 227; usefulness of fanaticism in, 227, 228. See also specific institutions

religion, doubleness in TBM's: public vs. private, 3, 221, 338, 349–352, 461; Christian but skeptic, 51, 99, 100; anticlerical Anglican, 302; belonging without believing, 314, 482; fast day dinner with Ellis, 349

religion, TBM's: civilization, liberty, and progress, 13; Christmas letter celebrating Jesus' birth, 41; acatalepsy, 44, 46; Ciceronian Anglicanism, 46; avowed Christianity in Leeds speech, 105–106; as Christian defined by Middleton, 173; England as surrogate for, 314; architecture's influence on, 351; primness as surrogate for, 353; respectability cultivated in lieu of, 358–364

religious intolerance toward the Jews, 330–331, 364–365

religious opinions, TBM's: modernized acatalepsy, 46; religious toleration, 82–83; on Bunyan's fervor, 91–92; apostates, 349; on Catholic militancy, 350; don't ask, don't tell policy, 350

religious pluralism, 234, 303, 305

"Report on the Indian Civil Service," 427–428

reputation, TBM's: historical, 1, 3–4, 301, 473–476, 478–484, 486–487; legacy in India, 1, 146; endurance of, 3–4; acceptance as a national sage, 3–4, 8; talents establish his political, 82; as a conversationalist, 87, 368; Edgar Allan Poe and, 249; as a liar, Churchill on, 312–313; the English historian, 324; as national icon, 473